Year Books of the Reign of King Edward the First

Michaelmas Term, Year XXXIII and Years XXXIV and XXXV

EDITED AND TRANSLATED BY
ALFRED J. HORWOOD

CAMBRIDGE
UNIVERSITY PRESS

CAMBRIDGE UNIVERSITY PRESS

Cambridge, New York, Melbourne, Madrid, Cape Town,
Singapore, São Paolo, Delhi, Mexico City

Published in the United States of America by Cambridge University Press, New York

www.cambridge.org
Information on this title: www.cambridge.org/9781108046954

This edition first published 1879
This digitally printed version 2012

ISBN 978-1-108-04695-4 Paperback

CAMBRIDGE LIBRARY COLLECTION

Books of enduring scholarly value

Rolls Series

Rerum Britannicarum Medii Aevi Scriptores, or The Chronicles and Memorials of Great Britain and Ireland during the Middle Ages, usually referred to as the 'Rolls Series', was an ambitious project first proposed to the British Treasury in 1857 by Sir John Romilly, the Master of the Rolls, and quickly approved for public funding. Its purpose was to publish historical source material covering the period from the arrival of the Romans to the reign of Henry VIII, 'without mutilation or abridgement', starting with the 'most scarce and valuable' texts. A 'correct text' of each work would be established by collating 'the best manuscripts', and information was to be included in every case about the manuscripts used, the life and times of the author, and the work's 'historical credibility', but there would be no additional annotation. The first books were published in 1858, and by the time it was completed in 1896 the series contained 99 titles and 255 volumes. Although many of the works have since been re-edited by modern scholars, the enterprise as a whole stands as a testament to the Victorian revival of interest in the middle ages.

Year Books of the Reign of King Edward the First

The records of the medieval English courts were compiled into manuscript 'year books', organised by regnal year of the monarch. The year books for the regnal years 20–2 and 30–5 of Edward I (1239–1307) were edited for the Rolls Series by Alfred Horwood (1821–81), and published in five volumes between 1863 and 1879, with translations provided for the Anglo-Norman text. Horwood notes that the quantity of cases is surprising given the size of the population. He attributes this to confidence among the people in the king's justice, but also points out that the law's delays during this period were notorious, and that in 1289 the king had effectively purged most of his judges on the grounds of corruption. This volume, published in 1879, contains cases from the four law terms of the years 1305–7, ending at the death of Edward I.

RERUM BRITANNICARUM MEDII ÆVI SCRIPTORES,

OR

CHRONICLES AND MEMORIALS OF GREAT BRITAIN AND IRELAND

DURING

THE MIDDLE AGES.

H 594. Wt. B 410.

THE CHRONICLES AND MEMORIALS

OF

GREAT BRITAIN AND IRELAND

DURING THE MIDDLE AGES.

PUBLISHED BY THE AUTHORITY OF HER MAJESTY'S TREASURY, UNDER THE DIRECTION OF THE MASTER OF THE ROLLS.

On the 26th of January 1857, the Master of the Rolls submitted to the Treasury a proposal for the publication of materials for the History of this Country from the Invasion of the Romans to the reign of Henry VIII.

The Master of the Rolls suggested that these materials should be selected for publication under competent editors without reference to periodical or chronological arrangement, without mutilation or abridgment, preference being given, in the first instance, to such materials as were most scarce and valuable.

He proposed that each chronicle or historical document to be edited should be treated in the same way as if the editor were engaged on an Editio Princeps; and for this purpose the most correct text should be formed from an accurate collation of the best MSS.

To render the work more generally useful, the Master of the Rolls suggested that the editor should give an account of the MSS. employed by him, of their age and their peculiarities; that he should add to the work a brief account of the life and times of the author, and any remarks necessary to explain the chronology; but no other note or comment was to be allowed, except what might be necessary to establish the correctness of the text.

The works to be published in octavo, separately, as they were finished; the whole responsibility of the task resting upon the editors, who were to be chosen by the Master of the Rolls with the sanction of the Treasury.

The Lords of Her Majesty's Treasury, after a careful consideration of the subject, expressed their opinion in a Treasury Minute, dated February 9, 1857, that the plan recommended by the Master of the Rolls "was well calculated for the accomplishment of this important national object, in an effectual and satisfactory manner, within a reasonable time, and provided proper attention be paid to economy, in making the detailed arrangements, without unnecessary expense."

They expressed their approbation of the proposal that each Chronicle and historical document should be edited in such a manner as to represent with all possible correctness the text of each writer, derived from a collation of the best MSS., and that no notes should be added, except such as were illustrative of the various readings. They suggested, however, that the preface to each work should contain, in addition to the particulars proposed by the Master of the Rolls, a biographical account of the author, so far as authentic materials existed for that purpose, and an estimate of his historical credibility and value.

Rolls House,
December 1857.

Year Books

OF THE REIGN OF

KING EDWARD THE FIRST.

MICHAELMAS TERM, Year XXXIII

AND

Years XXXIV and XXXV.

Year Books

OF THE REIGN OF

KING EDWARD THE FIRST.

MICHAELMAS TERM, YEAR XXXIII

AND

YEARS XXXIV AND XXXV.

EDITED AND TRANSLATED

BY

ALFRED J. HORWOOD,

OF THE MIDDLE TEMPLE, BARRISTER-AT-LAW.

PUBLISHED BY THE AUTHORITY OF THE LORDS COMMISSIONERS OF HER MAJESTY'S TREASURY, UNDER THE DIRECTION OF THE MASTER OF THE ROLLS.

LONDON:
LONGMAN & Co., PATERNOSTER ROW; TRÜBNER & Co., LUDGATE HILL:
ALSO BY
PARKER & Co., OXFORD; AND MACMILLAN & Co., CAMBRIDGE;
A. & C. BLACK, AND DOUGLAS & FOULIS, EDINBURGH;
AND A. THOM, DUBLIN.

1879

Printed by
Eyre and Spottiswoode, Her Majesty's Printers.
For Her Majesty's Stationery Office.

CONTENTS.

PREFACE.

PREFACE.

THE present volume contains reports of cases in Michaelmas Term, 33 Edw. I., in the four terms of the 34th and the three terms of the 35th year of the reign of Edw I. As that King died in the month of July 1307, Michaelmas term in that year falls within the reign of Edward II.

The reports are taken from the Additional MS. 5925 in the British Museum, described at p. lii. of the Preface to the volume containing reports of cases in the 30th and 31st years of Edward I.[1]

The judges of the Court of Common Pleas during the period comprised in the present volume were Ralph de Hengham, Lambert de Trikingham, William Howard, Hervey de Staunton, Peter Mallore, and William de Bereford. But at pp. 295, 539, and 573, HALES appears as a judge, whose name as a judge in this reign is not mentioned by Dugdale or Foss. The case beginning at p. 57 is before BRABAZON, who was of the King's Bench; and SPIGORNEL and ROUBYRI, who appear with him as judges in the case at p. 577, were also judges of the Court of King's Bench. The name of ROUBYRI appears also (seemingly as a judge) at pp. 51, 151, and 407, although the cases are in the Court of Common Pleas. The second case at p. 53 and the case at p. 55 are in the King's Bench. At p. 401 Warwick, the King's attorney-general, is stated to be "sitting in the Bench."

---

[1] In the passage describing the MS., the words "but there are no cases "of Novel Disseisin" should be erased.

A tendency to rely on cases previously decided appears in this volume. There are more than a dozen instances of reference to previous cases.

At p. 15 is an instance of the enfranchisement of a serf.

The references to Statutes are numerous, and at p. 83 HENGHAM claims to have been the draftsman of the celebrated Statute of Westminster 2, 13 Edw. I. At p. 57 the inquisitors of Trailbaston are mentioned.

The law and practice with regard to outlawry is discussed at pp. 55 and 417.

At p. 123 the judge tells a defendant what he ought to have done to save a default, when he found his journey to the Court obstructed by floods.

The number of acres in a carucate varied; at p. 353 it is said that at that time (A.D. 1306) the value of a carucate was at most 40*s.* per annum.

The judges were doubtless well acquainted with Bracton's treatise on the laws of England. At p. 205 the plaintiff in Replevin, whom the defendant alleged to be his vilein, was asked by BEREFORD, "And if pending his "writ he had found you in your nest, for what purpose "should he prosecute his writ?" Bracton, according to printed copies (Book 2, chap. 8, § 2), quotes a judgment by J. de Metingham, that if a naif should fly from his lord "within cities or the ancient demesne of the King "or elsewhere, and should return and be found in the "servile tenement whence he drew his origin, and should "be taken there by the lord *like a bird in its nest,* he "should be a serf for ever." But it may be remarked that this citation of Metingham's judgment was not written by Bracton, but probably by some early annotator; for Metingham was not a judge during the reign of Henry III., and the passage does not appear in two of the MSS. consulted for the new edition of Bracton (p. 204 *n.*) by Sir Travers Twiss.

A question arising whether the manor of Acle was of the Ancient Demesne (see p. 311), Domesday was examined, and the manor was found not to be of the Ancient Demesne. BEREFORD corrected the erroneous notion of HALES that a manor was Ancient Demesne because it was in the King's hands.

It appears from the case at p. 415 that the King could prosecute his rights in whatever Court he pleased.

The custom of Yarmouth with regard to deeds executed by married women is noticed at p. 77; the franchise of Colchester in cases of trespass or tort at p. 83; the process in the Court of Winchester at p. 117; and the custom of York regarding devises of land at p. 457.

At p. 471 is a passage of some importance regarding the means whereby the King was formerly made amenable to the claims of a subject. One of the counsel in the case says that in old times every writ, whether of right or of the possession, lay well against the King, but that now the King wills that one should sue against him by bill (or petition) where one formerly sued by by writ. Bracton (Book 1, chap. 8, and Book 5, chap. 4) lays it down that a writ does not run against the King, and (Book 4, chap. 10) that an Assise does not lie against the King, but that the proceeding must be by petition. But there are passages in the Year Books of Edward III. which are confirmed by the statement at p. 471 of this volume. In the Year Book of 22 Edward III. 3 b, it is said that in the time of King Henry and before the King was impleaded like any other man, but his son Edward ordained that one should sue the King by petition. In the Year Book of 24 Edward III. 55 b. Justice Wilbye said that he had seen a writ in these terms, "Præcipe Henrico regi Angliæ," instead whereof a petition is now given by reason of his prerogative. In the Year Book of 43 Edward III. 22 a, Cavendish said that in the time of King Henry the King was only as a common person, for then one might have a writ of Disseisin against the King and all other kinds of actions just as against any other person. The ordinance of the

Council and of the twelve chosen by the Commons made in the year 1258, and confirmed by Henry III. in the following year, seems plainly to give the subject the right to sue by writ against the King. *See* Rymer's Fœdera, i. 381, ed. 1816, and it may have been one of the writs issued after this provision that Wilbye saw. On this point *see* Mr. Brinton Coxe's note at p. 28 of his translation of Gutenbock's "Bracton, and his relation to "the Roman Law."

A. J. H.

ERRATA AND CORRIGENDA.

Page 154, last line, *for* he *read* she.
,, 200, line 12 from foot, *for* deed *read* died.
,, 204, ,, 8, *for* sue out *read* prosecute.
,, 208, ,, 8 from foot, *for* the writ *read* one writ.
,, 216, ,, 12 ,, *for Hervy read* HERVY.
,, 366, ,, 7 ,, *for* in parcenary disclaimed *read* disclaimed in the parcenary.
,, 425, line 6, *read* tient de nous.
,, 432, ,, 11 *for* vicars *read* vicar.
,, 474, last line, *for* forward ; judgment *read* before judgment.
,, 504, line 18, *for* issued *read* had to have been sued.
,, 579, ,, 14 from foot. S is probably a mistake for E.
554, ,, 7 ,, *for* for *read* so that.
,, 556, ,, 19, *for* our *read* [to] our.

TABLE OF NAMES.

TABLE OF NAMES.

A.

B.

C.

D.

E.

F.

G.

H.

N.

O.

P.

R.

CASES IN MICHAELMAS TERM

AT

THE END OF THE XXXIIIRD YEAR

OF THE

REIGN OF KING EDWARD.

CASES IN MICHAELMAS TERM AT THE END OF THE THIRTY-THIRD YEAR OF THE REIGN OF KING EDWARD.

A.D. 1305.

Dower unde nihil habet.

§ Agnes who was the wife of Reyner le Wodeward heretofore brought a writ of Dower against one William and M. his wife, who came into Court by attorney; and the attorney answered for M., that she had nothing and claimed nothing in the thing demanded against her; and for William, that he had nothing except jointly with one J., who was not named, &c.; and thereby he abated the writ. And Agnes anew brought a writ against the aforesaid William and J., who made default, so that the tenements were on the point of being lost. And thereupon came the aforesaid M., the wife of William, in her proper person.—*Hamptone* (for the demandant) prayed seisin of the land.—*Kinge.* Sir, you have here M., the wife of William, &c., who comes before judgment given, according to the Statute,[1] where her husband is going to let these tenements be lost, and prays to be received to defend her right.—*Hamptone.* You shall not get to that; for heretofore we brought the like writ against you and your husband, when you came into Court and claimed nothing in these tenements; wherefore your claim ought not now to avail you: and then your husband answered that he was enfeoffed of these tenements jointly with this J. against whom &c., and thereby abated our writ, and gave us this writ which we are now using and then freshly purchased, without any estate in those tenements being able to accrue to them; and moreover you are not named in the writ; wherefore

[1] 13 Edw. I. c. 3.

DE TERMINO SANCTI MICHAELIS ANNO REGNI REGIS EDWARDI XXXIII°. FINIENTE.

§ Agnes ke fu la femme Reyner le Wodeward autrefoiz porta bref de Dowere vers un Willeam e M. sa femme, ke viendrent en Court par attorne; e le *attorne* respundi pur M. qele navoit rienz en la demande vers lui fete ne rienz ne clama, e pur Willeam, qil ne avoit rienz si noun joint ove un J. nent nome, &c., e par tant abati le bref. Et Agnes derichief porta bref vers les avantdiz Willeam e J. qe fessoient defaute, ci qe les tenements furent en point de perdre. E sur ceo vient le avantdite M. la femme Willeam en propre persone.—*Hamptone* (pro petente) pria seisine de terre.—*Kinge.* Sire, vous avez icy M. la femme Willeam, &c., qe vient avant jugement rendu solom statut ou sun baron voleit ces tenementz perdre, e prie estre receu a defendre sun droit.—*Hamptone.* A ceo ne avendrez point; qe autrefoiz portames nous au tel bref vers vous e vostre baron, ou vous venistes en Court e rien ne clamastes en ces tenementz; par quei a ore ne vous deit vostre clame valer; e a donqes respondi vostre baron qil fut de ces tenementz joint feffe ove cesti J. vers qi, &c., e par tant abati nostre bref, e ceo bref nous dona qe a ore usoms, e frischement adonqes purchassames, sanz ceo qe a eux estat en ceux tenementz poeit acrestre; e ja plus tard vous ny estes mie nome en le bref; par quei, &c.—

A.D. 1305.
De Dote unde nihil habet.

A.D. 1305. &c.--*Kinge.* Although she disclaimed, yet that disclaimer was made by attorney, which can never oust a feme coverte from her estate; for she must be in Court in her proper person and be examined by the Court; and since she did not disclaim in her proper person &c., but by attorney, we pray judgment &c.—And the Rolls being examined, that was found to be so, and she was received, and vouched to warranty the aforesaid J. &c.

Right of advowson. § John le Rus brought the writ against the Abbat of Romney for the advowson of the tithes of two parts of the chapel of T.—*Hunte* counted of the seisin of his ancestor &c. who was seised of the entirety of the advowson of the chapel &c. in the time &c.—*Wescot* denied, and (said he) Sir, we do not think that to such a count he ought to be received; for you see well how he takes his title from the seisin of R. his ancestor, who he says was seised of the entirety of the advowson &c., and afterwards in the descent he lets go the entirety, and says that the right of two parts &c. descended to one Maud &c., in that respect varying from his title; and we pray judgment &c.—And the contrary was recorded.—*Wescote.* We pray the View.—*Hunte.* You shall not have it; for there is only a chapel and of a saint, and the tithes come by hazard from divers sources: of what will you then have the View?—HENGHAM. Hardly any of you ever before saw this case; let him have the View.

A little time afterwards the same Judge said to the counsel of the Abbat, Of what do you ask the View? of the tithes or of the place where you take them?—*Herle.* Of the place &c.—HENGHAM. Then have the View (thereby intimating that the View was not to be granted for the tithes).

Note. § In a writ of Monstravit de compoto &c. *Hamptone* said, Whereas he supposes by his writ that he has

Kinge. Coment qele desclama, cel desclamer fust fet par attorne, qe ne purra james ouster femme de baron coverte de sun estat; qar il la covendreit einz estre en propre persone, e examinie de Court; e de pus qele ne desclama en propre persone, &c., einz par attorne, demaundoms jogement, &c. Et scrutatis Rotulis compertum fuit illud idem, et illa admittitur, e voucha a garantie le avandit J. &c. A.D. 1305.

§ Johan le Rus porta le bref vers labbe de Rummeneye de lavoeson des dimes de deus parties de la chapele de T.—*Hunte* conta de la seisine sun auncestre &c., qe fust seisi del entier de lavoeson de la Chapele &c., en tenps &c.—*Wescot* defendi; e nentendoms pas Sire, qe a tele counte deive estre respondu; qar vous veez bien coment il prent sun title de la seisine R. sun auncestre, qi il dit estre seisi del entier de lavoeson &c., e pus en la descente entrelet cel entier, e dit qe le dreit de deus parties &c., descendi a une Maud &c., en tant variant de sun title; e demaundoms jugement &c. Et recordebatur contrarium. — *Wescote.* Nous demaundom la vewe. — *Hunte.* Vous ne la averez point; qar il ny ad fors qe une chapele e de un Seint, e les dimes venent aventurousement par divers forches: de quei voilliez donqes la vewe avoir?—HENGHAM. A peine si nul de vous onqe savant vist ceo cas; eit la vewe. IDEM parum post ad partem abbatis, De quei demandez vous la vewe, des dymes ou du lu ou vous les prendrez?—*Herle.* Du leu &c.—HENGHAM. Eiez donqes la vewe (quasi diceret non fore de decimis visus concedendus).

De Recto advocationis.

§ In brevi de monstravit de compoto &c—*Hamptone.* La ou il suppose par sun bref qil nad rienz ou il purra

Nota.

A.D. 1305. nothing where he may be summoned or attached to render this account, we tell you that he has assets in T. &c.—HENGHAM. Leave off your noise and deliver yourself from this account; and afterwards go to the Chancery and purchase a writ of Deceit; and consider this henceforth as a general rule.

Of parceners; that they wait the full age.

§ One T. brought his writ against four sisters, some of whom were under age; and they all came into Court.—*Hamptone* prayed their age.—BACOUN (having consulted HENGHAM). How much are they under age?—*Hamptone.* See, here is one who is only twelve years old; she is the youngest.—BACOUN. Adieu to all the others until she be 21 years old.

§ Note that, a man sued out a writ of trespass against four persons in these terms "why with force and arms "they entered his house, and his goods, &c." Two of the defendants were under age; the two who were of age came and said that they had recovered that house by judgment of the King's Court, and by that judgment had they entered, and not otherwise, nor by force, &c., ready, &c.—THE INQUEST was taken and passed for them in the aforesaid form: and the attorney sued on against the infants under age down to the Exigent. And when they were called in the County Court, they came and rendered themselves to the peace, and were brought into Court.—*Kinge* rehearsed the aforesaid facts. And because the attorney had sued against those who could not, on account of their tender age, bear the judgment (for even if it had been given it would have been reversible) the attorney was ordered to prison, and the children were bidden adieu, &c.

Taking of beasts.

§ Walter Randolf complained that John de Richmond tortiously took his beasts, namely so many sheep, &c.—*Passeley.* We avow the taking, &c., for the reason that estre somons ne attache de rendre ceste acounte, vous dioms qil ad assez en T. &c.—HENGHAM. Lessez vostre noyse e deliverez vous de ceste acounte, e pus alez a la chauncelerie e purchasez vous bref de desceite; e ceste reulle tiegnez desormes generale. A.D. 1305.

§ Un T. porta sun bref vers iiii. soers dount les unes furent denz age, e viendrent totes en Court.—*Hamptone* pria lour age.—BACOUN (consulto HENGHAM). Com bien sunt denz age?—*Hamptone.* Veez icy une qe nest mes de .xii. aunz, ele est punesce.—BACON. Aillent totes les autres a Deu tant qe ele soit de .xxi. an.

De participibus, quod servent ætatem.

§ Nota, qe un homme suist vers iv. bref de trespas, saver, "quare vi et armis domum suam intravit et bona &c."; dount les deus furent enfanz denz age; les deus dage autrefoiz viendrent e dissoient qe eux avoient cele meson recovery par jugement de la Court le Roi e par cel jugement furent eux entrez e noun pas autrement ne a force &c., prest &c.—*Lenqueste* prise e passa pur eux en ceste forme avantdite, e le attorne suy avant vers les enfanz denz age tant qe al exigend. Et quant eux furent en conte demaundez, eux viendrent e se rendirent a la pees, e furent amenez en Court.—*Kinge* repetiit prædicta.—Et pur ceo qe le attorne avoit suy vers eux qe ne poeient pur lour tendre age jugement porter, car tut eust il este rendu il eust este reversable, fust lattorne comande a la prisone, e dit a les enfanz qe eux alassent a Dieu, &c.

§ Wauter Randolf se pleint qe Johan de Richemond atort prist ces avers, nomement tant des berbiz, &c.—*Passeley.* Nous avowoms la prise, &c., par la resoun qe

Prise des avers.

A.D. 1305. we found them in the same place, &c., in our several pasture, where you ought not to common, pasturing in our several.—*Willuby.* We have in the same vill a virgate of land to which common is appendant, and we tell you that in the same place we have four acres of land where you took our sheep, and we pray judgment if you can claim in our several. And, together with this, we tell you that one Ralph le Rous lately held these tenements which we hold, by which Ralph we were enfeoffed thereof, and in that place he commoned in his lifetime, as in his common appendant &c., and we have always commoned there since we purchased that land of him, and we pray judgment. — *Passeley.* You cannot say that; for heretofore you would have commoned and we did not allow you; whereupon you brought the Disseisin before &c., by which assise it was found that you were never so seised thereof that you could be disseised; and we pray judgment if in opposition to that verdict, you can now claim common by any title of your seisin. —HOWARD. Is it not his soil? — *Hunt.* Many a man has soil where he ought not to common. I would rather than ten marks that I might common throughout my soil. — HOWARD. Then say it, if it be so regarding him. —*Passeley.* Nay, Sir, we think to be sufficiently aided by the verdict of this assise. — HOWARD. By common right a man may common in his own soil. —*Willuby.* He can not deny that it is our soil where the taking &c., and that we and our feoffor used that common; judgment. — *Hunt.* Nay, to a willing man no injury is done; and you yourself purchased the writ of Novel Disseisin and sued on until the assise passed in the form &c.; judgment if in opposition to that verdict &c.—HOWARD. His purchase was repugnant to his estate, for he supposed by his writ and his plaint that another was seised of the soil of which he was seised; and if you had then answered to his plaint that he was seised of the freehold and of the soil which he had put in his View, would you not have

nous les trovames en mesme le leu &c. en nostre several A.D. 1305.
de pasture ou vous ne devez comuner pessant nostre several. —*Willuby*. Nous avoms en mesme la ville une verge de terre a quei comune est apendant, e vous dioms qe en mesme tel leu si avoms iiii. acres de terre ou vous preistes nos berbiz, e demaundoms jugement si en nostre several puissez clamer. Et ovesqe ceo, vous dioms nous qe un Rauf le Rous jadis tient ceux tenementz qe nous tenoms, par le quel Rauf nous sumes de ces feffez, e en tiel leu communa en sa vie com en sa comune apendant, &c.; e nous pus qe cele terre de luy purchaames i avoms tut tenps comune, e demaundoms jugement.—*Passeley*. Ceo ne poez dire; qar autrefoiz vous voilliez aver comune, e nous ne vous suffrimes point; par quel vous portastes la disseisine devant &c., par quel assise fust trove qe vous ny estoiez unqes seisi si ne disseisi purriez estre; e demaundom jugement si encontre cele verdit par nul title de vostre seisine puissez a ore comune clamer. — HOWARD. Nest ceo sun soil?—*Hunt*. Meint homme ad soil ou il ne deit comuner. Jeo voley melz de .x. mars si jeo poei comuner par my mon soil.—HOWARD. Sil soit issi de ly dites le donqes.—*Passeley*. Nay, Sire, nous entendoms assez estre aide par le verdit de ceste assise.—HOWARD. De comune dreit homme purra comuner en sun soil demene. —*Willuby*. Il ne puet dedire qe ceo nest nostre soil ou la prise &c., e nous e nostre feoffor cele comune y avoms usee; jugement.—*Hunt*. Nay, volenti non fit injuria, e vous mesmes purchasates le bref de novele disseisine e suistes tant qe lassise passa en la forme &c.: jugement si encontre ceo verdist &c.—HOWARD. Sun purchaz fust repugnant a sun estat, car il supposa par sun bref e sa pleinte que autre fu seisi du soil de quel il estoit seisi; e si vous eussez a sa pleinte respundu adonqes qil fu seisi du franc-

A.D. 1305. abated his plaint? (intimating the affirmative :) so I tell you that that assise was null.

Ne vexes. § One R. brought the writ against the Abbat of St. Helen's. — *Asseby.* Sheweth unto you &c. tortiously troubles him, and causes him to be troubled in his free tenement which he holds of him in C., and in respect of it demands and causes to be demanded from him customs and services which he ought not nor has been used to do: and tortiously for this, that whereas he holds &c. by fealty and by the service of 3*s.* by the year for all services, the aforesaid Abbat troubles him and causes him to be troubled, and, besides these services, demands and causes to be demanded 5*s.* by the year, and to make him his foreman, and to tallage high and low at his will, and to compel him to do these things grievously distreins him, tortiously and to his damage &c.; and if he will deny it, he has good suit for it.—*Scrope.* The Abbat of St. Helen's denies tort and force and will deny &c.; and he tells you that R. ought not to be answered, for he is our vilein, and we are seised of him as of our vilein.—*Willuby.* Sir, he asserts what he wishes: he (R.) is a free man and of free condition, and his father Simon was free, and his grandfather was free; ready &c.—Afterwards on HENGHAM and HOWARD consulting together, HENGHAM said to *Willuby:* What do you intend to do by this writ? to discharge the tenements from the services &c. or to deliver the body (of R.) from serfdom &c.?—*Tiltone.* To discharge the tenements.—HENGHAM. Certainly then you plead dully, for the exception which he gives you is nothing to charge the tenements. On another day *Toudeby* repeated the matters aforesaid, and in conclusion said,—You have well heard that we said that he was our vilein, and that we were seised &c., and also our predecessor was seised of Simon his father and of his grandfather. And they said that they were free and of free condition &c.—HENGHAM to *Willuby.* Do you say that?—*Willoughby.*

tenement e du soil qil avoit mys en sa vewe, ne eussez sa pleinte abatue? quasi diceret sic: dount jeo vous dy qe cele assise fu nule. A.D. 1305.

§ Un R. porta le bref vers labbe de Seinte Eleyne.—*Asseby*. Ceo vous moustre &c., atort lui travaille e fet estre travaille de son franc-tenement qil tient de luy en C., e de ceo lui demaunde e fet estre demaunde coustumes e services qe faire ne luy deit ne soleit. E pur ceo atort, qe la ou il tyent &c. par fealte e par les services de treis soz par an pur touz services, le avandit abbe luy travaille e fet estre travaille, e estre ces services luy demaunde e fet estre demaunde v. soz par an, e a faire de luy sun provost, e a taillager haut e bas a sa volonte, e a ceo fere grevoussement lui destreine atort e a ces &c., e sil le voille dedire il en ad suite bone.—*Scrop*. Labbe de Seinte Eleyne defendi tort e force e defendra &c., e vous dit qe R. ne deit estre respondu, car il est nostre vilein, e nous seisi de lui com de nostre vilein.—*Willuby*. Sire, il dit sun talent; il est franc-homme e de franc estat, e sun pere Simon fu franc e ael franc; e prest, &c. Postea, consultis adinvicem HENGHAM e HOWARD,—HENGHAM a *Willuby*. Qe biez par ceo bref fere? le quel descharger les tenementz des services, &c. ou deliverer le corps de servage, &c.—*Tiltone*. Descharger les tenementz.—HENGHAM. Certes donqes pledez vous nicement, qar la excepcion qil vous donne nest nule rien a charger les tenements. Ad alium diem *Toudeby* repetiit prædicta, et in fine, e avez bien entendu qe nous deymes qil fust nostre vilein, e nous seisi, &c. e auxi nostre predecessor seisi de Simon sun pere e de sun ael, e eux disoient qe eux furent francs e de franc estat, &c.—HENGHAM a *Willuby*. Dites vous ceo?—*Willuby*. Nay

Ne vexes.

A.D. 1305. No sir, by God; we tell you that in this writ he ought not to use that exception; for this is a writ of right and is to be terminated by battle or the great assise.—HOWARD. Why can not they use this exception?—*Willuby.* Because this writ is to be terminated by battle or the great assise.—*Toudeby.* In a writ of right of plea of land, præcipe quod reddat &c., it would be a good exception to rebut the party from his action. And on the other hand if we were not admitted to this exception, our vilein would plead with us, by virtue of which pleading he would be enfranchised, and thus every vilein might enfranchise himself in spite of his lord.—HOWARD. You give no other reason why they ought not to use this exception except that this writ is to be terminated by battle or the great assise—[*Willuby.*] Sir, is not this a writ of right and is not the exception to the right? why then do they not accord?—*Toudeby.* They can not deny that he is our vilein and that we are seised of him &c. and our predecessors were seised of his father and grandfather and even great-great-grandfather, and we pray judgment &c.—HOWARD. Think you that even if you had brought him, and that your predecessors had brought his father, grandfather, or great-great-grandfather into servitude, and kept them in that condition by grievous distress while perchance their ancestors before them were free, he would be therefore a vilein? (intimating the negative.) —*Toudeby.* Sir, from time whereof there is no memory his ancestors were our vileins, and our predecessors were seised; ready &c.—On another day *Toudeby* repeated the aforesaid exception.—*Tiltone.* Nay, this is a writ of right, as high in the negative as a writ of land is in the affirmative, and is to be terminated by battle or the great assise, and we pray judgment if he can this exception &c.—HENGHAM. By the exception he makes you to be not answerable, and it is wholly to the person. Let the inquest run, and understand that it is at your equal risk, for if it pass against the Abbat the tenements sire noun Dieu; nous vous dioms qe il ne deit a cesti bref user ceste excepcion; car ceo est un bref de dreit, e voet estre trie e terminie par bataille e grante assise.—HOWARD. Pur quei ne pount eux user ceste excepcion?—*Willuby.* Pur ceo qe le bref voet estre termine par bataille ou grante assise.—*Toudeby,* En bref de dreit de play de terre præcipe quod reddat, &c., il serreit bone excepion a reboter la partie de accion, E dautre part, si nous ne fuissoms a ceste excepcion receux, si pledreit nostre vilein ove nous, par quel pleder il serreit enfranchi, e issi se enfranchereit chescon vilein maugre sun seignour.—HOWARD. Vous ne dites nule autre reson pur quei eux ne deivent user ceste excepion mes pur tant qe cestui bref voet estre terminie par bataille ou par grante assise. Sire, nest ceo bref de dreit e la excepcion de dreit? pur quei ne se acordent eux donqes.—*Toudeby.* Il ne poent dedire qil nest nostre vilein, e nous seisi de lui, &c., e nos predecessors seisi de sun pere ael e tresael uncore, e demaundoms jugement, &c.—HOWARD. Quidez vous qe tut fut il issi qe vous lui eussez mene e vos predecessors sun pere ael ou tresael en servage, e leynz tenu par grevouse destresse, e par aventure lour auncestres avant eux furent francs, qil en serra pur ceo vilein? quasi diceret nay.—*Toudeby.* Sire, du temps dount il ny ad memorie ces auncestres nos vileins, e nos predecessors seisi; prest, &c. Ad alium diem repetita excepcione prædicta de *Toudeby,*—*Tiltone.* Nay, ceo est un bref de dreit auxi haut en le negatif com bref de terre en le affirmatif, e voet estre termine par bataille e grante assise, e demaundoms jugement sil puisse ceste excepcion &c.—HENGHAM. Il vous fet par la excepcion noun responable, e est tut a la persone.—IDEM. Courge le enqueste, issi lentendez par ovel chupartie, qe si ele passe

A.D. 1305.

A.D. 1305. will be discharged for ever; but if it pass against R., then R. is a vilein &c.; and do not think that we shall enquire of the seisin by the Abbats of R. or of his father, grandfather, or great-great-grandfather, who perchance were by outrageous distress brought into servitude, but we will enquire of the rightful condition of R. He also said that prescription of time does not bring free blood to servitude, because it is impossible for a free man to procreate a serf.

A count on the form of the gift in a writ of right for the tenements given.

§ *Malmesthorp.* Sheweth unto you Roger de Suthcote, &c., that M., &c., tortiously deforces him, &c.; and tortiously for this, that it is his right and his heritage to him and to the heirs of his body begotten, and whereof he himself was seised to him and the heirs of his body begotten; and if he will deny, &c.—Neither battle nor the great assise can be joined because the mere right is not mentioned.

Fine drawn in a writ of Naif.

§ *Toudeby.* Whereas John Lovel brings this writ of Naif against Henry de Gyte, John acknowledges the said Henry to be a free man and of free condition, and releases and quit claims to him in this Court all manner of naiftys and vilein customs. And for this acknowledgment the said Henry will give forty pounds, and will pay them at such terms; and he specified the terms.

Essoin of being in the King's service falsely cast, &c.

The King's service.

§ The prior of Coventry, who was plaintiff in a plea of trespass, and Sir Robert de Mohaut had pleaded to the inquest; and at the day of the return of the Venire facias Sir Robert essoined himself as being in the King's service. — HENGHAM. Call for the essoigner, &c.—The essoigner answered. — HENGHAM. Do you cast this es-contre labbe les tenements serrount deschargez a touz jours, si encontre R. R. vilein, &c.; e ne entendez pas qe enquergoms de la seisine des abbes de R. ou de sun pere ael ou tresael, les queux par cas furent par outraciouse destresse mis en servage, mes nous enquerroms del estre R. de dreit. IDEM: prescriptio temporis non redigit sanguinem liberum in servitutem, quia esset inpossibile servum procreare liberum. A.D. 1305.

§ Narratio in brevi de recto de tenementis datis in forma donationis.—*Marmisthorp.* Ceo vous moustre Roger de Suthecote, &c., qe, R., &c. atort lui deforce, &c. E pur ceo atort qe ceo est sun droit e sun heritage a lui e a ces heirs de sun corps engendrez e dount il mesme fut seisi a luy e a ces heirs de sun corps engendrez, e si il voille dedire, &c.—Nec duellum nec magna assisa potest jungi quia de mero jure non loquitur, &c.

Pees retrete in bref de neifte.

§ *Toudeby.* La ou Johan Lovel porte cesti bref de neifte vers Henry de Gyte, Johan conust le avandit Henry estre franc homme e de franc estat, e lui relest e quite-cleyme en ceste Court totes maneres de neyftes e de villeines custumes. E pur ceste resconisance, le dit Henry lui dorra .xl. livres e paiera a teu termes, &c.: et nominavit terminos.

De essonio de servicio Regis de falso jacto, &c.

De servicio Regis.

§ Le priour de Coventrey, qe fu pleintif en play de trespas, e Sire Robert de Mohaut avoient plede al enqueste; e au jour del venire facias returne, Sire Robert se fesoit essoigner du service le Roi.—HENGHAM. Demandez le essonour, &c., qi respondit.—HENGHAM. Feites

A.D. 1305. soign for your lord?—*The essoyner.* Yes, sir.—HENGHAM. The essoign does not lie; for the King has sent us word that he is nowhere in his service: and because you have, to the delay of business in the King's Court, falsely cast this essoign, the Court adjudges that you go to prison, and that the said Robert be taken, &c.

That seisin is to be awarded after wager of law if the tenant make default, where the Petit Cape used to issue.

§ HENGHAM said to all the clerks in the Bench,—Take care that henceforth none of you, after the party has denied the summons and thereof waged his law and then at the day when he ought to make his law makes default, do enter the Petit Cape, but seisin of the land.—And this was done judicially a little time afterwards in this term. And the reason was because the first default was not yet done away with; for he did not come with his law, but made default; now the first default was not done away with, and there was default after default; so the judgment is naturally for seisin of the land.

Entry, where the demandant first used a writ of right.

§ A writ of entry was heretofore brought against a man and his wife for five marks of rent. The man made default, so that the tenements were on the point of being lost; the woman came before judgment, and was received, by form of the Statute.[1]—*Herle* (for the woman). We do not think that he ought to be answered, for we tell you that the tenements whence the rent arises are held of us in vileinage, so that we are seised of the demesne, and we pray judgment if against us who are tenants of the demesne, &c., you can demand this rent. Afterwards, this exception being written down, *Herle* said, We tell you that heretofore for these same tenements against our first husband and us you brought

---

[1] 13 Edw. I. c. 3.

vous jetter ceste essoin pur vostre seignour ?—*Essoniator*. Sire, oil.—HENGHAM. Lassoigne ne gist pas ; qar le Roi nous ad mande qil nest nulle parte en sun service. E pur ceo qe vous avez, en delayant les dreitures afere en la Court le Roi, ceste essoigne fausement jette, si agarde, &c., qe vous aillez a la prison e qe le dit Robert soit pris, &c. A.D. 1305.

§ Quod seisina consideretur post legem vadiatam si tenens fecerit defaltam, ubi parvum cape exire solebat. HENGHAM (omnibus clericis in Banco) : Gardez qe desormes nul de vous apres ceo qe la partie eit defendu la somonz, e de ceo gage la ley, e puis, au jour qil se devoit alaier, face defaute, ne entrez mes le petit cape einz seisine de terre. Et hoc factum fuit judicialiter parum post isto termino. Et la cause fust pur ceo ke la primere defaute ne fu pas uncore defete ; kar il ne se alaya mie, eynz fit defaute ; dount la primere defaute nent defete, il iad defaute apres defaute ; dount le jugement est naturelement seisine de terre. Nota.

De ingressu ubi petens primo utebatur brevi de recto.
§ Bref dentre autrefoiz fut porte vers un homme e sa femme de .v. marches de rente. Le homme fist defaute ci qe les tenements furent en point de perdre ; la femme vient avant jugement, e fut receu par forme de statut.—*Herle* (pro eadem). Nous ne entendoms point qil deive estre respondu, car nous vous dioms qe les tenements dount la rente surde sunt tenuz de nous en vileinage, ci qe nous sumes seisi del demeingne, e demaundom jugement si vers nous qe sumes tenans del demeingne, &c., puissez cele rente demaunder. Postea, scripta ista excepione,—*Idem*. Nous vous dioms qe autrefoiz de memes ceux tenements vers nostre primer baroun e nous avez porte vostre bref de droit, a quel bref nous respondimes

A.D. 1305. your writ of Right, to which writ we answered that we were enfeoffed of these tenements by our Lady the Queen, and that the King had confirmed that feoffment, and for that we showed their writings, and we prayed aid of the King, so the plea stayed, and this matter was laid before the Parliament, to which the King answered that he was not advised to render to them their demesne and recompense us to the value; wherefore they were bidden adieu and to wait the King's pleasure, and we were dismissed without day; and we do not think that, since the King is not yet of another way of thinking, we ought to answer them.—HENGHAM. Was the King bound to warranty?—*Herle.* He was bound by law to warrant us, for the tenements were given in exchange.—*Friskeney* His exception is made in two ways; one is that he thinks to abate our writ now, because heretofore we brought a writ of a higher nature; the other is in that he says that heretofore they prayed the King in aid, regarding which he has not yet expressed his pleasure: so it is fit that he hold to one of these ways. — *Herle.* I will have both; for the one shows how the other was used; the process shows that you used the said writ.—HENGHAM to *Herle.* He tells you the truth; you shall not have both.—*Herle.* Heretofore she used a writ of Right against us, and demanded the tenements with others; and we pray judgment if you can now use this writ against us.—*Friskeney.* How for the same tenements?—HENGHAM. He says enough; why should he tell you how? — *Friskeney.* Sir, I put the case that they had demanded from us a manor, within which manor those tenements were comprised; how would they aver that we brought a writ for these same tenements? — HENGHAM. You do not deny it; what need have they to aver it? — *Passeley.* How will he aver it? — *Herle.* By the record.—*Passeley.* Sir, it cannot be denied that a writ of Right was brought, in which writ the View was prayed; but those tenements were not put in View,

qe nous fumes de ceux tenements par madame la Reyne A.D. 1305.
feffez, e qe le Roi cel feffement avoit conferme, e de ceo mustrames leur escritz, e priames aide du Roi, dount la parole targa, e ceste chose fu mis avant au Parlement, a quei le Roi respondy qil ne fu pas avise de rendre a eux lour demesne e faire a nous a la vaillance; par quei dit lour fu qe eux alassent a Dieu attendanz la volonte le Roi, e nous sanz jour; e nentendoms pas, qe de pus qe le Roi nest uncore de autre volonte, qe devoms a eux respondre.—HENGHAM. Fut le Roi tenuz a la garantie? —*Herle.* Il nous devoit de lei garantir, car les tenementz furent donez en eschange. — *Friskeney.* Sa excepcion se prent par deus veies; la une est qil bie abatre nostre bref a ore pur ceo qe autrefoiz avoms porte bref de plus haute nature; lautre est de ceo qil dist qe autrefoiz ount il prie le Roi en aide, de quei il nen ad uncore dit sa volonte; dount il covendreit qil se preigne al une voie.—*Herle.* Jeo averay la une e lautre; qar la une moustre coment lautre fust use; qe le proces moustre qe vous usates le dit bref.—HENGHAM a *Herle.* Il vous dit verite; vous naverez mie la une a lautre.—*Herle.* Autrefoiz ad ele use bref de droit vers nous e demaunde les tenements ove altres; e demaundoms jugement si ceo bref vers nous a ore puissez user.—*Friskeney.* Coment de mesme les tenementz?—HENGHAM. Il dit assez; quei vous dirreit il coment?—*Friskeney.* Sire, jeo pose qe eux ussent demaunde vers nous par maner, de denz quel maner ceux tenements furent compris; coment le avereient eux qe nous portames bref de mesmes ceux tenementz?—HENGHAM. Vous ne le dedites point uncore; quel mester ount il de averer le? *Passeley.* Coment le voleit il averer?—*Herle.* Par record.—*Passeley.* Sire, ne puet estre dedit qil ny avoit un bref de droit porte, a quel bref la vewe fut demaunde; ceux tenements noun

A.D. 1305. ready, &c.—HENGHAM. That is a sophistry; and this place is designed for truth.

§ Mary de Breouse heretofore brought a writ of Dower against Hawise la Sauvage, who held a tenement for the term of her life, and recovered on default; and afterwards the said Hawise brought a writ founded on the Statute,[1] because she lost by default, and recovered on Mary's default; and Mary anew brought a writ, also founded on the Statute, against Hawise, and Hawise vouched to warranty the heir of William de Breouse, by the fine, &c.—*Willuby*, because the clerks would not make an entry that Hawise should hold in peace and that Mary should have from his [the heir's] tenements to the value, rehearsed the whole of the process, and prayed that thus it might be entered.—HENGHAM to *Bourne*. Enter it in those terms.

Formedon in the remainder, &c

§ Although the estates of the donee in writs of Formedon in the remainder and Formedon in the descender, and in Formedon in the reverter the estate of the donor ought regularly to be affirmed; to-wit of the donee, saying by what gift he was seised &c. the esplees &c.; and of the donor, saying which one S. father &c. who of these tenements was seised &c. gave &c., nevertheless one Lettice gave to one Isabel tenements for the term of Isabel's life, and granted that the same tenements which after the death of the said Isabel to her &c. should remain to one William, to have &c. to him and the heirs of his body begotten: and now comes William the son of William and brought a writ &c. in the remainder.—*Stapil.* &c. and for that &c. that Lettice &c. who was seised of these tenements in her demesne &c., the esplees &c., and thus affirming in this writ the estate of her who gave. And this was because she could only hold for term of life. And the writ ran

[1] 13 Edw. I. c. 4.

pas mys en vewe, prest, &c.—HENGHAM. Ceo est sofit- A.D. 1305.
erye; e ceste place est ordine pur verite.

§ Marie de Breouse autrefoiz porta bref de dowerie vers Hawyse la Sauvage, ke tient un tenement a terme de sa vie par vertue de une fin, e rescovery par defaute; e pus mesme ceste Hawyse porta bref par forme de Statut, pur ceo qe ele perdy par defaute, e rescovery par la defaute Marie; e Marie derichef porta bref vers Hawyse auxi par forme de Statut, e Hawyse voucha a garrantie le heir Willem de Breouse par la fin, &c.—*Willuby,* pur ceo qe les clers ne voleient entrer qe Hawyse tenist en pees, e qe Marie eut des tenements mesme celi a la vaillance, rehersa tut ceo proces e pria qe ensi fust entre.—HENGHAM a *Bourne.* Entrez le ensi.

De forma donationis in le remanere, &c.

§ Licet status donatorii in brevibus de forma donationis videlicet in le remanere et descendere et in le reverti status donatoris regulariter debeant affirmari sic, scilicet de donatorio dicendo par quel doun, il fu seisi &c., les esplez &c., et similiter de donatore les queux un S. pere &c. qe de ces tenements fu seisi &c. dona &c., tamen une Letice dona a une Isabele tenant a terme de la vie Isabele, e granta qe mesme les tenementz qe apres la mort Isabele a lui &c., remeinassent a un Willem, a aver &c. a lui e as heirs de son corps engendrez; e ore vient Willem le fiz Willem e porta bref &c. en la remanere.—*Stapill* &c., e pur ceo &c., qe Letice &c., qe de ces tenements fu seisi en sun demesne &c. les esplez &c., e issi afferme en ceo bref lestat cele qe dona. Et hoc fuit quia habere non potuit nisi ad terminum vitæ. Et fuit breve tale; quæ Letitia

A.D. 1305. thus;—which Lettice gave to Isabel for the term of her life; and which after the deaths of the said Isabel and of William father of the said William, whose heir &c., to the said William ought to remain, by the form of the aforesaid gift.—*Toudeby* challenged the writ, because it did not mention the form which entailed the tenements in the person of the father, and he claimed as heir of his father.—But the objection was not allowed, and the writ stood.

Note. An essoin quashed, before the King.

§ The Bishop of Durham had appointed his general attorney in the Chancery, and a special attorney in a plea of Trespass against the Prior of Durham; and that special attorney caused himself to be essoined.—*Herle.* We tell you that there is another general attorney who is not essoined; now, when there are two attorneys and one is essoined and the other is not, they both make default; and we pray judgment &c.; for it is not as if the general attorney had appointed the special attorney, for then the excuse of the latter would have been the excuse of the former, because he would have been in his place and have represented his person.—And the essoin was quashed. And the Bishop came.

Waste. § Piers Picot brought the writ against Heloise, and said that whereas she held, of his inheritance, the third part of the manor of Radeclif, she had committed waste, sale, and exile &c.—*Tiltone* denied &c., and (said he) We tell you that this same Heloise was from such a time to such a time under coverture of one S. formerly her husband, within which time if damage was done, it was not of her doing; and we pray judgment if for that time we ought to answer. And as to the remainder of the time, we say, No waste, ready &c.—*Willuby.* Then do you offer to say that the waste was committed in the time of your husband? let us be agreed as to that, and await dedit Isabellæ &c. ad terminum vitæ sue. Et que post mortem prefatæ Isabellæ et Willelmi patris prædicti Willelmi, cujus heres &c., prefato Willelmo &c. remanere debent per formam donationis prædictæ.—*Toudeby* chalanga le bref pur ceo qil ne parla mie de la forme qe se tailla en la persone sun pere, e il clama com heir sun pere. Et non allocatur, sed stetit breve. A.D. 1305.

De essonio cassato coram Rege.

§ Leveske de Durem avoit fet sun atturne general en la Chauncelerie, e un atturne especial en un play de trespas vers le Priour de Durem; e cele atturne especial se fit essoner.—*Herle.* Nous vous dioms qil ad un autre atturne general nent essone; dount quant deus atturnez sunt, e le un soit essone e lautre nent, il fount ambedeux defaute; e demaundoms jugement &c.; car il nest pas auxi com si le general atturne ust fet le especial atturne, qar adonqes la excusation de ly eust excuse lautre pur ceo qil fust en sun leu e representa sa persone. Et cassatum fuit essonium. Et episcopus venit. Nota.

§ Peres Picot porta le bref vers une Helewyse e dit qe la ou ele tyent de sun heritage la terce partie du maner de Radeclif, ele avoit fet wast, vente, e exil &c. —*Tiltone* defendi, e vous dioms qe mesme cele Helewyse fut de un S. jadis sun baroun de teu temps jekes a cel temps coverte, denz quel temps si damage fu fet ceo ne fu pas sun fet; e demaundom jugement si de cel temps deive respondre. E quant a tut le remenant du temps &c. nul wast, prest &c.—*Willuby.* Donqes volez vous dire qe le wast fu fet en temps vostre baroun? seoms a un de cel, e demoroms en De vasto.

A.D. 1305. judgment.—*Tiltone.* I have nothing to do with anything done during that time, for I ought not to answer for that time.—HENGHAM. A plea was pending for a long time in this Court, on the same exception, in the time of Sir John de Metingham, and the woman died before judgment could be given, so that no judgment was given. Therefore we wish to consider the matter.—*Wil-luby.* The case was not altogether the same, for in the other case the woman held for life by a limitation to her personally.

Warranty of charter.

§ One S. de B. brought the writ against one John de Sullinges &c., and counted that tortiously he did not warrant to him &c.; and tortiously for this, that whereas his father J. de Sullinges, whose heir &c., gave &c., and bound himself and his heirs &c., for which tenements one A. de B. brought the Assise of Novel Disseisin before &c. on such a day &c., in which time the aforesaid J. de Sullinges was dead; so this same S. often during that assise approached &c., and prayed him to warrant; but he would not, and refused, tortiously and to his damage &c.—*Passeley* denied &c., and (said he) We tell you that we ought not to warrant; for we tell you that the nine acres &c. were given in frank-marriage to our father &c. with our mother, and were by our father sold, so that we have an action to recover the same tenements. As to four acres, they were given in the like manner to our grandfather with our grandmother.—*Tiltone.* You can not oust us by that, for your mother is alive, and you can not in her lifetime have an action.—*Passeley* said as before, and (said he) Together with this we tell you that nothing has descended to us from our father by whose deed &c.—*Hamptone.* Assets have descended to you, ready &c.—And the other side said the contrary.—Therefore &c.—And here, as it is thought, *Hamptone* did too feintly hold to the exception which Tiltone took, jugement.—*Tiltone.* Jeo nay qe fere de nul fet fet en cel temps, car ne dey de cel temps respondre.—HENGHAM. Un plee pendy lungement en ceste Court pur mesme la excepcion en temps Sire J. de Methingham, e pus morust la femme einz qe jugement poeit estre rendu, ci qe nul jugement fust rendu. E pur ceo, nous voloms estre avise.—*Willuby.* Ne fu pas tot un cas, qar en lautre cas la femme tyent a terme de vie par une forme qe se tailla en sa persone. A.D. 1305.

De warantia cartæ.

§ Un S. de B. porta le bref vers un Johan de Sullingges &c., e conta ke atort ne lui garantist &c. E pur ceo atort, qe la ou sun pere J. de Sullyngges, qi heir &c., dona &c., e obliga lui e ces heirs &c., des queux tenementz un A. de B. porta lassise de novele disseisine devant &c., tiel jor &c., en queux temps lavandit J. de Sullyngges fu mort, dount mesme cesti S. sovent pendant cele assise aprocha &c., e pria qe ilui garantist, il ceo fere ne voleit, einz le dedit, atort e ces damages &c.—*Passeley* defendi &c., e vous dioms qe garantir ne devoms; qe nous vous dioms qe les ix. acres &c. furent donez en franc-mariage a nostre pere &c. ove nostre mere, e furent par nostre pere vendu, issi qe nous avoms accion de rescoverir mesme les tenements. En droit de .iiii. acres en meme la forme done a nostre ael ove nostre aele.—*Tiltone.* Par tant ne vous poez ouster, car vostre mere est en pleine vie, vivant qi accion ne poez aver.—*Passeley.* Idem quod prius, e ovesqe ceo vous dioms qe rienz nous est descenduz par nostre pere par my qi fet &c.—*Hamptone.* Assez vous est descenduz, prest &c. Et alii e contra. Ideo &c. Et hic ut creditur nimis ficte tenuit se Hamptone ad excepcionem quam Tiltone proposuit,

A.D. 1305. that during the life of the mother, who was a party to the gift, the issue could not have an action. Some are of the contrary opinion, because if he now warranted he would not have his recovery &c. And nevertheless he may have an action to recover.

A voucher shall not recover to the value of the tenement for which &c. in the state in which it was at the time of the alienation, although it be improved.

§ Elizabeth who was the wife of Thomas Gerberge by her attorney sued Roger Clerk for the moiety of a messuage with the appurtenances in Great Yarmouth, and sued Thomas Prentis for the moiety of a messuage with the appurtenances in the same vill. And Roger and Thomas came by attorney, and again vouched to warranty John son of Thomas Gerberge, who now came, on summons, by his attorney, and prayed that it might be shewn to him by virtue of what he was bound to warrant to them. And the said Roger and Thomas produce here two charters, in the name of the aforesaid Thomas the father &c., one of which witnesses that the said Thomas the father &c. gave to the said Roger a moiety of one rengiate of land with the buildings and appurtenances in the aforesaid vill; and the other witnesses that the said Thomas the father &c. gave to the said Thomas Prentiz a moiety of one rengiate of land with the buildings and appurtenances in the said vill, to hold to the said Roger and to Thomas Prentiz and to their respective heirs severally, and bound himself and his heirs to warranty &c. And John well acknowledged that the aforesaid charters are the deed of his said father Thomas, but he says that the said tenements were built and improved by the said tenants after the feoffments which the said Thomas &c. to them thereof made, &c., whereof he warrants to them in the same state in which the said Thomas the father &c. enfeoffed the said tenants of the said tenements, and by leave renders to the said Elizabeth quia vivente matre, parte dono, exitui nulla competit accio. Contraria est quorumdam oppinio quia si modo warantizaverit non poterit habere suum recuperationem &c. Et tamen recuperandi habeat accionem. A.D. 1305.

Quod vocator non recuperabit ad valentiam tenementorum unde &c. in statu in quo tempore alienacionis fuerint, licet meliorentur.

§ Elizabetha quæ fuit uxor Thome Gerberge per attornatum suum petit versus Rogerum le Clerk medietatem unius messuagii cum pertinentiis in Magna Jernemuth, et versus Thomam Prentiz medietatem unius mesuagii cum pertinentiis in eadem villa. Et Rogerus et Thomas per attornatum suum veniunt, et alias vocant inde ad warrantiam Johannem filium Thomæ Gerberge, qui modo venit per summonitionem per attornatum suum et petit sibi ostendi per quod eis warrentizare debeat. Et prædicti Rogerus et Thomas proferunt hic duas cartas sub nomine prædicti Thomæ patris &c. quarum una testatur quod idem Thomas pater &c. dedit eidem Rogero medietatem unius rengiate terræ cum edificiis et pertinentiis in prædicta villa. Et alia testatur quod idem Thomas pater &c. dedit predicto Thomæ Prentiz medietatem unius rengiate terre cum edificiis et pertinentiis in eadem villa, tenendas eidem Rogero et Thome Prentiz et heredibus suis sigillatim, et obligavit se et heredes suos ad warantiam, &c. Et Johannes bene cognovit prædictas cartas esse factum predicti Thome patris sui, sed dicit quod predicta tenementa edificata sunt et meliorata per ipsos tenentes post feoffamenta quæ predictus Thomas &c. eis inde fecit &c., unde in eodem statu quo prædictus Thomas pater, &c. ipsos tenentes de prædictis tenementis feoffavit eis warantizat; et per licentiam reddidit præ-

A.D. 1305. her said dower &c.—So it is considered that the said Roger and Thomas do hold in peace; and that the said Elizabeth shall have of the land of John, in a fit place, to the value of the said moieties, according to the state in which they were in the seisin of the said Thomas formerly her husband, of whose endowment, &c.

One delivered to the Bishop's prison, is not to be answered in the King's Court or in any plea until &c.

§ One William de Gerberge brought his writ of Account against one R.—*Este.* On this writ or on any other he ought not to be answered; for we tell you that he was arraigned for felony before Sir H. &c. justices &c., when he pleaded his clergy, and the said justices took an inquest on his condition, the better to know why he should be delivered to the Bishop; and we do not think that he ought in this Court or in any other to be answered.—*Herle.* At least you cannot say that he was condemned, or that he put himself on that inquest, or that by it he is condemnable; so by nothing that you have yet said can you rebut him. And on the other hand, if you do not answer him, there might be perchance damage to the King; for if he were to dereign against R. this account which may perchance be in arrear to him, thereby the King would have the advantage, for he would have his chattels, since he could not purge himself.—HENGHAM. This exception is equivalent to the exception of excommunication which rebuts until the time of absolution; and this rebuts until the time of purgation. Let R. go without day, and let William take nothing, &c.

Novel Disseisin. § One John, son of Giles de Breux, brought the assise of Novel disseisin against Ralph de Monthermer Earl of Gloucester and Joan his wife, and complained that he was disseised of certain tenements &c. Ralph and Joan came by bailiff, and claimed wardship in the tenements dictæ Elizabethe prædictam dotem suam, &c. Ideo consideratum est quod prædicti Rogerus et Thomas Prentiz teneant in pace. Et prædicta Elizabetha habeat de terra Johannis in loco competenti ad valentian prædictorum medietatum secundum statum in quo fuerint in sesina prædicti Thomæ quondam viri sui de cujus dotatione, &c. A.D. 1305.

Quod liberatus prisone Episcopi non est respondendus in curia Regis seu aliquo placito quousque, &c.

§ Un Willeam de Gerberge porta sun bref daccounte vers un R. — *Este.* Il ne deit a cestui bref ne a nul autre estre respondu; car nous vous dioms qil fut devant Sire H., &c., justices, &c. de felonie aresne, ou il se prist a sa clergie, ou mesmes cestes justices pristrent une enqueste de sun estre, de saver mon pur quei il serreit al eveske livere; e ne entendoms pas quil deive en ceste Court ne en nule autre estre respondu.—*Herle.* Au meins vous ne poez dire qil soit dampne, ou qe en cele enqueste se mist, ou par cele soit dampnable; dount par rienz qe vous avez uncore dit ne lui poez reboter. E dautre parte, si vous ne lui respondissez, il serreit par cas damage au Roi, car sil dereingnast vers R. ceste acounte qe serreit par cas en arrere vers luy, de tant averoit le Roi avantage qe averoit sun chateal, de pus qil ne se poeit purger. —Hengham. Ceste excepcion est equipollent a la excepcion de escomingement qe reboute taunt qe au temps de absolucion; e issi ceste taunt qe au temps de purgacion.—Idem. Aille R. sanz jour e Willeam rien ne preigne, &c.

§ Un Johan le fiz Giles de Breux porta lassise de novele disseisine vers Rauf de Mounthermer Counte de Gloucestre e Jone sa femme, e se pleint estre disseisi de certeinz tenementz &c. Rauf e Johane viendrent par baillif, e clamerent garde en les tenementz par resoun

Nova disseisina.

A.D. 1305. by reason of the nonage of the said John; for they said that his father Giles held of them those tenements by knight-service, and they said that they at that time claimed nothing else, and they would go to the assise.—THE ASSISE came and told how the tenements put in view were at a certain time in the seisin of one Nicholas de Meules, who held those tenements of Gilbert de Clare, formerly Earl of Gloucester, by knight-service; which Nicholas out of his seisin gave the same tenements to one William de Breux in frank-marriage with Agnes his daughter; William and Agnes were seised by virtue of that gift; Earl Gilbert came and distreined William de Breux so severely and often, that by reason of the force and the outrageous distress he attorned to him (the Earl) for his homage and for escuage; and they said that after the deaths of William and Agnes, Giles by extortion attorned to Gilbert for his homage, and afterwards of his own free will after the death of Gilbert, attorned for his fealty to Ralph de Monthermer the husband of Joan: and they said that, after Giles's death, Earl Ralph entered claiming the wardship of John son of Giles; and that John came and wished to have entered after his father's death, and that the Earl would not allow him. The parties, on this verdict, were adjourned into the Bench to hear their judgment. They came into the Bench before Sir RALPH DE HENGHAM and his companions.—*Herle.* (for the infant). Sir, we pray judgment for the infant under age; for we do not think that you have any warrant by the verdict to go to judgment as to him, since you have found that the tenements were in the seisin of Nicholas who held those tenements in chief of Earl Gilbert, and that Nicholas out of his seisin gave them to William &c. in frank-marriage, since a tenant in frank-marriage shall by common right hold always of him to whom the reversion belongs, if it be not said in his feoffment that he is to hold of some other; and by no attornment which William made to the Earl for his del noun age mesme celui Johan ; car il diseint qe sun A.D. 1305. pere Giles tient de eux ceux tenementz par service de chivaler, e disoient qe autre chose ne clamerent quant adonqes, e cheirent en la assise.—LASSISE vient e conta teu count, qe les tenementz qe furent mys en la vewe furent en ascon temps en la seisine un Nichole de Meules, qe ceux tenementz tient de Gilbert de Clare, jadis Counte de Gloucestre, par service de chivaler, le quel Nichole hors de sa seisine dona mesme les tenementz a un Willem de Breux en franc-mariage ove Agnes sa fille; Willem e Agnes seisi par cel doun; le Counte Gilbert vient e distreint si forte Willem de Breux e si sovent, qe par force e par outraciouse destresse il se atturna a lui e de son homage e escuage ; e disoient qe apres la mort Willem e Agnes, Giles se atturna de son homage a Gilbert par extorsion, e pus de sa bone volunte de sa fealte se atturna a Rauf de Monthermer baroun Jone apres la mort Gilbert : et diseint qe apres la mort Giles le Counte Rauf entra en clamant la garde de Johan le fiz Giles; Johan vient e voleit aver entre apres la mort sun pere, e le Counte ne le voleit suffrir. Les parties suz ceo verdit ajornez en baunk de oier lour jugement; viendrent en Baunk devant SIRE RAUF DE HENGHAM e ces compagnons.—*Herle* (pur lenfant). Sire, nous prioms jugement pur lenfant denz age ; car nous entendoms qe vous avez garant par le verdit de aler a jugement pur lui, del hour qe vous avez trove qe les tenementz furent en la seisine Nichole qe ceux tenementz tient en chief du Counte Gilbert, e qe Nichole hors de sa seisine les dona a Willem &c., en franc mariage, del houre qe tenant en franc mariage de comune droit tendra tut veirs de celui a qi la reversion apent si il ne soit assigne en sun feffement a tenir de autre ; qe par nul atturnement qe Willem fit au

A.D. 1305. service, which attornment was obtained by extortion and outrageous distress, can the present Earl claim wardship in the tenements.—*Hertepol.* If any judgment can be given now, it must be for the Earl, since it is found that Earl Gilbert was seised by the hand of William de Breux of his homage and his escuage, which are services which give wardship and marriage; and afterwards that Giles attorned to the present Earl for his fealty, in recognition of his seignory; but now we say that without other information you can not give judgment; for it is found that Giles attorned for his fealty to Ralph, and it was not enquired whether he attorned to Ralph in right of Ralph or in right of Joan his wife; wherefore it seems that, without your being informed as to that, you can not go on to give that judgment. — *Scoter.* There is no need for that; for you can not in any manner claim wardship of him; Nicholas de Meules remains still your tenant for the same tenements; wherefore you can not demand the wardship of us, if it be not by reason of wardship of wardship, and that you can not do.—BEREFORD. It is found &c. (and he rehearsed all the verdict), and it is found that Giles the father of John, whose heir he is, attorned for his fealty to Ralph, we know not why nor for what reason: wherefore it seems that we need information thereon.—*Wescote.* There is no need of it, since you have found by the verdict the main matter, that Nicholas de Meules held those tenements of Gilbert in chief, and that Nicholas out of his seisin gave them to William in frank-marriage, inasmuch as they can not have any other estate in the seignory than Gilbert had; and if they have Gilbert's estate, they have a way to demand the wardship and the marriage of the son of Nicholas if he be under age, by reason that Nicholas is their very tenant, and consequently claim no wardship of the heir of Giles; wherefore it seems that, inasmuch as the thing is found, there is no need of further information.—*Passeley.* If I have a tenant who holds of me, before he can

Counte de sun service qe fust par extorsion e par outra- A.D. 1305.
ciouse destresse puisse le Counte qe ore est garde en les tenementz clamer. —*Hertepol.* Si nul jugement se deust faire quant a ore, ceo serreit pur le Counte, del houre qe trove est qe le Counte Gilbert fu seisi par my la mayn Willem de Breux de son homage e de son escuage, qe sunt services qe donnent garde e mariage; e pus qe Giles se atturna a Counte qe ore est de sa fealte en resconisance de sa seignorye: mes ore dioms qe sanz autre avisement ne poez nent doner jugement; qar trove est qe Giles se atturna de sa fealte a Rauf, e ne fu pas enquis le quel il se atturna a Rauf com du droit Rauf ou com du droit Jone sa femme; par quei il semble qe sanz estre avise de ceo vous ne poez mie aler avant a cel jugement rendre.—*Scoter.* Ceo nest mie mestier, qar vous ne poez en nulle manere garde de lui clamer; qe Nichole de Meules si demoert uncore vostre tenant de mesmes les tenementz; par quei vous ne poez la garde de nous demaunder si il ne fust par reson de garde de garde, e ceo ne poez nent faire.—BEREFORD. Trove est &c., e rehersa tut le verdist, e trove est qe Giles le pere Johan, qi heir il est, se atturna de sa feaute a Rauf, nous ne savoms pur quei ne par quele reson; par quei il me semble qe mestier serreit de avisement de ceo.—*Wescote.* Ceo nest mie mestier, del houre qe vous avez trove par. verdit le gros, qe Nichole de Meules tyent ceux tenementz de Gilbert en chief, e qe Nichole hors de sa seisine les dona a Willem en franc mariage, tant com il ne pount autre estat aver en ceste seignorie qe Gilbert ne avoit, e sil eient lestat Gilbert il ount veie a demaunder la garde e le mariage del fiz Nichole sil soit denz age, par reson qe Nicole est lour verrei tenant, e par consequent nulle garde clamer del heir Giles; par quei il semble qil ne bosoigne mie tant com ceste chose est trove de autre avisement. -- *Passeley.* Si jeo ey un tenant qe tiegne

A.D. 1305. estrange himself, it is necessary that he devest himself and put another in his place, and that the other attorn on the assignment; but now we tell you that Nicholas remained always Gilbert's tenant, and did not put any other in his place to hold of the chief lord of the fee; and since he remains still their tenant, we have our acquittance against him as against a lord; and we pray judgment if he can claim the wardship of us. (On the same side.) In this case of frank-marriage, after it has come to the fourth degree, he to whom the reversion belongs will have an action to demand from the tenant the like services as are demanded from him, and the wardship and marriage of his son; wherefore it seems that notwithstanding that usurpation of services which he usurped he is wholly a stranger to that seignory which he now claims.—*Scrope.* If a man were enfeoffed in fee, before the Statute,[1] without mention being made of whom he is to hold, the law supposes that he shall hold of the feoffor rather than of any other; a multo fortiori then when the feoffment is in fee-tail.—BEREFORD. Do not rely too much on that maxim; for if the lord in the case you put can snatch the possession it will be very difficult to oust him.—*Herle.* Although those to whom the gift was made desired to have charged the tenements by a fine levied or by some other means, that would not be prejudicial to the infant, so as to prevent him from recovering the estate which was granted to him by the form.—BEREFORD. Is it not possible that the tenements were given in frank-marriage to hold of the chief &c.? we do not know this.—*Herle.* At the time we pleaded we put forward a charter which purported that they were not given &c.: join the deed with the verdict and then you

Judgment. have a full verdict.—[BEREFORD]. Because it is found by the verdict of the assise that Nicholas de Meules was rightfully the Earl's tenant of the tenements whereof Nicholas enfeoffed William and Agnes in frank-marriage;

---

[1] Quia emptores. 18 Edw. I. c. 1.

de moy, einz qil se puisse estranger il covent qil se demette e qil assigne un autre en sun leu e qe lautre se atturne par sun assignment; mes ore vous dioms qe Nichole demora tut veirs le tenant Gilbert e ne assigna nul autre en sun lu a tenir de chief seignorage du fee; e de pus qil demoert uncore lour tenant, nous avoms nostre aquitance vers lui com vers seignur; e demaundom jugement sil puisse la garde de nous clamer. (Ad idem). En ceo cas de franc-mariage, apres ceo qil est venu en le quarte degree celui a qi la reversion apent avera accion a demaunder du tenant autel services com sunt demaunde de lui, e garde e mariage de sun fiz; par quei il semble qe nent contre esteant cel acrochement des services qil acrocha qil est tut estrange a ceste seignorye qil cleime a ore.—*Scrop.* Si un homme soit feffe en fee avant statut sanz faire mencion de qi il tendra, ley suppose qil tendra plus tost du feffour qe de nul autre; a mult plus forte en fee taille.—BEREFORD. Ne vous fondez trop en cel maxime; qe si le seignur en le cas qe vous mettez puisse happer la possession il est mult forte de luy oster.—*Herle.* Me qe ceaux a qi le doun se fit voussissent aver charge les tenementz par fin leve ou en autre manere, ceo ne serreit mie prejudiciel al enfant qil ne rescovereit lestat qe grante lui est par my la forme.—BEREFORD. Nest il possible qe les tenementz furent donez en franc-mariage a tenir des chiefs &c.; e ceo ne savoms mye.—*Herle.* A cel houre qe nous pledames nous meymes avant une chartre qe voleit qil ne furent mie donez &c.; joinez le fet od le verdit e donqes avez plein verdit. E pur ceo qe trove est par verdit de assise qe Nichole de Meules fust le tenant le Counte de droit des tenementz des queles Nichole enfeffa Willem e Agnes en franc-mariage; tant com de comune droit

A.D. 1305.

Judicium.

A.D. 1305. and as by common right a tenant in frank-marriage ought to be quit of all manner of services until the third degree be passed, and the attornment procured by extortion and outrageous distress does not give a good title of seignory; this court adjudges that John do recover his seisin &c. and that the other be in mercy.

Before the King.

§ The King to the sheriff of Norfolk greeting. If Roger de Honeworth shall make you &c. then put &c. Roger Blesard that he be before &c. wheresoever &c. to answer as well us as the aforesaid Roger de Honeworth, why a certain writ of ours by means of a fine of 40s. paid to our use for getting that writ, in the names of the said Roger de Honeworthe and Alice formerly his wife who were totally ignorant of it, he fraudulently and maliciously obtained, to the deceit of our court and the heavy damage of the said R. de Honeworth. And have &c.

Quit-claim a bar in a writ of Right.

§ In a writ of Right the tenant put forward a quit-claim by the ancestor of the demandant from whom he took title &c.—*Hedone.* This is a writ of Right whereof the issue is naturally by battle or the great assise, and it may well be that after the quit-claim &c., which we do not admit, our ancestor was seised, which seisin is not denied; and we pray judgment &c. And notwithstanding this, he was driven by HENGHAM to answer to the quit-claim.

Ejectment from wardship: before BRABAZON.

§ Mary who was the wife of William de Breouse brought a writ against William de Breouse and others named &c., and counted that whereas the wardship of one messuage and two virgates of land with the appurtenances in Westgrenested, by reason of the nonage of the heir of one James de Byne, until the full age of the said heir belonged to her, because the said James &c. held the said messuage and two virgates of land of her by tenant en franc-mariage deit estre quites de totes maneres des services jeckes au tant qil soit passe le tiers degree, e tel attornement par extorsion e par outraciouse destresse ne fet pas dreit title de seignurye, agarde ceste Court qe Johan rescovere sa seisine &c. e lautre en la mercy. A.D. 1305.

§ Rex vicecomiti Norfolciensi salutem. Si Rogerus de Honeworthe fecerit te &c. tunc pone &c. Rogerum Blesard quod sit coram &c. ubicumque &c. ad respondendum, tam nobis quam præfato Rogero de Honeworthe, quare quoddam breve nostrum, per finem xl. *s.* pro brevi illo ad opus nostrum capiendam, nomine prædicti Rogeri de Honeworthe et Aliciæ quondam uxoris ejus hoc penitus ignorantium, fraudulenter et maliciose inpetravit in decepcionem curiæ nostræ et grave dampnum ipsius R. de Honeworthe. Et habeas &c. Coram Rege.

Quite-clamance barre en bref de droit.

§ Qe en un bref de droit le tenant mist avant quiteclamance del auncestre le demaundant de qi il prist title &c.—*Hedone.* Ceo est un bref de droit, dount naturelment est le issue par bataille ou graunte assise, e purra bien estre qe apres la quiteclamance &c., la quele nous ne grantoms point, nostre auncestre fu seisi, quele seisine nest nent dedite, e demaundoms jugement, &c. Et hoc non obstante fu chace a respondre a la quiteclamance par HENGHAM.

De ejectione custodiæ coram BRABAZONE.

§ Marie qe fu la femme Willem de Breouse porta bref vers Willem de Breouse e autres nomez &c., e conta qe com la garde de un mees e de deus verges de terre ove les appurtenances en Westgrenested par reson del noun age del heir un James de Byne jeckes al leal age le dit heir a lui aparteneit pur ceo qe le dit James &c. cel mees celes deus verges de terre tyent de luy par service de

A.D. 1305. knight-service, namely by fealty and by the services of the tenth part of a knight's fee, and the said Mary was in full and peaceable seisin of that wardship,—yet there came the aforesaid William &c. such a day &c., such a year &c., and the said Mary from that wardship with force and arms &c. namely &c. ejected, and cast out the goods (so many), and the goods and chattels of the said Mary, namely &c. to the value &c. there found took and carried away, and other damage &c.—And the writ ran thus "wherefore whereas "the wardship &c. by reason of the nonage of the heir of "James de Byne."—*Hunte.* Judgment of the writ; for it does not specify the baptismal name of the heir, which it was necessary to do since he is the cause of the wardship.—*Kinge.* There is good and there is better; this form is good enough.—*Wescote.* To our writ where we gave a certain name to the heir, you traversed that name, and thereby abated our writ here; now if in this writ we had given a certain name, you would also perchance have traversed it, and thereupon have offered an averment; so it seems that this form is better.—And note that the said Mary brought a similar writ against other persons, in which she named the heir by his proper name; and the defendants excepted that the ancestor had not an heir named W. but had an heir named R.; and she was not able to deny this, and the writ was quashed on the same day.—Roubyri adjudged the writ to be good, and told *Hunte* to answer over. — *Hunte.* We tell you that James de Byne held of our father William, whose heir &c., the aforesaid messuage and the land for which &c. by homage, fealty and knight-service, namely &c., of which services he was seised, and we ourselves after his death were seised. And we tell you that the said James died in our homage; after whose death we entered on the said tenements, as those the wardship whereof &c. by reason of the nonage &c., and we were seised, on which seisin this same Mary tried to abate, which abatement we did not permit; and other ejectment we did not

chivaler, nomement par fealte e par les services de la A.D. 1305.
dyme partie de un fee de chivaler, e mesme cele Marie en pleine e pesible seisine de cele garde estoit, La viendrent les avantdiz Willem &c. tel jour &c. tel an &c., e mesme ceste Marie de cele garde a force e as armes &c., nomement &c., la enjetterent, e les bens tant enjetterent, e les biens e les chateaux mesme ceste Marie nomement &c., a la vaillance &c. illoqes trovez pristrent e enporterent, altres leds &c. Et fuit breve tale, "quare cum custodia &c. "ratione minoris etatis heredis Jacobi de Byne."—*Hunte*. Jugement du bref; qar il ne nome mil certein noun de baptesme del heir, qe fere luy covendreit, de pus qil est cause de la garde.—*Kinge*. Il y ad bone e meillour, e ceste forme est assez bone. —*Wescote*. A nostre bref ou nous donames certein noun del heir vous estes traverse de cel noun, e par tant avez nostre bref ore einz abatu; dount si en ceo bref ussoms certein noun issi nome, ensi par cas vous eussez traverse, e sur ceo tendu averement, dount il semble ceste forme meuz valer. Et memorandum quod eadem Maria tulit consimile breve versus alias personas in quo nominavit hæredem proprio nomine. Et defendentes exceperunt quod antecessor non habuit hæredem W. nomine, immo R. Et illa hoc non posse dedicere; cassabatur breve eodem die. — ROUBYRI agarda le bref bon; e dit a *Hunte* qil respondesit outre. — *Hunte*. Nous vous dioms qe James de Byne entient de Willem nostre pere, qi heir &c., les avantdiz mees e la terre de quei &c., par homage, fealte, e par services de chivaler, nomement &c., des queux services il fu seisi, e nous mesmes apres sun deces seisi &c. Et vous dioms qe mesme cestui James morust en nostre homage; apres qi mort nous entrames mesmes ceux tenementz com ceux des queux la garde &c. par resoun del noun-age &c., e seisi fumes, sur quele seisine mesme ceste Marie voleit estre abatue, quel abatement nous ne suffrimes point, e

A.D. 1305. commit; ready &c.—*Wescote.* We will admit that his father William was seised &c. by the hand of James &c., and we tell you that after the death of the said William our lord the King seized the wardship of the lands of the said William by reason of the nonage of the heir of the said William, because he held of the King in chief; we sued out of the Chancery a writ to the escheator, on which writ the services of the said James were assigned to us by way of dower; on which assignment the said James attorned to us, and we were seised of his fealty and the other services which give wardship for 13 years; and he died in fealty to us; after whose death we entered those tenements as those &c. and were seised for five months and more, until &c.—*Hunte.* What have you to show the assignment?—*Wescote.* We have no need to answer as to that, for you do not deny it.—ROUBYRI. There seems to be no need for them to show what they have to prove the assignment, since you do not deny it; so the Court takes it for granted.—*Hunte.* Dower would be assigned to her by one of two ways, either by the heir of full age, or by a writ out of the Chancery; and we tell you that neither by one way nor by the other were these services assigned, ready &c.—*Wescote.* We are not pleading in a writ of right of wardship, but in a writ of ejectment, where it is sufficient for us to maintain that we were seised of the wardship.—*King.* He cannot counterplead the assignment, for see here his deed, by which, we being in seisin, he ratified the assignment; and we pray judgment if against that deed &c.—And the deed of confirmation being read, *Toudeby* said, Sir, we tell you that this same James de Byne held divers tenements in Westgrenested, namely a messuage, a virgate of land, about which there is no plea now, as appurtenant to the manor of Westgrenested, which to this same Mary were assigned &c., and another messuage and two virgates of land held of the honour of the castle of Brember whereof that William the father &c. was lord;

altre enjettement ne lui feimes point, e prest &c.—*Wescote.* Nous conussons bien qe Willem sun pere fu seisi &c. par my la mayn James &c., e vous dioms qe apres la mort mesme cestui Willem nostre seignur le Roi seisi la garde des terres le dit Willem par resoun del nonage le heir le dit Willem, pur ceo qil tient du Roi en chief; issi qe nous suymes bref hors de la Chancelerie al eschetor, par quel bref les services le dit James nous furent assignez en noun de dowere; par quel assignement meme cesti James se attorna a nous, e nous seisi de sa fealte e des altres services qe donnent garde par xiii. aunz, e morust en nostre fealte, apres qi mort nous entrames ceux tenementz com ceaux &c. e seisi fumes par v. moys e plus, taunt qe &c.—*Hunte.* Quei avez del assignement?—*Wescote.* A ceo navoms mester a respondre, qe vous ne le dedites point.—ROUBYRI (ad idem). Il ne semble mie estre mester a moustrer ceo qe eux ount del assignement, de pus qe vous ne le dedites point; dount la Court la tient agrante.—*Hunte.* Par un de deus veies lui serreit dowere assigne, ou par le heir de plein age ou par bref hors de la Chauncelerie; e vous dioms qe par la une voye ne par lautre luy furent ces services assignez, e prest &c.—*Wescote.* Nous ne pledoms pas au bref de droit de garde einz a lenjettement, ou assez nous est a meintenir qe nous fumes seisi de la garde.—*King.* Countrepleder le assignement ne puet il, car veez cy sun fet, par quel en nostre seisine il ratefia le assignement; e demaundoms jugement si encontre cel fet &c. Et lecto scripto confirmationis, *Toudeby.* Sire, nous vous dioms qe mesme cestui James de Byne entient divers tenementz en Westgrenested, nomement un mees, une verge de terre, dount il ny ad ore plee, com appurtenant au maner de Westegrenested, les queux a mesme ceste Marie furent assignez &c., et un altre mees e deus verges de terre del honor del chastel de Brember, dount mesme celui Willem pere &c. estoit seignur, apres qi mort mesme cesti A.D. 1305.

A.D. 1305. after whose death the said James to this said William did homage and the other services &c., and died in homage to him; which messuage and two virgates of land, of which the plea &c., are holden of the manor of Westgrenested and were assigned &c., and are not holden of the honour of the castle of Brember, ready &c. And the other side said the contrary. So &c.

Taking of beasts.

§ John Deyncourt complained that Joan who was the wife of John Wake tortiously took his beasts &c.—*Herle.* We avow the taking &c., and for the reason &c. that &c. holds the manor of Chesterton, in right of which manor she has the wapentake of N., and by reason of which wapentake she has the sheriff's aid. And because the vill of N. is assessed at three shillings yearly to the aid &c., at two terms &c., and whereof she herself and her husband and the other holders of that wapentake have for a long time been seised; and for that that aid was in arrear for the term &c., she avows &c. the taking &c., in such a place within the vill of N., and for the like cause in another place in another vill.—*Willuby* rehearsed the matter and said, You say that you hold the manor of Chesterton, in right of which manor &c.—*Herle.* Do not speak of the manor: we hold the manor of Chesterton, and we tell you that to that manor &c.—And this he said because a wapentake is not appurtenant to a manor.—*Friskeney.* For this aid she cannot make avowry; for we tell you that that wapentake was formerly in the hands of King John, which King gave it to William de Breouse; and we tell you that neither in the time of one nor in the time of the other were the aforesaid vills of N. & T. charged to that aid which they demand; ready &c.—BEREFORD. What answer you to their statement that Joan was seised and her husband &c.—*Friskeney.* They cannot be in a better condition than the King was in his time.—*Passeley.* We are pleading as high in the Right in discharging ourselves as if it were in a Ne Vexes.—

James a mesme cestui William fist homage e les autres services &c., e en sun homage morust; les queux mies & deus vergez de terre, dount play &c., sunt tenuz del maner de W. e assignez furent &c.; e ne mie tenuz del honor du chastel de Brember, e prest &c. Et alii e contra. Ideo &c. A.D. 1305.

Prise des Avers.

§ Johan Deyncurt se pleint qe Johane qe fu la femme Johan Wake atort prist ces avers &c.—*Herle.* Nous avowoms la prise &c., e par la resoun &c., qe &c. entient le maner de Cecestertoun, par resoun de queu maner ele ad le wappentake de N., par resoun de queu wappentake ele ad eide de viconte. E pur ceo qe la ville de N. si est arente a treis soz par an a eide &c. a deus termes &c., e dount ele mesme e sun baroun e les autres tenans de ceo wappentake de grant temps ount este seisi; e pur ceo qe cel aide fust arere du terme &c., si avowe &c. la prise &c. en teu leu denz la ville de N. E pur autele cause en un altre leu denz un autre ville. —*Willuby* rehercea, e dites qe vous tenez le maner de C., par resoun de queu maner.—*Herle.* Ne parlez nent du maner; nous tenoms le maner de C., e vous dioms a quel maner, &c. Et hoc dixit quia wappentake non est pertinens manerio.—*Friskeney.* Pur ceste aide ne puet ele avowerie [fere], qar nous vous dioms qe cel wappentake fust en akun tenps en la mayn le Roi Johan, la queu Roi dona a Willem de Breouse; e vous dioms qe en tenps de lun ne de lautre les avantdites villes de N. ne de T. ne furent nent charges de cel aide qe eux demaundent, e prest &c.—BEREFORD. Quei responez vous a ceo qe eux dient qe Johane ad este seisie e sun baroun &c ?—*Friskeney.* Il ne pount estre de meillour condicion qe ne fust le Roi en sun tenps.—*Passeley.* Nous pledoms auxi haut en le droit en deschargant nous com sil fust en un

A.D. 1305. BEREFORD. Nay, by my faith, you are not pleading in a Ne Vexes; they say that they have been seised, and also their husband and the other holders &c. for a great time; and (I will not lie) there escaped from one of them (I know not whom) a phrase about time whereof there is no memory, to which time they do not now hold; and you say that in the time of King John, who held the wapentake &c., and in the time of William de Breouse, to whom he gave it, neither the vill of N. nor the vill of T. was charged &c.: is this a sufficient answer to their avowry?—*Passeley.* The sheriff's aid belongs naturally to the sheriff; and since she is not sheriff nor holds the place of the sheriff, it does not appear that you can demand such an aid.—BEREFORD. Bailiffs of wapentakes and hundreds are in the habit thoughout the country of taking the sheriff's aid; and they say that they have been seised of that aid, and you do not loose or annul their seisin by anything that you have yet said.—*Friskeney.* We have said that they were discharged in the time of King &c. than whom they cannot be in a better condition.—BEREFORD. It may be that in the time of King &c. they were discharged, and they now think to charge them by their seisin.—*Friskeney.* Their seisin ought not to charge us; it was by extortion and grievous distress; they came once with four running horses to distrein.—*Herle.* Not by extortion, but by reasonable distress when it was in arrear, ready &c.—*Friskeney.* They have not nor can they have any other estate than the King had in whose time the vills were discharged; and we pray judgment.—BEREFORD. You have driven them to plead in another way, and you offered the same issue whereof they offer the contrary averment.

Quare non admisit.

§ The Abbat of Tewkesbury brought the writ against William Bishop of Worcester.—*Wescote* counted &c., that tortiously he did not receive, on his presentation, a fitting ne vexes.—BEREFORD. Nay, par foy, vous ne pledez nent vers un ne vexes; il diount qe eux ount este seisi e lour baroun e les autres tenans &c. de grant temps &c., e, ne mentrey point, il eschapa a un de eux, ne say a qi, une parole qe fust du temps dount il ny ad memorie, a queu temps il ne se pernent point ore; e vous dites qe en temps le Roi Johan qe tient le wappentake &c., e en temps Willem de Breouse a qi il le dona, ne furent les villes de N. ne de T. chargez, &c.; est ceo assez respons a lour avowerie?—*Passeley.* Aide du viconte apent naturelment a viconte; e de pus qe ele nest pas visconte ne leu de viconte ne tient, ne semble pas qe tele aide pussez demaunder.—BEREFORD. Baillifs de wappentake e de hundred assez par tote la terre pernent aide du viconte; e eux dient qe de cel aide ount eux este seisi, e vous ne delyez pas ne anentissez lour seisine par rien qe uncore avez dit.—*Friskeney.* Nous avom dist qe en temps le Roi &c. deschargez, de qi il ne serrount de meillour condicion.—BEREFORD. Il purra estre qe en temps le Roi &c. deschargez, e eux le byount a ore charger par lour seisine.—*Friskeney.* Lour seisine ne nous deit charger; qe ceo fust par extorsion e grevouse destresse, qe eux viendrent a la foiz a .iiii. chivals covers pur destreindre—*Herle.* Ne mie par extorsion, einz par renable destresse quant ele fust arere, e prest &c.—*Friskeney.* Eux ne ount ne aver ne pount altre estat qe le Roi ne avoit, en qi temps les villeez furent deschargez, e demaundoms jugement.—BEREFORD. Vous les avez chace de pleder par autre voie, e mesme le tendites issue dount il tendount le contrarie averement. A.D. 1305.

§ Labbe de Teukesbiri porta le bref vers Willem Eveske de Wyrcestre.—*Wescote* conta &c.; atort ne receut a sun presentement covenable persone al eglise Quare non admisit.

A.D. 1305. parson to the church of N.; and tortiously for this, that whereas the said Abbat in the Court of our lord the King, in a certain year on a certain day, by judgment recovered the presentation of the aforesaid church against the aforesaid William &c.; whereupon our lord the King ordered by his writ, that notwithstanding the claim of the aforesaid William &c., he should on the presentation by the said Abbat receive a fitting parson to the aforesaid church of N.; and the said Abbat delivered the said writ to the aforesaid William &c. in the presence of R., J. &c. in the church, and presented a fitting parson viz. one Nicholas Fermeband to the aforesaid church of N..; which presentation the aforesaid William &c. did not receive, but refused to do so, tortiously and in despite of the King and his Court and his command, and to the damage &c. —*Herle* denied tort and force, and that it was in despite of the King and his Court and command &c. And (said he) whereas he says that tortiously we did not receive him &c., he alleges what he wishes; we did not act tortiously, for we ought not to have received him, for the reason that the said Abbat is a man of holy church who cannot vary from his presentation; if once he present an incompetent parson, he cannot anew present another: for he ought to acknowledge his presentee. And because this same Abbat presented to us &c. an incompetent person, namely one Henry &c. who was guilty of simony and excommunicated so that he was not receivable, we gave it as of our collation, according to the ordinances and jurisdiction of Holy Church: and see here his deed, whereby he presented the said Henry.—*Kingesham.* Henry never accepted our presentation, ready &c.—*Warr.* Is it your deed or not?—*Kingesham* spoke as before.—HENGHAM. When the Abbat had presented he had done all that in him lay.—*Kingesham.* We tell you that the Abbat did not deliver that presentation to him, neither did he accept it, and neither did he or the Abbat deliver it to the Bishop.—HENGHAM. How then did it get to the Bishop?

de N. E pur ceo atort qe la ou mesme cestui Abbe A.D. 1305.
en la Cort nostre seignour le Roi, certein an e jour, par jugement rescovery le presentement del avantdite eglise vers lavantdit Willem &c., par quei nostre seignour le Roi manda par sun bref, qe ne mie contre esteant le cleim lavantdit Willem &c, al presentement mesme cestui abbe covenable persone al eglise de N. avantdite rescevereit, e mesme cestui abbe mesme cel bref al avandit Willem &c. en la presence R. J. &c. en la eglise &c. livera, e a la eglise de N. avantdite covenable persone, nomement un Nichole Fermeband, presenta, le quel presente lavantdit Willem &c. ne receut, einz fere le dedit, atort e en despit du Roi e sa Court e sun maundement, e a ces damages &c. — *Herle* defendi tort e force e quanc qe est en despit nostre seignour le Roi e sa Court e de sun mandement &c. E la ou il dit qe atort ne resceumes &c., il dist talent; noun pas atort, car resceyvre ne li devoymes; e par la resoun qe mesme celui abbe si est home de seinte eglise, qe ne puet mie varier de sun presentement; qe si un foiz noun able persone presente, il ne puet derichief autre presenter, car il deit conustre sun presente. E pur ceo qe mesme cestui abbe nous presenta &c. une persone noun able, nomement un Henri &c. qe fust simoniak e escomenge, dount il ne fust mie resceivable, si la donames de nostre collacion solom la ordinacion e jurisdiccion de seinte eglise; e veez icy sun fet par quei il presenta mesme celui Henri.— *Kingesham.* Qe Henri ne accepta onqes nostre presentement, prest etc.—*Warr.* Est ceo vostre fet ou noun?— *Kingesham,* ut prius. — Hengham. Quant labbe avoit presente il avoit fet ceo qe en lui fust.—*Kingesham.* Nous vous dioms qe labbe cel presentement ne luy livera, ne il ne la accepta ne al Eveske le livera, ne labbe ne le plus. — Hengham. Coment donques avient leveske?—

A.D. 1305. —*Kingesham.* We have nothing to do with that.—BEREFORD. If the bishop were to demand a debt from you by a writing which he put forward against you &c., would this be a good answer, We never delivered that writing to you? Ought we first to inquire of the acceptance of the deed by Henry, and of the delivery of it, and afterwards if there be such a deed?—*Malmesthorpe.* A fortiori ought one to inquire of the accepting.—*Passeley.* Although we had presented it and he would not receive it, and we presented another, we did not vary from our presentation; the first presentee he did not accept &c., and so there was only one presentee; the other was not followed by letter of inquiry nor by proffer of presentation to the Bishop.—BEREFORD. One ought to admit or deny the deed before pleading to the avoidance of it: wherefore it seems &c.—And at last they admitted the deed.—*Passeley.* We can not deny that this is our deed; but we tell you that we caused it to be made, and it remained at the abbey until we had sent to the said Henry &c. to know if he would take it up; and we tell you that the said Henry did not accept it nor would he take it up; so this presentation remained quietly at the abbey, without our delivering or sending it to the said Henry, or his accepting the presentation, or suing to the Bishop as presentee; then, although this presentation has without our knowledge come into the Bishop's hands, since we will aver, as before &c., we do not think that it should prevent us from presenting, or disturb our presentee.—*Warr.* And we pray judgment,—since you do not assign any tort or malice in the Bishop, and he has done nothing but what the ordinary ought to do, since he received your presentee, which is acknowledged,—if you can have an action against him: for suppose I were to put forward against you a quit-claim, it would be no answer to avoid it to say, this is my deed, but I never delivered it to you.—*Scoter.* It might be that one stole the Abbat's seal and sealed the writing: would he

Kingesham. De ceo navom qe faire.—BEREFORD. Si leveske vous demaundast une dette par un escrit qil mettroit contre vous &c., serreit il bien a dire, nous ne vous liverames onqes cel escrit?—IDEM. Devoms nous primes enquere del acceptement Henri du fet e du livere e pus si soit le fet.—*Malm.* De plus fort deit homme enquere e ceo est le acceptement.—*Passeley.* Tut lussoms presente e il ne la voleit mie resceivre, e nous presentames autre, nous ne variames nent de nostre presentement, qe le primer presente ne accepta point &c., e issi ne fust qe un presentement; qe lautre ne fu mie suy par lettre denqueste ne pas proffre del presentement al Eveske.—BEREFORD. Homme deit primes granter ou dedire le fet qe pleder a la voidance; par quei il semble &c. Et ad ultimum granterent le fet.—*Passeley.* Nous ne poms dedire qe ceo nest nostre fet, einz vous dioms qe nous le feimes faire, e demorra en labbeye tant qe nous aveymes mande al dit Henri &c. saver mon sil la voleit prendre, e vous dioms qe le dit Henri ne la accepta point ne prendre ne la voleit; dount cel presentement demorra en pees en labbeye, sanz ceo qe nous al dit Henri le liverames ou mandames ou qil le presentement accepta, ou al Eveske suyt cum presente; dount coment qe cel presentement soit sanz nostre su devenuz en la mayn leveske, de pus qe nous voloms averer ut prius &c., nentendoms qe obstacle nous serreit de presenter ou nostre presente destourber.—*Warr.* E nous jugement, de pus qe vous ne assignez nul tort ne malice en leveske, e il nad altre chose fet qe ordiner fere ne devoit, de pus qil receut vostre presente, qe conu est, si vers luy puissez accion aver; qar jeo pose qe jeo meisse encontre vous une quite-clamanz, il ne serreit mie respons de voider la, ceo est mon fet mes jeo ne vous liveray onqes.—*Scoter.* Il purra estre qe homme eust emble le seal A.D. 1305.

A.D. 1305. not.[1]—*Herle.* Yes he would; for then he could say that it was not his deed.—*Scoter.* Ink and parchment without delivery and acceptance do not make a presentation. —*Passeley.* It was not a presentation without the right of presentation, which the Abbat then had by some person presented by him, being completed and from him conveyed as far as the Bishop; but this was not done by that presentation, for he did not deliver &c., nor did the said Henry ever sue &c.; so the will on the one side and the assent on the other was not &c.; wherefore &c.—*Friskeney.* If the Abbat had been a purchaser, his estate would not have been affirmed by that presentation; wherefore &c.—*Passeley.* In an assise of "Dar-" rein presentement" he could not have taken title from that presentation.—*Herle.* Neither in one case nor in the other could his estate have been much blemished; for neither in the first did the Bishop give as claiming patronage, nor in the other as true patron.—*Hertepol.* All their endeavour is to defeat the presentation; and this they cannot do, since they have admitted this deed; for this deed is a witness of the fact, and in itself witnesses the presentation: and since the deed which they have admitted witnesses it, we pray judgment.—ROUBIRI. A charter is worth nothing without seisin; no more &c.—*Herle.* But what about a quit-claim?—*Malmesthorpe.* All the force which they have to affirm upon us this presentation is by reason of these words, "we have presented"; but thereby without a bodily act they cannot &c., any more than by the word "dedi" without seisin, affirm an estate &c.; and yet both words suppose the deed to be done; and nevertheless one shall be received to aver "not seised &c."; so &c.—*Herle.* If he had brought the "Quare Impedit" against us, and we had said that we did not claim anything in the advowson, and that you had presented &c., and thereupon

[1] This sentence seems imperfect.

labbe e ensele un escrist; ne le vodreit.—*Herle.* Si freit; qe adonqes poeit il dire nent sun fet.—*Scoter.* Enke e parchemyn sanz livere e le acceptement ne fet mie presentement.—*Passeley.* Presentement ne fut il point sanz ceo qe le droit de presentement, qe labbe adonqes avoit par aqune persone par lui presente, fut paremply e de luy tanke al Eveske conveye; mes ceo ne fu pas par cel presentement, qar il ne livera &c., ne le dit Henri onqes ne suy &c.; dount la volunte de une parte e dautre e lassente ne fu pas &c., par quei &c.—*Friskeney.* Si labbe eust este purchassour, sun estat ne eust pas este afferme par cel presentement; par quei &c.—*Passeley.* En lassise de drein presentement il ne poeit aver pris title de cel presentement.—*Herle.* En lun cas ne en lautre sun estat ne eust mie mult este blemie, car en le primer leveske ne dona mie com clamant patronage, ne en lautre come verey patron.—*Hertepol.* Tut lour force est a defere le presentement; e ceo ne pount eux, de pus qe eux ount ceo fet grante, qar ceo est fet e testmoignance du fet qe en luy meyme testmoigne le presentement; e de pus qe le fet qe eux ount grante le testmoigne, demaundoms jugement &c.—ROUBIRI. Chartre ne valt rienz sanz seisine, nent plus &c.—*Herle.* Mes quei quite-clamanz?—*Malm.* Tote lour force qil ount de affermer sur nous ceo presentement si est par ceste parole "presentames"; mes par tant sanz fet de corps de homme de pount eux &c., nent plus sanz seysine par le "dedi &c." affermer estat &c.; e la une parole e lautre suppose le fet estre fet; e ia plus tard homme serra receu de averer qe nent seisi &c., issi &c.—*Herle.* Sil ust porte vers nous le "quare impedit," e nous eussoms dist qe nous ne clamames rienz en lavoeson, e qe vous A.D. 1305.

A.D. 1305. we had offered an averment, we should not have been received without a letter, therefore in opposition to a letter you shall not have it.—*Scoter.* In the Quare Impedit you can not take title from a presentation alone, without you say that your ancestor or you presented &c. who was received and instituted &c.; wherefore &c. —And so to judgment.

Count in writ for the advowson of a third part.

§ *Malmesthorpe.* Tortiously deforces him of the advowson of the tithes of the third part of the church of N. And tortiously for this, that it is his right and his heritage, whereof his ancestor R. &c. was seised as of fee and of right, in time of peace, in the time of King &c., and in that time presented to the entirety of the church &c. his clerk, who on his presentation was received &c., the esplees &c., as in oblations, obventions &c., amounting &c.; and that such &c.—*Hedone* denied &c., and (said he) You see how he says that his ancestor presented to the entirety of the church &c. and that he took the esplees; thereby uniting the taking of the esplees with the advowson of the entirety of the church, and not with the parcel which is demanded; and we pray judgment. HENGHAM. If they were of the whole, they were also of the parcel, *Hedone.* We pray the View. —And he had it; to-wit of the place where &c.

Before the King. A judgment in an assise of Mordancester reversed.

ROUBYRI. John son of Avelyne brought a writ of Mordancester before SIR RALPH DE HENGHAM and his companions, on the death of John the clerk, his uncle, against Edmund of London, warden of the house of St. Thomas of Acre; and Edmund came and said that there ought not to be an assise; for he said that this is a writ which is to be brought on the death of the person last seised; and he said that after the death of John the aviez presente &c., e sur ceo tendimes averement, nous ne serrioms pas receu sanz lettre, ergo contre lettre vous naverez nent.—*Scoter.* En le "quare impedit" ne poez soulment de presentement prendre title sanz ceo qe vous diez qe vostre auncestre ou vous presentastes &c., qe fu receu e institut &c.; par quei.—Et sic ad judicium. A.D. 1305.

§ De advocacione tertiæ partis narratio.—*Malm.* Atort lui deforce lavoeson de dymes de la terce partie del eglise de N. Et pur ceo atort qe ceo son droit e sun heritage, e dount un son auncestre R. &c. fut seisi com de fee e de droit, en temps de pees, en temps le Roi &c., e en cel temps presenta a lenter de la eglise &c. un seon clerk qe a sun presentement fut receu &c., les esples &c., come en oblacions obvencions &c. montant &c., e qe tiel &c. —*Hedone* defendi &c., e vous veez bien coment il dist qe sun auncestre presenta a lenter del eglise &c., qe prist les esplez, en tant joyngnant le prendre des esplez al avoweson de lenter del eglise, e non pas a la parcele qe est demaunde; e demaundoms jugement.—HENGHAM. Si de tut ergo de parcele.—*Hedone.* La vewe. Et habuit. Videlicet de loco ubi &c.

Coram Rege de judicio in assisa mortis antecessoris reversato.

ROUBYRI. Johan le fiz Avelyne porta bref de Mortdauncestre devant SIRE RAUF DE HENGHAM e ces compaingnons, de la mort Johan le clerk sun oncle, vers Edmund de Londres gardeyn de la meson Seint Thomas de Acre; e Edmund vient e dist qe assise ne devoit estre; qar il dit qe ceo est un bref qe voet estre porte de la mort le drein seisi; e dist qe apres la mort Johan le clerk entra ceux tenementz unc Avelyne

A.D. 1305. clerk, there entered on those tenements one Avelyne, mother of the said John who brings &c., as sister and heir of the said John the clerk, and was seised, on whose death this John son of Avelyne might make use of the writ, and he prayed judgment of the writ; to which exception it was answered that Avelyne, after the death &c. did not enter and was not seised. And thereupon the Assise came and told this story;—that after the death of the said John the clerk, the said Avelyne, while the corpse was in the bier, entered and took possession, claiming as heir of John, and for half an hour in the day remained there, until, on the corpse being carried away, she still wishing to keep possession, came the said Edmund and ousted her. And because it appeared to the said Sir Ralph and his companions that that small seisin and at that time was nothing, they considered that, notwithstanding that abatement &c., the said John son of Avelyne might on the death of John his uncle well employ this writ, and they adjudged that John should recover his seisin. And because we see, as the verdict &c., that Avelyne, claiming &c., entered after the death of John and was seised until &c., on which seisin she might have employed the assise &c. and her heir after her death might have employed a writ of Entry founded &c., and thus the exception of the said Edmund is affirmed by the verdict of the Assise; and the cause of the judgment was the short time &c., and as to that we think that a mere placing of the foot conferred seisin on the true heir,—this Court adjudges that Edmund do have again his seisin &c. and his damages, and that John may have his recovery by another way if he will.

One indicted of procuring does not answer while one is unconvicted who is indicted of the fact. And what outlawry makes a convict and what not.

§ William de Gerberg, knight, was indicted before the coroners of the county of Norfolk that he had procured A., B., and C. to kill one S., of which indictment he was mere mesme cestui Johan qe porte &c., com soere e heir le dit Johan le clerk, e seisi fust, de qi mort mesme cesti Johan le fiz Avelyne poeit user ceo bref, e demaunda jugement du bref; a quele excepcion fust respondue qe Avelyne apres la nort &c. nentra point ne seisie ne fust. E sur ceo vient lassise e conta teu counte, qe apres la mort mesme celui Johan le clerk mesme ceste Avelyne, tant com le corps i fust en la bere, entra, e leinz fust, reclamant com heir Johan, e par un demi hour de jor y demora, tant qe sur lemportement du corps ou ele se voleit estre leinz tenuz vient le dist Emon e la osta. E pur ceo qe avis fust au ditz Sire Rauf e ce compaingnons qe cele petite seisine e en ceu tenps ne fut nule, si lour fut avis qe ne mie encontre esteant cele abatement &c. si empoeit le dit Johan fiz Avelyne de la mort Johan sun oncle ceo bref bien user, e agarderunt qe Johan recoverast sa seisine. E pur ceo qe nous veoms auxi com le verdist &c. qe Avelyne reclamant &c. entra apres la mort Johan, e seisi fust tanqe &c., de quele seisine ele poeit aver use lassise &c., e sun heir apres sa mort bref dentre fondu &c., e issi est la excepcion le dit Edmund afferme par veredit de lassise, e la cause de lour jugement fust pur le bref temps &c., et par de cea entendoms qe sola pedis posicio vero heredi seisinam contulit, si agarde la Court qe Edmund reeit sa seisine &c. e ces damages, e eit Johan sun rescoverir par autre veye sil voille. A.D. 1305.

Quod indictatus de procuratione inconvicto indictato de facto non respondet. Et quæ utlagaria facit convictum et quæ non.

§ Willem de Gerberg chivaler fust endite devant les coroners du counte de Norfolk qil endevoit aver procure un A. B. e C. de occir un S., de quel endite-

A.D. 1305. afraid, and fled to the church of the Minorites at Canterbury, and remained there full half a year, until the inquisitors of Trailbaston came into the country, before whom he was anew properly indicted, and thereupon he surrendered himself to prison, and was arraigned before the said inquisitors, and was asked how he would acquit himself of that procuration. And he said that he ought not then to answer regarding it; for he said that A., one of those indicted for the fact, was dead and was not attainted &c.; and that B., another of those indicted, was mainprised by writ until the Eyre and was not attainted &c.; and he said that, since those who were indicted of the fact were not attainted, it did not seem to him that he ought to answer concerning the procuration. And thereupon one of the standers by said that C., who he said then lived at &c. not attainted, was outlawed for the said fact, by which outlawry he was sufficiently attainted: of which thing the said inquisitors enquired of the coroners &c. of the said county, from whom they found that it was so: then the said inquisitors, because one of those indicted was outlawed &c. and thus attainted &c., as they considered, did drive him to answer as to the procuration. And William said that saving to himself the benefit of what he had previously said in that Court, he could not further answer, for he was a clerk &c.—And notwithstanding the aforesaid reasons they took an Inquest &c. the better to know for what he should be delivered &c., and that if it should be found &c.: which Inquest said that he was guilty of the procuration; and they were asked if William, after the indictment before the coroners, fled, and they said Yes; wherefore they delivered him &c. as attainted, and adjudged forfeiture of his goods; then the wife of the said William sued out a writ to cause to bring the record and the process &c. before the King. And the record being sent in those words, the Bishop was directed to cause the said William &c. to come on such

ment il se dota, e fuist al eglise de Freres Menours A.D. 1305.
de Cantirbiri, e la demora bien demi an, tanke les enquerours, saver Trayllebastone, viendrent en pays, devant queux il fust derichief en la manere endite, e sur ceo se rendi a la prisone, e arene fust devant les dis enquerours, e demaunde coment sil se voleit de cel procurement aquiter. Et il dit qil nen devoit de ceo adonqes respondre, qar il dit qe A. le un des enditez du fet fut mort nent atteint &c. Et B. lautre endite &c. si fust meinprise par bref tant qe en Eyre nent atteint &c.; e dit qe, de pus qe les enditez du fet ne furent nent atteinz, il ne lui sembloit pas quil en devoit respondre du procurement; e sur ceo un esteant de coste dit qe C. qil dit estre demorant a la foy &c. nent atteint, si enfust uthlaghe pur mesme le fet, par la quele utlagarie assez fut il atteint; de quele chose les diz enquerours enquistront des coroners &c. du dit counte, par queux il troverent qe ensi fust; dount les diz enquerors, pur ceo qe un des endites fust uthlaghe &c. e issi atteint &c., a ceo qe lour fut avis, lui chacerent a respondre du procurement. Et Willem dit qe, salve a lui ceo qe avant avoit dist en ceste Court, outre nen devoit nen poeit respondre, qar il enfust clerk &c. Et rationibus prædictis non obstantibus il pristrent enqueste &c. de saver mon pur quel il serreit livere &c. si trove fust &c.: la quele enqueste dit qil en fust coupable del procurement: e demaunde lour fust si Willem apres lenditement &c. devant coroners senfuist; qe disoient oil: par quei iluy livererount &c. come atteynt, e agarderent forfeiture de ces chateux; dount la femme le dit Willem suist bref de fere venir le record e le proces &c. devant le Roi. Et, recordo misso sub eisdem verbis, maunde fust al Eveske qil feist venir le dit Willem &c. teu jour &c.; a quel jour

A.D. 1305. a day &c.; on which day the Bishop returned that the writ came too late. On which day, BRABAZON said, We can do nothing with this record; for if there be any error therein, it should be shown to us by the party, who is not here.—*Toudeby.* He is here by attorney.—BRABAZON. When was he made attorney?—*Toudeby.* Since he was delivered to the Bishop.—BRABAZON. In prison he could not make an attorney; and nevertheless he is still as an attainted person and not at the common law; wherefore &c.—*Toudeby.* Sir, you see well how we have sued a writ to the Bishop &c. that he should cause to come &c., and what answer &c. he gives; and such answer he will give while we sue, for no law will in any wise force him to send or deliver the prisoner delivered to him without due purgation or without the principal cause of the attainder being defeated, to do which you are now sent, if any error &c. And since for certain causes, whereof you wish to be certified, this record has been brought before you, it belongs to you, without the showing by the party, to make examination &c., and, if error &c., undo the judgment.—BRABAZON the record being read as aforesaid fully, when he reached the errors, said, And because we find that they held to the record of the coroners of the outlawry of C., one of those indicted of the fact, to record which thing belonged to the whole commonalty of the county &c., and ought to have demanded it from that commonalty, we consider that there is error &c., because if by any false process there was falsely any outlawry in the county, and so falsely in that form in the Eyre recorded by the coroners &c., the amercement would fall on the whole commonalty. Again there is another error of more importance; which is that whereas the outlaw was returned to the peace by leave of the King, by his charter of pardon of the suit of his peace and of the outlawry, so that he would stand to law in his Court &c., by such an outlawry they thought him attainted of the fact, where the leveske retorna qe le bref vient trop tard. A quei jour,—BRABANZONE. Nous ne poms rienz faire de ceo record; car si errour i fust, ceo nous serreit monstre par la partie qe ny est point.—*Toudeby.* Il est cy par attorne.— BRABANZONE. Quant fet attorne?—*Toudeby.* Pus qil fust livere al Eveske.—BRABANZONE. En prisone ne poeit il fere attorne, e iatardeis il est uncore com atteint e nent a la comune lei; par quei &c.—*Toudeby.* Sire, vous veez bien coment nous avom suy bref al Eveske &c. qil feist venir &c., e quel respons &c. il donne; e tel respons dorra iatant suoms, qar il ne lui estovera mie par force de nule ley le prison a lui livere come atteint nule parte maunder ne deliverer sanz due purgacion ou sanz ceo qe la cause principale del atteyndre soit defete, a quei fere estes a ore enveye si errour &c.; et de pus qe pur certeines causes, des queles vous voillez estre acertez, si est ceo record fet venir devant vous, a vous estut sanz mustrance de partie de faire examinement &c. e si errour &c. le jugement defere.—BRABANZONE, lecto recordo ut predicitur particulatim, cum ad errores pervenerit, dixit: E pur ceo qe nous trovoms qil pristrent au record des coroners de la utlagerie C. un des enditez du fet, quele chose recorder aferoit a tote la comunalte du conte &c., e a cele comunalte devoit aver demaunde, si nous est il avis qe iluy ad errour &c., pur ceo qe si par faus proces fausement fust nule en Conte utlagherie e issi fausement en cele forme en Eyre recorde des coroners &c., la merciement chereit sur tote la comunalte; de richief iad il autre errour qe plus fet acharger, qe est la ou le utlaghe fust revenu a la pees de conge le Roi par sa chartre de pardoun de la suite de sa pees e de la uthlagerie, issi qe a droit estoit en sa Court &c., par tiel uthlagerie len entendirent eux estre atteint du fet A.D. 1305.

A.D. 1305. outlawry was only for his contumacy; but it would have been otherwise if he had remained without returning or being restored to the peace; then, since at the taking the Inquest they could not ex officio deal with the procurer, unless those indicted of the fact or one of them were attainted &c., and they held him to be by that outlawry attainted of the fact when in such a case it was only a judgment for contumacy, we are of opinion that there is an error. And there is reason for this; for if William as procurer &c., because the said C. who was indicted for it was outlawed, should be put to answer for the procuration, and perchance by the Inquest in which &c. he should be convicted &c., and before the said William should be convicted, C. should be restored to the peace by charter, and afterwards at the suit of some one should be inculpated for this fact, and perchance by the Inquest in which &c. acquitted, an inconvenience in law would follow, that he who was indicted of the procurement should be condemned &c. and he who was indicted of the fact &c.: wherefore we are of opinion that the said judgment is erroneous and therefore must be held null: and you shall have a writ to the Bishop to cause the said William to come on a certain day before us to find good mainprise &c., body for body, to answer as to the procuration, if it happen that the said B. and C. be convicted of the fact.—*Toudeby.* Sir, what is your will about our chattels.—BRABAZON. Let the chattels be confiscated, for the flight.—*Toudeby.* That forfeiture ought not be adjudged until the time comes for condemning or acquitting; now until that time when they shall enquire of the flight, it seems to us an error.—BRABAZON. We will send to the coroners of the county &c., and if we find by them that it was immediately after the indictment, we will adjudge a forfeiture of the chattels which he then had; but if it was not, then no forfeiture &c.—And note that they thought it an error that the aforesaid Justices had en-ou la uthlagerie ne fut mes pur sa contumacie; mes altre eust este sil fut demore sanz estre revenuz ou resuscite a la pees; dount de pus qe a lenqueste prendre de lour office aler ne poeint du procurour sanz ceo qe les enditez du fet ou un de eux fust atteint &c., e par cele uthlagerie luy tiendreit atteint du fet, ou en tiel cas ny est mes qe jugement de contumacie, si nous est il avis qe ily ad errour. Et piert par reson; car si Willem cum procurour &c., pur ceo qe le dit C. de ceo endite est uthlaghe, serroit mis a respondre del procurement, et par cas par enqueste en la quele &c. fust atteint &c., e avant ceo qe le dit Willem fut atteint C. fut resuscite a la pees par chartre, e pus a la suite de ascony de ceo fet acoupe en Court, e par cas par enqueste en la quele &c. aquite, ensuereit inconvenient de ley qe lendite du procurement dampne &c. e lendite du fet &c.; par quei avis est a la Court qe le dit jugement est erreroyne, e pur ceo soit tenuz a nul; e vous averez bref al Eveske de fere venir le dit Willem a certein jour devant nous a trover bon meinprise &c. corps pur corps a respondre del procurement, sil aviegne qe les dits B. ou C. du fet soient atteinz.—*Toudeby.* Sire, de nos chateux vostre volente.—BRABANZONE. Catalla pro fuga confiscantur.—*Toudeby.* Cele forfeiture ne serroit agarde tant qe temps dampnable ou aquittable avenist; dount tant qe a cel temps de ceo qil enquistrount de la sute [fuite ?] nous semble il errour.—BRABANZONE. Nous manderoms a les Coroners du Conte &c., e si par eux trovoms quil fust meintenant apres lenditement, nous agarderoms la forfeture des chateux qe a ceu tenps avoit, e si noun nule forfeture &c. Et memorandum quod reputaverunt illud erroneum quod

A.D. 1305.

A.D. 1305. quired of the Jury &c. concerning the flight &c.; since they ought to have been informed of that by the record of the coroners.

Debt: where two executors sued, omitting the other two who did not administer but who were named in the testament.

§ S. and T. executors &c. of the Bishop of London brought a writ against the Prior of St. Bartholomew's of London.—*Lanfar.* Show that you are executors. And the testament being exhibited it appeared that there were two others named &c. besides those two. —*Lanfar.* Judgment of the writ; for there are two other executors who are not named &c.—*Este.* It was not fit to name them; for one is dead and the other did not administer. —HENGHAM. Suppose that the Prior were to put forward an acquittance by one of them who is not named, who should be party to deny it? and their being demandants is not like the case of one demanding against them.—MALLORE. Suppose that he has never hitherto administered and now wished to administer, who should forbid him?—HENGHAM. Because we see by the testament that there are other executors &c. without whom &c. who are not named &c., this Court adjudges &c. take nothing by your writ.

Partition. § The writ was brought against one Robert de Hoyland who was by the law of England tenant &c., which tenancy was clearly stated in the writ.—*Tiltone.* Judgment of the writ; we have only an estate for term of life by the law &c., and we cannot be party to this partition which is to last for ever.—*Hedone.* You can pray aid.—*Tiltone.* You are not demanding our tenement.—TRIKINGHAM. He cannot now bring this writ against any one but you; and you may, on account of the weakness of your estate, pray aid: wherefore &c.—At another day, *Scrope* said, This is a writ of Right, and if partition be prædicti Justiciarii quesierunt de Jurata &c. de fuga &c. cum de hoc eis constare debet per recordum coronatorum. A.D. 1305.

De debito, ubi duo executores petierunt, omissis aliis duobus non administrantibus, in testamento tamen nominatis.

§ S. e T. executours &c. Leveske de Londres porterent bref vers le Priour de Seint Bartholemew de Londres.—*Lanfare.* Mustrez qe vous estes executours.--Et ostenso testamento fuerunt præter illos duos alii duo nominati &c. —*Lanfare.* Jugement du bref; qar ily sunt deus autres executours nent nomez &c.—*Este.* Il ne covendreit mie nomer, car lun est mort e lautre ne administra point. —HENGHAM. Jeo pose qe le Prior meist avant aquittance de un de eux qe nest mie nome, qi serreit partie a dedire la? e il nest mie semblable quant eux demaundent a homme demaunde vers eux.—MALLORE. Jeo pose qil ne ust onqes jekes en cea administre, e ore voleit administrer, qe lui vyereit?—HENGHAM. Pur ceo qe nous veoms par le testament qe ily sunt autres executours &c. sanz queux &c., nent nomez &c., si agarde la Court &c. ne preigne rienz par vostre bref &c.

De participatione facienda.

§ Le bref fust porte vers un Robert de Hoyland qe fust par la lei Dengletere tenant &c. quel tenant fust apertement mote en le bref.—*Tiltone.* Jugement del bref; qe nous ne avoms mes qe a terme de vie par la ley &c. e ne poms a ceste partison qe est a durer a touz jours estre partie.—*Hedone.* Vous poez prier aide.—*Tiltone.* Vous ne demaundez nent nostre tenement.—TRIKINGHAM. Il ne puet a ore vers autre qe vers vous ceo bref user; e vous poez pur la tendresce de vostre estat aide prier; par quei &c.—Ad alium diem, *Scrop.* Ceo est un

A.D. 1305. made it will be to last for ever, to which we in respect of the estate which we have cannot be party; judgment of the writ.—HENGHAM. This is not a writ of Right nor a writ of wrong; for of a truth we do not know what writ it is or on what law founded; it would be a wonderful thing if of a tenement which has descended to two parceners in common or has been purchased in common, one [parcener] in opposition to that descent, or one purchaser against the will of the other, should compel partition, since it descended to them or they were enfeoffed thereof in common: but I tell you that one of these apprentices has made the purchase to find out what judgment we shall give on this writ; so let your exception be entered and inrolled, and await judgment.—*Scrope*. Writs are ordained to remove wrong; but if he suffer him to have and to hold according to what has descended to him, he does him no wrong &c.; wherefore &c.

Dower unde nihil habet.

§ One Alice &c. brought the writ against one R. &c. of a freehold which was of Henry &c.—*Willuby*. She ought not to have dower, for Henry &c. never married her; ready &c.—*Hamptone*. That amounts to saying that she was never joined to him in lawful matrimony. —*Gildeford*. He tells you that she was not married in the face of the church, ready &c.—*Hamptone*. He ought not to get to that averment; for this same Alice heretofore brought a writ of Dower against one William &c., which William alleged in rebutting &c. that she was not &c. joined in &c., wherefore the Bishop was directed to convoke &c., which Bishop found &c. as he certified this Court, that she was joined &c.; and we pray judgment, since the contrary to his exception was formerly found by the Bishop's certificate, if he ought to get to that averment.—*Hales*. No more in this case than in case of bastardy ought one to send twice to the Bishop. —*Willuby*. We are not now pleading as William pleaded; we do not speak of not being joined &c., but we say bref de droit, e si partison se freit il serreit a durer a touz jours, a quei nous del estat qe nous sumes ne poms estre partie; jugement du bref.—HENGHAM. Ceo nest bref de droit ne bref de tort; qar nous ne savoms veirs quel bref ceo est, ne fondu sur quele ley; qe ceo serreit merveillouse chose qe de un tenement qe descendu fust a deus parceners en comune ou en comune purchase, qe le un contre cele descente on purchase contre gre lautre freit faire la partison, de pus qil lour est descendu ou feffez sunt en comune: mes jeo vous dy qe un de ceux aprentiz fist le purchaz pur fere quel jugement nous freoms sur ceo bref; dount soit vostre excepcion entre enroulle, e demorez a jugement.—*Scrop.* Brefs sunt ordinez de oster tort; mes si ily soeffre aver e tener solom ceo qe lui descendy, si ne le fit il nul tort &c.; par quei &c. A.D. 1305.

§ Une Alice &c. porta le bref vers un R. &c. del franc tenement qe fut a Henri &c.—*Willuby.* Dowere ne deit ele avoir, qe Henri &c. ne la esposa onqes; e prest. —*Hamptone* Tant amonte qe nent couple a lui en leal matrimoigne.—*Gildeford.* Il vous dit nent espose en face del eglise, e prest &c.—*Hamptone.* Al averement ne deit il avenir, car mesme ceste Alice altrefoiz porta bref de dowere vers un Willem &c., le quel Willem alegga en rebotant &c. qe ele ne estoit &c. couple &c., par quei fut mande al Eveske quod convocet &c., le quel Eveske trova &c., auxi com il certefia ceste Court, qele fust couple &c.; e demaundoms jugement, de pus qe le contrarie de sa excepcion si est autrefoiz trove par certificate leveske, si a tiel averement deive avenir.—*Hales.* Nent plus en ceo cas qe en bastardie deit homme deus foiz maunder al Eveske.—*Willuby.* Nous ne pledoms nent auxi com Willem pleda; qe nous ne parloms nent

De dote unde nihil habet.

A.D. 1305. that he never married her; of which the country may well have cognisance, and it may be tried in this Court. —HENGHAM. Certainly it can not; any more than that she was joined &c.—Afterwards, on another day, it being found by the record of the Roll that what *Hamptone* said was true, HENGHAM, having rehearsed the process &c. said, And because that heretofore the Court was certified by the Bishop &c. that Alice was joined to Henry &c., and we find also that it was adjudged that she should have a writ of resummons, this Court adjudges that she do recover &c.—And note that the tenant made default on the second day when the judgment was given, and yet the judgment was given in the principal &c.

Entry on disseisin.

§ One C. brought the writ against William de Peynbrigge &c. "into which he had not entry unless by one " R. who tortiously &c. disseised Robert his uncle &c. " whose heir &c."—*Lanfar.* You can not have an action, for this same Robert, one Nicholas &c. being in seisin, released and quit-claimed &c. to him and to his heirs; after whose death one S. heir to the said Nicholas, we being in seisin, released and quit-claimed [to us]; and see here the quit-claim; and we tell you that Robert after that time was never seised, ready &c., and we pray judgment.—*Passeley.* And we pray judgment, since this is a writ of entry in the degrees, and you have not denied them, but tacitly admitted them, and are not party to the quit-claim which you say our ancestor made to Nicholas, and could not be party to it if it were denied, and you do not show any specialty to witness that you are assignee of Nicholas,—if you can use that quit-claim as a bar against us. —BEREFORD (to *Lanfar*). Do you use the quit-claim?—*Lanfar.* Yes, Sir.—BEREFORD. What estate have you from Nicholas?—*Lanfar.* His heir released and quit-claimed to us while we were in seisin.—BEREFORD. How, you all entered by disseisin, both Nicholas and you de coupler &c., eynz dioms ne la esposa onqes, de quei pays puet bien aver conissance, e trie puet estre en ceste Cort.—HENGHAM. Certes noun puet, nent plus qele fu couple &c. Postea ad alium diem comperto per recordum Rotuli id forte [fore?] verum quod *Hamptone* dixit, HENGHAM,—reiterato processu &c., E pur ceo qe autrefoiz est la Court certefie par leveske &c. qe Alice fu couple a Henri &c. e trovoms uncore qe fust agarde qe ele out bref de resomonz, si agarde la Court qe ele rescovere &c. Et memorandum quod tenens fecit defaltam secundo die quod judicium fuit redditum et tamen reddebatur in principali &c. A.D. 1305.

§ Un C. porta le bref vers Willem de Peynbrigge &c., en les queux il ne avoit entre si noun par un R. qe atort &c. disseisi Robert sun oncle &c. qi heir &c.—*Lanfare.* Accion ne poez avoir, qar memes celui Robert en la seisine un Nichol &c. relessa e quiteclama &c. a lui e a ces heirs, apres qi mort un S., heir mesme celui Nichole, en nostre seisine relessa e quiteclama; e veez icy la quiteclamance; e vous dioms qe Robert unqes pus ceu tenps seisi, e prest &c., e demaundoms jugement.—*Passeley.* E nous jugement, de pus qe ceo est un bref dentre en les degrez, e vous ne les avez nent dedit, einz en teysant grantee, e nestes mie partie a la quiteclamance qe vous dites qe nostre auncestre fit a Nichol, ne partie estre ne purriez si ele fut dedite, ne especialte ne moustrez qe testmoigne qe vous seiez assigne Nichole, si vous cele quite-clamance com barre vers nous puissez user.—BEREFORD, a *Lanfare.* Usez vous la quite-clamance?—*Lanfar.* Sire, oil.—BEREFORD. Quel estat avez vous de Nichol?—*Lanfar.* Sun heir nous relessa e quite-clama en nostre seisine.—BEREFORD. Coment, vous estes touz entrez par disseisine, e Nichol e

De ingressu super disseisinam.

A.D. 1305. —*Wescote.* It may be that Robert, while Nicholas was in seisin, released and quit-claimed &c. and afterwards resumed his estate.—*Lanfar.* Never afterwards seised, ready &c.—*Passeley.* Nay, we are in a writ of entry in the degrees, and you have admitted them, and we pray judgment. And on the other hand you are not privy in blood to Nicholas, nor his assign, for anything that you show.—*Toudeby* (on the same side). The quit-claim does not bar; for if it was made before the seisin of the ancestor &c. it is worth nothing, nor does it any more avail Nicholas if it was after the seisin. — BEREFORD. There are many ways of pleading in a writ of Entry. One is by denying the entry; another is by denying the seisin of the ancestor &c.; and the third is by denying the right: and he abandons the first two and holds to the third; and if you were to bring against him a writ of Right, could he not join the mise to recognise the seisin of Robert, and, although Nicholas entered, say that he entered by Robert and that Robert leased to him &c., and thereupon in his seisin released and quit-claimed, and pray that it might be recognised &c. whether he had better right to hold &c. as those which the said Robert &c. leased to him and afterwards released &c., in his seisin &c?—*Passeley.* Then he would not use the quit-claim as a bar. — BEREFORD. One often takes issue by the Great Assise on a quit-claim, because one wishes to fall to an inquest; and many a one desires that the superiority of the right over the quit-claim which is put forward as a bar should be recognised by the assise; hereupon let the inquest join.—*Passeley.* It is for as much as a quit-claim is not a sufficient bar to a writ of Right.— BEREFORD. Does not the mise join on the words of the quitclaim?—ROUBYRI (on the same point). This is a mise based on the words of the quit-claim.

Debt, where an

§ One L. executrix &c. brought the writ &c.—*Rostone.* Show that you are executrix.—*Willuby.* Ready to aver vous.—*Wescote.* Il purra estre qe Robert en la seisine Nichol relessa e quite-clama &c. e pus reprist estat.—*Lanfare.* Unqes pus seisi, prest &c.—*Passeley.* Nay, nous sumes en bref dentre en les degreez, e vous les avez grante, e demaundoms jugement. Et dautre parte, vous nestes pas prive a Nichol du saunk ne sun assigne a ceo qe vous moustrez.—*Toudeby* (ad idem). La quiteclamance ne barre nent, qar si ele fust fete avant la seisine le auncestre &c. ele ne vaut point, ne Nichol pus la seisine nent plus.—BEREFORD. Ily ad mults des maners de pleder en bref dentre. Un a dedire lentre; un altre la seisine launcestre &c; e le tierce au droit: e il lest les deus veyes e prent au tierce; e vous si portissez vers lui bref de droit, ne poeit il joyndre la mise a conustrer la seisine Robert, e coment qe Nichol entra, dire qil entra par Robert e qe Robert lui lessa &c., e sur ceo en sa seisine relessa e quite-clama e prier qe conu fust &c. le quel il ad meaur droit a tenir &c. com ces qe le dit Robert &c. lui lessa e pus relessa &c. en sa seisine &c.?—*Passeley.* Adonqes ne usereit il mie la quite-clamanz, com barre.—BEREFORD. Homme prent sovent issue par grante Assise sur quite-clamanz, pur ceo qe homme hiet de cheier en enqueste; e moltz voet homme qe conuz soit la meaurte de droit sur la quite-clamanz par lassise qele mise pur barre: sur ceo joingne enqueste.—*Passeley.* Ceo par tant qe quite-clamanz nest pas suffissant barre au bref de droit.—BEREFORD. Ne se joyut la mise sur les paroles de quite-clamanz?—ROUBYRI (ad idem). Ceoest une myse taille des paroles de la quite-clamanz. A.D. 1305.

§ Une L. executrice &c. porta le bref &c.—*Rostone.* Mustrez qe vous estes executrice.—*Willuby.* Prest del De debito ubi executrix petiit.

A.D. 1305. that we are executrix and we have administered.—*Rostone.* An executrix must have a testament proved before the Ordinary which shall witness that she is executrix; and inasmuch as you have none such, judgment.

executrix sued.

Taking of beasts.

§ One R. complained that the Prioress of Markyate had tortiously taken his beasts &c. —*Willuby.* We avow the taking; and for the reason that one Eustace Domynge held those tenements which you hold, together with other tenements; which Eustace made himself bound to the Prioress and Nuns &c. of Markyate and to their successors in half a mark of yearly rent, to be paid every year at certain terms &c. for ever: of which rent one Joan &c. formerly Prioress, was seised &c. And see here the deed of Eustace which testifies that grant. And for that the rent was in arrear &c., and the writing showed that Eustace had granted, as aforesaid, and, besides this, had granted that if that rent was in arrear &c. it should be lawful for the Prioress or her successors, by the sheriff of the county or the bailiffs of the county of Gloucester, to distrein him and his heirs &c.—*Tiltone* rehearsed the avowry &c., and (said he) Since he avows by virtue of the writing &c. which intends only and grants power to distrein Eustace and his heirs, whose heir we are not, we pray judgment if on us &c. — *Hunte.* You are tenant of the land which Eustace held when he granted.—And he was [driven] to answer by HENGHAM as for the land &c., because tenements charged pass with the charge.—*Herle.* Eustace's heir has sufficient &c. of the same land &c.—HENGHAM. What of that? do you wish to limit the lady's power, and perchance the heir has only one acre, when 30 acres were charged, to what the heir holds which is only a parcel, when the whole being charged ought to answer?—*Herle.* Now ought they by secret contrivance to charge a parcel in the hands of a stranger and averer qe nous sumes executrice, e administre avoms.— *Rostone.* Executrice deit aver testament prove devant ordinere qe temoignera qil est executrice; e desicom vous ne avez point, jugement. A.D. 1305.

§ Un R. se pleint qe la Prioresse de Markyate atort avoit pris ces avers &c.—*Willuby.* Nous avouwoms la prise; e par la reson qe un Eustache Domynge tient ces tenementz qe vous tenez ensemblement ove altres tenementz; le quel Eustache se granta estre tenuz au Prioresse e a Noneignes &c. de M. e a ces successours en demi marc de annuele rente, a paier chescun an a teux termes &c. a touz jours; de quele rente une Johane &c. jadis Prioresse fu seisi &c. E veez ici le fet Eustace qe cel grante testmoigne. E pur ceo qe la rente fut arere &c., e lescrist voleit qe Eustace avoit grante, ut prædicitur, e estre ceo avoit grante qe si cele rent fust arere &c. bien lirreit au Priour ou a ces successours, vescounte del Conte, ou a Baillifs le Conte de Gloucestre destreindre luy e ces heirs &c.—*Tiltone* rehersa le avowerie &c.; e de pus qil avowe par vertue del escrist &c. qe voet soulement e grante poer a destreindre Eustace ou ces heirs, qi heir nous ne sumes point, e demaundoms jugement si sur nous &c.—*Hunte.* Vous estes tenant de la terre qe Eustace tient quant il granta; e il fust a respondre par HENGHAM, com de la terre &c. pur ceo qe tenement chargez passent oue la charge.—*Herle.* Le heir Eustace ad assez &c. de mesme la terre &c.—HENGHAM. De ceo quei? voillez restreyndre le poer la dame, e par aventure le heir nad qe une acre ou .xxx. acres furent chargez, [a] la tenance le heir qe nest fors qe parcele, ou lenter serroit de respondre chargez?—*Herle.* Ore areremeyn deyvent eux charger parcele en la tenance del estrange en

Prise des avers.

A.D. 1305. leave what the heir holds ?— HENGHAM. Neither one nor the other will be discharged. — *Herle.* Eustace &c. was not seised of that land when he granted &c., ready &c.

Quare impedit.

§ Three persons brought three writs of Quare Impedit, separately, against the Countess of Cornwall, for a church; one did not prosecute his writ.—BEREFORD (to the attorney of the said Countess). You shall have a writ, on the nonsuit of T., to the Bishop; but the execution of the judgment will stay until the others have pleaded.

Writ of Entry sur disseisin against an Abbat.

§ The writ was brought against the Abbat of Selby "into which he has not entry unless after the disseisin "which such an abbat effected on T. the uncle &c."—*Toudeby.* Judgment of the writ; for he supposes that the abbat had entry by his predecessor, and that an abbat makes a degree, which he does not.—GILDEFORD (having consulted with HENGHAM). The writ is good enough; it may be that your predecessor committed disseisin and enfeoffed a stranger, who enfeoffed the present abbat.—*Toudeby.* Again, judgment of the writ, for he says "after the disseisin which T. formerly abbat," and he does not say predecessor &c.—GILDEFORD. If he was abbat he was therefore predecessor &c.—*Toudeby* prayed the View, and he had it.

Case where the liberty of Lincoln was challenged.

§ Master R. de Bray, Chancellor of Lincoln, complained of the city &c., that John de Normanton had tortiously taken his beasts. John removed the plea &c. by a Recordari, of which the cause was "because he "distreined in the fee for customs and services &c." And the count being counted, the bailiff of Lincoln came and prayed the franchise, and said that the King had granted by his charter, which he showed, that the citizens of Lincoln should not plead or be impleaded anywhere lessant la tenance le heir.—HENGHAM. Ne lun ne lautre serra descharge.—*Herle.* Eustache &c. ne fut nient seisi de cele terre quant il granta &c., prest &c. A.D. 1305.

§ Treis porterent .iii. brefs de "quare impedit" diversement vers la Contesse de Cornwaille de une eglise; le un ne suist pas son bref.—BEREFORD (ad attornatum prædicte Comitisse). Vous averez bref par la nounsuite T. &c. al Eveske, mes la execucion du jugement targera tanke les altres eient pledez. De quare impedit.

§ Le bref fu porte vers labbe de Seleby "in quas non "habet ingressum nisi post dissesinam quam talis abbas "&c. fecit T. avunculo" &c.—*Toudeby.* Jugement du bref; qar il suppose qe labbe avoit entre par sun predecessour, e qe labbe face degre, ou il ne fet point.—GILDEFORD consulto HENGHAM. Le bref est assez bon; qil purra estre qe vostre predecessour eust disseisi e feffe un, estrange, e celui feffe labbe qe ore est.—*Toudeby.* Uncore jugement du bref, qar il dist post dissesinam quam T. quondam abbas, e ne dit predecessour &c.—GILDEFORD. Sil fust abbe ergo predecessour &c.—*Toudeby.* La vewe. Et habuit. Breve de ingressu super dissessinam versus abbatem.

§ Mestre R. de Bray, Chaunceler de Nicole, se fust pleint de la cite &c. qe Johan de Normantone atort avoit pris ces avers. Johan fit remuer la parole &c. par un Recordare dount fust la cause "quia distrinxit "in feodo pro consuetudinibus et serviciis" &c. Et narrata narratione vient le Baillif de Nicole e demaunda la franchise, e dit qe le Roi avoit grante par sa chartre, quil mustra, qe les citeseins de Nicole ne devoient Casus de libertate Lyncolniensi calumpniata.

A.D. 1305. except within the city &c., unless for foreign tenements and except with the ministers and serjeants of the King. —*Malmesthorpe.* They shall not have the franchise &c.; for they can not try that plea, and for this it was removed, and this is the cause of our Recordari.—*Herle.* Heretofore this plea was in your Court. And because the plea could not be terminated there, the King directed &c. that it should be recorded and the parties be &c. into the Bench; for if you had there disclaimed &c. we could not have had the advantage which is given to us by law &c., because that Court does not bear record: and therefore it was by Statute [1] ordained to cause to be recorded &c. and adjourned &c. out of the county courts and such like courts.—GILDEFORD. You fish before the net; the time for disclaiming has not yet arrived; wait until it comes, and then you can by resummons make the party come here to answer, because that Court has failed to do you right.—*Herle.* If he were to disclaim, judgment would be given &c.; after which judgment there would be no plea in the Court: how then would there be a resummons when the party would be without day?—GILDEFORD. One often sues out a resummons where the party is without day.—On another day he repeated his previous argument.—HENGHAM. Still he did not disclaim; what do you know of what he will do or say when &c. And when franchises are demanded here and allowed, the bailiff is ordered to do speedy right to the parties &c., otherwise that they (the parties) do return; then thus do you; for if this exception were allowed by law, every franchise might be taken away: for in a plea of land one alleges in that Court bastardy, of which they can not enquire &c.; and in a plea of Dower one may say that the demandant was not married &c., of which &c.; and thus take away these and

---

[1] 13 Edw. 1. c. 2. § 2.

nule parte pleder ne estre enpledez si noun denz la cite &c. si noun des tenementz foreins forpris oue les ministres e le mineors le Roi.—*Malm.* Il ne averont point la franchise &c.; qar il ne poient mie trier cel plee, e pur ceo est il remue, e ceo est la cause de nostre Recordare. — *Herle.* Autrefoiz fust ceste parole en vostre Court. E pur ceo qe le plee ne poeit estre leinz termine, le Roi manda &c. qele fust recorde e les parties &c. en Baunk; car si vous eussez leinz desclame &c., nous ne poeymes aver eu le avantage qe done nous est par ley &c., pur ceo qe cele Court ne porte nul record; e pur ceo par Statut ordeine de fere recorder &c. e ajorner &c. hors du contez e teles cours. --GILDEFORD. Vous peschez avant la reye; uncore ne avient pas le temps a desclamer; attendez tant qil viegne, e donqes par resomons poez faire la partie venir cienz a respondre pur ceo qe tele Court vous ad de droit failly.—*Herle.* Sil desclamast, jugement se freit &c.; apres queu jugement il ny avereit nule parole en la Court; quei donqes serreit resomons quant la partie serreit sanz jour?—GILDEFORD. Homme suist sovent resomons ou la partie est sanz jour.—Ad alium diem repetivit rationem quam prius dixit.—HENGHAM. Uncore desclama il point: qei savez vous ceo qil fra ou dirra quant &c. Et quant franchises sunt demaundez cienz e allowez, il est dit au Baillif qe hastive droit face a parties &c.; altrement qe eux returnent; dount issi fetes vous; qe si ceste excepcion fust allowable par luy poeit chescone fraunchise estre tolet; qe en play de terre homme alegge en cele Court bastardie, de quei eux ne pount conustre &c.; en play de dowere puet homme dire qe la demaundante nent espose &c. de A.D. 1305.

A.D. 1305. other their franchises.—HENGHAM (to the bailiff). Assign a day.—And the franchise was allowed &c.

A case upon the same matter.

§ Joan who was the wife of Roger Scot brought a writ of Dower against Ellen &c. for tenements in Yarmouth. The franchise of Yarmouth was challenged and allowed; and a day was assigned in the Court of Yarmouth to the parties &c.; where Joan came, and Ellen said that she ought not to have dower, for her husband Roger sold these tenements to the husband of the said Ellen by a charter, which she showed; and she said that Joan herself afterwards came into the Court of Yarmouth, and assented to that sale, which assent in the said Court was indorsed on the said charter; and she said that the customs of the vill of Yarmouth were such that if a woman thus assented she ought not to have dower.—And it was adjudged that she should take nothing. And Joan sued out a resummons.—*Toudeby.* Judgment is given; which judgment shall not be reversed by that resummons.—HENGHAM. Let Joan come and show in what the Court did her wrong, and wherefore she sued out the resummons.—*Mutford* repeated what he had previously said, and (said he) We tell you, Sir, that in this that Court did us a wrong, for no &c. whilst we were coverte &c. ought to oust us of dower which accrued to us after the death of our husband.—HENGHAM (having consulted with BEREFORD). Ellen, adieu &c., and do you (Joan) sue by writ of False Judgment &c.

Ejectment from wardship.

§ S. who was the wife of Roger Loveday brought the writ against Roger Bygod, Earl of &c., and counted that the wardship &c. belonged to her by reason that one R. father &c. held these tenements of her.—*Hunte* denied &c., and (said he) We tell you that R. &c. did not hold of her by knight-service.—*Friskeney.* Nay, you do quei &c.; e issi toler les e autres lour franchise. IDEM (ballivo). Assignez jour. Et allocata est libertas &c. A.D. 1305.

§ Johane qe fu la femme Roger Scot porta bref de dowere vers Eleyne &c. des tenementz en Jernemuthe. La franchise de Jernemuthe chalange, e allowe; e jour assigne en la Court de Jernemuth a les parties &c.; ou Johane vient, e Eleyne dist qe ele ne devoit dowere avoir, car sun baroun Roger ces tenementz vendy au baroun la dite Eleyne par une chartre qe ele moustra; e dit qe Johane mesme pus vient en la Court de Jernemuth, e a cele vente assenti, le quel assente en la dite Court fust endosse sur la dite chartre; e dit qe les usages de la ville de Jernemuth furent teles qe si femme issi assenti ele ne devoit dowere avoir. Et fust agarde quele ne preist rienz &c. e Johane suist la resomonz. —*Toudeby.* Jugement est[1] rendu, queu jugement ne serra pas reverse par cele resomonz.—HENGHAM. Viegne Johane e moustre ou la Court la fist tort par quei ele sui resomonz.—*Mutteford* repetivit illud quod predicitur: e vous dioms, Sire, qe en ceo nous fessoit &c. tort, qe pur nul &c. tant com nous fums covers &c. nous foringer de dowere qe nous acrust apres la mort nostre baroun. —HENGHAM consulto BEREFORD. Aille Eleyne a Deu &c., e vous suez par bref de faus jugement &c.

Casus super eodem casu.

§ S. qe fu la femme Roger Loveday porta le bref vers Roger Bygod counte &c. Et conta qe com la garde &c. a luy apent par la reson qe un R. pere &c. ces tenementz de luy tyent.—*Hunte* defendi &c. E vous dioms qe R. &c. ne tyent pas de luy par service de chivaler.—*Friskeney.* Nay, vous ne vous escussez point del tort &c.:

De ejectione custodiæ.

[1] MS. estre.

A.D. 1305. not excuse yourself from the tort; were we seised and did you oust us or not?—HENGHAM. He tells you enough, if he did not hold of you. What tort did he do you when you had no right therein?—*Friskeney.* The said R. held the said tenements of our husband Roger by the aforesaid services; after whose death A. son and heir of the said Roger assigned those tenements to us as Dower, and we were seised by virtue of the assignment, and without him we cannot bring them into judgment, and we pray aid.—*Hunte.* And we pray judgment of your writ, since by this you have heretofore supposed that R. held of you, in affirming your estate in this wardship, and now you open it up in right of the services; we pray judgment if you can employ this writ which supposes a simple right to the services: for you could have had a good writ stating "held &c. by assignment &c." *Friskeney* (not however being much driven to it), If the Court see that we can be party to this averment without the said A., we will be.—*Hunte* did not hold to the aforesaid exception, which however was thought valid, but said, He did not hold anything of you by assignment or by any other way, ready &c. —And the other side said the contrary.—So &c.

Taking of beasts.

§ John de Aumeye complained that an Abbat &c., had tortiously taken his beasts &c.—*Herle.* We avow the taking &c., and for the reason that the said John holds of us &c. by homage, fealty, suit every three weeks to our Court of Herdewyk in Devonshire, and by &c., of which services one C. our predecessor was seised &c. by the hand of W. father of John, as by the hand of &c. And, for that the homage &c. was in arrear, he avows the taking of so many beasts &c.: and for the fealty &c., of so many &c., and for the services &c., of so many &c.—And lo! that one may be bound for a tenement which is in one county to do suit in another county.—*Toudeby.* As to the homage we think that we have done it, for he fumes nous seisi e nous oustates vous ou noun ?—HENGHAM. Il vous dit assez sil ne tient pas de vous : quel tort vous fist il quant vous ny aviez nul droit ?—*Friskeney.* Mesme celuy R. tient les dits tenementz de Roger nostre baroun par les avantdiz services ; apres qi mort A. fiz e heir le dit Roger ceux tenementz nous assigna en dowere, e nous seisi par le assignement &c., sanz qi nous ne les poms mener en jugement, e prioms aide.—*Hunte.* E nous jugement de vostre bref, de pus qe par ceo einz ceo avez suppose qe R. tient de vous, en affermant vostre estat de ceste garde, e ore le desafeblez en droit du droit des services ; demaundoms jugement si ceo bref, qe suppose simple droit des services, puissez user ; qar vous puissez aver eu bon bref a dire "tenuit &c. ex "assignatione &c."—*Friskeney* (non tamen multum compulsus), Si la Court veye qe nous puissoms sanz le dist A. a ceste averement estre partie, nous le voloms. —*Hunte* non tenuit se super prædicta excepcione quæ tamen reputabatur valida. Il ne tient nent de vous par assignement ne par autre veye, prest &c. Et alii e contra. Ideo &c. A.D. 1305.

§ Johan de Aumeye se pleigna qe un Abbe &c. atort avoit pris ces avers &c.—*Herle.* Nous avowoms la prise &c., e par la reson qe mesme celui Johan entient de nous &c. par homage, fealte, suite de iii. semeyns a nostre Court de Herdewyk en Devenschyre e par &c., des queux services un C. nostre predecessour fu seisi &c., par my la mayn W. pere Johan, com par la mayn &c. E pur ceo qe le homage &c. est arere, avowe il la prise de tanz des bestes &c. ; e pur la fealte &c. de tanz &c., e pur la service &c. de tanz &c. Et ecce quod quis potest pro tenemento quod est in uno Comitatu potest teneri ad faciendam sectam curie in alio Comitatu.—*Toudeby.* En droit de homage nous entendoms qe nous lavoms fet, qar il fust

Prise des avers.

A.D. 1305. was in ward to the Abbat &c., and his mother told him that before the Abbat had the wardship he took his homage. And as to the fealty, we have tendered it to him, and are ready still to do it.—*Herle.* The homage is still in arrear, ready &c.; and you did not tender us the fealty, ready &c.—*Toudeby.* If you wish to have the homage renewed, we make no account of that.—HENGHAM. Will you have the fealty?—*Herle.* We will; but, to maintain the cause of our avowry, we are ready to aver that they did not tender it to us.—And John did fealty.—HENGHAM to *Toudeby.* Have you done the homage?—*Toudeby.* Our mother told us that we had done it; we ourselves do not know. HENGHAM. Where is the Abbot? *Herle.* He is here, by attorney. HENGHAM. He can not receive the homage: let John seek his lord and do homage to him. *Toudeby.* As to the suit, we do not hold by any suit; and we tell you that neither he nor any of his predecessors was, before the time which is given by the Statute of Marlbridge[1] to make distress for suit, which is before the the first passage of King Henry into Brittany, ever seised of that suit, ready &c. *Kingesham.* Then purchase a Prohibition, which forbids &c.; that writ is instituted for this. HENGHAM. The Statute says that no one shall be distreined for such suit unless he or his ancestors have been accustomed to do it before the first passage &c.; and you have distreined him. *Herle.* By that Statute he ought not to be aided; for we tell you that the second Statute of Westminster[2], which is of later date, gives power to distrein, on the seisin of the ancestor or predecessor from the time when the writ of Novel Disseisin runs, from which time we and our predecessors were seised &c., ready &c. *Malmesthorpe.* Although the Statute gives you power to distrein from that time &c., that is not in contradiction to the other Statute, but only postpones it

[1] 52 Hen. III. c. 9.

[2] 13 Edw. I. c. 2.

en la garde labbe &c., e sa mere lui dit qe einz qe labbe A.D.1305. avoit la garde il prist son homage. E en droit de la fealte, nous lui avoms tendue, e prest sumes uncore de la fere.—*Herle.* Le homage uncore arere, prest &c., e la fealte ne nous tendites point, prest &c.—*Toudeby.* Si vous volez aver le homage renovele, nous ne fessoms force. HENGHAM. Volez la fealte?—*Herle.* Nous la voloms; mes, a meintenir la cause de nostre avowerie, nous sumes prest del averer qil nous ne la tendirent. —Et fecit fidelitatem.—HENGHAM (a *Toudeby.*) Avez fet le homage?—*Tondeby.* Nostre mere nous dist qe nous le aveymes fet; nous ne savoms. HENGHAM. Ou est labbe?—*Herle.* Cy par atturne.—HENGHAM. Ne puet resceivre le homage; querge Johan son seignur e lui face homage.—*Toudeby.* En droit de la suite, nous ne tenoms par nule suite; e vous dioms qe lui ne nul de ces predecessours avant le tenps qe done est de fere destresse pur suite par lestatut de Marleberge, qest avant le primer passage le Roi Henri en Bretaigne, ne fust onqes de cele suite seisi, e prest &c.—*Kingesham.* Purchassez Prohibicioun donqes, qe defend &c. E pur ceo est ceo bref ordine.—HENGHAM. Le Statut voet " quod nullus distringatur pro hujusmodi secta nisi ipse vel antecessores sui facere consueverunt ante primam transfretationem " &c. a vous luy avez destreint.—*Herle.* Par cel Statut ne deit il estre eide; qe nous vous dioms qe le secunde estatut de Westminstre, qe de plus tardif temps est, donne poer a destreindre de la seisine le auncestre ou predecessour du temps qe le bref de novele disseisine curt, de queu nous e nos predecessours seisi &c., prest &c.—*Marm.* Tut vous doigne Statut poer a destreindre de ceu temps &c. ceo nest pas en ofension de autre Statut, einz fet attendre la

A.D. 1305. where you can legally make it do so; and that Statute was made because in a plea of taking of beasts one took title on a seisin so high up and in such a remote time before that Statute, that a jury could not perhaps have knowledge of it.—HENGHAM. Do not gloss the Statute; we understand it better then you do, for we made it: and it is often seen that one Statute extinguishes another.

False judgment.

§ The Abbat of St. Osyth brought the writ in the Court of Colchester, and the record was this; that the said abbat complained in the said Court against A., B., and C., for taking of beasts; and at the first court he was essoined, and at the second court he made default, wherefore a return of the beasts was adjudged to the said A., B., and C.; and the record being read in the same form, four men &c. of that Court &c. avowed that. —*Herle.* Although they now record and have forged that record, we tell you that it is true that the abbat complained against A., B., and C., as they say, and he pleaded with them &c., when they came and avowed the taking &c.; for they said that those of the town of Colchester had a franchise that if any one committed a trespass or tort against them out of their franchise, the misdoers should be attached, when they should come and be found within the town of Colchester, until they should make amends; and they said that because the said abbat had trespassed against P., L., and T., denizens of the town of Colchester, to wit, had tortiously taken toll of them, they took the beasts &c. of the said abbat in Colchester in order to make the amends &c. And the abbat said that by the common law no one could challenge amends for trespass commited on another. And inasmuch as they had acknowledged that the trespass for which they demanded the amends was committed on others than themselves, we pray judgment if for those amends they could make a distress. And on the other ou vous le poez faire de ley ; e fut fet cel Statut pur ceo qe homme prist title en play de prise des avers de si haute seisine e temps loynten avant cel Statut, de quele seisine pays ne poeit par cas aver conissance.—HENGHAM. Ne glosez point le Statut ; nous le savoms meuz de vous, qar nous les feimes ; e sovent veist homme qe un estatut deface un autre. A.D. 1305.

§ Labbe de Seint Osy porta le bref en la Court de Colcestre, e fut le record tel, qe le dit abbe se fu pleint en la dite Court vers A. B. e C. de play de prise des avers ; e [a] la primere Court fust essone, e a la secunde Court fist defaute, par quei return des avers fust agarde a dits A. B. e C. ; e, recordo lecto sub eadem forma, quatuor homines, &c. de Curia illa, &c. illud advocabant. — *Herle.* Coment qe eux recordent a ore, e eient forge cel record, nous vous dioms qe veirs est qe labbe se pleignoit vers A. B. C., auxi com eux dient, e pleda a eux &c., ou eux viendrent e avowerent la prise, &c. ; qar eux disoient qil ount une franchise ceux de la ville de Colecestre qe si homme lour face trespas ou tort hors de lour franchise, qe homme fra attacher ceux qe lour ayent meffet quant il vendrount e serrount trovez denz la ville de Colecestre tant qe eux eient fet les amendes ; e disoient qe pur ceo qe le dit abbe avoit trespasse a un P. L. e T. denzeins de la ville de Colecestre, nomement prise de eux torceneusement tonnue, si pristrent eux les avers &c. le dit abbe en Colecestre pur les amendes fere &c. E le abbe dit qe de comune ley nul ne poet de trespas fet a autri amendes dereigner. E desicom eux avoient conuz qe le trespas pur quei il demandoient les amendes fu fet a autres qe a eux, demaundoms jugement si pur celes amendes destresce poeient fere. Et dautre

De falso judicio.

F 2

A.D. 1305. hand, although there were such a franchise, which he did not admit &c., it was only to be understood of strangers and merchants passing, who had no lands or tenements whereby they might be distrained, if any tort, &c. And inasmuch as the abbat had sufficient lands and tenements whereby &c. if any tort &c., we pray judgment &c. And on the other hand, since he admitted that the trespass about which they spoke was committed out of their franchise, of which they had not power to take cognizance, we pray judgement, &c. And notwithstanding these reasons they adjudged the avowry to be good, and that the answer of the abbat was null, nor did they allow it, but adjudged the return to the said A., B., and C.; and this we are ready to aver by those who heard and saw where and howsoever this Court shall adjudge.—HENGHAM. I would deprive them of flesh and fish for a fortnight if I could see how you can aver it.[1]

Debt, by executors.

§ The executors of John the son of Simond brought a writ of debt against the Prior of the Trinity of London, and demanded from him 300*l.* which John the son of Simond, whose executors they are, delivered to him to be kept during his pleasure &c.; and to prove their persons to be answerable as executors, they put forward a testament which witnessed that one Walter was executor with them, who was not named in the writ; whereupon the prior prayed judgment of the writ. — *Este.* At the proving of the testament, because Walter would not administer, administration was granted by the Ordinary solely to those who are named; and this the testament proves, for it is indorsed by the Ordinary that this Walter never proved, ready &c. —*Toudeby.* His own seal is hanging to the testament which shows that he is executor, and that indorsement may as well be your act as the act of the Ordinary; wherefore we pray judgment

[1] Something seems wanting to the end of the original.

part, tut fut il issi qil en avoit tele franchise, qe il ne granta point &c., ceo ne fu pas a entendre mes qe de estranges e marchanz passanz qe nen avoient terre ne tenement par quei il poeient estre destreinz si nul tort &c. E desicom le abbe assez avoit de terre e tenement par quei &c. si nul tort &c., demaundoms jugement &c. E dautre part, de pus qil avoit conu qe le trespas de quei eux parlerent fut fet hors de lour franchise, de quei il nen avoient poer de conustrer, demaundoms jugement &c.—E ne mie contre esteanz cestes resons il agarderent lavowerie bone e qe le respons labbe ne fust nul, nel allowerent point, einz agarderent as dis A. B. e C. return &c.: e ceo sumes prest del averer par oyanz a veanz ou quanqe ceste Court agardera.—HENGHAM. Jeo voley deporter ces quinneze jours chare e pesson a iceles qe veie coment le purrez averer: fut ordine. A.D. 1305.

§ Les executours Johan le fiz Simond porterent bref de dette vers le Priour de la Trinite de Londre, e demaunderent vers luy .ccc. livres, les queux Johan le fiz Simon qi executours il sunt luy bailla a garder a sa volunte &c.; e [a] afermer lour persones responables com executours il mistrent avant un testament qe testmoigna qe un Wauter fust executour oveske eux, qe ne fu pas nome en le bref; par quei le Priour demaunda jugement del bref.—*Este.* Al prover del testament, pur ceo qe celui Wauter ne voleit fere administracion, soul bailla par ordinere a ces qe sunt nomez; e ceo prove le testament, qe est endosse par le ordinere issi, qe celui Wauter onqes ne administra, e prest &c.—*Toudeby.* Sun seal demeyne est pendant al testament qe testmoigne qil est executour, e cele endossure poeit auxi bien estre vostre fet com fet de ordinere; par quei nous demaundoms

De debito pro executoribus.

A.D. 1305. if you without him ought to be answered. Besides, if he had made an acquittance of this debt, that acquittance would bar them of an action; wherefore &c. —*Passeley.* If those who are named executors would not be executors or take out administration, by reason whereof the Ordinary had given the administration to others who were not named as executors, they would be answered and would answer as executors; wherefore administration makes the executor; since, then, Walter did not administer, it was not necessary that he should be named. —*Malmesthorpe.* If Walter wished to administer who should prevent him? (intimating that no one could).—HENGHAM. Although it be that executors can charge themselves by administration, they cannot demand by administration. Besides, if Walter had received the money and thereupon had made an acquittance, you could not try that acquittance without him; and he is not named: the Court adjudges that you take nothing by your writ: and you, prior, adieu.

§ A. and B., executors, brought a writ of debt against three persons by different præcipes. The one who was the principal debtor came into court, and said that they could not have an action for that he whose executors they were had ordered him to pay that debt to one R. to whom he was bound in a sum of money, and had granted that he should be quit of that debt to him and to his heirs and executors; and he put forward a deed which witnessed it. The executors denied the deed; wherefore it remained in the court. The executors nevertheless sued against the others as sureties and principal debtors, and they came into court.—*Herle.* You cannot have an action, for he who is the principal debtor has put forward the deed of him whose executors you are, to bar you of the action; which deed you have denied, and it is not yet tried; and we pray judgment if, before this deed be tried, we ought to answer about this jugement si vous devez sanz luy estre respondu. Estre A.D. 1305. ceo, sil eust fet aquitance de ceste dette, cele aquitance lour forcloreit de accion ; par quei &c.—*Passeley*. Si ceux qe sunt nomez executours ne voleient mie estre executours ne fere administracion, par quei le ordiner eust baille la administracion a autres qe ne furent pas nomez com executours, ceux serreient respondu com executours e respondre; par quei administracion fet executour; del houre donqe qe Wauter ne administra pas, mester nest pas qil fust nome.—*Malm*. Si Wauter vousit administrer qe luy vieroit? quasi diceret nemo.—HENGHAM. Tut soit il issi qe executours se pount charger par administracion, il ne pount mie demaunder par administracion. Estre ceo, si Wauter eust receu les deniers, e sur ceo eust fet aquitance vous ne porez mie trier cele aquitance sanz luy; e il nest pas nome: si agarde la Court qe vous ne preignez rien par vostre bref, &c.; e le Priour a Deu.

§ Un A. e B. executours porterent bref de dette vers treis par divers præcipes. Lun qe fut principal dettour vient en Court e dit qil ne poient accion avoir, car celuy qi executours il sunt lui avoit assigne a paier cele dette a un R. a qi il fut tenuz en deners, e avoit grante qil fut quites de cele dette vers luy e vers ces heirs e ces executours; e mist avant fet qe le testmoigna: les executours dedissoient le fet; par quei il demura a la Court; les executeurs jatardeys suyrent vers les autres com pleges e principals dettours, qe viendrent ore en Court.—*Herle*. Vous ne poez accion avoir; qar celuy qi est principal dettour ad mys avant le fet celui qi executour vous estes a forbarrer vous de accion, le quel fet vous avez dedit, e nest pas uncore trie; e demaundoms jugement si einz ceo qe ceo fet soit trie, devoms a ceste dette respondre: qe

A.D. 1305. debt : for let us suppose that we answer now, and perchance the debt be recovered against us, and then the deed be tried and be found good, and thus the principal acquitted &c., then they would recover against us whereas the principal was acquitted, which would be contrary to law; wherefore &c.—*Passeley*. If you ought not to answer, and afterwards the deed be found null, whereupon he would be condemned in the debt, and if he were not able to pay, by reason whereof we should sue you, you would again show that deed, wherefore &c.—*Herle* said No, because they were not party to the deed.—HENGHAM. We must inquire about this order to pay; for if it be good, you are all quit; if otherwise, you are all bound to the debt by the obligation; wherefore we must first know if the obligation is your deed &c.—*Herle* admitted the obligation.—HENGHAM. Then stay until the order to pay be tried.—Note, by *Warr.* that, if the deed be found null, as not being the deed of the testator, they will all, without any other answer, be condemned in the debt.

Replegiari. § Robert de Ecleshale complained that J. bishop of Norwich tortiously took his beasts.— *Willuby.* The bishop avows the taking &c., for the reason that he holds the half Wapentake of Newark of our lord the King in chief, within which Wapentake this Robert holds certain tenements which owe suit to that half Wapentake twice a year, after Easter and after Michaelmas, and afforcement of court when judgment is to be given or a thief is to be judged; of which suit one Oliver bishop of &c., predecessor of this bishop, was seised by the hand of one William Clarel, tenant of the same tenements: and for that he was summoned to be at the said Wappentake held next after Easter and after Michaelmas, and came not, it was adjudged first at one Wappentake and then at the other that he should be distreined: and so he avows, &c.—*Tiltone.* There are two kinds of suits; suit-posoms qe nous respondoms ore, e par aventure la dette fust rescovery vers nous, e pus le fet trie e trove pur bon, e issi le principal quite &c., donqe rescoverit il vers nous la ou le principal serreit quite, qe serreit contre lei par quei &c.—*Passeley.* Si vous ne devez ore respondre, e pus le fet soit trove pur nul, par quei il serreit condempne en la dette, e il ne fut pas suffissant, par quei nous suissoms vers vous, vous mustriez autrefoiz ceo fet; par quei &c.—*Herle* dit qe noun, pur ceo qil ne furent pas partie al fet.—HENGHAM. Il covent qe nous enquergoms de cest assignement; qe sil soit trove pur bon, vous estes touz quites, si pur autre, vous estes touz tenuz a la dette par la obligacion; par quei il covent primes qe nous sachoms si cele obligacion soit vostre fet &c.—*Herle* conust la obligacion.—HENGHAM. Donqe demorez ci la qe le assignment soit trie.—Et nota par *Warr.* qe si le fet soit trove pur nul qe ceo nest pas le fet le testator qil serrount touz, sanz autre respons, condempnez en la dette.

A.D. 1305.

Nota.

§ Robert de Ecleshale se pleint qe J. Eveske de Northwyc atort prist ces avers.—*Willuby.* Le Eveske avowe la prise &c., par la reson qil tient le demy Wapentake de Neuwerke de nostre seignur le Roi en chief, denz quel Wapentake cestui Robert tient certeinz tenementz qe deyvent la suite a cel demy Wappentake deus foiz par an, apres la Pasche e apres la Seint Michel, e aforcement de Court quant jugement est rendre ou laron ajugger, de quele suite un Oliver Eveske &c., predecessour cesti Eveske, fut seisi par my la mayn un W. Clarel tenant de mesme les tenements: e pur ceo qil fut somons de estre a mesme le Wappentake prochement tenuz apres la Pasche, e apres la Seint Michel, e ne vient nent, fut agarde a lun Wappentake e a lautre qil fut destreint, e issi avowe il &c.—*Tiltone.* Ily ad deus maneres

Replegiare.

A.D. 1305. service, which is due for tenements, and personal suit which is a coming for the peace; wherefore make your avowry certain, whether you avow for one or the other. —*Herle.* We avow for royal suit due for tenements, which is where a Wappentake or a hundred is holden in chief of the King, and suit is made by reason of tenements which are within the precinct &c.; that is royal suit and is not liable to be acquitted by the mesne.—*Tiltone.* Whereas they say that his predecessor was seised of such a kind of suit, we say that he was never seised except of one annual coming for the peace when he was resident, ready, &c.—And the other side said the contrary.

Note. § After the view of land was prayed, the tenant said that the demandant had parceners who were not named in the writ, and he prayed judgment of the writ.—*The demandant.* You have prayed the view and had it; judgment if you can now challenge omission of blood, since you have prayed the view against him as against the sole heir, accepting him to be the sole heir. —*Inge.* If he were to except against you that you were a bastard, would he not be received to that as well after the view as before? (intimating that he would).—*Malmesthorpe.* The case is not similar; for the exception of bastardy is to the action, and this exception is only to abate the writ. — *Toudeby.* If he wished to claim by the same descent, he would not be received after view prayed. And inasmuch as he might have given this exception before the view prayed, and did not, but prayed the view, accepting the person as solely answerable, we pray judgment.—*Scoter.* A party can not accept what the law will not accept; but the law does not allow that he solely shall be answerable in this action without his parceners; wherefore &c.—BEREFORD. You must answer this exception.—And because he could not deny that he had parceners not de suites; suite service qe est due des tenementz, e sute de persone qe est une venue pur la pees; par quei fetes vostre avowerie encertein, le quel vous avowez pur lun ou pur lautre.—*Herle.* Nous avowoms pur suite real qe est due des tenementz, qest la ou Wappentake ou hundred est tenu en chief du Roi e sute soit fete par reson des tenements qe sunt deinz la purceinte &c.; ceo est suite real e ne chiet mie en aquitance vers le mien.—*Tiltone.* La ou il dient qe sun predecessour fut seisi de une tele manere de suite, il ne fut onqes seisi fors qe de une venue par an pur la pees quant il fut reseant prest &c. Et alii contrarium. A.D. 1305. Nota.

§ Ke apres vewe de terre demaunde, le tenant dist qe le demaundant avoit parceners nent nomez en le bref, jugement del bref.—*Le demaundant.* Vous avez demaunde la vewe e la avez; jugement si a ore puissez omission de saunk chalanger, de pus qe vous avez demaunde le vewe vers lui com vers soul heir, en acceptant lui estre soul heir.—*Inge.* Sil excepcionast encontre vous qe vous fussez bastard, ne serreit il a cel receu auxi bien apres vewe com devant? quasi diceret sic.—*Malm.* Nest pas semblable; qe excepcion de bastardie est al accion, e ceste excepcion nest fors al abatement du bref. —*Toudeby.* Sil vousit clamer par mesme la descente, il ne serreit pas receu apres vewe demaunde. E desicom il poeit aver done ceste excepcion avant la vewe demaunde, e ne fit pas, einz demaunda la vewe en acceptant la persone estre responable soul, e demaundoms jugement.—*Scotre.* Partie ne puet pas accepter ceo qe ley ne acceptra pas; mes ley ne voet qil soul soit responable a ceste accion entere sanz ces parceners; par quei &c.—Bereford. Il vous covent respondre a ceste excepcion.—E pur ceo qil ne poeit dedire qil ne avoit parceners nent nomez en le bref, fut agarde qil ne preist Nota.

A.D. 1305. named in the writ, it was adjudged that he should take nothing. And this was in a writ of Cosinage where the demandant had made a resort to one on whose seisin he demanded, who had two sisters Julia and Elizabeth, from whom issued John and W. who were not named in the writ and who were as near in blood as was the demandant.

Note on debt.

§ Note, by HENGHAM. Where a debt is recovered in the King's Court, all the lands which he (the debtor) holds on the day of the recovery, and the lands which he shall afterwards purchase, shall be charged, into whose hands soever they come, until the judgment be executed and the debt fully levied &c.

Per quæ servitia.

§ One Robert de Leveriche sued out the "per quæ "servitia" against W., to ascertain by what services he held certain tenements of J. Bryan in Langetone, which services were granted to him. — *Lanfar.* These tenements were in the seisin of one G. father of J., who out of his seisin enfeoffed, since the Statute,[1] this W to him and his heirs, to hold of him and his heirs, and we pray judgment, since that feoffment is contrary to the Statute, if on his grant he ought to attorn.—HENGHAM. He ought not to hold of any other than the chief lord &c. since the Statute; whereas he is enfeoffed to hold of him &c. which is not allowable: wherefore as to that let W. go Adieu &c.

Admeasurement of pasture.

§ A writ of Admeasurement of pasture was brought against a man and his wife for tenements which they held in name of the wife's dower; they made default; wherefore the admeasurement was adjudged on their default, and the sheriff was directed to make the admeasurement and return it by a certain day; at which day, the admeasurement being returned, the wife came and prayed to be received to defend her right; and she was received; and she said that she had nothing

[1] Quia Emptores. 18 Edw. I.

rien. Et fut ceo en bref de Cosinage ou le demaundant avoit fet resorte a une de qi seisine il demaunda la quele avoit deus soers Julia e Elizabeth des queles isserent Johan e W. qe ne furent pas nomez en le bref, e les queles furent auxi proches du saunk com le demaundant. A.D. 1305.

§ Nota par HENGHAM. La ou dette est rescovery en la Court le Roi, totes les terres qil tient le jour del rescoverir e les terres qil purchacera apres serrount chargez, en qi meins qil devyegnent, deqes tant qe le jugement soit execute e la dette pleynement leve &c. Nota de debito.

§ Un Robert de Leveriche suist le "per que servi-"cia" vers W., a conustre par quel services il tient certeinz tenements de J. Bryan en Langetone, les queux services luy furent grantez.—*Lanfare.* Ces tenements furent en la seisine un G. pere J., qe hors de sa seisine enfeffa pus le Statut cestui W. a lui e ces heirs a tenir de lui e de ces heirs, e demaundom jugement, de pus qe cel feffement est contre Statut, si par sun grant se deive atturner.—HENGHAM. Il ne deit tenir de autre fors qe del chief seignur &c. pus le Statut, ou il est feffe a tenir de lui &c. qe nest pas suffrable: par quei quant a cel aille W. a Deu &c. Per quæ servicia.

§ Bref de Amesurement de pasture fut porte vers un homme e sa femme des tenementz qil tiendrent en noun de dowere la femme; il firent defaute; par quei le amesurement fut agarde par lour defaute, e mande al viconte qil feit le amesurement e returnast a certein jour; a quel jor, le amesurement returne, vient la femme e pria estre resceu a defendre sun droit; e fut Admesurement de pasture.

A.D. 1305. in the tenements except in name of dower, of the heritage of such an one, in whom &c., and she prayed aid &c., and it was granted. And summons was made &c., and now he does not come; wherefore the wife answers and says that she has no freehold to which common is appendant &c. The party said that to such an averment she ought not to be received, in opposition to the testimony of the sheriff who by warrant from this Court had made the admeasurement, and had returned into this Court that she had a messuage and a virgate of land to which common &c.—HENGHAM. If the sheriff return that I have land where I have none, shall not the party be received to an averment contrary to his return? (intimating that he shall). And the averment was received. Note this.

Appeal of robbery.

§ One R. the son of Nicholas sued out an Appeal of Robbery against Richard parson of the church of Cugworth and several other persons, saying that they feloniously robbed them of an ox &c.; and Richard came and said that he was a clerk, wherefore he could not answer without his Ordinary; and the others put themselves on the country that they were not guilty.—BEREFORD recorded, and said that although they had put themselves on the country for good and for evil, for the advantages which they thought to have by another way, and would not challenge this appeal, the Court ought not to receive the appeal if it be not receivable. And because we see well that he who sues the appeal is of so tender age that he knows not how to distinguish good from ill, and against whom this judgment can not be carried out, and who when he comes to full age may reverse the thing, therefore the Court adjudges that they shall be quit of this appeal. And because you, Nicholas, who are the infant's father, have acknowledged that you have procured and maintained this appeal, and what you have acknowledged it is not necessary should be resceu, e dit qe ele navoit riens en les tenements si noun en noun de doware, del heritage un tel en qi &c., e pria aide &c.; e fut grante. Et fut somons &c.; e ore ne vient pas, par quei la femme respont, e dit qele nad nul franc-tenement a quei comune est apendant &c.: la partie dit qe a tiel averement ne deust ele estre receu, contre testmoingnance de Viconte qe par garant de cienz ad fet le amesurement e returne cienz qele ad un mees e une vergee de terre a quei comune &c.—HENGHAM. Si le Viconte returne qe jeo ay terre la ou jeo nay nule, ne serra pas la partie receu al averement countre sun return? quasi diceret sic. E fut laverement receu; et sic nota. A.D. 1305. Nota.

§ Un R. le fiz Nichol suist un Appel de Roberie vers Richard persone del eglise de Cugworthe e plussours autres, qe eux felonessement le deussent aver robbe de un boef &c.; dount Richard vient e dit qil fust clerk, par quei il ne poeit respondre sanz ces ordiners; e les autres se mistrent en pais qil ne furent de rien coupable. — BEREFORD recorda, e dit qe coment il se sunt mis en pays de bien e de mal, pur les avantages qil entendont par autre veye aver, e ne volent chalenger cest appel, la Court ne deit nent resceivre le appel sil ne soit resceivable. E pur ceo qe nous veoms bien qe cestui qe suit le appel si est de si tendre age qil ne seet mie conustre bien ne mal, e vers qi ceo jugement ne se poet nent parfornir, e qi poet apres quant il vendra de plein age ceste chose purra repeller, par quei agarde la Court qil soient quites de cel apel. E pur ceo qe vous Nichol, qestes pere lenfant, si avez conu qe vous avez procure e meintenu cest appel, e ceo qe vous avez conu nest pas Appellum de Roberia.

A.D. 1305. inquired of by the country, the Court adjudges that you go to prison.—*Herle.* Since he has acknowledged that he is the procurer and abettor of this appeal, and it does not remain in us that we are not quit in due form, we pray our damages against him if the Court will allow it.—And he was told by BEREFORD that he must sue for his damages. And so whereas they put themselves on an Inquest, they passed quit at the suit of the King and of the party, and they had their damages without taking an Inquest.—Upon this Simon de Hibernia made these verses.[1]

Replegiari. § The Prior of Maiden-Bradley complained that Adam de la Forde tortiously took his beasts, namely two cows &c.—*Herle.* On this count he ought not to be answered; for heretofore, of this same taking he complained in this court, and assigned the taking to have been on a certain day in the high street, and afterwards made default, whereupon the return was adjudged; and now he assigns, in his count, that the taking was made in another place and on another day; so he varies from his first count as to the day and place; wherefore we do not think that on such a count he ought to be answered.—*Lanfar.* Before the Statute[2] a party might make default, and on each return adjudged on the default might sue an original writ for the deliverance, and on each deliverance count of divers takings; but now that process is abridged by statute, and the form of pleading is much changed. And inasmuch as we have counted against him of a tortious taking, and he answers not, we pray judgment.—*Herle.* On this same taking the return was adjudged, and that you yourselves have supposed by your writ which you have sued out of the Rolls; for of a new taking a new deliverance must be sued by original writ; then by this writ the nature of the first taking ought to be

[1] Here follow 17 Latin Leonine verses giving an abstract of the case; followed by 29 verses on a different subject.

[2] Westm. 2. 13 Edw. I. c. 2.

mester qe soit enquis par pays, si agarde la Court qe vous aillez a la prison.—*Herle.* Del hour qil ad conu qil est procurour e abbettour de cest apel, e en nous ne remeint mie qe nous ne sumes quites en due forme, e nous prioms nos damages vers luy si la Court le voet suffrir.—E dit luy fust par BEREFORD qil suit ces damages. Et issi la ou il se mistrent en enqueste si passerent il quites a la suite le Roi e la partie, e aveient lour damages sanz enqueste prendre. Unde versus per Simonem de Hibernia.[1] **A.D. 1305.**

§ Le Priour de Mayndenbradele se pleint qe Adam de la Forde atort prist ses avers, nomement deus vaches &c.—*Herle.* Il ne deit a cel counte estre respondu; qe autrefoiz a mesme ceste prise se pleint il en ceste court, e assingna la prise estre fete certein jour en le haute estret, e pus fit defaute, par quei return fut agarde; e ore assingne en son counte la prise estre fete en autre leu e par autre jour, par quei il varie de son primer counte de jour e del leu; par quei nentendoms pas qe a tel counte deive estre respondu.—*Lanfare.* Avant statut poeit partie fere defaute, e a chescon return agarde par defaute sure bref original pur fere la deliverance, e a chescone deliverance counter de divers prise; mes ore est cele suite abregge par statut, e la forme de pleder mut change. E desicom nous avoms conte vers luy de une torcenouse prise, e il ne respond nent, jugement.—*Herle.* De mesme ceste prise fut return agarde, e ceo avez mesmes suppose par votre bref qe vous suistes hors des Roulles; qe de novele prise covent novele deliverance estre suy par bref original; dount par cestui bref deit la nature de la primere prise estre trie; vous **Replegiari.**

[1] See note 1 at p. 96.

A.D. 1305. tried: you have counted of another day and another place, supposing that it was another taking, which cannot be tried by that warrant, and so you have varied from the first taking; we ask judgment and pray the return.—BEREFORD. He says that this writ serves him instead of an original, and nevertheless that would be a very weak reason for giving so high a judgment.—*Herle* (for Adam) avowed the taking &c., for the reason that the said Adam and J. his parcener are lords of the vill of Great Watford, by reason of which seignory they have view of frank-pledge twice a year, after Easter and after Michaelmas, to which leet there is a decennary called the decennary of Fancurt, who are the vileins of the said Prior, which decennary is assessed at the aforesaid leet at 6*s.* yearly, one half to be paid at Easter on the day when the leet is holden, and the other half at Michaelmas &c., of which rent one Walter uncle of this Adam and this John, whose heirs they are, was seised by the hands of the decennaries; and their ancestors before them were seised in like manner from time whereof there is no memory; and for that the rent was in arrear &c., he avows &c. in his own name and in the name of his parcener.—*Lanfar.* Judgment of the form of this avowry; they have avowed for rent, and have not said whether it is rent-seck or rent-service issuing from a freehold; and we pray judgment.—*Roistone.* It seems to me that the avowry is not according to law; for where there is a leet all the residents within the precinct of the leet ought to come for the peace; and they have made this avowry for rent, supposing that they ought not to come to the leet: judgment.—BEREFORD. The new law [1] made that fines be not given for pleading does not defeat rents which were anciently reserved.—*Roistone.* Still it appears that the avowry is defective; for they have avowed this taking in the soil of the Prior, and have not said that the Prior

[1] 3 Edw. I. c. 8., confirming 52 Hen. III. c. 11.

avez counte de altre jour e leu en supposant qe ceo est autre prise qe ne puet mie estre trie par cel garrant, e issi avez varie de la primere prise; demaundoms jugement e prioms return.—BEREFORD. Il dit qe cesti bref lui sert en leu de original, e jatardeys ceo serreit une mult feble cause a doner si haute jugement.—*Herle* (pur Adam) avowa la prise &c., par la reson qe mesme cesti Adam e J. son parcener sunt seignours de la ville de Grant Watteford, par reson de quele seignurye il ount vewe de franc plegge deus foiz par an, apres la Pasche e apres la Seint Michel, a quel lete il i ad une disseygne qe est apelle la disseyne du Fanecurt qe sunt les vileyns cestui Priour, la quele disseyne est arente a la lete avantdite a vi. soz par an, a paier la moite a Pasche le jour de la lete tenu, e lautre moite a la Seint Michel &c., de quele rente un Wauter oncle cestui Adam e cestui Johan, qi heirs il sunt, fust seisi par mi les meins de les diseners; e lour auncestre avant eux seisi en mesme la forme de temps dount memorie nest: e pur ceo ke la rente fut arere &c. si avowe il &c. en sun noun e en noun sun parcener.—*Lanfare.* Jugement de la forme de ceste avowerie; qil ount avowe pur rente, e noun pas dit le quel ceo est rente secke ou rente service issant de franc tenement; e demaundoms jugement. —*Roistone.* Il me semble qe le avowerie est hors de lei; qe la ou ily ad lete, touz les reseanz denz la purceinte de la lete y deyvont venir pur la pees; e il ount fet ceste avowerie pur rente, en supposant qil ne deyvent venir a la lete; jugement.—BEREFORD. La novele ley qest ordine qe fins ne seient pas donez pur pleder ne defet mie rentes qe sunt arentez auncienement.—*Roistone.* Uncore il piert qe lavoerie soit defectif, qil ont avowe ceste prise en le soil le Priour, e nount pas dit qe le A.D. 1305.

A.D. 1305. holds of them by those services, nor do they show any specialty which witnesses that the Prior charged that soil, nor that they were seised by the hand of the Prior, but only by the hands of these vileins who could not charge the freehold of the Prior; wherefore &c. And if the court adjudges, we will give a sufficient answer.—BEREFORD. Stop there, and you shall have your judgment; for the court will give only one judgment on your avowry.—*Lanfar.* They have avowed in the Prior's soil, and have not said that the vileins are reseant on that soil; and we pray judgment.—BEREFORD. If the rent be in arrear, they can distrein throughout the whole decennary as well in the high street as in any other place.—*Lanfar.* They have avowed in the name of their parcener as fully as in their own name, supposing that they can not be party to plead in the right without their parcener; wherefore we pray that their parcener may come in aid.—*Warr.* You have said nothing why we can not be party alone; if you will admit what we have said, there is no need that we should have aid.—And notwithstanding this it was adjudged that he should have aid &c.

Formedon in the reverter.

§ John de Ferrers brought a writ of Formedon in the reverter against William de Ferrers, and demanded certain tenements in the vill named in the writ, and said that W. Launcedene his great-grandfather was seised &c., and gave to Richard Mountfichet in frank-marriage with Agnes his daughter, and because they died &c. it reverted &c. to W. as donor; that from W. the right of the reversion descended to W. as son, from W. to R., and from R. to John who now demands &c. Besides this, he demanded another tenement in the said vill against the said W. by a writ of entry, and said "into which he has "not entry unless after the lease which W. his grand-"father made to Robert de Marchindene for a term "which is passed."—*Herle* (for W.). Sir, we tell you

Priour tyent de eux par teux service, ne especiaute ne moustrent qe testmoigne qe le Priour cel soil charga, ne qil furent seisi par my la mayn le Priour, fors qe par les meins ces vileins qe ne pount le franc tenement le Priour charger; par quei &c. Et si la court lagarde nous respondroms assez.—BEREFORD. Demorez la, e si averez vostre jugement; qar la court ne fra fors qe une agarde sur vostre avowerie.—*Lanfare.* Il ount avowe en le soil le Priour, e ne ount pas dit qe les vileins sunt reseanz sur tel soil; e demaundoms jugement.—BEREFORD. Si la rente soit arere, il pount destreindre par my tote la disseyne auxi bien en le haut estrete com en autre leu.—*Lanfare.* Il ount avowe en le noun lour parcener auxi avant com en lour noun, en supposant qil ne purrount mie estre partie a pleder en le droit sanz lour parcener; parquei nous prioms qe lour parcener viegne en aide.—*Warr.* Vous ne avez rien dit pur quei nous ne poms estre partie soul; qe si vous volez granter ceo qe nous avoms dit, nest mie mester qe nous eyoms eide.—Et, hoc non obstante, fust agarde qil eut eide &c. A.D. 1305.

§ Johan de Ferers porta bref de forme de doun en le reverti vers Willem de Ferers, e demaunda certeinz tenements en la ville nome en le bref, e dist qe W. Launcedene sun besael fut seisi &c., e dona a Richard Mountfichet en franc mariage ove Agnes sa fille, e pur ceo qil morerent &c. reverti &c. a W. com a donor; de W. descendi le droit de la reversion a W. com a fiz, de W. a R., de R. a Johan qe ore demaunde &c. Estre ceo il demaunda autre tenement en mesme la ville vers mesme celui W par bref dentre, e dit en les quels il nad entre si noun pus le lees qe W sun ael fit a Robert de Marchindene a terme qe

Forme de doun en le reverti.

A.D. 1305. that these tenements which he demands, specifying messuages and virgates in both writs, are the manor of Boultone with the appurtenances; and we tell you that that manor was in the seisin of Margaret de Ferrers his grandmother, who out of her seisin gave these tenements to W. our father and to the heirs of his body &c., to hold of her &c., and bound herself and her heirs &c.; and we tell you that we are in by that limitation, and if we were impleaded by a stranger, he as heir in bood to Margaret, would be bound to us in warranty; and in proof of that we tell you that Robert his father, whose heir he is, ratified and confirmed that deed; (and he put forward both deeds); and we pray judgment &c.—*Passeley.* You have put forward two deeds in bar of our action; to which do you hold?—HENGHAM. One is in confirmation of the other, therefore answer to both.—*Passeley.* Sir, at the time when the charter was made and when seisin was delivered of part of the tenements, she was not seised of those tenements which we demand by our writ of Formedon &c.—*Kinge.* If they ought to bar us, it would be by the warranty; but that they can not do, because the warranty extends to the gift; but she could not give that whereof she was not seised; consequently the warranty does not extend to that; wherefore &c.—*Herle.* That is not an answer; suppose I make you a charter of tenements whereof I am not seised, and a year afterwards purchase those tenements and put you in seisin by that charter, that charter is perfected, and it is no answer to say I was not seised on the day of the making of the charter. Besides this, suppose I give you portions of tenements whereof I am seised, and afterwards I am seised of other tenements by purchase or by some other means, and I put you in seisin of that parcel with the charter which comprises the whole, the gift is good enough, and yet I was not seised of that parcel at the time when seisin of the other parcel was delivered to you.—*Scoter* (on the same side). If I give to you cerpasse est.—*Herle* (pur W.). Sire, nous vous dioms qe ces tenements qil demaunde par mees e par vergeez en lun bref e en lautre, sount le maner de Boultone ove les appurtenances; e vous dioms qe cel maner fut en la seisine Margarete de Ferrers sa aele, qe hors de sa seisine dona ces tenements a W. nostre pere e a les heirs de sun corps &c. a tenir de lui &c., e obliga lui e ces heirs &c.; e vous dioms qe nous sumes einz par cele forme, e si nous fuissoms enpledez de un estrange, il com heir Margarete du saunke nous serreit tenuz a la garrantie; e en affermant cel vous dioms qe Robert sun pere, qi heir il est, cel fet ratefia e conferma; e mist avant lun fet e lautre; e demaundoms jugement &c. — *Passeley.* Vous avez mys avant deus fets en barre de nostre accion; a quele volez vous tenir?—Hengham. Lun est en affermant lautre, e pur ceo responez al un e al autre.—*Passeley.* Sire, a cel temps qe la chartre fu fete e qe la seisine fut livere de partie des tenements si ne fut ele mie seisi de ces tenements qe nous demaundoms par nostre bref de forme &c. —*Kinge.* Sil nous deivent barrer ceo serreit par la garrantie; mes ceo ne pount il fere, pur ceo qe la garrantie se estent al doun; mes ele ne poeit doner cel dount ele ne fu pas seisi; par quei a cel ne sestent pas la garrantie; par quei &c.—*Herle.* Ceo nest pas respons; qe posoms qe jeo vous face une chartre des tenements dount jeo ne sui mie seisi, un an apres jeo purchase ceux tenements e vous met en seisine par cele chartre, cele chartre si est pleyne, e si nest mie ceo respons jeo ne fu mei seisi le jour de la confeccion de la chartre. Estre ceo, jeo vous donne parties des tenements dount jeo sui seisi, puis jeo sui seisi de autre tenements par purchase ou en autre manere, jeo vous mette en seisine de cele parcele ove la chartre qe comprent lenter, le doun est assez bon, e si ne fu jeo pas seisi de cele parcele en temps quant la seisine del autre parcele vous fust livere. —*Scotre* (ad idem). Jeo vous A.D. 1305

A.D. 1305. tain tenements with my charter, and afterwards other tenements descend to me, and then I put you in seisin of those tenements, that gift is good and has relation to the first gift by the charter.—HENGHAM said that it was not.—*Toudeby.* Sir, we have said that his grandmother was seised and gave by that charter, to which it is first necessary that they should answer.—*Malmesthorpe* admitted the deed, and said, William Launcedene was seised of the manor wholly, and severed that parcel which we demand by our writ of Formedon from the manor, and gave it to Richard Mountfichet in frankmarriage with Agnes &c. William Launcedene was seised of the body of the manor and died seised, after whose death entered his son William husband of Margaret, and he leased that manor to Robert de Marchidene, to hold for his life; W died; Margaret argued so well with Robert that he rendered the manor to her; afterwards she gave that manor to W. her son &c., to wit those tenements which we demand by our writ of entry. Richard Montfichet was all along seised of the tenements which we demand by writ of Formedon as being severed from the manor by virtue of the first gift; and so she was not seised of those tenements at the time when the gift was made of the manor, ready &c.—HENGHAM. If she was not seised, then she could not give. Therefore tell us if she was seised at that time.—*Toudeby.* We have no need to answer as to the time, for we say that she was seised and gave &c., wherefore &c.; if he will traverse us, he must traverse us as simply as we state it, viz. that she was not seised.—BEREFORD. If you wish to have an averment on your statement, it is fit that you traverse him; and what you give in answer shall be in evidence that she was not seised, because Richard Montfichet was seised; and it shall be entered, and the inquest shall be charged thereon. And so to the country.—And as to the tenement which we demand by our writ of Entry, we do not donne certeinz tenements ove ma chartre, pus autre tenements me descendent, pus jeo vous met en seisine de ces tenements, cel doun est bon e ad relacion al primer doun par la chartre. — HENGHAM dixit quod non. —*Toudeby.* Sire, nous avoms dit qe sa aele fu seisi e dona par cele chartre, a quei il convent primes qil respoignent.—*Malm.* conust le fet, e dist qe Willem Launcedene fut seisi del maner enterement, e severa cele parcele qe nous demaundom par nostre bref de forme de doun del maner, e dona a Richard Montfichet en franc-mariage ove Agnes &c. Willem Launcedene seisi del corps del maner e morust seisi, apres qi mort entra W sun fiz, baroun Margarete, e lessa cel maner a Robert de Marchidene tenant a terme de sa vie : morust W. ; Margarete parla tant ove Robert qil la rendit le maner ; pus ele dona cel maner a W. sun fiz &c., saver ces tenements qe nous demaundoms par nostre bref dentre. Richard Montfichet tut tenps seisi des tenements qe nous demaundoms par nostre bref de forme de doun com severez del maner par vertu del primer doun, e issi ne fut ele mie seisie de ceux tenements a cel temps qe le doun se fit del maner, prest &c.—HENGHAM. Si ele ne fu pas seisie, donqe ne poeit ele pas doner. E pur ceo dites nous si ele fut seisie en cel temps.—*Toudeby.* Nous ne avoms mie mestier a respondre al temps ; qe nous dioms qele fut seisie e dona &c., par quei &c. ; sil nous voille traverser, il covent qil nous traverse auxi simplement com nous le dioms qe ele ne fu pas seisie.—BEREFORD. Si vous volez aver averement sur vostre dit, il covent qe vous luy seez travers ; e ceo qe vous donez pur respons serra en evidence qe ele ne fu pas seisie, pur ceo qe Richard Montfichet fut seisi, e serra entre, e sur cel serra lenqueste charge. Et sic ad patriam. E quant a tenement qe nous demaundoms par nostre bref dentre, A.D. 1305.

A.D. 1305. think that they can bar us, for the deed put forward is the deed of a female through whom we do not demand anything, and who is a total stranger to him on whose seisin we demand; and we do not think that by that deed of a stranger they can bar us.—HENGHAM. Are you heir in blood?—It was said that he was, but he had nothing by descent.—HENGHAM. You are not within the meaning of the Statute,[1] and at common law the heir in blood, whether he have anything by descent or not, would be barred in the Right, by the deed of his father and mother; wherefore as to that await your judgment &c.

[1] 6 Edw. I. c. 3.

nentendoms pas qil nous puissent barrer, qar le fet mys est fet de femele par my qi nous ne demaundom rien, e qe est tut estrange a celui de qi seisine nous demaundom; e nentendoms pas qe par cel fet de estrange nous puissent barrer.—HENGHAM. Estes vous heir du saunk? —Fut dit qe oil, mes il nad rien par descente.—HENGHAM. Vous ne estes mie en cas de Statut, e a la comune ley le heir du saunke, le quel qil eit par descente ou noun, serreit barre en le droit par le fet le pere e la mere; par quei quant a cel attendez vos jugement, &c. A.D. 1305.

PLACITA DE ANNO XXXIV°

REGIS EDWARDI.

HERE BEGIN THE PLEAS IN HILARY TERM OF THE XXXIVTH YEAR OF THE REIGN OF KING EDWARD.

A.D. 1306. Cui in vitâ. § A woman brought her writ of Cui in vita against a tenant.—*Lanfar.* We pray the View.—*Hamptone.* You ought not to be ignorant into what tenements you entered through our husband.—HENGHAM. You shall not have the View.

Entry. § A man brought his writ of entry Dum fuit infra ætatem against William de Henley and Isabel his wife, who said that he was of full age; whereupon an inquest was joined; and then the husband made default; whereupon the Petit Cape issued &c.; on which day the woman prayed to be received to defend her right.—*Lanfar.* She ought not to be received; for heretofore we brought the like writ against William alone, when he said that he had nothing in the tenements except in right of his wife who was not named in the writ, and prayed judgment; and we wished to have averred that he was sole tenant, and to that we could not be received, wherefore our writ abated, and this writ was given to us by the Court; and we are still ready to aver that she has nothing except as wife of William; judgment if she ought to be received. —*Este.* And since you have acknowledged that she has nothing in the tenements, and he supposes by his writ that she and her husband are joint tenants, judgment of the writ.—HENGHAM. I think that she is to be received. —*Lanfar.* Then let her show her right.—*Este.* Those tenements were given to us and to John our son, by this charter, and he is not named in the writ; judgment &c. —*Lanfar.* Heretofore you and your husband pleaded to the inquest, thereby supposing that that the entire

INCIPIUNT PLACITA DE TERMINO SANCTI HILLARII ANNO REGNI REGIS EDWARDI XXXIIII°.

§ Une femme porta sun bref 'cui in vita' vers un tenant.—*Lanfare.* Nous demaundoms la Vewe.—*Hamptone.* Vous ne devez mie mesconustre en queux tenements vous entrastes par nostre baroun.—Hengham. Vous ne averez mie la Vewe. **A.D. 1306.** Cui in vita.

§ Un home porta sun bref dentre "dum fuit infra "ætatem" vers Willem de Henley e Isabel sa femme, qe dissoient qil fust de plein age; par quei enqueste se joynt; e pus le baron fist defaute; par quei le petit cape issit &c.; a quel jour la femme pria de estre receu a defendre sun droit.—*Lanfare.* Receu ne deit ele estre; car autrefoiz si portames nous autiel bref vers Willem soul, ou il dist qil ne avoit rienz en les tenements si noun com del droit sa femme nent nome en le bref, e demaunda jugement; ou nous volioms aver averre qil fust soul tenant, e a ceo ne poms estre receu, par quei nostre bref se abati, e cestui bref nous fust done par la Court; e uncore sumes prest daverer qele nad rien si noun com femme Willem; jugement si ele deit estre receu.—*Este.* E de pus qe vous avez conue qele nad rien en les tenements, e par sun bref il suppose qele e sun baron sunt joint tenans, jugement del bref.—Hengham. Jeo loo qele soit receu.—*Lanfare.* Mustre donqe sun droit.—*Este.* Ceux tenements nous furent donez e a Jon nostre fiz, e par ceste chartre, nent nome en le bref; jugement &c.—*Lanfare.* Altrefoiz vous e vostre baroun pledastes al enqueste en supposant la Entre.

A.D. 1306. tenancy was in your persons; wherefore to this answer you ought not again to be received.—HENGHAM. Was she ever received before now?—*Lanfar.* No.—HENGHAM. Plead over.—*Lanfar.* Sole tenant, ready &c.—*Este.* To this averment we can not be party without our son, and he is not named; judgment, &c.—HENGHAM. Adieu, without day.

Dower. § One Clarissa who was the wife of Nicholas de Seytone brought a writ of Dower against John de Neville, and demanded the third part of a messuage, one acre of land and twenty shillings of rent &c.—*Willuby.* What you call a messuage is a garden appurtenant to our messuage, and we vouch to warranty Thomas son and heir of the said Nicholas, to be summoned &c.; and as to the remainder, we tell you that the wardship of the body of the said Thomas belongs to us, because his father held of us by priority of feoffment; and she has eloigned the body (of Thomas), and whenever she restores him to us, we will yield her dower.—*Tiltone* (for the other side) went out to imparl, and came back.—*Willuby.* We claim a moiety of the land by feoffment, and the other moiety as guardian, and we are not named guardian; judgment of the writ.—*Tiltone.* You can not get to that, for for part you have vouched, and as to the remainder you have given such an answer, whereupon we went out to imparl; judgment if now &c.—*Willuby.* This is a Præcipe, and if it abate in part, it abates wholly.—HENGHAM. He deforces the tenements as guardian, and he ought to have been named guardian, but is not; wherefore we abate the writ.

Restoration of writings. § John son of Mabel brought a Justicies in the county court against Piers de C., to compel him to give up a writing and a charter; the plea was afterwards removed into the Bench by a Pone at the suit of the defendant.—*Lanfar.* The original says "that he restore to him a "certain writing of agreement and a charter," and the tenance entier en vos persones, par quei a ceo respuns ne devez ore altrefoiz estre receu.—HENGHAM. Fust ele onqe receu avant ore?—*Lanfare.* Nanal.—HENGHAM. Dites outre.—*Lanfare.* Soul tenant, prest, &c.—*Este.* A ceste averement ne poms estre partie sanz nostre fiz, e il nent nome, jugement &c.—HENGHAM. Alez a Deu sanz jour. A.D. 1306.

§ Une Clarisse qe fust la femme Nichol de Seytone porta bref de dowere vers Johan de Neville, e demaunda la terce partie de une mies, une acre de terre, .xx. soz de rente &c.—*Willuby.* Ceo qe vous apellez mies ceo est un gardyn appurtenant a nostre mies, e vouchoms a garrantie Thomas fiz e heir meme cel Nichol, qe serra somons &c.; e en droit del remenant, vous dioms qe la garde del corps le avantdit Thomas a nous apent, pur ceo qe sun pere de nous tint par priorite de feffement; e ele ad alloigne le corps, e a quel houre qele nous lui rende, nous la rendroms sun dowere.—*Tiltone,* pur lautre partie, issit denparler e revyent.—*Willuby.* Nous clamons la moite de la terre par feffement, e lautre moite come gardein, nent nome gardein, jugement del bref.—*Tiltone.* A ceo ne poez avener, qe de partie si avez vouche, e del remenant done tiel respuns, sur quei nous sumes issu denparler; jugement si ore &c.—*Willubi.* Ceo est un præcipe, e sil abate en partie il abate en tut.—HENGHAM. Il est deforceor des tenements come gardein, ou il deust aver este gardein nome, e ceo nest il mie; par quei nous abatoms le bref. Dower.

§ Johan le fiz Mabille porta un Justicies en conte vers Peres de C., de ceo qe ilui rendesit un escrist e une chartre; pus la parole fust remue en Bank par un Pone a la suite le defendaunt.—*Lanfare.* Le original voet "quod reddat ei quoddam scriptum conventionale De scriptis reddendis.

A.D. 1306. Pone says "a certain writing obligatory and a charter"; judgment of the variance.—*Malmesthorpe.* It is your own purchase, wherefore &c.—*Hales.* The sheriff ought not to have done anything on that Pone.—*Friskeney.* It would be hard if he were to abate our writ by his own bad purchase.—HENGHAM. By what warrant shall we hold this plea?—*Friskeney.* We have seen before you that if a Replegiari was removed hither at the suit of the defendant, although it varied &c., the writ would not abate, but the plea would go on, since the original was here: so in the present case, since you have the original here.—HENGHAM. The original is a Justicies; how by that writ should we have warrant to hold this plea? (intimating that they should not).—*Malmesthorpe.* So he will always abate our writ.—HENGHAM. Do you purchase another Justicies; we will not intermeddle with this plea.

Darrein presentement. § An Assise of Darrein Presentement was brought against the Dean of the church of Lincoln.—*Herle.* The Dean has nothing in the church except jointly with the chapter who are not named in the writ; judgment.—*Willuby.* You solely disturb us and deforce us, ready to aver it by the assise.—HENGHAM. Did he find his deanery severally seised or not?—*Willuby.* He solely disturbs us and deforces us of the advowson; and although the chapter were named, yet since the chapter does not disturb us, we should have no advantage; wherefore &c.—HENGHAM. Keep your days until the Quinzein of Easter.

Replegiari. § An avowry was made thus:—Maude avows the taking good, &c., and for the reason that one W. was seised of the manor of A., and granted the same manor to Maude for the whole of Maude's life; on which grant, one R., tenant of the said manor by services which give wardship, attorned for these services to Maude; which R. died, and his son was under age, wherefore Maude

" et unam cartam," e le Pone voet "quoddam scrip- A.D. 1306.
" tum obligatorium et unam cartam"; jugement de la variance.—*Malm.* Ceo est vostre purchase demene, par quei &c. — *Hales.* Le viconte deust rien aver fet par ceo pone. — *Friskeney.* Ceo serreit duresce sil abatesit nostre bref par sun malvois purchaz.—HENGHAM. Par quel garant tendrioms nous ceo play? — *Friskeney.* Nous avoms veu devant vous si un replegiari fust remue cienz a la suite le defendant, tut y ust il varie &c. le bref ne se abatereit mie, einz home tendreit le play avant, de pus qe le original fust cienz: auxi par de cea, de pus qe vous avez le original cienz. HENGHAM. Le original si est un Justicies. Coment par ceo bref averioms nous garant a tener ceo play? quasi diceret nequaquam. *Malm.* Issint abatereit il touz jours nostre bref.—HENGHAM. Purchacez vous autre Justicies; qe nous ne nous entremettroms mes de ceo play.

Drein presentement.

§ Une assise de drein presentement fust porte vers le Deen del eglise de Nicole.—*Herle.* Le Deen nad rien en leglise si noun joint ovesqe le chapitre nent nome en le bref, jugement.—*Willuby.* Vous soul nous destourbez e nous deforcez, prest daverer par assise. —HENGHAM. Trova il sa Dene severalment seisi ou noun?—*Willuby.* Il soul nous destourbe e nous deforce lavoeson; e tut fust le chapitre nome, de pus qe le chapitre ne nous destourbe mie, nous naverioms nule avantage; par quei &c. HENGHAM. Agardez vos jours a la quinzeine de Pasche.

Replegiari.

§ Une tiele avoerie fust fete. — Maude conust la prise bone &c. e par la resoun qe un W. fust fete seisi del maner de A., e granta meime le maner a Maude a tote la vie Maude, par quel grant un R., tenant de meime le maner par services qe donnent garde, se atturna de ces services a Maude; le quel R. devya, e sun fiz denz age, par quei Maude seisi la garde. E pur ceo qe un

A.D. 1306. seized the wardship: and for that one William holds a messuage and a carucate of land within the same manor of the aforesaid R. by fealty and by the service of four marks and a half by the year, for the four marks and a half in arrear for one year before the day of the taking she distreined him, as well she might, on account of the said heir, and in the same place as in parcel of the tenements.

Default after default.

§ One Sarah Fetplace brought a writ against William, who made default after default; then came one William who said that he was tenant &c. —*Lanfar.* You are not that William against whom we bring our writ, but you are his son, and we pray judgment on the default.—*Hedone.* William who is here is tenant of the tenements demanded, and was so on the day when the writ was purchased, ready &c. —*Lanfar.* You had nothing in the tenements on the day when the writ was purchased, ready &c. —*Hedone.* We pray that he may find surety for the issues in the mesne time.—And he did so by judgment of the Court and of HENGHAM.

False judgment.

§ A writ of False judgment was brought against the suitors.—The *Sheriff* answered that he had distreined twenty-seven, and he named their names; and then the suitors were summoned. Twenty came, and the other seven did not come.—*Wescote.* See here the suitors ready to make their record.—*Willuby.* All the suitors are not come, wherefore we pray a writ to make the others come. —*Wescote.* There are no suitors in the Court of Winchester, but when a writ of right was brought, they summon the people of the town, but the serjeants do not come nor do the merchants who have to trade; so it would be hard if all the people of Winchester should have to come here; wherefore we pray that you will receive their record. — *Willuby.* Seven of those are wanting whom the sheriff testifies that he summoned and who are distreined.—HENGHAM. Sue out a writ to

Willem tient un mies e une carue de terre denz meime le maner del avantdit R. par fealte e par les services de .iiij. mars e demy par an, e pur le .iiij. mars e demi arere un an avant le jour de la prise si lui destreint ele come bien luy lust par reson del heir avantdit, e en mesme le leu com en parcel des tenements. **A.D. 1306.**

§ Une Sare Fetplace porta un bref vers Willem qe fist defaute apres defaute; survyent un Willem qe dist qil fust tenant &c. — *Lanfare.* Vous nestes mie celui Willem vers qi nous portoms nostre bref, einz estes sun fiz, e prioms jugement sur la defaute. — *Hedone.* Willem ke ci est est tenant des tenements demaundez, e fust le jour del bref purchace, prest &c. — *Lanfare.* Qe vous naviez rienz en les tenements le jour du bref purchace, prest &c. — *Hedone.* Nous prioms qil trove siurte des issues en le meen temps. Et ita fecit per considerationem curiæ et per HENGHAM. **Defaute [apres] defaute.**

§ Un bref de faux jugement fust porte vers les suiters. —*Le Viconte* respoundi qil avoit destreint .xxvii., e noma lour nouns, e pus les suiters furent demaundez. Les .xx. viendrent, les .vii. ne viendrent point. —*Wescote.* Veez ici les suiters prest a faire lour record.—*Willuby.* Touz les suitiers ne sunt mie venuz; par quei nous prioms bref a faire venir le remenant.—*Wescote.* Il ny sunt nuls suiters en la Court de Wyncestre; mes quant bref de droit est porte, home fra somondre les genz de la ville, mes les serjanz ne viendrent point, ne les marchanz qe ount a marchander; dont duresse serreit si touz les genz de Wyncestre vendreint cienz; par quei nous prioms qe vous recevez lour record.—*Willuby.* Ily faillent .vii. de ceux dount le viconte testmoigne la somons, e qe sunt destreint.—HENGHAM. Suiez bref a **Faux jugement.**

A.D. 1306. cause the others to come.—*Wescote.* Then we pray that you grant that they may make their record before Sir Piers when he shall come into the country, in like manner as we have seen you formerly do.—HENGHAM. You shall not have it.—A like plea and process was seen on the following day &c.

Cosinage where bastardy was alleged.

§ Hugh Chival brought his writ of Cosinage against Roger Chival, and counted of the seisin of Robert descending to Hugh as brother, from Hugh to John, from John to Hugh who now demands.—*Herle.* We are son of Robert and are in as heir; judgment if during our life you can have an action.—*Hedone.* Robert died without heir of his body, ready &c.—*Herle.* We do not claim, but we tell you that we are son of Robert and are in as heir; judgment &c. since you can not deny that we are son of Robert.—*Hedone.* You can not be heir; for you are a bastard, ready &c.—And the other side said the contrary.—So let them have a writ to the Bishop.—*Toudeby.* We pray judgment if in this possessory writ, which is of so tender a nature, he ought to be received to bastardise the tenant.—HENGHAM. As well in a possessory writ as in any other writ.

Mesne.

§ A man brought a writ of Mesne against one Walter, who demanded what he had to show the right to acquittance; and he put forward a deed which stated that the father of the defendant released and quit-claimed to him two shillings of rent, and to hold of him by the service of a rose every year, and bound himself and his heirs to warranty and acquittance against all persons &c.—*Rostone.* These same tenements were holden of A. our grandfather by the services of 4*s.* by the year, and 12 hens and two cocks; after whose death the said services descended to B. and to C. our father as one heir, by reason of Gavelkind, so that the tenant paid six hens and one cock and 2*s.* of rent to our father, and the like to his brother; afterwards our father released fere venir le remenant.—*Wescote.* Donqe prioms nous qe vous grantez qil puissont faire lour record devant Sire Peres quant il vendra en pays, sicom nous avom veu qe vous avez avant ces houres grante.—HENGHAM. Vous nel averez point.—Autel plai e proces fut veu lendemein &c. A.D. 1306.

§ Hughe Chival porta sun bref de Cosinage vers Roger Chival, e conta de la seisine Robert, descendant a Hughe com a frere, de Hughe a Johan, a Johan a Hughe qe ore demaunde. —*Herle.* Nous sumes fiz Robert e sumes einz com heir, jugement si, vivant nous, puissez accion avoir.—*Hedone.* Qe Robert morust sanz heir de sey, prest &c.—*Herle.* Nous ne clamoms mie, einz vous dioms qe nous sumes fiz Robert, e einz com heir; jugement &c., de pus qe vous ne poez dedire qe nous ne sumes fiz Robert.—*Hedone.* Heir ne poez estre, qe vous estes bastard, prest &c.—Et alii e contra.—Ideo habeant breve ad Episcopum.—*Toudeby.* Nous demaundoms jugement si en cestui bref de possession, qest de si tendre nature, deit il estre receu de bastarder le tenant. HENGHAM. Auxi bien en bref de possession com en autre bref &c. Cosinage [ou] bastardie [fut] alegge.

§ Un home porta bref de Meen vers un Wauter, qe demaunda ceo qil avoit de la quitance; e il mist avant un fet qe voleit qe le pere le defendant luy relessa e quiteclama .ii. soz de rente e a tener de luy par les services de une rose par an, e obligha luy e ces heirs a la garantie e a la quitance vers tote gent &c.—*Rostone.* Mesmes ces tenements furent tenuz de A. nostre ael par les services de .iiii. soz par an, .xii. gelins e .ii. cokes, apres qi mort mesmes les services descendirent a B. e a C. nostre pere come a un heir, par resoun de Gavelekynde, issint qe la tenant fist .vi. gelynis e un coke .ii. soz de rente a nostre pere, e autant a sun frere; pus nostre pere relessa les services qe a lui furent De Medio.

A.D. 1306. the services which were due to him excepting a rose to him yearly, and since that time our uncle died without heir of his body, so that the right to the other 2*s.* descended to us; then we acknowledge the services due and we will admit the acquittance. — *Malmesthorpe.* First admit this deed.—*Rostone.* I will admit it, but we pray that our statement may be noted on the roll, so that we be not foreclosed on another occasion from demanding the same services.—And it was granted by the Court.—And then he admitted the acquittance, saving to him the right to 2*s.* when he would demand them.

Replevin.

§ Oliver de la Souche avowed a taking of swans, for the reason that he had such a franchise in the water of Avon from the bridge of Donyngton to Christchurch, through whatever land the water goes, that no one ought to have swans without our permission, and of which we and all the tenants of the manor have been seised from the time of William the bastard down to the present time; and for that we found swans in the water without our permission we took them.—*King.* We are seised of having swans in the place without permission, and that before you had any thing therein, for you are a purchaser.—*Herle.* We and all the tenants of the manor have been seised &c. as above, and he also is a purchaser and has shown no title.—HENGHAM. He says that he was seised before you had anything &c. Is that not a good title as to you?—*Herle.* We and all the tenants of the manor have been seised, without this &c., as above.

Note.

§ Note, that at the day of the return of the writ to cause the four knights to come and choose &c., between Roger de Pengerskeke demandant and John de Leicester and Joan his wife tenants, on the first day of the Quinzein of St. Hilary, the default was recorded. On the next day John came to the bar and answered for his wife as attorney, and for himself in his own person, and said that that default ought not to hurt him, because dues, salve une rose a lui par an, e pus ceo temps nostre oncle morust sanz heir de sey, issint qe le droit des autres deus soz nous est pus descendu; donqes nous conissoms les services dues, e nous lui conustrom la quitance.—*Malm.* Conusez primes ceo fet.—*Rostone.* Jeo le conusse bien; mes nous prioms qe nostre dist soit touche en roulle, qe nous ne seoms mie forclos autrefoiz a demaunder mesmes les services.—Et concessum fuit a Curia.—E pus il conust la quitance, sauve a luy le droit de deus soz quant il les voudra demaunder. A.D. 1306.

§ Oliver de la Souche avowa une prise de cygnes par la resoun qe il avoit une tiele franchaise en lewe de Avene del Pount de Donyngton dekes a Cristes Chirche, par qi terre qe lewe se estent, qe nul home deit cygnes avoir sanz gre fere a nous, e dount nous avom este seisi e touz les tenans del maner de B. del temps Willem Bastard deke en cea; e pur ceo qe nous trovames ces cygnes en lewe sanz nostre gre, si le preymes.—*King.* Nous seisi de aver cygnes en lewe sanz gre faire, e ceo einz ceo qe vous rien i aviez, car vous estes purchasour.—*Herle.* Nous e touz les tenans del maner seisiz, ut supra; e il est auxi purchasour, e nule title ne a moustre.—HENGHAM. Il dist qil est seisi einz ceo qe vous rien. y aviez &c.; ne ceo bon title en droit de vous?—*Herle.* Nous e touz lez tenanz del maner seisi, sanz ceo, ut supra. Replegiari.

§ Nota ke al jour del bref returne de fere venir les iiii. chivalers de elyre &c. entre Roger de Pengerskeke demaundant e Johan de Leycestre e Jone sa femme tenans, al primer jour de la quinzeine de Seint Hillari la defaute fust recorde. Lendemein vient Johan a la barre e respondi com atturne sa femme, e luy meimes en propre persone, e dist qe cele defaute ne luy dust nure, Nota.

A.D. 1306. he was hindered by the rising of the waters.—*The demandant's attorney.* Where were you hindered?—*The tenant.* At Cesham.—MALLORE. At what hour of the day?—*The tenant.* At noon.—*The demandant's attorney.* And we pray judgment if from that time he could be here at the hour of pleading, since it is fifteen leagues away from here. Besides he began his journey too late. —*The tenant.* I travelled night and day.—MALLORE. What did you do when you came to the water and could not pass? Did you raise the hue and cry and the menée? for otherwise the country would have no knowledge of your hindrance.—*The tenant.* No, sir, I was not so much acquainted with the law, but I cried out and hallo'd.—*The demandant's attorney.* Judgment outright of his default, and we pray seisin of the land.—MALORE. Will you accept the averment that he was hindered as he says. — *The attorney.* If you adjudge so, sir; but since he has admitted that he did not raise the menée, judgment of his admission.—HENGHAM. Keep your days until to-morrow. — And on the morrow they were adjourned to the Quinzein of Trinity: which to some seemed strange.

Debt. § A man brought his writ of Debt in the county court; the defendant purchased a Pone to remove the plea; the sheriff returned the Pone without the original, and said that the cause in the writ was not true.—*Lanfar.* The cause is and was true, ready &c., and we pray a writ to cause the sheriff to come and answer for his false return.—And he could not be received to this, but he was told that he must return to the county court.

§ Note that in a Cui in vitâ the tenant said that he from whose gift the woman took her title was not ever so seised that he could make the gift.—And it is a good issue that she had nothing except as wife of the man. And he was received to the averment.

Entry. § One Robert and one Agnes brought their writ of Entry "ad terminum qui præteriit," into which he had qil fust destourbe par crecin de ewe.—*Latturne le demaundant.* Ou destourbe?—*Le tenant.* A Cesham. —MALLORE. A quel houre de jour?—*Le tenant.* A houre de mydy.—*Latturne le demaundant.* E nous jugement, si de cel houre poeit estre ici a houre de plee, de pus qe ceo est xv. lues de veie de ci. Estre ceo il comensa ces journez trop tard.—*Le tenant.* Jeo alay nuyt e jour.—MALLORE. Quei feistes vous quant vous venistes al ewe e ne poeites passer? levates hu e cri e la mene? qe autrement le pays navereit point de conissance de vostre destourbance.—*Le tenant.* Sire, nay, qe jeo ne savoye mie tant de ley, mes jeo criay e brayay. —*Latturne le demandant.* Jugement de sa defaute tut atrenche, e prioms seisine de terre.—MALORE. Volez laverement qil fust destourbe com il dist.—*Latturne.* Sire, si vous agardez; mes de pus qil ad conu qil ne leva mie la mene, jugement de sa conissance.—HENGHAM. Agardez vos jours a demein.—E pus lendemein furent ajornez a la quinezeine de la Trinite: quod tunc videtur quibusdam mirabile. A.D. 1306.

§ Un homme porta sun bref de dette en conte; le defendant purchasa un Pone a remuer la parole; le viconte returna le Pone sanz le original, e dist "quod "causa non in brevi vera."—*Lanfare.* Quod causa est et fuit vera, prest &c.; e prioms bref a fere venir le viconte a respondre de sun faux return. Et non potuit admitti. Immo dictum est ei quod redeat ad comitatum. Dette.

§ Nota ke en un "cui in vita" le tenant dist qe cel de qi doun la femme prist sun title ne fust unkes seisi qe doun poet fere. Et exitus est bonus quod nil habuit nisi ut uxor viri. E fut resceu al averement.

§ Un Robert e une Agnes porterent lour bref dentre "ad terminum qui preteriit," en les queux il navoit

A.D. 1306. not entry unless after the lease which the great-grandfather of the said Walter and Agnes thereof made &c.; and in counting he made the common ancestor great-grandfather to one and great-great-great-grandfather to the other, and of this variance *Friskeney* prayed judgment.—HENGHAM. The proximity of one parcener draws to itself the other parcener who is of a further degree, and makes the writ good, as in a writ of Mordancester and in other possessory writs according to the statute.[1]—*Friskeney.* Although we were in a writ of Mordancester, it would be right to make the parceners such as they really are, farther off or nearer to the ancestors in the degrees.—HENGHAM. We shall not have a writ in the Chancery of the seisin of the great-great-great-grandfather.—*Friskeney.* What is that to us? we pray judgment of this writ.—*Hegham.* Of two hardships the less is to be chosen; but it is a less hardship to maintain this writ in this case, than to drive us to our writ of Right, since our action is mixed in the possession, and we can not have any other writ in the Chancery.—HENGHAM. The Mordancester was made to avoid battle.—And so to judgment.

Intrusion. § Command Henry de Verdone and Matilda his wife that &c. they yield up to Stephen son of Nicholas one messuage &c. into which the said Henry and Matilda have not entry unless after the intrusion which W. de B. made on them after the death of R. de W and Matilda his wife who held them for their lives by grant from Roger Attehale, uncle of the said Stephen, by a fine thereof in our court at &c. before Roger de Seyton and his companions justices of the Bench, levied between the said Roger and Robert and Matilda his wife, and which after the deaths of the said Robert and Matilda ought to revert to the said Stephen by the limitation of the said fine.—And he prayed the View, and had it.

[1] 6 Edw. I. st. 1. c. 6.

entre si noun pus le lees [qe le] besael les avantdiz Wauter e Agnes de ceo enfist &c.; e en contant si fist il le comune auncestre besael al un e quartael al autre, e de ceo demaunda jugement. *Friskeney* de la variance. —HENGHAM. La procheinete del un parcener atret a sei lautre parcener qest en plus lointein degre, e fet le bref bon, come en le mortdancestre e en autre bref de possession solom lestatut.—*Frisqeney.* Tut fuissoms en le mortdancestre il covendreit fere les parceners al auncestres tiels com il fuissont plus loinz ou pres en les degrez.—HENGHAM. Nous naveroms nul tel bref en la Chancelerie de la seisine le quart ael.—*Friskeney.* Quei est ceo a nous? nous demaundoms jugement de cestui bref. — *Hegham.* De deus duresces la meindre est a lire; mes meindre duresce est a meintenir ceo bref en ceo cas qe nous chacer a nostre bref de droit, de pus qe nostre accion est mixt en la possession e nous ne poms autre bref avoir en la Chancelerie. — HENGHAM. Le Mortdancestre fust fet pur eschuyre bataille. Et sic sunt ad judicium.

A.D. 1306

Entre

De intrusione.

§ Precipe Henrico de Verdone et Matilde uxori ejus quod &c. reddant Stephano filio Nicholai unum mesuagium &c. in quibus iidem Henricus et Matilda non habent ingressum nisi post intrusionem quam W. de B. in illas fecit post mortem R. de W. et M. uxoris ejus, qui illas tenuerunt ad vitam suam ex concessione Rogeri Attehale, avunculi prædicti Stephani, per finem inde in curia nostra apud &c. coram Rogero de Seytone et sociis suis Justiciariis de Banco levatam inter ipsum Rogerum et Robertum e Matildam uxorem, et quæ post mortem prædictorum R[oberti] et M[atilde] præfato Stephano reverti debent per formam finis ejusdem. Petiit Visum et habuit.

A.D. 1306. Formedon in the reverter.

Robert de Osgoteby and Agnes his wife brought a writ of Formedon against one Robert, and counted that one A. was seised as of fee and of right &c., the esplees &c., which A. gave the said tenements to one Nicholas and to the heirs &c.; then because the said Nicholas died without heir &c. the right reverted to A. as donor, and from A. descended to Agnes as daughter and heir, and which &c., and because &c.; and the writ stated that Andrew the great-grandfather of Agnes whose heir &c. gave &c., and which after the death of the said Nicholas to the said Robert and Agnes ought to revert &c.; judgment of the writ.—And afterwards the writ abated.

§ The executors of Richard Foliot sued so far against one Thomas &c., who was bound to Richard the testator by a statute[1] in 200*l.*, that his body was taken and sent to prison; and they had another writ to know if he could say anything why they ought not to have his lands; and Thomas came into court by a writ which he had out of Chancery at his suggestion. — *Toudeby* (for the executors). You were taken and imprisoned at our suit for 200*l.* which you owed to our testator Richard Foliot, and we do not know how at your suggestion or in any other manner you got out of prison, and we pray seisin of your lands according to the statute. —*Malmesthorpe.* It was agreed between Richard your testator and us by his writing, which is here, that if I could so speak or do that the lands of W. de B. should remain to Richard Foliot in fee by feoffment, he would release me from that debt and that that acknowledgment of the statute should be null; and we tell you that we so managed that he had that manor in fee, and was seised thereof in his life, and you for two years since his death have been and now are seised; judgment &c.: and see here the deed of Richard which witnesses this. —*Hedone.* Since he has admitted the debt

[1] 13 Edw. I. st. 3.

§ Robert de Osgoteby e Agnes sa femme porterent un bref de forme de doun vers un Robert, e conta qe un A. fust seisi come de fee e de droit &c., les esplez &c., le quel A. dona mesmes les tenements a un Nichol e a les heirs &c.; dount pur ceo qe Nichol morust sanz heir &c. reverti le droit a A. com a donor, e de A. descendi &c. a Agneis com a fille e heir, e les queux &c., e pur ceo &c.; e fist le bref qe Andreas proavus Agnetis cujus heres &c. dedit &c., et quæ post mortem prædicti Nicholai ad prefatos Robertum et Agnetem reverti debent &c.: jugement del bref. E pus le bref se abati &c.

A.D. 1306.

Forme de doun en le reverti.

§ Les executours Richard Foliot suierent tant en vers un Thomas qe fust oblighe a Richard le testatour par lestatut en cc. livres tant qe sun corps fust pris e livere a la prisone; e autre bref a saver sil sout rienz dire pur quei il ne deust aver ces terres, qe vient en court par bref qil avoit hors de la Chancelerie a sa suggestion.—*Toudeby* (pur les executours). Vous fustes pris e en prisone a nostre suite pur cc. livres qe vous deviez a nostre testatour Richard Foliot, e nous ne savioms coment a vostre suggestion ou en autre manere estes issue de la prison, e prioms seysine de vos terres solom statut. — *Malm.* Il acovyent entre Richard vostre testatour e nous par sun escrit, qe ci est, qe si jeo puisse tant parler ou fere qe les terres W. de B. remeinassent a Richard Foliot en fee par feffement, qil me relerreit cele dette, e qe cele conissance del estatut fust nulle; e vous deymes qe nous feimės tant qil avoit cel maner en fee, e fust seisi en sa vie, e vous fustes deus anz seisi apres sa mort, e estes hui ceo jour; jugement &c.: e veez ici le fet Richard qe ceo testmoigne.—*Hedone.* De pus qil ad conu la dette e nad

A.D. 1306. and has no specialty to show payment, we pray judgment &c. — HENGHAM. Is this your testator's deed or not ?—*Hedone.* Not his deed; ready &c.—And the other side said the contrary.

§ One Robert prayed seisin of land by the default of one William, who came by attorney and said that he held the tenements jointly with his son Thomas who was not named in the writ, and he prayed judgment of the writ.—*Roistone.* You ought not to be received to that; for when the Grand Cape was returned, you came into court and denied the summons, affirming the tenancy to be wholly in your person, and you were essoined de malo veniendi, and we had a day at the quinzein of Michaelmas, at which day you were essoined as being in the king's service, and you had a day until now, and you have not your warrant; judgment.—*Malmesthorpe.* See here the charter which is sufficient evidence to the court and shows the joint-tenancy, and we can not lose any other tenancy; judgment of the writ. — *Roistone.* As before.—*Malmesthorpe.* See here is Thomas in whose person the fee and the right repose, who holds jointly with William, and prays that no default which William makes may oust him from his tenancy; and we pray judgment of the writ, since he is not joined in the writ.—*Roistone.* As before.—HENGHAM. Would it be right that Thomas who is joint owner of the inheritance should lose by the default of William who wishes to lose gratis in order to oust Thomas from the freehold which he holds jointly with him ?—*Willuby.* If he prays to be received, as he in whose person the fee and the right repose &c., to abate the writ, he ought not to be received to this, for he is not named in the writ.—HENGHAM. He can not singly yield up, because he is jointly tenant, nor consequently by his default ought Thomas to be ousted from his tenancy. — *Roistone.* He has his recovery by assise. — HENGHAM. That would be a hardship.—*Roistone.* William

nulle especialte qe testmoigne la paie, jugement. — A.D. 1306.
HENGHAM. Est ceo le fet vostre testatour ou noun ?—*Hedone.* Nent sun fet ; prest &c. Et alii e contra.

§ Un Robert pria seisine de terre par la defaute un Willem, qe vient par atturne e dist quil teneit les tenements joynt ove Thomas sun fiz nent nome en le bref, jugement del bref. — *Roistone.* A ceo ne devez estre receu, qe quant le grant cape fust returne vous venistes en Court e defendistes la somonse, en affermant la tenance entierment en vostre persone, e fustes essone de mal de venue, e avioms jour a la quinzeine de Seint Michel, a quel jour vous fustes essone de service le Roi, e aviez jour a ore, e navez mie vostre garant ; jugement.—*Malm.* Veez ici la chartre qe est assez evidence a la Court qe testmoigne le jointe, ne nous poms autre tenance perdre ; jugement del bref. —*Roistone.* Ut supra.—*Malm.* Veez icy Thomas en qi persone le fee e le droit repose, qe tient joint ove Willem, e prie qe nulle defaute qe Willem fet nel hoste de sa tenance ; e demaundom jugement del bref, de pus qil est jointe en le bref.—*Roistone.* Ut prius. —HENGHAM. Serroit ceo reson qe Thomas qe est enherite e est joint qe par la defaute Willem qe de gre voet perdre pur oster Thomas del franc-tenement qil tient ove luy joyntement, qil dust perdre ?—*Willuby.* Si il prie de estre receu come celuy en qi persone le fee e le droit repose &c., si a bref abatre, a ceo ne deit il estre receu, qil nest mie nome en le bref.—HENGHAM. Il ne puet soul rendre, quia conjunctim tenens, ne par consequens par sa defaute si ne deit Thomas estre oste de sa tenance.—*Roistone.* Il ad sun rescoverer par assise.—HENGHAM. Ceo serreit duresce.—*Roistone.* Qe Willem fust soul tenant e soul pleda, e

A.D. 1306. was sole tenant and he pleaded solely and solely wageo his law, ready &c.; judgment, as above; and Thomas had nothing, ready &c., if he will receive this averment. —HENGHAM. Against whom will you join that averment?—*Roistone.* Against Thomas who says that he has an estate in the tenements and wishes to abate our writ. —*Malmesthorpe.* If the inquest pass against Thomas would he thereby be ousted from the tenancy? (intimating that he would not be).

Formedon. § A formedon in the remainder was brought against a tenant, and the writ ran thus, "which one A. gave to "one B. and the heirs of his body begotten, and if &c. "that the tenements should remain to A. and the heirs "&c., and if &c. that the tenements should remain to "the aforesaid D. &c., and which after the deaths of B. "and A. ought to remain to the said D. by the form of "the gift aforesaid, because the aforesaid B. and A. died "without heirs of their bodies."—*Herle.* First the gift contained a limitation to B. severally and afterwards to A. severally, and at the close of the writ it says "and "which after the deaths of B. and A. ought to remain "to D., because the aforesaid B. and A. died without "heirs of their bodies," supposing the gift to be made to B. and A. jointly; judgment of the writ; for it ought to have said in the close, "because the aforesaid B. died "without heir of his body and the aforesaid A. died without heir of his body."—HENGHAM adjudged the first form to be good.—*Herle.* A. is alive; judgment if during his life &c.—*Malmesthorpe.* He is dead, as to the law.—*Herle.* How dead?—*Malmesthorpe.* He has entered into religion, and is professed.—*Herle.* And we pray judgment since you have not made any mention of his entry or profession; judgment of the writ.—*Malmesthorpe.* We can not have any other writ in the Chancery.—HENGHAM. There are several kinds of Mordancester; one where it says "the day on which he died"; another which says "on the day when he took the habit of religion"; a soul gaia la ley, prest, &c.; jugement ut supra; e qe Thomas rien navoit, prest &c., si la voudra ceste averement receiver. — HENGHAM. Envers qi joyndrez cel averement? — *Roistone.* Envers Thomas qe dist qil ad estat en les tenements qe voet nostre bref abatre. —*Malm.* Si lenqueste passast contre Thomas, serreit il par tant oste de la tenance? (quasi diceret non). A.D. 1306.

§ Un forme de doun en le remanere fust porte vers un tenant, e fust le bref tiel, les queux un A. dona a un B. e a les heirs de sun corps engendrez, e si &c., qe les tenements remeindreynt a A. e a les heirs &c., e si &c., qe les tenements reimeindreynt al avantdit D. &c., e les queux apres la mort B. e A. al avantdit D. remeindre deyvent par la forme du doun avantdit, pur ceo qe le avantdit B. e A. devierent sanz heir de lour corps. — *Herle.* Primes le doun se tailla a B severalment e pus a A. severalment, e en la perclos del bref si dist il e les queux apres la mort B. e A., a C. remeindre deivent, pur ceo qe les avantdiz B. e A. devyeront sanz heir de lour corps, en suppossant le doun estre fete jointement a B. e A.; jugement del bref; car il deust dire en la perclose, pur ceo qe lavantdit B. sanz heir de sun corps, e le avantdit A. sanz heir de sun corps devierent.—HENGHAM agarda la primere forme bone.—*Herle.* A. est en pleine vie, jugement si vivant lui &c.—*Malm.* Mort quant a la ley.—*Herle.* Coment mort? — *Malm.* Entre en religion e professe.—*Herle.* E nous jugement, de pus qe vous navez fet nule mencion del entre, ne de la profession, jugement del bref.—*Malm.* Nous ne poms autre bref avoir en la Chauncelerie.—HENGHAM. Ilui sunt plussours maneres de Mortdancestre, un, a dire "die quo "obiit," un autre "die quo habitum religionis assumpsit," [Forme] de doun.

A.D. 1306. third which says "on the day when he set out on a "pilgrimage"; now if you bring one writ when you ought to have brought another, the writ does not lie. And since you have admitted that he has entered into religion, and no mention is made thereof, the Court adjudges that you take nothing by the writ.

Replevin. § A Replegiari was brought against the Bishop of Ely by a lady: they pleaded so far on that by the nonsuit of the lady a Return was adjudged. *The lady's attorney* now sued out a judicial writ according to the Statute,[1] and the sheriff returned that he had sent orders to the bailiffs of the liberty of such a place, who had done nothing thereon. The lady's attorney sued out the "omit not on account of any liberty," and that the Bishop should be attached to answer the lady. —*Toudeby.* When the Return was adjudged to us, the lady's attorney sued out the writ to have the Return in our name, in deceit of the Court, and we pray that he may be convicted thereof.—*The lady's attorney.* When the Return was adjudged to you, the lady caused the beasts to be driven to the Bishop's manor, and the Bishop's bailiff would not receive them, wherefore we sued out a judicial writ according to the Statute.—*Toudeby.* And we pray judgment of your admission, since you have admitted that you drove the beasts to the Bishop's manor, supposing thereby that you sued out the writ of Return in our name in deceit of us and the Court; judgment.—*Herle.* I have found on examination that, when the Return was awarded to the Bishop, the lady ordered her attorney to sue out a judicial writ according to the Statute; and he did so; the sheriff returned as above, wherefore we sued out the "omit not" which is now returned; and you are in Court; wherefore we wish to know if you will answer, or if not we pray our damages.—*Toudeby.* Your judi-

[1] 13 Edw. I. st. 1, c. 2. § 3.

la terce "die quo iter peregrinationis arripuit;" dount si vous portez le un bref, la ou vous duissez porter lautre, le bref ne gist mie. E de pus qe vous avez conu qil est entre en religion, e nulle mencion de ceo fet, si agarde &c. qe vous ne preignez rien del bref. A.D. 1306.

§ Un Replegiare fust porte vers leveske de Ely par une dame; tant plederent qe par la noun suite la dame return fust agarde. *Latturne la dame* meintenant suy bref de jugement solom lestatut; le visconte returna quod mandavit ballivis libertatis de tel leu qui nihil inde fecerunt. Latturne la dame suist le "non omittas propter libertatem," e qe leveske fust attache a respondre a la dame.—*Toudeby.* Quant return nous fust agarde, latturne la dame suist bref de aver return en nostre noun en deceite de la Court, e prioms qil seit de ceo atteint.—*Latturne la dame.* Quant return vous fust agarde, la dame fist chacer meismes les avers al maner levescke, e le baillif levescke ne les voleit resceivere, par quei nous suymes bref de jugement solom lestatut. —*Toudeby.* E nous jugement de vostre conissance, de pus qe vous avez conu qe vous chaceates les avers la dame al maner levescke, en suppossant qe vous suistes bref de return en nostre noun, e par tant en desceite de nous e de la Court; jugement. — *Herle.* Jeo ay trove par examinement qe quant return fust agarde a leveske, la dame comanda a sun atturne quil suisit bref de jugement solom lestatut; e auxi fist il: le Viconte returna ut prius, par quei nous suymes le non omittas qest ore returne; e vous estes en Court, par quei nous voloms saver si volez respondre, ou si noun nous prioms nos damages. — *Toudeby.* Vostre bref de jugement suppose Replegiare.

A.D. 1306. cial writ supposes that we had the Return; and that is false; for we did not sue out the Return; judgment &c. —*Herle.* And although you will not sue out a writ to have the Return, nevertheless when the Return is adjudged we should have our recovery by a judicial writ according to the Statute; and you are in Court and answer nothing; judgment, and we pray our damages.—*Toudeby.* Count, then.—And then he counted the like count as in the first Replegiari for the same taking on the same day and year and in the same place.—*Malmesthorpe.* We avow the taking &c., and for the reason that the lady holds one messuage, 300 acres of land &c. of the Bishop by homage, fealty, and suit to his court of W. every three weeks &c., and by suit to his court of D. every three weeks &c., and by the service of enclosing 20 perches of the Bishop's wood round the Bishop's park at the lady's expense, and 20 perches round the Bishop's wood in the same manor, and of enclosing 10 perches round the site of the Bishop's manor &c., and when the vill of B. is assessed at 20*s.* at each creation of a Bishop the lady shall pay 16½*d.*, and when at more, more &c.; of which services one Geoffrey our predecessor was seised by the hand of the lady as by the hand of his very tenant; and because she was warned to enclose 20 perches round the park, and she did not, we avow &c. the taking of two horses and the taking of two oxen, for the wood not enclosed &c., and of two cows for the 10 perches round the site of the manor not enclosed, and for 17*s.* 0½*d.* which was her assessed portion when the vill was assessed at 20 marks, we avow the taking of three horses &c. — *Herle.* We admit that we hold of him one messuage and one carucate of land in the manner which we will tell you, namely, by suit to his court of B. every three weeks &c. and by suit to his hundred of D. every three weeks &c., and by the service of enclosing 20 perches of the Bishop's wood round the Bishop's park, so that we ought to have the

qe nous avioms return; e ceo est faux, qe nous ne A.D. 1306
suymes unkes return; jugement &c.—*Herle.* E tut ne volez vous suyr bref de aver return, nepurquant quant return est agarde nous averioms nostre rescoverir par bref de jugement solom lestatut; e vous estes en Court, e rien ne respondez: jugement, e prioms nos damages.—*Toudeby.* Contez donqes. Et postea narravit autiel counte com en le primer replegiare de meime la prise, de meime le jour, an e leu.—*Malm.* Nous avowoms la prise &c. par la reson qe la dame tient del Eveske un mies treis cent acres de terre &c. del Evescke par homage fealte e suite a sa court de W de treis semeines &c., e par suite a sa court de D. de treis semeines &c., e par les services denclore xx. perchez entour le parke leveske del boys leveske a les custages la dame, e xx. perches entour le boys leveske en meyme la maner, e denclore x. perchez entour le site del maner leveske &c.; e a quel houre qe la ville de B. fust assis a xx. soz a chescone creacion de Eveske, la dame paiera xvi. deners obole, e quant a plus, plus &c.; des queux services un Geoffrey nostre predecessor fust seisi par la mayn la dame com par la mayn sun verrey tenant; e pur ceo qele fust garny denclore xx. perches entour le parke, e ele ne fist mie, si avowoms &c. la prise de deus chivaux e la prise de deus boefs pur le boys desclos &c., e de deus vaches pur x. perches entour le site del maner desclose, e pur xvii. soz obole qe lui afferoit a sa porcioun quant la ville fust asis a xx. mars si avowoms la prise de treis chivaux &c.—*Herle.* Nous conussoms qe nous tenoms de lui un mies e une carue de terre en la manere qe nous vous dirroms, saver par suite a sa court de B. de treis semeines &c., e par suite a sun hundred de D. de treis semeines &c. e de enclore xx. perches entour le parke leveske del bois leveske meimes, issint

A.D. 1306. old fencing, and also 20 perches round his wood; and because the old fencing was carried away before we came, and so we could not have the profit which we ought to have had for our labour, we would not enclose; judgment. And as to what he says of our being liable to enclose ten perches round the site of the manor &c., we say that his predecessor was never seised &c.; and as to the 17*s.* 0½*d.* since he has admitted by his avowry that we are a free tenant, we pray judgment if for any tallage at your pleasure you can make avowry.—*Malmesthorpe.* Admit then our seisin &c.—*Herle.* I have no need; but since your avowry is against common right, we have no need to answer to your seisin, unless you affirm it by alleging it from time of which there is no memory; and this you do not; judgment &c.

Covenant. § Two persons brought a writ of Covenant against the parson of the church of St. Mary of East Salenam bidding "that he perform to them the agreement made "between them, namely that he would keep the said "Thomas and A. harmless in respect of the fruits of the "tithes of the church of such a place bought by them, as "they say;" and they counted how he sold to them the fruits of the church of C., and that he was to save them harmless against all people; and how there came the bishop of such a place and sequestered the said tithes from such a day to such a day; whereupon the said Thomas and A. came to the aforesaid Piers and prayed him that he would hold them harmless, but he would not do this &c. — *Hedone.* One ought not to have "as he says" or "as they say" in a writ of covenant; but he has those words in this writ; judgment of the writ. —HENGHAM. One may have them in a writ of covenant as well as in any other writ. — *Hedone.* One of the two is non-suit and severed by judgment; and we do not think that in this writ of covenant the other singly ought to be answered; and such a judgment we saw qe nous devoms aver la veille enclosture, autresi xx. perches entour sun bois; e pur ceo qe la veille enclosture fust enporte einz ceo qe nous venimes, e issint ne poeimes aver le profit qe aver duissoms pur nostre travaille, si ne voilloms point enclore; jugement: e de ceo qil dist qe nous duissoms enclore x. perches entour le site del maner &c. qe sun predecessor ne fust unqes seisi &c.: e en droit de les xvii. soz obole, de pus qil nous ad conu franc tenant par sa vouerie, demaundoms jugement si pur nule taillage a vostre volente puissez avowerie faire.—*Malm.* Conussez donqes nostre seisine &c. — *Herle.* Jeo nay mestier; mes de pus qe vostre avowerie si est encontre comune dreit, nous navoms mester a vostre seisine respondre sanz ceo qe vous ne lafermez par tens dount ny ad memorie; e ceo ne fetes mie; jugement &c. A.D. 1306.

§ Deux porterent un bref de Covenant de Seint Marye persone del eglise de Estsalenam "quod teneat "eis convencionem inter eos factam de eo quod prefatos "Thomam et A. de fructibus decimarum ecclesiæ de tel "leu ab eodem emptis conservaret indempnes ut dicunt;" et conterent coment il lour vendi les fruis del eglise de C. e qil lour sauvereit sanz damage vers tote gente, la vient levescke de tel leu e sequestra meimes les dymes de tiel jour deke a tiel jour, par quei les avantdiz Thomas e A. viendrent al avantdit Peres, e lui pria qil lour salvast de damage, il ceo fere ne voleit &c. — *Hedone.* Homme navera mie "ut dicit" ne "ut dicunt" en bref de covenant, e il le unt en cestui bref; jugement del bref.—HENGHAM. Homme le puet avoir en bref de covenant come en autre bref.—*Hedone.* Un de deus est noun suy, e severe par jugement; e nentendoms mie qe [a] cestui bref de covenant lautre Covenant.

A.D. 1306. given in the case between such an one and such an one; judgment &c. — HENGHAM. What was the covenant about?—*Hedone.* I think it was about land.—HENGHAM. This covenant is not about land. Have you any thing else to say?—*Hedone.* What have they to show the covenant. — *Willuby* put forward an indenture made between Thomas and A., who were the plaintiffs, and one B. who was the proctor of Master Piers.—*Hedone.* Judgment if by the deed of another person we ought to be holden to answer this covenant.—*Willuby.* He had power to sell and to bind in all things &c. Besides, heretofore on a certain day in a certain year you brought a writ of debt against us, and by the other part of that indenture you challenged the debt against us; judgment if by this part of it you ought not to be bound to this covenant.—*Hedone.* This is not our deed; judgment if by the deed of another we ought to be bound to this covenant.—HENGHAM. This indenture and the other are all one deed.—HENGHAM. Did you recover the debt against him as he has said, or not?—*Hedone.* Since it is not our deed, we do not think we have any need to answer that.—HENGHAM. You can not deny it: therefore the Court adjudges that they do recover their damages, &c., and that you be in mercy.—*Master Piers.* We pray that our arguments be entered on the roll, or if not see here is a bill and we pray you to seal it.—HENGHAM refused to do this, and afterwards Master Piers brought a writ to cause the record and the process to come before the king, and he delivered another writ directing that Sir Ralph should in person appear before the king to show why he would not seal the Bill according to the form of the Statute,[1] &c.

§ A writ was brought against a man and his wife; they vouched to warranty one B., who entered into war-

---

[1] 13 Edw. I. c. 31.

soul deit estre respondu; e autiel jugement si veymes nous entre un tiel e un tiel; jugement &c.—HENGHAM. De quei fust le covenant?—*Hedone.* Jeo crey qe de terre.—HENGHAM. Ceo covenant ne mie de terre: volez autre chose dire?—*Hedone.* Quei ount il del covenant?—*Willuby* mist avant une endenture qe fust fete entre Thomas e A. qe furent pleintifs, e un B. qe fust le procuratour mestre Peres.—*Hedone.* Jugement si par autri fet devoms a ceo covenant estre tenuz a respondre.—*Willuby.* Il avoit poer a vendre, e a obliger en totes choses &c. Estre ceo, autrefoiz certein jour e an si portastes bref de dette vers nous, e par lautre partie de cel endenture si dereignates vous la dette vers nous; jugement si par ceste partie ne devez a ceo covenant estre lie.—*Hedone.* Ceo nest pas nostre fet; jugement si par autri fet a ceo covenant devoms estre lie.—HENGHAM. Ceste endenture e lautre sunt tut un fet.—HENGHAM. Rescoverastes vous la dette vers luy com il ad dist ou noun?—*Hedone.* De pus qe ceo nest mie nostre fet nentendoms mie qe nous eoms mestier a ceo respondre.—HENGHAM. Vous ne poez ceo dedire, par quei agarde &c. qil rescovere ces damages, &c. e vous en la mercie.—*Mestre Peres.* Nous prioms qe nos resons seient entre en Roulle; ou si noun veez ici Bille e prioms qe vous lenselez.—HENGHAM hoc facere recusavit, e pus meintenant mestre Peres porta un bref a faire venir le record e le proces devant le Roi, e delivera un autre bref qe Sire Rauf meimes fust en propre persone devant le corps le Roi a mustrer pur quei il ne voleit enseler la bille solom forme de estatut &c. A.D. 1306.

§ Un bref fust porte vers un homme e sa femme; eux voucherent a garantie un B., qe entra en la ga-

A.D. 1306. ranty and vouched the husband of the woman, who made default after default; the woman came before judgment given, and prayed to be received to defend her right.—*Friskeney.* She and her husband have vouched and put their answer in the mouth of another, and they are warranted; and if they lose they will have to the value against their warrantor; wherefore &c. Besides, in order that a woman may be received &c., it is necessary that she have a day in Court; but she is without a day, because she is warranted; wherefore she ought not to be received.—HENGHAM. She is named in the writ, and her husband, by default, is about to lose the tenements; wherefore let her be received. And afterwards she vouched to warranty.

Covenant

§ A., B., and C. brought their writ of Covenant against one D., bidding him perform to them his covenant about the manor of B., whom she and her husband formerly vouched to warranty: and they counted that it was agreed between them that if the son of A. should marry the daughter of D., D. should enfeoff the son and the daughter of the said manor in fee tail; and that afterwards the son of A. did marry the daughter of D.; whereupon he prayed D. to enfeoff them; but that D. would not, tortiously and to their damage of 200 marks &c.—*Toudeby.* They have counted that the feoffment was to be made to C. and his wife only, and in the close of the count they say "tortiously and to their damage," thereby supposing that each has equal damage, which is false by their own count; judgment of the count.—*Malmesthorpe.* The covenant was made with those three that the third should be enfeoffed; then inasmuch as you did not enfeoff the third you broke the covenant. with the three; and such is the covenant.—*Toudeby* That one only is damaged who is to receive the profits &c.—*Malmesthorpe.* Such was the covenant wherefore &c.—*Toudeby.* The writing which they put forward states that when they should be enfeoffed in fee rantie e voucha le baroun la femme, qe fist defaute apres defaute; la femme vient avant jugement rendu, e pria de estre receu a defendre sun droit.—*Friskeney.* Ele e sun baroun ount vouchez e mis lour respons en autri bouche, e sunt garanti; e sil perdent il averont a la value vers lour garant; par quei &c. Estre ceo, a ceo qe femme deit estre receu &c. il covyent qele eit jour en Court; mes ele est sanz jour, pur ceo qele est garanti; par quei ele ne deit estre receu.—HENGHAM. Ele est nome en le bref, e son baroun par defaute voet perdre les tenements; par quei soit ele receu. Et postea vocavit ad warrantiam. A.D. 1306.

§ Un A. B. e C. porterent lour bref de Covenant vers un D. quil lour tensit covenaunt del maner de B. quem ipsa et vir suus prius vocaverunt ad warrantiam, e conterent qil acovient entre eux qe si le fiz A. esposat la fille D., qe D. enfeffereit le fiz e la fille de meime le maner en fee taille; e pus le fiz A. esposa la fille D., par quei i lui pria qil lour enfeffat: D. ceo faire ne voleit, atort e a lour damage de c. c. mars &c.—*Toudeby.* Il ont conte qe le feffement se dust faire a C. e a sa femme tant soulement; e en la perclose del counte, il dyent, atort e a lour damage, en supposant qe chescon ad owelement damage, quod est falsum par sun conte demene, jugement del counte.—*Malm.* Le covenant se fist a eux treis qe le terce deust estre enfeffe; dount en tant com vous ne enfeffastes mie le terce, si enfrenites le covenant a les treis, e tiel est le covenaunt. —*Toudeby.* Celuy soulement est endamage qe dust resceiver les profiz &c. — *Malm.* Tiel fust le covenant, par quei &c. — *Toudeby.* Lescrist quil mettont avant voet qe quant il serreient enfeffez en fee taille Covenant.

A.D. 1306. tail they would re-enfeoff us for the term of our life, and of this they have made no mention in their count; judgment of the count.—*Herle.* Specify yourself what works to your advantage; what works to our advantage we have specified; wherefore &c.—*Toudeby.* The writing states that at the time when we should enfeoff them in fee tail, they should find us such security as we should fix; and we tell you that on a certain day in a certain place we prayed them to find security before SIR WILLIAM INGE and W. DE ORMESBY, justices assigned; and they would not, ready &c.—HENGHAM. The law does not allow a tenant in fee tail to enfeoff any one either for life or in fee; and your covenant is such; wherefore we will never award you damages by reason of that covenant.—*Herle.* The party has tendered an issue of the plea, and says that he warned us to find him surety, and that we would not; he did not warn us, but we were always ready to find him surety and to keep the covenants, and the wrong was in him and not in us; ready &c.

Note. Quod permittat.

§ Note that in a Quod permittat vileins to make suit to a mill, where the defendant prayed the view, *Herle* said, We count of our seisin, and we say that you yourselves have disturbed them, judgment if of your own wrong &c. Besides, there is only one mill in the said vill; judgment.—*Hales.* How shall he know of what tenements you ask the suit, without he has the view.—HENGHAM. Let him have the view.—And he had it.

Dower.

§ A woman brought her writ of Dower; the tenant vouched to warranty one A., who warranted, and pleaded over that the woman ought not to have dower, for she has made allowance to the heir of her husband who held of us certain tenements by services which give wardship; judgment; for we have a writ pending against her for the same wardship.—*Hedone.* Our husband did not hold of you by services which give wardship; ready &c.—

qil nous refeffeit a tote nostre vie, e de ceo ne ount A.D. 1306.
il nul mencion fet en contant; jugement del counte.—*Herle.* Ceo qe chiet en vostre avantage demene nomez le meyme, e ceo qe chiet en nostre avantage nous le avom nome; par quei &c.—*Toudeby.* Lescrist voet qe ai celes qe nous les enfeffasoms en fee taille, qil nous troverereient au tele suirte com nous voillioms ordiner; e vous dioms qe certein jour e leu si les priames qil nous trovasseut siurte devant. SIR WILLEM INGE e W. DE ORMESBY Justices assignez; il ceo faire ne voleint, prest &c. — HENGHAM. Ley ne soeffre mie qe tenant en fee taille puisse feffer aqun homme ne a terme de vie ne en fee; e vostre covenant est tele; par quei nous ne vous agarderoms jammes damages par encheson de ceo covenant.—*Herle.* La partie ad tendu issue de play, e dist qil nous garny de luy trover suyrte, e ceo fere ne voilloms; qil ne nous garny point, mes qe nous touz jours sumes prest de luy trover suirte, e a tener les covenanz, e qe en luy renust e nent en nous; prest, &c.

§ Nota ke en un "quod permittat villanos facere sectam ad molendinum," ou le defendant demaunda le vewe,—*Herle.* Nous contoms de nostre seisine demene, e dioms qe vous meymes les avez destourbe; jugement si de vostre tort demene &c. Estre ceo, il ny ad qe un molin en meime la ville; jugement.—*Hales.* Coment savera il des queux tenementz vous demaundez la suite sanz aver la vewe.—HENGHAM. Eit la Vewe.—Et habuit.

Nota, quod permittat.

§ Une femme porta sun bref de Dowere; le tenant voucha a garantie un A., qe garantist e dist outre qe la femme ne dust dowere avoir, car ele ad allowe le heir sun baroun, qe de nous tient certeinz tenements par services qe donnent garde; jugement, car nous avoms bref pendant vers luy de meyme la garde.—*Hedone.* Qe nostre baroun ne tient mie de vous par services qe donnent garde; prest &c. Et alii e contra.

Dowere.

A.D. 1306. And the other side said the contrary.—*Hedone.* We pray a common day of plea of dower.—*Herle.* Since we have a writ of wardship pending against her, and she of her malice made default at the Quinzein of St. Hilary, whereupon we had a day for that plea at the Quinzein of Trinity, we pray you to adjourn this plea until the same day.—*Hedone.* We pray a day for the dower.

Annuity.

§ A writ of Annuity was brought against an abbat.—*Tiltone.* The writing says, "until we have provided "him with a fitting benefice;" and we tell you that we tendered him the presentation to the church of B., and he would not receive it; judgment.—*Passeley.* Say on what day; for thereby you shall not extinguish the arrears of the time aforesaid.—*Tiltone* named a day which was long past, and said that all the arrears were extinguished.—*Passeley.* You ought not to get to that averment, for see here a writing which witnesses that the abbat has recited and affirmed the first writing, and paid to us 10*s.* of the arrears of the said annuity; and this writing is of later date than the day which you name of the presentation; judgment.—*Hales.* This writing is not sealed with the seal of the convent, but only with the abbat's seal; so that does not prove your statement. Do you accept the averment?—*Passeley* granted it.

Dower.

§ A woman brought her writ of Dower against a tenant; the lord of a liberty came and demanded the liberty, and he had it, and he gave a day to the parties, within the liberty; at which day the tenant vouched to warranty three persons, of whom one was foreign and the other two within; and because that they had not power to make the foreigner come, the demandant sued out a resummons to resummon the parties to be before the justices at a certain day, and then before the same justices the tenant challenged the warranty of the vouchees.—*Roistone,* for the lord of the liberty, again prayed his franchise.

—*Hedone.* Nous prioms comune jour de play de dowere. **A.D. 1306.** —*Herle.* De pus qe nous avoms bref de garde pendant vers luy, e ele de sa malice fist defaute a la quinzeine de Seint Hillari, par quei nous avoms jour de cel play a la quinzeine de la Trinite, e prioms qe vous ajornez ceo play deke a meyne ceo jour.—*Hedone.* Nous prioms jour de dowere.

§ Un bref de Annuyte fust porte vers un abbe.— **Annuelte.** *Tiltone.* Lescrist voet ci la qe nous luy eoms purveu de covenable benefice; e vous dioms ke nous luy tendymes le presentement del eglise de B., e il resceiver ne le voleit; jugement.—*Passeley.* Dites quel jour; qe par tant ne esteindrez vous mie les arrerages del temps avantdit.—*Tiltone* noma tel jour qe fu loinz passe, qe touz les arrerages furent esteinz. — *Passeley.* A cel averement ne devez avenir, qe veez ici un escrist qe testmoigne qe labbe ad reherce e afferme le primer escrist e paie a nous .x. soz des arrerages de meime lannuite, e cest escrist est de pusne date qe nest le jour qe vous nomez del presentement; jugement.—*Hales.* Cest escrist ne mie ensele del seal le covent, mes del seal labbe tant soulement; par quei ceo ne mie proeve de vostre dit; volez laverement?—*Passeley* concessit.

§ Une femme porta sun bref de dowere vers un **Dowere.** tenant; vient le seignour de une franchise e demaunda la franchise; et habuit; e dona jour a les parties denz la franchise; a quel jour le tenant voucha a garantie treis, dount un fust forein e les deus einz; e pur ceo qe eux navoient mie poer de faire venir le forein, le demaundant suist une resomons de resomondre les parties de estre devant justices a certein jour, e puis devant meymes les justices le tenant derena la garantie des vouchez. — *Roistone,* pur le seignour de la

A.D. 1306. —*Hales.* For want of power in your liberty the plea is now in this court; wherefore you shall never again in this plea have your franchise.

Writ of right close. § A little writ of Right close was brought against an abbat in the ancient demesne of the king. The abbat put forward the charter which testified that the king had given the said tenements to the abbat and his church; wherefore he ought not to answer without the king. Then the demandant sued out a writ to the sheriff to cause the record and the process to come before the Justices of the Bench. — *Toudeby* (for the tenant). You can not in this court hold a plea of our freehold without the king's writ; but now you have not the little writ in this court, for the writ which went to the sheriff to make record of the plea says only at the end of the writ "and "have there this writ," without saying "and the other "writ;" wherefore we pray that this plea be extinguished. —And the writ was read, and the words "other writ" were wanting; wherefore the plea was extinguished.

Replegiare. § An avowry was made for a relief, and he said that the father of the plaintiff held of him by certain services, and by escuage, to wit &c.; whereof he was seised by his hand &c., and for 100*s.* for relief, which is in arrear, he avows &c. —*Hedone.* Not seised of the homage &c.— *Lanfar.* That is no more an answer in this writ than in a writ of wardship; wherefore &c. — HENGHAM. Do you hold of him by escuage, or not?—*Hedone.* He has made an avowry and said that he was seised of the escuage, and we say that he was not seised, ready &c.— HENGHAM. If escuage did not run in his time, yet ought he to have the wardship and relief; therefore, do you hold of him by escuage or not?— *Hedone.* We hold of him by the service of 7*s.*; and of that we vouch the record of the roll (and so it was found in the roll.)— [*Lanfar*]. You hold of us by escuage besides, ready, &c.— And the other side said the contrary.

franchise, pria altre foiz sa franchise. —*Hales*. Par defaute de noun poer de vostre franchise la parole est ore cienz; par quei jammes autrefoiz naverez de ceo plai vostre franchise &c. A.D. 1306.

§ Un petit bref de droit clos porte vers un abbe en les aunciens demeines le roi. — *Labbe* mist avant la chartre qe testmoigne qe le roy avoit done meyme les tenements al abbe e a sa eglise, par quei il ne duist saunz le roi respundre. Puis le demaundant suist bref al visconte de fere venir le record e le proces devant les Justices du Baunk.—*Toudeby* (pur le tenant). Vous ne poez tenir play cienz de nostre franc-tenement sanz bref le roi; mes ore navez mie le petit bref cienz, car le bref qe ala a visconte de faire recorder la parole dist tant soulment a la fin del bref, "et habeas ibi "hoc breve" sanz dire "et aliud breve," par quei nous prioms qe cest plee soit amorti.—E le bref fust lu e le "aliud breve" defaillist; par quei la parole se amorty.

Bref de droit clos.

§ Une avowerie fust faite pur relef, e dist qe le pere le pleintif tient de lui par certein services, e par escuage, saver &c.; dount il fust seisi par sa mayn &c., e pur .c. soz de relef qe arere [est] si avowe il &c.—*Hedone*. Nent seisi del homage &c.—*Lanfar*. Ceo nest nent plus respons en ceo bref qen bref de garde; par quei &c.—HENGHAM. Tenez vous de lui par escuage ou noun? —*Hedone*. Il ad fet avowerie, e dist qil fut seisi del escuage; e nous dioms qe nent seisi, prest &c. —HENGHAM. E si escuage ne currit mie en sun tenps, si deit il garde e relef avoir; par quei, tenez vous de ly par escuage ou noun? — *Hedone*. Nous tenoms de lui par les services de .vii. soz; e de ceo vouchom record de roulle; e issint fust trove en roulle; e qe vous tenez de nous estre ceo par escuage, prest &c. Et alii e contra.

Replegiare.

A.D. 1306. Entry on disseisin. § One A. brought a writ of Entry founded on disseisin done to himself. — *Hedone.* The tenements put in the View are meadow, and were so twenty years before the writ was purchased, and you demand them as land; judgment &c.—*Lanfar.* While they were in our seisin they were land, ready &c. — *Hedone.* If it was ever in your seisin it was as meadow and not as land, ready &c.; not however admitting your seisin. — *Lanfar.* By your exception you admit our seisin. — BEREFORD. He demands the tenements as land, and you say it is meadow and if you have changed them from land to meadow, ought he not to demand them in the condition in which he was seised of them ? (intimating that he ought). And he offers to aver that in his seisin it was land, and you say it was not; on that point then have an averment. — *Hedone.* He says that it was land while it was in his seisin; we say it was not, ready &c.

§ A man and his wife purchased certain tenements, to the man and his wife and to the heirs of the man; and they afterwards leased the tenements to another for the term of his life: a stranger brought a writ of Covenant against the man and his wife and the tenant for term of life, for the same tenements: the case was disclosed to the court and then the concord was drawn in this form,—the man and his wife and the tenant for term of his life acknowledged the tenements comprised in the writ to be the right of the stranger, and rendered them to him &c.: and the woman was examined.

Replegiari. § A Replegiari was brought against the abbat of C. &c.—*Hegham.* The abbat tells you that as to two cows they are not your beasts, ready &c.—And the other side said the contrary.—And as to the remainder the abbat avows the taking to be good &c., and for the reason that one C. granted to one D. 16 marks of rent issuing out of the manor of B., which was holden of him in vilenage, for a term of six years, and whereof D. was

§ Un A. porta bref dentre founde sur disseisine fet a luy meymes.—*Hedone.* Les tenements mis en la Vewe sunt pree, e furent xx. anz avant le bref purchace, e vous le demaundez com terre, jugement &c.—*Lanfare.* Tant come il furent en nostre seisine si furent il terre, prest &c.—*Hedone.* Si ceo fust unqes en vostre seisine si fust ceo pree, e nent terre, prest &c., e nent en grantant vostre seisine.—*Lanfare.* Par vostre excepcion si grantez vous nostre seisine.—BEREFORD. Il demaunde les tenements come terre, e vous dites qe ceo est pree; e si vous les eez change de terre en pree, ne les deit il demaunder solom ceo qil fust mesme seisi? (quasi diceret sic debet) e il voet averer qe en sa seisine si fust ceo terre; e vous dites qe noun; seez donqes par la al averement.—*Hedone.*[1] Il dist qe ceo fust terre en sa seysine; qe noun, prest &c. A.D. 1306. Entre founde sur la disseisine.

§ Un homme e sa femme purchacerent certeinz tenements al homme e sa femme e a les heirs le homme; e pus lesserent les tenements a un autre a terme de vie; un estrange porta un bref de Covenant vers le homme e sa femme e le tenant a terme de vie de meyme les tenements: le cas fust desclos a la court, e pus la pees tret en ceste forme, — le homme e sa femme e le tenant a terme de vie conissoient les tenements contenuz en le bref estre le droit celui estrange, e ceo luy rendirent &c.; e la femme fust examine.

§ Un Replegiare fust porte vers labbe de C. &c.—*Hegham.* Labbe vous dist qen droit de deus vaches, nent vos avers, prest &c. — Et alii e contra.—En droit del remenant labbe avowe le prise bone &c., e par la reson qe un C. granta a un D. xvi. mars de rente issant del maner de B., qe de luy fust tenuz en vileynage, a terme de vi. anz, e dount D. fust seisi &c., e granta Replegiare.

[1] MS. Hengham.

A.D. 1306. seised &c. and granted the same rent to the abbat for the same term, and the abbat was afterwards seised; and for one mark in arrear for such a year, and for 100*s*. for another term afterwards and before the day of the taking, he avows &c. in the same place, as in parcel of the tenements &c.; and he put forward the two deeds.—*Tiltone*. It is forbidden by statute[1] that tenements should come into mortmain; and he is an abbat and we do not think that he is able to make that avowry. — ROUBYRI. Will you grant him the rent and then say that he ought not to have it? Plead something else.—*Tiltone*. The contract was not made between him and us, wherefore &c. — HENGHAM. He only claims a term.—*Tiltone*. The writing which he puts forward does not give him power to distrein; judgment if he can avow a distress. — ROUBYRI. Ought he not to have what you have granted to him?—*Tiltone*. The writing only states that he is to receive sixteen marks in the manor of B.; wherefore although he had a freehold in the thing, yet he could not avow a distress.—ROUBIRI. How ought he to have it then?—*Tiltone*. Never; we pray judgment of the avowry; for the specialty which he puts forward states that D. is to receive sixteen marks in the aforesaid manor, to wit so much from this free man, so much from that free man, so much from this vilein and so much from that vilein, so that every one is specified and every tenant particularly charged, and he has avowed for the whole in the vilenage, and that jointly, whereas every tenant is severally charged; judgment. — TRIKYNGHAM. The court adjudges that you have your beasts quit and your damages.

Debt. § A writ of Debt was brought, and demanded ten quarters of wheat which he bought of him, to be paid on a certain day, and he did not &c.—*Lanfar*. You did not buy any wheat of us, ready &c.—*Tiltone*. And if your

---

[1] Magna Charta, c. 36. and 7 Edw. I. st. 2.

meyme la rente al abbe a meyme le terme, e labbe pus seisi; e pur un mark arere de tel an, e pur c. soz de un autre terme pus, e avant le jour de la prise, si avowe il &c. en meyme le leu, com en parcele de tenement &c.; e mist avant les deus fetz.—*Tiltone.* Defendue est par estatut qe tenements ne viegnent a mort mein; e il est abbe, e nentendoms pas qil soit able de fere cele avowerie.—ROUBYRI. Le volez vous granter la rente e il ne deit mie aver? dites autre.—*Tiltone.* Le contracte ne se prist pas entre luy e nous, par quei &c. —HENGHAM. Il ne cleim qe terme. — *Tiltone.* Lescrist qil met avant ne lui grante mie powere a destreindre; jugement si il puisse destresse avower. — ROUBYRI. Ne deit il aver ceo qe vous luy avez grante?—*Tiltone.* Lescrist ne voet fors qil receive xvi. mars en le maner de B.; par quei tut ust il franc-tenement en la chose, il ne puet mie destresse avower.—ROUBIRI. Coment le deit il aver donkes? — *Tiltone.* Unkes; jugement de lavoerie, ke lespeciaute qil met avant si voet qe D. deust receivere xvi. mars en le maner avantdit, saver tant de tel franc homme, e tant de tel franc homme, tant de tiel vilein, e tant de tiel vilein, issint qe chestcon est mis en certein e chescone tenant charge en certein; e il ad avowe pur le tut en le vilenage, e ceo joint, par la ou chesconi tenant est severalment charge; jugement. — TRYKYNGHAM. Si agarde &c. qe vous eez vos avers quites e vos damages. A.D. 1306.

§ Un bref de dette fust porte, e demaund x. quarters de forment, les queux il achata de lui, a paier a certein jour, e ne fist point &c.—*Lanfare.* Vous ne achatates[1] nul blee de nous, prest &c.—*Tiltone.* E si Dette.

[1] MS. achatames.

A.D. 1306. bailiff has received our money in your name and for your profit, ought you not to answer?—*Lanfar.* We acknowledge that you bought of us so much wheat to be paid on a certain day, on which day you were fully paid, and on the same day you received forty shillings worth of timber for the forty shillings, ready &c.—*Tiltone.* Since you have admitted the debt, and do not show any acquittance, judgment &c.—HENGHAM. Do you accept the averment?—*Tiltone.* As before.—HENGHAM. Do you accept the averment?—*Tiltone.* Not paid, ready &c.—But he was not driven to that by judgment; nor ought he to be, as appears by a similar plea in Michaelmas Term in the xxth year of King Edward.

Cosinage. § A writ of Cosinage was brought, and it made a resort to one A.; from A. descending to B. as sister and heir.—*The tenant.* A. had no sister named B., ready &c. —*Hedone.* Heretofore we counted of the seisin of the same A., and made the same descent, when you pleaded to the action and joined the inquest, and thereby affirmed the descent; whereby &c.; and for this we vouch the record.—*The tenant.* You ought not to be received to that, for you were nonsuit in that writ, and of your own nonsuit you cannot vouch the record.—*Hedone.* As before.—HENGHAM. Do you accept the averment?—*Hedone.* A. had a sister named B., as we have counted, ready &c. —And the other side said the contrary.

Right. § A. and B. brought a writ of Right against one C. in the liberty of York.—*The tenant,* for a cause, removed the plea by a Recordari, and left out the names of the demandants; the sheriff removed the plea into the Bench at a certain day, at which day the demandants wished to have been essoined, and when the essoin should have been adjudged, *Hales* looked at the Recordari and saw that the demandants were not named, and said, we have no power to hold this plea.—*Hedone.* What the tenant vostre baillif eit receu nos deners en vostre noun e a vostre profit, ne devez mie respondre ?—*Lanfare.* Nous conissoms qe vous achatates de nous tant de forment a paier a certein jour, a quel jour vous fustes pleynement paie, e a meyme le jour si resceutes vous xl. soz de meryn pur les xl. soz prest &c.—*Tiltone.* De pus qe vous avez conu la dette e rien ne mustrez de la quitance, jugement &c.—HENGHAM. Volez laverement ?—*Tiltone.* Ut prius.—HENGHAM. Volez laverement ?—*Tiltone.* Qe noun, prest &c.—Sed non per judicium compulsus nec deberet compelli prout visum est in consimili placito in termino Sancti Michaelis anno regni Regis Edwardi xx. A.D. 1306.

§ Un bref de Cosinage fust porte, e fist un resort a un A.; de A. descendant a B. come a soere e heir.—*Le tenant.* Qe A. navoit nulle soere B. par noun, prest &c.—*Hedone.* Altrefoiz contames de la seisine mesme celui A. en fessant mesme la descente, ou vous pledastes al accion, e joingnates lenqueste, e par tant affermastes la descente, par quei &c.; e de ceo vouchom record.—*Le tenant.* A ceo ne devez estre receu, qe vous fustes noun suy de cel bref, e de vostre noun suite demene ne poez record voucher.—*Hedone.* Ut supra.—HENGHAM. Volez laverement ?—*Hedone.* Qe A. avoit une soere B. par noun sicom nous avom conte, prest &c. Et alii e contra. Cosinage.

§ Un A. e B. porterent un bref de Droit vers un C. en la franchise de Everwyke.—*Le tenant* par cause fit remuer la parole par un recordari, e entrelessa les nouns del demaundanz; le viconte remua la parole en Bank a certein jour, a quel jour les demaundanz voleient aver este essoines, e quant lassoigne duist estre ajuge, *Hales* regarda le recordari e vist qe les demaundanz ne furent mie nomez, e dist, nous navom pas poer a tenir ceo play.—*Hedone.* Le purchas le tenant De Droit.

A.D. 1306. purchased shall not abate our writ; and see here the patent whereby you have power &c., and we pray that something may be entered on the roll that we be not without day.—HENGHAM. The whole affair is without warrant.

§ One William owed 10*l.* to a merchant, and for fear of that debt bound himself to his father in a statute for 1,000*l.*: when the merchant brought an action against William, his father sued according to the form of the statute; whereby he had all the lands of William, and consequently the merchant goes without his debt.

Replegiari. § One Robert avowed a taking for a chantry on the Abbat of &c.—*Lanfar* (for the plaintiff). We hold these tenements in vilenage of the Master of the Temple, and we pray aid of him.—*Hedone.* He is not a party to our avowry, wherefore &c.—And by judgment he had [the aid] on account of the weakness of his estate.

Note. § Note by *Warr.* If the uncle enter as heir apparent while the true heir is out of the kingdom, and die seised, and his son be seised, although the true heir comes back he shall never recover by English law.

Oath in Account. § This hear, ye Justices, that I will loyally charge myself with the moneys which I have received from W. in the vill of N. from the time when I became his bailiff, and will render a loyal account, and will not allege any outlays or expenses that are not true; so help me God and the Saints.

Mesne. § A woman brought her writ of Mesne against John, and said that tortiously he does not acquit her of services which B. demands from her for a tenement which she holds in dower of the heritage of the said John, inasmuch as &c. And the writ was in accordance with the count.

Dum fuit infra ætatem. § John de B. and M. his wife brought a writ of Entry "while he was under age" against William, "into which ne abatera mie nostre bref; e veez icy la patente par quei vous avez poer &c., e prioms qe akune chose soit touche en roulle qe nous ne seom mie sanz jour.—HENGHAM.—Tut est sanz garrant. A.D. 1306.

§ Un Willem devoit x. livres a un marchant, e pur doute de cele dette si se obliga a sun pere en ley en lestatut de M. livres; quant le marchant mova accion vers Willem sun pere suy solom forme de estatut, par quei qil avoit totes les terres Willem, par quei qe le marschant est sanz sa dette.

§ Un Robert avowa une prise pur chanterie sur labbe de celui &c.—*Lanfare* (pur le pleintif). Nous tenoms ces tenements en vilenage del Mestre du Temple, e a sa volunte, e prioms aide de luy.—*Hedone.* Il nest mie partie a nostre avowerie, par quei &c. E par agarde il avoit pur la feblesse de sun estat. Replegiare.

Nota par *Warr.* Si le oncle entre com heir, apparant tant com le verrey heir est hors del realme, e devie seisi, e sun fiz seisi, tut viegne la verrei heir il ne rescovera jammes par ley de Engleterre. Nota.

§ Ceo oiez vous Justices qe jeo lealment me chargera de deners qe jeo ay receu de W. en la ville de N. del temps je jeo esteye son bailif, e leale acounte renderay, e nules mises ne despenses noun verreys ne allegeray, si Dieu moy aide e les Seins. Juramentum in compoto.

§ Une femme porta sun bref de Meen vers Johan, e dist qe atort ne lui aquite des services qe B. de luy demaunde de franc-tenement qil tient en dowere del heritage meyme celuy Johan, desicom &c. E le bref fust acordant al counte. Meen.

§ Johan de B. e M. sa femme porterent un bref dentre "dum fuit infra ætatem" vers Willem, en les queux Dum fuit infra ætatem.

A.D. 1306. " the said William has not entry unless by the aforesaid " M. while she was under age."—*Roistone.* If Maud had any estate in these tenements, it was jointly with her parcener Joan who is not named [in the writ], judgment. —*Hedone.* Heretofore we named Joan together with ourselves in a writ, when the writ abated because the lease by Maud could not give a title to Joan; wherefore &c. since she solely alienated.—LAMBERT. If they were jointly seised when Maud alienated, one ought not to be received without the other; wherefore answer if she was jointly seised or not.—*Hedone.* We have no need to do that, since the naming her heretofore abated our writ, and our alienation does not give her a title; and if we be ousted from this writ, perchance we are without recovery.—LAMBERT. Answer if she were solely seised or not.—*Hedone.* Solely seised and she alienated.—*Roistone.* The reverse.

Entry, on the Statute of Gloucester.

§ A man and his wife brought a writ of Entry, on the Statute of Gloucester,[1] for tenements held for a term of life, which had been alienated in fee.—*The tenant* said that he claimed nothing except for the term of the life of his lessor; and he showed a deed which witnessed it; wherefore it was adjudged that they should take nothing by their writ.—*Toudeby.* Let the claim of the tenant be entered.

Formedon.

§ One Beatrix brought a writ of Formedon in the remainder against the heir of the donor; and the case was that Robert the father of the tenant gave to John in fee tail, and if &c. to Thomas in fee tail, and if &c. to Beatrix the demandant. And the writ ran thus, "and " which to the aforesaid Beatrix ought to remain by the " form &c. because the aforesaid John &c.;"—and she put forward a deed which showed the form.—*Hedone.* By the deed, during the life of Thomas nothing ought to remain to Beatrix, and Thomas is not mentioned in the

[1] 6 Edw. I.

mesme Willem nad entre si noun par lavant dite M. tant com ele fust de denz age.—*Roistone.* Si Maud nul estat en ces tenements avoit, ceo fust joynt ove sa parcenere, nent nome; jugement. — *Hedone.* Autrefoiz nomames Johan ovesqe nous en un bref, ou le bref se abati, pur ceo qe le lees Maude ne poeit mie doner title a Jone; par quei &c., de pus quele soule aliena.—LAMBERT.[1] Si il furent jointz seisi quant Maud aliena, la une ne deit estre receu sanz lautre; par quei responez si ele fust joint seisi ou noun.—*Hedone.* A ceo navom mestier, de pus qe son nomer autrefez abati nostre bref, e nostre alienacion ne la donne mie title; e si nous seoms oste de cesti bref, par cas nous sumes sanz rescoverir.—LAMBERT. Responez si ele fust soule seisi ou noun.—*Hedone.* Soule seisi, e aliena.—*Roistone.* Le revers. A.D. 1306.

§ Un home e sa femme porterent un bref dentre sur lestatut de Gloucestre de tenements a terme de vie alienez en fee.—*Le tenant* dist qil ne clama si noun a terme de la vie sun lessour; e mustra fet qe ceo testmoigna; par quei fust agarde qil ne preist rienz par son bref.—*Toudeby.* Soit le clame le tenaunt entre.

Entre sur Statut de Gloucestre.

§ Une Beatrix porta une forme de doun en le remanere vers le heir le donour; et fuit casus qe Robert pere le tenant dona a Johan en fee taille, e si &c. a Thomas en fee taille, e si &c. a Beatrix ke demaunde. E fut le bref tiel, e les queux al avantdit Beatrix remeindre deivent par la forme &c. e pur ceo qe lavantdit Johan &c.; e mist avant fet qe testmoigna la forme.—*Hedone.* Par le fet vivaunt Thomas rien deust remeindre a Beatrix, e

Forme de doun.

[1] Lambert de Trikingham.

A.D. 1306. writ; judgment.—*Roistone.* That ought not to trouble us; John survived Thomas who died without heir &c.—*Hedône.* That does not prove that you ought not to mention him.—LAMBERT adjudged the writ good as to that, and said Plead over.—*Hedone.* It is not the deed of our father, ready &c.—*Roistone.* You tacitly did now admit it.—*Hedone.* I did not; I will aver that he never had any estate by the charter.—*Warr.* Answer to the form; the charter is only the witness of a fact; he does not put it forward except as evidence; for without the charter he ought to be answered.—*Hedone.* John never had anything such as he states, by means of the form; ready &c.—And the other side said the contrary.

Note. § Note, that a fine can not be levied by a man and his son acknowledging to R., and R. granting to the father for the term of his life, either by render or without render, because R. was not tenant.

Quare impedit. § Henry of Lancaster and Isabel his wife brought a Quare Impedit against the prior of Gloucester, and said that William de Valence, guardian of Isabel by gift from the king, by reason of the manor of N. presented the last parson, who on his &c., wherefore &c., to wit John &c.—*King.* His presentee was never instituted, ready &c.—*Herle.* He does not deny that John was presented; and we will aver that he died parson imparsonee.—*King* was driven to answer if John was presented or not by the guardian, and if he died parson imparsonee, without anwering to the institution: and he answered No.—And so they went to the country.—And the case was this, that the said John who was presented was under age, and had a tutor and died under age &c.

Eschete. § The prioress of Markyate brought a writ of Escheat against one John: they pleaded down to the inquest; then the plea remained, by a protection. Then the nule mencion fet de Thomas en le bref; jugement.—*Roistone.* Ceo ne nous deit grever; qe Johan survesquist Thomas qe morust sanz heir &c.—*Hedone.* Ceo ne prove mie qe vous ne freez nule mencion de lui.—LAMBERT. agarda le bref bon en ceo; e dit[es] outre.—*Hedone.* Nent le fet nostre pere, prest &c.—*Roistone.* En teysant or le grantastes.—*Hedone.* Noun fesei; jeo voille averer qe unkes estat par la chartre navoit.—*Warr.* Responez a la forme; qe la chartre nest forsqe testmoignance de un fet, si ne la met il avant si noun en evidence; car sanz la chartre si deust il estre respoundu.—*Hedone.* Johan navoit onqes rien par my la forme auxi com il dist, prest &c.—Et alii e contra. A.D. 1306.

§ Nota, ke une fine ne se puet lever par la ou un homme e sun fiz conussoient a R., e R. grantereit al pere a terme de sa vie, ne par rendre ne sanz rendre, pur ceo que R. ne fust pas en tenance. Nota.

§ Henri de Lancastre e Isabele sa femme porterent un "quare impedit" vers le Priour de Gloucestre, e disoient ke Willem de Valence, gardein Isabele del doun le roy, par reson del maner de N. presenta la dreine persone, qe a sun &c., par quei &c., saver Johan &c. —*King.* Sun presente ne fust unkes institut; prest &c. —*Herle.* Il ne dedit mie qe Johan ne fust presente; e nous voloms averer qil morust persone e enpersone.—*King* fust chace si Johan fust presente ou noun par gardein, e si il morust persone e enpersone, sanz respondre al institucioun: qi respondi qe noun. Et sic ad patriam.—Et fust le cas tel, qe meimes celui Johan qe fust presente si fust denz age, e avoit tutour, e morust denz age &c. Quare impedit.

§ La Prioueresce de Markyate porta bref deschete vers un Johan: plederent al enqueste: pus demora la parole par proteccioun: puis la priouresce suist une reso- Eschete.

A.D. 1306. prioress sued out a re-summons, in which no mention was made of the inquest. And it was said by HENGHAM and TRIKINGHAM that the demandant should have a writ out of the Rolls to make the inquest come: and the re-summons was adjudged good.

Note. § Note, a man was purchaser of a lordship, and a tenant died leaving his son under age; the purchaser brought his writ of Wardship.—*Lanfar* (for the deforceant). He holds of us and of our ancestors by an older feoffment than yours or your ancestors', ready &c.—*King*. He holds of us and of our feoffor and of his ancestors by an older feoffment than yours &c.—*Lanfar*. And we pray judgment, since he has admitted that he held rather of our ancestors than of his ancestors, and the statute [1] only speaks of the ancestors of those who are parties to the plea.—LAMBERT drove *Lanfar* by judgment to answer if he held rather of his feoffor.

Note. § Note, that four persons were impleaded by one præcipe, and they vouched one John, who asked by virtue of what &c. A man and his wife had a specialty, but the other two had not; wherefore they made default.—*Lanfar*. We pray first to be acquitted as to those who do not come.—And he was acquitted before he was driven to answer the other two.

---

[1] 13 Edw. I. (Westm. 2) c. 16.

mons, en la quele nule mencion fut del enqueste. E fut dist par HENGHAM e TRIKENGHAM qe le demaundant avereit bref hors des Roulles de fere venir lenqueste; e la resomons agarde bone. A.D. 1306.

§ Nota, la ou un homme fust purchasour de la seignorye un tenant qe morust e sun fiz denz age, le purchassour porta son bref de garde.—*Lanfare* (pur le deforceour). Il tient de nous e de nos auncestres par eygne feffement qe de vous ou de vos auncestres; prest &c.—*King.* Il tient de nous e de nostre feffour e de ces auncestres par eigne feffement qe de vous, ou &c. — *Lanfare.* E nous jugement, de pus qil ad conu qil tient plus tost de nos auncestres qe de ces auncestres, e lestatut ne parle si noun des auncestres de ceux qe sunt partie al plee.—LAMBERT chasa *Lanfare* par agarde sil tint plus tost de sun feffour. Nota.

§ Nota qe iiii. furent enpledez par un precipe, qe voucherent un Johan, qe demaunda par quei &c. Un homme e sa femme avoit especiaute, mes les autres deus navoient point, par quei il fesseient defaute.—*Lanfare.* Nous prioms estre assouz primes en droit de ceux qe ne viegnent point. E fust assouz einz ceo qil fust chace a respondre as altres deus. Nota.

PLEAS IN EASTER TERM.

XXXIV. EDWARD I.

PLEAS IN EASTER TERM IN THE XXXIVTH YEAR OF THE REIGN OF KING EDWARD.

Dower. § I have only a term for three years by lease from B., ready &c. And he was not driven to vouch.

Dower. § A guardian de facto vouched a guardian de facto.—*Hervy.* Wardship does not make a degree; wherefore answer.—And the reason is because the thing passes with the honour &c.

§ The demandant claimed against the tenants as holding over a term which had passed: the man and his wife said they held in fee, ready &c. And the other side said the contrary. — THE INQUEST. The father of the demandant leased the land to the father of the woman for a term of three years, to hold to him his heirs and assigns &c. At Nisi Prius the woman prayed to be received, but she was not. On another day in the Bench she prayed as before.—BEREFORD. To do what?—*Scrope.* To defend her term.—BEREFORD. She and her husband heretofore claimed the fee; and the reverse of your statement is found.—*Scrope.* That was her husband's pleading; but on the day of the taking of the Inquest Alice put forward a writing which witnessed the term, and what the Inquest said, and prayed to be received; and so she does still; for otherwise she is without remedy.—BEREFORD. The term is only a chattel, and belongs to the husband and not to the wife; and if she were received she would defend what she cannot have: wherefore the Court adjudges that the demandant do recover.—BEREFORD. A woman shall never be received while her husband is in court.

DE TERMINO PASCHE ANNO REGNI REGIS EDWARDI XXXIIII^{TO}.

§ Jeo nay ke terme de iii. anz del lees B. prest &c.: e ne fust mie chace a voucher. Dowere.

§ Un gardein de fet voucha un gardein de fet.—*Hervy*. Gardein ne fet mie degre; par quei responez. Et est ratio quia res transit cum honore &c. Dowere.

§ Ad terminum qui preteriit; le homme e sa femme, En fee, prest &c. Et alii e contra.—*Lenqueste*. Le pere le demandant lessa la terre al pere la femme a terme de treis anz a tener a ly e ces heirs e a ces assignez &c.: al nisi prius la femme pria de estre receu; et non fuit. Ad alium diem in banco ele pria ut supra.—BEREFORD. A quei fere?—*Scrop*. A defendre sun terme. BEREFORD. Luy e sun baroun einz ces houres ount clame fee; e trove est le revers de vostre dist.—*Scrop*. Ceo fut le pleder sun baroun; mes le jour del enqueste prise Alice mist avant lescrist qe testmoigna le terme, e ceo qe lenqueste dist, e pria de estre receu, e auxi fust ele uncore, qar autrement est sine remedio.—BEREFORD. Le terme nest qe chatel, e est al baroun e nent a la femme; e si ele fust receu ele defendreit ceo qele ne peut mie avoir; par quei agarde qe le demaundant rescovere.—BEREFORD. Femme ne serra jammes receu e sun baroun en court.

A.D. 1306.

Quare impedit.

§ In a Quare Impedit against vicars.—*Passeley.* It is full by our patronage, to our own use, for thirty years before your writ was purchased, by the gift of one John Peche, and by this deed and this other deed of the ordinary.—*Malmesthorpe.* They are secular persons and not regulars like persons in religion; wherefore they can not hold to their own use. — HENGHAM. Why not? since the thing is given them to hold thus.—*Malmesthorpe.* John Peche never had anything in the vill &c., so that he could confer an estate on them, ready &c.—HENGHAM. Ought we now to plead a writ of right, whereas they allege plenarty? (intimating the negative); therefore sue out a writ to the bishop, &c.

Darrein presentement.

§ A prior brought a writ of Darrein Presentement against Philip de Kyme.—*Toudeby* did not counterplead the seisin, because the Prior had many charters from the ancestors of Philip, nor did he make to himself a title from ancestors or feoffors to the manor whereof he was tenant to which he said the advowson belonged.—*The Prior.* B. our predecessor presented his clerk &c., and C. our predecessor presented another before him.—*Toudeby* W. Wake, tenant of the manor of N., whereof we are seised, presented &c. W. who &c. — *Passeley.* This W. le Wake released and quit-claimed in the Prior's seisin; and by this deed. And he put forward many deeds of other lords who made claims on the advowson. And *Passeley* would have pleaded to Simond's title, but could not, because the Assise was awarded.—BEREFORD. Good people, you have nothing more to inquire than if any of the predecessors of the aforesaid Prior presented the last parson by whose death &c., and if they did not, tell us who did.—THE ASSISE. None of the predecessors of the Prior nor this le Wake presented the last parson, but Hugh father of Randolph Earl of Chester did, and all the presentations for the time since past the Bishops have given, on account of the great controversy which

A.D. 1306.

Quare impedit.

§ Quare impedit vers vikeres. — *Passeley.* Ele est pleyne de nostre avowerie en propres us xxx. anz avant vostre bref purchace, del doun un Johan Peche, e par ceo fet, e ceo autre fet le ordiner.—*Malm.* Il sunt seculers genz e nent reulers com gent de religion; par quei en propres us ne la pount tener.—HENGHAM. Pur quei noun? de pus qe la chose lor est done a tener issint.—*Malm.* Johan Peche navoit unkes rien en la ville &c. e issint qil poet estat a eux faire, prest &c.—HENGHAM. Devoms ore pleder un bref de droit par la ou il alleggent plenerete? quasi dicerit non; e pur ceo suiez bref al eveske &c.

Drein present.

§ Un Priour porta un drein presentement ver Phillippe de Kyme.—*Toudeby* ne contrepleda mie lassise [la seisine ?], quia Prior habuit plura monumenta de antecessoribus Philippi, nec fecit ei titulum ab antecessoribus nec feoffatoribus de manerio unde fuit tenens ad quod dicebat advocationem pertinere.—*Le Priour.* B. nostre predecessour presenta un seon clerk &c., e C. nostre predecessour un autre avant ly.—*Toudeby.* W. Wake tenant del maner de N., dount nous sumes seisi, presenta &c. W. qi &c. —*Passeley.* Celui W. le Wake relessa e quiteclama en la seisine le Priour, e par ceo fet; e mist avant plussors fez de autre seignors qe mistrent debat en la avoeson.—E *Passelei* voleit aver plede al title Simound, et non potuit, pur ceo qe lassise fust agarde. — BEREFORD. Bones genz, vous navez plus denquerre fors si nul des predecessours le Priour avantdit nomez presenterent la dreine persone par qi mort &c., e si noun dites nous qi.—LASSISE. Nul des predecessours le Priour ne celui le Wake ne presenterent mie la dreine persone, einz fist Hughe pere Randolf Count de Cestre, e touz les presentements pus ount les Eveskes donez pur tens passe pur le grant

A.D. 1306. there was about it.—And they were driven to name the clerk who was presented: and they did so.—*Toudeby.* We pray our damages because the prior has troubled us. —BEREFORD. The assise has said nothing on your behalf; wherefore &c.—*Warr.* The Assise has sung for the King.

Toudeby. Whereas Michel de Meldoun brought a writ of Customs &c., (and he said &c. and named the services which he demanded,) Sir, B. acknowledges that he holds the aforesaid tenements of Michel by homage &c., for all services; and for that acknowledgment Michel released and quit-claimed to W. 12*d* of yearly rent for which Michel made his demand against him.

A View was granted to two jointly, and they did not sue out any writ.—On another day one of them was essoined, and the other again prayed the View, and prayed a writ to the Sheriff; and he did not have it, because his joint-tenant was essoined; but it was adjourned to the same day with the essoin; but he proffered himself against the plaintiff, who did not come, so he and his pledges &c.

Voucher. § John de Wra brought six Præcipes against six tenants; one of whom vouched an infant under age. So let him await &c. The five vouched one A. and did not sue out any writ. On another day they entered a Postea; on another day another Postea; and on the third day he was essoined; wherefore the demandant made a statement showing how he was delayed; and now, said he, he is essoined, and he has appeared twice since the voucher. — BEREFORD. Were they ever before now essoined after the voucher? — *The demandant.* No. — BEREFORD. Then let it stand.—*The demandant* prayed that the justices would adjudge the tenants that they should sue at their peril; and because the essoin was not received on such a command &c. no writ was debat qe ilui avoit. E furent chacez a nomer le clerk qe fust presente: et sic fecerunt.—*Toudeby.* Nous prioms nos damages de ceo qe le Priour nous ad travaille. BEREFORD.—Lassise nad rien dist pur vous, par quei &c. —*Warr.* Lassise ad chante pur le Roi. A.D. 1306.

§ *Toudeby.* Par la ou Michel de Meldoun porta bref de custumes &c. e dist &c. noma les services qil demaunda, Sire, B. conust a tener les avantdiz tenements de Michel par homage &c. pur touz services, e pur cele reconissance Michel relest e quiteclamast a W. xii. deners de annuele rente de la quele Michel fist sa demaunde vers luy.

§ Une Vewe fust grante a deus jointement, e il ne suyrent nul bref.—Ad alium diem le un fust essone, e lautre demaunda autrefoiz la Vewe e pria bref a Viconte; et non habuit, quia sun jointe fust essone; einz fust ajorne a meyme tiel jour come le essone: sed optulit se contra petentem, qui non venit, ideo ipse et plegii sui &c.

§ Johan de Wra porta vi. Precipes vers vi. tenans; Voucher. le un vouche enfant denz age. Ideo expectet &c. Les v. voucherent un A. e ne suierent nul bref. Ad alium diem il entrerent un postea. Et ad alium diem un autre postea; et ad tertium diem si fust il essone; par quei le demaundant fist sa demostranz coment il fist delaie; e ore est essone, et apparuit bis pus le voucher.—BEREFORD. Furent il essone onqes puis le voucher avant ore?—*Le demaundant.* Nanil.—BEREFORD. Estoise donqes.—*Le demaundant* pria qe les Justices agarderent al tenans qil suissont a lour peril; e pur ceo qe lessone ne fust pas de tel mandement receyve &c., nullum breve

A.D. 1306. returned, the demandant was told to sue out a writ to summon the warrantor. And, according to some, the tenant can keep the writ in his purse: and on another day he will sue at his peril; and on another day the voucher may be essoined; but to quash the delays the demandant sues out writs.

Voucher to warranty by a charter where the "dedi" was void.

§ Theobald de Verdun vouched the Earl of Hereford, and said that one Humphrey his father gave the tenements demanded to Robert de W. in frank-marriage with Margery his daughter, and bound himself; and by this deed.—*King.* For fifteen years before this charter was made Humphrey our father had nothing in the tenements, so that by the gift which that charter witnesses they never had anything; judgment if by a charter where the "dedi" is void &c.—*Friskeney.* We do not think to bind you to the warranty by the "dedi," but by the clause of warranty which is simple; and the deed is admitted, judgment.—*King.* I make void the "dedi" on which the warranty depends; for at the making of this deed Margery was seised and Humphrey had nothing, so that into the person of Theobald nothing could pass by that charter; judgment &c.—MALORE. Is not Theobald tenant, and the charter containing the warranty in his hands?—*King.* The charter is void; nothing passed by the gift.—MALORE. See if that follows; therefore take care.—*Friskeney.* Since the deed is admitted, and Theobald and Margery were seised on the day of the making thereof, and Robert was never seised, and it states a simple warranty &c., judgment &c.

Dower.

§ In a writ of Dower [the tenant said that] after the death of her husband she [the demandant] was seised of her dower, and alienated it to such an one, by whom we entered; judgment.—*Hamptone.* By whose assignment?—*Passeley.* There is no need to say, for although a tenant by disseisin had assigned to you, that would not suffice.—HENGHAM. You must say by whose assign-fuit retornatum, dictum fuit al demaundant qil suissit bref de somondre le garrant. Et secundum quosdam le tenant puet tener ceo bref en sa bours. Et ad alium diem il suiera a sun peril: et [ad] alium diem le voucher put estre essone; sed ad cassandum dilationes sequitur petens brevia. A.D. 1306.

Voucher a garrantie par chartre ou le dedi fut voi[de].

§ Tebaud de Verdone voucha le Counte de Hereford, e dist qe un Umfrey sun pere dona les tenements demaundez a Robert de W. en franc-mariage ove Margerie sa fille, e se obligha &c., e par ceo fet. — *King.* XV. anz avant ceste chartre fet si avoit Umfrey nostre pere rien en les tenements, issint qe [par] le doun qe cele chartre testmoigne unqes rien navoient; jugement si par chartre ou le "dedi" est voide &c.—*Friskeney.* Nous ne vous byoms point a lier a la garantie par le "dedi," einz par la clause de garantie qest simple; e le fet conu; jugement. — *Kyng.* Jeo voide le "dedi" de qi la garantie depent; qar a la confeccion de ceo fet Margerie fust seisie, e Umfrey rien navoit; issint qen la persone Tibaud par cele chartre rien ne pout passer, jugement &c. — MALLORRE. Nest Tibaud en tenance e la chartre trove en sa mein qe voet garrantie?—*King.* La chartre est voide; qe rien ne passa par my le doun.—MALLORRE. Veez si il ensuit, e pur ceo pernez garde.—*Friskeney.* De pus qe le fet est conu, e Tibaud e Margerie seisi le jour de la confeccion, e Robert unqes seisi, e voet garrante simple &c., jugement &c.

Dowere.

§ En un bref de dowere, apres la mort sun baroun ele fust seisi de sun dowere e aliena a un tiel par qi nous sumes entre en, jugement. — *Hamptone.* De qi assignement?—*Passeley.* Non oportet, qe tut vous eust un tenant par disseisine assigne hoc non sufficeret. — HENGHAM. Oportet dicere de qi assignement.—*Passeley.*

A.D. 1306. ment.—*Passeley.* By G.'s assignment.—*Hamptone.* Never seised of dower by his assignment, ready &c. — HENGHAM. By whose assignment then? You must tell that or traverse the seisin.—*Hamptone.* Never seised, ready &c.

Right. § A man in the Chancery made a suggestion that, whereas he was impleaded for certain tenements for which he is now impleaded, he vouched the person who is now demandant; and because there was a foreign plea pending in the Eyre of that warranty, therefore he caused the plea to be recorded.—*The demandant.* The cause is insufficient to remove the plea; judgment. — THE JUSTICE. Plead over. — *The tenant.* We pray the View. — *Lanfar.* Heretofore in the liberty you had the View. Moreover, by your own purchase you supposed that you were certified by the View of what you vouched for; judgment. — And because it was found in the first record that he had the View, he was ousted from the View.

Wardship. § Showeth unto you Lettice, who was the wife of John de Burtone &c., that Adam de Irland tortiously deforces her &c. of the wardship of the lands of Richard de Scozetone, the wardship of which belongs to her, for the reason that the said Richard held of her by services which give &c.: and tortiously for this, that the said Richard held a messuage &c. in the vill &c., of John de Burtone formerly husband of the said &c., by homage and by escuage, to wit &c.; of which services John was seised by the hand of &c. as by the hand &c. the day when he endowed her at the church-door when he married her, and died seised of his homage; after whose death Roger Bigod, Earl &c. guardian of the lands and of the heir of John de Burton assigned to the aforesaid Lettice the services of the said Richard de Scozetone, in dower; on which assignment Richard attorned to her, and she was seised of his services by his hand

Par le assignement G. — *Hamptone.* Onqes seisi de dowere de sun assignement, prest &c.—HENGHAM. Par qi assignement donqes? il covent ceo dire ou traverser la seisine.—*Hamptone.* Unqes seisi, prest &c. A.D. 1306.

§ Un homme en la Chancelerie fist une suggescion qe la ou il fust enplede de certeinz tenementz des queux il est ore enplede il voucha mesme celui qe est demaundant, e pur ceo qil fust forein play pendant en Eyre de cele garrantie, e pur ceo fit recorder la parole. —*Le demandaunt.* La cause est insufficient a remuer la parole; jugement. — LA JUSTICE. Dites outre.—*Le tenant.* Nous demaundoms la Vewe. — *Lanfare.* Autrefoiz en fraunchise aviez la Vewe. Estre ceo, par vostre purchaz demene de ceo qe vous vouchez si supposastes estre acerte de la Vewe, jugement. Et quia inveniebatur quod in primo recordo quod habuit visum, fust oste de la Vewe. De recto.

§ Ceo vous moustre Letice qe fu la femme Johan de Burtone &c., qe Adam de Irland atort la deforce &c. la garde des terres le heir Richard de Scozetone qi garde a lui apent par la reson qe mesme celui Richard sa terre de luy tient par services qe donnent &c. E pur ceo atort, qe le avantdit Richard tient un mies &c. en la ville &c., de Johan de Burtone jadis baroun meme ceste &c. par homage e par escuage, saver &c.; des queux services meime celui Jon fust seisi par la main &c., com par la main &c., le jour qil la dowa al huis de moustrer quant il la esposa, e morust seisi de sun homage; apres qi mort, Roger Bygod counte &c., gardein des terres e del heir Johan de Burtone, assigna al avantdit Letice les services meymes celuy Richard de Scozetone en dowere; par quel assignement Richard se attorna a luy, e ele seisi de ces services par sa mayn, com par De garde.

A.D. 1306. as by the hands of her very tenant, and so he died tenant to her as dowress.—And at the end of her count she said—tortiously deforces her of the wardship, to her damage &c.—*Toudeby.* In the tenements we have only a term of years by lease from Roger Bigod, and we vouch him.—*Friskeney.* Roger was never seised of these tenements, after the assignment which he made to us of the services, in such a manner that he could make a lease of them, ready &c.—And the other side said the contrary.

Ravishment of ward.

§ Tortiously &c. the body of John son and heir of W de N. being under age, the wardship of whom belongs to him by reason that the aforesaid W., father of &c., whose heir &c., his land &c. by services &c. found in such a place, with force and arms ravished, against the peace and to his damage &c. — *Toudeby* denied the coming &c.; and (said he) he has not counted that he was seised; judgment.—*Lanfar.* The writ does not state that.—*Toudeby.* The statute[1] requires it, wherefore &c.—And the statute was read, and it did not require it; and the count was adjudged good. — *Toudeby.* The writ is given against him who has no right; and the father of the infant held of us; wherefore judgment. — *Wescote.* He held of us by an elder feoffment.—*Toudeby.* Bring your writ and it shall be tried there and not here.—HENGHAM. Why not in this writ; does not the writ state "which belongs to him"? and this is a writ of trespass where one can not try the tort without trying the right: wherefore answer over.—*Toudeby.* The tenements which he held of us were the first tenements which his ancestors ever purchased to hold by knight-service &c.—And the other side said the contrary.

Dower

§ A woman was received on the default of her husband, and prayed aid of her parceners and had it; and they then all said that the joint feoffee with her husband survived him, wherefore &c.—*Toudeby.* He had a fee in

[1] 13 Edw. I. (Westm. 2) c. 35.

la mayn sun verrei tenant, e issint morust sun tenant come en dowere: et in fine la deforce la garde a tort e ces damages &c. — *Toudeby.* Nous navom en les tenements si noun terme des anz du lees Roger Bygot e lui vouchom.—*Friskeney.* Roger ne fust unqes seisi de ces tenements pus le assignement qil fist a nous des services saver qil poeit lees faire, prest &c. Et alii e contra. A.D. 1306.

§ Atort &c. le corps Johan fiz e heir W. de N. denz age esteant, qi garde a luy apent par la reson qe le avantdit W. pere le &c. qi heir &c. sa terre &c. par service &c. en tel leu trove a force e armes ravissent encontre la pees e a ces damages &c. — *Toudeby* defendi le venir &c.: il nad mie conte kil fust seisi, jugement.—*Lanfare.* Le bref ne voet mie ceo.—*Toudeby.* Le statut le voet, par quei &c. E fut lestatut lu, et noluit hoc, e fust le counte agarde bon.—*Toudeby.* Le bref est done vers celui qe nul droit nad, e le pere lenfant tient de nous &c.; par quei jugement.—*Wescote.* Il tient de nous par eigne feffement.—*Toudeby.* Portez vostre bref e la serra ceo trie e nent icy.--HENGHAM. Pur quei nent en cestui bref; ne voet mie le bref "quod "ad ipsum pertinet;" e ceo est un bref de trespas, ou homme ne puet mie trier qe ad le tort sanz trier le droit; par quei responez outre.--*Toudeby.* Les tenements qil tient de nous si furent les primers tenements qe unkes ces auncestres purchacerent par service de chivaler &c. Et alii e contra.

Ravissement de garde.

§ Une femme receu par la defaute sun baroun, qe pria eyde de ces parceners, et habuit; e pus disoient touz qe le joint feffe sun baroun lui survesqui, par quei &c.--*Toudeby.* Il avoit fee en les tenements le jour qil les

Dowere.

A.D. 1306. the tenements on the day when he alienated them to such an one; judgment.—*Friskeney.* Never solely seised, but jointly with such an one who is alive; judgment.—*Toudeby.* What have you to show it?—*Friskeney.* Ready &c.; for the charter remains with our feoffor who is liable to warrant us; and see here the charter whereby we purchased. — *Toudeby.* Since you have admitted the seisin of our husband, and have nothing to show the joint-tenancy, judgment. — *Friskeney.* Admit what we state and let us abide judgment.—*Toudeby.* We will aver that our husband had the fee on the day when he alienated; and you have admitted his seisin, at least of a moiety, and of that we pray seisin, and we will go to an averment as to the remainder. — MALORE. By the alienation their right was equally extinct, and each one was seised as of fee on the same day; wherefore some think that the joint-feoffment which existed previously was very weak after the alienation.—*Friskeney.* If they had been disseised jointly would not the heir of him who is alive have an action for the entirety without naming the heir of her husband? (intimating that he would.)—MALORE. When a woman has an action to demand dower, the husband can not bar her by any act except by his felony; but a joint tenant does not by felony forfeit anything; wherefore &c.—And so to judgment.

Quod permittat. § In a Quod permittat to throw down a mill, the defendant vouched, and on another day made default.—*Hamptone.* — We pray that the mill may be thrown down.—HENGHAM. Let the great distress run; and you, vouchee, adieu without day: and he did not say "quit "of the warranty &c."

Non compos mentis. § In a Non compos mentis, *Lanfar.* Of sound memory, ready &c. — HENGHAM. Sue out a writ to the sheriff where he was resident, and not to the sheriff where the land is.

aliena a un tiel; jugement.—*Friskeney.* Onqes soul seisi einz[1] jointe ove un tel qest en pleine vie; jugement.—*Toudeby.* Quei avez de ceo?—*Friskeney.* Prest &c., qar la chartre demoert vers nostre feffour qe nous dust garantir; e veez icy la chartre par quei nous purchasames.—*Toudeby.* De pus qe vous avez conu la seisine nostre baroun, e rien navez del joint, jugement. —*Frisqeney.* Conussez ceo qe nous dioms, e demoroms en jugement.—*Toudeby.* Nous voloms averer qe nostre baroun avoit fee le jour qil aliena; e vous avez conu sa seisine a meinz de la moite, e de ceo prioms seisine, e al averement del remenant.—MALORRE. Par lalienacion lour dreit fust owelment esteint, e chescon fust seisi come de fee meime le jour; par quei les unes entendent qe le joynt feffement qe fut avant apres le alienacion si fust mult feble.—*Friskeney.* Sil ussent este disseisi jointement navereit le heir celuy qe vist accion a lentier sanz nomer le heir sun baroun? quasi dicerit sic.—MALORE. Quant femme ad accion a demaunder dowere, le baroun ne la puet [barrer] par nul fet si [noun] par felonie; mes joynt par felonie rien ne forfet; par quei &c. Et sic ad judicium. A.D. 1306.

§ En un "quod permittat prosternere molendinum," *le defendant* voucha, et ad alium diem fist defaute.—*Hamptone.* Nous prioms qe le molin soit abatu. — HENGHAM. Courge la grante destresse, e vous vouche alez a Dieu sanz jour. Et non dixit quites de la garantie &c. Quod permittat.

§ Non compos mentis.—*Lanfare.* De bone memorie prest &c.—HENGHAM. Suez bref a viconte ou il fust reseant, e noun pas a viconte ou la terre est. Non compos mentis.

[1] MS. sanz.

A.D. 1306.

Entry.

§ In a writ of entry one of the parties alleged imprisonment, to save a default, and then quit-claimed from a time after the default, and the witnesses were all of different counties; and for suspicion of the matter he had a day, of grace.

Darrein presentment.

§ Nicholas Daune brought a writ of Darrein presentement against the Abbat of Tavistock, and said that the said abbat, as guardian, presented the last &c. and his grandfather before him. — *Hegham.* The church is full by our patronage, and of him by whose resignation he says the church is vacant.—*Toudeby.* By what right?—*Malmesthorpe.* In this possessory writ it is sufficient to allege plenarty by the writ. — *Toudeby.* By the statute [1] a presentation in time of nonage does not give a title against the infant when he is of full age; and we are seised of the manor to which the advowson &c., and he does not show any right, and he is a man in religion. — HENGHAM. They have answered sufficiently to each point of your writ for the purpose of abating the writ; the writ states "which is vacant." — *Idle.* He is not pleading to your title, but to abate the writ; and he does not claim the advowson to his own use, for then it would be necessary to make a title; and your answer on the statute is to be understood when the church is vacant; and they allege plenarty for 20 years before the writ was purchased: wherefore, do you wish a writ to the bishop?—*Toudeby,* by way of compromise, agreed. But (said he) I protest that we do not grant him any presentation by his patronage.— HENGHAM. Sue out a writ to the bishop.

Voucher.

§ An averment, according to the form of the statute,[2] to oust a man from his voucher, sounded against the demandant. And the writ was not quashed, but he was amerced.

---

[1] 13 Edw. I. (Westm. 2), c. 5.

[2] 3 Edw. I. c. 40.

§ Entre, ou il allegga enprisonement pur saver une defaute e pus quite-clama de tens pus la defaute, e les testmoigne touz de divers countez, e pur suspecion il avoit jour de grace. A.D. 1306. Entre.

§ Nichol Daune porta un drein presentement vers labbe de Tavystoke, e dist qe meyme labbe com gardein presenta la dreyne &c. e sun ael avant luy.—*Hegham.* Leglise est pleine de nostre avowerie e de celui par qi resignement il dist leglise estre voide.—*Toudeby.* Par quel droit?—*Malm.* En cestui bref de possession il suffit de allegger plenerete pur bref.—*Toudeby.* Par statut presentement en tenps de noun age ne donne mie title encontre lenfant quant il est de plein age; e nous sumes seisi del maner a quei la avoeson &c., e il ne moustra nul droit, e est homme de religion.—HENGHAM. Il unt respondu assez a chescon point de vostre bref pur bref abatre, qe le bref voet "quæ vacat."—*Idle.* Il ne plede mie a vostre title, einz a bref abatre; e il ne cleime lavoeson en propre us, qe donqe covendrey de fere title; e vostre respons sur statut fet a entendre la ou eglise est voide; e il alleggent plenerete de .xx. anz avant le bref purchace; par quei volez bref al eveske?—*Toudeby,* de contractu concessit: tamen protestor qe luy grantoms nulle presentement de savowerie.—HENGHAM. Suez bref al eveske. Drein presente.

§ Un averement solom forme de statut, de oster homme de son voucher, chanta contre le demandaunt. Et breve non cassatur sed amerciatur.

A.D. 1306. Voucher.

§ In a Cui in vitâ the tenant vouched B. the heir of the husband.—*Lanfar.* Our husband had no son named B., ready &c.—And the other side said the contrary.—*Moyne.* For one acre we say that we did not enter by her husband, but by C., ready, &c.—*Lanfar.* What do you answer as to the remainder.—*Moygne.* This is a præcipe.—And by HALES and MALORE he was driven to answer as to the remainder; and then he vouched G. son and heir of the husband.—*Lanfar.* He has vouched him as if he were of full age, whereas he is under age; judgment.—*Moygne.* That is nothing to you; it only concerns the voucher.—*Lanfar.* He is under age, ready &c.; and we pray seisin now according to the statute.[1]—HALES. He shall be first seen by the Court, and then &c.—*Moygne.* Now she has admitted that her husband had a son named B., but he is under age; judgment &c.—HALES. You shall be in the like condition as if the averment had sounded against him; and therefore let the voucher stand; and we absolve you from the inquest.—And so the tenant abridged his delays by his own folly.

Ael.

§ John de Boys brought a writ of Ael against Thomas Peche.—*King.* Wronow, the father of John, released &c. to Amory Peche, in whose seisin &c.; which Amory Peche enfeoffed us &c.; judgment if in opposition to the deed of your father &c.—*Malmesthorpe.* Then you put forward this exception as assign of Amory.—*King.* We give it as tenant of the tenements; therefore admit this deed first.—*Toudeby* was driven to do this: and (said he) We tell you that at the same time when the quitclaim was made to Amory who held those tenements by the law of England, Amory had leased the manor of N. to Wranow for the term of his life, paying to him yearly 20*l.* and acquitting Amory and all his tenants of the same manor against the chief lord from all manner of

[1] 13 Edw. I. (Westm. 2), c. 40.

§ Cui in vita. Le tenant voucha B. heir le baroun. A.D. 1306.
—*Lanfare.* Nostre baroun navoit nul fiz B. par noun, Voucher.
prest &c.—Et alius e contra.—*Moyne.* Pur un acre[1] nous ne entrames mie par son baroun einz par C., prest &c.—*Lanfare.* Quei responz en droit del remenant.—*Moygne.* Ceo est un præcipe:—e par HALES e MALORRE il fust chace a respondre del remenant; e pus voucha G. fiz e heir le baroun.—*Lanfare.* Il luy ad vouche com de plein age, la ou il est de denz age; jugement.—*Moygne.* Ceo nest rien a vous einz al voucher.—*Lanfare.* Qe il est denz age, prest &c.; e prioms seisine meintenant solom statut.—HALES. Il serra prime veu de court, e pus &c.—*Moygne.* Ore ad ele conu qe sun baroun ad un fiz B., mes il est denz age, jugement &c. — HALES. Vous serrez en autiel estat com si le averement ust chante contre luy; e pur ceo estoise le voucher; e nous vous assoloms del enqueste: e issint abregga le tenant ces delaies par sa folie demeine.

§ Johan de Boys porta bref de Ael vers Thomas Ael.
Peche. — *King.* Wronou pere Johan relessa &c. a Amorie Peche, en qi seisine &c.; le quel Amorie Peche nous enfeffa &c.; jugement si encontre le fet vostre pere &c. — *Malm.* Donkes mettez vous avant ceste excepcion com assigne Amourie.—*King.* Nous com tenant des tenements la donomes; e pur ceo connussez ceo fet primes. — *Toudeby* fust chace a ceo fere, e vous dioms qe a meime ceo tenps qe la quite clamanz fust fete a Amorie qe ceux tenements tient par la ley Engleterre, si avoit Amorie lesse le maner de N. a Wranou a terme de sa vie fessant a luy xx. livres par an, e acquistrent Amorie e touz ces tenans de meime le maner vers le chef seignur de tote ma-

[1] MS. autre.

A.D. 1306. service, and a writing embodying this agreement was made between them in this form, viz. that, if Wranow should do that thing as aforesaid, Amory would not alienate the tenements now in demand nor do any other thing which should grow to the disturbance of the reversion, and that the quit-claim made to Amory should be holden as null &c. to Wranow; and this writing is as a condition in the quit-claim, and we will aver that the condition is fulfilled by Wranow; wherefore we do not think that by this quit-claim we ought to be barred.—*Friskeney.* The quit-claim is simple, without condition, and admitted; judgment &c.—*Scrope.* If a man make a simple charter of certain tenements, and also a separate writing which states that if he pay a sum of money at a certain day he shall have again the tenements, if he pay the money at the day, the gift made by the charter is null: but now the quit-claim and the writing amount to this condition viz., that, if we keep our agreement with him, he neither ought to nor can alienate the tenements; wherefore we pray judgment since we will aver the condition which has been performed by us.—*Herte.* The case is not similar: for by the quit-claim the simple right accrues immediately to him to whom it is made, and the other is clearly ousted; but in the case of a charter it is necessary that there be seisin and other things; wherefore &c.—*Scrope.* If the force of the condition in the writing had been at the end of the quit-claim we should now annul the quit-claim by the condition having been performed: why not under the present circumstances since the writing was made at the same time?—BEREFORD. There was too wise a head on one side and too weak a one on the other.

Dower. § A woman brought her writ of Dower.—*The tenant.* You were never joined to him in lawful matrimony.—*Passeley.* The reverse.—BEREFORD. In what bishoprick?—*Passeley.* In the bishoprick of Lincoln.—BEREFORD.

nere de service, e un escrist de ceo covenant fet entre eux en ceste forme qe, si Wranou feit ceste chose com avant est dist, qe Amorie ne alienereit les tenements qe ore sunt en demaunde, ne nulle autre chose ne freit qe cherreit en desturbance de la revercion, e qe la quite-clamanz fet a Amorie fut tenu pur nul &c. a Wranou; e cest escrist est com une condicion en la quite clamanz, e nous voloms averer la condicion paremply par Wranou; par quei nentendoms pas qe par ceste quite clamanz devom estre barre.—*Friskeney.* La quite clamanz est simple sanz condicion e conu; jugement &c.—*Scrop.* Si un homme ust fet une chartre simple de certeinz tenements, e un escrist de cost qe voet si il payast une summe de deners a certein jour qe il reust ces tenements, si il luy paie les deners al jour, le doun qe se fist par la chartre si est nule; mes ore amonte la quite-clamanz e lescrist a tele condicion qe voet si nous lui tenoms covenant qil ne deive ne ne puisse les tenements aliener; par quei nous demaundom jugement de pus qe nous voloms averer la condicion par nous acomply.—*Herte.* Non est simile; qe par la quite-clamanz si acreste le droit simple meintenant a celuy a qi ele est fete, e lautre oste de net; mes a chartre si covent qe luy eit seisine e autre chose; par quei &c.—*Scrop.* Si la force de la condicion del escrist fust en la fin de la quite-clamanz nous lanenteroms meintenant la quite-clamanz par la condicion paremply; par quei nent de ceste parte de pus qe lescrist fet a meime ceo tens.—BEREFORD. Ilui avoit trop sage parte de une parte e trop feble de autre parte. A.D. 1306.

§ Une femme porta sun bref de dowere.—*Le tenant.* Onqes acouple a lui en leal matrimoigne. —*Passeley.* Le revers. — BEREFORD. En quel evesche ? — *Passeley.* En le evesche de Nicol. — BEREFORD. Ele ne vient Dowere.

A.D. 1306. She never came into England, so you have lost all.—*Passeley.* Not so; for at the suggestion of him who sues for the woman, they will have a writ to the bishop of the place where they say that the espousals were had, although it be out of the realm, to certify him thereof, and then he will send to this court in the same form: this is the law of England.

Jure de utrum.

§ In a Jure de utrum the prior of Bradstoke vouched the prior of Wandragese by reason of exchanges of tenements beyond the sea which he gave for the same tenements which are in demand, and he showed a charter witnessing this, and the King's charter which witnessed the exchanges.—*Toudeby.* The charter supposes by itself that it was made out of the realm, wherefore &c.—*Malmesthorpe.* You can not deny it, for the King's charter witnesses the exchanges and ratifies them; wherefore &c.—BEREFORD. Have you seen the plea between the King of Scotland and one B., where a charter could not be denied because the King's charter was put forward in evidence of that deed, just as now?—*Toudeby.* When the exchanges were effected we delivered to him all the muniments of those tenements which we had, by which muniments we ought to vouch; wherefore we ought not to warrant. Moreover, they have from us a charter which William the Conqueror made to us, by which he can bar him; judgment &c.—BEREFORD. That is your own foolishness.—*Toudeby.* According to the exchanges we enter into warranty.—*King.* Our predecessor was seised in the time of the present King, and he alienated; and we pray the Jury.—*Toudeby.* The exchanges were made in the time of King Henry, wherefore we pray aid of what was said before he vouched us, and as if he had said nothing.—*Warr.* Since the parson has allowed the voucher which is more . . . of his action, we do not think that he ought to have the Jury from a lower time than our seisin onqes en Engleterre, par quei vous avez tut perdue.— *Passeley.* Nanil, car a la suggestion celui qe seust pur la femme si averont il bref al Eveske del leu ou il dient les esposailles estre fetes, tut seit ceo hors del realme, de lui certefier, e puis il mandera a ceste court en mesme la forme; e ceo voet lei Dengleterre. A.D. 1306.

§ En une "jure de utrum" le priour de Bradestoke voucha le priour de Wandragese par reson des eschanges des tenements dela la mer qil dona pur meyme les tenements qe sunt en demaunde, e moustra chartre qe ceo testmoigne, e la chartre le Roy qe testmoigna ces eschanges. — *Toudeby.* La chartre en sey suppose estre fete hors de roialme, par quei &c. — *Malm.* Vous nel poez dedire, car la chartre le Roy testmoigne les eschanges, e les ratefie; par quei &c.—BEREFORD. Veistes le plee entre le Roy de Escoce e un B. ou une chartre ne poeit estre dedit pur ceo qe la chartre le Roi fust mis avant en testmoignance de ceo fet, auxi com ore? — *Toudeby.* Quant les eschanges se pristrent nous lui liverames touz les monumenz qe nous avioms de ces tenements, e par queux monumenz nous duissoms voucher; par quei garantir ne devoms. Estre ceo il ount une chartre de nous qe William le Conquerour nous fist, par la quele il le puet barrer; jugement &c. — BEREFORD. Ceo est vostre folie demene. — *Toudeby.* Solom les eschanges entroms en la garantie. — *King.* Nostre predecessour seisi en tenps le Roi qe ore est, e aliena, e prioms la Jure. — *Toudeby.* Les eschanges se pristrent en tenps le Roi Henri, par quei nous prioms aide de ceo qe fust dist einz ceo qil nous voucha, e si ne avoit il rien dist.—*Warr.* De pus qe la persone ad suffert le voucher qe est plus[1] de sa accion, nentendoms mie qil deive aver la Jure de plus bas temps qe nostre Jure de utrum.

(1) Some word seems omitted here.

A.D. 1306. was.—And it was not allowed.—*Toudeby.* We pray that the Jury may be examined of the form of the first gift. —And this was granted.

Escheat. § Note that, in a writ of Escheat against Nicholas Malemeinz, who put forward the King's charter which said "saving every one's right,"—*Toudeby.* We have right; for he by whose felony the King had the escheat held of us these same tenements by certain services.— And because Nicholas could not be a party to try this, the plea awaited until communication with the King &c.

§ One Walter avowed, for the reason that B. held certain tenements of A. by the services &c., of which &c., which A. granted that rent to C. and M., by which grant &c., for all their lives, and that after their deaths the services should remain to the aforesaid Walter and the heirs of his body &c.; and for so much &c.—*Toudeby.* He makes himself a purchaser, and does not say that he was seised, judgment.—*Passeley* showed a deed witnessing the seisin; and C. and M. were seised, wherefore &c.—*Scotre.* Either the abbat or we ought to distrein.—*Inge.* The abbat has no right; for the right vested, by the attornment to C. and M., and this gives him title.—*Toudeby* was driven to answer over.—*Toudeby.* C. and M. had an estate in fee simple, ready &c. —And the other side said the contrary.

Dower. § A woman brought a writ of Dower. *The tenant* said that her husband was never joined to her in lawful matrimony; whereupon a writ was sent to the Bishop returnable at the quinzein of Easter; at which day the Bishop sent word that he was joined to her in lawful matrimony. The tenant was called for and did not come; wherefore the lady recovered her dower without the Petit Cape being awarded.

seisine ne fust.—Et non allocatur. — *Toudeby.* Nous A.D. 1306.
prioms qe la Jure soit examine sur la forme del primer doun.—Et concessum fuit.

§ Nota ken un bref deschete vers Nichol Malmeinz Eschete.
qe mist avant la chartre le Roi qe voleit sauve chescony droit,—*Toudeby.* Nous avoms droit, car celui par qi felonie le Roi avoit leschete si tient de nous mesmes ces tenements par certein services. E pur ceo qe Nichol ne poeit estre partie a ceo trier, si demora la parole ad interloquendum cum Rege &c.

Un Wauter avowa par la reson qe B. tient certeinz tenements de A. par les services &c., des queux &c., le quel A. granta cele rente C. e M., par queu grant &c., a tote lour deus vies, e qe apres lour deces les services remeindreint al avantdit Wauter e a les heirs de sun corps &c., e pur tant &c.—*Toudeby.* Il se fet purchasour e ne dist mie qil fust seisi ; jugement. *Passeley* moustra fet qe testmoigna la seisine, e C. e M. si furent seisiz ; par quei &c.—*Scotre.* Ou le abbe ou nous devoms destreindre. — *Inge.* Labbe nad nul droit, car le droit se vesti par latturnement a C. e M., e ceo luy donne title. — *Toudeby* fust chace outre.— *Toudeby.* Qe C. e M. avoient estat simple, prest &c.— Et alii e contra.

§ Une femme porta sun bref de Dowere. *Le tenant* Dowere.
dist qe sun baroun ne fust unkes acouple a luy en leale matrimoingne, par quei bref fust mande al Evescke &c. returnable a la quinzeine de Pasches, a queu jour leveske manda qil fust acouple a luy en leale matrimoigne. Le tenant fust demaunde e ne vient point ; par quei la dame rescovery sun dowere, sanz agarder le petit cape.

A.D. 1306. Dower. § A woman brought her writ of Dower against one A., who said that the tenements whereof &c., were given to A. and B. and the heirs of B.: and (said he) B. is dead leaving a daughter C. in whose person the fee and the right repose, without whom &c., and we pray aid of her.—*Hedone.* Vouch her; for you ought not to have aid.—*Middiltone.* We can not vouch without her. —*Hedone.* You can, well enough.—HENGHAM. Vouch if you will, for you shall not have aid.

Scire facias. § A Scire facias for an annuity was sued out against a parson of a church, asking if he could say anything why &c. — *Toudeby.* We found our church discharged, and we can not charge it without the Bishop and the patron, and we pray aid of them. — *Herle.* We have been always seised by the hand of Sir John de Godele formerly parson of the same church, your predecessor; and until you yourself withdrew it; wherefore you did not find your church discharged; and consequently you ought not to have aid. Besides, see here a fine which witnesses that the Patron and the Bishop with the assent of the parson granted the said annuity, and we formerly sued out execution against Sir John de Godeley your predecessor, and had execution, by judgment.—*Toudeby.* The execution which you had against our predecessor, seeing that he could not have aid of the patron or the Ordinary, ought not to trouble us or charge our church. Besides, it may be that you have released and quit-claimed to the patron; wherefore we pray aid.—And he had it, by judgment.

Scire facias where the writ abated because the heir of the disseisor was not named. § A man brought an assise of Novel disseisin and recovered; the disseisor died; the plaintiff sued out a Scire facias against the tenant for the time of the disseisor, from the day when the disseisin was found, to know if he could say anything why &c.—*Passeley.* The heir of the disseisor who owed the damages is not named in this writ; judgment.—*Wescote.* The heir has no inheri-

A.D. 1306.

Dowere.

§ Une femme porta sun bref de Dowere vers un A. qe dist qe les tenements dount &c. si furent donez a A. e B. e les heirs B.; B. est mort e ad une fille C. en qi persone le fee e le droit repose, sanz qi &c., e prioms aide de lui.—*Hedone.* Vouchez, car aide ne devez avoir.—*Middiltone.* Nous ne poums sanz lui voucher. —*Hedone.* Si poez assez bien. — HENGHAM. Vouchez si vous volez, car aide naverez mie.

Scire facias.

§ Un scire facias de une Annuelte fust suy vers une persone de une eglise, si il savoit rienz dire pur quei &c. —*Toudeby.* Nous trovames nostre eglise descharge, e ne la poms charger sanz leveske e le Patron; e prioms aide de eux.—*Herle.* Nous seisi touz jors par la main Sire Johan de Godele jadis persone de mesme la eglise, predecessour, e ci la qe vous meymes avez sustret; par quei vous ne trovastes mie vostre eglise descharge, e par consequens vous ne devez eide avoir. Estre ceo, veez icy fin qe testmoigne qe le Patron e le Eveske, par assente de la persone, granterent meyme lannuyte, e nous autrefoiz suymes execucion vers Sire Johan de Godeley vostre predecessour, e avioms execucion par agard.—*Toudeby.* Le execucion qe vous aviez vers nostre predecessour, la ou il ne purra mie aide del Patron ne del ordiner, ne nous deit grever ne nostre eglise charger. Estre ceo, puet estre qe vous avez relesse e quiteclame a Patron; par quei nous prioms aide.—Et habuit par agarde.

Scire facias ou le bref se abati pur ceo qe le heir le disseisor ne fut mie nome.

§ Un homme porta une assise de novele disseisine, e rescovery; le disseisor morust; le pleintif suy une scire facias vers le tenant del tens le disseisor le jour de la disseisine atteint, a saver mou sil savoit rienz dire pur quei &c.—*Passeley.* Le heir le disseisor qe devoit les damages ne[st] pas nome en cestui bref; jugement. — *Wescote.* Le heir nad rienz par descente de

A.D. 1306. tance by descent, ready &c.—BRABAZON. Who owes the damages? (intimating that the heir did); but on the heir's default the tenant of the tenements ought to pay the damages: because he is not named, sue out another writ.

Scire facias.

§ The King sued out a Scire facias against one A. and B. his wife, and against one D. to know if &c., he ought not to present a fit parson to the church of B. whereof the aforesaid A. and B. his wife and D. heretofore granted their right of presentation to the King, in an assise of Darrein presentement, A. and D. did not come.—*Kingesham.* See here F. the wife of D. who is joint feoffee with him of the advowson of the church aforesaid, and she has come before judgment, and she prays to be received &c. —*Warr.* She is not named in the original writ out of which this Scire facias issued; wherefore she ought not to be received.—*Kingesham.* Heretofore the King brought a Quare impedit against D. and F. his wife, supposing a joint estate in their persons; judgment if she ought not to be received.—*Warr.* As before. And what do A. and B. his wife answer?—*Kingesham.* A. makes default; and B. tells you that she has come before judgment given, and she will tell you now how it belongs to her to present.—*Warr.* You shall not get to that, for heretofore in an assise of Darrein presentement you granted the presentation to the king, saving to yourself your right, and thereby you are driven to your writ of right.—*Kingesham.* We only granted to the king the presentation for that turn; wherefore &c.—*Warr.* It is not one and the same to say saving to us our turn and saving to us our right; for by the one you oust yourself from the possession, and by the other you save to yourself the possession; wherefore &c.—HENGHAM. Cause the rolls to be brought so that we may see how the affair went.—Then they found by the record that at the octaves of St. Michael the assise of Darrein presentement was adjudged and was adjourned to the octaves of St. Hilary; and also they found heritage, prest &c.—BRABAZOUN. Qi deit les damages? (quasi diceret le heir); mes par defaute le heir si deit le tenant des tenementz paier les damages; pur ceo qil ne[st] mie nome, suez autre bref. A.D. 1306.

§ Le Roi suy un scire facias vers un A. e B. sa femme e vers un D., a saver mon sil &c. il ne dust presenter covenable persone al eglise de B., e dount les avantdiz A. e B. sa femme e D. graunterent al Roi sun presentement autrefoiz, en une assise de drein present. A. e D. ne viendrent point.—*Kingesham.* Veez icy F. la femme D. qest joynt feffe ovescke luy de lavoeson del eglise avantdite, e est venuz avant jugement &c., e prie de estre receu &c.—*Warr.* Ele nest mie nome en le bref original dunt cest scire facias est issu, par quei ele ne deit estre receu.—*Kingesham.* Autre foiz porta le Roi un quare impedit vers D. e F. sa femme, en supposant joint estat en lour persone; jugement si ele ne deit estre receu.—*Warr.* Ut supra, e quei responent A. e B. sa femme?—*Kinge.* A. fet defaute, e B. vous dist qele est venue avant jugement rendue, e vous dirra coment a lui apent a presenter quant a ore.—*Warr.* A ceo ne avendrez mie, car autrefoiz en lassise de drein present vous grantastes le presentement al Roi, sauve a vous vostre droit, e par tant estes chace a vostre bref de droit.—*Kinge.* Nous ne grantames au Roi fors le presentement a cel foiz; par quei, &c.—*Warr.* Il nest mie tut un a dire sauve a nous nostre turn, e sauve a nous nostre droit; qe par le un vous vous ostez de la possession, e par lautre vous vous savez la possession; par quei, &c.—HENGHAM. Fetes venir les roulles qe nous puissoms vere coment la chose est ale. Puis troverent par record qe a les utaves de Seint Michel lassise de drein present fust agarde, e ajorne as utaves de la Seint Hillari; e auxi troverent en un autre record de

Scire facias.

A.D. 1306. in another record of the same Michaelmus term that the defendants' attorneys granted the presentation to the King.—*Kingesham.* When the assise was adjourned &c., the power of the justices and of the court over this plea remained asleep until Hilary term.—HENGHAM. Because it is thus found, the court adjudges that all the Scire facias be annulled, and the plea &c.

While he was under age.

§ One Geoffrey brought a Dum fuit infra ætatem against one William. — *Toudeby.* The demandant received a messuage &c. in exchange.—*Toudeby.* You are seised, if you have not alienated it.—HENGHAM. You must say that he was seised of the subject of exchange after he was of full age, and agreed &c.—*Toudeby.* After he was of full age he alienated the tenements which he received in exchange, ready &c.—*Hedone.* We were not seised after we attained full age, ready &c. —*Toudeby.* And if you were under age at the time of alienation, you have your recovery, judgment &c.; for it is not right that you should have both —MALORE. Answer if you received certain tenements in exchange, or not.—*Este.* We are pleading to that which they have given us, for they have said that we were of full age and consenting &c., and we say Not so, ready &c.—MALORE. Answer to this statement, that you received certain tenements in exchange.—*Hedone.* We did not receive any tenements in exchange, ready &c. — And the other side said the contrary.

Quare impedit.

§ John del Ospyn brought his Quare impedit against one Robert, who always made default; and when the great distress was returned, by judgment John had a writ to the bishop, and, on his presentation, the ordinary received his clerk; whereupon Robert sued out a writ of Deceit, and by the summoners and by the pledges and the mainpernors examined it was found that Robert was not summoned or attached or distreined according to the meime le terme de Seint Michel qe les attornez le defendant granterent au Roi le presentement.--*Kinge.* Quant lassise fust ajorne &c. si demora le poer des Justices e de la court de ceo plee tut endormy deke a la Seint Hillari.--HENGHAM. Par ceo qe issint est trove, si agarde &c. qe tut le scire facias soit anenti, e le play &c. A.D. 1306.

§ Un Geoffrey porta un Dum fuit infra etatem vers un Willem.--*Toudeby.* Le demandant receust un mies &c. en eschanges. — *Toudeby.* Vous estes seisi si vous nel eiez aliene. — HENGHAM. Il vous covent dire qil fust seisi des eschanges pus qil esteit de plein age, e se agrea &c. — *Toudeby.* Qil aliena pus qil esteit de plein age les tenements qil receust en eschange, prest &c.—*Hedone.* Qe nous ne fumes mie seisi pus nostre plein age, prest &c. — *Toudeby.* E si vous fustes denz age en temps del alienacion, vous avez vostre rescoverir; jugement &c., car il nest mie reson qe vous eez le un e lautre. — MALORRE. Responz si vous resceutes certeinz tenements en eschanges ou noun.—*Este.* Nous pledoms a ceo qil nous ount done, car il ount dist qe nous de plein age en agreant &c., e qe noun, prest &c. —MALORRE. Responez a ceo qe vouz resceutes certeinz tenements en eschange. — *Hedone.* Qe nules tenements ne resceumes en eschanges, prest &c. Et alii e contra.

Dum fuit infra etatem.

§ Johan del Ospyn porta son quare impedit vers un Robert, qe touz jours fist defaute; e quant la grant destresse fust returne, par agard Johan avoit bref al eveske, e a sun presentement le ordiner receust sun clerk; dount Robert suy bref de desceite, e par les somoners e les pleges e les maynpernors examinez fust trove qe Robert ne fust mie somons ne attache ne

Quare impedit.

A.D. 1306. law of the land; wherefore it was adjudged that John del Ospyn should be in the same condition as he was the first day when his original writ was returnable. Then Robert was told to answer to the Quare impedit; and John did not count, but made a declaration how the presentation belonged to him.—*Hedone.* By the judgment given on the writ of Deceit the Quare impedit is terminated, and as it were abated; judgment if to that same writ we ought to answer.—HENGHAM. Plead over.—But the cause was because the six months time was past, and if this writ had been quashed the plaintiff would not have had remedy by a possessory writ.—*Hedone.* Then we grant him the presentation as to the present, saving to us our turn again. And he showed how by reason of the turn the presentation on the next voidance belonged to him, for he had the estate of a parcener in the tenements to which the advowson was appendant.—*Friskeney.* That we do not admit. — HENGHAM. At the next voidance you must come to an agreement.—*Friskeney.* —We pray our damages.—HALES. You shall not have them; for this is like the first day, and he acknowledged that the presentation was yours, without your being in any way delayed.—And he did not have damages.

Dower. § In a writ of Dower,—*Roistone.* We vouch to warranty &c. R. de C. and E. his wife one of the heirs of William de E., and A. de E. and Idonea his wife another of the heirs &c., whose lands by reason of the nonage of the husband are in ward to the king, and E. de F. and G. his wife one of the heirs &c., whose lands are in ward to such an one by reason of the nonage &c., to be summoned &c.

Entry. § One A. brought a writ of Entry against B., saying " into which he has not entry unless by the king to whom " Alexander demised them, who thereof &c. disseised " the said A."—*Lanfar.* Alexander died seised; after whose death Robert entered as son and heir, and enfeoffed one Eustace, who re-enfeoffed Robert and Isabel destreint solom ley de terre; par quei fust agarde qe Johan del Ospyn fust en autiel estat come il fust le primer jour quant sun bref original fust returnable. Dount fust dit a Robert qil respondesit al quare impedit; e Johan ne conta mie, mes fist une demoustraunce coment le presentement a luy apent. — *Hedone.* Par le jugement qe se fet sur le bref de deceyte le Quare impedit est termine, e com se fust abatu, jugement si a meyme ceo bref devoms respondre.— HENGHAM. Dites outre.—Causa autem fuit quia tempus semestre fuit transactum, et si hoc breve fuisset cassatum petens non haberet remedium per breve de possessione. — *Hedone.* Donqes nous luy grantoms le presentement quant a ore, sauve a nous autrefoiz nostre turn; e moustra coment par reson de turn le presentement a luy apent a la prochein voydance, car il aveit estat de parcener des tenements a quei lavoeson fust apendant. — *Friskeney.* Ceo ne grantoms nous mie. — HENGHAM. A la prochein voidance bien vous acoviene. —*Friskeney.* Nous prioms nos damages.—HALES. Vous ne les averez point, qe ceo est auxi com le primer jour; e il vous conust le presentement sanz ceo qe vous seez ren delaie.—Et non habuit dampna. A.D. 1306.

§ A un bref de Dowere,—*Roistone.* Nous vouchoms a garantie &c. R. de C. e E. sa femme un des heirs William de E., e A. de E. e Idoigne sa femme, un altre des heirs &c., qi terres par reson de noun age le baroun sunt en la garde le Roi, e E. de F. e G. sa femme un des heirs &c., qi terres sunt en la garde un tiel &c. par reson del noun age &c., qe serrunt somons &c. Dowere.

§ Un A. porta sun bref dentre vers B., "in quas non "habet ingressum nisi per Regem cui Alexander illa "dimisit qui inde &c. disseisivit prædictum A."—*Lanfare.* Alissandre morust seisi, apres qi mort Robert entra come fiz e heir e enfeffa un Eustace qe refeffa Robert e

N 2

A.D. 1306. his wife in fee-tale, which Robert and Isabel granted the same tenements to W for the term of his life, against whom this writ is brought; and since the degrees are past, judgment of the writ.—*Hampton.* And since you have admitted that B. entered by you, and you by Alexander,[1] and our writ supposes that, judgment if any retaking by you in the mesne time ought to prejudice us, since you are in your first estate.—*Kingesham.* By his entering into warranty he is as it were in the estate which he received by the feoffment by Eustace, and of that estate he pleads, and he says it was by Eustace.—BEREFORD. By your entering into warranty alone you are in your first estate and have affirmed the writ to be good.—And the writ stood.

§ Note that the reversion of the tenements which Sir Ralph de Hengham holds for his life was granted to a stranger by a fine levied.—HENGHAM. I ought not to do any fealty, for the conusor held the same tenements of me by the service of one penny, and he leased to me the same tenements for the term of my life, and thereby the penny is extinguished; wherefore I ought not to do him any fealty.—And this was said on the day when the fine was first levied.

§ Note that the reversion of certain tenements was granted to an infant under age. *Herle* (for the tenant). He is under age and can not bind himself to warranty or acquittance; judgment if we ought to attorn. (And he put forward a deed which witnessed that his feoffor was bound to him in warranty and acquittance.)—*Scotre.* No service has been granted; therefore of the acquittance we have no need to speak.—HENGHAM. If he were to attorn to you, and the chief lord were to distrein him for another service, from whom should he have his acquittance? (intimating that he would not have it from the infant.)—*Herle.* He can not bind himself to warranty, wherefore &c.—*Scotre.* His right to warranty from his feoffor remains to him; wherefore &c. *Herle.* If we

[1] According to the writ (see p. 195) it should be "that you entered by "R.; and R. by Alexander."

Isabele sa femme en fee taille, les queux Robert e Isabele granterent meymes les tenements a W. a terme de sa vie, vers qi cestui bref est porte; e de pus qe les degrez sunt passez, jugement de cestui bref.—*Hamptone.* E de pus qe vous avez conu qe B. entra par vous, e vous par Alexandre, e ceo suppose nostre bref, jugement si nulle repris par vous fet en le meen temps nous deit grever, de pus qe vous estes en vostre primer estat.—*Kingesham.* Par sun entre en la garantie si est il come en lestat qil receust par le feffement Eustace, e de tel estat plede il, e dist qe ceo fust par Eustace.—BERREFORD. Par vostre entre en la garantie soul si estes en vostre primer estat e avez afferme le bref bon. Et stetit breve. A.D. 1306.

§ Nota qe la reversion des tenements qe Sire Rauf de Hengham tient a terme de sa vie fust grante a un estrange par fin leve.—HENGHAM. Jeo ne dey nule fealte faire; car le conissour tient mesme les tenements de moy par les services de un dener, e il me lessa meyme les tenements a terme de ma vie, e par tant le dener esteynt; par quei jeo ne luy dey nule fealte faire. Et hoc dictum fuit die quo finis primo levabat.

§ Nota ke la reversion de certeinz tenements fust grante a un enfant denz age.—*Herle* (pur le tenant). Il est denz age e ne se puet obliger a la garantie ne a la quitance; jugement si nous devoms atturner: e mist avant fet qe testmoigna qe sun feffour luy fust tenu a la garantie e a la quitance.—*Scotre.* Ny ad nul service grante, par quei de la quitance ny avom qe parler.—HENGHAM. Si il se atturnast a vous, e le chef seignor luy destrensit pur autre service, vers qi avereit il la quitance? quasi diceret non versus infantem.—*Herle.* A la garantie ne se puet il obliger, par quei &c.—*Scotre.* Sa garantie luy demoert vers sun feffour, par quei &c.—

A.D. 1306. were to attorn to the infant, and were afterwards impleaded and were to vouch the feoffor, the infant would enter because our voucher would be to his disheritance.

Replegiari. § Note in a Replegiari the defendant said that he did not take the beasts, and he was driven, by judgment, to answer to the detenue.

§ An Assise of Darrein presentement was brought against the Dean of Lincoln, who said that he had nothing in that church except jointly with the chapter who were not named in the writ, and he prayed judgment.—*Willuby.* You are the sole deforceant, ready &c.—*Herle.* That which they call a church is a chapel appendant to the church of Chesterfield which is appendant to our deanery; and we have nothing in the deanery except by the election of the chapter, without whom &c., and we pray aid of the chapter.—*Passeley.* We shall recover damages because you deforce us &c., which is a personal act as far on as in a Quare impedit; wherefore &c.—BEREFORD. And if a Mordancester were brought against the Dean for tenements, and he were to say that he found his church seised and his predecessor before him seised, should he not have aid? (intimating that he should.) So (said he) in this case.—And he had the aid.

Dower where the husband committed felony, and they alleged several felonies. § Sybil who was the wife of John de Trimyng by her attorney demanded against Robert de Harwdoun and Simon son of Gerard the third part of one messuage &c. in Kelestone, as her dower. And Robert and Simon come and say that the aforesaid Sybil can not claim anything by way of dower of the endowment of the said John formerly her husband &c. For they say that the said John was outlawed in the county of Southampton, to-wit on Monday in the feast of the Assumption of the Blessed Mary at Southampton for divers robberies whereof the said John was indicted, and for this they

Herle. Si nous atturnassoms al enfant, e pus fumes enplede e vouchassoms nostre feffour, lenfant entrereit pur ceo qe nostre voucher fust a sa desheritance. A.D. 1306.

§ Nota ken un replegiare le defendant dist qil ne prist rien les avers, e par agarde fust chace a respondre a la detenue. Replegiare.

§ Une Assise de drein present fust porte vers le Deen de Nichol, qe dist qil navoit ren en cele eglise si noun joyne ove le chapitre nent nome en le bref, jugement. — *Willuby.* Vous estes soul deforceour prest &c. — *Herle.* Ceo qil apelent eglise est une chapele apendant al eglise de Cestrefeld qest apendant a nostre Denee; dount nous avoms rien en la Denee si noun par eleccion del Chapitre, sanz qi &c., e prioms aide de chapitre.—*Passeley.* Nous rescoveroms damages pur ceo qe vous nous deforceoms &c. qest une personel fet tant avaunt come en un Quare impedit par quei &c.—Bereford. E si un mortdauncestre fust porte des tenements vers le Deen, e il deit qil trova sa eglise seisi, e sun predecessour avant luy seisi, navereit il mie aide? quasi diceret sic: auxi dist il de ceste parte: par quei habeat auxilium.

§ Sibilla que fuit uxor Johannis de Trimyng per attornatum suum petiit versus Robertum de Harwdoun et Simonem filium Gerardi tertiam partem unius messuagii &c. in Kelestone ut dotem. Et Robertus et Simon veniunt et dicunt quod prædicta Sibilla nichil clamare potest nomine dotis ex dotacione prædicti Johanis quondam viri &c. Dicunt enim quod idem Johanes fuit utlagatus in comitatu Suthamptone, scilicet die Lunæ in festo Assumptionis beatæ Mariæ apud Suthamptone pro diversis roberiis, unde idem Johanes De dote ubi vir fecit feloniam et allegabant felonias.

A.D. 1306. put themselves on the record of the rolls of the said county and of the coroner of the said county. And the said Sybil does the same. So it was commanded to the sheriff and coroner &c. that in full county court they should make record of the said outlawry, and send the record under their seals to the justices here, in the octaves of St. Michael, at the prayer of the demandant.—*Willuby* (in the same plea). Where and for what felony?—*Passeley.* In the county of Southampton. — *Willuby.* Before what justices was the exigent awarded?—BEREFORD. What can he know about it? it was not perhaps at his suit.—*Willuby.* For what felony?—BEREFORD. If he say it was for one felony and it be found that it was not for that felony but for another, still the voucher would be good enough: wherefore let the voucher stand.

Dower. § Robert, son of Richard, and Margery his wife brought their writ of Dower against Robert son of Henry of Wersk. Robert vouched Richard son of Henry de Brokles, and said that Henry, father of Richard, whose heir he is, by fine levied gave and rendered the same tenements to him, and bound himself &c. to warranty. And so &c. — *Herle.* Henry our father held the same tenements by lease from us for term of life, and of that estate deed seised, and we after his death entered, as upon our reversion, and Robert disseised us, so that the estate which he has up to this time is by his disseisin; judgment if we ought to warrant.—*Passeley.* Your father rendered to us and we are in possession; judgment; for their answer goes to avoid the fine.—*Herle.* Although we were to recover by assise, yet you would have your recovery by Scire facias; for if after battle waged you were to enter without a judicial writ, I should recover against you by assise; and still you can have execution out of the first judgment.—BEREFORD. He says that your father rendered to him by fine &c.,

rettatus fuit, et de hoc ponit se super recordo Rotulorum Comitatus prædicti et Coronatoris ejusdem Comitatus. Et prædicta Sibilla similiter. Ideo preceptum est vicecomiti et coronatori &c. quod in pleno comitatu recordari facerent utlagariam prædictam, et recordum mittant Justiciariis hic sub sigillis suis in octavis Sancti Michaelis prece petentis.—*Willuby* (in eodem placito). Ou e pur quele felonie ?—*Passeley.* En le conte de Suthamptone.—*Willuby.* Devant queles justices fust le exigend agarde ?—BEREFORD. Qe puet il saver, ceo ne fust par cas a sa suite.—*Willuby.* Pur quel felonie ?—BEREFORD. Si il deit pur une felonie, e trove fust qe nent pur cele felonie einz pur un autre, uncore le voucher serreit assez bon; par quei estoise le voucher. A.D. 1306.

§ Robert le fiz Richard e Margerie sa femme porterent lour bref de Dowere vers Robert fiz Henri de Wersk. Robert voucha Richard fiz Henri de Brokles, e dist qe Henri pere Richard, qi heir il est, par fin leve luy dona mesme les tenements e lui rendi, e obligha lui &c. a la garantie. Et sic &c.—*Herle.* Henri nostre pere tient meime les tenements de nostre lees a terme de vie, e de tiel estat morust seisi, e nous apres sa mort entrames come en nostre reversion, e Robert nous disseisi, issint qe lestat qil ad hui ceo jour si est par sa disseisine; jugement si nous ne devoms garantir *Passeley.* Vostre pere nous rendi e nous sumes einz; jugement, car lour respons chiet en voydance de la fin.—*Herle.* Tut rescoveryoms nous par assise, uncore avez vostre rescoverer par le scire facias; car si vous entretes apres bataille gage sanz bref de jugement, jeo rescoveray vers vous par assise; e uncore poez aver execucion hors du primer jugement. — BEREFORD. Il dist qe vostre pere luy rendy par fin &c., Dowere.

A.D. 1306. and he is in possession; now to try if he be in possession by judicial writ or not, does not this go to avoid the fine?—*Middeltone.* Although I enter without judicial writ you shall never recover by assise.—*Herle.* Of what use then is a judicial writ? (intimating of none).

Quare vi et armis.

§ Note; in a Quare vi et armis for his corn trampled down and his two harnessed horses, it was said that the plaintiff granted to one Maud 10*l.* of rent, and bound the tenements where the taking was made, in whose hands soever they should be, to distress, and that he as bailiff of Maud distreined for the same rent in arrear &c. —*Hedone.* We will aver that it was with force and arms, as our writ supposes.—BEREFORD. He says that the distress was by virtue of your own deed; what answer you to that?—*Hedone.* Maud enfeoffed us of certain tenements in fee simple, and for security we bound the same tenements to distress by her for 10*l.*, and we granted to her 20*l.* to be paid at a certain day on the same condition; and she executed to us a writing stating that whenever we should enfeoff her of the same tenements for term of life the 10*l.* and the 20*l.* should be extinguished; now we say that this same [defendant] as Maud's executor demanded from us the 20*l.*, and we put forward the writing which we have mentioned annulling the security for the 20*l.*, and at that time he denied the writing; wherefore the writing remained before the Court and it still does.—The writing was found, and the defendant wished again to deny the writing.—*Hedone.* Heretofore as executor you denied this writing, and therefore you were received to do it; but now you are as a stranger; wherefore you can not now be received to deny the writing.—HENGHAM. The writing is denied by him, and before it be tried we can not go on.—And so the case is pending.

Replegiari.

§ Note; in a Replegiari it was said "he is our "vilein and we are seised of him as of &c.; judgment e il est einz; dount a trier sil soit einz par bref de jugement ou noun, ne chiet mie ceo cy en voidance de la fin?—*Middeltone.* Tut entre jeo sanz bref de jugement vous ne rescoverez jammes par assise.—*Herle.* E dount cert bref de jugement donqe? quasi diceret nil. A.D. 1306.

§ Nota en un 'quare vi et armis' de ces blees defolez e de ces deus chivaux armes fust dist qe le pleintif granta a une Maude x. livres de rente, e obligha les tenements ou la prise fust fete a la destresse en qi meinz &c., e il com baillif Maude pur meyme la rente arere destreina &c. — *Hedone.* Nous voloms averer qe a force e as armes, solom ceo qe nostre bref suppose.—BEREFORD. Il dist qe par vertu de vostre fet demeyne si fist il la destresse; quei responez vous a ceo?—*Hedone.* Maude nous enfeffa de certeinz tenements en fee simple, e pur suirte aver si obligames meymes les tenements a sa destresse pur x. livres, e luy grantames xx. livres a paier a certein jour sur meyme la condicion; e ele nous fist un escrist qe a quele houre qe nous luy enfeffassoms de meyme les tenements a terme de vie qe les x. livres e les xx. livres fuissont esteintz; dont nous dioms qe mesme cestui com executour Maude nous demaunda les xx. livres, ou nous meymes avant lescrist dount nous parloms, en anentissant lescrist de xx. livres, e a cel houre il dedit cel lescrist; par quei lescrist demora vers la court e uncore fet. Lescrist fust trove e la partie defendant voleit aver autrefoiz dedit lescrist.—*Hedone.* Autrefoiz come executour dedeites ceste escrist, e pur ceo a ceo fustes receu; mes ore estes com estrange, par quei a dedire lescrist ne poez ore estre receu.—HENGHAM. Lescrist par luy est dedist, e einz ceo qil soit trie nous ne poms avant aler.—Et sic pendet.

Quare vi et armis.

§ Nota ken un Replegiare fust dist il est nostre vilein e nous seisi de luy come de &c., jugement &c.

Replegiare.

A.D. 1306. " &c."—*Passeley.* You can not say that; for heretofore at a certain day &c. you brought a writ of Naif against us, and by so doing you supposed that you were out of possession; and we do not think that you can say that you are seised of us as of your vilein without you show a later title. — BEREFORD. And if while his writ was pending he had found you in your nest, for what purpose should he sue out his writ?—*Passeley.* How seised? *Wescote.* Seised of him and of his father and of his grandfather, by tallaging &c. — BEREFORD. You say that you are seised of him as of your vilein, and were so on the day when your writ was purchased; is not that enough?—*Wescote.* We are seised of him as of our vilein, as by tallaging high &c., and were so on the day of the purchase of the writ, without going higher.—*Friskeney.* You could not have maintained what you first said, because you are a purchaser &c. — *Friskeney.* We are a free man and of free estate, and you are not seised of us as of your &c., ready &c. — And the other side said the contrary.

Quare vi et armis. § A prior brought a writ of Quare vi et armis, for his land dug into.—*Scotre.* We are lord of the manor of B., and we and our ancestors and the feoffors of our ancestors, from time whereof there is no memory, throughout all the lands within the precinct of the same manor have mined at their pleasure by the custom of the country; and so we mined as it was well lawful for us to do.—*Hertepol.* The place where &c. is out of your seignory; wherefore by reason of your seignory you can not claim anything. — *Scotre.* We and our ancestors and their feoffors have been seised &c. from time whereof there is no memory, ready &c.—BEREFORD. Do you claim the right to mine by reason of your seignory or by reason of usage?—*Scotre.* We can not divide one from the other. —*Hertlepol.* See here the charter of their feoffor whereby he gave to us the same tenements where &c. in pure and perpetual alms; and you can not be in a better situation

—*Passeley.* Ceo ne poez dire; qe autrefoiz certein jour &c. portastes bref de Neyfte vers nous, e par tant supposastes qe vous fustes hors de possession; e nententendoms mie qe vous poez dire qe vous estes seisi de nous com de vostre vilein sanz plus tardif title moustrer. —BEREFORD. E si pendant sun bref il vous eust trove en vostre ny, la quei fere suyreit il sun bref?—*Passe.* Coment seisi?—*Wescote.* Seisi de luy e de sun pere e de son ael, com a tailler &c.—BEREFORD. Vous dites qe vous estes seisi de lui com de vostre vilein e fustes le jour de vostre bref purchace: ne est ceo assez?—*Wescote.* Nous seisi de lui come de nostre vilein com a tailler haut &c., e fumes le jour del bref purchace, sanz parler plus haut—*Friskeney.* Vous ne purriez aver meintenu ceo qe vous primes deites, pur ceo qe vous estes purchassour &c.—*Friskeney.* Nous sumes franc homme e de franc estat, e vous nent seisi de nous come de vostre &c., prest &c.—Et alii e contra. A.D. 1306.

Quare vi et armis.

§ Un priour porta un "quare vi et armis" de sa terre fowe.—*Scotre.* Nous sumes seignor del maner de B., e nous e nos auncestres e les feffors nos auncestres du temps dount ny ad memorie par my totes les terres denz la purceynte de meyme le maner ont myne a lour volunte par usage du pays, e issint minames nous com bien nous lust.—*Hertepol.* Le leu ou &c. hors de vostre seignorie, par quei par reson de vostre seignorie ne poez rien clamer.—*Scotre.* Nous e nos auncestres e lour feffours seisi &c. du tenps dount ny ad memorie, prest &c.—BEREFORD. Le quel clamez vous la myne par reson de vostre seignorye ou par reson de usage. —*Scotre.* Nous ne poms mie severer le un del autre. —*Hertlepol.* Veez icy la chartre lour feffour par quei il nous dona meyme les tenements on &c. en pure e perpetuele aumoigne; e vous ne poez estre de meillour

A.D. 1306. than your feoffor; wherefore &c.—*Scotre.* By that charter he did not bar himself of the right to mine.—BEREFORD. When I enfeoff you in pure and perpetual alms what do I reserve to myself? I bar myself from all kinds of services and customs; for while I myself am seised of a manor I can dig and mine at my pleasure; but if I enfeoff you of a parcel of the manor to hold of me by the service of a penny for all services, I can not afterwards dig as before; so it is in this case; your feoffor, as long as he held the manor in demesne, was at liberty to mine; and he then enfeoffed the prior of one parcel in frank almoigne &c., and afterwards enfeoffed you of what remained in his hands: ought you in right of that to mine in their land? (intimating the negative.)—*Scotre.* We and our ancestors and their feoffors have been seised of the right of mining from time whereof there is no memory, ready &c.; judgment.—BRABAZON. There is a mesne continuance of seisin, the origin whereof is tortious, and for which one can not have a writ under the circumstances suitable for discharging oneself; but if the thing perchance come to be pleaded, and he can show how he ought to be discharged the court will then by law discharge him; and therefore I advise that you agree between yourselves &c.

Dower. § In a writ of Dower the heir said that she had eight of his charters, wherefore &c.—*Lanfar.* We have muniments in a box, but we do not know how many, and we pray a day to produce them.—*The heir.* And since she has not them ready, we pray judgment how we ought to depart.—*The woman.* They were never demanded in pais, ready &c.—HENGHAM gave the woman a day to produce the charters.—Quære if she shall have damages.

§ A Cessavit was brought against a vilein for tenements which he had purchased before his lord put his hand &c.; the vilein prayed the View &c. and then said that nothing was in arrear, and did not counterplead the quantity of estat qe vostre feffour; par quei &c.—*Scotre.* Par cele chartre ne se forclost il mie de miner.—BEREFORD. Quant jeo vous feffe en pure e perpetuele almoigne quei me reservè jeo? jeo me forclose de tote manere des services e coustoumes; car tant come jeo suy meymes seisin de un maner jeo puisse fower miner a ma volunte; mes si jeo vous enfeffe de parcel del maner a tenir de moy par les services de un dener pur touz services, jeo ne puisse mie apres fower come avant; auxi est il ceste parte; vostre feffour tant com il fust seisi del maner en demene poeit miner; e pus enfeffa le priour de une parcele en franche almoigne &c., e pus vous enfeffa de ceo qe remist en sa mayn; devez vous par tant miner en lour terre? quasi diceret non.—*Scotre.* Nous e nos auncestres e lour feffours seisi de miner del temps dount ny ad memorie prest &c. jugement.—BRABANZOUN. I luy ad meyn continuance de seisine dount le foundement est torcenouse e dount homme ne puet bref aver en le cas acordant a sey descharger; mes si la chose par cas viegne en plee, e il puisse moustrer coment il deit estre decharge, la court alafoiz de ley luy deschargera; e pur ceo jeo loo qe vous acordez entre vous &c. A.D. 1306.

§ En un [bref de] dowere le heir dist qele avoit viii. de ces chartres, par quei &c.—*Lanfare.* Nous avoms monumenz en une boyste, mes ne savom com bien, e prioms jour de les faire venir.—*Le heir.*[1] E de pus qe ele ne ad mie prist, jugement coment nous devom departir. —*La femme.* Il ne furent unkes demaundez en pays, prest &c.—HENGHAM dona jour ala femme de faire venir les chartres. Queritur si habebit dampna. Dowere.

§ Un Cessavit fust porte vers un vilein des tenementz qil avoit purchace einz ceo qe sun seignour mist la mayn, qe demaunda la Vewe &c., e pus dist rien arere, nent contre pledant la quantite des services; e al pro-

[1] MS. *Lanfare.*

A.D. 1306. the services; and on the next day the vilein made default; the Petit Cape issued &c.; at which day the vilein alleged imprisonment, wherefore &c.; it was found that such was not the case; he had a day to hear his judgment; at which day the vilein tendered eight marks.—*The demandant* said that the arrears amounted to nine marks, and prayed judgment since he (the vilein) had not the arrears ready.—Another person rose up who said that he who was impleaded was the vilein of his lord, and prayed that no pleading which he had made should turn to the prejudice of his lord.—MALORE. You have come very late; but if the tenant have the arrears I advise him to put them forward.—On the morrow the tenant tendered the eight marks, and offered to aver that he did not hold of the demandant by so much service as he had counted.—*The demandant.* When you pleaded that nothing was in arrear you tacitly admitted the services; wherefore &c.—And because he had not all the arrears, and was wanting in a surety, the tenements were lost, by judgment &c.

§ A Quid juris clamat was sued out against an infant under age and against others: and *Hervy* saw that the infant who was to acknowledge what estate he had was under age, and said that he neither could nor ought to, before his age, acknowledge anything or attorn. And this was in the presence of HENGHAM. But as to the others they acknowledged and attorned. And it was asked if the fine might be engrossed as to them and the note be valid as to the infant, since they were named in the writ. —But to this HERVY did not answer. Therefore *quære.*

§ Whereas Thomas de Apiltone held of Adam de Kinge and Lucy his wife certain tenements hy homage, fealty and escuage, to wit by the fourth part of a knight's fee, and by the service of six marks by the year, they granted to John de B. and his heirs the six marks, to be received from the hands of Thomas, except one half-penny chein jour le vilein fyst defaute; le petit cape issit &c; a queu jour le vilein alegga enprisonement, par quei &c.: trove fust qe noun; avoit jour de oier sun jugement, a quel jour le vilein tendi .viii. mars.—*Le demaundant* dist qe les arrerages amonterent a .ix. mars, e pria jugement de pus qil navoit mie les arrerages prist. Survyent un autre qe dist qe celuy qe fust enplede fust le vilein sun seignor, e pria qe nul pleder qil avoit fet ne turnast en prejudice sun seignour.—MALLORE. Vous estes venuz mo tard; mes si le tenant eit les arrerages le met avaunt jeo loo. Lendemain le tenant tendi les .viii. mars, e tendi de averer qil ne tient pas del demaundant par tant de service come il avoit conte.—*Le demaundant.* Quant vous deites rien arere en teissant grantastes les services; par quei &c. E pur ceo qil navoit mie enter les arrerages, e la suirte lui failly, si furent les tenements encoruz par jugement &c. A.D. 1306.

§ Un "quid juris clamat" fust suy vers un enfant denz age e vers altres; e HERVY vist qe lenfant qe deust conustre quel estat il avoit si fust denz age, dist qil ne poeit ne ne devoit avaunt sun age rien conustre ne atturner, et hoc in presentia HENGHAM. Mes en dreit des altres si conustrent il e se atturnerent. E fust demaunde si la fin poet engrosser en droit de eux, e la note valer en droit del enfant, de pus qe ceux furent nomez en un bref. Et ad hoc non respondebat HERVY. Ideo quere.

§ Par la ou Thomas de Apiltone tient de Adam de Kinge e Luce sa femme certeinz tenements par homage fealte e escuage, saver par la quarte partie de un fee de chivaler e par les services de .vi. mars par an, si grantent il a Johan de B. e a ces heirs les .vi. mars, a res-

A.D. 1306. and the homage and the fealty and the knight-service; and Adam and Lucy and the heirs of Adam were to warrant &c.—BEREFORD. What you have granted is not a service but a charge.—BEREFORD. How shall he get what you have granted to him?—And, because of the doubt, Adam and Lucy granted to him the services and the seignory, and the other gave him six marks.

§ A writ was brought against an Abbat, not by his certain name, and he was deposed, and the writ stood: and he afterwards died, and the writ was quashed &c.

§ One John, before the Statute,[1] by fine levied granted and rendered tenements to W., to be holden of him, and gave seisin to him out of Court by virtue of the Statute; who came freshly and did the services to the chief lord, namely the Bishop of Lincoln. The fine not being engrossed John sued out a writ to B. that he might retain his part of the fine.—*B.* If the fine be engrossed it will be according to the form of the note, and that is in opposition to the Statute; wherefore &c. Besides, there is now only one mesne between the king and the tenant of the demesne, namely the Bishop. And if the fine were engrossed there would be two mesnes; wherefore &c. HENGHAM. Since the note always bears record until the fine be engrossed let the fine be engrossed.—And the reason why John sued out a writ was that he might have the seignory.

---

[1] 18 Edw. I. Quia Emptores.

ceivere par la mayn Thomas forpris une maille e le homage e la fealte e les services de chivaler; e Adam e Luce e les heirs Adam garranterent &c.—BEREFORD. Ceo qe vous avez grante nest mie service einz charge.—BEREFORD. Coment avendra il a ceo qe vous luy avez grante? Et propter dubium si granta A. e Luce les services e la seignorye, e lautre luy dona .vi. mars. A.D. 1306.

§ Un bref fust porte vers un Abbe nent par certein noun, e fust depose; et breve stetit: et postea obiit, et breve cassatur &c.

§ Un Johan granta e rendy tenements a W. par fin leve, a tenir de luy avaunt lestatut; e luy livera la seisine hors de Court par vertu del estatut; qe vient frischement, si fist les services al chief seignor, saver al Eveske de Nicol; la fin nent engrosse, Johan suy bref a B. qil reteyne sa parte de la fin.—*B.* si la fin engrosse ceo serra solom la forme de la moite [note ?], ceo est countre lestatut; par quei &c. Estre ceo, il ny ad ore si noun un mien entre le Roi e le tenant del demeine, saver le Eveske. E si la fin fust engrosse iluy avereient deus meens, par quei &c.—HENGHAM. De pus qe la note porte record touz jors ci la qe la fin soit engrosse, soit la fin engrosse. Et fuit causa quare Johan sequeretur breve pur aver la seignourye.

PLEAS IN TRINITY TERM

XXXIV. EDWARD I.

HERE BEGIN THE PLEAS IN TRINITY TERM IN THE XXXIVTH YEAR OF THE REIGN OF KING EDWARD.

A.D. 1306. Note.

§ Note that *Toudeby* advised an attorney who doubted whether it was the deed of his client who was plaintiff, that if it was not the deed of his lord he might be non-suit without danger.

Note, Warwick said that one shall not in one day have judgment on non-suit by the king.

§ A. acknowledged &c. to be the right of C., and for that &c. C. granted and rendered &c. to A. to have &c. for the whole of his life, and that after his death it should remain to B. his wife for the whole of her life, and that after her death the tenements should remain to the right heirs of A.—This fine was not admitted because B. was the wife of A. and was not named in the writ of covenant. And then he would have levied the fine in this form, viz. that after the death of A. the tenements should remain to B. the daughter of J. de S. —HALES. Since the Court has heard that this is the wife of A. and is not named in the writ, we do not admit it.—*Lanfar*. Such a fine has often been received,--HALES. The Court could not have known the facts.

§ John acknowledged &c. to be the right of Richard, and for &c. Richard grants and renders to William and to John and to the heirs of the body of William begotten, and if &c. the &c. to the right heirs of John. And it was not allowed, because William who was party to the writ and to the render was not present by attorney or

INCIPIUNT PLACITA DE TERMINO SANCTE TRINITATIS. ANNO REGNI REGIS EDWARDI XXXIIII^TO.

§ Nota ke *Toudeby* consela un atturne ke mesconusoit si ceo fust le fet sun client ke fust pleintif, quod si non esset factum domini sui posset esse non prosecutus sine periculo. A.D. 1306. Nota.

§ Nota homme navera mie jugement de la noun suite le roi a un jour, par Warrewyke.

§ A. conust &c. estre le droit C. e pur cele &c. E. granta e rendist &c. a A. a aver &c. a tote sa vie, e apres sun deces qil remeint a B. sa femme a tote sa vie, e apres sun deces qe les tenements remeignent a droit heirs A. Non admittitur finis iste, pur ceo qe B. fust femme A. et non nominabatur in brevi de convencione: e puis voleit il aver leve la fin en ceste forme, qe apres la mort A. les tenements remeignent a B. fille J. de S. — *Hales.* De pus qe la Court ad entendue qe ceste est la femme A. e nent nome en le bref non admittemus.—*Lanfare.* Tele fin ad este reseu sovent.—HALES. Ceo fust noun sachant la Court.

§ Johan conust &c. estre le droit Richard, e pur &c. Richard grante e rende a Willem e a Johan e as heirs du corps Willem engendrez, e si &c., qe les &c. a droit heir Johan. Non admittitur, quia Willelmus qui fuit pars brevi et reddicioni non fuit per attornatum

A.D. 1306. in person; but it was said by the Court that John should sue out a judicial writ that William should sue, to wit when &c.

§ John acknowledged &c. to be the right of William, and rendered it to William and Maud his wife and the heirs of William; and for that acknowledgment William granted, for him and his heirs, twenty shillings to John for his life out of the same tenements.—It was not allowed, because Maud was not personally present &c.

Replegiare. § John complained of his horse being taken within the house.—*Robert.* We are lord of the manor of N., in right of our wife, in which there is a leet twice a year, to which every reseant within the manor ought to come on being warned; and because John holds a messuage within the manor and was warned &c. and did not come, therefore he was amerced in 12*d.*, and for that we avow &c.—*John.* Where did you take them?—*Robert.* At the door of the house.—*John.* The high street adjoins the door.—*Robert.* When we took it, two of its feet were within the door, and two were outside: and since he does not hold any other thing of us, judgment if our avowry &c.—*John.* Since it is not lawful for any one to distrein within a house except for the king's debt, judgment; and we pray our damages.—*Hervy.* Will you abide there for judgment?—*John.* If the Court sees that he can distrein inside the house, we will give a sufficient answer.—LAMBERT. Plead over if you will, or the plea will take an issue on the judgment.—And John dared not demur there, and said, Out of his fee, ready &c.—And the other side said the contrary.

Cosinage. § In a writ of Cosinage, *Willuby.* The writ says "Command John son of Walter &c.," supposing that Walter was the father of John, which is false, for one William is.—*Lanfar.* He is known by that name.—*Willuby.* Filio Walteri in Latin supposes that Walter was the nec in propria persona; sed ex parte curie dictum fuit A.D. 1306. qe Johan suissit un bref de jugement quod Willelmus sequeretur, silicet cum &c.

§ Johan conust &c. estre le droit Willem, e ceo lui rendist a Willem e Maude sa femme e as heirs Willem, e pur cele reconisance Willem grante pur luy e ces heirs .xx. soz a Johan a tote sa vie de meyme les tenements. Non admittitur, quia Maude non fuit in propria persona &c.

§ Johan se pleint de sun chival pris denz la meson.— Replegiare. *Robert.* Nous sumes seignor del maner de N. par reson de nostre femme, denz quel iad lete deus foiz par an, a quei chescon reseant denz le maner deive venir par garnissement; e pur ceo qe Johan tient un mies denz le maner, e fust garny &c., e ne vient point, par quei il fust amercie a .xii. deners, e pur ceo avowoms &c. — *Johan.* Ou les pristes vous? -- *Robert.* Al huis del mies. -- *Johan.* Le haute estret passe joignant al huis. — *Robert.* Quant nous le prymes les deus peez furent de denz le huis e les deus de hors; e de pus qil ne tient autre chose de nous, jugement si nostre avowerie &c. — *Johan.* De pus qe ne list a nully a destreindre denz meson si noun pur la dette le roi, jugement, e prioms nos damages.—HERVY. Volez demorer la en jugement? — *Johan.* Si la Court veist qil puisse destreindre en la meson, nous respondroms assez.—LAMBERT. Dites outre si vous volez, ou le play prendra issue sour le jugement.— E *Johan* ne osa pas demorer la, e dist hors de son fee prest &c. Et alii e contra.

§ En un bref de Cosinage, *Willuby.* Le bref voet, Cosinage. Præcipe Johanni filio Walteri, en supposant qe Wauter fust le pere Johan, quod est falsum, einz un Willem.— *Lanfare.* Conu par tel noun. -- *Willuby.* Filio Walteri en Latin suppose Wauter estre sun pere; mes si le

A.D. 1306. father ; but if the writ had said Johan fiz-Wautier in French, the writ would have been good.--*Hedone.* Was William his father, or not ?—*Lanfar* could not deny this, and he prayed leave &c.

§ In a Cui in vitâ, *Passeley.* John, from whom she takes her title, was her husband ; judgment. — *Hedone* He gave them to us seven years before he married us, and we were in peaceable possession for seven years. — *Passeley.* Not seised for seven years, ready &c.—*Lanfar.* Did he give us the tenements or not ?—*Passeley.* I traverse your statement.—And he was not received to do this. — *Passeley.* She had nothing in these tenements except as wife, ready &c.—And the other side said the contrary.

Dower. § *Passeley.* John her husband assigned to her certain tenements in dower, with the assent and will of his uncle Robert; judgment if such a common writ &c.—*Lanfar.* The exception is not full if he do not say that she was seised after the death of her husband and assented thereto. — And HERVY agreed with this. — *Hamptone.* She was seised and she assented after the death of her husband, ready &c.—*Lanfar.* He can not say that we were seised as of dower ; for John Tiltone by fine granted these tenements to our husband and us for the term of our two lives; judgment. — *Passeley.* The two things may stand together ; wherefore &c.—*Lanfar.* Still, he can not say that; for after the death of our husband, John Tiltone granted these tenements to us by fine for the whole of our life; wherefore &c. — HERVY. It may be that the reason for his granting that estate to you was on account of the estate in dower assigned which you had : therefore answer if you were seised after &c. or not. — *Lanfar.* No ; ready &c. —And the other side said the contrary.

bref deit Johanni fiz Wauter en Franceys le bref fust bon. — *Hedone.* Fust Wauter [Willem ?] sun pere ou noun ?—*Lanfar* ne poeit ceo dedire, e pria conge &c. A.D. 1306.

§ En un "cui in vita," *Passeley.* Johan, de qi ele prent sun title, fust sun baroun, jugement. — *Hedone.* Il nous les dona vii. anz[1] avant qil nous esposa, e en pesible seisine fumes nous vii. anz. — *Passeley.* Nent seisi vii. anz, prest &c. — *Lanfare.* Nous dona il les tenements ou noun ?—*Passeley.* Jeo traverse vostre dist. Et ad hoc non admittebatur.—*Passeley.* Ele navoit ren en ces tenements si noun com femme, prest &c. -- Et alii e contra.

§ *Passeley.* Johan sun baroun la assigna certeinz tenements en dowere, del assente e la volunte Robert sun oncle, jugement si tiel comune bref &c.—*Lanfare.* La excepcion ne mie pleine, sil ne die qele fust seisi apres la mort sun baroun e se agrea: et ad hoc concordabat HERVY. — *Hamptone.* Seisi e se agrea apres la mort sun baroun, prest &c. — *Lanfare.* Qe nous fumes seisi come de dowere ne puet il dire, qe Johan Tiltone par fin granta meimes ces tenements a nostre baroun e a nous a terme de nos deus vies, jugement. -- *Passeley.* Il pout ester ensemble, par quei &c. — *Lanfare.* Uncore ne puet il ceo dire, qe apres la mort nostre baroun, Johan Tiltone nous granta meyme ces tenements par fin a tote nostre vie; par quei &c. -- HERVY. Puet estre qe la cause pur quei il vous granta cel estat fust pur lestat de dowere assigne qe vous aviez; e pur ceo responez si vous fustes seisi apres &c. ou noun.—*Lanfare.* Qe noun, prest &c.—Et alii e contra. Dowere.

---

[1] MS. mars.

A.D. 1306.

Quid juris clamat.

§ In a Quid juris clamat, the woman said, We are impleaded, and have entered into warranty, and we will attorn.—And the other side agreed, and the woman attorned.

Entry on disseisin.

§ Entry on disseisin committed on John de S. grandfather of the demandant. — *Justice.* There never was any such person, ready &c. — *Passeley.* Was there one John, as we say? — *Friskeney.* There never was such a grandfather John.—*Passeley.* You ought not to be received to traverse the surname.—And *Friskeney* could not get to the averment, and he said that John his grandfather was never disseised since the limitation, ready &c.—And the other side said the contrary.

Replegiari.

§ Replegiari for a bull.—*Roistone.* The place &c. is of the ancient demesne &c., judgment &c. — HERVY. In a plea of taking of beasts your exception, without saying more, is of no avail; therefore answer over. — *Roistone* avowed, as being in his property doing damage. — *Malmesthorpe.* We are lord of a moiety of the vill of N., by reason of which moiety we and our ancestors and all the tenants of that moiety have had a free bull in the whole of the vill; judgment. — *Roistone.* The place where &c. is out of his fee &c.; judgment if without a specialty &c.; wherefore answer our statement.—*Roistone.* The place &c. is of the ancient demesne &c., and the King gave these tenements to his brother Edmund in tail, and the reversion is in the King; judgment if you can allege any prescription of time which may turn to the King's prejudice. — HERVY. You must grant whether the taking was made in the ancient demesne or not.—*Malmesthorpe* admitted it, and alleged prescription of time, as before.—HERVY to *Roistone.* And since they have admitted that the taking was made in the ancient demesne &c., but plead, for title, &c., you must either admit their seisin in the form &c. and thereupon abide judgment, which course ought not to injure you,

§ En un "quid juris clamat," la femme Nous sumes enplede e entre en la garantie, e nous atturneroms. Et alius concessit, e la femme se atturna. A.D. 1306. Quid juris clamat.

§ Entre sour disseisine fet a un Johan de S. ael le demaundant.—*Justice.* Il ny avoit unkes nul tiel, prest &c. — *Passeley.* Y avoit il un Johan sicom nous dioms? — *Friskeney.* Il navoit onqes tiel ael Johan.— *Passeley.* Vous ne devez estre reseu a traverser le surnoun?—E *Friskeney* ne poeit avenir a laverement e dist qe Johan sun ael ne fust onqes disseisi pus la limitacion, prest &c.—Et alii e contra. Entre sur disseisine.

§ Replegiare de un tor.---*Roistone.* Le leu &c. est des aunciene demene &c. jugement &c. — HERVY. En prise des avers vostre excepcion sanz plus dire de mie chargant; e pur ceo dites outre.—*Roistone* avowa en sun [terre] damage fesant.—*Malm.* Nous sumes seignor de la moite de la ville de N., par resoun de quele moite nous e nos auncestres e touz cele moite tenans ount eu franc tor par tote la ville; jugement. — *Roistone.* Le leu ou &c. hors de sun fee &c.; jugement si sanz especialte &c.; par quei responez a nostre dist.—*Roistone.* Le leu &c. est del aunciene demene &c., e le Roi dona ceux tenements a Edmund sun frere en forme taille, e la reversion al Roi; jugement si nule prescripcion de temps qe puisse turner en desavantage le Roi puissez allegger. — HERVY. Il covyent granter la prise estre fete en launciene demene ou noun.— *Malm.* le conust, e alegga prescripcion de temps ut prius. — HERVY a *Roistone.* E de pus qil ount conu la prise estre fete en les auncienes demenes &c. mes dient pur title &c., il covent qe vous conussez lour seisine en la forme &c. e sur ceo demorerez en jugement, qe ceo ne vous deit grever, ou qe vous dedites le title qil alegent. Replegiare.

A.D. 1306. or deny the title which they allege.—*Roistone*. We aid ourselves by two reasons. One is that the tenements are out of their fee &c. The other is that the tenements are of the ancient demesne, which thing they do not deny, and we pray judgment.—HERVY to *Malmesthorpe*. What estate do you claim in the moiety of the manor?—*Malmesthorpe*. For term of life, and the reversion belongs to one M. — HERVY. Let M. come; the averment goes up higher than your estate.

Right. § Writ of Right for a manor. — *Toudeby*. For one carucate of land within the said manor we vouch one B., and join the mise as to the remainder.—*Herle*. Neither B. nor any of his ancestors was ever seised &c., ready &c.—*Toudeby*. We do not wish to be in Honewardby's case.—And he would have joined &c. the mise. And at last they held to one mise for the whole &c.

Right. § One A. brought a writ of Right against Gilbert de Gaunt, and demanded the manor of Honewardby. And the case was that part of the demesne, which was in the seisin of the ancestor of the demandant, was alienated, to be holden of Gilbert, and so charged with services. Gilbert said that he could not render the entire manor, because such an one holds so much, and such and one so much, to wit certain parcels alienated.—*The demandant*. You hold the manor wholly in demesne as in demesne, in service as in service. — *The tenant*. As before. — And upon this there was an inquest.—And the tenant saw that he had unadvisedly joined the Jury, and he came before the Jury, and disclosed the case, and that he did not hold the entire manor as it was in the seisin of the ancestor of the demandant; and he prayed that the other side might understand that he had put himself upon the jury in that form. — *The demandant*. We are at a certain issue; wherefore you can not replead.—And the Inquest gave verdict against the tenant, whereby the demandant re-

—*Roistone*. Nous nous eidoms par deus resons. La une est de ceo qe les tenements si sunt hors de lour fee &c.: lautre de ceo qe les tenements sunt del aunciene demene, la quele chose il ne dedient point, e demaundoms jugement.—HERVY a *Malm*. Quel estat clamez en la moite del maner?—*Malm*. A terme de vie, e la reversion a un M.—HERVY. Viegne M.; qe laverement se estent plus haut qe vostre estat. A.D. 1306.

§ Bref de droit de un maner.—*Toudeby*. De une carue de terre denz meyme le maner nous vouchoms &c. un B., e joint la mise del remenant.—*Herle*. B. ne nul de ces auncestres ne fust unkes seisi &c., prest &c.—*Toudeby*. Nolimus esse in casu Honewardby; e voleit aver joint &c. la mise: e au drein il se tiendrent a la une mise pur lentier &c. De droit.

§ Un A. porta bref de droit vers Gilbert de Gaunt, e demaunda le maner de Honewardby. Et fuit casus qe partie del demene, qe fust en la seisine le auncestre le demaundant, fust aliene, a tenir de Gilbert, e issint charge en service. Gilbert dist qil ne poeit le maner entier rendre, quia talis tenet tantum et talis tantum secundum particulas alienatas.—*Petens*. Vous tenez le maner enterement en demeine com en demeine, en service com en service.—*Tenens*. Ut prius: et super hoc inquisitio: e le tenant vist qil avoit malement joynt la Jure, e vient avant la Jure e descloa le cas; et sic non tenuit manerium integrum secundum quod fuit in seisina antecessoris petentis, e pria qe lautre entendesit issint qil se avoit mis en cele forme en la Jure.—*Petens*. Nous sumes a certein issue; par quei vous ne poez repleder.—Et inquisitio dixit contra te- De droit.

A.D. 1306. covered. And then Gilbert caused the record and the process to come before the King, to redress the error therein, in that the Court had received that issue by averment of the jurors, whereas the parties were not opposed in the issue; for it might well be that Gilbert de Gaunt held the entire manor in demesne as in demesne, in service as in service, on the day when the writ was purchased, as the demandant said, and yet that of the same manor, according to the state in which it was in the seisin of the ancestor of the demandant, such an one held so much, and such an one so much, on the day when the writ was purchased, those parcels having been alienated, as the tenant says.—And afterwards Gilbert died, the error not being corrected.

§ In a writ of Right for tenements in the vill of N. the tenant joined the mise by means of a deed, and said that the tenements demanded were in B. which was within the vill of N., to make the place agree with the specialty.

Replegiari. § In a Replegiari, *Herle.* One John held of us the tenements where the taking &c. by such a service, in right of our wife; of which services &c. as by the hand of &c., and which John enfeoffed Robert, who complains, according to the form of the Statute;[1] by which feoffment we are seised of the rent by the hand of Robert; and for so much in arrear &c. on Robert as on our very tenant. — *Middeltone.* We do not hold or claim to hold anything of him; judgment.—*Herle.* Did John hold of us or not? — *Middeltone.* To that we have no need to answer; for you have simply avowed on me &c.; and I disclaim &c.—*Herle.* We did not say that you had attorned to us for your fealty; therefore acknowledge if John &c. (as above) and let us abide judgment.—HERVY. It is great folly in such a case to avow on the feoffee before he has fully attorned.—*Herle.* And if I make

[1] 18 Edw. I. Quia Emptores.

nentem, per quod petens recuperavit. E pus Gilbert fist venir le record e le proces devant le roi de redresser le errour qe ly avoit, en ceo qe la court avoit reseu tel issu par averement des jorours, par la ou les parties ne furent mie contraries en le isseu; qil poeint ensemble ester qe Gilbert de Gaunt tient le maner enter en demeyne com en demeyne, en service com en service, le jour del bref purchace, sicom le demaundant dist, e ialemeinz de mesme le maner, solom lestat qil fust en la seisine le auncestre le demaundant, si tient un tiel tant e un tiel tant le jour del bref purchace, quæ perticulariter alienatæ, sicom le tenant dist. Et postea Gilbertus obiit, errore non correcto. A.D. 1306.

§ En un bref de droit en la ville de N., le tenant joynt la mise par my fet, e dist qe les tenements demaundez si furent en B. qe fust denz la ville de N., a fere le leu acordant al especialte.

§ En un Replegiare, *Herle.* Un Johan tint de nous les tenements ou la prise &c. par tel service, come del droit nostre femme, des queux services &c. come par la mayn &c., e le quel Johan enfeffa Robert qe se pleint solom forme de statut;[1] par quel feffement nous sumes seisi de la rente par my la mayn Robert, e pur tant arere &c. sur Robert come sur nostre verrey tenant.—*Middeltone.* Nous tenoms ne ne clamoms rien a tenir de luy; jugement. — *Herle.* Tyent Johan de nous ou noun?—*Middeltone.* A ceo navoms mester a respondre; car vous avez simplement avowe sur moy &c.; e jeo descleim &c. — *Herle.* Nous ne deymes mie qe vous estes atturne a nous de vostre fealte, e pur ceo conusez[2] si Johan, ut supra, e demoroms en jugement.—HERVY. Ceo grant folie en tiel cas de avower sur le feffe avant qil soit pleynement atturne. — *Herle.* E si jeo face Replegiari.

[1] Quia Emptores, 18 Edw. I.

[2] MS. contez.

A.D. 1306. avowry on the feoffor, he will join with the feoffee and will do the services to me, and will always remain mesne; which is against the Statute. — BEREFORD. He says that you never attorned to him and that John was his very tenant, and on that account your disclaimer is not receivable: therefore answer if John held of him or not. -- *Middeltone*. Out of his fee, ready &c.--And the other side said the contrary.

§ In a writ of Trespass the writ was returned in the liberty of Bristol that they did nothing because the plaintiff did not find pledges to them when he had found pledges to the sheriff, the bailiffs returned to the sheriff that they had done nothing; then the sheriff returned that he sent orders to the bailiffs of the liberty &c. who answered as above; wherefore it was adjudged, notwithstanding the liberty &c.

Replegiari. § In a Replegiari brought against three, the Protection was put forward for the principal, and that avowry should not be made: it was not known who was the principal, and consequently two were distreined: on another day the name of the third being known and the Protection, it was adjudged that the plea should remain without day &c.

Replegiari. § In a Replegiari, for Sir John de St. John the plaintiff a Protection was put forward.—HOWARD. Shall he sue out a writ to resummon himself? (intimating that he could not.)—*Toudeby*. Judgment of his non-suit.—HALES showed this to BEREFORD.—BEREFORD. Since the plaintiff has put the protection &c., go, Sir Robert de Mohaut, adieu, without there being a return, and quit of damages.

§ A woman who was received vouched A. and B., one for one moiety, and the other for the other moiety; and she sued out a writ to summon them. On another day the Protection was avowed for A. The woman, understanding by this that the whole was put off, went to her inn; and then was called for, and lost seisin of a moiety on account of the double default which she made.

avowerie sur le feffour, e se joindra al feffe e me fra les services e touz jours demora meen; quod est contra statutum.—BEREFORD. Il dist qe vous nestes mye atturne a luy, e qe Johan fust sun verray tenant, e par tant vostre descleym nent receivable; e pur ceo tient Johan de luy ou noun?—*Middeltone.* Hors de son fee, prest &c. Et alii e contra. A.D. 1306.

§ En un bref de Trespas le bref fut returne en la franchise de Bristul quod nil fecere quia querens non invenit eis plegios, quia invenit plegios vicecomiti: les baillifs turnerent a vicomte quod nihil [1] pus vicomte returna quod mandavit ballivis libertatis &c. qui respondebant ut supra; par quei fust agarde non obstante libertate &c.

§ En un Replegiare porte vers treis, la proteccion fust mis avant pur le principal, et quod non fiebat advocacio; ignorabant quis fuit principalis, et per considerationem duo fuerunt districti: ad alium diem, cognito nomine tertii et proteccione tota loquela remaneat sine die &c. Replegiare.

§ Replegiare; pur sire Johan de Seint Johan pleintif la proteccion fust mis.—HOWARD. Suira il de resomondre luy meime? quasi diceret non potest.—*Toudeby.* Jugement de sa nounsuite.—HALES demostra ceo a BEREFORD.—BEREFORD. De pus qe le pleintif ad mis la proteccion &c., aille Sire Robert de Mohaut a Deu, sanz return aver, e quite de damage. Replegiare.

§ Une femme receu voucha A. e B., un de la moite e lautre del autre moite, e suist bref de les somondre. Ad alium diem la proteccion fust avowe pur A. Mulier intellexit totam loquelam per hoc tardari, e ala a lostel, e pus fust demaunde, e perdi seisine de la moite propter dupplicem defaltam quam fecit.

[1] A blank in the MS.

A.D. 1306.

Formedon in the descender.

§ In a Formedon,—*Friskeney.* The donor died seised, ready, &c.—And he was not received to this.—*Friskeney.* The donor devised the tenements to the ancestor of the demandant in fee simple, and by this testament which witnesses it, and their writ is by virtue of the special law; judgment of the writ.—*Lanfar.* We will aver the form.—And they went to the country.

Quid juris clamat.

§ In a Quid juris clamat, *The woman.* We hold of the heritage of John, who acknowledges it.—Then came one Jordan who said, John entered after the death of his father and enfeoffed us of the entirety, and we assigned dower to our mother, and so the reversion belongs to us; judgment &c.—*The woman.* John assigned dower to us, and we never attorned to Jordan.—*Jordan.* We will aver our statement.—HERVY. You are not a party.—HERVY. If Jordan says truth he can enter safely without there being any recovery for the woman.—And the woman by judgment attorned to the other.

Cui in vita.

§ In a Cui in vitâ where the woman's dower had been alienated by the second husband, she counted that it was her freehold in dower. And she had her delays as in a writ of Entry, and not as in a writ of Dower.

Suit to a mill.

§ The prior of Lancaster against John son of Peter; —to his mill in Lancaster, of all corn baked or brewed in his house in Lancaster, to wit wheat &c. to the twentieth vessel.—*Malmesthorpe.* The Justicies says, such an one and such an one and such an one, and the Pone only says John son of Peter; judgment of the variance. And because it was his own purchase, thereof he had no advantage.—*Malmesthorpe.* He does not say that we hold of him, and you do not show any specialty; judgment.—*Hegham.* Answer to our seisin.—*Lanfar.* You think to recover the suit for ever; and to do this you have not laid your claim through seignory or by specialty; judgment.—HERVY. If you have a spe-

§ En une forme de doun.—*Friskeney.* Le donour morust seisi, prest &c. Et ad hoc non admittebatur. —*Friskeney.* Le donour devisa les tenements al auncestre le demaundant en fee simple, e par ceo testament qe ceo testmoigne, e lour bref est a la ley especiale; jugement del bref. —*Lanfare.* Nous voloms averer la forme. Et sunt ad patriam. A.D. 1306. Forma donationis en le descendere.

§ En un "quid juris clamat,"—*La femme.* Nous tenoms del heritage Johan qe conust.—Un Jordan survyent e dist qe Johan apres la mort sun pere entra e nous enfeffa del entier, e nous assignames dowere a nostre mere, e issint la revercion a nous; jugement &c. —*La femme.* Johan a nous assigna dowere, e a Jordan onqes naturnames.—*Jordan.* Nous voloms averer nostre dist. — HERVY. Vous navez mie partie. — HERVY. Si Jordan dist voire il puet entrer sauvement sanz rescoverir a la femme. Et mulier per considerationem se attornavit alteri. Quid juris clamat.

§ En un "cui in vita" ou le dowere la femme fust aliene par le secunde baroun, e ele conta qe ceo est sun franc-tenement de dowere. Et habuit dilationes sicut in brevi de ingressu et non sicut in brevi de dote. Cui in vita.

§ Le priour de Lancastre vers Johan le fiz Peres:[1]— a sun molyn en Lancastre de tous les blees forniz e bracez en sa meson en Lancastre saver forment &c. a xx. vesseal.—*Malm.* Le justicies voet talem e talem e talem, e le pone ne voet fors Johan le fiz Peres, jugement de la variance: e ceo est pur ceo qe ceo fust son purchaz, dont il navoit nule avantage. — *Malm.* Il ne dist mie qe nous tenoms de luy, e nulle especialte ne moustrez; jugement. —*Hegham.* Responez a nostre seisine.—*Lanfare.* Vous byez a rescoverer la suite pur touz jours; e a ceo fere si navez lye par mye seignurye ne par especialte; jugement.—HERVY. Si De secta ad molendinum.

[1] The first part of the count seems wanting.

A.D. 1306. cialty or anything to aid you, put it forward.—*King.* Edmund earl of Cornwall gave us the mill and the suit, and the king confirmed it, and we are thereby seised, and so was our predecessor, and by this deed.—And the charter said "the mill" only.—*Malm.* The king has a mill in the town, and so also have other persons, to which we are accustomed to go at our pleasure to grind our corn as well as to the prior's mill: and so he is not seised except at our pleasure &c.—And the other side said the contrary.

§ The king brought a Quare impedit against the prior of C., and the prior alleged that he presented four times successively since the presentation by king John on whose presentation &c., and because the Darrein presentement is an answer to the Quare impedit, and to plead in good faith, he showed charters which state that one Alein, earl &c., gave them that advowson, and that king John confirmed it.—*Warr.* Do you hold to the deeds or to the presentation?—And *Toudeby* held to the presentation.—*Warr.* And since the presentation whereof &c. is acknowledged, and kings are under age so that no time can run in respect of a thing annexed to the crown, judgment.—HENGHAM. Did the prior present as he says he did?—*The King's Clerk.* Yes.—HENGHAM adjudged that the prior should have a writ to the bishop.

§ Note. If a common be in three vills, and beasts be taken therein, he may put in his plaint whichever vill he pleases, because the defendant must say Not in such a vill.

§ Debt against several executors was delayed by the Protection of one, notwithstanding that it was said that the plea was concerning the goods of the testator and not the goods of the executors.

Admeasurement.

§ In an Admeasurement, because it was testified that the View had been had of the common but not of the vous eez especialte ou chose qe vous eide, botez le avant.—*King*, Edmound counte de Cornwaille nous dona le molin ove la suite, e le roy ceo confirma, e nous par ceo seisi e nostre predecessour, e par ceo fez. E voleit la chartre molendinum tantum.—*Malm.* Le roi ad un molyn en la ville, e autres autresi, a qi nous solioms aler a nostre volunte pur moudre nostre blee auxi com al molyn le priour: et sic ne seisi si noun a nostre volunte &c. Et alii e contra. A.D. 1306.

§ Le roi porta un "quare impedit" vers le priour de C., e alegga qil presenta quatre foiz successive pus le presentement le roi Johan de qi presentement &c., ceo qe le drein present est respons al "quare impedit" e pur pleder en bone fey mustra[1] chartres qe un Alein conte &c. les dona cele avoweson e le roi Johan le conferma.—*Warr.* Tenez vous al fees ou al presentement?—E *Toudeby* se tint al presentement.—*Warr.* E de pus qe le presentement dount &c. est conu, e les roys sunt denz age issint qe nul tenps purra courer de chose annex a la corone, jugement.—HENGHAM. Presenta le priour sicom il dist?—*Le Clerk le Roi.* Oil. —HENGHAM agarda qe le priour ust bref al evescke.

§ Nota Si une comune soit en treis villes, e avers seient leinz pris, il se purra pleindre en quele ville qil voudra, pur ceo qil covient qe le defendant dye nent en tiele ville.

§ Dette vers plussors executurs fust delaye par la proteccion le un, non obstante qe fust dit quod placitum fuit de bonis testatoris et non de bonis executorum.

§ En amesurement pur ceo ke la vewe fust testmoigne de la comune e nent del franc tenement, pars iterum Amesurement.

[1] MS. mustrez.

A.D. 1306. freehold, the party again had the View, because the writ said that he should have the View of the common and of the land to which &c.

Dower. § Dower, where the woman demanded a moiety according to custom.—*Willuby.* The custom is not such, ready &c.—HERVY. What answer you as to the third part?—*Willuby.* Her husband was never seised in such wise that he could endow her.—HENGHAM. That answer goes to the whole of her demand; therefore render the third part or keep to this answer to the whole.—*Willuby* would not render; and held to this,—Never seised in such wise &c., ready &c.—And the other side said the contrary.

Dower. § Dower.—*Lanfar.* Three charters still are wanting, ready &c.; (and the other side said the contrary:) and, (for excuse for damages,) She did not tender them to us, ready &c. And the other side said the contrary.—HERVY. You shall not by your simple assertion delay her from having seisin of the tenements whereof her husband died seised. And therefore, lady, find us surety, at the peril pertaining thereto.—And she did so.—And HERVY adjudged that she should recover seisin: and as to the damages let the inquest remain. And let the inquest be charged to find if she had previously tendered the charters or not.

§ Two men and their wives brought a writ of Covenant against the bishop of Durham, who granted one moiety to one man and his wife and the heirs of the wife, and the other moiety to the other man and his wife in like manner.

§ A bishop makes return about a distress on a clerk, He is not beneficed; and otherwise did not deny it. So let him return to his original writ.

Præcipe. § A Præcipe was brought against two joint-feoffees, who made default, whereupon the Grand Cape issued, habuit visum, quia breve dixit quod habeat visum de comuna et de terra ad quam &c. A.D. 1306.

§ Dowere, ou ele demaunda la moite soulom usage.—*Willuby*. Consuetudo non est talis, prest &c.—HERVY. Quei responez de la terce partie?—*Willuby*. Sun baroun ne fust unqes seisi issint qe dowere la pout.—HENGHAM. Ceo respons se extende al enter de sa demaunde, e pur ceo rendez la terce partie ou tenez vous a ceo respons pur lenter.—*Willuby* noluit reddere, e ceo tient, onqes seisi issint &c., prest &c.—Et alii e contra. Dowere.

§ Dowere.—*Lanfare*. I luy faillent treis chartres uncore, prest &c.; et alii e contra: e pur escuse de damage, qele ne les nous tendy point, prest &c.; et alii e contra.—HERVY. Des tenements dont sun baroun morust seisi vous ne la targerez mie par vostre simple vente qele navera seisine; e pur ceo, dame, trovez nous suirte a peril qe apent. Et sic fecit. E HERVY agarda qele rescoversit seisine: e pur les damages demore lenqueste, et inquisitio oneretur si ele la tendy avant ore les chartres ou noun. Dowere.

§ Deus hommes e lour femmes porterent bref de Covenant vers le Eveske de Derem, ke granta a une moite al un homme e sa femme e as heirs la femme, et sic de alia medietate alteri homini et mulieri.

§ Episcopus returnavit de distringendo clericum, non est beneficiatus, et aliter vero non dedixit; ideo redeat ad suum originale.

§ Un præcipe fust porte vers deus joynt feffees qe firent defaute, par quei le grant cape issit returnable Præcipe.

A.D. 1306. returnable the &c., at which day they waged their law for non-summons, and at another day they were essoined: and at the next day one of them came not, and the other made his law for the non-summons. *The demandant* prayed seisin of a moiety of the land.—HERVY. It is adjudged that the demandant do take nothing by his writ, but be &c.—And the reason was that the Præcipe was one and the summons was one, and it was defeated in part and consequently as to the whole.

§ A writ of Right was removed out of the court of York into the Bench, the cause being that the tenant asserted that he entered the tenements demanded by judgment of the court of our lord the king &c.—*Roistone*. The original has Margery, and the Recordari has Margaret; judgment of the variance.—*Hedone* (for the plaintiff). It is your own purchase; wherefore &c.—*Roistone* waived that exception gratis, and said, We will plead, if the court will permit it. — HOWARD and STAUNTON. The court has no warrant to entertain this plea, and if we were to do so the whole would be reversible *coram rege:* neither can you return, because you have come here without warrant and process. So, adieu without day, and bring your writ of False judgment against the suitors, if you think it proper.

Note, about a writ for scutage.

§ Note that one shall have a writ to levy scutage if he himself do his service to the king. And this may be found in the Canterbury register: and one writ suffices for all the sisters.

Right.

§ A writ of Right was removed into the Bench by a Recordari; because the tenant made default after default, came C. and showed a fine testifying that the tenant held for life of him, and that the reversion belonged to him, and prayed to be received &c. BEREFORD. The sheriff has himself found that the tenant was not there, but made default, and the sheriff says "I

&c., a quel jour il gagerent lour ley de la noun somons, e al autre jour furent assoignes; e al prochein jour apres le un ne vient point; lautre fist sa ley de la noun somons. *Le demaundant* pria seisine de terre de la moite. — HERVY. Ideo consideratum est quod petens nil capiat per breve suum, sed sit &c. Et fuit causa le præcipe fust un, e la somons fust un, e defet en partie e par consequens en tut. A.D. 1306.

§ Un .bref de droit fust remue hors de la court de Everwyk en Bank; causa quia tenens asserit se intrasse tenementa petentis per judicium curiæ domini regis &c. —*Roistone.* Le original voet Margeria, e le recordare Margereta; jugement de la variance.—*Hedone* (pro petente). Ceo est vostre purchas demeyne; par quei &c.—*Roistone* gratis weyva cele excepcion, e dist, nous pledroms si la court voet suffrir. — HOWARD STANTONE. La court nad mie garant a tenir ceo plee, e si nous le feissoms, tut serreit reversable coram rege; ne retourner ne poez, quia sine warranto et processu estes venuz cienz. Ideo alez a Deu sanz jour, e portez vostre bref de faux jugement versus sectatores si videret expedire.

§ Nota ke nul homme avera bref de lever escuage sil meime fet sun service al roi: et hoc in registro Cantuariensi inveniatur, et unum breve pro omnibus sororibus sufficit. Nota de brevi pro scutagio.

§ Un bref de droit remue en Bank par record; pur ceo qe le tenant fist defaute apres defaute, survyent C. e mostra fin qe le tenant tient a terme de sa vie de luy, e la reversion a luy, e pria de estre receu &c.—BEREFORD. Le viconte ad atteint luy meyme qe la partie tenant ne fust mie, einz fist defaute, e le De droit.

A.D. 1306. "fixed a day for the parties"; but that he could not do except in the presence of the parties. — *Friskeney.* This Recordari says, And let him tell such an one that be there &c.—And he was received, and vouched that tenant.—And it was allowed &c.

Right. § A writ of Right was removed out of the Ancient demesne by Recordari because the tenants asserted that they were tenants of the demandant by the common law of England, and not according to the custom of the manor.

Ael. § A. and B. brought their writ of Ael on the death of W., and made their descent from W. to two sisters as daughters and one heir, and from the two sisters to themselves.—*Toudeby.* We admit the seisin of W., after whose death the tenements descended to W. as son, from W. to Robert as son, and from Robert to us as son; judgment if through the daughters anything can descend &c. while the male blood, which is the more worthy blood, exists, and of which blood we are the issue.—So, by *Friskeney,* the other side was non-suit.

§ Note about B. who avowed on D. son of C. for relief after the death of E. — *Toudeby.* The same tenements were given to us and to E. our husband and to the heirs of our husband, to hold of you who are chief lord (and he put forward one part of a fine testifying it); judgment if, while I live who am very tenant by the fine and without whom E. our husband had nothing in the tenements, you can demand relief.—*Herle.* You have admitted that you have nothing but a freehold, and consequently ought to hold of him in whom the fee reposes; and you have admitted sufficient to enable us to avow for relief; judgment.—*Toudeby.* As before. And you by our hand have received escuage since the death of our husband.—And because the aforesaid [A.] holds the said tenements jointly with the aforesaid E. according to the aforesaid fine, viconte dist "diem prefixi partibus"; car ceo ne puet il fere si noun in presentia partium. *Friskeney.* Ceo record voet "Et dicat prefato tali quod tunc sit ibi &c." —E fust receu e voucha celuy tenant. Et admittitur &c. A.D. 1306.

§ Un bref de droit receu hors del aunciene demene par record quia tenentes se asserunt tenentes petentis per comunem legem Angliæ et non secundum consuetudinem manerii. De droit.

§ A. e B. porterent lour bref dael de la mort W., e firent lour descente de W. a deus soers come a filles e un heir, de deus soers a eux.— *Toudeby.* Nous grauntoms la seisine W., post cujus mortem les tenements descendirent a W. com a fiz, de W. a Robert com a fiz, de Robert a nous come a fiz; jugement si par les filles rien puet descender &c. tant come iluy ad del saunk mal, qe est plus digne del sank, de la quele nous sumes issu.—Ideo par *Friskeney* lautre fust nounsuy. De ael.

§ Nota de B. qi avowa sur D. fiz C. pur relef apres la mort E. — *Toudeby.* Mesme les tenements si furent donez a nous e a E. nostre baroun e as heirs nostre baroun, a tenir de vous qestes chief seignur (et proposuit partem finis hoc testantem); jugement si vivant moy qe suy verrey tenant e par la fin, e sanz qi E.[1] nostre baroun nout rien en les tenements, puissez relef demaunder. — *Herle.* Vous avez conue qe vous navez qe franc tenement, e par consequens devez tenir de celuy en qi le fee repose; a avez grante quant ke a nous apent avower pur relef; jugement. — *Toudeby.* Ut prius; e vous par my nostre mayn avez receu lescuage pus la mort nostre baroun. — Et quia predictus tenet predicta tenementa conjunctim cum predicto E.[2] scilicet secundum finem prædictam, considera-

[1] MS. D.

[2] MS. D. un'.

A.D. 1306. it is adjudged that &c. have his beasts quit and his damages and that B. be in mercy

Debt. § Two executors brought a writ of Debt, and one of them came not, wherefore he was severed. The other counted and demanded the whole debt.—*Roistone.* John your co-executor who is named in the writ is dead; judgment of the writ.—*Hedone.* He is severed; wherefore &c. —HOWARD. He is severed; and he (*Hedone*) ought not to name the executors of him who is dead; and you can not give him any other writ; wherefore, &c.—*Roistone.* If a writ be brought against an abbat, and pending the plea the abbat be deposed and other be created in his place, if the deposed abbat die, the writ will abate; so in the present case.—STAUNTON. Since he is severed his death will not abate the writ; wherefore answer over.—*Roistone.* He has counted that they delivered to us the said silver to be kept for the use of Alice the daughter of B. until she was of full age, and that if she should die under age he should redeliver the said silver to the said executors; and because she died under age &c., by the delivery to us of the silver, the property therein remained in the person of the daughter; wherefore as executor he can not demand it. — HERVY. Answer over. — *Roistone.* She died of full age according to the custom of York, ready &c.—*Hedone.* The custom does not extend to a debt.—*Roistone.* She could alienate; wherefore &c.—*Hedone.* Of full age, ready &c.—And the other side &c.

§ A dean and chapter complained of their beasts being taken within their messuage by Roger de Mortimer.—*Toudeby.* We have a leet within our manor of B., and the dean and chapter have purchased three virgates of land within the precinct of the said leet; and because it was presented at our leet that the dean and chapter had made an encroachment on the king's highway, they were amerced, and for that amercement &c. — *Herle.* You have no kind of seignory or jurisdiction over us, and we tum est quod &c. habeat averia sua quieta et dampna, et B.[1] in misericordia. A.D. 1306.

§ Deux executours porterent bref de dette, e le un ne vient point, par quei il fust severe. *Lautre* conta e demaunda lentier.—*Roistone.* Johan vostre co-executour qe est nome en le bref est mort; jugement del bref. — *Hedone.* Il est severe, par quei &c.—HOWARD. Il est severe, e il ne diet mie nomer les executours celuy qe mort est; e vous ne poez doner luy autre bref; par quei &c.—*Roistone.* Si bref soit porte vers un Abbe, e pendant le play labbe soit depose e autre en sun leu cree, si celui Abbe depose devye, le bref se abatreit; auxi par de cea. — STANTONE. De pus qil est severe sa mort ne abatera mie le bref; par quei respone outre. — *Roistone.* Il ad conte qe eux nous livererent meyme largent a garder al oes Alice la fille B. tant qele fust de plein age, e si ele devyast denz age qil rebaudereint meyme largent a mesmes les executours; e pur ceo qele deviast denz age &c. par la liverie a nous fet del argent si demora meintenant la proprete en la persone la fille; par quei com executour ne puet il demaunder. — HERVY. Responez outre. — *Roystone.* Il morust de plein age solom les usage de Everwyk, prest, &c.—*Hedone.* Usage ne se estent mie a dette.—*Roistone.* Ele poiet aliener; par quei &c.— *Hedone.* De plein age prest &c. Et alii &c. Dette.

§ Le deen e le chapitre se pleindrent de lour avers prises denz lour mies, e par Roger de Mortimer. — *Toudeby.* Nous avoms lete denz nostre maner de B., e le deen e le chapitre ount purchase treis vergeez de terre denz la purceint de mesme la lete; e pur ceo qe presente fust a nostre lete qe le deen e le chapitre aveient fet purpresture sur le real chemyn, si fust il amercie, e pur cele amerciement &c. — *Herle.* Vous navez nulle manere de seignurye ne jurisdiccion sur

[1] MS. A.

A.D. 1306. have a leet within the same manor which was allowed in the Eyre; judgment &c.—*Toudeby.* You can not present your own encroachment.—HERVY. If he have a leet and make an encroachment on the king's highway, that shall be presented in the Eyre.—*Toudeby.* See here the king's charter showing that we have a leet, and the three acres which they have purchased are within the precinct of our leet; judgment.—BEREFORD. He says that he does not hold anything of your fee or of your seignory; and he says that he has a leet and that it was allowed &c. Has he a leet or not?—And at last seeing that he must need answer to this, *Toudeby* said No, ready &c.—*Herle.* He has, ready &c. by the record. — BEREFORD. He was not present when your leet was allowed in the Eyre; therefore let there be a good jury.—In the same plea *Toudeby* avowed, in another place than that in which the taking was made, and would have traversed the place.—And *Herle* and *Willuby* always pleaded to the avowry.—*Toudeby.* They plead to our avowry made in another place than that of which they have counted, thus waiving their count; judgment. — HOWARD. It is for them to agree as to the place; and if you make the avowry upon a false cause, why ought he not to be received to plead to your false cause? specially in this case, for, for such an amercement one may avow in the king's highway: so whether the taking was made within the close or without, that is not a traverse.—And he was ousted by judgment &c.

Darrein presentement.

§ A prior brought a writ of Darrein presentement against John. — *Passeley.* William our predecessor presented the last parson, A. &c., by whose death &c., and before him this same William presented C. de D. who on his presentation &c.—*Toudeby.* John well admits the last presentation by the prior, but that ought not to damage him, for at that time his grandfather was under age. And as to the next previous presentation we tell you that our grandfather, and not your predecessor W., nous, e si avoms nous lete denz meyme le maner, e allowe en Eyre; jugement &c.—*Toudeby.* Vous ne poez mie presenter de vostre purpresture demene.—HERVY Si il eit lete e face purpresture sur le real chemyn, de ceo presentera homme en Eyre.—*Toudeby.* Veez icy la chartre le Roi ke nous avoms lete, e les treis acres de terre kil ount purchace si sunt denz la purceinte de nostre lete; jugement.—BEREFORD. Il dist qil ne tient rien de vostre fee ne de vostre seignurie, e il dist qil ad lete e allowe &c.: ad il lete ou noun?—et de necessitate oportebat ipsum ad hoc respondere.—*Toudeby.* Qe noun, prest &c.—*Herle.* Qe si, prest &c. par record.—BEREFORD. Il ne fust mie quant vostre lete vous fust allowe en Eyre; par quei courge bon pays.—En meisme ceo play,—*Toudeby* avowa en autre leu qe la prise ne fust fete, e voleit aver traverse le luy. Et *Herle* e *Willuby* touz jours plederent al avowerie.—*Toudeby.* Il pledent a nostre avowerie fet en autre leu qe il ne ount conte, e en weyvant lour conte; jugement.—HOWARD. En eux est de acorder a lui; e si vous facez lavowerie sur une faux cause, pur quei ne deit il estre receu de pleder a vostre faux cause? e nomement en ceo cas, car pur tiel amerciement si puet homme avowere en le real chemyn; dount le quel qe la prise se fist de denz le clos ou de hors, ceo nest mie travers. E fust oste par agarde &c. A.D. 1306.

§ Un priour porta un drein present vers Johan.—*Passeley.* Willem nostre predecessour presenta la dreine persone A. &c., par qi mort &c., e devant luy si presenta meyme celuy Willem C. de S.,[1] qi a sun presentement &c.—*Toudeby.* Johan conust bien le drein presentement le priour, mes ceo ne luy deit grever, qe a cel temps sun ael fust denz age. Et quant al presentement devant prochein, nous vous dioms qe nostre ael pre- Drein presentement.

[1] MS. D.

A.D. 1306. presented the said C., and this he did by reason of the manor to which &c., (and he alleged two other previous presentations;) judgment &c.—*Passeley*. We are in a plea of assise, and we will aver that your grandfather was of full age in the time of &c.; and if it be found that he was under age, we will aver that William our predecessor presented C. de S., and that your grandfather did not.—*Toudeby*. You who bring the writ ought not to plead by "if it be found," and particularly in this case; for to inquire if our grandfather was of full age or not does not fall to an assise but to a jury; and to inquire whether your predecessor or our grandfather presented C. de S. the last presentee falls to the assise; judgment if after what you have pleaded on the seisin you can plead to the assise.—BEREFORD. He has acknowledged to you the last presentation, but he says that his grandfather was under age; so to inquire about his age is to inquire about the seisin.—*Passeley*. We hold to that presentation: our predecessor, and not his grandfather, presented C. de S.; and we pray the assise.—So let the assise be taken.

Replegiari. § In a Replegiari, the count named a day later than the date of the writ, and the distreinor did not challenge it, and made avowry against the statute.—The COURT told the plaintiff to change the day, as otherwise they would have no warrant.—And he did so; and afterwards prayed aid, and had it.

Cui in vitâ. § An infant under age was vouched in a Cui in vitâ in the post.—*Mutford*. We pray seisin, according to the statute,[1] which says, "let the purchaser tarry" &c.—*Toudeby*. That is to be understood of the first purchaser, against the heir of the husband, although the statute does not say so expressly: for otherwise the infant would lose his free law when he was resummoned at his

[1] Westm. 2. 13 Edw. I. c. 40.

senta mesme celui C. e nent W. vostre predecessour, A.D. 1306.
e ceo par reson del maner, a quei &c.; e alegga deu autres presentemenz devant; jugement &c. —*Passeley.* Nous sumes en plee de assise, e voloms averer qe vostre ael fust de plein age en temps &c., e si trove soit denz age, nous voloms averer qe Willem nostre predecessour presenta C. de S. e nent vostre ael. — *Toudeby.* Vous qe portez le bref ne devez mie pleder par si trove soit, e nomement en ceo cas; qe denquere si nostre ael fust de plein age ou noun, ceo ne chiet mie en assise einz en une jure; e si vostre predecessour presenta C. de S. le drein presente ou nostre ael, ceo chet al assise; jugement si apres ceo qe vous avez plede de la seisine puissez al assise pleder.—BEREFORD. Il vous ad conu le drein presentement, mes il dist qe sun ael fust denz age, dount denquere de sun age si est de la seisine. — *Passeley.* Nous tenoms a cel presentement, qe nostre predecessour presenta C. de S. e nent sun ael, e prioms lassise.—Ideo capiatur assisa.

§ En un replegiare fust conte de jour pusne de la Replegiare.
date du bref, e le destresse ne chalenga mie e fist lavowerie contra statutum.—LA COURT dist al pleintif qil changast le jour, qe autrement il navoient point de garantie.- Et fecit: postea petiit auxilium, et habuit.

§ La ou un enfant denz age fust vouche en un "cui Cui in vita.
"in vita" en le post.—*Mutteford.* Nous prioms seisine solom statut qe dit "expectet emptor &c." — *Toudeby.* Ceo fet a entendre del primer akatour vers leir le baroun, tut nel dye le statut expressement; car autrement si perdreit lenfant franche ley quant il fust re-

A.D. 1306. full age to warrant without suit of the party demandant, and would give to the value without having his answer to the party demandant or his voucher entered.—And notwithstanding that the demandant showed a roll where previously in the same case the woman recovered, and the purchaser tarried &c., it was adjudged that the whole plea should remain until the age of &c.

Mesne. § In a writ of Mesne,—judgment if aid for the marriage of the king's daughter, which was something like the fifteenth or tenth penny, or other common tallage by common grant collected, ought to fall within the acquittance.—And it was adjudged that it did; because although it was not granted yet it should be levied: for this thing is due and issuing out of the freehold, and the charter which you have admitted contains an acquittance; and if you will, you yourself shall have aid to marry your daughter.

§ In a plea of land, A. the tenant vouched B., who immediately came into court and asked by virtue of what.—And because A. had not his charter ready, he prayed leave in that respect. Because the aforesaid A. departed in contempt of the court, it was adjudged that the demandant should recover his seisin &c.

Waste. § A. brought a writ of Waste against B., who said that on the day when the writ was purchased he was not tenant of the tenements, ready &c., but that L. was. —*Friskeney*. Our father leased the tenements to you for the term of your life, and down to this day you hold them of us in that manner; wherefore although you may have in the mesne time leased the tenements over, our writ against you is good enough.—*Toudeby*. That is so in Dower, where he to whom the lady has leased her estate can not hold of you in dower as the lady held: it is otherwise here where we have a term for life by lease from your father.—But this writ was adjudged somons a sun plein age a garrantie sanz suite de partie A.D. 1306. demaundant, e freit a la value sanz aver sun respons a la partie demaundant ou sun voucher entre.—Et non obstante qe le demaundant moustra roulle ou prius en meime le cas la femme rescovera, et emptor expectavit &c., consideratum fuit quod tota loquela remaneat usque ad ætatem &c.

§ En un bref de meen, jugement si ayde a la fille Meen. le roi, qe fust auxi com quinsin ou dime denier, ou autre comune taillage par comune grant coylle, deive coure en aquitance. Et consideratur quod sic, quia tut ne fust il grante jatardeys il serreit leve; car ceste chose est due e issant de franc tenement, e la chartre qe vous avez conu voet aquitance; e si volez vous meymes aver[ez] aide a vostre fille marier.

§ In placito terræ, A. tenant voucha B., qe meintenant vient en court e demaunda par quei.—Et quia A. non habuit cartam promptam petiit inde licentiam. Quia predictus A. recessit in contemptu curiæ, consideratum est quod petens recuperet inde seisinam suam &c.

§ A. porta bref de waste vers B., qe dist qe le jour Waste. del bref purchase il ne fust mie tenant de tenements, prest &c., einz un L.—*Frisqeney.* Nostre pere vous lessa les tenements a terme de vostre vie, e hui ceo jour le tenez de nous en la manere; par quei tut ussez vous en le meen tenps lesse les tenements outre, e assez est nostre bref vers vous.—*Toudeby.* Un en dower ou celuy a qi la dame lest sun estat ne puet tenir de vous en dowere come la femme tyent; secus est hic, ou nous avoms terme de vie du lees vostre

A.D. 1306. good. — *Toudeby.* No waste has been done since the death of your father, and your writ proves this answer to be good; for the writ says to the disheritance of the aforesaid A.; and disherited he could not be before the right descended to him.—Notwithstanding this he was driven to say, No waste was committed, simply, for the waste which you have assigned was committed in the time of your father before the tenements were leased to us, ready &c.—And the other side said the contrary.

Quare non admisit.

§ Edward Charles brought a Quare non admisit against the bishop of Norwich saying that whereas he in the Bench &c. recovered the presentation against A. by an assise of Darrein presentement, and on that day &c., and he brought a writ &c., that notwithstanding the reclaim of A. the same the parson &c., and together with this, we presented to him one J.; but he would not receive him &c. — *Herle.* After the voidance of the church, on such a day came the said A. and presented to us one Robert his clerk &c. The inquest was taken in due form &c., and it was found that he was the true patron and that the clerk was fitting for the church; wherefore we gave institution, and so the church was full at the time when you brought the king's writ, and presented one &c. before you or anyone else had raised any debate about any one except him. — *Toudeby.* You have admitted that we recovered, and that we presented within the six months, and within the six months time no time can run against the true patron; judgment &c. And the recovery by Edward in the Darrein presentement was such that he brought the writ against the said A., who granted the presentation to him for that turn.

Formedon in the reverter.

§ In a Formedon in the reverter it was said that A. gave to Robert fitz Hurs in frank-marriage with his daughter Matilda. And the "his" was challenged; for the "his" ought to be referred to the last named person, and that was Robert, and consequently he married his pere ; sed hoc consideratum est breve bonum. — *Tou-deby.* Puis la mort vostre pere nul waste fet, e vostre bref prove ceo respons bon ; car le bref voet ad exheredacionem prædicti A. e disioint ne puet il estre einz ceo qe droit luy soit descendue : et hoc non obstante si fust il chace a dire nul waste fet, simplement, qe le waste qe vous avez assigne si fust fet en temps vostre pere avant qe les tenements nous furent lessez, prest &c. Et alii e contra. A.D. 1306.

Quare non admisit.

§ Edward Charles porta le "quare non admisit" versus episcopum Nortfolciensem, e dist qe la ou il in banco &c. rescoverist le presentement vers A. per assisam drein present e cel jour &c. e cely porta bref &c. quod non obstante reclamatione A. idem personam &c., e ovescke un tel J. luy presentames, il resceivre ne le voleit &c.—*Herle.* Pus la voidance del eglise tel jour vient meyme celui A. e nous presenta un Robert sun clerk &c. Lenqueste prise modo debito &c. ; trove fust quil fust verrey patron, le clerk able leglise,[1] par quei nous donames institucion, et sic fu leglise pleyne en temps qe vous aportastes le bref le roi e presentates un &c., e avant qe vous ou nul autre debat y aviez mis forsk ly.—*Toudeby.* Vous avez grante nostre rescoverir e qe nous presentames denz les vi. moys, et infra tempus semestre versus verum patronem non potest aliquod tempus labi, jugement &c. E si fust le rescovre Edward en le drein present tel qil porta le bref vers le dist A., qi luy granta le presentement illa vice.

Forme de doun en le reverti.

§ En une forme de doun en le reverti qe A. dedit Roberto fiz Hurs in liberum maritagium cum Matilda filia sua. E fu le "sua" chalenge, qe le "sua" debet referri ultimo prenominato, e ceo fust le "Roberto," e

[1] The words "neyt litig" follow the word "leglise," but have the marks of deletion.

A.D. 1306. own daughter: so it ought to have said, "with Matilda "daughter of the aforesaid A." Nevertheless the writ was held good, because the "his" ought to be construed in the fittest way by which it could be understood.

Replegiari. § In a Replegiari brought against B. who said, At that time I was bailiff of the abbat of C.; and moreover admitted the taking, for service, — *Friskeney* said, Wage the deliverance. — *Toudeby.* Not so; for they remained impounded for your default, ready &c. — *Friskeney.* Never seised. — *Toudeby.* We cannot be a party to that without the present abbat; for we have admitted the taking in the name of the abbat who is dead, whose estate J. the present [abbat] has, and of whom we pray aid. — And he had it, because he had it not previously.

Quare impedit. § William Touchet brought a Quare impedit against Roger de Nevylle, and counted that Thomas de Luda was seised of the manor of Hoppewelle to which the advowson was appendant, who presented to the same one M., by whose death &c., which Thomas enfeoffed the said W. Tochet of the said manor, to wit &c.; and he says that he afterwards demised the said manor, reserving to himself the said advowson, to J. de Bassingborne and Alice his wife for a term of years; and for that reason it belongs to the said W now to present. — *Toudeby.* It belongs to us to present; for we are seised of the manor of Roddeborne, to which &c.; and we tell you that the said Thomas de Luda at the time when he presented was seised of our manor of Roddeborne for the term of ten years, and before that presentation one Richard Dalazon who had the said manor of Roddeborne in ward, by reason of the non-age of J., presented to the same church as appendant to the said manor of Roddeborne; judgment if the presentation by Thomas, while our manor of Roddeborne to which &c. was in his hands, can give you any title of right. — *Friskeney.* We par consequens il esposereit sa fille demene. Ideo debet dixisse cum Matilda filia predicti A. Tamen consideratum fuit breve bonum quia le "sua" debet sumi aptissimo modo quo potest intelligi. A.D. 1306.

§ En un replegiare porte vers B. qe dist en ceu temps jeo esteye baillif labbe de C. e conussoit outre la prise pur service, — *Friskeney.* Gagez la deliverance.—*Toudeby.* Noun fra qil morerent enparke pur vostre defaute prest &c. — *Friskeney.* Unqes seisi. — *Toudeby.* A ceo ne poms estre partie sanz labbe qe ore est; car nous avoms conu la prise en noun labbe qe mort est, qi estat J. ad qe ore est, e de qi nous prioms ayde. Et habuit quia non prius. Replegiare.

§ Willelmus Touchet porta le 'quare impedit' vers Roger de Nevylle, e conta qe Thomas de Luda fust seisi del maner del Hoppewelle a quei lavoeson apent, qui ad eandem presentavit M., per cujus mortem &c., qui de eodem manerio silicet &c. feoffavit prædictum W. Tochet; et dicit quod ipse post dimisit prædictum manerium, retenta sibi advocatione prædicta, cuidam J. de Basyngborne et Alicie uxori ejus ad terminum annorum; et ea ratione ad prædictum W. pertinet modo presentare. — *Toudeby.* A nous apent a presenter, qe nous sumes seisi del maner de Roddeborne a quei &c., e vous dioms qe mesme celui Thomas de Luda en temps de sun presentement seisi fust de nostre maner de Roddeborne a terme de x. anz, e avant cel presentement un Richard Dalazon qe avoit le dit maner de Roddeborne en garde par le noun age J., qe presenta a mesme cel eglise com apendant a meime le maner de Roddeborne; jugement si le presentement Thomas, tant com nostre maner de Roddeborne a quei &c. fust en sa mayn, vous puisse title de dreit doner. — *Friskeney.* Nous contames lavoeson Quare impedit.

A.D. 1306. counted that the advowson was appendant to our manor of Hoppewelle, and you say that it is appendant to your manor of Roddeborne; we are sufficiently at issue, and we will aver our statement. — *Toudeby.* You shall not get to the country; for we have shown our title of right, to wit the presentation by Dalazon earlier than the presentation which you take for title; wherefore insomuch as that presentation by reason of the manor of Roddeborne is not denied nor annulled, the presentation which Thomas made while he was seised of our manor of Roddeborne for the term of ten years ought rather to be held our presentation than yours. — *Friskeney.* We have no need to answer higher up than the estate of our feoffor; and we will aver it to be appendant to our manor of Hoppewelle, which averment you refuse; judgment. Nor do you show how you are privy to H. J. K. by whose non-age you say that Dalyson presented as guardian of the manor of Roddeborne; judgment. — *Toudeby.* Although we were to say that we were the son of one the sisters you would not be received to deny it, but you must plead on the appendancy; and since we are seised of the manor &c., therefore, unless we came to it by disseisin, that is sufficient.—Afterwards, to ease the court, he said that he was the son of H.—BEREFORD. Roger shows his right to be earlier than you make your title, and insomuch as he says that Thomas your feoffor was seised of the manor of Roddeborne for a term of years when he presented, the law supposes that presentation to be a continuance of Roger's right; wherefore you must show how it was severed from the manor of Roddeborne, or defeat the presentation by Dalazon in the manner stated by him &c. — *Friskeney.* The same person whom he says that Dalazon presented by reason of non-age, our feoffor presented in right of our manor of Hoppewelle, ready &c.—And the other side said the contrary.

estre apendant a nostre maner de Hoppewelle, e vous dites qe ceo est apendant a vostre maner de Roddeborne; assez sumes a travers, e voloms averer nostre dist. — *Toudeby.* Al pays ne avendrez mie; qe nous avoms mustre nostre title de dreit, saver le presentement Dalazon eygne del presentement qe vous pernez pur title; par quei en tant cel presentement par resoun del maner de Roddeborne non dedicta nec adnullata, le presentement qe Thomas out tant com il fust seisi de nostre maner de Roddeborne a terme des anz potius debet teneri nostre presentement qe le vostre. — *Friskeney.* Plus haut qe lestat nostre feffour navom mester respondre; e nous voloms averer lapendance a nostre maner de Hoppewelle, le quel averement vous refussez; jugement; ne vous ne mustrez coment vous seez prive a H. J. K. par qi noun age vous dites qe Dalyson presénta com gardein del maner de Roddeborne; jugement. — *Toudeby.* Me ke nous deissoms qe nous fuissoms fiz la une soere vous ne serriez mie reseu a dedire le, eynz covendreit pleder sur lapendanz; e de pus qe nous sumes seisi del maner &c., par quei mes qe nous fuissoms avenuz par disseisine il suffit.—Pus pur eser la court il dist quil fust fiz H. — BEREFORD. Roger mustre sun droit eigne qe vous fetes vostre title, e par tant com il dist qe Thomas vostre feffour seisi del maner de Roddeborne a terme des anz quant il presenta, ley suppose cel presentement estre continuance del dreit Roger; par quei il vous covent mustrer coment severe del maner de Roddeborne, ou de faire le presentement Dalazone en la manere quil dist &c. — *Friskeney.* Meimes la persone qil dist qe Dalazon presenta par reson del noun age nostre feffour presenta par reson de nostre maner de Hoppewelle prest &c. — Et alii e contra. A.D. 1306.

A.D. 1306. Dower. § In a writ of Dower brought against B., who said, We hold the tenements by the endowment of C. the father of your husband, and so by an older endowment, judgment &c.,—*Friskeney* (for A.). After our husband endowed you after the death of his father &c., he was afterwards seised so that he was able to endow us, ready &c. And because she acknowledged that B. was at some time endowed of the said tenement by an earlier &c., and still was tenant, she was driven to show title how her husband was seised, and she said that it was by render of B.—*Toudeby*. You cannot say that we rendered to him, for in this court he granted by fine the reversion of the same tenement which we hold in dower to one L., on which grant we attorned.—And she wished to vouch this. And because A. could not be party to the fine, she was received to aver that her husband was seised, after he assigned dower to the said B., by the render of the said W.

Dower. § A. brought a writ against B., who said, We hold these tenements for life by a lease from C., and we pray aid of him. —*Malmesthorpe*. You can vouch; wherefore &c.—Notwithstanding this she had the aid by order of the Court.

§ In a distress on a bishop to have a clerk &c., the *Attorney of Bishop* said, He is not beneficed.—And the other side could not deny this.—So let him return to his original writ.

§ A. brought a writ of Trespass against B. according to the statute[1] "why his beasts out of the county &c.;" and B. said, We did nothing against the peace, but with the peace &c. we made such a taking &c. according to the common law, as bailiff of the abbat of W., for services to him due &c.—*Toudeby*. You cannot say that; for that same abbat is also named in this writ, and he heretofore

[1] 52 Hen. III. c. 4.

§ En un bref de dowere porte vers B. qe dist nous tenoms les tenements del dowement C. pere vostre baroun, et sic eygne, jugement &c., — *Friskeney* (pur A.). Pus qe nostre baroun vous oust dowe post mortem patris &c. il fust pus seisi issint qe dowere nous pout prest &c. Et quia cognovit quod B. aliquo tempore fust dowe de mesme ceo tenement de eygne &c., e uncore est tenant, fust chace a moustrer title coment sun baroun fust seisi; e dist qe par rendre in B.—*Toudeby.* Qe nous luy rendimes ne poez dire; qar il granta cienz par fin la reversion de meyme ceo tenement le quel nous tenoms en dowere a un L., par quel grant nous attournames. Et hoc voluit vocare. Et quia A. non potest esse pars fini, ele fust rescu de averer qe sun baroun fust seisi, puis qil assigna dowere a mesme ceste B., par le rendre mesme ceste W. A.D. 1306. Dowere.

§ A. porta bref vers B. qe dist nous tenoms ces tenements a terme de vie del lees C. e prioms aide de luy. —*Malm.* Vous poez vocher, par quei &c.: hoc non obstante habuit auxilium per curiam. Dowere.

§ Distringere episcopum ad habendum clericum.—*Latturne Leveske.* Non est beneficiatus: et alius non potest hoc dedicere: ideo redeat ad suum originale.

A. porta bref vers B. de trespas secundum statutum "quare averia extra comitatum &c," qe dist, Nous ne feymes rien contra pacem, einz ove la pees &c. feymes une tele prise &c. secundum communem legem cum ballif labbe de W. pur services a luy dues &c.—*Toudeby.* Ceo ne poez dire; qe meyme celui abbe est auxi nome en cestui bref, qe autrefoiz ad plede e dist Transgressio.

A.D. 1306. pleaded and said Not guilty; and since he in whose name you have acknowledged the taking has disavowed it, we pray judgment and damages.—*Herle.* You shall not get to that, to wit, to convict us of this trespass against the peace; for if we shall be convicted of that by his disavowal, it must needs be that we should have acknowledged it in his name: but now we wholly denied at first the trespass against the peace, and thereby we were so contrary to your writ that you can plead nothing to what we said over, nor do any other thing except maintain your writ.—HOWARD said the same thing.—*Toudeby.* Whereas you say that at the time of the said taking you were bailiff for the said abbat of the manor of H. which extends as far as the said vill of R., as well in demesne as in service, in the county of Derby, so that the said abbat has tenants in the said vill of R., which is on the confines of the counties of Derby and Leicester, and you say that a certain &c. holds of the aforesaid abbat one messuage in the aforesaid vill of R. by fealty and the service of one penny by the year, and making two attendances in the year to the said manor of H.; and whereof the said abbat was seised &c.; and for that the service of one penny &c. he took the aforesaid beasts as bailiff &c. in the fee of the said abbat in the aforesaid county of Derby, which is a member of the said manor of H., and drove them as far as the said manor, and lawfully impounded them there, as it was well lawful for him to do according to the custom hitherto used by the said abbat and convent and their predecessors, —we tell you that you maliciously and injuriously took the said beasts in the said county of Derby and drove them into the county of Leicester, against the peace and against the statute, ready &c. —And the other side said the contrary.

§ In a writ of account brought against B., who went without day by a Protection and was afterwards reattached, A. counted a new count.—*Friskeney.* Judgment of the variance between the count counted with the de rien coupable; e de pus qe celuy en qi noun vous avez conu la prise lad desavowe, jugement et dampna. —*Herle.* A ceo ne avendrez mie de nous atteyndre de ceo trespas contra pacem, car si nous serroms de ceo atteint par sun desavowement, il covendra qe nous lussoms conu en sun noun; mes ore lavoms dedit tut a deprimes le trespas contra pacem, e par tant fumes si contraries a nostre bref ke vous ne poez rien pleder a ceo qe nous deymes outre, ne altre chose forske meyntenir vostre bref:—idem dicit HOWARD.—*Toudeby.* La ou vous dites qe "tempore capcionis predicti fuisti "ballivus predicti abbatis de manerio de H., quod se "extendit usque ad prædictam villam de R. tam in "dominico quam in servicio in comitatu Derbiensi, ita "quod idem abbas habet tenentes in eadem villa de R. "quæ est in confinio utriusque comitatus Derbiensis et "Leycestrensis, et dicit quod quidam &c. tenet de præ-"dicto abbate unum messuagium in prædicta villa de "R. par fealte e service un dener par an, et faciendo "duos adventus ad prædictum manerium de H. par an. "Et unde idem abbas fuit seisitus &c. Et quia servicia "unius denarii &c. cepit prædicta averia tanquam bal-"livus &c. in feodo ipsius abbatis in prædicto comitatu "Derbiensi quod est membrum prædicti manerii de H., "et ea fugavit usque ad prædictum manerium, et ea "ibidem legaliter inparcavit sicut ei bene licuit se-"cundum consuetudinem per prædictos abbatem et "conventum et prædecessores suos hucusque usitatam," vous dioms qe vous maliciose de injuria sua propria cepisti averia prædicta in prædicto comitatu Derbiensi, et illos fugavistis usque in comitatum Leycestrensem contra pacem et contra statutum, prest &c.—Et alii e contra.

A.D. 1306.

§ A un bref de accounte vers B. qe ala sine die per proteccionem, pus reattache, A. conta nouveau conte. —*Friskeney.* Jugement de la variance entre le counte

A.D. 1306. Protection and this count; for the other count said that we were his bailiff in the 32nd and 33rd years, and this count says in the 31st and 32nd years.—And this being found so, the writ was quashed.—*Toudeby.* If I were to count in accordance with the first count, I should do ill, for then I should charge him for a time after the suing out of the writ.

Resummons. § When ecclesiastical persons would not have the king's Protection, the king ousted them from his protection[1] in cases where they were plaintiffs &c. their went without day: and now they sued out resummons.—*Toudeby.* This resummons ought not to hold good, for the parol demurred without day by discontinuance; for you do not find on the roll any cause of the discontinuance, such as a Protection or the like; and consequently a resummons can not serve him, because all the pleas of persons of Holy Church were in a manner without day, and this by the king's will, and they now have the king's will in place of a resummons.

Entry. § A. against B., "into which he has not entry unless "by C., to whom D. father of the said A. demised it for "a term which has passed."—*Toudeby.* The said D. your father gave us these same tenements, and bound himself and his heirs to warranty by this deed; judgment &c.—*Herle.* This is contrary to our writ, and we will aver that you entered by C. as our writ supposes.—Howard. He pleads higher than to the degrees and better; for if you do not defeat his warranty, he defeats your action.—*Herle* and *King.* He never had anything by gift from our father, nor did he take anything by that charter, ready &c.—Bereford. Then that is not an answer to the warranty; for it is possible that your father made the deed to him while he was in seisin.—*Herle.* Then this deed would be worth nothing; "I have given, granted,

[1] I suppose that this refers to the king's proceedings in 1297.

conte oveske la proteccion e ceo conte ; car lautre conte voleit qe nous esteymes sun baillif anno .xxxii. et .xxxiii., e ceo counte voet anno .xxxi. et anno .xxxii. : et hoc comperto quassatur breve. —*Toudeby.* Et si computassem accordant al primer conte, ergo male, quia tunc onerarem eum de tempore post impetracionem brevis. A.D. 1306.

§ Quant totes les persones ecclesiastice qe ne voleient aver la proteccion le roi, le roi les osta de sa proteccion par la ou il furent pleintif &c., lour . . . .[1] ala sanz jour; ore suient resomons.—*Toudeby.* Ceste resomons ne deit lu tenir, car la parole demorra sine die par discontinuance; car vous ne trovez en roulle nule cause de la discontinuaunce, saver protexion vel hujusmodi ; e par consequens, resomons ne luy poet servir, pur ceo qe touz les pleez des persones de seynte eglise furent en la manere sine die, et hoc per voluntatem regis, et ipsi nunc habent voluntatem regis [quæ] locum teneat resummonitionis. Resomons

§ A. vers B., "in quod non habet ingressum nisi per "C. cui D. pater prædicti A. illud dimisit ad terminum "qui preteriit."—*Toudeby.* Mesme celui D. vostre pere nous dona meymes ces tenements, e obligha luy e ces heirs a la garantie par ceo fet; jugement &c.—*Herle.* Ceo est contrarie a nostre bref e nous voloms averer qe vous entrastes par C. auxi com nostre bref suppose. —Howard. Il plede plus haut qe a les degreez e meuz; car si vous ne defacez sa garantie, il defet vostre accion.—*Herle, King.* Il nout unkes rien del doun nostre pere, ne rien par cele chartre, prest &c.—Bereford. Donqe nest ceo mie respons a la garantie; car possibile est qe vostre pere luy fist le fet en sa seisine.—*Herle.* Donke ne vaudreit ceo fet rien, "dedi concessi et hac Entre.

[1] A blank in the MS.

A.D. 1306. " and by this present charter have confirmed " and all the rest, are as one charter; for if the " dedi " be void then what follows is void.—BEREFORD. You are wrong; but the deed will be good to rebut you if he was seised at the time of the making thereof; wherefore admit the deed or &c.—*King.* We admit it, but he took nothing by that charter, judgment.—HERVY. And because you have admitted this deed which contains a warranty, the court adjudges that you take nothing by your writ &c.

§ A. has complained to us that B. has raised a certain covert to the nuisance &c. And tortiously for this that whereas the said A. has his land adjoining to B.'s land on the north, B. has planted in his soil trees so that by reason of the shade &c. the corn of A. can not ripen.—*Toudeby.* Any one can make a covert except for birds, judgment of the writ.

Dower. § A. brought a writ of Dower against B., and the Cape said Cestretone, and the original writ said Castretone.—HERVY. The tenements are not in the vill named in the original; wherefore sue out a Cape, sicut alias.

§ A. avowed by reason that B. held of him certain tenements by &c., of which services he was seised by the hand of C. father of W., and for so much &c. on the said B. &c.—*D.* B. enfeoffed us to hold of the chief lord &c., and we by that feoffment attorned to you for our fealty; and we tell you that the tenements are not holden by such services as you say, but by the service of one penny, and we tendered it to you &c.; judgment if on any other than on us &c. — *Friskeney.* He says that he does not hold of us by such services. I will aver that we were seised of those services &c.—HERVY. He says that you can not avow on any other than him &c., and you say that you were seised of the services &c. and that you will aver it: he can not aver the reverse unless you make him party to your avowry; wherefore answer if you "presenti carta confirmavi," et totum com chartre; qar si le "dedi" soit voide ergo quanke ensuit.—BEREFORD. Vous dites mal; mes le fet serreit bon de vous reboter sil fust seisi tempore confeccionis: par quei conussez ceo fet ou &c.—*Kyng*. Nous le conussoms, mes il navoit unkes rien par ceste chartre, jugement. —HERVY. E pur ceo qe vous avez conu ceo fet qe voet garrantie, si agarde &c. qe vous ne preignez rien par vostre bref &c. A.D. 1306.

§ Questus est nobis A. quod B. levavit quoddam volatum ad nocumentum &c. E pur ceo atort, qe la ou A. ad sa terre joignant a la terre B. de parte le Northe, B. ad plante en sun soil arbres, issi qe pur lombre &c. le blees A. ne pount en meurer.—*Toudeby*. Nul home puet faire volee fors oysel, jugement del bref. Nussance de volee.

§ A. porta bref de dowere vers B., e le Cape voleit Cestretone e le bref original Castretone.—HERVY. Les tenements ne sunt mie en la ville nome en le original; par quei suez Cape sicut alias. Dowere.

§ A avowa par la reson qe B. tient de luy certeinz tenements par &c., des queux services il fust seisi par la mayn C. pere W., e pur tant &c. sur mesme cestui B. &c.—*D*. B. nous enfeffa a tenir de chief seignur &c., e nous par ceo feffement a vous atturnames de nostre fealte; e vous dioms qe les tenements ne sunt mie tenuz par teux services com vous dites, einz par les services de un dener, e ceo vous tendimes &c., jugement si sur autre qe sur nous &c.—*Friskeney*. Il dist qil ne tient mie de nous par teux services; jeo voille averer qe nous fumes seisi de teux services &c.—HERVY. Il dist qe vous ne poez sur autre qe sur luy avower &c., e vous dites qe vous fustes seisi des services &c., e ceo volez averer: il ne puet mie averer le revers si vous ne lui ussez fet partie a vostre avowerie; par

A.D. 1306. be seised of his fealty or not.—*Friskeney.* Not seised, ready &c.

Replegiare. § A prior avowed on A. for certain services of which he was seised by the hand of B. father of A.—*Hedone.* We hold these tenements in parcenary with D., after the death of C. our great-grandfather, and we pray aid of him.—*Herle.* We have laid our seisin by the hand of your father, wherefore by reason of parcenary higher up you ought not to have aid.—And he was ousted from aid.—*Hedone.* We hold these tenements in chief of the king, by certain services, and the king is to this day seised of our services and of our homage for the same tenements; wherefore, without the king &c.—And he was ousted from that.—*Hedone.* You can not avow upon us; for King Henry the elder gave certain tenements, whereof the place where the taking &c., to C. our great-grandfather by a charter which you will find there on the roll, and afterwards King John confirmed the same gift by this charter; judgment if he can avow upon us &c.— *Kinge.* W. our predecessor gave the tenements where the taking &c. together [with &c.] to C. his great-grandfather, to hold of him &c. by the services aforesaid, and they have continued that estate down to this time, ready &c.; judgment.—*Hedone.* What have you to show that?— BEREFORD. The charter is with you and not with him. — *Hedone.* And since we show the king's charters which witness our statement, and they show nothing but an assertion, we do not think &c.—BEREFORD. Will you abide judgment there?—*Hedone.* C. our great-grandfather never had anything of the gift of W. your predecessor since the gift by King Henry.—BEREFORD. Did his predecessor give or not?—*Hedone.* He did not ever give since &c.—BEREFORD. You shall not have that averment. Did his predecessor give or not? —*Hedone.* The estate which we have at this day we have by gift from King Henry, and not by gift from his predecessor, ready &c. —And the other side said the contrary.

quei responez vous si vous seez seisi de sa fealte ou noun.—*Friskeney.* Qe noun, prest &c. A.D. 1306.

§ Un priour avowa sur A. pur certein services des queux il fust seisi par la mayn B. pere A.—*Hedone.* Nous tenoms ces tenements en parcenerie ove D. apres la mort C. nostre besael, e prioms eide de luy.—*Herle.* Nous avoms lye nostre seisine par la mayn vostre pere, par quei de parcenerie plus haut ne devez aide avoir.—E fust oste del eyde.—*Hedone.* Nous tenoms ces tenements en chief du roi par certein services, e le roi huy ceo jour seisi de nos services e de nostre homage pur meyme les tenements, par quei sanz le roi &c.—E de ceo fust oste.—*Hedone.* Sur nous ne poez avower; qe le Roi Henri le eigne dona certeinz tenements, dunt le leu ou la prise &c., a C. nostre besael par une chartre qe vous troverez la en roulle, e pus le Roi Johan meyme le doun conferma par ceste chartre; jugement si sur nous puet il avower &c.—*Kinge.* W. nostre predecessour dona les tenements ou la prise &c. ensemblement a C. sun besael, a tenir de luy &c. par les services avantdiz, e cel estat ount il continue deke en cea, prest &c.; jugement.—*Hedone.* Quei avez de ceo?—Bereford. La chartre demoert vers vous e noun pas vers luy.—*Hedone.* E de pus qe nous moustroms les chartres le roy qe testmoignent nostre dist, e il ne moustrent forske vente, nentendoms mie &c.—Bereford. Volez demorer par la en jugement?—*Hedone.* Qe C. nostre besael unqes rien navoit del doun W. vostre predecessour pus le doun le Roi Henri.—Bereford. Dona sun predecessour ou noun?—*Hedone.* Il ne dona onqes pus &c.—Bereford. Cel averement naverez mie; dona sun predecessour ou noun?—*Hedone.* Lestat qe nous avoms huy ceo jour nous le avoms del doun le Roy Henri, e noun pas del doun sun predecessour, prest &c.—Et alii e contra. Replegiare.

A.D. 1306.
Taking of beasts.

§ A parson complained that one B. had tortiously taken his beasts. B. acknowledged the taking in the name of the earl of Warren deceased, for the reason that one Richard held three hundred acres of land of the earl by certain services &c., of which &c. he was seised by the hand of W. father of Richard, and for &c. he avows on Richard since the earl is dead, judgment of the writ.—HENGHAM. Before you go you shall excuse the tort which he lays upon you.—*Hedone.* We can not plead in the name of him who is dead.—HENGHAM. Answer over. — *Hedone* acknowledged the taking, as before.—*Kinge.* We recovered the same tenements against W the father of Richard, as frank-almoign of our church, where it is not lawful for any one to distrein; judgment.—*Hedone.* We avow upon Richard, and you say that you answer against William: what is that to us?—HENGHAM. Did he recover these tenements as his frank-almoign or not?—*Hedone.* The tenements which he recovered are not the tenements where the taking was made.—*Kingesham.* Is it the frank-almoign of our church or not? — HENGHAM. Is it the tenement which you recovered or not?—*Hegham.* Yes, ready &c.—And the other side said the contrary.—*Hegham.* Wage the deliverance. —*Hedone.* We are not seised of the beasts; for when we took them we put them into the park of the earl who is dead; wherefore &c.—HENGHAM. You alone took the beasts, and against you alone is the writ brought; and if the bailiff were here in court he should not depart before he had waged the deliverance; therefore take care of the attorney until he has waged the deliverance. — And this was done. — Afterwards *Hedone* (for the attorney) said, He himself is seised of these beasts, ready &c.—And the other side said the contrary.

§ A Cessavit was brought against R. and the writ said, "B. who was the great-grandfather of the said A. "gave to D. prior of the preaching friars of L. to cele- "brate divine &c., and which to the said A. ought to re- "vert &c."—*Toudeby.* The writ says Command R. prior

§ Une persone se pleint qe un B. atort prist ces avers. B. conussoit la prise en noun le counte de Gar. qe mort est, par la reson qe un Richard tient .ccc. acres de terre del counte par certeine services &c., des queux &c. il fust seisi par la mayn W pere Richard, e pur &c. si avowe sur Richard de pus qe le counte est mort, jugement del bref. — HENGHAM. Vous escusserez vostre tort qil vous surmet einz ceo qe vous alez. —*Hedone*. Nous ne poms mie pleder en le noun celuy qe mort est.—HENGHAM. Responez outre.—*Hedone* conussoit la prise ut prius. — *King*. Nous rescoverames mesme les tenements come la franche almoigne de nostre eglise vers W pere Richard, ou ne list a nul homme a destreindre; jugement.—*Hedone*. Nous avowoms sur Richard, e vous dites qe vous responez vers Willem: quei est ceo a nous?—HENGHAM. Rescovera il ceo tenements come sa franche almoingne ou noun? —*Hedone*. Les tenements qil rescovera ne sunt mie les tenements ou la prise fust fete.—*Kingesham*. Est ceo la franche almoigne de nostre eglise ou noun?—HENGHAM. Est ceo le tenement qe vous rescoverastes ou noun? — *Hegham*. Oil, prest &c. — Et alii e contra. — *Hegham*. Gagez la deliverance.—*Hedone*. Nous ne sumes mie seisi des avers; qar quant nous le prymes nous les meymes en le parke le conte qe mort est; par quei &c.—HENGHAM. Vous soul preistes les avers, e vers vous soul le bref porte; e si le baillif fust ore cienz il ne departireit mie einz ceo qui ust gage la deliverance; e pur ceo pernez garde del atturne ci la qil eit gage la deliverance.—Et sic factum fuit. Postea *Hedone* (pur latturne). Il est meymes seisi de ces avers, prest &c. Et alii e contra.

A.D. 1306. Pris des avers.

§ A un cessavit vers [R. ou le bref dist] B. qui est proavus prædicti A. contulit D. priori fratrum Prædicatorum de L. celebrandi divina &c. et ad prædictum A. reverti debet &c.—*Toudeby*. Le bref voet "præcipe R. priori

A.D. 1360. of the Friars &c., and does not say "brother R.;" judgment. — And he was ousted from that.—*Toudeby.* The writ says "into which the said &c. has not entry" supposing thereby that he had entry into these tenements as one of the people; whereas his entry was by election, and therefore the writ ought to have said "into which &c. "the said prior &c.;" judgment.—*Scotre.* The writ says "Command Richard the prior," and afterwards the writ says "into which the said &c.;" wherefore that is sufficiently certain.—And the writ was adjudged good.—And the tenant wished to find surety to offer the arrears; and the demandant made his demand for the cesser for four years of a yearly chaplain.—Afterwards they came to terms.

Dower.

§ Cecily who was the wife of Richard de Mohaut demands against Peter, parson of the church of Brokynholme, the third part of twelve acres &c. as her dower &c. And Peter by his attorney comes, and as to three roods of the aforesaid tenements whereof &c., he says she ought not to have dower thereof, because he says that the aforesaid &c. formerly her husband never was seised of the said tenements &c. in such wise that he could endow her thereof. And as to that he puts himself upon the country.—And Cecily does the same.—So &c.—And as to the residue of the said tenements whereof she demands dower, he says that the aforesaid Richard granted delivered and to farm let them to the said Peter, to hold to him and his heirs for the term of twenty years, whereof ten have passed, and bound himself and his heirs to warranty; and in the form aforesaid he vouches to warranty James son and heir of the said Richard, who is present and asks by virtue of what he is bound to warrant. And the said Peter says that the said Richard did grant the said tenements in the form aforesaid, and he puts forward one part of an indenture under the name of the said Richard which witnesses the lease and warranty aforesaid. And James

" fratrum" &c. e ne dist mie fratri R. jugement. E de ceo fust oste.—*Toudeby.* Le bref voet " in quas idem &c. " non habet ingressum " en supposant luy aver lentre en ces tenements com home del poeple, la ou sun entre est par eleccion; e pur ceo le bref dust dire " in quas &c. " idem prior &c." jugement.—*Scotre.* Le bref dist primes " præcipe Ricardo priori," e pus le bref dist "in quas " idem &c.;" par quei ceo est assez certein. E fust le bref agarde bon.—Pus le tenant voleit trover suirte a [1] tendre les arrerages, e le demaundant demaunde pur le cesser par quatre anz de un chapelein par an. Postea concordati fuerunt. A.D. 1306.

§ Cecilia quæ uit uxor Ricardi de Mohaut petit versus Petrum personam ecclesiæ de Brokynholme tertiam partem xii. acrarum &c. ut dotem &c. Et Petrus per attornatum suum venit et quoad tres rodas terræ de prædictis tenementis unde &c. dicit quod non debet inde dotem habere, quia dicit quod prædictus &c., quondam vir suus, nunquam fuit seisitus de prædictis tenementis &c. ita quod ipsam inde dotare potuit. Et de hoc ponit se super patriam, et Cecilia similiter. Ideo &c. Et quoad residuum prædictorum tenementorum unde petit dotem, dicit quod prædictus Ricardus concessit tradidit et ad firmam dimisit eidem Petro, tenendum sibi et heredibus suis ad terminum xx. annorum, unde x. sunt elapsi, et obligavit se et heredes suos ad warrantiam; et in forma prædicta vocat inde ad warrantiam Jacobum filium et heredem prædicti Ricardi, qui presens est et petit per quod ei warrantizare debeat. Et prædictus Petrus dicit quod prædictus Ricardus concessit [2] prædicta tenementa in forma prædicta, et profert partem scripti indentati sub nomine prædicti Ricardi, qui dimissionem et warrantiam prædictas tes- De dote.

[1] MS. e.

[2] MS. non concessit.

A.D. 1306. well admits the said writing to be the deed of the said Richard &c., and that he is the heir in blood of the said Richard, and he warrants to him and renders to the said Cecily her said dower &c.; but he says that he has nothing by descent from the said Richard his father &c., whereby he can make recompense in value to the said Peter &c. And he says that he purchased the said tenements whereof &c. from the said Richard his father after the said demise for the term &c., on which the said Peter attorned to the said James in respect of his term. And because the said James well admits the said demise for the term &c.; and the said Richard bound himself and his heirs to warranty; and the said Richard could not alienate the said tenements except saving to the said Peter his farmer &c. his said term, it is adjudged that the said Cecily do recover her seisin against the said Peter of the third part of the said tenements &c.: and that the said Peter do hold the said two parts of the said tenements until the end of the term aforesaid, and afterwards until he shall have received to the value of the third part lost.

Dower. § Robert the son of Richard de Radeclif and Margaret his wife by their attorney demand against Robert son of Henry de Werake the third part of one hundred acres of land, of twenty acres of meadow, of two hundred acres of wood, of two hundred and nine acres of pasture, with the appurtenances in W.; and against Jordan de W. the third part of six messuages, of a hundred acres of land, of eighteen acres of meadow, of two hundred acres of wood, and of a hundred acres of pasture with the appurtenances in the said vill, as the dower of the said Margaret, by the gift of Henry de W. her first husband &c. And Robert the son of Henry and Jordan come by attorney, and Jordan vouches to warranty Richard son of Henry de W., who comes by his attorney tatur. Et Jacobus bene cognoscit prædictum scriptum esse factum prædicti Ricardi &c., et quod ipse est heres prædicti Ricardi de sanguine, et ei warrantizat et reddit prædictæ Ceciliæ prædictam dotem suam &c., sed dicit quod ipse non habet aliquid per descensum de prædicto Ricardo patre &c. unde facere potest præfate Ceceliæ [Petro ?] ad valentiam &c. Dicit etiam quod ipse perquisivit prædicta tenementa unde &c. de prædicto Ricardo patre suo post prædictam dimissionem ad terminum &c., per quod prædictus Petrus se attornavit prædicto Jacobo de termino suo. Et quia idem Jacobus bene cognoscit prædictam dimissionem ad terminum &c., Et quia[1] prædictus Ricardus obligavit se et heredes suos ad warrantiam, Et quia[1] prædictus Ricardus tenementa prædicta alienare non potuit nisi salvo prædicto Petro firmario &c. termino suo prædicto, Consideratum est quod prædicta Cecilia recuperet seisinam suam versus prædictum Petrum de tertia parte prædictorum tenementorum &c.; et idem Petrus teneat prædictas duas partes eorumdem tenementorum usque ad finem termini prædicti et ulterius usque ad valentiam tertiæ partis amissæ. A.D. 1306.

§ Robertus filius Ricardi de Radeclif et Margareta uxor ejus per attornatum suum petunt versus Robertum filium Henrici de Werake tertiam partem .c. acrarum terræ .xx. acrarum prati, .cc. acrarum bosci, .ccix. acrarum pasturæ, cum pertinentiis in W., et versus Jordanum de W. tertiam partem .vi. messuagiorum .c. acrarum terræ, decem et octo acrarum prati, .cc. acrarum bosci, et .c. acrarum pasturæ, cum pertinentiis in eadem villa, ut dotem ipsius Margaretæ, ex donacione Henrici de W primi viri &c. Et Robertus filius Henrici et Jordanus veniunt per attornatum, et Jordanus[2] vocat inde ad warrantiam Ricardum filium Henrici de W. Dowere.

[1] MS. quod.

[2] MS. Abbas.

A.D. 1306. and asks that it may be shown to him by virtue of what he ought to warrant. And the said Jordan, as to the third part demanded against him, says that the said Richard son of Henry, whom he vouches to warranty, the said tenements whereof dower &c. being in his seisin, by his writing granted released and quit-claimed to the said Jordan and his heirs all the right and claim which he had in the said tenements, and bound himself and his heirs to warranty &c.; and he puts forward the writing of the said Richard son of Henry witnessing this &c.; and asks that he may warrant to him &c. And the said Richard acknowledges that the said writing is his deed, and he warrants to him &c. And the said Robert son of Henry as to a hundred acres of land, twenty acres of meadow, a hundred acres of wood, and twenty acres of pasture of the aforesaid tenements in the said vill whereof she demands dower against him, says that heretofore before J. de Metingham and his companions, justices at York, in the morrow of St. John the Baptist in the 27th year of the reign of the present king, a certain fine was levied between a certain Richard son of Henry de W. the younger, brother of the said Robert son of Henry, whose heir he is, plaintiff, and the said Henry de W., father of the said Richard whom the said Richard vouches &c., deforciant &c., of the said tenements with the appurtenances, by which fine the said Henry acknowledged the said tenements to be the right of the said Richard the younger, son of the said Henry, and rendered them in the said court, to have and to hold to the said Richard the younger and his heirs for ever, and bound himself and his heirs to warranty; and he puts forward one part of the said fine which witnesses this; and for the same reason he says that the said Richard and the heirs of the said Henry are bound to the said Robert son of Henry, brother and heir of the said Richard son of Henry the younger, to warrant the third part of the said tenements &c. And as to one hundred qui venit per attornatum suum et petit sibi ostendi per quod warrantizare debeat. Et prædictus Jordanus quoad tertiam partem versus eum[1] petitam, dicit quod iste idem Ricardus filius Henrici quem vocat ad warrantiam, prædictis tenementis unde dos &c. in seisina sua existentibus, per scriptum suum concessit remisit et quieteclamavit eidem Jordano et heredibus suis totum jus et clameum quod habuit in prædictis tenementis, et obligavit se et heredes suos ad warrantiam &c. Et profert scriptum ipsius Ricardi filii Henrici quod hoc testatur &c. Et petit quod ei warrantizare &c. Et idem Ricardus cognoscit prædictum scriptum esse factum suum et ei warrantizat &c. Et prædictus Robertus filius Henrici quoad .c. acras terræ, .xx. acras prati, .c. acras bosci, et .xx. acras pasturæ de prædictis tenementis in prædicta villa unde petit dotem versus eum, dicit quod alias, coram J. de Methingham et sociis suis justiciariis apud Eboracum in crastino Sancti Johannis Baptiste anno regni regis nunc .xxvii., levavit quedam finis inter quemdam Ricardum filium Henrici de W. juniorem fratrem ipsius Roberti filii Henrici, cujus heres ipse est, querentem, et prædictum Henricum de W. patrem ipsius Ricardi quem idem Ricardus vocat &c., deforceantem &c., de eisdem tenementis cum pertinentiis, per quem finem idem Henricus recognovit eadem tenementa cum pertinentiis esse jus ipsius Ricardi filii Henrici junioris, et illa reddidit in eadem curia, habenda et tenenda eidem Ricardo juniori et heredibus suis imperpetuum, et obligavit se et heredes suos ad warrantiam; et profert partem prædictæ finis que hoc testatur; et ea ratione dixit quod prædictus Ricardus et heres ipsius Henrici tenetur eidem Roberto filio Henrici fratre et heredi prædicti Ricardi filii Henrici junioris tertiam partem eorumdem tenementorum warrantizare &c. Et quoad .c. acras bosci, .cc. A.D. 1306.

[1] MS. eam.

A.D. 1306. acres of wood and two hundred acres of pasture of the said tenements in the said vill, whereof dower &c., he says that a certain other fine heretofore before the said J. de Metingham and his companions &c. there at York was levied in the morrow of St. John the Baptist in the 29th year of the said present king, between the said Robert son of Henry, plaintiff, and the said Henry father of the said Richard son of Henry, whose heir he is, deforciant, of the said woods and meadows &c., whereof a plea of covenant &c., by which fine the said Henry acknowledged the said tenements with the appurtenances to be the right of the said Robert, and rendered them to him &c., to have and to hold to the said Robert and his heirs &c. for ever: and he bound himself and his heirs to warranty &c. And he puts forward one part of a certain other fine which witnesses this &c.: and for that reason he says that the said Richard son and heir of the said Henry is bound to warrant to him the said third part of the wood and pasture &c. And Richard son of Henry says that in this matter &c. he ought not to be compelled to warrant to the said Robert; because he says that the said Henry the father &c. had nothing else in the aforesaid tenements than a term for his life by grant from the said Richard son of Henry, to whom after his death the reversion belonged &c. And he says that he, after the death of the said Henry, entered into the said tenements and was in seisin thereof as his right until the said Robert son of Henry, ejecting thence the said Richard who was so seised, intruded himself on the aforesaid tenements whereof he now asks warranty; and this he is ready to aver &c. Whence he says that an action accrues to him in respect of the injuries and intrusion &c. to dereign the said tenements and the seisin of the said Robert. And he prays judgment if the aforesaid tenements into which the said Robert by intrusion and not by render entered, as he is ready to aver, he to the said Robert acras pasture, de prædictis tenementis in prædicta villa, unde dos &c., dicit quod quidem alius finis alias coram præfato J. de Methingham et sociis suis &c. ibidem apud Eboracum levavit in crastino Sancti Johannis Baptiste anno ejusdem regis nunc .xxix., inter ipsum Robertum filium Henrici querentem et prædictum Henricum patrem ipsius Ricardi filii Henrici cujus heres ipse est deforcientem, de prædictis boscis et pasturis &c. unde placitum convencionis &c., et per quem finem idem Henricus recognovit prædicta tenementa cum pertinentiis esse jus ipsius Roberti, et illa ei reddidit &c., habenda et tenenda eidem Roberto et heredibus suis &c. imperpetuum : et obligavit se et heredes suos ad warrantiam &c. Et profert partem cujusdam alterius finis que hoc testatur &c. : et ea ratione dicit quod prædictus Ricardus filius et heres ipsius Henrici tenetur ei prædictam tertiam partem bosci et pasture warrantizare &c. Et Ricardus filius Henrici dicit quod ad prædictam warrantiam prædicto Roberto filio Henrici faciendam &c. artari non debet in hac parte &c., quia dicit quod prædictus Henricus pater &c. nichil aliud habuit in prædictis tenementis nisi terminum ad terminum vite sue ex concessione ipsius Ricardi filii Henrici, ad quem post mortem ejusdem spectabat reversio &c. Et dicit quod ipse post mortem prædicti Henrici intravit in prædictis tenementis et inde fuit in seisina ut de jure suo quousque prædictus Robertus filius Henrici ejiciendo inde ipsum Ricardum sic seisitum intrusit se in prædictis tenementis unde modo exigit warrantiam. Et hoc paratus est verificare &c. Unde dicit quod accio competit ei super injurias et intrusionem &c. eadem tenementa et seisinam ipsius Roberti disrationandi. Et petit judicium si prædicta tenementa in quibus idem Robertus per hujusmodi intrusionem et non per reddicionem sic intravit, prout paratus est verificare, eidem

A.D. 1306

A.D. 1306. ought to warrant &c. And Robert says that the aforesaid Richard ought not to get to an averment by the country on this point, because he says that when he puts forward here in court &c. the parts of fines &c. one of which witnesses the render of the said hundred acres of wood and two hundred acres of pasture to the said Robert his brother, as aforesaid, and the other witnesses a certain other render made by the said Henry the father &c. to the said Richard son of Henry the younger, brother of the said Robert son of Henry, whose heir he is, of the entire residue of the said tenements whereof dower &c., into which tenements the said Robert son of Henry after the death of the said Richard his brother entered as heir &c. in form aforesaid; and the averment which the said Richard son of Henry offers, that the said Robert intruded himself &c. is directly opposed to the render of the said fines, which fines the said Richard has not denied, and which averment if it were admitted would clearly go to avoid the fines, which is not permissible &c., nor does the said Richard show that he ever after a render of this kind had any estate in the same by which he could be intruded &c., he prays judgment if the said Richard ought not to warrant to him, especially since he is ready to aver by the country that the said Richard has lands and tenements by descent from the said Henry sufficient to make answer to him for the value &c. And Richard says that, howsoever the said fines may witness the render &c., the said Robert son of Henry never obtained seisin of the said tenements by virtue of that render, but altogether by intrusion which he made upon them as aforesaid, for which tenements an action &c. accrues to him for that reason, which intrusion he is ready to aver, if the court will permit him to do this in opposition to the said fines; and he prays judgment &c. Afterwards, saving

Roberto warrantizare debeat &c. Et Robertus dicit quod prædictus Ricardus ad verificationem patriæ super hoc attingere non debet; quia dicit quod cum ipse proferat hic in curia &c. partes finium[1] &c., quarum una testatur redditionem prædictarum c. acrarum bosci et cc. acrarum pasturæ ipsi Roberto factam ut prædictum est, et alia pars finis testatur quamdam aliam redditionem factam per ipsum Henricum patrem &c. præfato Ricardo filio Henrici juniori fratri ipsius Roberti filii Henrici, cujus heres ipse est, de toto residuo prædictorum tenementorum unde dos &c.; in quibus tenementis idem Robertus filius Henrici post mortem ejusdem Ricardi fratris sui intravit ut heres &c. in forma prædicta; et verificacio quam idem Ricardus filius Henrici pretendit, quod idem Robertus intrusit se &c., directe opponitur testificacioni reddicionis finium prædictorum, quos quidem fines prædictus Ricardus non dedixit, et quæ verificacio si admittatur manifeste esset ad fines illos evacuandos, cum hoc non liceat &c., nec idem Ricardus ostendit quod ipse nunquam post hujusmodi reddicionis aliquam habuit statum in eisdem per quod posset intrudi &c., petit judicium si idem Ricardus ei warrantizare non debeat, maxime cum ipse paratus sit verificare per patriam per quod idem Ricardus terras habeat et tenementa per descensum de ipso Henrico pro valentia inde sibi facienda ad sufficens &c. Et Ricardus dicit quod qualitercumque fines prædicti testantur redditionem &c., idem Robertus filius Henrici nunquam adeptus fuit seisinam prædictorum tenementorum per hujusmodi redditionem, omnino penitus per intrusionem quam fecit in eisdem ut prædictum est; de quibus tenementis ea ratione competit ei accio &c., quam quidem intrusionem ipse paratus est verificare si curia ista ipsum ad hoc contra fines prædictos velit admittere; et petit judicium &c. Postea salvis sibi alias pro loco et

A.D. 1306.

[1] MS. sum.

A.D. 1306. to himself his action therefor when place and time occur, he now warrants to him &c. And as well as to the third part of the tenements which he warrants to the said Jordan as to the said third part of the tenements warranted to the said Robert as aforesaid, he says that the said Margaret ought not to have dower thereof, because he says that the said Henry formerly the husband &c., by whose endowment &c., was not on the day when he married her or ever afterwards seised of the said tenements in his demesne as of fee in such wise that he could endow her thereof: and in respect of this he puts himself upon the country. And Robert son of Richard and Margaret does the like. So it is commanded to the sheriff that he cause to come here at the Quinzein of Trinity twelve &c. by whom &c. who neither &c., who as well &c.

Quare vi et armis.

§ Joan, prioress of Swyne, and others were in mercy for several defaults; the said prioress and others were attached to answer Robert de Ros in a plea why with force and arms they broke up and consumed the turves of the said Robert de Ros in the common turbary, and did other grievous things to him, to the damage &c. and against the peace &c. And whereof the said Robert de Ros, by his attorney, complains that the said Joan and others, with force and arms, to wit with arrows and bows and swords, the turves of the said Robert in his common turbary at East Byngham to the value &c. broke up, consumed &c. And Joan and the others come and defend, and say that they did no trespass to the said Robert de Ros against the peace; but the said prioress says that she has a certain several turbary in the vill of East Byngham in which the said Robert de Ros ought not to dig any turves; and she says that the said Robert on the day and year aforesaid came into the said vill of East Byngham wishing to dig turves in the several turbary of the said prioress; the said prioress hindered him from doing it, as it was well lawful for her to do;

tempore inde accione sua, ei ad presens warrantizat &c. Et tam quoad tertiam partem tenementorum quam prædicto Jordano warrantizat quam quoad prædictam tertiam partem tenementorum prædicto Roberto in forma prædicta warantizatam, dicit quod prædicta Margareta non debet inde dotem habere, quia dicit quod prædictus Henricus quondam vir &c., de cujus dotacione &c., die quo ipsam disponsavit nec unquam postea fuit seisitus de prædictis tenementis in dominico suo ut de feodo ita quod ipsam inde dotare potuit. Et de hoc ponit se super patriam. Et Robertus filius Ricardi et Margareta similiter: ideo præceptum est vicecomiti quod venire faciat hic a die Sanctæ Trinitatis in xv. dies xii. &c. per quos &c. qui nec &c., qui tam &c. A.D. 1306.

§ Johanna priorissa de Swyne et alii in misericordia pro pluribus defaltis; idem priorissa et alii attachiati fuerunt ad respondendum Roberto de Ros de placito quare vi et armis turbare ipsius Roberti de Ros in communi turbaria comminuere, consumpserunt, et alia enormia ei intulerunt, ad dampnum &c. et contra pacem &c. Et unde idem Robertus de Ros per attornatum suum queritur quod prædicta Johanna et alii vi et armis, scilicet sagittis et arcubus et gladiis, turbas ipsius Roberti in communi turbaria sua apud Estbyngham inventas ad valentiam &c. comminuere, consumpserunt &c. Et Johanna et alii veniunt et defendunt, et dicunt quod nullam transgressionem fecerunt eidem Roberto de Ros contra pacem, sed prædicta priorissa dicit quod ipsa habet quamdam seperalem turbariam in villa de Estbyngham in quam prædictus Robertus de Ros aliquas turbas fodere non debet; et dicit quod idem Robertus die et anno prædictis venit in prædicta villa de Estbyngham volens turbas in seperali turbaria ipsius priorissæ fodere; eadem priorissa ipsum inde inpedivit

Quare vi et armis.

A.D. 1306. wherefore as well the said prioress as the said Simon well deny that they on the said day and year did break up or consume the turves of the said Robert in W. as is laid to their charge. And she asks that this may be inquired of. And the said Robert does the like &c.

Replegiare. § The master of the Hospital of St. John the Evangelist at Cambridge was summoned to answer Adam Elyot in a plea why he took the chattels of the said Adam and them unjustly &c. And whereof the said Adam, by his attorney, complains that the said master of the Hospital on the day &c. and year &c. at Cambridge took two swine of the said Adam and them unjustly &c., in respect whereof he says &c. And the master of the Hospital comes and defends &c.; for he says that one Robert Scherman did lately in the king's court at Cambridge, before J. de Willuby &c., implead a certain Nicholas then master of the said Hospital, predecessor &c., for a messuage with the appurtenances in Cambridge, which said master &c. vouched to warranty thereof William Scherman and Margaret his wife, who warranted to him &c.; and afterwards by judgment of the court they lost that messuage: so that it was adjudged that the said Robert should recover his seisin of the said messuage which was valued at five shillings, and that the said master of the Hospital should have of the land of the said William and Margaret to the value of &c. And he says that the sheriff by the king's command was to give for the said value to the said master of the Hospital &c. five shillings by the year to be taken out of three messuages which the said William and Margaret held in the said vill of Cambridge by the hands of the tenants of the said messuages, by the assent and will of the said William and Margaret, for the said value of the messuage lost &c. And he says that the said Nicholas, predecessor &c., was seised of the said five shillings by the year by the hands of the said William and Margaret, who paid that rent and accepted sic ei bene licuit; unde tam prædicta priorissa quam prædictus Simon bene defendunt quod ipsi prædictis die et anno turbas prædicti Roberti in W. non comminuere nec consumpserunt sicut eis inponitur. Et hoc petit quod inquiratur, et Robertus similiter &c. A.D. 1306.

§ Magister Hospitalis Sancti Johannis Ewangeliste Cantebregiensis sumonitus fuit ad respondendum Ade Elyot de placito quare cepit catalla ipsius Ade, et ea injuste &c. Et unde idem Adam per attornatum suum queritur quod prædictus magister Hospitalis die &c. et anno &c. apud Cantebrigiam cepit duas porcas ipsius Ade et eas injuste &c., unde dicit &c. Et magister hospitalis venit et defendit &c. Dicit enim quod quidem Robertus Scherman nuper in curia regis apud Cantebrigiam coram J. de Willuby &c. inplacitavit quemdam Nicholaum tunc magistrum hospitalis prædicti, prædecessorem &c., de uno messuagio cum pertinentis in Cantebrigia, qui quidem magister &c. vocavit inde ad warrantiam Willelmum Scherman et Margaretam uxorem ejus, qui ei warrantizaverunt &c.; et postea per judicium curiæ amiserunt mesuagium illud. Ita quod consideratum fuit quod prædictus Robertus recuperet seisinam suam de prædicto mesuagio, quod extendebatur ad v. s., et quod prædictus magister hospitalis haberet de terra prædictorum Willelmi et Margaretæ ad valentiam &c.: et dicit quod vicecomes per preceptum domini regis ad valentiam prædictam faceret prædicto magistro hospitali &c. v. s. per annum percipiendos de iii. mesuagiis quæ iidem Willelmus et Margareta tenuere in eadem villa Cant. per manus tenentium ipsorum mesuagiorum ex assensu et voluntate ipsorum Willelmi et Margaretæ pro valentia prædicta mesuagii amissi &c. Et dicit quod prædictus Nicholaus prædecessor &c. fuit seisitus de prædictis v. s. per annum per manus prædictorum Willelmi et Margaretæ qui redditum illum solverunt et assigna- Replegiare.

A.D. 1306. the said assignment &c. And likewise William, predecessor &c., was seised of the said five shillings by the hands of the said William and Margaret. Afterwards a master, predecessor &c., was seised of the said rent by the hands of one John son and heir of the said M., which said John alienated the said messuages charged with the said rent in form aforesaid to the said Adam &c. And because 5s. of the said rent for one year were in arrear on the day of the taking, he took the said swine as was well lawful for him &c. And Adam says that the said master of the said Hospital cannot avow the taking to be just; for he says that although the said sheriff had power to assign to the said master, predecessor &c., of the lands of the said W. and M. to the value of &c., yet he had no warrant to burden with the said rent the said tenements which were previously exonerated, and in doing so exceeded his warrant &c., nor ought the ratification or acceptance by the said William of the inheritance of the said M. to prejudice the said Margaret, because the said M. died in the lifetime of the said W.; nor ought the acceptance by the said John son and heir of the said M. to avail anything &c., since the said John is still under age &c., and he prays judgment &c. And the master of the Hospital says that inasmuch as he is ready to aver the seisin of his predecessors in form aforesaid &c. and the said Adam is a stranger purchaser and can not be in a better condition in this matter than his feoffor who accepted the said assignment, and who paid the rent by his hands, he prays judgment. A day is given them to hear judgment at the Quinzein of the Holy Trinity &c.

Enrolment. § Simon de Hoo and William Baude were attached to answer Adam son of John de Westone in a plea why when the said Adam lately sent some of his men with his horses and carts as far as Westele to carry his corn there collected to the value of 20*l.* to his house at Westele, the said Simon tionem prædictam acceptaverunt &c. Et similiter quidem Willelmus prædecessor &c. fuit seisitus per manus prædictorum Willelmi et Margaretæ de prædictis v. s. Et postea quidem magister predecessor &c. fuit seisitus de predicto redditu per manus cujusdam Johannis filii et heredis predicti M., qui quidem Johannes predicta messuagia onerata de predicto redditu in forma predicta &c. alienavit predicto Ade &c. Et quia v. solidi de predicto redditu de uno anno a retro fuit die captionis, cepit ipse predictas porcas &c. sicut ei bene licuit &c. Et Adam dicit quod predictus magister hospitalis predictæ captam justam advocare non potest; dicit enim quod licet idem vicecomes auctoritatem habuisset assignandi predicto magistro predecessori &c. de terris predictorum W. et M. ad valentiam &c., tamen non habuit warantum onerandi de predicto redditu predicta tenementa quæ prius exonerata fuerunt, modo in facto predicto excedebat warantum suum &c., nec etiam ratificatio seu acceptatio predicti Willelmi de hereditate predictæ M. eidem Margaretæ prejudicare debet, quia eadem M. obiit vivente predicto W., nec acceptatio predicti Johannis filii et heredis predictæ M. aliquid valere debet &c., cum idem Johannes adhue sit infra etatem &c., tamen petit judicium &c. Et magister hospitalis dicit quod ex quo ipse paratus est verificare seisinam predecessorum suorum in forma predicta &c., et idem Adam extraneus perquisitor, nec potest esse melioris conditionis in hac parte quam suus feoffator qui predictam assignationem accepit, qui redditum predictum per manus suas soluit, petit judicium &c. Dies datus est eis de andiendo judicio a die Sanctæ Trinitatis in xv. dies &c. A.D. 1306.

§ Simon de Hoo et Willelmus Baude attachiati fuerunt ad respondendum Ade filio Johannis de Westone de placito quare cum predictus Adam nuper quosdam homines suos cum equis et carectis suis usque Westele misisset ad blada sua ad valentiam xx. librarum ibidem **Irrotulatio.**

A.D. 1306. and others took the said horses out of the carts and led them away, and with a great part of the said corn fed the beasts of the said Simon, and trampled down and consumed, not permitting him to carry elsewhere the residue of the said corn and make his profit thereof, by reason whereof the said corn perished and rotted; and other grievous things &c. to the damage &c. And whereof the said Adam by his attorney complains that the said Simon and others, on Wednesday next after the feast of the Assumption of the Blessed Mary in the 31st year, in the vill of Westele caput which is called Suffled, took four horses out of the said cart with force and arms, swords, bows &c.; and with a great part of the corn fed their beasts, in form aforesaid, and other grievous things &c. against the peace &c., whereby he says he is made worse and is damaged to the value of &c. and thereof &c. And Simon and William by their attorney come and deny force and injury &c. when &c., and they well deny that they have committed any trespass on the said Adam &c. against the peace &c. And Simon says that he on the aforesaid day and year took the said horses justly &c.: for he says that the said Adam granted and by his writing confirmed to a certain Matilda, who was the wife of Richard son of Ranulf of Saxham, 10*l.* of yearly rent, to be taken for the whole of the life of the said Matilda at two terms of the year, half at Pentecost and the other half at Michaelmas, and for himself and his heirs bound all his lands and tenements in Westele and elsewhere within the liberty of St. Edmund to distress by the said Matilda, and that whenever the said rent should be in arrear, she might at her pleasure distrein for the rent in those tenements. And he says that he, in the name of the said Matilda then his wife, made the said distress of the said four horses in the tenements charged &c., for 20*l.* of the said yearly rent, in arrear on the day of the taking. And Adam says that the said Simon can not avow the distress for the said collecta ad domum suam in Westele carianda misisset, predictus Simon et alii equos predictos extra carectas &c. ceperunt et abduxerunt, et magnam partem bladorum illorum cum averiis ipsius Simonis depasti fuerunt, conculcaverunt et consumpserunt, non permittentes ipsum ad residua bladorum illorum aliunde asportare et comodum suum inde facere, per quod blada illa perierunt et putruerunt, et alia enormia &c. ad dampna &c. Et unde idem Adam per attornatum suum queritur quod predictus Simon et alii die Mercurii[1] proxima post festum Assumptionis Beatæ Mariæ anno xxxi° in villa de Westele capt qui vocatur suffled ceperunt iiij. equos extra carectam predictam vi et armis gladiis arcubus &c., et magnam partem bladorum scilicet cum averiis suis depasti fuerunt in forma predicta, et alia enormia &c. contra pacem &c.: unde dicit quod deterioratus est et dampnum habet ad valentiam &c., et inde &c. Et Simon et Willelmus per attornatum suum veniunt et defendunt vim et injuriam quando &c., et bene defendunt quod ipsi nullum transgressionem eidem Adæ &c. contra pacem &c. inde fecerunt. Et Simon revera dicit quod ipse predictis die et anno cepit predictos equos juste &c.: dicit enim quod predictus Adam concessit et scripto suo confirmavit cuidam Matildæ, quæ fuit uxor Ricardi filii Ranulfi de Saxham, x. libras annui redditus percipiendas tota vita ipsius M. ad duos anni terminos, usque ad festum Pentecostes et aliam medietatem ad festum Sancti Michaelis, et obligavit pro se et heredibus suis omnes terras et tenementa sua in Westele et alibi infra libertatem Sancti Edmundi ad districtionem predictæ M. quandocunque redditus ille a retro fuerit, quod pro redditu illo pro voluntate sua in tenementis illis distringere possit. Et dicit quod ipse nomine predictæ Matildæ tunc uxoris suæ fecit predictam districtionem predictorum quatuor equorum in tenementis oneratis &c. pro xx. libris a retro existentibus die captionis de predicto annuo redditu. Et Adam dicit quod predictus Simon districtionem A.D. 1306.

[1] MS. in curia.

A.D. 1306. yearly rent; for he says that after the making of the said obligatory writing it was agreed between the said Matilda and Adam that as soon as Adam should enfeoff Matilda for the term of her life of certain tenements in Wetham which the said Adam purchased from the said Matilda in court by a fine levied, then the said obligatory writing for the said rent should be of no force: and he says that the said writing for annulling the said rent by reason of the aforesaid agreement was brought here into court in a plea of a certain debt contained in the said writing &c. between the said Adam and the said Simon executor of the testament of the said Matilda who claimed the said debt &c., and remained in the keeping of the court &c., which writing being afterwards searched for, the contents were found to be so. And he says that, since he afterwards re-enfeoffed the said M. of the said tenements according to the form of the agreement, the said obligatory writing ought to be of no force or virtue: and he prays judgment. And because this plea cannot be further proceeded with until it be proved whether the said written agreement is or is not the deed of the said Matilda who is dead, and in the aforesaid plea of debt the parties have a day here fifteen days next after the day of the Holy Trinity, therefore the same day is given to the said Adam and Simon in the Bench &c.

pro predicto annuo redditu advocare non potest; dicit enim quod post predictum scriptum obligatorium factum convenit inter predictam Matildam et Adam, scilicet quod quam cito idem Adam feoffaret predictam Matildam ad terminum vitæ ipsius Matildæ de quibusdam tenementis in Wetham quæ idem Adam de eadem Matilda perquisivit in curia per finem relevatum, scilicet tunc predictum scriptum obligatorium de dicto redditu nullius esset vigoris; et dicit quod predictum scriptum de predicto redditu adnullando ratione predictæ conventionis illas in curia hic super placito cujusdam debiti in eodem scripto contenti &c. inter ipsum Adam et predictum Simonem executorem testamenti predictæ Matildæ predictum debitum exigentem &c. deductum fuit, et in custodia curiæ remansit &c., quo scripto postea quesito, et in scripto idem compertum est. Et dicit quod ipse postea refeoffavit predictam M. de predictis tenementis juxta formam conventionis, predictum scriptum obligatorium nullius debet esse vigoris nec virtutis, unde petit judicium. Et quia in placito isto ulterius procedere non potest quousque convincatur utrum predictum scriptum conventionis sit factum predictæ M. quæ mortua est nec ne, et in placito predicto de debito partes habent diem hic a die Sanctæ Trinitatis in xv. dies proximos futuros, ideo idem dies datus est predictis Adæ et Simoni in Banco &c. A.D. 1306.

PLEAS IN MICHAELMAS TERM

XXXIV. EDWARD I.

PLEAS IN MICHAELMAS TERM IN THE XXXIVTH YEAR OF THE REIGN OF KING EDWARD.

A.D. 1306. Record in Dower.

§ One A. brought a writ of Dower against B. and demanded &c. B. said that she ought not to have dower, for that her husband was not seised &c. on the day when he married her or ever afterwards, in such wise &c.; and on that the averment was joined. A jury came before Sir Elias de Bekyngham, and said that the husband of the woman &c. was at a certain time seised of the said tenements, and that he took a wife, and because he wished his wife to have an estate in the said tenements, he enfeoffed one G. of these tenements, who thereof enfeoffed one D., which D. gave the said tenements to the husband and his wife and the heirs of their bodies together, and this was before the statute[1] &c., by whom he had issue; which wife died, and the husband married this woman who now brings the writ, and it was before the statute. And because it was found that the husband was seised &c. in his demesne as of fee, for, before the statute, after he had issue he could have alienated, the court adjudges that she do recover &c.

Note, of a view previously had.

§ In a writ of Entry, after the View, the parol demurred without day by a Protection, and the demandant did not sue out the resummons, but purchased a new writ.—*Herle* prayed the view. —*Lanfar.* You shall not have it, for you had it in another writ.—STAUNTON. How and in what writ? —*Lanfar.* He formerly brought a like writ where he had the view; but the parol demurred

[1] 13 Edw. I. De donis.

DE TERMINO SANCTI MICHAELIS ANNO REGNI REGIS EDWARDI XXXIIII°.

§ Un A. porta bref de dowere vers B. e demanda &c.: e *B.* dist qele ne devoit dowere avoir, kar sun baron ne fu mie seisi &c. le jour qil la esposa ne unkes pus issi &c., e sur ceo se joynt le averement. Pays vient devant Sire Elis de Bekyngham qe dit qe le baron la femme &c. en asqun temps fust seisi de mesmes ceux tenements, qe prist femme, e pur ceo qil voleit qe sa femme ust estat en mesmes les tenements, il enfeffa de ces tenements un G. qe de ces enfeffa un D., le quel D. dona mesmes ceux tenements au baron e a sa femme e a les heirs de lour corps engendrez, e avant statut &c., de qi il avoit issue; la quele femme devya, e le baron prist mesme ceste qe ore porte sun bref, e avant statut. E pur ceo qe trove est qe le baron fust seisi &c. en sun demene come de fee, qar apres ceo qil out issue avant statut il poeit aver aliene, si agarde &c. qele rescovere &c. A.D. 1306. Recordum de dote.

§ En un bref dentre apres la vewe, la parole remist sanz jour par proteccion, e le demandant ne suist point la resumons einz purchasa novel bref.—*Herle* demanda la vewe.—*Lanfare.* Vous ne la averez point, qar vous la aviez a un altre bref.—STANTONE. Coment, e a quel bref?—*Lanfare.* Il porta autrefoiz autiel bref ou il Nota de visu prius habito.

A.D. 1306. without day.—*Herle.* Judgment then if we ought not to have the view.—And he had the view &c. Nor is the statute in the way, for the statute[1] speaks of where a writ is quashed in which &c. by the answer of the tenant.

Per quæ servitia.

§ Philip de Gaytone was made to come to acknowledge by what services he held his tenements of Hugh de Thorham in Cravesle and in Flore, which services the said Hugh had granted to William de Ros &c., who came. —*Herle.* We do not hold of Hugh anything in Cravesle, and what we hold in Flore we hold jointly with one John our son, who is under age, and by this charter, and without him we cannot make any acknowledgment.—STAUNTON. Where is John?—*Herle.* He is not here, nor has he at present any day.—STAUNTON (to William de Ros). Answer.—*Este.* We cannot be party to that charter, for it is not the deed of Hugh nor is it the deed of any of our ancestors, and Hugh ought well to know his tenant.—TRIKINGHAM (having looked at the note). We cannot by this note make John come, wherefore you must needs begin again and have a new note.—STAUNTON. Let Philip go without day for the present. And note, by TRIKINGHAM, that even if John had been named in the note, the acknowledgment could not have been made until he was of full age.

Nuper obiit.

§ A. and B. brought the writ against C., D., and E. his wife.—*Stapilford.* &c. he tortiously deforces from them the moiety &c.: and tortiously for this that it is their right and ought to be their rightful part which belongs to them of the heritage which belonged to T. father of the aforesaid A. B. C. and E. whose heirs &c.: and whereof that same T. was seised of the entirety of that messuage &c. in his demesne as of fee and of right, in time &c., the esplees &c., and lately died: from T. descended &c. to A. B. C. and E. as daughters &c.; and

[1] Westm. 2. 13 Edw. I. c. 48.

avoit la vewe, mes la parole demora sanz jour.—*Herle.* Jugement donqes si nous ne devoms la vewe avoir. Et habuit visum &c. Nec hoc obest Statuto, quia Statutum loquitur ubi breve cassatur in quo &c. per responsum tenentis. **A.D. 1306.**

Per quæ servicia.

§ Phelip de Gaytone fust fet venir a conustre par queux services il tient ces tenements de Hughe de Thorham en Cravesle e en Flore, queux services mesme cestui Hughe avoit grante a Willem de Ros &c., qe vient. — *Herle.* Nous ne tenoms de Hughe riens en Cravesle, e ceo qe nous tenoms en Flore si tenoms joint ove un Johan nostre fiz denz age, e par ceste chartre, sanz qi nous ne poms nule conissance fere. — STANTONE. Ou est Johan?—*Herle.* Il ny est pas, ne il ne ad mie jor a ore. — STANTONE (a Willem de Ros). Responez. — *Este.* Nous ne poms estre partie a cele chartre, qe ceo nest le fet Hughe, ne ceo ne est le fet nul de nos auncestres, e Hughe devoit bien conustre sun tenant. — TRIKINGHAM (inspecta nota). Nous ne poms nent faire venir Johan par ceste note, par quei il vous covent recomencer e aver novel note. — STANTONE. Aille Phelip sanz jour ad presens.—Et nota per TRIKINGHAM qe tut eust Johan este nome en la note, la conissance ne se poeit fere tant qil fust de plein age. **Nota.**

Nuper obiit.

§ Un A. e B. porterent le bref vers C. D. e E. sa femme.—*Stapilford.* &c. atort lour deforce la moite &c. E pur ceo atort, qe ceo est lour droit e lour resnable partie estre deit qe a eux affiert del heritage qe fust a T. pere les avantdiz A. B. C. e E., qi heirs &c. E dount mesme cestui T. fust seisi del entier de cel mies &c. en sun demene come de fee e de droit en temps &c., les esplez &c., e morust nadgers; de T. descendi &c. a A. B. C. e E. come a filles &c. Et dount mesme

A.D. 1306. whereof these same C. and D. and E. his wife hold the whole, and the aforesaid A. and B. have nothing thereof; and if &c. suit &c.—*Kingesham* defended &c. and (said he), We tell you, as to a moiety of the tenements &c., that one F. leased that moiety to the said D. and E. his wife for the term of their two lives, and we vouch to warranty &c.—STAUNTON reproved *Stapilford* because he understood that he had counted against them as against strangers, because they vouched, and he told him to go and seek more advice. —*Willuby* and *Este* came with him and said that the count was good, and they asked that the party should make her challenges if she would. *Kinge.* again vouched as before.—STAUNTON. Then, according to you, T. did not die seised.—*Willuby.* We will aver that he died seised, and although it were the fact that after his death they had feigned that feoffment to put away their bad tenancy, that would not avail anything; for by the law of the land neither view nor voucher lie in this writ.—*Warr.* (on the same side). If you disclaim now in the parcenary, you shall not at another time have aid of the parceners; and if perchance those feoffments be made between you and F., and you were now to vouch F. and he were to revouch you, you will not have aid of your parceners since you formerly disclaimed; and nevertheless this is not a Mordancester, and if the tenant be the first who entered after the death of the ancestor on whose seisin the demandant &c., and the demandant will aver this, by Statute[1] the voucher will not be received.—STAUNTON. Will you have the voucher at your peril? Know that if the court see that the voucher does not lie &c. you will lose.—*King.* waived it &c., and said, As to A. she ought not to have a share, for our ancestor T. on whose seisin &c. gave her in frank-marriage a virgate of land in K.; so unless she put that land into hotchpot she shall not have a share.—*Stapil-*

---

[1] Westm. 1. 3 Edw. I. c. 40.

cestes C. D. e E. sa femme tut entenent, e les avant- A.D. 1306.
dites A. e B. ren ne ount, e si &c. suite &c. —*Kingesham* defendi &c. E vous dioms quant a la moite des tenements &c. qe un F. cele moite lessa a mesme ceux D. e E. sa femme a terme de lour deux vies, e vouchoms a garantie &c. — STANTONE reprova *Stapilford* pur ceo qil entendi qil avoit conte vers eux com vers estranges, pur ceo qe eux voucherent, e luy dit qil se alast quere plus de consail. — *Willuby* e *Este* viendrent ove luy e diseient qe le conte fust bon, e demanderent qe la partie deit ces chalanges si ele voleit. — *Kinge* autrefoiz voucha com avant.— STANTONE. Donqes par vous G. [T.?] ne morust mie seisi.— *Willuby*. Nous voloms averer qil morust seisi, e tut fust il issi qe apres sa mort il ussent feint cel feffement pur eloigner lour malveise tenance, ceo ne vaudreit rienz, qar de ley de terre ne la vewe ne voucher ne gisent en ceo bref. — Ad idem *Warr.* Si vous desclamez ore en la parcenerie, vous ne averez mie autrefoiz de parceners aide; e si par cas teux feffemenz seient fez entre vous e F., e vous vouchissez ore F., e il vous revouchast, vous ne averez mie aide de vos parceners del houre qe autrefoiz desclamastes, e jatardeis ne est ceo le mortdancestre, e si le tenant soit le primer qe entra apres la mort le auncestre, de qi seisine le demandant &c., e le demandant ceo voille averer, le voucher ne serra mie receu par Statut.— STANTONE. Volez le voucher a vostre peril? qe sachez qe si la Court veie qe le voucher ne gise mie &c. vous perdrez.— *King* le weyva &c. E en droit de A. ele ne deit partie aver, qar nostre auncestre G. [T.?], de qi seisine &c., la dona en franc mariage une vergee de terre en K.; dount sanz ceo qele mette cele terre

A.D. 1306. *ford.* Nothing in frank-marriage, ready &c.—And the other side said the contrary. And as to E. &c. they rendered &c. And it is to be noted that *King.* said, in the examination of his client at the bar, that if they had disclaimed in the parcenary, and the others had again brought the Mordancester against them, they could not have claimed in the parcenary, and thereby the others would have recovered the entirety &c.

A case of dower.

A woman does not lose her dower for any acknowledgment by her husband of a debt by statute.

§ One A. had formerly recovered her dower against S. of the manor of T., and was seised; and afterwards the said S., because B. the husband of A. by statute[1] &c. was bound to S. in a certain sum of money, recovered the said manor of T. by statute, to be held &c.; and thereupon the said A. sued a writ out of the rolls, in which writ was set forth all her recovery, and the recovery by S., and in the end of the writ the sheriff was directed to warn S. that he should be &c. to show if he could say anything why the said A. ought not to have her dower according as she had recovered it.—*King.* This writ is only to make execution of a judgment, and we tell you that execution was fully done, for she was seised; and we pray judgment; for a Scire facias supposes that execution is not done.—*Lanfar.* This is not purely a Scire facias, but it is a writ framed for our case.—STAUNTON (to *King.*, having examined the writ). Answer.—*King.* We freely grant that she may have that third part, but we must have the other two parts at an apportioned value until we have &c. by statute &c.; and that third part is not to be taken into allowance: and we pray that it may be so entered on the roll.—*Lanfar.* We pray the issues &c. for the mesne time.—STAUNTON. I know not if he be warned to do this.—And in reading the writ it was found &c. and to do and receive what the court may adjudge.—STAUNTON. You shall have them.—*King.*

[1] 13 Edw. I. st. 3.

en hochepot ele navera nule partie.—*Stapilford.* Riens en franc mariage, prest &c. Et alius e contra. Et quoad E. &c. reddiderunt &c. Et memorandum qe *King* dist, en examinement de sun clyent a la barre, qe si eux eussent desclame en la parcenerie e les autres ussent autrefoiz porte lour mordancestre vers eux, il ne poeient mie aver clame en la parcenerie, e par tant les autres ussent rescovery lenter &c. A.D. 1306.

Mulier non amittet dotem pro aliqua recognitione viri sui de debito per statutum. Casus de dote.

§ Une A. avoit altrefoiz rescovere sun dowere vers S. du maner de T., e seisie fust; e pus mesme cestui S., pur ceo qe B. baron A. par statut &c. fust tenuz a S. en une summe de avoir, rescovery le dist maner de T. par statut, a tenir &c.; e sur ceo mesme ceste A. suist bref hors de roulles, denz quel bref fust contenuz tut sun rescoverir e le rescoverir S.; e, en la fin du bref, qe le viconte feist garnir S. qil fust &c. a monstrer sil savoit rienz dire- pur quei mesme ceste A. solom ceo qele avoit rescovery sun dowere aver ne deust.—*King.* Ceo bref ne est autre mes a faire execucion de une jugement, e vous dioms qe execucion est pleynement faite, kar ele fust seisie; e demaundom jugement; ke scire facias suppose ke execucion ne est mie faite.—*Lanfare.* Ceo nest pas purement un scire facias, einz est bref forme sur nostre cas.—STANTONE inspecto brevi, a *King.* Responez.—*King.* Nous grantoms bien qele eit cele terce partie, mes qe nous eoms donqes les deus parties par estente apportione, tanqe nous eoms &c., par statut &c. E qe cele terce partie ne courge mie en allowance, e prioms quil seit issi entre en roulle.—*Lanfare.* Nous prioms les issues &c. del meen tenps. —STANTONE. Jeo ne say sil soit a ceo garny.—Et lecto brevi, conpertum est &c., et ad faciendum et recipiendum quod curia consideret.—STANTONE. Vous les averez.

A.D. 1306. Then we pray that we may take so much out of the two parts before they go out of our hands, and that it may be so entered.—HALES. So it shall be.

Debt, for executors.

§ Two executors of John de Lutegre brought the writ against Christine de Meyvelle.—*Willuby.* Show that you are executors.—*Hedone* showed the testament where they two and two others were named executors.—*Willuby.* There are two other &c. who are not named in the writ; judgment &c.—*Hedone.* Those two never administered; wherefore &c.—And notwithstanding this, the writ was abated by HOWARD and MALORE.—And some were of opinion that in this case it was not necessary to show the testament, if they could aver that they were executors; and thus the writ might have been saved.

Account.

§ One A. brought the writ against B. "for the time during which the said B. was receiver of the moneys of the said A. from whatever source and contract for the common profit of the said A. and B." and charged him with the receipt of twenty pounds &c.—*Lanfar.* What have you to show what we received from you ?—*Hampton.* Ready &c.—*Lanfar.* We only received from you ten pounds, and to those ten pounds we put another sum of ten pounds to trade with for our common profit, so that the gain and loss should fall in common &c.: we with those twenty pounds bought goods, namely &c., and put them on board of a ship to pass into &c., which ship was lost at sea, and we pray judgment if you can demand anything.—*Hampton.* We handed you twenty pounds in manner as we have counted, ready &c. And as to the loss you speak of, we have nothing to do with that, for we handed them to you to trade with in the vill of Lynn, and not elsewhere, ready &c.—And the other side said the contrary.—So &c.

Challenge of essoin.

§ John Baldwyn brought the Ne vexes against one Master Alexander, and at the first day John caused himself to be essoined.—*Passeley* rehearsed what is

King. Donqes prioms qe nous puissoms tant prendre de deus parties einz qe eux aillent hors de nostre meyn, e qil soit issi entre.—HALES. Issi serra il. A.D. 1306.

De debito pro executoribus.

§ Deus executours Johan de Lutegre porterent le bref vers Cristiene de Meyvelle. — *Willuby.* Moustrez qe vous estes executour.—*Hedone* moustra le testament ou teux deus e deus autres furent nomez executours.—*Willuby.* Iluy sunt deus autres &c. nent nomez en le bref; jugement &c.—*Hedone.* Ceus deus ne administrerent unqes; par quei &c.; et hoc non obstante le bref se abatist par HOWARD e MALORRE.—Et fuit quorumdam opinio quod in hoc casu non esset necesse testamentum monstrare, dummodo verificare poterant quod fuerunt executores, et sic posset salvari breve &c.

De composto.

§ Un A. porta le bref vers B. de tempore quo idem B. fuit receptor denariorum ipsius A. ex quacumque causa et contractu ad comunem utilitatem ipsorum A. et B. proveniencium, e lui charga de la receite de xx. livres &c.—*Lanfare.* Qei avez de ceo qe nous ressumes &c. de vous?—*Hamptone.* Prest &c.—*Lanfare.* Nous ne ressumes de vous mes qe x. livres, e a ces x. livres meimes autre x. livres a marchander a nostre comune profit, issi qe le gaigne e la perte cherreit en comune &c.; nous de ces xx. livres achatames mers, nomement &c., e le feymes charger en une neef, pur passer &c., la quele neef peri en mer, e demandom jugement si rienz puissez demander. — *Hamptone.* Nous vous baillames xx. livres solom ceo qe nous avoms conte, e prest &c. Et quaunt a la perte dount vous parlez, navom qe fere, qar nous les vous baillames a marchander denz la ville de Leen, e noun pas aillours, prest &c. Et alius e contra. Ideo &c.

Nota de calumpnia essonii.

§ Johan Baldewyn porta le ne vexes vers un mestre Alexandre, e au primer jour Johan se fist essoner.—*Passeley* rehersa idem quod prædicitur; e chalangoms

A.D. 1306. before stated, and said, Sir, we challenge this essoin, for John is our vilein, and we pray that our challenge may be entered, so that he may not enjoy the benefit of freedom without being reclaimed.--STAUNTON ordered that their challenge should be entered on the essoin, and that the essoin should be adjourned.—And so it was done.

Trespass.

How a lord is to defend himself against his naif.

§ One John brought the writ [against R.], and counted that R. tortiously &c. took him and imprisoned him &c. and assaulted, beat &c., and his goods &c. took and carried away.—*Roistone* denied tort and force, and as to its being against the peace of our lord the King, and (said he), We tell you that John ought not to be answered, for he is our vilein, and we were seised of him on the day of which he complains; and as to any thing done against the peace &c. we say Not guilty &c. -- *Herle.* Be avowed.—And he was avowed. — *Herle.* We are at issue in the plea; we have counted that he imprisoned us &c., beat &c., and our goods &c., and he says that he is not guilty; we are ready to aver our plaint.—*Roistone.* As to the chattels you ought not to be answered.--*Herle.* Nay, you entirely negatived our plaint, for you said Not guilty.—Here *Roistone* pleaded badly, at least in answering after his defence, because he ought rather to have distinguished his second exception, and to have avowed the goods carried away, because it is lawful for a lord &c. And nevertheless at length it was so enrolled &c. And *Herle*, considering this, thus protested,—Since you will thus enter it, we make protestation that we do not admit their exception of vileinage, but oppose it, and we pray that it may be so entered. — And it was so. — On another day BEREFORD and HOWARD being in the bench,--*Herle* rehearsed the process, and at the end said, And, sir, since he in commencing his argument by his exception of vileinage endeavoured to rebut us from an action, and then, waiving that, answered us, and took an issue in the plea, we pray that that exception of

Sire ceste essone, qar Johan est nostre vileyn, e prioms A.D. 1306.
qe nostre chalange soit entre qil ne enjoye benefice de franchise sanz estre reclame. -- STANTONE comanda qe lour chalange fust entre sur le essone, e lassone ajorne. —Et ita fuit.

Qualiter defendendum sit contra nativum per dominum. Transgressio.

Un Johan porta le bref, e conta qe R. atort &c. lui prist e lenprisona &c. e le assailly, bati &c., e ces biens &c. prist e enporta.—*Rostone* defendi tort e force e quanqe est encountre la pees nostre seignour le Roi, e vous dioms qe Johan ne deit estre respondu, qar il est nostre vilein, e nous seisi de luy &c. le jour qil se pleint; e quant a chose faite encontre la pees &c., de riens copable &c. — *Herle.* Seez avowe: et advocabatur. -- *Herle.* Nous sumes a issue de plee; nous avoms conte qil nous enprisona &c. bati &c. e nos biens &c., e il dist qil nest de rien copable; prest daverer nostre pleinte. — *Roistone.* Quant a chateux vous ne devez estre respondu.—*Herle.* Nay, vous estes enterement a la negative de nostre pleinte, qar vous deistes de rienz coupable. — Et hic male placitavit *Rostone*, saltem respondendo post defensum, quia magis debuit distinguisse secundum excepcionem suam [et] advocasse bona asportata, quia licitum est domino &c. Et tamen ad ultimum sic fuit irrotulatum &c.—Et *Herle,* hoc perpendens, protestabatur sic, del houre qe vous la volez issi entrer nous fessoms protestacion qe nous ne conussoms point lour excepcion de villenage, einz la reclamoms e prioms qe issi soit entre &c. Et fuit.—Ad alium diem BEREFORD HOWARD existentibus in Banco, -- *Herle* rehersa ces proces, et in fine, Et del houre sire qil en comensaunt sa reson par sa excepcion de villenage se afforsa de reboter nous de accion, e pus en wayvant tiele nous respondy e prist issue de plee, prioms qe cele excepcion de villenage ne soit entre

A.D. 1306. vileinage be not entered on the roll, since he waived it. —*Ròistone.* Nay, you did not deny it, wherefore it is admitted, and so it only remains to inquire of that trespass committed against the peace, which it is not lawful for a lord to do to his vilein.—BEREFORD. When you at first took an exception to the person, and afterwards answered him, your first exception was worth no more than if you had kept it in your purse, and only amounts to your saying You ought not to be answered, and then answering.—STAUNTON (privately, between him and BEREFORD). He charges him with a trespass, which is not avowable on a vilein, wherefore &c.—BEREFORD. Then he might have said thus, Neither as to the carrying off the chattels nor as to what he says of the imprisonment, ought he to be answered, for he is our vilein and we were seised &c., and because he wished to flee from us, or did some other thing against our will, we put him in the stocks and took his chattels as our &c.: and as to the beating and wounding we did it not, ready &c.—*Herle.* For the issue which he took he is avowed, and if he will now avow the carrying off the chattels, let him do so.—And he said this because he understood that the said A. was enfranchised from servitude by the answer which *Roistone* first made, by reason of which he could not avow the carrying off the chattels.—STAUNTON to *Roistone.* Will you still avow the carrying off the chattels?—*Roistone.* We hold to what we have said; you will do as you please.—*Herle* prayed that the exception of vileinage might be ousted.—And so it was; and the roll was amended by BEREFORD.

Replegiari. Where a stranger purchaser, seised of part of the services, avowed for the remainder &c.

§ One A. complained that B. tortiously &c. namely eight oxen and three horses.—*Friskeney.* We avow the taking &c. on this same A., and for the reason that one R. and Joan his wife &c. in right of Joan &c. whose heir A.

en roulle del houre qil la weyva. — *Roistone.* Nay, vous ne le dedites point, par quei ele est graunte, e si ne remeint a enquere mes qe de teu trespas fete encontre la pees, qe ne list mie seignour fere a sun vileyn.—BEREFORD. Quant vous excepcionastes primes a la persone e pus a mesme celuy respondites, tant vous vaut vostre primer excepcion com vous la eussez tenu en vostre burse, e nent plus ne fet a dire qe nest vous ne devez estre respoundu e pus respondre.—STANTONE. (privement entre luy e BEREFORD.) Iluy surmist trespas qe nest pas avowable de fere a vilein, par quei, &c.—BEREFORD. Adonqe poeit il aver issi dist; quant a lenporter des chateux ne a ceo qil parle denprisonement il ne deit estre respondu, qar il est nostre vilein e nous seisi &c., e pur ceo qil nous voleit defure ou autre chose fist contre nostre gree, si luy meymes en ceps e les chateus prymes com nos &c. Et quant al batre e au player nous ne le feymes point, prest &c. — *Herle.* Del issue qil prist si est il avowe, e sil voudra ore avower lenporter des chateux, face. Et hoc dixit quia intellexit predictum A. liberare a servitute per responsum quem Roistone primo fecit, per quod catalla sua asportata advocare non potuit. —STANTONE a *Roistone.* Volez uncore avower lenporter des chateux? — *Roistone.* A ceo qe nous avoms dist nous tenoms; vous freez vos volentez. — *Herle* pria qe la excepcion de vileynage fust oste. Et ita fuit, et rotulus emendebatur per BEREFORD. A.D. 1306.

Ubi extraneus perquisitor seisitus de parte servitiorum advocavit pro remanente &c. Replegiare.

§ Un A. se pleint ke B. atort &c., nomement .viii. boefs e treis chivals. — *Friskeney.* Nous avowoms la prise &c. sur mesme cestui A., e par la reson qe un R. e Johane sa femme &c., qi heir A. est, tyendrent

A.D. 1306. is, held &c. of one James de Byroun, by homage fealty and the service of one knight's fee and ten shillings by the year for the guard of the castle of Richmond, of which services James &c. was seised &c. by the hands of R. and Joan, as &c.; then from James the right of the manor of T. together with the services of R. and Joan descended to one Robert, and from Robert to John, which John gave and granted to this same B. the manor of T. together with the aforesaid services &c., on which grant the said A., in acknowledgment of all the other services, attorned to B. for the rent of ten shillings; and because that rent &c. was in arrear for one year on the day of the taking, we avow &c. for the four (three ?) horses, and because the homage of the said A. was in arrear &c. we avow for the eight oxen.—*Passeley.* You avow this taking as a stranger purchaser, who must by force of law avow of his own seisin; and we tell you that you were never seised of the services for which you make the avowry, ready &c.—*Friskeney.* We were seised of the rent, in acknowledgment of the rest, ready &c.—HOWARD to *Passeley.* If you hold of me by the service of ten marks, and I grant your services to Roger Scotre, and you attorn to him and in acknowledgment deliver to him one penny, can he not distrein for the remainder of the services ? (intimating that he could).—*Passeley.* Never seised of the rent &c.—And the other side said the contrary.—So &c.—And note that *Passeley* in rehearsing the avowry said that *Friskeney* had said that John &c. had granted to B. against whom &c. only the services &c., whereas he said, the manor of T. with the services &c. — *Friskeney* challenged it and amended it in that point, and the reason was because the services were comprised in the gross of the manor.

§ One W. brought the Attaint &c. to attaint the twelve who passed against him with the abbat of Ramsey: eleven came, and the twelfth did not come.—*Toudeby* put forward for him a Protection, and prayed that

&c. de un James de Byroun, come du droit Johane &c., A.D. 1306.
par homage fealte e le service de un fee de chivaler e dis soz par an, a la garde du chastel de Richemond, des queux services James &c. seisi &c. par my les meins R. e Johane, cum &c.; dount de James descendi le droit du maner de T., ensemblement ove les services R., e Johane, a un Robert; de Robert a Johan; le quel Johan dona e granta a mesme cestui B. le maner de T. ensemblement ove les avantdiz services &c., e par quel graunt mesme celuy A., en resconissance de touz les autres services, se atturna a B. de la rente de dis soz; e pur ceo ke cele rente &c. arere par un an le jour de la prise, si avowoms &c. de quatre chivals, e pur ceo qe le homage mesme celui A. nous est arere &c., si avowoms &c. de huit boefs. — *Passeley.* Vous avowez ceste prise com estraunge purchassour, qi covent par force de ley avower de sa seisine demene; e vous dioms qe vous ne estoiez unqes seisi des services pur queux vous fetes lavowerie, prest &c. — *Friskeney.* Seisi de la rente en resconissance del remenant, prest &c. —Howard a *Passeley.* Vous tenez de moy par service de dis mars; jeo graunte vos services a Roger Scotre, vous atturnez a lui e en resconissance ly baillez un denier, ne vous purra il destreindre pur tant pur le eel des services? quasi diceret sic. — *Passeley.* Unqes seisi de la rente &c.—Et alius e contra; ideo &c.—Et memorandum qe *Passeley* en rehersant lavowerie dist qe *Frisqeney* avoit dit qe Johan &c. avoit grante a B., vers qi &c., soulement les services &c., ou il dit le maner de T. ove les services &c.—*Frisqeney* lui chalenga e luy amenda de tant, e la cause fust pur ceo qe les services furent compris del gros du maner.

§ Un W. porta latteinte &c. de atteyndre les .xii. qe Nota ubi pro.
passerent contre lui ove la abbe de Rameseye; les .xi. viendrent, le .xiime ve vient point.—*Toudeby* mist &c. pur luy la proteccion, e pria qe sur luy qe fust en le

A.D. 1306. upon him who was in the service of our lord the king no distress should run.—And upon this, the Justices having long conferred together, STAUNTON said, You William and you, abbat, keep your days at three weeks of Easter, and you eleven &c. the same day, and let the twelfth remain without day &c.

Cosinage. § Edmund Castelyn brought the writ against Thomas Corbet, and counted of the seisin of John his cousin &c., and that from John the fee and the demesne resorted to Geoffrey as cousin, he being brother of Denise mother of Roger father of John; and that from Geoffrey it descended to Edmund as son &c. And Thomas formerly had prayed aid of the king, and he put forward the king's charter which witnessed that the tenements demanded, after the death of John &c., came into the hands of the king, as his escheat for default of blood, and that the king had restored those tenements to Thomas as next heir of John: and notwithstanding the royal charter it was adjudged that Thomas should answer over: and this without consulting the king. — *Toudeby.* He demands the tenements as cousin and heir of John, and for us it is sufficient to affirm our estate in the tenancy; then since the king testifies by his deed that we are heir to John, and the tenements &c. as heir &c. restored to us, we pray judgment &c.—This was not allowed.—*Toudeby.* He can not make a resort in the blood of Denise, for these tenements were at a certain time in the seisin of Reymond de Luke, who held them in chief of the king; from Reymond they descended to Isabel as daughter &c., which Isabel Roger married; so that Roger never had anything but as husband of Isabel; from Isabel they descended to John, and we pray judgment if anything in these tenements ought to resort in the blood of Denise; for that blood is totally foreign to this heritage.—*Passeley.* These tenements were the right of Roger, ready &c.—*Toudeby.* Still your answer is not full; say if Roger and Maud after him had any-service nostre seignour le Roi destresce ne cursit. Et A.D. 1306. super hoc, justiciariis diu consultis, STANTONE. Vous Willeam, e vous abbe, gardez vos jours a treis semeines de Pasche, e vous .xi. &c. meme le jour, e le .xiime remeigne sanz jour &c.

§ Edmound Castelyn porta le bref vers Thomas Corbet, e conta de la seisine Johan sun cosin &c., de Johan resorti le fee e le demene a Geffrey come a cosin, frere Dyonise mere Roger pere Johan; de Geffrey descendi a Emon come a fiz &c. Et Thomas autrefoiz avoit prie aide du Roi, e mist avant la chartre le Roi qe testmoigna qe les tenements demandes apres la mort Johan &c. devyendrent en la mayn le Roi com sa eschete par defaute de saunke, e qe le Roi avoit mesmes ceux tenements renduz a Thomas com a prochein heir Johan: et non obstante illa litera regia fust agarde qe Thomas respondesit outre, R[ege] super hoc inconsulto.—*Toudeby.* Il demaunde ces tenements come cosin e heir Johan, e a nous suffit nostre estat affermer en la tenance; dount del houre qe le Roi nous testmoigne par sun fet estre heir Johan, e les tenements &c. com heir &c. nous rendi, demandoms jugement &c.: nec allocatur. — *Toudeby.* En le saunke Dyonise ne puet il resort faire, car ces tenements furent en ascon temps en la seisine Reymond de Luke qe ces tenementz tient en chief du Roy; de Reymond descendi a Isabele come a fille &c., la quel Isabele Roges esposa, issi qe Roges rien ne avoit mes com baroun Isabele; de Isabele descendi a Johan; e demandoms jugement si de ces tenementz en le saunke Dyonyse deyve renz resortir, qe cel saunke est tut estraunge a ceste heritage. — *Passeley.* Ces tenements furent le droit Roges, prest &c. — *Toudeby.* Uncore nest pas vostre respons plein; dites si Reymond e Maude apres luy avoient

Cosinage.

A.D. 1306. thing or not. And although it were as you say, yet you do not show that the tenements ought to resort in the blood of Denise.--*Passeley.* These tenements were &c. the right of Roger, and Roger inherited them, without Isabel, of whom you speak, having anything therein except as wife of Roger, ready &c.—*Toudeby.* Still you do not answer sufficiently; for we defeat your resort, and you do not maintain it at all, nor do you say anything to show why these tenements ought to resort in the blood of Denise; wherefore &c.; and for affirming our estate, we say that the king was seised and gave to Reymond; and in this case we are pleading for the king, for if we should lose, he would recompense us in value &c.; wherefore &c.--*Passeley.* The tenements &c. were the right of Denise, and from her descended to Roger, and from Roger to John, ready &c.—*Toudeby.* Had not Reymond anything? I will aver my statement by the rolls of the Chancery, and if it can not be sufficiently averred by those, ready to aver it by the country.—*Passeley.* I have nothing to do with him.—BEREFORD confirmed this.—On another day *Toudeby* said, We will aver by record of the Chancery that King Henry was seised and gave to Reymond who was seised, after whose death the right descended &c. to Isabel as daughter, from Isabel to John as son, of which John the blood failed, wherefore the present king for default of the blood was, as chief lord, seised of the tenements as his escheat, out of whose seisin we have the same tenements, and now we are to plead as if the tenements were in the king's seisin; and we pray judgment, since he does not deny that King Henry was seised thereof &c., and gave them to Reymond from whom the right lineally descended to John, if he can make any resort in the blood of Denise.--*Friskeney.* The tenements descended to John through Roger whose heritage &c., and not through Isabel, ready &c.--BEREFORD. What answer you to their statement that King Henry was seised and gave &c. to Reymond?—*Friskeney.* It is rien ou noun. Idem; e tut fust il issi come vous dites, uncore ne mustrez point qe les tenements devoient resortir en le saunk Dyonise.—*Passeley.* Ces tenements &c. le droit Roges, e Roges de ces enherite, sanz ceo qe Isabele de qi vous parlez rien en out mes come femme Roges, prest &c.—*Toudeby.* Uncore ne responez pas assez; qar nous defessomes vostre resort e vous ne le meintenez nent, ne riens ne dites pur quei ces tenements deivent en le saunk Dionise resortir; par quei &c.; e en affermant nostre estat, dioms qe le Roi fust seisi e dona a Reymond, e pur le Roi en ceo cas pledoms, qar si nous perdissoms il nous freit a la value &c.; par quei &c.—*Passeley.* Les tenements &c. furent le droit Dyonise e de luy descendirent a Roges, e de Roges a Johan, prest &c.—*Toudeby.* Ne avoit Reymond rienz? jeo voille averer mon dit par roulles de la Chauncelerie, e si par ces assez ne purra estre avere, prest del averer par pays.—*Passeley.* Jeo nay qe faire de luy.—Bereford hoc affirmavit.—*Toudeby,* ad alium diem. Nous voloms averer par record de la Chancelerie qe le Roi Henri fust seisi, e dona a Reymond qe devya seisi, apres qi mort descendi &c. a Isabele come a fille, de Isabele a Johan come a fiz, a queu Johan le saunk failly, par quei le Roi qe ore est, en defaute de saunk, ses tenements seisi com chief seignour e com sa eschete, hors de qi seisine nous avoms mesmes les tenements; e ore sumes a pleder auxi come les tenements fuissount en la seisine le Roi; e demaundoms jugement, de pus qil ne dedit point qe le Roi Henri en fu seisi &c., e dona a Reymond de qi linealiter descendi a Johan, sil puisse nul resort en le saunk Dyonise faire—*Friskeney.* Les tenements descendirent a Johan par my Roges qi heritage &c., e noun pas par my Isabele, prest &c.—Bereford. Quei responez vous a ceo qe eux dient qe le Roi Henri fust seisi e dona &c. a Reymond?—*Fris-* A.D. 1306.

A.D. 1306. not for us to take cognizance of the estate of Reymond; it is sufficient for us to maintain our action; and we will aver that Denise was seised &c., after whose death it descended to Roger and from Roger to John.—BEREFORD. At what time was Denise seised? After the seisin of King Henry or before? for since we find that King Henry was seised and gave, we will not defeat that obstacle which he alleges against you, and by those evidences, unless you say something else.—*Friskeney*. We tell you that King Henry was seised, and gave to Reymond; Reymond enfeoffed &c. Denise; from Denise who died seised it descended to Roger, and from Roger to John.—*Toudeby*. Now we pray judgment for the king; since you have admitted that Reymond held in chief of the king &c., and you say that of these tenements he enfeoffed Denise, without showing a deed by the king giving him license to do this, we pray judgment.—HENGHAM. Why could he not enfeoff? Was he not seised in his demesne as of fee? — *Toudeby*. If the heir of Reymond had got seisin of these tenements, and they were to demand them against him on the seisin of their ancestor Denise, and it was admitted on both sides that Reymond being tenant in chief of the king enfeoffed Denise without the king's license, that enfeoffment would be of no value, nor would it give any estate to Denise &c.

Quid juris. § John Gerberge brought the writ against one J. &c., to acknowledge what right &c. in those tenements, of which tenements Roger de Boys had granted to the said John the reversion after the death of J. &c.; and J. came and said by *Lanfar* that she claimed a fee in those tenements.—*Passeley*. By what title?—*Lanfar*. She has no need to answer to that; she was made to come here to acknowledge what right &c., and she has acknowledged, so she has nothing more to do. — BEREFORD. There are forty fools here who think that as soon as one has in such a case acknowledged, there is nothing more *keney*. A nous nest pas a conustre del estat Reymond; il nous suffit a meyntenir nostre accion; e voloms averer qe Dyonise fust seisi &c., apres qi mort descendi a Roges, de Roges a Johan.—BEREFORD. En queux temps fust Dionise seisie? apres la seisine le Roi Henri ou avant? qe de pus qe nous trovoms qe le Roi Henri fust seisi e dona, nous ne defroms pas cele obstacle qil alegge contre vous, e par celes evidences, sanz ceo qe vous diez altre chose.—*Friskeney*. Nous vous dioms qe le Roi Henri fust seisi, e dona a Reymond; Reymond enfeffa &c. Dionise; Deonise devya seisie, descendi a Roges, de Roges a Johan.—*Toudeby*. Ore demandoms jugement pur le Roi; de pus ke vous avez conu ke Reymond tient en chief du Roi &c., e dites qil de ces tenements enfeffa Dionise sanz moustrer fet du Roi qe ceo fere conge luy donast; demandoms jugement.—HENGHAM. Pur quei ne poeit il feffer? ne fust il seisi en sun demene com de fee?—*Toudeby*. Si le heir Reymond est happe seisine de ces tenements, e eus fussent a demander les vers luy e de la seisine lour auncestre Dionise, e conu fust de ambepars qe Reymond tenant en chief du Roi enfeffa Dionise sanz conge le Roi, cel feffement serreit de nule value, ne nul estat ne durreit a Dionise &c. A.D. 1306

§ Johan Gerberge le porta vers une J. &c., a conustre quel droit &c. en teux tenements, des queux tenements Roger de Boys a mesme celui Johan avoit la reversion graunte apres le deces J. &c.: e J. vient e dist par *Lanfare* qe ele clama en ces tenements fee &c.—*Passeley*. Par quel title?—*Lanfare*. A ceo nad ele mestier a respondre; ele est fete venir a conustre quel droit &c., e ele ad conue, dount ele ad nent plus a faire.—BEREFORD. Iluy sunt xl. fous seinz qe quident qe a plus tost qe homme eit en teu cas conu qil ny est nent plus Quid juris.

A.D. 1306. to do, although the tenant claim an estate other than that which he has; this would be a great hardship: (to *Lanfar*) Answer, by what title do you claim the fee?—*Lanfar.* Roger de Boys released and quit-claimed &c. to us and our heirs for ever, by this deed &c., in our seisin, before the grant &c.—*Passeley.* At the time when he granted to us you held in dower without his then having released to you &c., ready &c.—And the other side said the contrary.—So &c.

Quid juris.

§ William de Ingwardeby and Aubrey his wife were made to come to acknowledge what right they claimed in the view of frankpledge, three messuages &c., which tenements one Aleyn had granted to R. by fine &c.—*Tiltone.* We claim a tenancy for the term of our two lives, and we tell you that we ought not to attorn &c.; for this same Aleyn before he made this grant to R. gave two pence of rent to one Alein his son, and granted the reversion of these things to him, on which grant we attorned to Alein the son of Alein, and we pray judgment &c.—*Herle.* It is fit that you say that the attornment on the grant made to Alein son of Alein was made before the grant made to us.—*Toudeby.* So we say.—*Passeley.* The acknowledgment and the grant were made on such a day &c., on which day they held for term of life of Aleyn the elder without having attorned to any other person, ready &c.—So &c.

Monstraverunt for men of the ancient demesne.

§ B. C. and D. &c. brought the writ against the abbat of Tyntern.—*Malmesthorpe.* Show unto you &c. the abbat's men of the manor of Acle which is of the ancient demesne of the crown of our lord the King, that the abbat of Tyntern &c. tortiously demands of them other customs and other services than they ought to do and than their ancestors tenants of the said manor were used to do in the time when the said manor of Acle was in the hands of your progenitors Kings of England. And for that whereas each one of them sepaa faire, tut cleime le tenant autre estat qil nad; a ceo serreit graunt duresce. IDEM a *Lanfare*. Responez par quel title clamez vous fee.—*Lanfare*. Roger de Boys nous relessa e quiteclama &c. a nous e a nos heirs a touz jours par ceo fet &c. en nostre seisine avaunt le graunt &c.—*Passeley*. A tens qil nous graunta e vous tenistes &c. en dowere, sanz ceo qil adonqes vous eust relesse &c., prest &c.—Et alii e contra.—Ideo &c. A.D. 1306.

§ Willeam de Ingwardeby e Aubrey sa femme furent fetz venir a conustre queu dreit il clamerent en la vewe de franc plegges, treis mes &c., queux tenements un Aleyn avoit graunte a R. par fin &c.—*Tiltone*. Nous clamoms tenance a terme de nos deus vies, e vous dioms qe attourner ne devoms &c., qar mesme cestui Alein avant ceo qil fist ceo graunt a R., dona une darre de rente a un Alein sun fiz, e de cestes choses lui graunta la reversion, par quel graunt nous atturnames a Alein le fiz Alein, e demandoms jugement &c.—*Herle*. Il vous covendra dire qe par my le graunt fet a Alein le fiz Alein le atturnement se fist avant le grant fet a nous.—*Toudeby*. Ensi dioms nous.—*Passeley*. La conissance e le grant se fist seins a teu jour &c., a quel jour il tiendrent a terme de vie de Aleyn leygne sanz estre atturne a nul autre, prest &c. Ideo &c. Quid juris.

§ B. C. D. &c. porterent le bref vers labbe de Tynterne—*Marmesthorpe*. Ceo vous moustre &c. hommes le abbe du maner de Acle qest del aunciene demene de la corone nostre seignour le Roi, qe le abbe de Tynterne &c. atort lour demaunde autres coustumes e autres services qe fere deyent e lour auncestres tenant de mesme le maner fere soleient au temps qe le dit maner de Acle fust en meins de vos progenitours Rois dEngleterre. E pur ceo qe la ou chescon de eux Monstraverunt pro hominibus de antiquo dominico.

A.D. 1306. rately holds of the said abbat one messuage and eight acres of land within the said manor by these services, (and he named the services) and ought not to do, neither were their ancestors &c. used to do, any other service in the time of &c. Kings of England, that is to say in the time of King William the Conqueror &c., this same abbat, besides these services, demands of them the redemption of flesh and blood &c., and to compel them to it he distreins them &c., so that they can not till their land; so the said B. &c. on such a day in such a year at such a place and in the presence of &c. delivered to him the Prohibition of our lord the King, and forbad him &c.; but he for that did not leave off distreining them as before, tortiously and against the Prohibition &c., and to their damage &c. — *Toudeby* denied tort and force, and as to its being against the Prohibition &c., and will deny &c.; and we tell you that they ought not to be answered, for they are our vileins, and we were seised of them &c. on the day when the writ &c. — *Hunt.* Are we of the ancient demesne or not, and so of those to whom recovery is given by this writ? — *Toudeby.* That is no business of mine. Certify the court if you can that you are of the ancient demesne, to affirm your estate. — *Kingesham.* We will send to the Exchequer to find out in Domesday.—And when this was done it was found by the Domesday that they were not of the ancient demesne &c. — So it was adjudged by HENGHAM that they should take nothing by their writ &c. And note that in this plea it was found that the entry in Domesday was "Acle; earl so and so holds," and that the manor afterwards fell into the King's hands. On that account HALES thought that it was of the ancient demesne.—BEREFORD. Nay, there are a hundred manors in the land which have been in the King's hands by escheat, which are not of the ancient demesne; I have seen a manor fall twice by escheat into the King's hands &c.

aparly entent del dit abbe un mies viii. acres de terre denz mesme le maner par teux services, et nominavit servicia, e autres services faire ne deveient ne lour auncestres &c. fere soleyent, au temps &c. Rois dEngleterre, cest a saver au temps le Roi William le Conquerour &c., mesme celuy abbe, estre ces services, lour demande redempcion de chare de saunke &c., e a ceo fere lour destreint &c., issi qe eux ne pount lour terre gaigner; dount mesmes ceux B. &c. tiel jour, tiel an, tiel leu, e en la presence de teux, lui liverent la prohibicion nostre seignour le Roi e luy defendirent &c.; il purceo ne lessa qil ne lour destreignast come avant, a tort e encontre la prohibicion &c., e a lour damage &c.—*Toudeby* defendi tort e force e quant qe est encontre la prohibicion &c., e defendra &c., e vous dioms qe eux ne deivent estre respondu, qar eux sunt nos vileyns, e nous seisi de eux &c. le jour du bref &c. — *Hunte.* Sumes nous del aunciene demene ou noun, a queux rescoverir est done par cesti bref?—*Toudeby.* Ceo nest mie a moy, acertez vous la court si vous poez qe vous estes del aunciene demene en affermant vostre estat.—*Kingesham.* Nous manderoms al Eschekere pur quere en le Domesday. Et hoc facto, inventum est par le Domesday illos non extitisse de antiquo &c. Ideo consideratum est per HENGHAM quod nil capiant per breve &c. Et memorandum qe en ceo plee fust trove en le Domesday sic, "Acle talis comes "tenet," e qe cel maner pus fust cheu en la main le Roi.—HALES pur ceo entendi qe ceo eust este aunciene demene. — BEREFORD. Nay, iluy sunt cent maners en la terre qe ount este en la main le Roi escheux qe ne sunt pas del aunciene demene; qe jeo ay veu un maner par deus fez par eschete cheir en la mayn le Roi &c. A.D. 1306.

A.D. 1306.
Debt.

§ A writ of Debt was brought against a man and his wife.—*Wescote.* The demand is for a chattel, and supposes that the property in a chattel may be in the wife during the life of her husband, which the law does not allow; judgment. And they might have had a good writ naming the man, and might have counted of the delivery to the woman if such had been the case.—And notwithstanding this, he answered over, but not by judgment.

When the vouchee has nothing but a fee-tail &c.

§ The tenant in a plea of Dower vouched to warranty the heir of the husband of the woman.—*Hunt* (for the vouchee). We warrant as heir in blood &c., and we render &c.; but we ought not to recompence to the value, for nothing has descended to us except in fee tail by the form of this charter; judgment &c.—*Hampton.* Assets have descended to you, ready &c.—BEREFORD. Other than these tenements named in the charter?—*Hampton.* Yes, Sir.—*Hunt.* Where and in what vill?—*Hampton* named the vill.—*Hunt.* The contrary.—So &c.

Where the debtor came by the great distress.

§ In a plea of Debt, *Hunt*, for the defendant, to avoid damages, said that before the purchase of the writ, and often since, he had tendered to the plaintiff the debt, and he again tendered the money at the bar.—MALORE. You come into court by the great distress, and so, as it appears, against your will; now if the truth be as you state, why did not you come on the first day &c.? And he adjudged damages &c. to the plaintiff.

Entry.

Where a tenant under age had the view, and notwithstanding this had the view when he came of age.

§ A writ of Entry was brought against an infant under age, who came &c. and prayed the view &c.; and at another day he came and said that his father died seised of those tenements, after whose death he entered &c., and he prayed his age, and he had it &c.; and the parol demurred without day &c. And now, being of full age, he was resummoned, and came.—*Kingesham.* &c. the

§ Qe bref de dette fust porte vers un home e sa femme.—*Wescote.* La demande est de chatel, e suppose qe proprete de chatel puisse estre a la femme vivant sun baroun, qe nest pas suffrable de ley; jugement; e il poeint aver eu bon bref a nomer le prodhomme meme, e aver conte du baille la femme, si le cas ust este tel. Et hoc non obstante il respondy outre, sed non per judicium. A.D. 1306. Nota de debito.

§ Le tenant en play de dowere voucha a garant le heir le baroun la femme.—*Hunte* (pro vocato,) Nous garantoms come heir du saunk &c., e rendoms &c.; mes a la vaillance ne devoms faire, qe rienz nous est descenduz si noun a tenir par la forme de ceste chartre en fee taille; jugement &c.—*Hamptone.* Assez vous est descendu, prest &c. — BEREFORD. Autres qe ces tenements nomez en la chartre?—*Hamptone.* Oil, Sire. —*Hunte.* Ou e en quele ville?—*Hamptone* nominavit villam.—*Hunte.* Contra.—Ideo &c. Ubi vocatus nil habet nisi feodum talliatum &c.

§ En un play de dette, *Hunte,* pur le defendant, pur esturtre des damages, dist qe avant le bref purchace e puis sovent avoit il tendue au pleintif la dette, e uncore tendi les deners a la barre.—MALLORE. Vous venez en court par la graunte destresse, e issi, a ceo qil piert, encontre vostre volunte; dount si vostre verite soit tele, qe ne ussez venuz au primer jour &c.; e agarda damages &c. au pleintif. Ubi debitor venit per magnam districtionem &c.

Ubi tenens infra etatem habuit visum, et hoc non obstante habuit visum cum ad etatem pervenit. Entre.

§ Un bref dentre fust porte vers un enfant denz age, qe vient &c. e demanda la vewe &c., e a un autre jour vient e dist qe sun pere morust seisi de ces tenements, apres qi mort il entra &c., e pria sun age &c. et habuit &c.; e la parole demorra sanz jour &c. Et ore fust il resumons de plein age, e vient.—*King.* &c. la vewe &c. — *Passeley.* Vous laviez. —

A.D. 1300. view &c.—*Passeley.* You have had it.—*Kingesham.* The parol demurred without day by reason of our nonage, and then we were resummoned, after which resummons we never had the view, and we cannot take cognizance of the previous time, for we were under age.—HOWARD. Then will you say that you had the view, but were then under age, wherefore &c.?—*Kingesham.* I do not admit it, for I have no cognizance of that time.—*Passeley.* By statute,[1] if you had had the View in another writ which had abated, you would not have it in this, therefore a fortiori if once in this writ &c. you shall not have it again.—*War.* The court was deceived. Can a guardian ask the view? (intimating that he could not).—And, by HOWARD's order, he had the view.

Quid juris. Where the tenant would not acknowledge &c., and so was committed to the Fleet gaol.

§ William of Cambridge heretofore brought the writ against Walter de Risle and his wife &c., to acknowledge what right &c. in certain tenements in Scheltone, of which tenements John de Croxton had granted to him the reversion; they came, and the wife of Walter de Risle claimed the fee simple; and William wished to join an averment with them that she had not &c. but for the term of life. And because the court was not then advised that an averment could be joined between them by that judicial writ, it was adjudged that Walter and his wife should go without day. And William anew sued the Quid juris out of the note, returnable now.—*Herle.* On another such writ which issued by that note we went without day; wherefore we do not think that in this we are bound to claim or to disclaim. And on the other hand, this matter does not set out by a good process; for since the note once reposed without continuance of process, if it is to be resumed, John de Croxtone,

---

[1] 13 Ed. I. (Westm. 2.) c. 48.

Kingesham. La parole remist sanz jour pur nostre noun-age, e pus fumes resomons, apres quele resumons nous ne aveymes onqes la vewe, e du temps avant nous ne poms conustre, qar nous esteoms denz age.—HOWARD. Donqes volez vous dire qe vous aviez la vewe, mes adonqes vous fustes denz age, par quei &c.—*Kingesham.* Jeo ne le grant mie, qe jeo nay conissance de ceu temps.—*Passeley.* Par statut si vous eussez eu la Vewe en un autre bref qe ust abatu vous ne la averiez mie en cestui: ergo per locum a majore, si une foiz en ceo bref &c. vous ne la averez mie autrefoiz.—*War.* La court fust deceu; purra gardein demander la vewe? quasi diceret nay. Et habuit visum per HOWARD. A.D. 1306.

Ubi tenens noluit cognoscere &c. Ideo committebatur gaole de Flete. Quid juris.

§ Willeam de Cantebruge autrefoiz porta le bref vers Wauter de Risle e sa femme &c., a conustre queu droit &c. en certein tenements en Scheltone, des queux tenements Johan de Croxtone luy avoit grante la reversion; qe adonqe viendrent, e la femme Wauter de Risle clama fee simple; e Willem voleit ove eux averement joint qele nout &c. mes qe a terme de vie. E pur ceo qe adonqes a la court ne estoit pas avis qe tiel averement par ceo bref de jugement entre eux point [poieit?] joindre, fust agarde qe Wauter e sa femme alassent sanz jour &c. Et Willem derechief suist le Quid juris hors de la note, a ore retournable.—*Herle.* A un autre tel bref qe issi par cele note nous alames sanz jour; par quei nentendoms point qe a cestui seoms tenuz a clamer ou desclamer. E dautre parte, ceste chose ne se vest mie par bon proces; qar de pus qe la note une foiz repose sanz continuance de proces, si ele devoit estre resume, Johan de Croxtone, qe a

A.D. 1306. who is party to that note, should be summoned or warned and he is not; wherefore &c.—BEREFORD. The judgment given was not final, nor did it defeat the estate of William: for I have seen a note sleep five years, and yet out of that one has sued a Quid juris. And so it may be where the tenant who should acknowledge at the time of the grant is under age.—On another day they were asked by the court what right they claimed &c.—*Herle* would not further answer for them, because the truth was that they had nothing &c. but for the term of the woman's life, and formerly they had claimed the fee; wherefore to claim now a term for life &c. seemed to him to be a dangerous thing; nor would Walter and his wife answer anything else than that they had formerly claimed in a writ which issued out of that note and had gone without day, wherefore &c. And they were asked by the court what right &c., and they would not answer; wherefore they were committed to the Fleet. And after the rising of the justices they were mainprised until the morrow; and on the morrow they came and claimed only for the term of the woman's life, and they both attorned and did fealty.

Dum non fuit compos mentis.

Case where he in whose person the fee and the right &c. prayed to be received &c.

§ One Ralph, while he was not of sound mind &c., gave certain tenements to one Piers and Agnes his wife, to have and to hold to them and to their heirs in fee simple. Piers survived Agnes, and was ousted from the tenements by Hugh de Courtney, in whose seisin Ralph the first donor released and quit-claimed &c. Hugh enfeoffed &c. William de Braumpton. William re-enfeoffed Piers and one Emma his wife, to have and to hold to Piers and Emma and the heirs of Emma. Emma died without heir of her body; Piers held the freehold; the right descended to Alice as sister of Emma; and from Alice to William her cousin, as son &c. And now comes cele note est partie, serreit sumons ou garny, ou il nest pas, par quei &c. BEREFORD. Le jugement qe se fist ne fust pas final, ne defet pas lestat Willem; qe jeo ay veu une note dormir cink anz, e uncore hors de cele hom ad suy le Quid juris. Et sic potuit esse ubi tenens qui cognosceret tempore concessionis est infra etatem.—A un autre jour demande lour fust par la court quel droit il clama &c.—*Herle* noluit ulterius pro eis respondere, pur ceo qe la verite fust qe eux ne avoient rienz &c. mes qe a terme de la vie la femme, e autre foiz avoient clame fee; par quei a clamer ore a terme de vie &c. iluy sembloit perilleuse chose; ne les avantdiz Wauter e sa femme autre chose ne voleient respondre, mes qe eus disoient qe autre foiz avoient eux clame par bref qe issit hors de cele note e alerent sanz jour, par quei &c. Et eux furent sovent demandez par la court quel droit &c., e eux ne voleient respondre; par quei eux furent commis a Flete. Et apres le lever des justices meinpris tant qe lendemain; e viendrent lendemain e clamerent mes qe a terme de la vie la femme, e se atturnerent e fessoient fealte ambedeux. A.D 1306.

Casus ubi ille in cujus persona feodum et jus &c. petiit admitti &c. Dum non fuit compos mentis, &c.

§ Un Rauf, dum non fuit compos mentis &c., dona certeinz tenementz a un Perys e Agnes sa femme a aver e a tenir a eux e a lour heirs simplement. Peres survesqui Agnes, e fust de mesmes les tenements oste par Hughe de Corteney, en qi seisine Rauf le primer donour relessa e quiteclama &c. Hughe enfeffa &c. Willem de Braumptone. Willem refeffa Piers e une Emme sa femme, a aver e a tenir a Peres e a Emme e a les heirs Emme; Emme devya sanz heir de sun corps; Peres tient le franc tenement; le droit descendi a Alice come a soere Emme; de Alice a Willem cosin come a fiz &c. Et ore vient le fiz Rauf le primer

A.D. 1306. the son of Ralph the first donor, and brings a writ of Dum non fuit compos mentis &c. And *Piers* said that he (Ralph) was of sound memory, ready &c.—THE INQUEST said that Ralph was not of sound memory; and thereupon came William, cousin and heir of Emma, in whose person the fee &c., and prayed to be received &c., and said that at a certain time the tenements were in the seisin of William de Braumpton, who thereof enfeoffed Piers and Emma, to have and to hold to Piers and Emma and the heirs of Emma; and he said that he was the heir of Emma, and as Piers had nothing in the tenements except for term of life, and wished to lose them, he prayed to be received &c.—*Lanfar.* You ought not to be received; it would abate our writ; and we have pleaded to the Inquest with Piers, and the Inquest has passed, and we pray judgment on the verdict &c.—*Kingesham* (on the same side). William de Braumpton is not in the degrees of the entry; wherefore on the strength of his deed you shall not be received.—BEREFORD. If you, on what you state, were received, that would be to defeat their writ and action and whatever they have, and that by the deed of William de Braumpton who is out of the degrees already affirmed by the Inquest; and perchance it may be that Ralph while not of sound memory enfeoffed Piers, and afterwards, because Piers thought his estate was weak, enfeoffed &c. William de Braumpton, and afterwards William de Braumptone re-enfeoffed them by that charter &c., and so under cover of that trick you wish now to be received: now it would be different if Emma the wife of Piers had prayed to be received, for she was party to that deed: wherefore on no account shall you be received.—*Friskeney.* We tell you that Piers had no estate in those tenements on the day of the purchase of the writ unless by the gift of William de Braumpton, by this charter, jointly &c.—BEREFORD. It may still be by such fraudulent feoffments, as I have said.—*Friskeney.* We will tell

donour e porte bref "dum non fuit compos mentis &c." A.D. 1306.
Et *Peres* dit qil fust de seyne memorie, prest &c.—LENQUESTE dit qe Rauf ne fust pas de seyn memorie; e sur ceo vient Willem, cosin e heir Emme[1] en qi persone le fee &c., e pria estre receu &c., e dit qe ces tenements furent en ascon temps en la seisine Willem de Braumptone, qi de ces enfeffa Pieres e Emme, a aver e tenir a Peres e a Emme e a les heirs Emme; e dist qil fust heir Emme, e coment qe Peres rienz navoit en ces tenements si noun a terme de vie e les voleit perdre, il pria estre receu &c.—*Lanfare.* Receu ne devez estre, qe serreit de abatre nostre bref, e nous avoms plede al enqueste ove Peres, e lenqueste est passe, e prioms jugement sur le verdit &c.—*Kinge.* (ad idem). Willem de Braumptone nest mie en les degres del entre; par quei par force de sun fet ne serrez receu.—BEREFORD. Si vous, sur ceo qe vous dites, fuissez receu, ceo serreit a defere lour bref e accion; e quant qe il ont, e ceo par le fet Willem de Braumptone qest hors de les degrez ia affermez par enqueste; e poeit estre par cas qe Rauf, nent de seyne memorie, enfeffa Peres, e puis, pur ceo qe le dit Peres entendi sun estat estre febles, enfeffa &c. Willem de Braumptone, e puis Willem de Braumptone lour refeffa solom cele chartre &c., e issi suz la coverture de ceste faucyne voillez ore estre receu; dount uncore autre serreit si Emme la femme Peres ust prie estre receu, qe ele fust partie a ceo fet; par quei par nule verite ne serrez receu.—*Friskeney* Nous vous dioms ke Peres ne avoit nul estat en ces tenements le jour du bref purchace si noun par le doun Willem de Braumptone, par ceste chartre, joynt &c.—BEREFORD. Ceo poeit estre uncore par teus faus feffementz com jeo ay dit.—*Friskeney.*

[1] MS. Maude.

A.D. 1306. you the truth: Ralph enfeoffed Piers and Agnes &c. to them and theirs in fee simple; Piers survived and was ousted by Hugh de Courtney, to whom, in his seisin &c., Ralph released and quit-claimed; Hugh enfeoffed William de Braumpton, and William enfeoffed Piers and Emma, whose heir we are, by that charter &c. And see here that quit-claim which Ralph made to Hugh, and the charter which Hugh made to William de Braumpton.—BEREFORD. In God's name! now this is good; now you counterplead them in the degrees by the quit-claim &c.—*Kingesham.* Still, he shall not be received; for if Piers would have vouched William de Braumpton out of the degrees, he would not have been received thereto, since he had admitted the degrees; no more shall he be now received, by the deed of one who is out of the degrees, and so affirmed by the Inquest; wherefore &c.—BEREFORD. Piers might have traversed the entry and thereupon have joined the averment; and although he had done so and the Inquest had passed against him, yet William the cousin would be in the state in which he is now, and now he is pleading in the degrees, by the quit-claim; wherefore if you do not know how to say anything else, he shall be received.—And he was received, and the quit-claim was denied &c.—So &c.

Formedon in the descender. § Ralph de Grenham brought the writ against A., and the writ ran thus, "which R. &c. gave to Ralph de " Grenham and Mabel his wife and to the heirs of the " bodies of the said R. and M. issuing, and which after " the deaths of the said Ralph & Mabel and Peter son " of the said Ralph and Mabel, to the said Ralph son of " the said Peter and cousin and heir of the said Ralph " and Mabel, ought to descend &c."—*Roistone.* Judgment of the form of the writ; for this action is given wholly to the heir lineal, whereas it makes Ralph heir collateral; so the writ ought to have said "and which, " after the deaths of Ralph and Mabel and Peter son and " heir of the said &c., to the said Ralph son and heir of

Nous vous dirroms la verite: Rauf enfeffa Peres e Agnes &c. a eux e a lour heirs simplement; Perys survesqui e fust oste par Hughe de Corteney, a qi Rauf, de qi seisine &c., relessa e quiteclama: Hughe feffa Willem de Braumptone, e Willem Peres e Emme, qi heirs nous sumes, par cele chartre &c. Et veez icy cele quiteclamanz qe Rauf fist a Hughe, e la chartre qe Hughe fist a Willem de Braumptone.—BEREFORD. Noun Deu! ore est bien: ore les contre pledez vous en les degrez par la quiteclamanz &c.—*Kingesham.* Uncore ne serra il receu; qar si Peres voleit aver vouche Willem de Braumptone hors de les degrez, il ne ust mie este receu, del houre qil avoit grante les degreez; nent plus ne serra il a ore receu par le fet un qe est hors de les degreez par enqueste affermez; par quei &c.—BEREFORD. Peres poeit aver traverse lentre, e sur ceo joint le averement; e tut ust il issi fee, e enqueste ust chante contre luy, uncore serreit Willem cosin en lestat qil est ore, e ore plede il en les degrez par la quiteclamanz; par quei si vous ne sachez autre chose dire il serra receu. E fust receu, e la quiteclamanz dedite &c.—Ideo &c. A.D. 1306.

§ Rauf de Grenham porta le bref vers A., et fuit breve tale "quæ R. &c. dedit Radolfo de Grenham et "Mabillæ uxori sue et heredibus de corporibus ipsorum "R. et M. exeuntibus, et quæ post mortem prædictorum "Radulfi et Mabillæ et Petri filii eorumdem Radulfi et "Mabillæ prefato Radulfo filio predicti Petri et consan-"guineo et heredi predictorum Radulfi et Mabillæ "descendere debent &c."—*Roistone.* Jugement de la forme du bref; qar ceste accion est done enterement al heir lineal, ou il fet Rauf heir collateral; dount le bref devoit dire issi, "Et quæ post mortem Radulfi et "Mabillæ et Petri filii et heredis eorumdem &c. prefato

Forma donacionis en le descendre.

A.D. 1306. "the said Peter, and cousin &c." and so have made him heir to Ralph and Mabel lineally.—And notwithstanding this, HENGHAM and STAUNTON adjudged that the writ was in good form, and of a better form than that given by *Roistone;* because it is sufficient to call the demandant the heir of those on whose seisin he demands &c.

Ael, where a tenant claimed nothing in the freehold.

§ The writ was brought against three persons by several præcipes: two of them denied the seisin of the grandfather. — *Stapilford* (for the third). We do not claim anything in the freehold nor had we anything on the day when the writ was purchased; but we hold these tenements at the will of one T. &c.; judgment of the writ.—*Willuby.* Tenant of the freehold on the day when the writ was purchased, ready &c. — *Stapilford.* Nay, purchase a writ against the tenant of the freehold; I can not join any averment in respect of these tenements. —*Willuby.* Perchance Thomas when he shall come would give a like answer, and so ad infinitum; and by God! the bishop of London was the other day received to that answer.—*Friskeney.* If you do not fear what he claims in the freehold, then put yourself in possession.—*Willuby.* Nay, I can not, for I have no power to do so.—BEREFORD withdrew with HENGHAM and STAUNTON [and said to them], I saw a writ &c. brought against one T. &c., and T. said that he claimed nothing in the freehold but that he held at will of the dean and chapter of &c.; the demandant said that he was tenant of the freehold on the day when the writ &c., and thereupon they joined the averment, which passed for the demandant, and he recovered seissin; and thereupon the dean and chapter &c. brought the assise of novel disseisin and recovered.—BEREFORD to *Willuby.* The way which he offers to you is worth more than that which you wish to have; nevertheless that which you ask I have seen received, and thereby many fine tenements have been lost.

"Radulfo filio et heredi predicti Petri et con- A.D. 1306.
"sanguineo &c.," e issi lui ust il fet heir Rauf e Mabille linealiter. Et, hoc non obstante, le bref fust agarde de bone forme e de meillour forme qe Roistone ne dona, par HENGHAM e STANTONE, quia sufficit petenti nominare heredem illorum de cujus seisina petit &c.

Ael ou un tenant ne clama rens en le franc tenement.

§ Le bref fust porte vers treis par divers precipes; les deus dedissoient la seisine le ael.—*Stapilford*, pur le tierz, Nous ne clamoms rienz en le franc tenement ne riens ne avioms le jour du bref purchace, einz ces tenements tenoms a la volente un T. &c.; jugement du bref.—*Willuby*. Tenant du franc tenement le jour du bref purchace, prest &c. — *Stapilford*. Nay, purchasez vous bref vers le tenant du franc tenement; jeo ne puisse de ceux tenements nul averement joyndre. — *Willuby*. Au teu respons durreit Thomas par cas quant il vendreit, e issi usque in infinitum; e par Deu! leveske de Londres fust lautre jour receu a tel respons. —*Friskeney*. Si vous ne crossez qi cleime en le franc tenement, mettez vous leinz donqes. — *Willuby*. Nay, jeo ne puisse mie, qar jeo ne sui mie de poer.—BEREFORD se retret a HENGHAM e STANTONE. Jeo vy qe en bref &c. fut porte vers un T. &c., e T. dist qil ne clama rienz en le franc tenement, einz tient a la volente le deen e le chapitre &c.; le demandant dit qil fust tenant del franc tenement le jour du bref &c., e sur ceo joyndrent laverement, qe passa pur le demandant, e il rescovery seisine; e sur ceo le deen e le chapitre &c. porterent lassise de novele disseisine e rescovererent. —IDEM a *Willuby*. La veye qil vous tent vaut meux qe cele qe vous volez avoir; ne purquant cele qe vous demandez ay jeo bien veu estre receu, e par cele perdre mult beaus tenements.

X 2

A.D. 1306.
Avowry in the king's highway.

Writ founded on the statute[1] forbidding any one to distrein out of his fee or in the king's highway.

§ One Simond de Berton brought the writ against Walter &c. and two others who did not come. — *Lanfar* counted in accordance with the writ. — *Willuby* (for Walter) denied &c., and (said he) We admit the taking &c., in the place of which he complains, as bailiff of Ralph earl of Gloucester, and for the reason that the said earl is lord of the said &c., and has there his leet and whatever to a leet belongs, which he holds once every year, to wit after the feast of St. Michael, at which time the whole vill of E. pays him twenty shillings as an ancient fine and fixed rent. And for that the twenty shillings for such a term &c. were in arrear to his lord, he acknowledges the taking in the market place of the said vill of E. &c., which belongs to his lord, and in the place where he takes his tolls and stallage and whatever belongs to the seignory of the market, as in his lord's fee. —*Lanfar*. He admits the taking in the highway; judgment &c.—HENGHAM. He says that he has the view &c., and for a thing which pertains to the view he made the distress, and to that extent he was the king's servant, so he might well do it.—MALORE. In many places some vills are assessed to the sheriff's aid at four shillings, others at three; and think you not that for that aid the sheriff can distrein wherever he pleases ?—*Lanfar*. Not in the highway.—MALORE. Certainly he can.—And with this agreed HENGHAM and HOWARD.—*Lanfar*. Judgment of this admission; for still he does not say that Simon is of the vill of E. or within the leet.—*Toudeby*. Say that you are not: it was not fit to say [that he was] when you could deny it by way of replication, if that were the truth.—*Lanfar*. Still he has not said that any of his ancestors or himself was seised of that rent by the hand of us or of any other; judgment &c. — This was not

[1] 52 Hen. III. c. 15.

Breve fundatum super statutum de hoc quod non licet alicui districtiones facere extra feodum vel in regia via. A.D. 1306. Advocatio in regia strata.

§ Un Simond de Bertone porta le bref vers Wauter &c. e deus autres qe ne viendrent point. — *Lanfare* conta acordant au bref.—*Willuby*, pur Wauter, defendi &c., e conussoms la prise &c. en le leu ou il se pleint, com baillif Rauf &c. counte de Glocestre, e par la reson qe le dit counte si est seignour de mesme la &c., e illoeke ad sa lete e quant qe a lete apent, la quele il tent chescon an une foiz, saver apres la feste Seint Michel, a quel temps de aunciene fin e rente arente tote la ville de E. lui fera xx. soz. E pur ceo qe les xx. soz. de tiel terme &c. furent arere a sun seignour, si conust il la prise en le marche de mesme la ville de E. &c., qe a sun seignour est, e en leu ou il prent ces tonnuz e stallage, e quant qe a seignourye de marche apent, com en le fee sun seignour.—*Lanfare.* Il conust la prise en le haute estre[te]; jugement &c.—HENGHAM. Il dist qil ad la vewe &c., e pur chose qe apent a la vewe fist il la destresse, e de taunt fust il ministre le roi, dount il le poeit ben faire.—MALORRE. Il sunt en mults des lues les unes villes arentez a eide de vesconte en quatre soz, les autres en treis; e ne quidez point qe pur cele aide le viscont purra destreindre quele parte il voudra? —*Lanfare.* Noun pas en le haute estre[te].—MALLORE. Certes si purra. Et huic concordebant HENGHAM e HOWARD.—*Lanfare.* Jugement de ceste conissance; qe uncore ne dist il pas qe Simoun est de la ville de E. ne denz sa lete. — *Toudeby.* Dites qe vous ne estes pas; dount il ne covent pas dire quant vous le poez dedire par voie de replicacion si tele fust la verite.—*Lanfare.* Uncore nad il pas dist qe nul de ces auncestres ne lui meimes fust de cele rente par nostre meyn ne nuly autre seisi; jugement &c.: nec allocatur.—*Lanfare.* Il ne les prist

A.D. 1306. allowed.—*Lanfar.* He did not take them for that cause but for another, ready &c.—HOWARD. For what cause then ? can you know their intention ?—*Toudeby.* You do not deny that that cause is true; judgment &c.—And *Lanfar* being laughed at by the court on account of his last answer, said, Neither Simon nor any of his ancestors ever paid anything towards that rent, ready &c. —HENGHAM to *Lanfar.* You must say more than that; you must say that no tenant of that land which he holds &c.—*Lanfar* added that.—*Warr.* This rent and present is given by reason of the person and by not reason of land; wherefore &c.—MALORE. Certainly it is not. For suppose that you have a leet in A. where you take such a rent fixed &c., now I shall pay you nothing of that rent nor am I bound to anything; and if I purchase an acre of land in the vill, immediately after the purchase I shall be charged &c.—And the averment was received &c.

Voucher. Voucher to warranty where the vouchee said that he had a right to claim the tenements in demesne &c.

§ In a plea of Dower the tenant vouched to warranty one R. &c. the son of Robert le Ku, who came and asked by virtue of what the tenant wished to bind him to warranty: and the tenant put forward the deed of his father Robert on whose endowment the dower was demanded, which witnessed that Robert had given &c. and bound himself and his heirs &c. — *Roistone.* By virtue of that deed I ought not to warrant, for I have an action to demand the same tenements in demesne. And on the other hand nothing has descended to me from Robert &c. — *Lanfar.* That answer lies after you have warranted; so warrant first. — STAUNTON to *Roistone.* You must say more; for you must say by what right you have an action to demand these tenements.—*Roistone.* It was the heritage of our mother, after whose death our father Robert had nothing point par tele encheson, einz par autre, prest &c. — HOWARD. Par quele encheson donqe, poez vous conustre lour volunte ?—*Toudeby.* Vous ne dedites point qe cele cause nest verroie, jugement &c. Et *Lanfare* propter ultimam responsionem derisus a curia, — *Idem.* Simon ne nul de ces auncestres onqes a cele rente rien ne paya, prest &.—HENGHAM a *Lanfare.* Il covent plus dire; qar il covent dire ne nul tenant de cele terre qil tient &c.—*Lanfare* hoc addidit.—*Warr.* Ceste rente e prestacion est done par reson de persone e noun pas de terre; par quei &c.—MALLORRE. Certes noun est: qe jeo pose qe vous eiez lete en E. ou vous pernez une tele rente arente &c., ore ne vous feray jeo rienz a cele rente ne de rienz suy tenuz; e si jeo purchace une acre de terre en la ville, meintenant apres le purchaz jeo serray charge &c.—Et admittitur verificatio &c. A.D. 1306.

Vocatio ad warrentiam ubi vocatus dixit se habere jus petendi tenementa in dominico &c. **Voucher.**

§ En un ple de dower le tenant voucha a garantie un &c. le fiz Robert le Ku, qe vient e demanda par quei le tenant lui voleit a la garantie lier: e le tenant mist avant le fet sun pere Robert, de qi dowement le dowere fut demande, le quel fet testmoigna qe Robert avoit done &c. e oblige li e ces heirs &c.—*Roistone.* Par cel fet ne dei jeo garantir; qe jeo ay accion a demander mesmes les tenements en demene. E dautre parte, rienz ne me est descendue par Robert &c.—*Lanfare.* Ceo respouns gist apres ceo qe vous aviez garanty; dont primes garrantez.—STANTONE a *Roistone.* Il vous covendra plus dire; qar il vous covendra dire par quele reson vous avez accion de ces tenements demander.—*Roistone.* Ceo fut le heritage nostre mere,

A.D. 1306. therein but as tenant by the law of England.—STAUNTON. Then you can rebut her from dower.—*Roistone*. Yes, Sir; but if I were to warrant now, my action would thereby be extinct.—HOWARD. You bring the Mordancester on the death of your mother, and the tenant will vouch you by virtue of the charter of your father from whom nothing has descended to you; you shall warant to him as heir of blood; and nevertheless you shall have the assise. And on the other hand, before the Statute of Gloucester[1] the son in such a case would have been foreclosed from his mother's heritage by the deed of his father from whom nothing descended to him, because he was heir of blood; for amendment of which it is provided by that statute that he shall not be foreclosed, except for as much as he has by descent from his father, and that if nothing has descended to him, then, notwithstanding the deed of his father, he shall recover the whole, and that yet he shall warrant, as heir of blood, because something may descend to him: wherefore you must warrant, since you have admitted the deed.—*Roistone* (being put to this by the court). We warrant, saving to us our action; and we pray that it may be so entered.—STAUNTON. It shall be so.—*Roistone* answered over to the demandant, Our father Robert &c., was never seised in such wise that he could endow her.—*Lanfar*. Nay, you shall not get to that; for heretofore you said that nothing had descended to you; and we tell you that assets have descended to you, ready &c.—STAUNTON. That answer was not accepted, wherefore &c.—And the averment stood in the form in which *Roistone* last tendered it.

Cui in vitâ. Where the tenant, as it was presumed by the plea, entered by the woman, the husband being far away.

[1] 6 Edw. I.

apres qi desces Robert nostre pere nen avoit rienz mes com tenant par la ley dEngleterre.—STANTONE. Donqe la poez vous reboter de dowere.—*Roistone.* Oil, Sire; mes si jeo garantisse ore, ma accion par tant se esteindreit.—HOWARD. Vous portez le mortdauncestre de la mort vostre mere, le tenant vous vouchera par la chartre vostre pere de qi rienz vous est descendu; vous lui garanterez com heir du saunke, e jatardeis vous averez la assise. Et dautre parte, avant statut de Gloucestre le fiz en tiel cas serreit forclos del heritage sa mere par la fet sun pere de qi rienz ne lui fust descendue, pur ceo qil estoit heir du saunke, de quei en amendement par cel statut est done qil ne serra forclos mes qe de tant come il avera par descente del pere, e si rienz ne eit par descente, non obstante le fet sun pere il rescovera tut, e uncore garantera il com heir du saunke, pur ceo qe iluy purra descendre: par quei il vous covent garantir, del houre qe vous avez conu le fet.—*Roistone,* ad hoc positus per curiam, Nous garantoms sauve a nous nostre accion, e prioms qe issi soit entre. — STANTONE. Issi serra il. — *Roistone* respondit ultra petenti, Robert &c. ne fust onqes seisi issi qe dower la pout.—*Lanfare.* Nay, vous ne avendrez mie; e qe autre foiz deistes vous qe rienz vous fust descendu; e vous dioms qe assez vous est descendue, e prest &c.—STANTONE. Cel respons ne fut mie accepte, par quei &c.--Et stetit verificatio eodem modo quo Roistone ultimo tendebat. A.D. 1306.

Ubi tenens, ut presumebatur per placitum, intravit per mulierem viro existente in remotis. Cui in vita.

A.D. 1306. § One C. de L. brought the writ.—*Hamptone.* We did not enter by D. your husband, but by one C. de L., ready &c.—*Lanfar.* That is ourself by whom you say you entered; and we tell you that at the time of your entry we were under coverture.—*Hamptone.* Now we pray judgment of your admission and of your writ: for you admit that we entered by you, which does not accord with your writ.—STAUNTON. It may be that you have the deed of her husband and of her, and you think to be aided thereby; and we think that if she was coverte when you entered, anything that she did in that case was not her own act, but the act of her husband; so you shall tell us if she leased it to you while she was sole or not.—*Hamptone.* Sole, ready &c.—So &c.

Debt. Debt, where the defendant wished, against the writing obligatory, to aver payment by satisfaction.

§ The abbat of Grace-Dieu brought the writ for twenty-four marks against one R., and counted of a contract made between his predecessor and the said R., and put forward the deed of R. which witnessed &c.—*Roistone.* As to four marks he can not demand anything, for his predecessor was fully paid them; and see here the acquittance &c.: and as to the remainder he cannot demand anything, for we delivered to the said A. his predecessor eight bovates of land and a quarry where he gets stone to enclose his park of T., in satisfaction of the said twenty marks, of which land he himself is still seised; and we pray judgment if he can demand anything.—*Hedone.* What have you to evidence what you have stated?—*Roistone.* Ready &c.—*Hedone.* As to the acquittance, we can not deny it &c.; as to the remainder we pray judgment, since we have your deed which you have admitted and which binds you in that debt, and you to loose yourself from that debt have no acquittance but only an assertion; we

Un C. de L. porta le bref.—*Hamptone.* Nous ne entrames nent par D. vostre baroun, einz par une C. de L., prest &c.—*Lanfare.* Ceo est nous mesme, par qi vous dites qe vous entrastes; e vous dioms qe au temps de vostre entre nous esteymes coverte de baroun.—*Hamptone.* Ore demaundoms jugement de vostre conissance, e de vostre bref; qar vous conissez qe nous entrames par vous, qe ne acorde pas a vostre bref.—STANTONE. Il purra estre qe vous eez le fet sun baroun e de li, e par tant quidez estre aide; e nous entendoms qe si ele fust coverte quant vous entrastes, rienz qele fist en teu cas ne estoit sun fet, einz le fet sun baroun; dount vous nous dirrez si ele vous lessa tant com ele fut sole ou ne mie.—*Hamptoune.* Sole, prest &c. Ideo &c. A.D. 1306.

De debito, ubi defendens voluit contra scriptum obligatorium verificare solutionem per allocationem.

§ Labbe de Grascedeue porta le bref de .xxiiii. marcs vers un R., e conta de contracte fet entre sun predecessour e le dit R., e mist avant le fet R. qe testmoigna &c.—*Roistone.* Quant a les iiii. marcs il ne purra rienz demander; qar sun predecessour de ces fust pleinement paie; e veez icy laquitance &c.: e du remenant ne purra il rienz demander, qar nous baillames al avantdit A. sun predecessour .viii. boveez de terre e une quarrere ou il prist perre pur sun parc de T. enclore, en allowance des dits .xx. marcs, e de quele terre il meme en est uncore seisi; e demandoms jugement si il purra rienz demander.—*Hedone.* Quei avez de ceo qe vous aviez dit?—*Roistone.* Prest &c.—*Hedone.* En droit del aquitance nous ne le poums dedire &c.; en droit du remenant demandoms jugement, del houre qe nous avoms vostre fet le quel vous avez conu qe en cele dette vous lie, e a vous delier de cele dette aquitance ne rienz ne avez mes qe De debito.

A.D. 1306. pray judgment. — *Roistone.* We put forward against you a thing which is worth as much as an acquittance, since the country can have cognizance of it; and we plead on our truth, whereto the court ought to have regard.—STAUNTON. Although you plead on your truth, he wishes to plead according as the law allows them: and when you were bound to him by deed, why did you deliver your land to him without a deed. You have admitted the deed &c., and you have nothing which unlooses you: the court adjudges that he do recover &c. twenty marks and his damages of a hundred shillings taxed by the court, and as to the four marks that he take nothing, but be in mercy &c.

Voucher. Voucher to warranty where the vouchor had no seisin by the charter of the tenements comprised in the charter &c.

§ One Christiana, against whom one A. who was the wife of Henry &c. brought the Cui in vitâ, vouched to warranty Philip de Kyme, and, to bind him to warranty, put forward the charter of the said Philip, which witnessed that he had given and granted to the said Christiana &c., and bound himself and his heirs &c.—*Toudeby.* By virtue of that deed we ought not to warrant; for by that charter you never had any seisin of or estate in those tenements, ready &c.; nor had Philip ever anything in those tenements so that he could make a gift, ready &c.; and we will aver whichever of these two ways you will &c.—*Roistone.* Nay, you shall not get to that; for you have admitted the deed, which of itself witnesses that the gift was made to us; and in addition, we hold those tenements of you by homage and escuage, of which homage you are seised; and nevertheless there is in the charter the clause of warranty, which alone, without any thing else, binds you; wherefore &c.—*Malmesthorpe.* Then waive the charter and hold to the homage.—*Toudeby.*

vente; demandoms jugement. — *Roistone.* Nous mettoms contre vous chose qe tant vaut come aquitance, del houre qe pais de ceo puet aver conissance, e nous pledoms a nostre verite dount la court deit aver regard. — STANTONE. Coment qe vous pledez a verite, il voet pleder a ceo qe lei lur donne; e quant vous estoiez oblige a lui par fet, quei lui baillastes vous vostre terre sanz fet. — IDEM. Vous avez conu le fet &c. e rienz ne avez qe vous delie; si agard &c. qil rescovere &c. .xx. mars e ces damages de cent soz taxez par la court, e des .iiii. mars rienz ne preigne, einz soit en la mercy &c. A.D. 1306.

Vocatio ad warrentiam ubi vocator nullam seisinam habuit per cartam de tenementis in carta contentis &c. Voucher.

§ Une Cristiene, vers qi une A. qe fut la femme Henri &c. porta le Cui in vita, voucha a garantie Philippe de Kyme, e de lier li a la garantie mist avant la chartre le dit Phillippe, qe testmoigna qil avoit done e graunte a la dite Cristiene &c., e oblige lui e ces heirs &c.—*Toudeby.* Par cel fet ne devoms garantir; qar vous ne aviez onqes de ceux tenements par cele chartre seisine ne estat, prest &c.; ne Phillippe onqes en ceux tenements rienz ne avoit ci qil poeit doun fere, prest &c.; e voloms averer la quele veye de cestes deus qe vous voudrez &c.—*Roistone.* Nay, vous ne avendrez mie; qe vous avez le fet conu, qe en lui mesme testmoigne doun estre fet a nous; e oveske ceo nous tenoms ceux tenements de vous par homage e escuage, de quel homage vous estes seisi; e jatardeis ilui ad en la chartre la clause de garantie, qe tut sanz autre chose vous lie; par quei &c. — *Marmisthorpe.* Weyvez donqes la chartre, e pernez al homage. —

A.D. 1306. Do you think that that homage binds us to warranty? (intimating the negative, because of the deed.) If you had not any seisin by the said charter, then the charter is not full; wherefore &c.—At another day, *Toudeby.* Philip never had anything &c. so that he could make a gift.—BEREFORD. You have admitted the deed, and there is more in the charter than the "I have given," for there is "I have granted and by this my present "charter have confirmed," and there is the clause of warranty.—*Toudeby.* When the clause of warranty is in a charter containing "I have given," it is to be understood that it binds the donor and his heirs to the warranty &c. of the tenements given; but here there were no tenements given. And we often see that a specialty which has not the words "I have "given" or any livery of seisin, but has a clause of warranty, binds the feoffors and their heirs thereby to warranty, as if the chief lord had bound himself and his heirs to warrant to his tenant &c. the tenement which he held of him, where the clause of warranty is made on a release or a quit-claim, but not by a void charter as this is.—BEREFORD. He does not say in the clause of warranty in this charter "I will warrant "the tenements which I have given." And I have seen that Adam de Strattone bought tenements, whereof he had a charter without warranty, and he fancied he might be impleaded for those tenements, and he gave to his feoffor 100*s.* to make him a charter with a clause of warranty, without ever changing his estate or taking seisin by virtue of the latter charter; and he made him such a charter; and I tell you that Adam was impleaded and vouched &c. by that latter charter with the clause of warranty, and his vendor was bound to the warranty in spite of himself, not for the reason which you give.—*Toudeby.* Sir, if you adjudge &c.—BEREFORD. If we give judgment we shall give it with the benefit attaching.—And at last he warranted.

Toudeby. Quidez vous qe cel homage nous lie a la garantie? quasi diceret nai quia de facto. — *Idem.* Si vous ne eussez nule seisine par la dite chartre, donqe nest pas la chartre pleine; par quei &c. — Ad alium diem, *Toudeby.* Phillippe ny avoit unqes rienz &c. ci qil poeit doun fere.—BEREFORD. Vous avez conu le fet, e iluy ad plus en la chartre qe le "dedi," qe iluy ad "concessi et hac presenti cartâ meâ confirmavi," e la clause de garantie. — *Toudeby.* La clause de garantie en chartre ou ilui ad "dedi" fet a entendre qil lie le donour e ces heirs a la garantie &c. de les tenements donez; e il ny avoient nuls tenements donez. Et nous veoms sovent qe especialte en quei cele parole "dedi" ni est pas, ne nule livere de seisine, en ces especialtes nest einz clause de garantie, les feffours de ces especialtes e lour heirs par ces estre a la garantie liez, auxi com le chief seignour se obligha e ces heirs [a] garantir sun tenant &c. tenement qil tient de luy, la ou la clause de garantie est fete sur reles e quiteclamanz, mes noun pas par chartre voide cum ceste est. —BEREFORD. Il ne dist pas en la clause de garantie de ceste chartre "warantizabo tenementa quæ dedi." Et jeo vy qe Adam de Strattone avoit achate tenements des quels il avoit une chartre sanz garantie, e il se dota estre enplede de ceux tenements; il dona a sun feffour cent soz de fere lui une chartre ove la clause de garantie sanz ceo qe onqes chaunga sun estat ou par cele dreine chartre seisine prist; e ilui fist une tele chartre; e vous dy qe Adam fust enplede e voucha &c., e par cele dreine chartre ove la clause de garantie, e fut lie a la garantie maugre le soen, noun pas par cele reson qe vous dites. — *Toudeby.* Sire, si vous agardez &c. — BEREFORD. Si nous froms agard nous le froms ove la salz qe iapent. Et ad ultimum warantizavit.

A.D. 1306.

A.D. 1306. Cui in vitâ.

Where the demandant brought the writ against a man and his wife, the wife making default after default.

§ Henry Gog and Agnes his wife brought the Cui in vitâ against one A. and E. his wife; and A. came.—*Herle.* We brought our writ &c. and they were summoned to be here on the morrow of last St. Martin &c.; on which day they were essoined, and had a day until three weeks of Easter, at which day E. made default; we sued out the Grand Cape returnable now at the quinzein &c.; and now she makes default, and we pray seisin &c.—*Roistone* (for the husband). One R. leased to us those tenements for the term of our life, and we are sole tenant thereof, and were so on the day when the writ was purchased, and we ought not to lose our tenancy by her default.—And he put forward the deed which witnessed this.—*Herle.* If she make default you make default, for she is your wife, and the law of the land supposes that she is at your bidding and that you can bring her at your pleasure; so you ought not to be received to the answer that you are the tenant of the entirety unless she were here.—*Passeley* (on the same side). If Henry and Agnes were now to dereign these tenements against A. singly, she could after the death of A. have her Cui in vitâ, and so the recovery of Henry and Agnes would not avail; now it is otherwise than if they were two strangers.—BEREFORD. We well see that E. made default, and for that default you shall have as much as you can have; but plead now with A.—*Passeley.* Then pray we seisin as to a moiety &c.—STAUNTON. Nay, he tells you that he is tenant of the entirety.—*Roistone.* Yes, Sir; and we vouch to warranty J. the son of R. &c.—*Passeley.* Nay, that would be for the abatement of our writ; and we will aver that you and E. your wife entered as our writ supposes, and so held on the day when the writ was purchased.—*Roistone.* We are sole tenant &c.—So &c.

Ubi petens tulit breve versus virum et uxorem suam, uxore faciente defaltam post defaltam. A.D. 1306.

Cui in vita.

§ Henri Gog e Agnes sa femme porterent le "cui "in vita" vers un A. e E. sa femme; e A. vient.—*Herle.* Nous portames nostre bref &c., e furent somons destre ci a lendemeyn de Seint Martin drein &c., a quel jour eux furent essone, e avoient jour tant qe treis semeynes de Pasche, a quel jour E. fist defaute; nous suymes le grant cape returnable a ore a la quinezeine &c., e ore fet ele defaute, e prioms seisine &c.—*Roistone* (pro viro). Un R. nous lessa ceux tenements a terme de nostre vie, e sumes de ceo soul tenant, e fumes le jour du bref purchace, e nous ne devoms perdre nostre tenance par sa defaute: e mist avant le fet qe ceo testmoigna. —*Herle.* Si ele face defaute vous fetes defaute, qar ele est vostre femme, e ley de terre suppose qele soit a vostre volunte, e qe vous la puissez mener a vostre volunte; dount vous ne devez estre receu a tel respons qe vous estes tenant del enter sanz ceo qele ifut.—*Passeley* (ad idem). Si Henri e Agnes dreygnassent a ore ces tenements vers A. soulement, ele poeit apres le desces A. aver sun "cui in vita;" e issi ne vaudreit le rescoverir Henri e Agnes; dount autre est qe sil ne fuissount deus estraunges.—BEREFORD. Noüs veoms bien qe E. fet defaute, e pur cele defaute vous averez quant qe vous poez aver; mes pledez ore ove A. —*Passeley.* Donqe prioms nous seisine en droit de la moite &c. — STANTONE. Nai, il vous dist qil est tenant del enter.—*Roistone.* Oil, Sire; e vouchoms a garantie J. le fiz R. &c.—*Passeley.* Nay, ceo serreit al abatement de nostre bref; e nous voloms averer qe vous e E. vostre femme entrastes come nostre bref suppose, e issi tenistes le jour du bref purchace. *Roistone.* Nous soul tenant prest &c. Ideo &c.

A.D. 1306.

Taking of beasts.

§ Isabella Atteholdehalle heretofore complained that the bishop of Ely had tortiously taken her beasts &c. The bishop avowed the taking &c., for the reason that the said Isabella held of him &c. by homage, fealty &c., and after the creation of every bishop, when the vill of C. was assessed at 20*s.*, 16*d.*, and when more more, and when less less; of which services his predecessor Hugh de Balsham was seised by the hand of this same &c., and also his predecessor William was seised by the hand of this same Isabella &c.: and for that after his creation all the vill of C. was assessed at 20*s.*, he avowed the taking for 16*d.* And Isabella prayed judgment if he could make such an avowry upon her, since she freely inherited the land where the taking was made, and if, since she was free and of free estate, he could for tallage high and low at his pleasure make avowry on them. And upon this they remained a long time for judgment.—And in this term HOWARD rehearsed &c. And we are of opinion that they can well make avowry in such form as they have done by such a seisin &c. And therefore plead something else, if you will. — *Herle.* They take their title from two seisins: in this plea of taking of beasts the title must be certain; therefore let them hold to one of the two. — *Hunte.* Hugh de Balsham was seised. — *Herle.* And do you take that seisin as title and avow thereon?—*Friskeney.* We tell you that in the time of king Henry, father of the present king, our grandfather held these tenements of one Hugh de Northwold your predecessor by such services &c., discharged from the service &c. of making at every creation &c. And we tell you that during the whole of the time of Hugh de Balsham your predecessor we were under coverture of such an one, our husband, and we pray judgment if any seisin during that time ought to hurt us. — *Toudeby.* We said that Hugh de Balsham and William, both one and the other, were seised. —

§ Isabele Atteholdehalle autrefoiz se pleint qe le eveske de Ely atort avoit pris ces avers &c.—*Leveske* avowa la prise &c. par la reson qe mesme ceste entient de luy &c. par homage fealte &c., e apres la creacion de chescon eveske quant la ville de C. fust assis a .xx. soz .xvi. deniers, e a plus plus, e au meinz meinz; des queux services un sun predecessor Hughe de Balsham fust seisi par mi la main mesme ceste &c., e auxi un sun predecessor Willem seisi par my la mayn mesme ceste Isabele &c. E pur ceo qe apres sa creacion tote la ville de C. fust mis a .xx. soz, si avowa il la prise pur .xvi. deniers. Et Isabele demanda jugement sil poeit sur lui tiele avowerie faire, del houre qele estoit de la terre ou la prise fust fete enherite, franc e de franc estat fut, sil poeit pur taillage a haut e bas a sa volunte sur eux avowerie faire: e sur ceo demorerent long temps en jugement.—Et isto termino HOWARD rehersa &c.: e avis est a nous qe eux poent bien avowerie fere en tele forme qe eux ount fet par tel seisine &c. E pur ceo dites autre chose si vous volez. —*Herle.* Il pernent lour title de deus seisines; en ceo play de prise des avers le title serra en certein, e pur ceo se pernent al une des deus. — *Hunte.* Hughe de Balsham fust seisi.—*Herle.* E cele seisine pernez vous com title e de cel avowez? — *Friskeney.* Nous vous dioms qen temps le roi Henri, pere le roi qe ore est, nostre ael entient ces tenements de un Hughe de Northwold vostre predecessor par teu service &c., descharge de tiel service &c. de fere a chescone creacion &c. Et vous dioms qe tut le temps Hughe de Balsham vostre predecessor nous esteymes coverte de un tel nostre baroun, e demandoms jugement si nule seisine de ceu temps nous deive grever. — *Toudeby.* Nous deymes qe Hughe de Balsham e Willem, lun e lautre,

A.D. 1306. Prise des avers.

A.D. 1306. *Herle.* Nay, you shall hold to one; and you have done so, and we have answered thereto. — *Toudeby.* Do you hold of us or not? for you have admitted the seisin. — *Herle.* We have not admitted it: but we make no account, even if it be, in the way in which we say, admitted, that he had the aid of us in the time of our husband. — *Toudeby.* William our predecessor was seised by your own hands while you were single, and John de Kirkeby our predecessor, and Ralf &c. also seised. — *Herle.* Nay, you held to the seisin of Hugh de Balsham, to which we have answered in discharge of our tenancy from time before &c.—STAUNTON. Was any of your ancestors seised since the time limited for avowry? — *Toudeby.* As before. William our predecessor &c. was seised. — HOWARD. Were your ancestors seised before the limitation?—*Malmesthorpe.* There is no need to say; the seisin of our predecessor is admitted, and we will aver that she holds of us by those services &c. — STAUNTON. The seisin of Hugh de Balsham your predecessor is admitted, but it is so admitted that it does not give you a true title; for Isabel was coverte; now seisin by the hand of the husband was not a title in right of the wife.—*Malmesthorpe.* We will aver that she holds of us by those services; and even if all the tenants had been females, and always, each one after the other, had been under coverture, so that no tenancy was at any time without a coverture, yet that would not defeat our estate.—*Toudeby* (on the same side). And again we say that William was seised &c. by your own hand being sole. —STAUNTON. Before the limitation or not? — *Toudeby.* There is no need to say that.—HOWARD. Yes there is: she discharges her tenancy from these services from a time before: she says that in the time of Hugh de Northwold your predecessor, which was in the time of king Henry, father &c., her grandfather held &c. discharged from that service. At last *Toudeby* said, All furent seisiz.—*Herle.* Nay, vous prendrez al un, e issi avez fet, a quel nous avoms respondue. — *Toudeby.* Tenez vous de nous ou noun? qar la seisine avez grante.—*Herle.* Uncore ne la grantames point; mes nous ne fessoms force, tut soit ele solom manere qe nous dioms grante, qe il ust de nous[1] aide en temps de nostre baroun. — *Toudeby.* Willem nostre predecessor seisi fu par vos meins demene sole, e Johan de Kirkeby nostre predecessor auxi, e Rauf &c. auxi seisi. — *Herle.* Nay, vous pristes a la seisine Hughe de Balsham, a quel nous avoms respondue en descharge nostre tenance du temps avaunt &c.—STANTONE. Fust nul de vos auncestres seisi pus le temps limite de avowerie?—*Toudeby.* Ut prius. Willem nostre predecessor &c. seisiz.—HOWARD. Furent vos auncestres seisiz avant la limitation? — *Marmisthorpe.* Coe ne covent nent dire; qe la seisine nostre predecessor est conue, e nous voloms averer qil tient de nous par tieux services &c. — STANTONE. La seisine Hughe de Balsham vostre predecessor est conue, mes ele est issi conue qele ne vous doigne veray title, qe Isabele fu coverte; dount seisine par la mein le baroun ne ert pas title du droit la femme. — *Marmisthorpe.* Nous voloms averer qele tyent de nous par tieux services; e tut fust il issi qe totes les tenaunts ussent este femeles, e tut temps chescon apres autre coverte de baroun, issi qe nule tenaunte en nul temps fust sanz coverture, ceo ne defreit pas nostre estat.—*Toudeby* (ad idem). E uncore dioms qe Willem seisi &c. par vostre mein demene, sole.—STANTONE. Avant la limitation ou noun?—*Toudeby.* Ceo ne covent pas dire.—HOWARD. Si fet; qele descharge sa tenaunce de ces services du temps avant; kele dist qen temps Hughe de Northwold vostre predecessor qe fust en temps le roi Henri, pere &c., si tient sun ael &c. descharge de cel service.—Ad ultimum, *Toudeby.* Touz nos prede- A.D. 1306.

[1] MS. qe ele nous nust ne vous.

A.D. 1306. our predecessors were seised, before the time limited for making an avowry, by the hands of all your ancestors, ready &c.: and afterwards Hugh de Balsham and William, John and Ralph; ready &c. — HOWARD. If she had a charter by one of your predecessors which made mention of certain services, and she were to put it forward against you in this avowry, then because the service which you demand is not comprised in that charter, she would on that account bar you, unless you could aver that you or your ancestors were seised before the first passage to Brittany, according to the statute of Marlbridge.[1] — *Toudeby.* It would be right if she had a charter which unbound her; but since she has none, we marvel that you put us to plead so high.—*Herle.* Again we pray judgment,—since it is not denied that in the time of king Henry, father &c., which is since the time limited &c., our grandfather held &c. discharged &c. of your predecessor Hugh de Northwold, and so the seisin of your predecessors was interrupted, and this you tacitly admit,—if you can make such an avowry &c.—On another day the aforesaid process being rehearsed by HOWARD, BEREFORD blamed the avowry, because they said that when the vill of C. was rated at 20*s*. they paid 16*d*., and at more more, and at less less: because he said that by the first words of their avowry it seems that Isabel did not pay them anything except when the vill was assessed at 20*s*., and that when they said afterwards, at more more, and at less less &c., they suppose that, even although the vill of C. paid less than 20*s*., she paid &c. according &c.—*Toudeby.* Can it not well be in this case as in the case of escuage? and if the vill of C. were assessed at 10*s*., she would have to pay 8*d*.—And notwithstanding all that, they changed their avowry, by omitting the phrase "and at less &c.," and laid it thus,

---

[1] 52 Hen. III. c. 9.

cessors seisiz, avant le temps limite de fere avowerie, A.D. 1306. par meinz de touz vos auncestres, prest &c.; et pus Hughe de Balsham, Willem, Johan a Rauf; prest &c. —HOWARD. Si ele ust chartre un de vos predecessors qe feist mencion de certeines services, e ele la meist contre vous en ceste avowerie, pur ceo qe cel service qe vous demandez a ore nest pas compris en cele chartre, ele vous forbarreit par tant, sanz ceo qe vous puissez averer qe vous ou vos auncestres fuissent seisiz avant le primer passage en Bretaigne, solom lestatut de Marleberg.—*Toudeby.* Ceo serreit reson si ele ust chartre qe se deliast; mes del houre qele nad nulle, il nous merveille qe vous nous metez de pleder si haut.—*Herle.* Uncore demandom nous jugement—del houre qe nest pas dedit qen temps le roi Henri, pere &c., qe est pus le temps limite &c., nostre ael tyent &c. descharge &c. de vostre predecessor Hughe de Northwold, e issi la seisine de vos predecessors interrupt, e ceo grauntez enteissant,—si vous puissez tiele avowerie faire &c.—Altera die processu predicto reiterato par HOWARD, BEREFORD blama la avowerie pur ceo qe eux disoient qe quant la ville de C. fust mis a .xx. soz eux paieront .xvi. deniers, e a plus plus, e au meins meinz; pur coe qil dit qe par les primeres paroles de lour advowerie semble qe Isabele ne lour paya renz mes quant la ville fust mis a .xx. soz, e par tant qe eux dissoient pus a plus plus e au meinz &c., suppossent eux qe tut payast la ville de C. meinz de .xx. soz ele paya &c. solom &c.—*Toudeby.* Ne purra il estre bien auxi en droit de ceo com de escuage, e si la ville de C. fust assis a dis soz ele fereit .viii. deniers.—Et nent pur tant il changerent lour avowerie en tant qil osterent cele parole e au meinz &c., e le pristrent issint, a chescone livere

A.D. 1306. "for every pound, 16*d.* &c. And, as it seemed to many, this was not necessary, for since they could tallage at their will in the more, so it seemed that they could in the less.—At another day the process being again rehearsed, *Toudeby* said, We will aver that Hugh de Balsham our predecessor was seised of these services by your hand, and so were also William, John and Ralph &c. — BEREFORD. And what answer you to his discharging himself in a previous time?—*Toudeby.* By what does he discharge himself? What has he to show for it? (intimating that he had nothing because he had not a charter &c.). And on the other hand we are not pleading in a writ of Customs and services. — HOWARD. We have seen in a plea of taking of beasts pleading as high up as in a writ of Customs and services (and he named the parties to the case &c.). — *Toudeby.* Yes, Sir, he had a charter &c. (as before mentioned). — BEREFORD. He says that from a time before that when you take your title the tenements were holden of Hugh de Northwold your predecessor discharged &c., and you do not deny it.—*Toudeby.* What has he to show it? — *Herle.* We are tenants of the demesne, and the fee is yours; so I shall be in as good a condition to discharge my tenancy, as you will be to charge your fee, and I will aver that in the time of Hugh de Northwold, our grandfather &c. discharged &c.—BEREFORD (to the same purport). He wishes to aver his statement if it should be denied. — *Toudeby.* That would not avail him, nor shall he get to it without a charter.—BEREFORD. Yes he will, in God's name; if you think not, abide judgment: and whoever would have well pleaded this plea, he would have taken title from the seisin of the last predecessor, and there have remained until he was driven to go higher, and this is the natural course of pleading in a plea of taking of beasts; so if you are damaged, lay it to your mispleading.—Afterwards *Toudeby* said,

.xvi. deniers &c. Et ut videbatur pluribus hoc non fuit necesse, qar del houre qil lour poeient tailler a lour volunte en le plus, bene videtur qe en le meinz. —Ad alium diem iterum iterato processu, — *Toudeby.* Nous voloms averer qe Hughe de Balsham nostre predecessor fu seisi de ces services par my vostre meyn, e Willem, Johan e Rauf &c.—BEREFORD. E quei responez vous a ceo qil se delye par temps avant?—*Toudeby.* Par quei se delye il? qei ad il de ceo &c.? (quasi diceret nichil, quia non habuit cartam &c.) Et dautre parte, nous ne sumes point a pleder bref de coustumes e de services. — HOWARD. Nous avom bien veu en play de prise des avers pleder auxi haut com en bref de coustumes e de services; et nominavit inter quos &c.—*Toudeby.* Oil, Sire, il avoit chartre &c., sicut predicitur.—BEREFORD. Il dit qe de temps avant qe vous pernez vostre title les tenements tenuz de Hughe de Northwold vostre predecessor deschargez &c., e vous ne le dedites point. — *Toudeby.* Qei ad il de ceo? — *Herle.* Nous sumes tenans del demene, e le fee est le vostre; dount de auxi bone condicion serray jeo a descharger ma tenance come vous serrez a vostre fee charger; e voille averer qe en temps Hughe de Northwold, nostre ael &c. descharge &c.—BEREFORD (ad idem). Il voet sun dist sil fust dedit averer.—*Toudeby.* Ceo ne lui vaudreit mie, ne a ceo ne avendra il sanz chartre.—BEREFORD. Si fra noun Deu; si vous quidez qe noun, demorez a jugement; e qi eust bien plede ceo plee il ust pris title de la seisine le drein predecessor, e illoeke demore tant qil eust este chace a plus haut; e issi est il a pleder naturement en prise des avers; dount si vous seez anguise, rettez le a vostre mespleder —Postea *Toudeby.* Hughe de Balsham prede- A.D. 1306.

A.D. 1306. Hugh de Balsham, our predecessor, was seised &c. by your hands &c., and all our predecessors in times previous, as well at the time from which the writ of Novel disseisin runs as before, were seised by the hands of your ancestors, ready &c.—*Herle.* Which of your predecessors was seised, and by the hands of which of our ancestors? for as we offer an averment specially, so shall you do and not generally; and I will aver that Hugh de Northwold was not seised. — *Toudeby.* We know not in what time[1] Hugh de Northwold was; and we offer an averment which is receivable and you refuse it, judgment &c.—HOWARD to *Herle.* They take their title from the seisin of Hugh de Balsham by your hands &c., which seisin you have admitted, and that title you attack and think to defeat because you were under coverture &c.; and they to maintain that title offer to aver the seisin of their predecessors since the time that the writ of Novel disseisin runs and previously; it would not be a good answer to say that Hugh de Northwold was not ever seised; wherefore we think that the averment is receivable. — *Herle.* Before the time of Hugh de Balsham never was any ancestor of theirs seised &c. — *Toudeby.* We do not know in what time he was.—BEREFORD. Then if I were pleading against you I would pray judgment against you, since you take title from his seisin and do not know in what time he was; and a certain time is given for making avowry.—*Herle* did so, but did not hold to it. — BEREFORD to *Herle.* He tells you that from a time before Hugh de Balsham his predecessors were always seised &c.: and if Hugh de Northwold was not seised, then what he says is false. — *Friskeney.* Our father, grandfather, great-grandfather, great-great-grandfather, great-great-great-grandfather, and great-great-great-great-grandfather never did these services to the

[1] He was bishop of Ely from 10 June 1229 to his death, 6 Aug. 1254.

cessor seisi &c. par my vostre meyn &c., a touz nos predecessors du temps avant tant qe au temps qe bref de novele disseisine curt, e avant, seisi par my les meins de vos auncestres, e prest &c.—*Herle.* Qi vostre predecessour, e par qi mein de nos auncestres? qe auxi come nous tendoms averement in specie, auxi freez vous, e noun pas in genere; e jeo voille averer qe Hughe de Northwold ne fu pas seisi.—*Toudeby.* Nous ne savoms en quel temps Hughe de Northwold fu, e nous tendoms averement resceivable, e vous le refussez; jugement &c.—HOWARD a *Herle.* Il pernent lour title de la seisine Hughe de Balsham par my vos meinz &c., quele seisine vous avez conue, e cel title afforcez vouz e biez a defere pur ceo qe vous estoiez coverte de baroun &c.; e eux a meyntenir cel title tendent de averer seisine de lour predecessours pus le temps qe bref de novele disseisine curut e avaunt; il ne serreit pas bon respons a dire qe Hughe de Northwold ne fust onqes seisi, par quei nous entendoms qe lavere-ment est resceivable.—*Herle.* Avant le temps Hughe de Balsham onqes auncestre qil eurent seisi, prest &c.—*Toudeby.* Nous ne savoms en quel temps il estoit.—BEREFORD. Donqe demanderay jeo de vous jugement si jeo fusse pledour contre vous, del hour qe vous pernez title de sa seisine e ne savez en queu temps il fust, e certein temps est done de fere avowerie.—*Herle* ita fecit sed ad hoc non se tenuit.—BEREFORD a *Herle.* Il vous dist qe de temps avant Hughe de Balsham ces predecessours seisiz &c. de touz jours. Et si Hughe de Northwold ne estoit point seisi, donqe est il faux ceo qil dit.—*Friskeney.* Nostre pere, ael, besael, tresael, quart ael, quint ael, ces services onqes ne fessoient as predecessours qil eurent, prest &c.—

A.D. 1306

A.D. 1306. predecessors which they had, ready &c.—HOWARD. Then what they say is false. Nevertheless, on what you have now fallen, and in the condition in which you are in the plea, the averment which they offer is receivable: do you accept it?—*Herle.* If the court adjudges it &c —HOWARD. We will make no judgment thereon: do you accept it &c.?—At length *Herle* averred the contrary to what *Toudeby* said.—So &c.

Writ of dower.

In a plea of dower where the wife of the possessor by fraud recovered dower; and this because the plea was badly pleaded as appears,

§ MALORE.—A. who was the wife of D. brought a writ, &c., and demanded the third part &c. against E. &c. —E. came and said that she ought not to have dower; for he said that D. her husband was not seised of the tenements on the day when he married her, or ever afterwards, in such wise that he could endow her. And A. said that he was &c.—And on that they went to the country. The jury came before me &c., and said that one J. at a certain time held these tenements by the law of England; which J. sold the same tenements to D. the husband of A. in fee; whereupon one P., to whom the reversion of those tenements belonged, by a writ of Entry recovered the said tenements against D., on account of the alienation in fee by the tenant for life. And because we find that the husband of the woman was seised in his demesne as of fee, although his estate was other than what is found by this verdict, and we can not give judgment on the plea otherwise than in the form in which it is pleaded, this court doth adjudge that she do recover seisin; and shame to him who pleaded this plea.—And this he said because if he had disclosed the case and prayed judgment,—inasmuch as he recovered these tenements as his right by judgment &c., and the estate which her husband had was fully defeated—

HOWARD. Donqe est ceo faux qil dyent. Nepurquant, sur ceo qe vous estes chieux a ore, e en lestat qe vous estes en le plee, laverement qe eux tendent est resceivable: le volez vous?—*Herle.* Si la court lagarde &c.—HOWARD. Nous ne froms nule agard de ceo: le volez vous &c.? Ad ultimum *Herle* contrarium dictum de *Toudeby.*—Ideo &c. A.D. 1306.

In placito dotis ubi uxor possessoris male fidei recuperavit dotem; et hoc quia placitum male placitabatur prout patet, Breve de dote.

§ MALORRE. Une A. qe fu la femme D. porta bref &c. e demanda la terce partie &c. vers E. &c. E. vient e dit qele ne devoit dower avoir; qar il dist qe D. sun baroun ne fut pas seisi de ces tenements le jour qil la esposa, ne onqes pus, issi qe dowere la pout. Et A. dist qe si &c.: e sur ceo descendirent en pais. Pays vient devant moy &c., qe dist qe un J. ascon temps tient ces tenements par la lei dEngleterre, le quel J. vendy mesme le tenement a D. baroun A. en fee; parquei un P., a qi la reversion de ceux tenements fust, par bref dentre recovery les diz tenements vers D. pur le alienacion par le tenant a terme de vie fet en fee. E pur ceo qe nous trovoms qe le baroun la femme fust seisie en sun demene com de fee, tut fust sun estat autre qe par ceo verdist est trove, autrement qe play en la forme qele est plede ne poums jugger, si agard la Court qele rescovere seisine; e hounte eit il qe ceo ple pleda. E ceo dit il pur ceo qe sil ust desclos le cas e prie jugement, desicom il rescovery mesme ces tenements come sun droit par jugement &c., quel estat qe sun baroun avoit pleinement fust defete, si ele devoit de ceux tene-

A.D. 1306. if she ought to have dower of those tenements, thereby of a truth he might have barred her &c.

Taking of beasts.

§ One A. complained that the abbat of Robertsbridge had tortiously taken his beasts.—*Passeley.* We avow the taking &c., and for the reason that this same A. holds of us &c. by fealty and by the services of 4*l.* by the year &c., and relief after the death of every tenant, according to the custom of Kent viz., double the rent; and for the relief &c. after the death of John, the plaintiff's brother, he avows &c. for the remainder.—*Willuby.* He can not make avowry for the relief; for we tell you that at a certain time there was a dispute about the land between one T. formerly abbat of Robertsbridge, his predecessor, and one S., abbat of Treport, when the said abbat of Treport by fine levied before so and so justices, at such a place &c., granted and gave to the said abbat of Robertsbridge and his successors for ever 4*l.* of annual rent issuing out of the same land, to have and to hold &c. for all other services customs and demands; and this is a demand; judgment if, against the form of the fine, he can make avowry for that relief.—*Passeley.* And we pray judgment, since you admit the services which naturally according to the custom of Kent draw to themselves relief in the manner, &c. as by common law escuage brings relief, if by those words "for all other demands," since it is comprised in the gross which is admitted, you can bar us of that relief.—*Willuby.* And we pray judgment, since certain services are granted to you by the fine, which fine restrains you from excess of all other services and demands, if you can make avowry for other services than those mentioned in the fine: and together with this we tell you that at the time of levying that fine and ever since and previously we held those tenements at fee-farm; judgment if for relief &c.—At another day *Passeley* briefly rehearsed what had been before said, and ended by saying, We pray judgment,—since they

Note that for a tenement holden at fee farm relief shall not be given.

mentz dowere avoir, e par tant en sa verite la poeit aver forbarre &c. A.D. 1306.

Prise des avers.

§ Un A. se pleint qe labbe de Pount Robert atort avoit pris ces avers.—*Passeley.* Nous avowoms la prise &c., e par la reson qe meme cestui A. entient de nous &c. par fealte e par les services de .iiij. livres par an &c., e apres chescon desces de tenaunt relef solom le usage de Kente, nomement le doubler de la rente; e pur relef &c. apres la mort Johan frere le pleintif si avowe il &c. de remenant. — *Willuby.* Avowerie pur relef ne puet il faire, qar nous vous dioms qe ascon temps de mesme la terre si fust debat entre un T. jadis abbe de Pont Robert sun predecessour, e un S. abbe de Treyporz, ou le dist abbe de Treypors par fin leve devant tieles justices tel leu &c. granta e dona al dist abbe de Pont Robert e ces successors a touz jors iiij. livres de annuele rente issaunt de mesme la terre, aver e a tenir &c. pur touz altres services coustumes e demandes; e ceo est une demande; jugement si encontre la forme de la fin pur cel relef puisse avoerie fere. — *Passeley.* E nous jugement, del hour qe vous grantez les services qe naturelement solom le usage de Kente atrent a sey relef en la manere &c., auxi com de comune ley escuage fet relef solom lei comune, si par cele parole pur totes altres demandes, del houre, qil est compris en le gros grante, nous puissez de cel relef forbarrer.—*Willuby.* E nous jugement del houre qe certeins services vous sunt par la fin grantez, quele fin vous restreint de exces de tut altres services e demandes, si vous puissez pur altres services qen la fin sunt motez avowerie fere: e oveske ceo vous dioms qen temps de lever de cele fin e tut tens pus e avant nous tenimes ceux tenements a fee ferme; jugement si pur relef &c.—Ad alium diem *Passeley* breviter rehersa ceo qe avant fust dit, e in fine, E demandoms jugement, del houre

Nota quod de tenemento tento ad feodi firmam non dabitur relevium.

A.D. 1306. have put forward a fine which witnesses that they hold of us by the services which we have stated, and which naturally according to the custom &c. draw to themselves the like relief for which we avow,—if they can bar us of that relief; and we pray the return.—*Friskeney.* Nay, you do not rehearse that we said we held &c. at fee-farm, and that we put forward the fine to show our tenancy, which fine witnesses that the tenements in our tenancy are charged with 4*l.*; now by that fine our statement is proved, for there is only one carucate of land, and commonly a carucate of land is not at most worth more than 40*s.* by the year.—BEREFORD. You would better have been silent when you spoke of the fine, and have pleaded in the last course which you took; and nevertheless they have one part of the fine I am certain; and if you had been silent and said that you held these tenements in fee farm, they would then have well proved to you by the fine that this was a rent-service; then since they by the putting forward and by the fine had proved this, and it seems that you by the putting forward &c. have admitted it, God help you. Are fee-farm and rent-service the same thing? (intimating the negative.)—*Friskeney* saw that judgment would go against him, and said, Sir I have answered to only one relief.—BEREFORD. Answer then to the other: to which have you answered?—*Friskeney.* To the relief on the death of the father &c. And as to the relief on the death of the brother &c we think that this relief should properly be given out of the chattels of the dead man, and naturally this thing should be demanded against the executors &c.—BEREFORD. Nay, certainly never except in certainc ases; therefore an action is given in certain cases to the executors to demand the relief, but in what case I will not say, for perchance I might cause many suits to

Judgment. be raised.—HOWARD recorded the whole and said, And because you say that you held at fee-farm, and the fine which you laid before the court witnesses that it is a qe eux ount mys avant une fin qe testmoigne qe eux tiegnent de nous par les services qe nous avoms dit, e qe naturelement solom le usage &c. atret a sey tiel relef pur quel nous avowoms, sil nous puissount de cel relef forbarrer, e prioms retourn.—*Friskeney.* Nay, vous ne rehercez point quant qe nous deymes qe nous tenymes &c. a fee ferme, e meymes avaunt la fin pur nostre tenaunce mustrer, quele fin testmoigne qe les tenements en nostre tenaunce sunt chargez de .iiij. livres; dount par cele fin est nostre dit provee, qil ny ad mes qe une carue de terre, e comunement une carue de terre ne valt mes qe xl. soz par an au plus. —Bereford. Il vous vaudra plus aver tu quant vous parlastes de la fin, e pledo par la dreigne coster qe vous dites; e nepurquant il ount la partie de la fin jeo sui certein, e si vous eussez tu e dit qe vous tenistes ces tenements en fee ferme, eux vous eussent donqes bien provee par la fin qe ceo fu rente service; dount del houre qe eux par le mettre avant par la fin ceo eussent prove, e semble qe vous par le mettre avaunt &c. le avez grante, e si vous aide Deux. Est il tut un fee ferme e rente service? (quasi diceret non). —*Friskeney* vidit quod judicium iret contra illum, dixit, Sire jeo nay respondu mes qe al un relef.— Bereford. Responez donqes a lautre: a quel avez respondue?—*Friskeney.* Au relef de la mort le pere &c.: e quant a relef de la mort le frere &c., nous entendoms qe tiel relef voet estre done proprement des chateux le mort, e naturelement serreit ceste chose demande vers les executours &c.—Bereford. Nay, certes jaimes mes par cas; ergo accion est done par cas as executours a demander relef, e en quel cas ne dirray jeo point, qe jeo feisse par cas mult des pleez estre meuz.— Howard recorda tut. E pur ceo qe vous dites qe vous tenistes a fee ferme, e la fin qe vous meistes a la court testmoigne qe ceo est rente service e issi

A.D. 1306.

Judicium.

A.D. 1306. rent service, and so disproves your statement, the Court adjudges &c. that the abbat has the return &c.

Waste. Of waste, where the tenant claimed the fee and the right &c.

§ One Eleanor brought the writ against one Adam &c. and John le Botiler and Joan his wife. Adam came, John and Joan made default, and the great distress was now returned on all three &c. And the writ was for tenements which the said Joan holds in dower, of the inheritance &c. — *Kinge.* She can not use this writ againt us ; for it is very true that that Joan at a certain time held these tenements in dower, of the inheritance of this Eleanor, which Eleanor granted the reversion of these tenements to one Henry her brother, to whom Joan attorned &c. From Henry the right descended to three sisters, two of whom granted the reversion to Richard, father of Adam, and thereupon the said John and Joan yielded up these tenements to the said Richard, so that he was seised of the fee and of the demesne thereof, and died seised of that estate; after whose death we entered and are in possession as son and heir; and we pray judgment if this writ &c. — *Hunte.* Eleanor was always seised in fee, without making a grant thereof to any other person &c.; and even although there were contrivances between John and Joan and you, yet not for that shall this waste be unpunished.—*Kynge.* Our father Richard died seised in his demesne as of fee, and we are in possession as his heir ; judgment if this writ &c.—Bereford. They say that Joan holds these tenements in dower of the inheritance of Eleanor, and Joan is still alive and is named in their writ. And if a woman who holds tenements in dower lease them to another for her life or for a term of years, and the lessee commit waste, he to whom the reversion belongs will bring the writ of desprove vostre dist, si agarde la cort &c. qe labbe eit retourn &c. A.D. 1306.

De vasto, ubi tenens clamabat feodum et jus &c.

§ Une Elianore porta bref vers un Adam &c. e Johan le Botiler e Jone sa femme. Adam vient, Johan e Johane fessoient defaute, e la graunte destresse returne fust a ore sur touz treis &c. Et fuit breve de tenementis que eadem Johanna tenet in dotem de hereditate &c.—*Kinge.* Ele ne puet ceo bref vers nous user; qar bien est verite qe cele Johane en ascon temps ceux tenements tient en dowere del heritage ceste Elyanore, la quele Elianore la reversion de ces tenements graunta a un Henri sun frere, a qi Johane se atturna &c. De Henri descendit le droit a treis soers, dount les deus cele reversion granterent a Richard pere Adam, e sur ceo mesmes ceux Johan e Johane ces tenements rendirent au dit Richard, issi qil en fu seisi del fee e del demene, e de tiel estat seisi devya, apres qi mort nous entrames e einz sumes come fiz e heir; e demaundoms jugement si ceo bref &c.—*Hunte.* Elyanore tut veyrs seisi del fee sanz fere grant de ceo a nul autre &c; e tut fust il issi qe makemenz soient fez entre Johan e Jone e vous, par tant ne serra mie cel waste despuny.—*Kynge.* Nostre pere Richard devya seisi en sun demene come de fee, e nous einz come sun heir; jugement si ceo bref &c. — BEREFORD. Eux dient qe Jone tyent ces tenements en dower del heritage Elianore, e Johane uncore en vie e nome en lour bref. Et si femme ke tyent tenements en dowere les lesse a altre a terme de sa vie ou a terme des anz, e il face waste, celui a qi la reversion est portera le bref de waste vers la femme

A.D. 1306. waste against the woman, although she be not tenant, and against him to whom she has leased them, and shall recover against both ; and he tells you that Eleanor did not devest herself nor did she ever grant her estate to another : do you accept the averment ?—At last *Kinge* said, She granted the reversion to Henry, as before, ready &c.—So &c.—*Hunte*. As to John and Joan, the great distress is now returned : they come not ; we pray the inquest by their default.—BEREFORD. Nay, that shall wait until this be taken. And this was because, if the averment which *Kinge* offered was true, the writ did not lie.

Of Entry sur disseisin, where the tenant made use of a quitclaim made to a stranger who was not named in the degrees of the writ, and of whom the tenant was not the assign.

Entry. § One A. brought the writ against William &c. saying " into which he had not entry unless by Matilda &c. " who thereof unjustly &c. disseised Robert &c. uncle " &c. whose heir &c."—*Lanfar*. We tell you that your uncle Robert, of whose &c., released and quitclaimed to one Nicholas by this deed &c. ; after whose death one R. son and heir of Nicholas, in our seisin released and quitclaimed ; judgment if in opposition to this deed you can have an action.—*Passeley*. And we pray judgment, since you do not deny the degrees of the entry, but tacitly admit them ; we pray judgment &c.—BEREFORD to *Lanfar*. How did Nicholas first and afterwards William enter ? Were they all disseisors ? (As much was said at another time).—And in that term *Toudeby* rehearsed &c., and (said he) We tell you that A. can not have an action, for Robert &c. his uncle from whom he takes his title, during the seisin of Nicholas &c., whose estate we have, released and quitclaimed by this deed ; judgment.—*Passeley* said as before &c.—BEREFORD. You have heretofore spoken of two quitclaims

tut ne soit ele tenante, e vers celui a qi ele ad lesse, A.D. 1306.
e rescovera vers ambedeux; e il vous dist qe Elianore ne se demist ne a altre granta onqes sun estat: volez laverement?—Ad ultimum *Kinge*, Ele granta la reversion a Henri, ut prius, prest &c.—Ideo &c.—*Hunte*. Quant a Johan e Johane la grante destresse est ore returne; il ne viegnent pas; nous prioms lenqueste par lour defaute.—BEREFORD. Nay, cele attendra tanke ceste soit prise. Et hoc quia, si verificatio quæ Kinge prætendebat fuerit vera, breve non jacet.

De ingressu super disseisinam ubi tenens utebatur quieteclamantia facta extraneo qui non erat in gradibus brevis nominatus, cujus etiam et assignatus idem tenens non extitit.

§ Un A. porta bref vers Willem &c. "in quas idem Entre.
"W. non habuit ingressum nisi per Matillam &c. qui "inde injuste &c. disseisivit Robertum &c. avunculum "&c. cujus heres &c.— *Lanfare*. Nous vous dioms qe vostre uncle Robert, de qi &c., relessa e quiteclama a un Nicol par ceo fet &c.; apres qi mort un R., fiz e heir Nichol, en nostre seisine relessa e quiteclama; jugement si encontre ceo fet accion puissez avoir.—*Passelei*. E nous jugement, del houre qe vous ne dedites point les degrez del entre, einz en teissant les grantez; demaundoms jugement &c.—BEREFORD a *Lanfare*. Coment entra primes Nichol e pus Willem? furent eux touz disseisors? tantum alias dictum fuit. Et in isto termino *Toudeby* rehersa &c., e vous dioms[1] qe A. ne puet accion avoir, qe Robert &c. sun uncle de qi il prent sun title en la seisine Nichol &c., qi estat nous avoms, relessa e quiteclama par ceo fet; jugement.—*Passeley* idem dixit quod prius &c.—BEREFORD. Avant ces houres avez parle de deus quiteclamances, e

---

[1] MS. dient.

A.D. 1306. and you shall not have two staffs.—*Toudeby.* We hold to this deed to Nicholas whose estate &c. —*Wescote.* Nicholas is out of the degrees ; and if he wished to vouch him, he would not be received to do that, no more will he be received to this answer &c. ; and again, he does not show that he is the assign of Nicholas.—*Toudeby.* I have his estate, ready &c. if you will deny it.—BEREFORD to STAUNTON. There is some scruple in their affair ; nevertheless since the ancestor once deprived himself of right by his quitclaim, without its being revived by a new estate, he and his heirs in right of him have lost the action.—BEREFORD to *Toudeby.* You must in your exception say more.—*Toudeby.* As before. Robert &c. released &c. to Nicholas during his seisin, whose estate &c., without Robert being ever afterwards seised, ready &c.—*Passeley.* As before &c. : and you do not show that you are the assign of Nicholas. — BEREFORD. He is tenant of the land and defends his tenancy, and I tell you that if Robert released &c. to Nicholas during the seisin of Nicholas, whose estate &c. as they say, without you show that he retook an estate later on, he will rebut you from the action.—*Passeley.* Nicholas &c. was not ever seised &c., ready &c.—And the other side said the contrary.—So &c.—The circumstances of this plea were that Maud first of all disseised Robert while she was sole, and then took a husband, and that husband aliened &c. to Nicholas ; Nicholas was seised ; Robert released and quitclaimed to Nicholas ; Maud's husband died, and she dereigned these tenements &c. from Nicholas by the Cui in vitâ &c., and died seised ; after her death her son and heir William entered, to whom Robert, son and heir of Nicholas, released and quitclaimed &c.

Formedon in the reverter.

Formedon in the reverter, where the donee had two sons, and only one was named in the writ.

§ One John the son of Robert de Ferrers heretofore brought this writ against Clemence who was the wife vous ne averez point deus bastons. — *Toudeby.* Nous pernoms a ceo fet a Nichol qi estat.—*Wescote.* Nichol est hors de les degrez; e sil lui voleit voucher il ne serreit mie receu a ceo faire, nent plus a ceo respons &c.; e jatardeys uncore ne mustre il point qil soit le assigne Nichol.—*Toudeby.* Jeo ay sun estat, e prest &c. si vous le voillez dedire. — BEREFORD (inter ipsum et STANTONE), Il y a en lour afere ascon scruble; nepurquant del houre qe launcestre se osta une foiz du droit par sa quiteclamance sanz ceo qe ceo dreit par novel estat fust revivifie, il e ces heirs en droit de luy ont accion perdu. — IDEM a *Toudeby.* Il covendra plus dire en vostre excepcion.—*Toudeby.* Ut prius. Robert &c. relessa &c. a Nichol en sa seisine, qi estat &c., sanz ceo qe Robert estoit onqes pus seisi, prest &c. —*Passeley.* Ut prius &c.: e vous ne mustrez pas qe vous estes assigne Nichol. — BEREFORD. Il est tenaunt de la terre, e defend sa tenance, e vous dy qe si Robert relessa &c. a Nichol en la seisine Nichol qi estat &c., a ceo qe eus dient, sanz ceo qe vous poez mustrer qil reprist estat de plus tard, il vous rebotera de accion. — *Passeley.* Nichol &c. ne esteit onqes seisi &c., prest &c.—Et alii e contra. Ideo &c.—Et fuit casus istius placiti qe Maude primes disseisi Robert tant come ele fu sole, e pus prist baroun, e celui baroun aliena &c. a Nichol; Nichol seisi; Robert relessa e quiteclama a Nichol; le baroun Maude morust, e ele dreigna ces tenements &c. de Nichol par le Cui in vita &c., e morust seisi; apres sun deces entra sun fiz e heir Willem, a qi Robert fiz e heir Nichol relessa e quiteclama &c. A.D. 1306.

Forma donacionis en le reverti ubi donatorius habuit duos filios, et in brevi non nominatur nisi unus illorum: causa subest. **Forma donacionis en le reverti.**

§ Un Johan le fiz Robert de Freres autrefoiz porta ceo bref vers Clemens qe fu la femme Johan de Vescy

A.D. 1306. of John de Vescy &c. And Clemence heretofore said that she held &c. for the term of her life, and that the reversion belonged to one William de Vescy of Kildale, without whom &c., and she prayed aid &c. And William was summoned and did not come; wherefore she answered singly.—*Wercote.* She tortiously deforces him of the manor of Stapelford with the appurtenances, except one messuage eight bovates of land and the advowson of the church of the same vill: and tortiously for this, that it is his right, for the reason that one William de Ferrers his grandfather was seised of these tenements in his demesne as of fee and of right, except as aforesaid, in time of peace, in the time of king &c., the esplees &c., as in homage, fealty, rent, the services of free men and of vileins, corn, herbage and other kinds &c. amounting &c., as of fee and of right, except &c.; which William gave this same manor, except &c., to one William de Vescy with Agnes his daughter in frank-marriage; by virtue of which gift the aforesaid William de Vescy and Agnes were seised of the aforesaid manor, except &c., according to the form &c.; and from which William de Vescy and Agnes issued one William, to whom the same manor with the appurtenances, except &c., descended, according to the form &c., and which William the son of William de Vescy died without heir of his body; so the right of these tenements reverted and ought to revert to William de Ferrers as the first donor; from William de Ferrers the right of the reversion descended and ought to descend to Robert as son, and from Robert to John the present demandant, as son, and which after the deaths of William de Vescy and Agnes his wife and William the son of William de Vescy and Agnes, to the aforesaid John son of Robert &c. ought to revert by the form of the aforesaid gift, because the aforesaid William, son of William de Vescy &c., died without heir of his body begotten; and if he

&c. Et Clemens autrefoiz dist qele tient &c. a terme A.D. 1306. de sa vie, dount la reversion fust a un Willem de Vescy de Kildale, sanz qi &c., e pria aide &c. Et Willem fust somons e ne vient pas, par quei ele respondi soule.—*Wescote.* Atort lui deforce le maner de Stapelford ove les appurtenans forpris un mies .viii. bovez de terre e le avoweson de la eglise de mesme la ville: e pur ceo atort, qe ceo est sun droit, e par la reson qe un Willem de Fereres sun ael de ces tenements fu seisi en sun demeyne come de fee e de droit, forspris la forprise, en temps de pees, en temps le roi &c., les espleez &c., come en homage, fealte, rente, services des francs e des villeins, bleez e en herbage e altre manere &c., montant &c., come de fee e de droit, forspris &c.; le quel Willem mesme cel maner, forpris &c., dona a un Willem de Vescy ove Agnes sa fille en franc mariage; par quel doun les avantdiz Willem de Vescy e Agnes furent seisiz de lavaundit maner, forpris &c., solom la forme &c.; e des queux Willem de Vescy e Agnes issit un Willem, a qi le dist maner ove les appurtenans, forpris &c., descendi solom la forme &c.; e le quel Willem le fiz Willem de Vescy morust sanz heir de sun corps; dount reverti le droit de ces tenements e devoit revertir a Willem de Fereres com au primer donour; de Willem de Fereres descendi le droit de la reversion e devoit descendre a Robert com a fiz, de Robert a Johan qe ore demaunde com a fiz, e le quel apres la mort Willem de Vescy e Agnes sa femme e Willem le fiz Willam de Vesci e Agnes, al avantdit Johan fiz Robert &c. revertir deit par la forme du doun avantdite, pur ceo qe le avantdit Willem le fiz Willem de Vescy &c. morust sanz heir de son corps

A.D. 1306. will &c.—*Friskeney* denied, and briefly rehearsed, and said, We tell you that from the said William de Vescy to whom the gift &c., and Agnes there issued one John of whom the writ does not make mention; judgment.—BEREFORD. Was he son and heir of William and Agnes? —*Friskeney* was silent, because unless he was son and heir &c., and at last had died seised &c., the right after his death did not revert to William the first donor, and consequently he ought not to have been named in the writ.—*Kinge* spoke to the same purport as BEREFORD'S remark, and added, Nevertheless he shall not now get to challenge the form &c., for he has demanded the view and prayed aid &c.—*Herle.* The tenements were given to William de Vescy and Agnes, to have and to hold to William and to Agnes and to the heirs of Agnes, ready &c.—BEREFORD. See that there is no deceit in your pleading; for from what you have said we understand that the tenements &c. were given to William and Agnes and to the heirs and assigns of Agnes, and there is no force in that word "assigns" but simply in those words "heirs of Agnes."—*Herle.* That say we; and in a fine no one puts the word "assigns;" and yet an assign can vouch him or the heirs of him who granted &c. by fine &c., and bound himself and his heirs to warrant only his feoffee and his heirs, and will bind him &c.—*Passeley.* You have not traversed the gross of our action, which is that the tenements were given in frank-marriage; now if you wish to traverse us, you shall give the negative to that.—*Herle.* We have sufficiently traversed him, since we say that the gift was in fee simple.—HOWARD. You shall say "and not in frank-marriage;" for that is the mode of enrolment, and we will not vary the form on your account, for it would not be good.—*Herle.* The tenements were given to William and to Agnes and to the heirs of Agnes, and not in the form which they state &c.—And the other side said the conengendrez ; e sil voille &c.—*Friskeney* defendi, et breviter repetiit ; e vous dioms qe des dis Willem de Vescy a qi le doun &c. e Agnes issit un Johan, de qi le bref ne fet nule mencion ; jugement. — BEREFORD. Fust il fiz e heir Willem e Agnes? — *Friskeney* tacuit, quia nisi fuerat filius et heres &c. et ultimo obierat seisitus &c. jus post ejus mortem non revertebatur Willelmo primo donatori, et per consequens non debet in brevi nominari.—*Kinge.* (ad idem quod BEREFORD dixit). Et jatardeis il ne avendra pas a ore de chalanger la forme &c., qar il ad demande la vewe e prie aide &c. —*Herle.* Les tenements furent donez a Willem de Vescy e Agnes, aver e a tenir a Willem e a Agnes e as heirs Agnes, prest &c. — BEREFORD. Veez kil ne soit mie desceyte en vostre pleder ; kar, de ceo ke vous avez dist, entendoms issi qe les tenements &c. furent donez a Willem e Agnes e as heirs e as assignes Angnes, e si ne ad il pas force en cele parole assignes mes as heirs Agnes simplement.—*Herle.* Ceo dioms nous, e en fin ne mette home jaimes assigne ; e uncore purra un assigne voucher celui ou ces heirs qe granta &c. par fin &c., e obliga lui e ces heirs a garantir soulement sun feffour e ces heirs, e lui liera &c.—*Passeley.* Vous ne estes pas a travers du gros de nostre accion, qe est qe les tenements furent donez en franc mariage ; dount si vous nous voillez traverser vous serrez a la negative de ceo. — *Herle.* Assez le avoms traverse del houre qe nous dioms en fee simple. — HOWARD. Vous dirrez e mye en franc mariage ; qar ceo est manere de enrouller, e nous ne froms altre manere pur vous, qar ele ne serreit pas bone.—*Herle.* Les tenements furent donez a Willem e a Agnes e a les heirs Agnes, e ne mie en la forme qe eus dient &c.—Et alii e contra.— Ideo &c. A.D. 1306.

A.D. 1306. trary.—So &c.—And it is to be noted that, after the deaths of William and Agnes, John the son of the said William and Agnes entered on the said tenements, to whom succeeded William as brother &c. of whom the writ speaks; but nevertheless there is not any mention made of the said John in the writ, because after his death, his brother William being alive, there could not be a resort in the blood of the donee, nor is any mention made of him in the count, because the demandant does not demand by means of the blood in tail as in the descender, but in truth of the seisin and by means of the blood of the donor, in which blood it is not fitting to omit any degree. Neither did it say of William de Ferrers to whom the tenements reverted, "the right of "the reversion descended except &c." but only "the "right of the reversion." But it seems better to say "except &c." But it was not challenged.

Waste, against three, where one died before the inquest was taken.

Writ of waste.

§ One A. brought the writ against three &c., who came and said that they had not committed any waste, ready &c.—The sheriff was ordered to inquire &c., and before the inquest was taken one of the three died; and nevertheless the sheriff went on to take the inquest, and found that waste was committed, and he returned the inquisition.—*Herle.* You can make no judgment by virtue of that inquest or that verdict, for it was taken without warrant, since there was no party thereto, but one of the defendants was then dead.—*Passeley.* The party pleaded with us down to the inquest, and the inquest is now taken, and waste is found, which waste shall not be unpunished, and we pray judgment.—MALORE. Against whom will you recover the tenements wasted?—By God, not against the dead man.—Wherefore it was adjudged that the writ abated &c.

Et memorandum quod post mortem Willielmi et Agnetis Johannes filius eorumdem Willelmi [et] Agnetis intravit dicta tenementa; cui successit Willelmus ut frater &c. de quo loquitur breve; nec tamen de eodem Johanne in brevi fit mencio, quia post ejus mortem Willelmo fratre suo superstite non potuit fieri resorcio in sanguine donatorii, nec de eodem in narrando fit mencio, quia petens non petit per medium sanguinis talliati ut in le descendere, immo de seisina et per medium sanguinis donatoris, in quo sanguine aliquem gradum omittere non est oportunum. Nec etiam dixit de Willelmo le Ferers a qi les tenements revertirent, descendi le dreit de la reversion, forpris &c., sed solummodo le dreit de la reversion. Tamen videtur melius dicere forspris &c. Nec fuit calumpniatum. A.D. 1306. Casus placiti.

De vasto versus iii., ubi unus obiit ante inquisitionem captam.

§ Un A. porta bref vers treis &c., qe viendrent e dissoient qe eux ne avoient nul waste fet, prest &c. Maunde fust a viconte qil enqueist &c.; e einz ceo qe la enqueste fu prise &c. un des treis morust; e jatardeis le viconte ala a prendre lenqueste, e trova qe waste fu fete, e retourna lenqueste.—*Herle.* Par cele enqueste ne cel verdit ne poez faire nul jugement, qar ele fu prise sanz garante del houre qe il ny avoit point de partie, einz adonqes fu mort. — *Passeley.* La partie pleda ove nous a lenqueste, e la enqueste est ore prise, e wast trove, le quel wast ne serra mie despuny, e prioms jugement. — MALORRE. Vers qi rescoverez vous le tenement wastes? per du, noun pas vers le mort: par quei fut agarde qe le bref fust abatu &c. Breve de vasto.

A.D. 1306. Entry sur disseisin, where it was objected to the demandant that he was under age &c.

§ One A. brought the writ for tenements in Fenny Stratford, to wit "whereof the said &c. disseised such "an one, his father &c.—*Toudeby.* A. is under age, and counts of the seisin of his ancestor; we pray that he may be seen by the court.—And he was viewed by the court, to whom it seemed that he was of full age; and yet he was the demandant. — *Toudeby.* He can not demand anything, for A. his father, of whose seisin &c., gave to us the same tenements by his charter, which is here, and bound himself and his heirs to warranty; then, if we were impleaded by another &c.—*Hampton.* Although there be a clause of warranty yet that will not hurt us, since we have an action to demand the tenements.—HENGHAM. Is it your father's deed &c.?—*Hampton.* Not his deed, ready &c.—And here *Hampton* pleaded too craftily; because he might have offered to aver the entry, and have made the party answer direct to the entry seeing that the party did not deny it. And yet it is thought that at last it would not avail, because although the said tenant did not obtain his estate or seisin by the charter of A. the father of the demandant, yet by the clause of warranty alone he is bound to warrant; consequently his action would be null, as appears before, where Phillip de Kyme was vouched &c.

Nuper obiit. Nuper obiit, where the tenant in parcenary disclaimed &c.

§ One A. brought the writ against B., and counted of the seisin of D., great-grandfather of the said A. and grandfather of B., who lately died seised.—*Kinge.* This writ lies only between parceners, and we claim nothing in the parcenary; judgment.—STAUNTON. Why

De ingressu super disseisinam, ubi objicitur petenti quod fuit infra etatem &c. A.D. 1306.

§ Un A. porta bref des tenements en Fenny Stretteford, scilicet, de quibus idem talis disseisivit talem patrem suum &c. — *Toudeby*. A. est denz age, e counte de la seisine sun auncestre; nous prioms qil soit veu de court. Et fuit visus a curia, cui videbatur se fore plenæ ætatis, et tamen fuit petens. — *Toudeby*. Il ne purra rienz demander, qar A. sun pere, de qi seisine &c., nous dona mesmes les tenements par sa chartre, qe ci est, e obliga luy e ces heirs a la garantie; dount si nous fuissoms de un altre enplede. — *Hamptone*. Tut jeit il clause de garantie cele nous nuyra point, del houre qe nous avioms accion a demander les tenements. —HENGHAM. Est ceo le fet vostre pere &c.? — *Hamtone*. Nent sun fet, prest &c. Et hic nimis ficte placitavit *Hamptone*, pur ceo qil poeit aver tendue daverer le entre, e aver fet la partie a respondre directe al entre ou la partie ne le dedit. Et tamen creditur ad ultimum non valere, quia licet idem tenens statum seu seisinam per cartam A. patris petentis non consequebatur, per clausulam tantum warantiæ tenetur warantizare; per consequens nulla foret ejus actio, ut patet ante ubi Phillippus de Kyme vocabatur &c. Nota.

Nuper obiit, ou le tenant desclama en la parcenerie &c. Nuper obiit.

§ Un A. porta bref vers B. e conta de la seisine D. besael le avantdit A., e ael B. qe nadgers morust seisi. — *Kinge*. Ceo bref gist soulement entre parceners, e nous ne clamoms riens en la parcenerie; jugement.— STANTONE. Pur quei ne clamez vous rienz &c.? coment

A.D. 1306. do you not claim anything &c. ? How then do you claim ?—*Kinge.* Whereas he makes me parcener by the blood of my mother, I do not claim anything &c. by my mother ; but I tell you that my father Thomas died seised &c. of these tenements in his demesne as of fee, after whose death I entered as his heir; judgment &c. — *Willuby.* Our great-grandfather was seised &c. and died seised &c. — *Kinge.* Whereas you make us parcener &c., we disclaim &c. ; and this is your advantage, for thereby you may recover the entirety &c. —STAUNTON explained the case to HOWARD, and he said that they did not abate the writ by the disclaimer. —STAUNTON to *Kingesham.* How came your father Thomas by these tenements ? — *Kingesham.* By the feoffment of John, bishop of T. — STAUNTON. How did the bishop come by them ? — *Kingesham.* They were the right of his church.—STAUNTON. Did D. their ancestor die seised or not ? — *Kingesham.* This writ does not lie between us, as before &c.—HENGHAM. You do not answer to what is asked of you, viz. if D., of whose seisin &c., died seised or not; wherefore the court takes it for granted if you will not deny it.—Afterwards *Kingesham,* being put to this by the court, viz. if D. the ancestor of whose seisin &c., said, He had not any estate except a tenancy in vilenage of J. bishop of &c., who of these tenements enfeoffed Thomas our father, so that D. did not die seised in his demesne &c. —And note that in this writ, it should be said at the end of the count, "and whereof the said B. holds the " whole and the said D. has nothing"; and not "and " deforces the said A. of his rightful part."—But there seems no reason for this except use only.—To another like writ *Toudeby* said, T., of whose seisin &c., did not die seised, ready &c. ; judgment of the writ.—*Bacon.* You do not deny that he was seised ?—*Toudeby.* When he shall bring a writ of a higher nature, where we shall have to answer wholly to the seisin of the ancestor donqes clamez vous.—*Kinge.* La ou il me fet parcener A.D. 1306. par le saunk ma mere jeo ne cleyme rienz &c. par ma mere ; einz vous dy qe mon pere Thomas de ces tenements devya seisi &c. en sun demene come de fee, apres qi mort jeo sui entre come sun heir ; jugement &c.—*Willuby.* Nostre besael seisi &c. e morust seisi &c., prest &c.—*Kinge.* La ou vous nous fetes parcener &c. nous desclamoms &c., e ceo est vostre avantage, qar par tant poez rescoverer lentier &c.—STANTONE moustra le cas a HOWARD, e il dist qe eux ne abatirent point le bref par le desclamer.—STANTONE a *Kingesham.* Coment avyent Thomas vostre pere a ces tenements ?—*Kingesham.* Par le feffement Johan eveske de T. —STANTONE. Coment leveske ?—*Kingesham.* Ceux furent le droit de sa eglise. — STANTONE. Morust D. lour auncestre eisi ou noun ?—*Kingesham.* Ceo bref ne gist parentre nous, ut prius &c.—HENGHAM. Vous ne responez nent a ceo qe home vous demande, si D., de qi seisine &c., morust seisi ou noun ; par quei la court le tient a grante, si vous ne le volez dedire. Postea *Kingesham,* ad hoc positus per curiam, si D. le auncestre de qi seisine &c., ne avoit nul estat si noun tenance en villeynage de J. eveske &c. qe de ces tenements enfeffa Thomas nostre pere issi qe D. ne morust mie seisi en sun demene &c. — Et nota quod in hoc brevi sic est dicendum in fine narrationis, Et dount mesme celui B. tut entient e le avantdit A. rienz nad, et non sic, E a le avantdit A. sa renable partie deforce. Nulla tamen videtur ratio nisi solus usus. A un altre tieu bref, *Toudeby,* T. de qi seisine &c. ne morust mie seisi, prest &c. ; jugement du bref.—*Bacone.* Vous ne dedites pas qil ne fu seisi.—*Toudeby.* Quant il portera plus haut bref, ou il nous covendra entier-

A.D. 1306. from whom he takes his title, we will give sufficient answer.

Saving a default.

§ Note that, to the return of a Petit Cape the tenant said that he made such an one his attorney, who at such a place, while he was coming to the court, went mad, and there was taken and bound, and remained there until his friends took charge of him, and still continues mad; and he prays judgment if such a default &c.—And thereby he saved the default &c.

Record.

It was found by the inquest that the charter denied was not the deed of him against whom it was used; and nevertheless it was not cancelled.

§ STAUNTON. One D. brought a writ of Ael &c. against C., who put forward against him the charter of his grandfather, of whose seisin &c., whereby he had of the tenements &c. enfeoffed &c. in fee-tail, and prayed judgment &c. And D. said that it was not his ancestor's deed &c. And C. said that it was his deed &c. and that he would aver it by the witnesses named and by a good jury &c. The jury came before &c., and none of the witnesses &c. were alive except one whose testimony was worthless because he was formerly perjured, and the jury said by their oath that it was not the deed &c.; so the court adjudges that D. do recover &c. And because perchance C. may have the Attaint, let the charter &c. remain whole in quiet in the king's keeping &c.

Writ of wardship.

Of wardship of right, where the defendant first vouched the husband of the woman to whom the wardship by law belonged, and that husband being dead &c.

§ John de Hastings brought the writ against Hugh de Pepham, and demanded the wardship of the body of the ment a la seisine le auncestre de qi il prent sun title respundre, nous respondroms assez. A.D. 1306.

§ Nota ke a un petit cape retourne le tenant dist qil fist sun attourne un tiel, qen venant vers la court tiel leu se arraga, e illoeke fu pris e lye, e demorra illoke tant qe ces amis laquistrent, e uncore demoert en cele rage, e demande jugement si tele defaute &c.; e par tant sava la defaute &c. Saver de defaute.

Compertum est per inquisitionem quod carta dedicta non fuit factum illius versus quem utebatur; et tamen non cancellatur. Recordum.

§ STAUNTONE. Un D. porta bref dael &c. vers C., qe mist contre lui la chartre sun ael de qi seisine &c., qe iluy avoit des tenements &c. feffe &c. en fee taille, e demanda jugement &c. Et D. dist qe ceo ne estoit le fet sun auncestre &c. Et C. dit qe ceo fu sun fet &c., e ceo voleit averer par les testmoignes nomez, &c. e par bon pays &c. Pays vient devant &c., e nul des temoignes &c. ne fust en vie, estre un qe la testmoingnance de celuy un ne fust nule pur ceo qil estoit autrefoiz perjurs, qe disoient par lour serement qe ceo ne fu mie le fet &c.; si agarde &c. qe D. rescovere &c. E pur ceo qe par cas C. puet aver latteinte, demoerge la chartre &c. entiere en pees en la garde le roi &c.

De custodia de recto ubi defendens primo vocavit virum mulieris cui custodia jure pertinuit, et illo viro mortuo &c. Breve [de] custodia.

§ Johan de Hastingg porta bref vers Hughe de Pepham, e demanda la garde du corps e del heir Giles

A.D. 1306. heir of Giles son of William de Cugenholle, which Hugh formerly vouched to warranty James de la Planche, which James died &c.—*Herle* rehearsed this &c., and said, Wherefore let Hugh revouch or say something else. — *Willuby.* We say that this wardship was the right of Maud the wife of James at the time when he gave it to us, and that it still is so, and without her &c., and we pray aid.—*Herle.* You shall not have aid of her, for you had not the wardship by lease from her, nor by the lease of any of her ancestors. — *Friskeney.* William of Cugenholle held of James de la Planche and Maud his wife one messuage, one carucate of land and the advowson of the church of Cugenholle by knight-service, as in right of Maud, so that this wardship is the right of Maud for this reason, and we pray aid. — *Herle.* You shall not go out of the course which you began; you heretofore vouched James &c.; so revouch his heir &c. if you will &c.—*Friskeney.* William de Cugenholle held that messuage &c. of James and of Maud &c. by knight-service in right of Maud, without holding any other tenements of any other person by knight-service, ready. — *Herle.* He held of us two knights' fees in Cugenholle, ready &c.—Afterwards HINGHAM came into the bench, and STAUNTON rehearsed the plea to him, who said that the aid was not grantable &c., but that Maud should be summoned to hear the jury; for although she had come before the issue of the plea, she could not have pleaded otherwise.—Yet the contrary seems possible, for she might have alleged priority of feoffment, &c.

Replevin. Replegiari, where the tenant held by knight-service and alienated portion of his tenancy to another to be holden in socage of him &c.; and that tenant being dead, the lord and guardian of his son wholly acknowledged &c. that for a certain service he had the tenement in socage &c.

§ John de la Croys complained against William Penres. — *Passeley.* We admit the taking &c. and for fiz Willem de Cugenholle, le quel Hughe autrefoiz voucha a garantie Jake de la Planche, le quel Jake morust &c. — *Herle* ceo rehersa &c., par quei revouche Hughe ou die altre chose.—*Willuby*. Nous dioms qe ceste garde fu le droit Maude la femme Jake au temps qil la nous dona, e uncore est, sanz quele &c., e prioms aide.—*Herle*. Aide de lui ne averez pas, qar vous ne aviez point la garde de sun lees ne du lees nul de ces auncestres.—*Friskeney*. Willem de Cugenholle tient de Jakes de la Planche e Maude sa femme un mies une carue de terre· e le avoeson del eglise de Cugenholle, par service du chivaler, com du droit Maude, issi qe ceste garde est le droit Maude par ceste reson, e prioms aide. — *Herle*. Vous ne irrez pas hors de la veye qe vous comenceastes ; autrefoiz vouchiez vous Jakes &c., dount revouchez sun heir si vous volez &c.—*Friskeney*. Willem de Cugenholle tient ceu mies &c. de Jakes e de Maude &c. par service de chivaler come du droit Maude, sanz tenir nuls autres tenements de nul autre par service de chivaler, prest.—*Herle*. Qil tient de nous deus feez de chivaler en Cugenholle, prest &c.—Postea venit in banco HENGHAM, et STANTONE recitavit sibi placitum, qe dit que eide ne fu pas grauntable &c., mes qe Maude serreit somons de oier la jure ; qar tut eust ele venue avant le issue du plee, ele ne poeit autrement aver plede : cujus contrarium videtur, qele poeit aver alegge priorite de feffement &c. A.D. 1306.

Replegiare ubi tenens tenuit per servicium militare et partem tenenciæ suæ alienavit altero tenendam in socagio de illo &c., et mortuo illo tenente integre dominus et custos filii sui cognovit &c. pro servicio tenementum habere in socagio &c. Replegiare.

§ Johan de la Croys se pleint vers Willem Penres. —*Passeley*. Nous conissons la prise &c., e par la reson

A.D. 1306. the reason that one John de Gernoun held of us &c. by homage &c. and escuage, and died in our homage; after whose death John, his son and heir, fell into our ward, and is there still: and because this same John holds of the aforesaid John de Gernoun one carucate &c. by fealty and by the service of 40*s.*, of which services the said John was seised &c. by the hand of Richard de la Croys father of John &c., and which John, for his fealty and 2*s.* in acknowledgment &c. attorned to us as guardian of John son and heir of John &c.; and because the remainder of the said rent was in arrear &c., we acknowledge the taking &c.—*Willuby.* You can not do that, for we hold &c. in free socage; judgment if you as guardian of right &c. can claim anything in that rent.—*Passeley.* What of that? We shall have while the infant is under age and in ward to us as much as he ought to have if he were of full age, by reason of the tenancy which he holds of us; and you can not deny that you hold of him by those services; judgment &c. And, nevertheless, we are seised of your fealty and of 2*s.* of rent in acknowledgment &c., and what you hold is of our fee.—STAUNTON. Be first agreed as to that: (to *Willuby*). Is it of their fee?—*Willuby.* Yes, Sir, certainly it belongs to John de Gernoun, our mesne, of whom we hold in socage.—STAUNTON. Did you attorn to William for your fealty and the rent of 2*s.*?—*Tilton.* There is no need to answer to that; since we put forward against them an exception of law, there is no need to answer to any exception of fact.—STAUNTON to *Passeley.* If Richard de la Croys were under age you would not have his wardship or marriage, neither would you have the rent.—*Willuby* (to the same purport). John de Gernoun &c. enfeoffed John our father, whose heir &c. by 40*s.* for all services, in socage, and before the Statute;[1] which

[1] 18 Edw. I. Quia emptores.

qe un Johan de Gernoun entient de nous &c. par homage &c. e escuage, e morust en nostre homage ; apres qi mort Johan sun fiz heir chey en nostre garde, e leinz est uncore. E pur ceo qe mesme cestui Johan entient del avantdit Johan de Gernoun une carue &c. par fealte e par les services de .xl. soz, des queles services mesme celuy Johan fu seisi &c. par la mayn Richard de la Croys pere Johan &c., e le quel Johan de sa fealte e de deus soz en resconissance &c. a nous se atturna come au gardein Johan fiz e heir Johan &c. E pur ceo qe le remenant de la dite rente fust arere &c. si conissoms la prise &c.—*Willuby.* Ceo ne poez faire, kar nous tenoms &c. en franc socage ; jugement si vous come gardein du droit &c. en cele rente puissez rien demander.—*Passeley.* De ceo quei ? nous averoms quant qe lenfant esteant denz age e en nostre garde deust aver sil fust de age, par reson de la tenance qil tient de nous ; e vous ne poez pas dedire qe vous ne tenez de luy &c. par teux services, jugement &c. ; e jatardeys nous sumes seisi de vostre fealte e de deus soz de rente en resconisance &c., e ceo qe vous tenez est de nostre fee.—STAUNTONE. La seez primes a un. IDEM a *Willuby.* Est ceo de lour fee ?—*Willuby.* Certes Sire oil, a Johan de Gernoun nostre meen de qi nous tenoms en socage. — STAUNTONE. Estes vous atturne a Willem de vostre fealte e de la rente de deus soz ?—*Tiltone.* A ceo ne covent pas respondre ; del hour qe nous mettoms contre eux excepcion de ley, ne covyent a nule excepcion de fet respondre. — STAUNTONE a *Passeley.* Si Richard de la Croys fust denz age vous ne averez pas sa garde ne sun mariage, nent plus la rente.—Ad idem *Willuby.* Johan de Gernoun &c. enfeffa Johan nostre pere, qi heir &c., par .xl. soz pur touz services en socage e avant statut ; quele rente est

A.D. 1306. rent is naturally the profit of the heir of the said John de Gernoun who shall fall into the ward of his next friend to whom &c., who, on his coming of age, shall according to the statute[1] render to him an account; and we pray judgment &c.—*Passeley.* Although that parcel of land be not holden of us by knight-service, the 40*s.* which we demand are holden of us by those services, and we have heretofore learned that the tenant in demesne can hold in socage of his mesne, and his mesne hold by knight-service of his lord paramount, and the lord paramount by serjeanty &c.—*Willuby.* These 40*s.* were never holden of you.—*Passeley.* Yes they are; for if John who is in ward to us were of full age and were to commit felony, we should have these 40*s.* by escheat; therefore he does hold them of us. And on the other hand, if John de Gernoun had died seised of that land &c., we should have the wardship thereof; consequently of the rent which issues from that land.—Afterwards the said John was non-suit &c. And it is to be remembered that he was not willingly non-suit, for the opinion of *Willuby* and *Tilton* was that the law was on his side, but *Passeley* was of the contrary opinion &c.

That one under age cannot disclaim &c.

§ A woman heretofore complained that William Giffard tortiously took her beasts. And William avowed the taking &c. on one T. &c.; and the woman said that she held &c. in dower of the inheritance of the said T., and prayed aid of him. T., who was under age, came and joined himself. — *Willuby* (for T.). We do not claim to hold anything of him &c. — *Kinge.* You can not disclaim any more than you can render.—STAUNTON to *Willuby.* You know well that the court will not take such an answer from you.—*Willuby.* If we should deny the seisin &c. we should thereby admit the tenancy:

---

[1] 52 Hen. III. c. 17.

naturelment le profit leir le dit Johan Gernoun qi chera A.D. 1306.
en la garde sun plus prochein amy a qi &c., qe a sun age de cel profit solom statut luy rendra acounte; e demandoms jugement &c.—*Passeley.* Tut ne soit pas cele parcele de terre tenuz de nous par service de chivaler, les .xl. soz qe nous demandoms sunt tenuz de nous par teux services, e einz ces houres avoms apris qe le tenant en demeyne purra tenir en socage de sun meen, e sun meen par service de chivaler de sun seignour par amonte, e celuy par amounte par serjantie &c.—*Willuby.* Ces .xl. soz ne furent onqes tenuz de vous.—*Passeley.* Si sunt; qar si Johan qest en nostre garde fust de plein age e feit felonie, nous en averoms ces .xl. soz par eschete; ergo il les tient de nous. E dautre parte, si Johan Gernoun ust devye seisi de cele terre &c., nous averioms de cele la garde, ergo de la rente qe de cele terre surde.—Postea predictus Johannes non est prosecutus &c. Et memorandum qil ne fist pas la noun suite de gre, qe la oppinion de *Willuby* e de *Tiltone* fust kil avoit ley pur luy, e *Passeley* en le oppinion contrarie &c.

Quod existens infra etatem non potest disclamare &c.

§ Une femme autrefoiz sey pleyne qe Willem Giffard atort prist ces avers. Et *W.* avowa la prise &c. sur un T. &c. e la *femme* dist qil tient &c. en dowere del heritage celui T., e pria aide de lui. T. denz age vient, e se joint.—*Willuby* (pur T.) Nous ne clamoms rienz tenir de luy &c.—*Kinge.* Vous ne poez desclamer nent plus qe rendre.—STAUNTONE a *Willuby.* Vous savez bien qe la court ne prendra point teu respons de vous.—*Willuby.* Si nous dedeissoms la seisine &c., en tant grantames le tenance; par quei, si la court le

A.D. 1306. wherefore, if the court will allow it, we will disclaim. —STAUNTON. Even if you had now admitted the seisin, you might hereafter, when of full age, disclaim; wherefore &c.—*Willuby*. Never seised of the homage, ready &c.—So &c.

Cosinage. Cosinage, where the tenant in another like writ had the view, which writ was not abated. So he again had the view &c.

§ Roger the son of Piers Corbychoun brought the writ against B., and counted of the seisin of the sister of the grandfather who died without heir &c. — *Herle*. We pray the view &c.—*Tiltone*. You shall not have it; for we heretofore brought the like writ against you for the same tenements, to which writ you alleged non-tenure, wherefore we took out another writ &c.—*Herle*. Was that writ abated by judgment?—STAUNTON asked the same question.—*Willuby*. Surely no; and that was foolish &c.—STAUNTON. Therefore let him have the view &c.

Entry. Of Entry on disseisin in the degrees, where the tenant by the equity of the law and on account of the hardship &c. vouched out of the degrees.

§ One A. brought the writ against one Avelyne, thus, "into which she has not entry unless by Hugh " Husee, who thereof unjustly and without judgment " disseised the said A. &c."—*Friskeney*. We vouch &c. John de Pabornham &c. — *Hunte*. You can not do that, for our writ is in the degrees, in which neither he nor any of his ancestors is named; judgment &c.—And, the writ being looked at by the court, STAUNTON asserted what *Hunte* said to be true. — *Friskeney*. By force of law we ought to have this voucher, for we tell you voille suffrir, nous voloms desclamer.—STANTONE. Tut eussez vous a ore la seisine grante, vous puissez apres ces houres de plein age desclamer; par quei &c. — *Willuby.* Onqes seisi del homage, prest &c. Ideo, &c. A.D. 1306.

Cosinage, ou le tenant a un autre teu bref avoit la vewe, le quel bref ne fust pas abatu. Ideo habeat visum alias &c. Cosinage.

§ Roger le fiz Peres Corbychoun porta bref vers B., e conta de la seisine la soere le ael qe morust sanz heir &c.—*Herle.* Nous demandoms la vewe &c. — *Tiltone.* Vous ne laverez pas; qe altrefoiz portames autiel bref vers vous mesme de mesmes les tenements, a queu bref vous allegastes nountenure, par quei nous preymes altre bref &c.; jugement &c. — *Herle.* Fust ceo bref abatu par jugement?—STANTONE idem dixit *Willuby.* Certes nay; e ceo fu folie &c.—STANTONE. Ideo habeat visum &c.

De ingressu super disseisinam in gradibus ubi tenens equietate lege et ob duritiam &c. vocavit extra gradus. De ingressu.

§ Un A. porta le bref vers une Avelyne sic, "In "quas non habet ingressum nisi per Hughe Husee "qui inde injuste et sine judicio disseisivit predictam "A. &c." — *Friskeney.* Nous vouchoms &c. Johan de Pabornham &c.—*Hunte.* Ceo ne poez pas; qe nostre bref est en les degreez, des queux il ne nul de ces auncestres est nome; jugement &c.—Et breve a curia inspecto, STANTONE asserebat dictum de *Hunte* esse verum.—*Friskeney.* Il nous covendra de force de ley

A.D. 1306. that these same tenements were at a certain time in the seisin of the said Hugh Husee, after whose death the tenements now demanded were assigned in dower to this Avelyne his wife by Isabel, daughter and heir of the said Hugh; which Isabel, with one Henry de Tychemerche her husband, did by fine &c. grant the reversion of the same tenements to the said John de Pabornham, who sued out the Quid juris against the said Avelyne, whereupon she attorned; and which John then in court bound himself and his heirs to warrant &c. to the said Avelyne; (and he mentioned the number of the roll where Avelyne attorned to John, and the said John bound himself and his heirs to warranty;) and we pray judgment &c. — *Hunte.* The statute[1] expressly says that one shall not be received to vouch out of the degrees; wherefore &c.—STAUNTON (HENGHAM, HOWARD, and he having consulted together). Whatever be the words of the statute, yet, because of the hard case which would otherwise ensue, the voucher is receivable; and it shall not destroy your writ, which shall be always in the *per*, for this John is the assign of the heir of him who is within the degrees, and they shall be as one degree.—And the voucher was received.—And *Hunte* prayed that the reason why it was received, and the counterplea, should be entered on the roll. And he did this lest the warrantor at another time might quash his writ by reason that neither he nor any of his ancestors was named in the degrees in the writ &c.

Of Entry ad terminum qui præteriit where the ancestor of the demandant demised for the term of his life.

Entry. § One A. brought the writ against B. thus, "into "which &c. unless by D. father of the said A., whose "heir &c., who demised them to him for a term

[1] 3 Edw. I. (Westm. I.) c. 40.

aver ceo voucher, qar nous vous dioms qe mesmes A.D. 1306.
ceux tenements furent en ascon temps en la seisine le dit Hughe Husee, apres qi mort les tenements a ore Nota.
demaundez furent assignez en dowere a ceste Avelyne sa femme par Isabele, fille e heir mesme celuy Hughe; la quele Isabele, ove un Henri de Tychemerche sun baroun, la reversion de mesmes les tenements par fin &c. granterent au dit Johan de Pabornham, qe suist le quid juris vers mesme ceste Avelyne, par quei ele se atturna, e le quel Johan adonqes en court obliga lui e ces heirs a garantir &c. a mesme ceste Avelyne; et nominavit numerum rotuli ubi Avelina attornavit Johanni, et idem Johannes obligavit se et heredes ad warrantiam &c.; e demandoms jugement &c.—*Hunte.* Statut dit expressement qe homme ne serra mie receu a voucher hors de les degreez; par quei &c.—STANTONE (HENGHAM HOWARD et illo adinvicem consultis). Coment qe statut parle, pur la duresse qe autrement suereit le voucher est resceivable; e si ne deperira point vostre bref, en serra tut veirs en le per, car cestui Johan assigne le heir celui qest en les degreez, e celuy serront come un degre.—Et admissa fuit vocatio.—Et *Hunte* pria qe la cause pur quei ele fu receu e le contrepleder fust entre en roulle. Et hoc fecit ne warrantus alias posset breve suum cassare per hoc quod ille nec aliquis suorum antecessorum nominabatur in gradibus brevis &c.

De ingressu ad terminum qui preteriit ubi antecessor petentis dimisit ad terminum vitæ suæ.

§ Un A. porta le bref vers B. sic "In quas &c. nisi De ingressu.
" per D. patrem predicti A., cujus heres &c., qui illas

A.D. 1306. " which has passed."—*Hedone.* That cannot be, for we ourselves heretofore before so and so &c. Justices, brought an assise of Novel disseisin against this same D. his father for the same tenements, by which assise we recovered &c. against him as against a disseisor, and that estate have we ever since continued; judgment.—STAUNTON. Then did he not lease to you for a term &c.? — *Hedone.* Let A. answer to what I state.—*Lanfar.* True it is that D. our father leased to you these tenements for the term of his life, and after that ousted you &c., whereupon &c., whereby you recovered against him by an assise &c. your first estate. And D. is now dead, and so consequently the term is passed &c., judgment &c.—*Hedone.* He leased to us in fee, ready &c.—So &c.

Scire facias for an annuity, where a grant with the assent of the bishop but without the assent of the parson was valid.

Scire facias. The prior of Stoke brought the writ against Nicholas, parson of the church of Foxerde &c., that he should be &c. if he knew what to say why twenty-six marks which were in arrear to him for an annuity of four marks, according to the purport of a fine, ought not to be levied &c.—And the fine was in this form, Between such an one demandant and such an one deforceant &c., to wit that the said prior granted to such an one the aforesaid advowson with the appurtenances, saving to himself and his successors the yearly rent of four marks per annum &c.: to wit so that the clerk whom the said prior should present to the said church should pay those four marks yearly—*Toudeby.* We do not think that he can by that fine demand that annuity; for before any church can be charged it must be so by the patron of the church and by the parson thereof who has therein an estate for the term of his

" ei dimisit ad terminum qui preteriit."—*Hedone.* Ceo ne puet estre, qar nous mesme altrefoiz devaunt teux &c. Justices, portames assise de novele disseisine vers mesme cestui D. sun pere de mesmes ces tenements, par quel assise nous rescoverymes &c. vers luy come vers disseisour, e cel estat sumes tut temps pus continue, jugement.—STANTONE. Donqe ne vous lessa il pas a terme &c.—*Hedone.* Respoigne A. a ceo qe jeo dy.—*Lanfare.* Veirs est D.[1] nostre pere vous lessa ces tenements a terme de sa vie, e apres ceo vous ousta &c., par quei &c., par quei vous rescoveristes vers lui [2] par assise &c. vostre primer estat. Et D.[1] est ore mort, e issi par consequent le terme passe &c., jugement &c.—*Hedone.* Il nous lessa en fee, prest &c.—Ideo &c. A.D. 1306.

Scire facias de une annuelte, ubi concessio cum assensu episcopi sine assensu personæ satis valuit.

§ Le priour de Stoke porta le bref vers Nichol persone de la eglise de Foxerde &c. qil ifut &c. sil savoit renz dire pur quei .xxvi. mars qe arere lui furent de une annuelte de .iiii. mars solom le purport de un fin ne devoient estre levez &c. Et fuit finis ille de tali forma, inter talem petentem et talem deforcientem &c., videlicet quod idem prior concessit tali advocacionem predictam cum pertinentiis, salvo sibi et successoribus suis annuo redditu .iiii. marcarum per annum &c. Ita scilicet quod ille clericus quem idem prior ad eandem ecclesiam presentaverit illas iiii. marcas annuatim solvat.—*Toudeby.* Ne entendoms point qil puisse par cele fin cele annuelte demander; qar einz ceo qe nule eglise soit charge il covent qil soit par patron e persone de la eglise qi en cele ad estat a terme Scire facias.

[1] MS. A.

[2] MS. loo.

A.D. 1306. life, and with the assent of the bishop, or by judgment of court; now since that fine does not witness that the patron &c. charged it, nor in that fine is any one named as patron, and also the said fine supposes that at the time of levying that fine there was not any parson, and consequently it was not then charged by any parson, nor did any parson assent to that charge, nor do they show that it was charged by judgment of court, we pray judgment if by that fine he can &c.—BEREFORD. The fine says "between such an one and such an one "for the advowson &c."; then it well seems that there was a patron; wherefore on that point no more is to be said.—*Toudeby.* This writ is given to do execution of a fine; now this fine is executed; for it speaks throughout of the advowson and not of this annuity; no more in case I release and quit-claim to you &c. saving to me &c. an annual rent, is a title to that rent given to me by that quit-claim.—BEREFORD. The chief cause for which the king's Prohibition lies in this case is the fine; and for making a lease a fine is levied of those things, because otherwise it would not be pleadable in the king's court. And know that we have seen a church divided into two by a fine.—*Herle.* Since he has not shown a deed by the parson &c., neither by way of charge nor assent, nor does the fine in itself say that that annuity was granted, for in the fine there are no such words as "such an one has granted &c.," [judgment]. —BEREFORD. What of that? he reserved that annuity to himself by the fine, which is equivalent.—*Herle.* Still, he has not the assent of any parson of that church. —BEREFORD. No; but he has the assent of the patron and of the ordinary (intimating that that was sufficient). —*Rostone.* Neither the ordinary nor the patron can alienate any land annexed to the parsonage; no more without him, [the parson], can they charge it &c.—And at length the fine, which was the deed of the patron with the assent of the bishop, was adjudged a good de vie, e par assent de eveske, ou par jugement de court; dount de pus qe cele fin ne testmoigne point qe le patron &c. ne la charge, ne en cele fin nest nul com patron nome, et auxi suppose meme la fin qe au temps de lever de cele fin nule persone ifust, e par consequent par nule persone adonqes charge, ne nule persone a cele charge se assenti, ne par jugement de court ne moustrent qele soit charge, e demandoms jugement si par cele fin puisse &c.—BEREFORD. La fin dist inter talem et talem de advocacione &c.; donqe semble il bien qe iluy avoit patron; par quei de cel costere nestut il mes parler.—*Toudeby.* Ceo bref est done de fere execucion de fin; dount ceste fin est execute, car ele parle tut del avoeson e ne mie de ceste annuite, nent plus qe en cas ou jeo vous relesse e quiteclame &c. sauve a moi &c. une annuele rente, title de cele rente ne me est done par cele quiteclamanz.—BEREFORD. Ceo est la greignure cause pur quei la prohibicion le roi gist en ceo cas la fin. E pur les fet kem sur celes choses lever, pur ceo qe autrement ne serreit il mie pledable en la court le roi. Et sachez qe nous avoms veu une eglise partie en deus par fin.—*Herle.* Del houre qil ne mustre fet la persone &c. ne de la charge ne de lassent, ne la fin en luy mesme ne dit point qe cele annuite fust grante, qar il ny ad en la fin nule tele parole "tales concessit &c." —BEREFORD. De ceo quei? mes il lui sauva par la fin cele annuite, qe tant vaut.—*Herle.* Uncore ne ad il le assent de nule persone de cele eglise.—BEREFORD. Noun, mes il ad de patron e de ordiner (quasi diceret hoc sufficit).—*Roistone.* Ordinare ne patron ne poet sanz la parsone nulle terre annexe au parsonage aliener, nent plus sanz lui charger &c.—Et ad ultimum la fin qe fut fet le patron oveske le assente leveske fust

A.D. 1306.

A.D. 1306. title to recover this annuity.—*Toudeby.* He has said that he was seised by the hand of &c.—*Passeley.* We and all our predecessors have been seised always &c., except for six years before the writ &c.—HOWARD (to the party of the parson). What do you answer?—*Herle.* We have pleaded to a thing which we think falls into a question of law; we will not offer any averment without our client; he is here in his own person; let him answer for himself.—And this he said because he knew that to offer an averment was of no avail, since by it the fine was not quashed.—And the parson himself came and said that they were never seised, ready &c.—*Toudeby* (to aid him). This he says for the arrears, and for this writ which is badly worded; it ought to have said "to show if he knows what to say why he ought not to "have four marks &c."; for he should have been seised, and afterwards if the annuity were in arrear then have had such a writ as he has now; for one shall never have arrears of that whereof he was not ever seised.—*Passeley.* He shall not get to the averment; for heretofore we brought a writ against such an one, his predecessor &c., who, because he saw that judgment would go against him, came into court and granted that annuity; judgment then if he ought by averment to defeat our seisin.—*Herle.* How did he grant it? It was not by judgment (intimating that otherwise it was worth nothing).—And the averment was not received because that would be to avoid the fine.—Afterwards, terms being come to, the parson came and admitted the seisin of the prior &c.

Record. Formedon in the descender.

§ STAUNTON. One A. brought a writ of formedon in the descender against *B.*, who came into court and said that he could not have an action, for he said that A.'s father, whose heir &c., enfeoffed him of the same tenements and bound himself and his heirs &c. And he said that if he were impleaded by a stranger, he as agarde bon title pur ceste annuyte rescoverer. — *Toudeby*. Il ad dist qil fut seisi par my la main &c. — *Passeley*. Nous e touz nos predecessours seisi de tut temps &c. estre seis anz avant le bref &c.—HOWARD (ad partem personæ). Quei responez vous ?—*Herle*. Nous avoms plede de chose qe nous entendoms qe chete en ley; nous ne tendroms nul averement sanz nostre client; il est cy en propre persone, respoigne de ceo mesm*Passeley*.hoc dixit quia novit verificationem pretendere non valere cum per eam finis non cassabatur. Et vient la persone mesmes e dit qil ne estoient unqes seisiz, prest &c.—*Toudeby* (in ejus auxilium). Ceo dit il pur les arreres, e pur ceo bref qe est malement conceu, qil devoit issi dire &c. a moustrer sil savoit reinz dire pur quei il ne deust aver .iiii. mars &c.; qar ilui covendra estre seisi, e pus si la annuyte fust arere, adonqes aver tel bref com il ad ore, qe homme navera jaimes arreres de ceo qe homme nestoit unqes seisi.—*Passeley*. Al averement ne vendra il mie, qe autrefoiz nous portames bref vers un tel sun predecessour &c., qe pur ceo qil vist qe jugement se freit encountre lui vient en court e granta cele annuelte; jugement sil deyve donqes par averement nostre seisine defere.—*Herle*. Coment le granta il ceo? ne fut pas par jugement (quasi diceret aliter non valuit).—Et non fuit admissa verificacio quia hoc esset in evacuatione finis. Postea, concordia facta, persona venit et cognovit seisinam prioris &c. A.D. 1306.

§ STAUNTONE. Un A. porta bref de forme de doun en le descendere vers B., qe vient en court e dit qe accion ne poeit il avoir, qar il dit qe le pere A., qi heir &c., lui enfeffa de mesme ceux tenements e obligha luy e ces heirs &c. Et dit qe sil fust enplede de un estrange, il com heir &c. luy serreit lye a la garantie, Recordum. Forma donacionis en le descendere.

A.D. 1306. heir &c. would be bound to him in warranty; and he prayed judgment if the action &c. And A. said that this would not bar him from demanding by the form; for he said that nothing had descended to him &c.; and the other side said the contrary. A jury came before SIR W. HOWARD &c., who said on their oaths that one C., father of the said A. did, three days before his death, enfeoff A. his son of certain tenements, which tenements ought to have descended to him by heritable succession &c.; and they said that he enfeoffed him fraudulently and by collusion, because he thought that his son after his death could escape from the warranty to B., by saying that nothing had descended to him, because he was a purchaser &c. And because it is found that his father enfeoffed him of those tenements which &c. fraudulently and by collusion, in order to make him escape from the warranty, and fraud and craft ought to be of advantage to no one, the court doth adjudge that A. do take nothing by his writ, but be barred through the warranty, and be in mercy. And B., adieu &c.

Record in novel disseisin.

§ Mary who was the wife of William de Breouse brought an assise of Novel disseisin against William the son of William de Breouse, Henry Beljambe and others named &c., and put in her view certain tenements &c. William the son of William came and said that he neither had anything nor claimed anything therein, nor any tort &c. Henry Beljambe came and answered as tenant, and said nothing to put off the assise; wherefore it was awarded &c. Which assise came and said that William de Breouse, husband of the said Mary, was seised of the manor of T. with the appurtenances in his demesne as of fee and of right, and died seised; of which manor the same tenements of which she claims to be disseised are parcel; after whose death the king seized the said manor &c., because the said William e demanda jugement si accion &c. Et A. dist qe ceo ne lui serreit barre a demander par la forme; qar il dit qe rien ne luy fut descendu &c.; e alius e contra. Pais vient devant Sire W. HOWARD &c., qe dissoient par lour sermenz qe un C. pere le dit A., treis jors avant sa mort, enfeffa de certein tenements A. sun fiz, les queux tenements li devereient aver descendu par succession de heritage &c., e dissoient qe en fraude e en collusion lui enfeffa il, pur ceo qil entendi qe sun fiz apres sun desces esturtereit de la garantie vers B. en dissant qe rien ne lui fut descendu pur ceo qil fut purchassour &c. Et pur ceo qe trove est qe sun pere lui enfeffa de ceux tenements les queux &c. en fraude e en collusion pur luy fere esturtre de la garantie, et fraus et dolus nemini debent patrocinari, si agarde &c. qe A. ne preigne rien par sun bref, einz soit barre par my la garantie, e soit en la mercy; e B. a Deu &c. A.D. 1306.

§ Marie ke fust la femme Willem de Breouse porta une assise de novele disseisine vers Willem le fiz Willeam de Breouse, Henri Belejambe e autres nomez &c., e mist en sa vewe &c. certeinz tenements &c. Willem le fiz Willem vient e dist qil nen avoit rienz ne rienz ne clama, ne nul tort &c. Henri Belejambe vient e respondi com tenant, e rien ne dit a targer la assise; par quei ele fut agarde &c. La quele assise vient e dit qe Willem de Breouse, baroun la dite Marie, fut seisi del maner de T. ove les appurtenans en sun demene come de fee e de droit, e morust seisi, de quel maner mesmes les tenements dount ele se pleint estre disseisi sunt parcele; apres qi mort le roi seisi le dit maner &c., pur ceo qe le dit Willem tient de luy en Recordum in nova disseisina.

A.D. 1306. held of him in chief; and they said that the said William, husband &c., had leased the said tenements put in view &c. to the said Henry Beljambe, to hold of him at his will, and that afterwards William the son of William de Breouse, while the manor was in the king's hands, executed a charter of these same tenements to the said Henry in fee simple. But they said that the king did not seize into his hands the tenements put in view &c.; and they said moreover that the king out of his seisin assigned the said manor of T. with the appurtenances to the said Mary to hold in name of dower of the endowment of her husband. Mary came after she was seised of the gross of the manor &c., and wished to enter that parcel whereof the said Henry was tenant, to wit the tenements whereof she complains &c. Henry would not allow &c.; whereupon she brought the assise; and other things &c., and they prayed the advice of the justices. And because it is found &c. that William the husband &c. was seised of the manor &c. in such wise that he could endow her; and whatever charter William the son of William executed to the said Henry during the time when the manor was in the king's hands was null and shall not turn to the prejudice of the king or of the woman; and since Mary was seised of the gross of the manor by the assignment by the king and the endowment by her husband, and wished to have entered the tenements in respect of which she brought the assise against Henry as parcel of the manor assigned to her, and was not allowed to do so, it seems to us that she was sufficiently disseised. And therefore this court doth adjudge that she do recover her seisin by the view &c. and her damages &c.—And so note that because she was seised of the gross of the manor &c. thereby they thought that she was sufficiently seised of the parcel into which she was prevented from entering &c.

chief; e disoient qe le dit Willem, baron &c., avoit lesse les dits tenements mis en vewe &c. al dit Henri Belejambe a tenir de lui a sa volunte, e pus Willem le fiz Willem de Breouse, tant come le maner fut en la mayn le roi, fyst al dit Henri une chartre en fee simple de mesmes ces tenements; mes il disoient qe le roi ne seisi point en sa mein les tenements mis en vewe &c.; e disoint outre qe le roi hors de sa seisine assigna le dit maner de T. ove les appurtenans a la dite Marie, a tenir en noun de dowere del dowement sun baroun. Marie vient, apres ceo qele fust seisie del gros du maner &c., e voleit entrer cele parcele dount le dit Henri fust en tenance, saver les tenements dount ele se pleint &c. Henri ne voleit suffrir &c.; par quei ele porta la assise; e autre chose &c.; e prierent discrecion des justices. E pur ceo ke trove est &c. ke Willem baroun &c. fust seisi del dit maner &c. issi qe dowere la pout; e quele chartre ke Willem le fiz Willem fit al dit Henri en temps ke le maner fut en le mein le roi ne fust nule, ne ne tournera en prejudice du roy ne de la femme; e de pus qe Marie fust seisi del gros du maner par my lassignement le roi e del dowement sun baroun, e voleit aver entre les tenements dount ele porta la assise vers Henri com en parcele du maner a luy assigne, e ne fu pas sufferte, il nous semble qe assez fust ele disseisie. E pur ceo agarde &c. qele rescovere sa seisine par vewe &c. e ces damages &c.—Et sic nota qe pur ceo qele fust seisie del gros du maner &c. par tant la entendirent il assez estre seisie de la parcele dount ele fust destourbe dentrer &c.

A.D. 1306.

Nota.

A.D. 1306. Ael.

§ John [Sewal] and John Swetyng brought the writ against the bishop of London. And the writ ran thus: "Command &c. that he yield up &c. the keeping of the "park of T. of which G. the grandfather of the said "John Swetyng and the great grandfather of John "Sewal, whose heirs &c. was seised in his demesne "as of fee &c. on the day &c."—*Toudeby.* Judgment of the writ; for whereas it says "Command that he "yield up the keeping," since the keeping is a thing which is not capable of being handled, it would better have said "that he permit &c. to have the keeping &c. —*Malmesthorpe.* The advowson of a church is not capable of being handled, and yet a writ says "Com-"mand that he yield up the advowson &c.;" wherefore &c. — *Passeley.* Still we pray judgment of the writ, for the having the keeping &c. does not lie in demesne, and the writ says "in demesne"; judgment. —STAUNTON. As to that, the writ is good enough.—*Toudeby.* If the writ were brought against a stranger who was a deforceant of the keeping, then it would well say "that he yield up &c."; but now we tell you that the bishop himself is tenant of the park, and has the keeping of the park.—*Herle.* Now we pray judgment of your own admission; for you admit that you deforce us of the keeping; wherefore &c.

§ Johan e Johan Swetyng porterent le bref vers leveske de Londres. Et fuit breve tale "Precipe &c. "quod reddat &c. custodiam parci de T. de qua G. avus "predicti Johannis Swetting et proavus Johannis "Sewal, cujus heredes &c., fuit seisitus in dominico "suo ut de feodo &c. die &c."—*Toudeby.* Jugement du bref; qe la ou il dit "precipe quod reddat custodiam," del houre qe garde est chose qe nest mie maniable il serreit meuz dit "quod permittat &c. habere custodiam "&c."—*Malm.* Avoweson de eglise nest mie maniable, e si dit hoc "precipe quod reddat advocacionem &c.," par quei &c.—*Passeley.* Uncore jugement du bref, qar de aver garde &c. ne chet mie en demene, e le bref voet "in dominico"; jugement.—Stantone. Quant a ceo le bref est assez bon.—*Toudeby.* Si le bref fust porte vers un estrange qe fut deforceor de la garde, dount dirreit il bien "quod reddat" &c.; mes ore vous dioms qe leveske mesme est tenant du park e ad la garde du park.—*Herle.* Ore demandoms nous jugement de vostre conissance demeine; qe vous mesme grantez qe vous nous deforcez la garde; par quei &c.

A.D. 1306.
Ael.

PLACITA DE ANNO XXXV° REGIS EDWARDI.

PLEAS IN HILARY TERM IN THE THIRTY-FIFTH YEAR OF KING EDWARD THE FIRST.

A.D. 1307.

Debt. Note.

§ In a plea of Debt, after wager of law the defendant made default; wherefore it was adjudged that the plaintiff should recover his debt &c. and his damages stated in his plaint &c., and not damages taxed by the court, &c.

Account. Note.

§ In a plea of Account, the writ was brought to the sheriff of Gloucester, when the plaintiff charged the defendant only with a receipt (of moneys) in London; wherefore the writ abated, by judgment of the court, for the reason that if the defendant had denied the receipt &c., it must have been sent to the sheriff to whom the original came, and a jury of the county of Gloucester could not have cognizance thereof.

Dower. Note.

Where the demandant in dower married after wager of law of non-summons.

§ In a plea of Dower, after the return of the Grand Cape, the tenant waged his law &c.: at the day which was given to him to make his law he came ready with his law &c., but he alleged that the demandant was after the purchase of the writ under coverture; and she was compelled by the court to make answer to this; and she said that she was still sole, ready &c.; and the tenant found surety for the issues in the mesne time &c.

Formedon in the descender.

Where the hereditary succession is given to heir of the woman only of tenements given in frank-marriage.

§ The writ ran "which such an one gave to William "&c. in frank-marriage with Sibil his sister and the "heirs of the body of the said Sibil, and which after the "deaths of the aforesaid William and Sibil and Michael, "son of the said William and Sibil, ought according to "the form &c. to descend to the said Alice daughter "of Michael and cousin and heir of the said William

INCIPIUNT PLACITA DE TERMINO SANCTI HILLARII ANNO TRICESIMO QUINTO.

§ En play de dette, apres la lei agage, le defendant fit defaute; par quei fust agarde qe le pleintif recoverast sa dette &c. e ces damages nomez en sa querele, et non per taxacionem curiæ &c. A.D. 1307. Nota de dette.

§ En play dacounte le bref fust porte au vicomte de Gloucestre, ou le pleintif charge le defendant soulement de receite qil receut en Loundres; par quei le bref se abati par agard, pur ceo qe si le defendant ust dedit la receite &c., il covendra aver mande au viscount a qi le original vient, e de ceo ne poeit pays del counte de Gloucestre aver conissance. Nota de compoto.

Ubi petens dotem post legem de non summonitione vadiatam maritat.

§ En play de dowere, apres le grant cape returne, le tenant gaga la lei &c.; au jour qe done ly fust de fere sa lei il vient prest ove sa lei &c., mes il alegga qe la demandante pus le bref purchace fust coverte de baron; a quei ele fut chace a respondre par la court; e dit qele fust uncore sole, e prest &c.: e le tenant trova suirte des issues en le meen temps &c. Nota de dote.

Ubi successio hereditaria conceditur heredi mulieris tantum de tenementis datis in liberum maritagium.

Et fuit breve tale, "Quæ talis dedit Willielmo "&c. in liberum maritagium cum Sibilla sorore sua "et heredibus de corpore ipsius Sibillæ exeuntibus, "et quæ post mortem predictorum Willielmi et Sibillæ "et Michaelis filii eorundem Willielmi et Sibillæ, pre-"dictæ Aliciæ filiæ Michaelis et consanguineæ et heredi "predictorum Willielmi et Sibillæ descendere debent Forma donacionis en le descendere.

A.D. 1307. "and Sibil." And the count was in accordance with the writ. — *Lanfar.* We pray judgment of this writ; for when the writ says "and to the heirs of the body of "the said Sibil," it is to be supposed that she demands them only as heir of Sibil; and then when it says "and "which after the deaths of the said William and Sibil," it is to be supposed that she demands them as heir of both: judgment &c. — *Hunt* (on the same side). The writ is self-repugnant. For of tenements given in frank-marriage the heir is, naturally, the issue of him to whom the land is given with his wife who is the moving cause of the gift: for otherwise, if the first husband of the woman should have a daughter (by her) and the second husband should have a son (by her), that son would take the inheritance. And inasmuch as the writ says "and "to the heirs of the body of the said Sibil," the writ indicates that the heirs of the woman only are inheritors; and that is against the form of frank-marriage. — HOWARD. Why so? If I give you a tenement in frank-marriage, can I not frame the entail as I please? (intimating that he could). And she can not have any other writ according to her case and her charter.—And the writ was adjudged good.—And *The Tenant* said that Sibil survived William and alienated before the statute[1] &c.—And because the court was not certain whether she could alone before the statute alienate in such a case, because the statute says "hitherto feoffees in this wise "had the power &c." and does not say "either of "them &c.," the plea remained.

Where the tenant for life aliened in fee, and afterwards recovered the same tenements by judgment of the king's court.

Entry, by the Stat. of Gloucester.

§ The writ was brought against the tenant, who made default, by reason whereof the tenements were on the point of being lost: and thereupon came she who aliened the tenements and whom the demandant supposed

---

[1] 13 Edw. I. De donis.

"per formam &c.;" et narracio brevi concordat.—*Lanfare.* Jugement de cesti bref; qar primes, par tant qe le bref dist "et heredibus de corpore ipsius Sibillæ "exeuntibus," fet a supposer qe ele les demande solement com heir Sibille; e puis par tant qil dist "et que "post mortem predictorum Willielmi et Sibillæ" fet a supposer qe ele les demaunde com heir le un e lautre; jugement &c.—*Hunte* (ad idem). Le bref est en lui meyme repugnant; qar des tenements donez en franc mariage est naturement heir le issu celi a qi le doun se fet ove sa femme, qe de ceo est cause; car autrement, si le primer baron la femme &c. out une fille, e le secunde baron un fiz, celui fiz avereit cel heritage. E en tant com le bref dit "et heredibus de corpore "ipsius Sibillæ exeuntibus" voet le bref qe les heirs la femme solement seient enheritez; e ceo est encontre forme de franc mariage.—HOWARD. Pur quei? si jeo vous doigne tenement en franc mariage, ne purra jeo fere la taille a ma volente? (quasi diceret sic). E ele ne poet aver autre bref mes solom sun cas e sa chartre.—Et fut le bref agarde bon.—E *le tenant* dit qe Sibille survesqui Willem e aliena devant statut &c.—E pur ceo qe la court ne fut pas ascerte si ele sole poeit en tiel cas aliener avant statut, pur ceo qe lestatut dit "hucusque habuerunt hujusmodi feoffati potestatem "&c." et non dicit "alter eorum" &c. demura. A.D. 1307.

De ingressu per statutum Gloucestriæ ubi tenens ad terminum vitæ alienavit in feodum, et postea eadem tenementa per judicium curiæ domini regis recuperavit.

§ Le bref fust porte vers le tenant, qe fist defaute; par quei ces tenements furent en point de perdre; e sur ceo vient ele qe ces tenements aliena, e qe, a ceo qe le demaundant supposa, fut tenant a terme de vie, Entre sur statut de Gloucestre.

A.D. 1307. to be tenant for life, and said that she brought a writ, for cause of matrimony treated between them, against him whom the demandant has now made tenant, and recovered the tenement, on default after default; and that she was seised of them in her demesne; and she prayed that she might not be, by any default of him who was not now tenant of those tenements, ousted from her frank tenement &c. — *Herle.* Nay! whatever you may talk of recovery; we tell you that you held of us &c. for term of life, and you alienated in fee: and although you have since, by collusion between you and the tenant, recovered, yet that alienation shall not be unpunished: and also our writ is of older date than your writ was by which you recovered. — *Passeley.* What of that? Why when we recovered did you not come and disclose your case to the court? But you then made no objection: wherefore &c. — *Este.* We were not in a position to make any objection; for we knew nothing about the matter; nor had we then any day in the court. — STAUNTON to *Passeley.* What do you ask? — *Passeley.* That we may be received to abate this writ, since we are the tenants &c., and not he against whom the writ is brought. — *Herle.* If she is to be received it must be by virtue of the statute: but she is not within any particular of the statute[1]: wherefore &c. — HENGHAM. We see plainly that she is tenant now; and we receive her to defend her tenancy, and not to abate the writ. And before the statute she was receivable in such a case. — *Passeley.* The tenements &c. were given to our husband and us in fee simple, to us and our heirs; we survived, and alienated as we were well able to do. — *Herle.* The tenements were given to your husband whose heir &c.; and they were given to you and the heirs of your husband; so that you had nothing in the tenements but a tenancy for life; ready &c.—And the other side said the contrary.—Therefore &c.

[1] 13 Edw. I. (Westm. 2.) c. 3.

e dit qe ele porta bref "causa matrimonii inter eos "prelocuti" vers celui qe le demaundant a ore fet tenant, e ces tenements &c. rescovery par defaute apres defaute, e ele de ces seisie en demene, e pria qe ele ne fust, par nule defaute de celui qe de ceux tenements a ore ne fut tenant, de son franc tenement oste. —*Herle.* Nay! coment qe vous parlez de rescoverir, nous vous dioms qe vous tenistes de nous &c. a terme de vie, e alienastes en fee; e coment ke vous eez pus, dar collusion entre vous e le tenant, rescoveri, cele alienacion ne serra mie despuni; e jatardeis nostre bref est de eigne date qe ne fust le vostre par quel vous rescoveristes.—*Passeley.* De ceo quei? quant nous rescoverames qe ne fuissez vous venuz e desclos vostre cas a la cort? mes vous a donqes nul debat ne feistes; par quei &c. — *Este.* Nous ne poeimes debat fere, car nous de ceo rienz ne savoimes, ne nul jour en court a donqes ne avoimes.—STANTONE a *Passeley.* Qe priez vous? — *Passeley.* Estre receu de abatre ceo bref, del hour qe nous sumes tenans &c. e noun pas celuy vers qi il porte sun bref. — *Herle.* Si ele serreit receu ceo serroit par statut; mes ele nest en nul point del statut; par quei &c. — HENGHAM. Nous veoms bien qele est tenant a ore, e la resceivoms a defendre sa tenance, e noun pas a bref abatre: e avant statut ele fut resceivable en tiel cas. — *Passeley.* Les tenements &c. furent donez a nostre baron e a nous en fee simple, a nous, e a nos heirs; nous survesquimes e alienames com bien nous lust. —*Herle.* Les tenements furent donez a vostre baroun, qi heir &c., e a vous e as heirs vostre baron; issi qe vous en ces tenements rien ny aviez mes qe tenance a terme de vie; prest &c. Et alii e contra Ideo &c.

A.D. 1307.

A.D. 1307. Note.

§ A writ was brought against a man for tenements which were the joint purchase of the tenant and his wife, and she was not named in the writ. Piers, the demandant, seeing this, purchased another writ of the same kind against the tenant and his wife; and it was challenged, because it was purchased pending the other writ. —*Passeley.* In order to make that exception hold, two things are necessary, viz., that the writ should be between the same persons and in respect of the same tenements; but now we tell you that there are other persons in this writ, &c.—That answer was not allowed, but the writ was quashed.

Essoin of "In the king's service."

§ R. de Chaumpaigne, who was vouched &c., made default after appearance; whereupon the Petit Cape issued &c.; and at the day when it was returned he essoined himself as in the king's service; and at the day given to him &c. the demandant insisted on the default &c.; and there was nothing said as to the warrant for his essoin. And Robert said that he could not make a default, by reason that he was imprisoned &c.; and on that the inquest joined and passed against him *in pais* before &c. And on the day which was given to him to hear his judgment &c., he again essoined himself as in the king's service: and this was challenged by *Herle* for two reasons; 1st because the essoin did not contain the name of the person who answered as essoiner; and 2nd because the first essoiner was not warranted.—And it was quashed for the reasons aforesaid by HENGHAM, and the demandant recovered seisin.

For a yearly rent granted for service performed and to be performed, where the defendant alleged particulars of the plaintiff's refusal to do the service.

Annual rent.

§ One A. brought a writ of Annuity, and demanded ten marks, as arrears of an annuity of 13*s.* 4*d.*; and put forward a writing granting the annuity.—*Lanfar.* We

Un bref fust porte vers un home des tenements qe furent le joint purchas le tenant e sa femme qe ne fu pas nome en bref. Piris le demandant si aperceut, e purchassa autre bref de mesme tiele forme vers celui tenant e sa femme, qe fut chalange pur ceo qil fu purchace pendant lautre bref. — *Passeley.* De fere tele excepcion bone covendreit deus choses; saver, entre mesme les persones e de mesme les tenements; mes ore vous dioms qe ily sunt autres persones en ceo bref &c. Et non allocatur, sed breve cassabatur. A.D. 1307. Nota.

§ R. de Chaumpaigne ke fust vouche &c. fit defaute apres apparance, par quei le petit cape &c.; e au jour qe fut returne sei fit essoigner de service le roi; et au jour a lui done &c. le demandant se prist a la defaute &c. Et nichil loquebatur de warrento essonii sui. Et Robert dit qil ne poeit defaute fere, car il fut enprisone &c.; e de ceo joint enqueste, qe passa encontre lui en pays devant &c.: e au jour qe done lui fust de oier sun jugement &c., autrefoiz se fit essoigner de service le roi; qe fust chalange par deus resons par *Herle,* la une pur ceo quil ny avoit mie en le assoigne le noun celui qe respondi com essoner; et lautre reson pur ceo qe le primer essoner ne fut pas garanti. Et fuit cassatum predictis rationibus per Hengham: et petens recuperavit seisinam. Nota. De essonio de servicio regis.

De annuo redditu, concesso pro servicio inpenso et inpensuro, allegante defendente in certis quod querens servicium ei nolebat inpendere. De annuo redditu.

§ Un A. porta le bref, e demanda .x. mars qe arere luy furent de une annuite de .xiii. soz .iiii. deniers; e mist avant escrist de cele annuite. — *Lanfare.* Nous

A.D. 1307. readily admit the writing to be our deed; but we tell you that you cannot demand anything in respect of that annuity; for the writing runs thus—"for service &c. "performed and to be performed," and we tell you that on such a day we had to plead in a plea &c. in such a county against &c. with the said A.: and we prayed him to serve us in that plea, and he would not: therefore since he has failed to do the thing which is the cause of the grant of the annuity, we do not think that he can demand it.—*Willoughby.* And we pray judgment, since the specialty is admitted which witnesses the cause to be as well the service done as service to be done (by the words "for "service performed") if he can, by anything which he has pleaded, bar us of the annuity,—HOWARD rehearsed the entire process, and concluded by saying, And since you have admitted the writing which binds you to pay the annuity to them, and have pleaded nothing relieving you from the liability, this court doth adjudge that he do recover the ten marks accrued due before the writ issued, and also the amount which has since accrued due, and also his damages &c.

Where the avowry was made on one under age for scutage in tenements holden in dower.

Replevin. § The wife of Geoffrey Lucian complained that the abbat of Peterborough tortiously took her plough-beasts &c.—*Willoughby.* We avow the taking &c. on Geoffrey the son of Geoffrey Lucian; and for the reason that the said Geoffrey holds of us the manor of Ayllynton (whereof the place where the taking was made is part) by fealty and homage and the service of 30*s.* yearly, and the service of one knight's fee; of which services, viz. the fealty and homage and rent &c., we ourselves were seised, by the hand of his father Geoffrey &c.; and our predecessor William was seised of the service of one knight's fee viz. of escuage, as by the hand of &c. And for that the escuage for the 28th and 31st years [of the king], namely 40*s.*

conussoms bien lescrist estre nostre fet; mes nous vous dioms qe vous ne poez de cele annuite rien demander; car lescrist voet "pro servicio &c. inpenso et "inpensuro:" e vous dioms qe a teu jour aveimes nous a pleder en play &c. a teu counte vers &c. ou mesme cestui A., e nous lui priames qil nous servit en tel plee; e il ne voleit: par quei de lour qil nous ad failli de fere cele chose qe est cause du graunt del annuite, nentendoms mie qil le puisse demander.—*Willuby.* E nous jugement, de lour qe lespecialte est grante qe temoigne la cause estre autresibien pur service fez com pur service a faire, par tant qil dit "pro servicio "inpenso," sil puisse par rienz qil ad dit nous forbarrer de cele anuite. — HOWARD repetiit totum processum, et in fine, E pur ceo qe vous avez graunte lescrist qe vous lie a eux en cele annuite, e rienz ne dites qe de cel vous delye, si agarde &c. qil rescovere les dis mars encoruz avant le bref &c., e ceo qe pus est encoru, e ces damages &c. A.D. 1307.

Facta advocacione super existente infra etatem pro scutagio in tenementis tentis in dotem.

§ La femme Geffrey Luciane se pleint qe labbe de Burghe Seint Pere atort prist ces avers &c.—*Willuby.* Nous avowoms la prise &c. sur Geffrey le fiz Geffrey Luciane; e par la reson qe mesme celui Geffrey entient de nous le maner de Ayllyntone, de quei le leu de prise est parcele, par feaute, homage, e par les services de .xxx. soz par an, e par les services de un fee de chivaler; des queux services, nomement fealte, homage, e rente &c., nous mesme en fu seisi par la main Geffrey sun pere &c.; e Willem nostre predecessour seisi del service de un fee de chivaler, cest a saver de escuage, com par my la main &c.: et pur ceo qe lescuage nous fut arere &c. del an &c. .xxviii. e del an .xxxi., Replegiare.

A.D. 1307. for every year, was in arrear to us, we avow the taking &c., and we have brought a writ to the sheriff that he should assist us in levying the escuage from our fees; and the king is seised of our services for the same.—*Passeley.* You can not avow for the escuage upon him; for he is under age; and his body and his lands and tenements and all that he has are in ward of the king: judgment &c.; and we can not plead anything to your avowry.—*Herle.* What of that? then pray aid of him.—ROUBURY. Of whom should she pray aid? of the king? (intimating that she could not) and the infant is under age.—*Herle.* If she will not pray aid or plead anything else, we pray a return.—ROUBURY. The king is so prerogative in his lands that he will have none above him. —HOWARD. What will you have us do? She holds the manor in dower by assignment from the king, and the infant on whom you avow is under age and his body and lands are in ward of the king.—*Herle.* I have seen a similar case where the defendant had the return, and the woman plaintiff was put to her writ of Mesne when the infant should come to his full age.—*Warwick.* If Geoffrey were in the ward of any other person than the king, you would have the wardship of the lands which are holden of you: and if you had the wardship you would not have the escuage: and nothing ousts you from the wardship but the prerogative of the king.—*Herle.* For all his prerogative, we shall not be ousted of our services; for by reason of our having them nothing is withdrawn from him, since he is not seised of the tenements &c.—STAUNTON rehearsed the process, and said, And for that you have avowed &c. on an infant under age, whose body and whose lands are in ward of the king, who as it seems to the court will not pay escuage, the court adjudges that you take nothing by your writ, and that she (the plaintiff) do recover her damages taxed &c.

saver de chascon an .xl. soz, si avowoms la prise &c., e si avom porte bref a visconte qil nous fut en aide de lever escuage de nos feez, e le roi en est seisi de nos services.—*Passeley*. Sur lui ne poez avowerie fere pur escuage, qar il est denz age, e sun corps e terres e tenements e quant qil ad en la garde le roi; jugement &c.; e nous ne poms rienz pleder a vostre avowerie.—*Herle*. De ceo quei? priez donqes eide de luy.—ROUBYRI. De qi priereit ele aide? du roi? (quasi diceret nay); e lenfant est denz age.—*Herle*. Si ele ne voille eide prier, ou autre chose dire, nous prioms return.—ROUBIRI. Le roi est en sa terre si prerogatif qil ne voet aver nul sur luy.—HOWARD. Qe voillez qe nous feissoms? qe ele tient ceu maner en dowere del assignement le roi, e lenfant sur qi vous avowez denz age, e sun corps e ces terres en la garde le roi.—*Herle*. Jeo ay veu en teu cas, qe home ad agarde return al defendant, e qe la femme pleintive ad este mise a son bref de meen quant lenfant serroit de age.—*Warr*. Si Geffrey fust en autri garde qe en la garde le roi vous averiez la garde des terres qe sunt tenuz de vous; e si vous eussez la garde, vous naveriez escuage; e rienz ne vous ouste de la garde meqe la prerogatif del roi. *Herle*. Pur sa prerogativete ne serrioms mie oustez de nos services; ke par tant ke nous les eomes rien lui descret del hour qil nest mie seisi del tenement &c.—STANTONE repetiit processum: E pur ceo qe vous avez avowe &c. sur un enfant denz age, qi corps e terres sunt en la garde le roi, qe a ceo qil semble a la court nul escuage paiera, si agarde &c. qe vous ne preignez rien par vostre bref, e rescovere ces damages taxez &c.

A.D. 1307.

A.D. 1307.
Quare non admisit.

§ Edward Charles brought a writ of Darrein presentement against one William, who came into court and granted the presentation to the said Edward: whereupon Edward had the writ &c. "that notwithstanding the "reclamation," addressed to the bishop of Norwich, who did nothing thereon; whereupon he brought the Quare non admisit &c.—*Passeley.* We tell you that we are bishop of the place, and that one William &c. did, after the death of the last parson &c., as true patron present to us &c., in whose behalf we made a letter of inquiry, on which inquiry it was found that the church &c. was void and that William was the true patron, and that the parson presented was fit &c.; and no other person did as patron oppose him; therefore we gave him a letter of institution, and of him, down to the time when the writ "notwithstanding the reclamation" came to us, the church was full: so this other we could not receive.—*Herle.* Now we pray judgment, since the law gives a lay patron six months to ascertain and dereign his right, within which time nothing is to prejudice him; and you have acknowledged that you received the king's writ before the six months were passed: we pray judgment.—*Passeley.* We did that which a bishop ought rightfully to do; now, if you wanted to have disputed the matter you should have brought the Prohibition; or why did you not oppose the taking an inquest, for your right?—*Kinge.* We brought a writ to the sheriff within three weeks after the death of the last parson; so it clearly appears that we did dispute the matter.—*Passeley.* We could not have any knowledge by that writ: for many writs go to the sheriff of which we know nothing.—*Kinge.* No more can we know when you took your inquest.—*Passeley.* The writ which you had out of this court was by William's grant, and it was after he had presented to us his clerk, who was received and instituted; and this was by collusion between you and him: and this we will aver; and we pray judgment &c.—*Herle.* You

§ Edward Charles porta le drein present vers un Willem, qe vient en court e granta le presentement au dit Edward; par quei Edward avoit bref &c. quod non obstante reclamatione al eveske de Norwyche, qe rienz ne fit; par quei il porta le quare non admisit &c.—*Passeley.* Nous vous dioms qe nous sumes eveske du leu, a qi un Willem &c., apres la mort la dreine persone &c., com verrey patron presenta &c., a qi nous feimes lettre denqueste, par quele enqueste trove fust qe la eglise &c. fut voide, e qe Willem fut verrei patrone, e la persone presente able &c.; e nul autre com patron se opposa, par quei nous lui feimes lettre de institution, e de qi a ceu temps qe ceo bref nous vient non obstante reclamatione la eglise &c. fu pleine; par quei a cele autre resceivre ne poeimes.—*Herle.* Ore demandoms jugement, del houre qe a lay patron pur sun droit conustre e dereigner est de ley done temps de vi. moys, denz queux temps rienz ne le serra en prejudice, e vous avez conue qe vous resceutes le bref le roi, e ceo avant les vi. moys passez, demandom jugement. — *Passeley.* Nous feimes ceo qil convendra eveske fere de reson; dount si vous voillez aver mys debat, qe nous eussez porte prohibicion, ou qe ne vous eussez oppose a lenqueste prendre pur vostre droit.—*Kinge.* Nous portames bref au viconte denz treis semeynes apres la mort la dreine persone; par quei il parust bien qe nous meymes debat.—*Passeley.* Par ceo bref ne poems nous aver nule conissance; car mults des brefs viegnent au viconte dount nous ne savom rienz.—*Kinge.* Nent plus ne poums nous saver quant vous preistes vostre enqueste. — *Passeley.* Le bref qe vous aviez hors de cienz ceo fu par le grant Willem, e ceo apres ceo qil nous avoit presente sun clerk, qe fu receu e institut, e ceo par collusion entre vous e luy; e ceo voloms averer, e demandoms jugement &c. —*Herle.* Alaverement ne avendrez point; car home

A.D. 1307.

Quare non admisit.

A.D. 1307. shall not get to the averment: for it will be found here by the record that William granted the presentation to us at that time, thereby supposing that the church was void: now you shall not go against that record by averring, by the country, that the church was full of William's presente e. *Warwick.* If a bishop institute within the six months it is at his peril; and therefore he had a command here what he was to do, and not without peril to deliver corporal possession to the presentee.—*Passeley.* It was by collusion between William and Edward, &c.; and a quarter of a year after the institution of William's presentee, Edward, with William's assent, brought the assise and dereigned &c., on the default of William and not by the assise; ready to aver it was by collusion &c., if the court will permit it. On the other hand, when Edward presented to us &c., it was before the feast of St. Andrew: and we at once made for him our letter of inquest, which he did not sue out until Mid-Lent: so it was his fault in allowing the time to pass &c.

Right. § The prior of St. Katherine brought the writ open to the bailiff of the town &c.; and in that court was non-suit; and after the non-suit had a Tolt in the county court, and then brought the Pone, and the plea was removed. — *Heydon.* Tortiously he deforces him of a messuage &c.; and tortiously for this, that it is his right and the right of his church of Saint Katherine aforesaid, by reason that one William holds of him by fealty and by the services of 2*s.* 6*d.* yearly; of which services the said prior was seised by the hand of the said William, as by the hand of his very tenant &c., namely of the fealty, as of fee and of right and the right of his church &c., in time of peace &c., in the time of king &c., and which prior, because the said rent was in arrear, distreined in that house (and he set out the particulars) which distress Walter &c., who was also named in the writ as tenant with William, replevied &c.; and in this court before you, on such a day in such a year, they trovera cienz par record qe Willem nous granta le presentement adonqes, en tant supposant qe la eglise fust voide; dount encontre ceo record ne avendrez point de averer par pays qe la eglise fu pleine du presente Willem.—*Warr.* Si eveske face institucion denz les vi. mois ceo est a sun peril; e pur ceo ad il commande issi qil puet fere, e ne mie liverer au presente corporele possession sanz peril.—*Passeley.* Ceo fu par collusion entre Willem Edward &c., e un quarte dan[1] apres ceo qe la institution fu fete del presente Willem Edward porta le assise del assente Willem e dereigna &c. par defaute Willem et non per assisam; e prest del averer qe ceo par collusion &c. si la cort la puisse suffrir: dautre part, quant Edward nous presenta &c. ceo fu avant la feste Seint Andreu; e nous meintenant lui feimes &c. lettre denqueste, la quele il ne suy pas tant qe a my Quareme: issi qe ceo fu sa[2] defaute qe suffri le temps passer &c. A.D. 1307.

§ Le priour de Seinte Katerine porta le bref overt au baillif de la ville &c. E en cele court fist une noun suite; e jatardeis apres la nounsuite fist la toute en conte, e pus porta le pone, e la parole remue.—*Hedone.* Atort luy deforce un mies &c., e pur ceo atort, qe ceo est sun droit e le droit de sa eglise de Seinte Katerine avantdit, par la reson qe un Willem de ceu mies en tient de luy par feaute e par les services de deus soz e seis deners par an, des queux services mesme cestui priour en fu seisi par my la main mesme celi Willem, com par my la mein &c., nomement de la feaute, com de fee e de droit e le droit de sa eglise &c., en temps de pees &c., en temps le roi &c., e le quel priour, pur ceo qe la dite rente luy fust arere, en ceu mees fist une destresse (et nominavit de quei) la quele destresse Wauter &c., qe auxi fut nome en bref com tenant ov Willem, fist replever &c., e en ceste court devant De recto.

[1] MS. del.

[2] MS. la.

A.D. 1307. complained that tortiously he had taken &c.; which taking in that messuage the prior avowed as having been made in his fee for the aforesaid rent in arrear for one year before the day of the taking &c.; at which plea the aforesaid William came and joined with Walter &c., and disavowed and disclaimed holding that messuage of the said prior of his church &c.; by which disavowal and disclaimer an action accrued to the said prior to demand the messuage in demesne; and if they will deny it, here is good suit and proof. — *Willoughby.* This writ was brought to the bailiffs of L., and by that writ this plea is attached to the hustings of that place, where this said Prior was non-suit; wherefore we do not think that by this writ the plea can be begun again. —STAUNTON. We find by the sheriff's return that the sheriff gave you a day in this court; and so it seems that the plea was in the county court, and it is now continued so that you have a day here; therefore it is not good for you to demur there.—*Willuby* defended, and demanded the view.—*Friskeney.* You ought not to be ignorant what house it is that you disclaim holding of us: therefore you shall not have the view.—Notwithstanding this, the court allowed him the view.

Quare impedit.

§ N. de Warwick,[1] who sued &c. [said] that Henry de Lancaster and Maud his wife &c. tortiously disturb &c. from presenting a fit person to the church of St. Ismael in Wales &c., and tortiously for this that it belongs to him to present, by reason that one A. late abbat of Gloucester presented to that church as of right &c., in time of peace &c., by whose death the church &c. became void during the time that the abbey was in the hands of our lord the king; so &c. tortiously &c. And the writ ran thus "that he do permit him to present to the "church of St. Ismael." — *Friskeney.* We pray judgment of the writ; for every Quare impedit should contain the name of the town where the church is: but in this writ there is none, but it must needs be supposed

[1] N. de Warwick was the king's Attorney general.

vous meisme, nomement tiel jour e tel an, se pleignerent atort avoit pris &c., de quele prise le priour fist avowerie en cel mees come sun fee pur le avantdite rente arere de un an avant le jour de la prise &c.; a queu plee le avantdit Willem vient e se joint a Wauter &c., e desavowa e desclama tenir ceu mees del avantdit priour e de sa eglise &c.; par quel desavowement e desclamanz accion acrust al avantdit priour a demander cel mees en demene; e sil le voillent dedire &c. suite bone e dreigne. — *Willuby.* Cestui bref fust porte au baillifs de L. e par ceo bref ceo plee illoke attame en lour hustenge, ou meisme cestui prieur fist une noun suite; par quei nentendoms mie qe par cestui bref purra plee derichief estre comence. — STANTONE. Nous trovoms par return del visconte, qe le viconte vous dona jour cy; e entant semble il qe la parole fust en conte, e ore continue ci qe vous avez jour cienz; par quei il ne vous est pas pur bon a demorer la. — *Willuby* defendi e demanda la vewe. — *Friskeney.* Deconustre ne devez quele mees vous desclamez de nous tenir; par quei vous ne averez mie la Vewe.—Et hoc non obstante habuit per curiam visum &c. A.D. 1307.

§ N. de Warr. qe seust &c. qe Henri de Lancastre e Maude sa femme &c. atort lui destourbent &c. presenter covenable persone a la eglise de Seint Ismael en Gales &c., e pur ceo atort qe a luy apent a presenter par la reson qe un A. jadis abbe de Gloucestre a cele eglise presenta com du droit &c. en temps. &c., par qi mort la eglise &c. se voida en temps qe le abbeie fu en la mayn nostre seignur le roi, issi &c. atort &c. Et fuit breve tale "quod permittat presentare ad ecclesiam de Sancto Ismael." — *Friskeney.* Jugement du bref; car il covent en chescun quare impedit estre noun de la ville ou la eglise est; mes en ceo bref Quare impedit.

A.D. 1307. that by St. Ismael is meant the name of the saint by whom the church was founded; now he might have a good writ running "of the vill of St. Ismael."—*Warwick.* The vill has not any name except St. Ismael, just like Warwick. And it would not be a good form to say "to "the church of the town of Warwick;" no more &c.—HOWARD. A writ which says "to the church of St. Mary" is not good: neither is one which says "to St. Ismael's "church."—*Warwick.* Nay; our writ says "to the "church of St. Ismael."—The writ was at length held good by HOWARD because it said "of St. Ismael" and not "St. Ismael's;" this diversity making it supposed that it was rather the name of a town than the name of some saint.—*Friskeney.* Yet again we pray judgment &c., because the writ says "in Wales," which is out of the county &c., and the writ goes to the sheriff.—STAUNTON. You shall take no advantage of that; for the king chooses to plead here.—*Friskeney* defended &c., and (said he) we tell you that that advowson is appendant to the manor of T. which is the heritage of the said Maud; and we tell you that while she was under age and in ward of the king, one William who held the manor under commission from the king, did to that church present one S. who was the last parson imparsonee and who died parson, and we pray judgment.—STAUNTON. Nay; you must say more than that.—*Friskeney.* So that if the abbat had any presentation, it was while we were under age.—*Warwick.* At least you admit that he presented.—*Friskeney.* Yes, by my faith, while Maud was under age.—*Warwick.* Now we pray a writ to the bishop, since you have admitted that the king found the abbat seised, and he during his time ought by reason of his prerogative to have and to hold it in the state in which he found it, we pray judgment &c., for we have no need to plead about Maud's condition.—*Friskeney.* You have to uphold the presentation by the abbat from whom you derive title.—*Warwick.* No, we ny iad il nule, einz fet meuz a supposer par tant qil A.D. 1307. dit de Sancto Ismaele le noun seinte de la eglise de qi ele est fondue, dount il poeit aver bon bref "villæ "de Sancto Ismael." — *Warr.* La ville nad autre noun mes Seint Ismael auxi com Warr[1] e il ne serreit pas de forme a dire "ad ecclesiam villæ de Warr.," nent plus &c.— HOWARD. A dire "ad ecclesiam beatæ Ma-"riæ" nest pas bon bref; nent plus "ad ecclesiam Sancti "Ismaele." — *Warr.* Nay, nostre bref dit "ad eccle-"siam de Sancto Ismaeli."—Postea breve consideratum fore bonum par HOWARD, Quia dicit de Sancto Ismaeli et non Sancti Ismaelis; eo quod per hoc diversificatur, et supponitur quod magis est proprium nomen villæ quam alicujus sancti. — *Frisqeney.* Uncore jugement &c. qe le bref dist en Gales qe est hors du counte &c., e vest le bref a viconte &c.—STANTONE. De ceo ne prendrez nule avantage, qe le roi voet pleder cy. — *Friskeney* defendi &c.; e vous dioms qe cele avoweson si est apendant au maner de T. qest le heritage la dite Maude; e vous dioms qe tant com ele fu denz age e en la garde le roi, un Willem qe ceu maner tient par comission le roi, a cele eglise presenta un S. qe fut la dreigne persone enpersonee e morust persone, e demandom jugement. — STANTONE. Nay, il vous covendra dire plus. — *Friskeney.* Issi qe si labbe eust nul presentement, ceo fut taunt com nous fumes denz age. — *Warr.* Au meinz vous grantez qil presenta.—*Frisqeney.* May foi, oil; Maude esteant denz age.— *War.* Ore prioms bref al eveske, del houre qe nous avez grante qe le roi trova labbe seisi, e il en sun temps la deit aver e tenir par reson de sa prerogativete en tiel estat qil la trova, demaundoms jugement &c.; car nous ne avoms nent a pleder del estre Maude.—*Friskeney.* Vous avez a meintenir le presentement le abbe de quei vous pernez title. — *Warr.* Noun avom pas; qar tut eust

[1] The word *Warr.* is repeated.

A.D. 1307. have not. For albeit the abbat had mistaken the advowson, which we who are suing for the king do not admit, that must be arranged between you and the present abbat; and therefore the statute[1] says "let him have the "same action and exception &c."

Outlawry promulgated by order of justices for gaol-delivery is erroneous.

Outlawry promulgated by a justice for gaol-delivery is erroneous.

§ Note that, against a woman who brought a writ of Dower it was alleged that she ought not to have dower, by reason that her husband who endowed her &c. was outlawed in the county of &c.; whereupon the sheriff was commanded to record in the full county court &c., and that he should send the record &c.; and he did so, and sent word that as he was directed by certain justices appointed for gaol-delivery, to order a certain S. husband of the woman &c. to be at the county court, and if he appeared to take him, and that if he did not appear &c.; and that by virtue of the order he was cried for at three county courts and did not appear, and that at the fourth county court he was mainprised, and that at the fifth he did not come; whereupon he was outlawed.—HOWARD (after looking at the record). We find by this record that he is an outlaw by command of justices assigned &c. who have no power to make such a command; so that outlawry may be quashed.—*The attorney for the tenant.* We have pleaded, in bar to the demandant, that her husband &c. was outlawed; and you find that to be the case by the record: we pray judgment.—The justices consulted together, and then STAUNTON said, Whatever the case may be, we find by this record that he was outlawed; and although there may be an error we can not now upset it, and we have not now to sit in judgment on the case of the outlawry; therefore this court adjudges that the tenant do go without day, and that the demandant do take nothing by her writ.

---

[1] 13 Edw. I. (Westm. 2.) c. 5, § 1.

le abbe mespris le avoeson, qe nous qe pur le roi suoms ne grantoms point, de ceo bien vous coviegne entre vous e labbe qe ore est; e pur ceo dist lestatut "habeat ean-" dem actionem et exceptionem &c. A.D. 1307.

Quod uthlagaria per preceptum justiciariorum assignatorum ad gaolam deliberandam promulgata est erronea.

§ Nota, en countre une femme qe porta bref de dowere fut alegge qele ne devoit dowere avoir, car sun baron de qi dowement ele &c. fust utlaghe en tiel conte &c., par quei mande fust au viconte qil feit recorder en plein conte &c. e qil mandast le record &c., qe ensi fit, e manda qe com lui fust par certeinz justices assignez a la gaole deliverer de fere mander un tiel S., baron la femme &c., en conte, e sil aparust qe ilui preist, e si noun &c., par quel comandement il fut demande a treis contez e ne aparust pas, e au quarte conte meinprise, e a quinte ne vient pas, par quei il fut utlaghe.—Howard (inspecto recordo). Nous trovoms par ceo record qil est uthlage par comande des justic s assignez qe ne ount pas poer de fere tiel comande, do nt cele utlagarie est anyentissable. — *Attorne* [*le*] *tenant.* Nous avoms dit, en rebotant la demandante, qe sun baron &c. est utlaghe; e vous ceo trovez par record ; jugement. — Postea justiciariis consultis adinvicem, — Stantone. Coment qil soit, nous trovoms par ceo record qil est utlaghe; e tut isoit il errour, ne ne la poums nent a ore repeller, ne la cause de la uthlagarie nest pas a nous ore ajuger, si agarde &c. qe le tenant &c. sanz jour, e la demandante rienz ne preigne par sun bref &c.

A.D. 1307.

Note, voucher to warranty.

§ A tenant vouched to warranty one William the son of W. de la Lande, to be summoned, for the purpose of voucher, in the county of Nottingham: and now William came by virtue of the voucher.—*Royston.* We pray judgment of the bad voucher; for we are under age, and he has vouched us as if we were of full age.—The court said that he was of full age.—*Roistone.* By virtue of what do you vouch us?—*The Tenant's attorney.* See here the deed of your father whose heir you are, which witnesses &c. — *Roistone.* We will enter into warranty as heir in blood; but we are not bound to make satisfaction in value, because by heritable succession from him by whom the deed was executed nothing has descended to us except in tail.—STAUNTON. How in tail?—*Roistone.* One C. gave those tenements in L. to our father whose heir we are, to hold to him and the heirs of his body begotten; and they descended to us &c., and these we have and none else. — *The Attorney.* Assets in the county of Lincoln have descended to you in fee simple.—STAUNTON. Where and in what vill?—The attorney did not know. — Then said STAUNTON. If you can not tell in what vill, your assertion is worthless.—And afterwards he (the attorney) named the vill, and offered an averment by the country where the voucher was.—And note that the better course was to name the vill, because it is always thus said in the Venire facias "ten men &c. of the neighbourhood of such a vill "&c."; and if he should not name any vill it would not be known of what neighbourhood the inquest should be &c.

Cui in vitâ, where the estate of the donor was counter-pleaded.

§ The writ said that he should answer A. &c., which she claims to be her right, by the gift of M. who thereof enfeoffed the aforesaid W., her late husband, and the said A., and into which he has not entry except after a demise which the aforesaid W. the late husband &c. thereof made to L. — *Lanfar* counted, and took title from the seisin of her who made the gift.— *Willoughby*

A.D. 1307.

§ Un tenant voucha a garantie Willeam le fiz W. de la Lande, qe serreit somons a ceo qil en son voucher en le counte de Notingham, e Willem meintenant souz le voucher vient. — *Roistone.* Jugement del malvois voucher; qe nous sumes denz age, e il nous ad vouche com de plein age. — E la court lui dit qil fust dage. —*Roistone.* Par quei nous vouchez vous? — *Attorne [le] tenant.* Veez ici le fet vostre pere qi heir &c. qe testmoigne &c.—*Roistone.* Nous garantissoms com heir du saunk, mes fere a la vaillance ne devoms, car par succession de heritage de celui par qi le fet &c. rienz nous est descendu si noun en forme taille.—STANTONE. Coment en forme taille? — *Roistone.* Un C. dona a nostre pere, qi heir &c., ceux tenementz en L. a luy e a ces heirs de sun corps engendrez; les queux tenements nous descendirent &c., e ces avoms nous e nuls autres.—*Attorne.* Assez vous est descendue en le conte de Nichole en fee simple. — *Roistone.* A ceo ne avendrez point, car nous vous vouchastes soulment en le conte de Notingham, pur quei &c. — *Attorne.* Assez vous est descendue en le conte de Notingham.—STANTONE. Ou e en quele ville?—Et attornatus ignoravit. STANTONE. Si vous ne sachez dire en quele ville, vostre dit ne vaut rienz.—Et postea dixit nomen villæ et pretendit verificationem patriæ qua vocatum. Et nota quod optimum fuit nominare villam, quia dicitur sic semper in le venire facias, " x. homines &c. de visneto " de tali villa &c." Et si non nominaret aliquam villam ignoraretur de quo visneto inquisitio foret &c.

Nota voucher a garant.

§ Breve sic, quod respondeat A. &c. quod clamat esse jus suum de dono M. quæ inde predictum W. quondam virum suum et ipsum A inde feoffavit, et in quod non habeat ingressum nisi post dimissionem quam predictus W. quondam vir &c. inde fecit L.—*Lanfar* conta, e prist title de la seisine la doneresce.—*Willuby* de-

Cui in vita ubi status donatoris contrapla citatur.

A.D. 1307. defended &c.; and (said he) We tell you that this M. never had any such interest in the tenements that she could make a gift thereof, nor had she any estate except as wife of her husband, one T., whose tenements they were: ready &c.—*Lanfar*. The gift is not denied: and even though she had not had any other estate than what you allege, and had enfeoffed us, and we had had seisin on that feoffment, in that case we should have this action.—STAUNTON. Then [say] that it was so.—And he would not, but negatively joined an averment to Willuby's plea.—However, *Lanfar* held himself too feintly here, since the writ is mixed, to wit, in the possession and in the right; nor is the right nor the possession of the demandant denied: it seems however that the averment offered by *Willuby* is receivable, since it wholly destroys the title of the demandant, namely the seisin of the donor. Nor did she in counting take any title from her own seisin, because neither her sole seisin nor her seisin jointly with her husband nor the seisin of her husband conferred any title on her; nor could any title be taken from her seisin, since it was not entire and sole.

Ael. § An infant under age brought the writ and sued by his guardian, and demanded a messuage and eight acres of land and six acres of meadow. — *Roistone*. What you call [acres] are the bounds of selions of the land comprised in this fine; and we tell you that he can not demand anything of these tenements through his grandfather, of whose seisin he counts; [for his said grandfather] in this court &c. acknowledged the same tenements to be our right, and gave them up to us &c. to have and to hold for ever; and see here one part of the fine which shows this: we pray judgment &c.—*Hedone*. The meadow is a separate thing, as our writ supposes. And as to the remainder the infant is under age and cannot be a party to the fine any more than we can.—HOWARD. If you wish to have the land, you must give fendi &c., e vous dioms qe ceste M. en ces tenements unkes rienz ne avoit issint qele les poeit doner, ne nul estat mes com femme un T. sun baron qi tenements ces furent; e prest.—*Lanfare.* Le doun ne pas dedit; e tut ne eust ele eu altre estat qe vous dites, e ele nous eust feffe, e nous eussoms par cel feffement seisi, en ceo cas nous averioms ceste accion. —STANTONE. Donqes qil fust issi. Et noluit, set negative ad dictum de *Willuby* junxit verificationem. Nimis tamen ficte[1] hic se tenuit *Lanfare,* cum breve sit mixtum, scilicet in possessione et jure, nec jus nec possessio petentis dedicitur; apparet tamen verificatio pretensa per *Willuby* fore acceptabilis, cum omnino titulum petentis, videlicet seisinam donatoris, destruat. Nec de seisina sua propria cepit titulum in narrando, quia solam seisinam immo viro suo conjunctim nec seisina viri sibi contulit titulum, nec de seisina sua cum non fuit integra et sola, titulus capi potest. A.D. 1307.

§ Un enfant denz age porta le bref e suit par gardein, e demanda un mes viii. acres de terre e vi. acres de pree.—*Roistone.* Ceo qe vous apellez [acres] sunt chenes a bones des seliouns e de la terre comprise en ceste fin; e vous dioms qil ne puet en ces tenements rienz demander par sun ael de qi seisine, en ceste court &c. conust mesmes les tenements estre nostre droit e vous nous rendi &c., aver e tenir a touz jours; veez icy la partie de la fin qe ceo temoigne; jugement &c. —*Hedone.* Le pree est un gros, auxicom nostre bref suppose. Et quant al remenant lenfant est denz age. e ne se puet mie fere partie a la fin, ne nous le plus. HOWARD. Si vous volez aver la tere vous respondrez De avo.

[1] MS. fiat.

A.D. 1307. answer to the fine. (And afterwards he was compelled by the court to do so.)—*Hedone.* The meadow is a separate thing; and as to the remainder, the tenements put in our view are not comprised in the fine.—STAUNTON. Nay! You shall not have those two pleas; your first, by saying that the meadow is a separate thing, supposes that the remainder of the tenements are comprised in the fine; but if you insist on pleading that the tenements put in view are not comprised in the fine, that will serve for the meadow and everything.—*Hedone* did so.—So &c.

Ael. Note, that a woman named in the writ, a stranger to the tenant named in the writ, was received on the default of that tenant.

§ A writ of Ael was brought against a woman, who made default after default; wherefore &c.: thereupon came one J. and, by *Willoughby* said that she was joint purchaser of the said tenements, and that the tenements were given to her who made default after default and to the said J., to have and to hold to them two and to the heirs of J.: and she put forward a charter and prayed judgment of the writ.—STAUNTON. Do you, who supervene, think to abate their writ?—*Willoughby.* In a similar case in this court, that has been done. (And he named the parties.)—STAUNTON (after consulting with HENGHAM). Plead with them, if you please; but you shall not abate the writ.—And she being admitted only to defend her right, pleaded that the grandfather did not die seised.

Mesne, where the writing whereby the mesne was bound to acquittance did not specify the tenement which the plaintiff claimed to hold of him &c.

Mesne. § A. brought a writ of Mesne against B.—*Westcote.* Tortiously he does not acquit him (and he counted the ordinary count).—*Lanfar.* What have you to show the liability to acquit?—*Westcote* put forward B.'s own deed

a la fin.—Et postea per curiam fust a ceo chace.— A.D. 1307.
Hedone. Le pree est un gros &c., prest; e quant al eel, le tenement mis en nostre vewe ne sunt mie compris en la fin. — STANTONE. Nay ces deus naverez point; car vostre primer dist ke vous dites, ke le pree est un gros &c., fet a supposer qe le eel des tenements sunt compris en la fin; mes si vous volez dire qe les tenements mys en vewe ne sunt compris en la fin, ceo vous servira pur pree e pur tut. — *Hedone* sic fecit.— Ideo &c.

De avo.

Nota quod nominata in brevi et extranea tenenti in brevi nominato admittitur in defalta illius tenentis.[1]

§ Bref dael fust porte vers une femme qe fist defaute apres defaute, par quei &c.; e sur ceo vient un J., e dit par *Willuby* qe ele de mesme les tenements joint purchasere, e dist qe les tenements furent donez a cele qe fit defaute apres defaute e a ceste J., aver e a tenir a celes deus e as heirs J.: e mist avant une chartre, e demanda jugement du bref.--STANTONE. Quidez vous superveniens de abatre lour bref?—*Willuby.* Ensi ad homme avant en ceste curt &c.; et nominavit inter quas personas. — STANTONE consulto HENGHAM. Pledez ove eux si vous volez; qe le bref ne abaterez point. —Et admissa pro jure suo defendendo solummodo, dicit quod avus non obiit seisitus.

De medio.

De medio ubi in scripto per quod medius ligaretur ad aquietanciam non specificatur tenementum quod querens de eo tenere clamavit &c.

§ A. porta le bref vers B. — *Wescote.* Atort ne lui aquite; et narravit communem narrationem.—*Lanfar.* Quei avez de la quitance?—*Wescote* mist avant sun fet

[1] The word "admittitur" is repeated here.

A.D. 1307, to this purport, "Know &c. that whereas Agnes my "mother gave to me an annual rent of 12 shillings to be "received and taken of T., and the said T. attorned to "me for the same, I am bound to acquit the said T. "against all chief lords of the fee and others."—After the writing had been read, *Lanfar* said, He has counted that he holds of us certain tenements whereof he says that we are mesne lord between &c., and he urges by his count that we are to acquit him as tenant; and in order to bind us to that acquittance he puts forward a deed which is not in accordance with his count: judgment if by that deed &c., which deed does not specify any tenement.—*Westcote.* The deed states that you are bound to acquit us, and you do not deny that it is your deed: we pray judgment. And in addition to this you are seised of our services for these tenements &c.—BEREFORD. For what tenements?—*Westcote.* For the two virgates of land.—BEREFORD. This is your writing: and the usage has heretofore been that where a writing is to affirm a count, the two must accord.—HOWARD. If this writing should bind him to acquit, it would just as well bind him for all the tenements which you hold in England as for those two virgates of land.—*Westcote.* What does it matter to us if he solemnly bound himself?—BEREFORD. What land does he bind himself to acquit? (intimating not any). What kind of rent are the 12 shillings which you say he takes from you?—*Westcote.* Rent service. —BEREFORD. Out of what tenement issuing?—*Westcote.* Out of these two virgates of land.—BEREFORD. Does your writing say so? (intimating that it did not).—*Passeley.* The writ of warranty of charter says, "which he "holds and claims to hold of him, and in respect of "which he has his charter &c.;" and although the charter does not testify that the land &c. is holden of him &c., nevertheless he shall warrant. Wherefore it seems that so he shall in this case.—BEREFORD. The cases of warranty and of acquittance are not similar:

demene, cujus effectus fuit "Noverint &c. quod cum A.D. 1307.
"Agnes mater mea mihi donavit .xii. annui redditus "percipiendos de T., ac idem T. inde se mihi attor- "naverit, me teneri &c. prædictam T. contra omnes "capitales dominos feodi et alios aquietare."—*Lanfare* (lecto scripto). Il ad conte qil tient nous certeins tenements, des queux tenements il dit qe nous sumes meen entre &c., e voet par sun counte qe nous les aquitoms en sa tenance, e pur nous lier a cele aquitance met avant fet qe ne acorde mie a sun counte: jugement si par teu fet &c. quel fet ne especefie nule tenement.—*Wescote.* Le fet voet qe vous estes tenuz de aquiter nous, e vous nel dedites point qil ne est vostre fet; jugement; e oveske ceo vous estes seisi de nos services pur ces tenements &c.—BEREFORD. Par queux tenements.—*Wescote.* Pur les deus vergez de tere.—BEREFORD. Ceo vostre escrist; e home ad use einz ces houres qe la ou escrist affermera counte il serreient acordanz.—HOWARD. Si ceste escrist lui liast a la quitance, tant bien li liereit il pur touz les tenements qe vous tenez en Engletere qe pur cestes deus vergez de tere.—*Wescote.* Qei est ceo a nous sil se seit solemnetes lye. BEREFORD. A la quitancc de quele tere se lye il? (quasi diceret de nule). IDEM. Quele rente sunt ces .xii. soz qe vous dites qil prent de vous?—*Wescote.* Rente service.—BEREFORD. Issant de queu tenement?—*Wescote.* De ces deus verges de terre.—BEREFORD. Temoigne ceo vostre escrist? (quasi diceret non).—*Passeley.* Bref de garantie de chartre dit "quam tenet et de eo tenere "clamat, et unde cartam suam habet &c."; e tut ne temoigne mie la chartre qe la terre &c. est tenuz de lui &c., jatardeis il garantira; par quei semble issi &c.—BEREFORD. Nest pas semblable de garantie e de aqui-

A.D. 1307. for if you have a charter from your mesne lord which testifies warranty, defence and acquittance, and he grants over your services to John de Westcote, and on that grant you attorn to him, he shall not be bound to acquit you although you have his deed whereby he is bound to acquittance: and yet notwithstanding he shall warrant you &c.

Entry, by reason of the alienation in fee made by the tenant for life, where he who claimed by the remainder brought the writ thus :—

§ Command Alice who was the wife of Walter de Beauchamp that justly &c. she yield up to Laurence de Saint Michael the younger &c. into which she has not entry unless after the demise which Laurence de Saint Michael the elder, to whom W &c. granted them to be holden to the said Laurence &c. the elder and Eve his wife for the lives of the said Laurence and Eve, so that after the deaths of the said Laurence &c. the elder and Eve the said tenement should remain to the heirs of the said Laurence &c. the elder whom he should beget on the aforesaid [Eve], by a fine &c., and which after the demise thereof in fee made to T. by the said Laurence &c. the elder, ought to remain to the said Laurence de Saint Michael the younger son and heir of the said Laurence &c. the elder, by the terms of the statute of Gloucester[1] &c. — *Middleton.* Tortiously &c.; for it is his right, and for the reason that one W., who was seised of these tenements, granted them to Laurence, to hold to the said Laurence &c. and Eve his wife &c., so that &c., by virtue of which gift the said Laurence &c. and Eve were seised &c. in their demesne as of freehold, in time of peace &c., the esplees &c. as of freehold (and so he went on in accordance with the writ).—*Passeley* defended &c., and (said he) we do not think that the statute of

[1] 6 Edw. I.

tance; qar si vous eiez chartre de vostre meen qe testmoigne garantie defense e aquitance, e il graunte vos services a *Johan de Wescote*, par queu graunt vous attornez a luy, il ne vous serra mes tenuz de aquiter, tut eiez vous sun fet par quei il est lye a laquitance: et jatardeis vous garantira &c. A.D. 1307.

De ingressu causa alienationis in feodo factæ per tenentem ad terminum vitæ, ubi clamans per le remanere tulit breve sic:—

§ Precipe Aliciæ que fuit uxor Walteri de Bellocampo quod juste &c. reddat Laurentio de Seint Michel juniori &c. in quas non habet ingressum nisi post dimissionem quam Laurentius de Seint Michel senior cui W. &c. illa concessit tenenda predicto Laurentio &c. seniori et Evæ uxori sue ad terminum vitæ ipsorum Laurentii et Evæ; ita quod post mortem ipsorum Laurentii &c. senioris et Evæ predictum tenementum heredibus ipsius Laurentii &c. senioris quos de predicta procreavit remaneret per finem &c., et quæ post dimissionem per prefatum Laurentium &c. seniorem T. inde factum in feodo ad prefatum Laurentium de Seint Michel juniorem filium et heredem prefati Laurentii &c. senioris remanere debent per formam statuti Gloucestriæ &c. — *Middelton.* Atort &c., qe ceo sun droit, e par la reson qe un W., qe de ces tenements fu seisi, ces tenements granta a Laurence, a tenir al avantdit Laurence &c. et Eve sa femme &c., issi &c., par quel doun mesme ceux Laurence &c. e Eve furent seisis &c. en lour demene come de franc tenement en temps de pees &c., les esplees &c., com de franc tenement, et post totum brevi concordans.—*Passeley* defendi &c., e nentendoms pas qe lestatut de Gloucestre soit garant de

A.D. 1307. Gloucester is a warrant for this writ; for the statute speaks of a lease in fee made by a tenant for life; but Laurence &c., according to their own statement had a fee tail; wherefore &c.— BEREFORD. Does the statute run exactly as you state? — *Willoughby.* It only speaks of tenancy in dower; and the second statute of Westminster[1] directs that in a similar case, where a remedy is needed, a similar remedy is to be given; therefore this writ is warranted by the two statutes; for since Laurence &c. who alienated had only a tenancy for life, it is a case sufficiently similar to the case where a tenant in dower, who has only a life estate, aliens &c. And on the other hand you have passed the time for challenging the form of the writ; for you have prayed the view &c.— HOWARD. Could not the warrantor, if he had vouched, challenge the form of the writ? (intimating that he could).—*Herle.* He does not stand in the place of a warrantor. — BEREFORD affirmed this; and asked if the Laurence the elder survived And he put this question because [if he were dead] Laurence &c. the younger would have an action by writ of Formedon in the remainder, but if he were alive, not.—*Passeley.* There is yet another great defect in the writ, which says, "which "ought to remain, by the form of the statute of Glou- "cester," whereas the statute does not suppose a remainder but supposes only a reversion. And even though we were to abandon these challenges, the court would not entertain a plea on a writ framed in terms not warranted.—BEREFORD. If you hold to that and do not challenge it, we shall not abate the writ. — On a future day HOWARD briefly recapitulated the points and said that the statute was not a warrant &c., for the statute speaks not of a fee tail. — *Herle.* We have nothing to do with the entail; we claim only as a stranger by virtue of the remainder. — BEREFORD (to

---

[1] 13 Edw. I.

ceo bref; qe statut parle du lees en fee fet par tenant qe tient a terme de vie; mes Laurence &c. a ceo qe eux mesme dient avoit fee taille; par quei &c.--Bereford. Parle le statut tut droit com vous dites? --*Willuby*. Il ne parle fors qe de tenance en dowere, e le secunde estatut de Westminstre voet qe en semblable cas ou remedie faut soit done semblable remedie; par quei ceo bref est garanti par le un statut e lautre; car del houre qe Laurence &c. qe aliena ne avoit mes qe tenance a terme de vie, assez est il semblable a cas ou tenant en dowere, qe nad mes ke terme de vie, aliene &c.: e dautre part vous estes passe le pase de chalanger forme du bref, car vous avez demande la vewe.—Howard. E sil eust vouche, ne poeit le garant &c. chalanger la forme? (quasi diceret sic).—*Herle*. Il nest pas en leu de garantie.—Bereford hoc affirmavit et petiit si Laurentius senior fuerat superstes: et hoc petiit quia ipse Laurentius &c. junior haberet actionem per breve de forma donacionis in le remanere, ipso autem vivente non.—*Passeley*. Uncore iad il un autre grant defaute en le bref, qe dist "remanere debet per "formam statuti Gloucestre" ou le statut ne suppose nent de remeyndre einz solummodo de reversione; e tut fut il issi qe nous lessasoms teux chalanges, la court ne tendreit mie plee sur bref conceu sanz garant. —Bereford. Si vous vous tenez, e ne chalengez pas, ne abatroms ia le bref. — Alio die Howard breviter repetiit, e dit qe le statut ne fust mie garant &c. qe le statut ne parle mie de fee taille.—*Herle*. Nous ne avoms rienz a fere de la taille, nous demandom com estraunge par le remanere. -- Bereford a *Herle*. Si

A.D. 1307.

A.D. 1307. *Herle*). If your father and mother were both dead, would you demand by this writ or by writ of Formedon?—*Herle*. That is a question which I will not answer. And they have passed the time for challenging the form.—HOWARD. There may be an exception to the form &c., and there may be an exception to the form and the matter; now, the force of his exception is that you have not an action for the employment of this writ; and thus his exception goes to the matter.—*Herle*. Then it is given to our action.—*Passeley*. What we are pleading is to the court and not to you.—*Herle*. Then we pray judgment of you as undefended, since you do not answer us.—*Passeley*. If the court sees that it has warrant and a good base for entertaining this plea, notwithstanding what we have urged, we will fully answer.—And he said, Your writ says "ought to remain to the said Laurence &c. son "and heir of Laurence &c.;" now you cannot have an action as heir of Laurence &c. until he be dead.—*Herle*. Our action is good; for Laurence &c. holds for the term of his life, and the fee and the right are ours by virtue of the remainder which was limited to us; now by the forfeiture incurred by the alienation in fee by the tenant for life who held of us, there has accrued to us an action to demand the tenements in demesne.—HOWARD. The statute of Gloucester only says where the reversion &c.; and the statute of Westminster 2nd directs that in a similar case there shall be a similar remedy; but these two things, reversions and remainders, are not similar.—After the justices had examined the statutes, HENGHAM rehearsed the process &c., and said, For that we see clearly that the statute of Gloucester, which is cited as a warrant for this writ, has no reference to a fee tail &c., this court doth adjudge that Laurence &c. do take nothing &c.

Cosinage. § STAUNTON. T. brought the writ against one J., who was summoned &c. and appeared &c., and after that appearance made default, whereupon the Petit Cape &c.; and because J. came &c. and was under age, T. could not vostre pere e vostre mere fuissont mors le un e lautre, demandriez vous par cestui bref ou par bref de forme de doun ?—*Herle.* Ceste est une question a quele jeo ne respondray mie: e eux sunt ore passez de chalanger la forme. — HOWARD. Il ad excepcion soulment a la forme &c., e excepcion a la forme e au matir ; dount la force de sa excepcion est qe vous ne avez mie accion de user ceo bref; e issi est ele au matir partie. —*Herle.* Donqe est ele done a nostre accion.—*Passeley.* Quant qe nous pledoms est a la court e ne mie a vous.—*Herle.* Donqe demandom nous jugement de vous com de noun defendu, del houre qe vous ne responez nent a nous.—*Passeley.* Si la court veie qe ele eit garant e bon foundement de tenir cel plee, non obstante ceo qe nous avoms dit nous respondroms assez.—*Idem.* Vostre bref dit "predicto Laurentio &c. filio et heredi " Laurentii &c. remanere debet;" dount vous ne purriez mie [accion] aver come heir Laurence &c. tant qil soit mort.—*Herle.* Nostre accion est bone ; qar Laurence &c. tient a terme de vie, e le fee e le dreit le nostre par le remanere qe se tailla a nous ; dount par cele forfeture qe nostre tenant qe a terme de vie de nous tient aliena en fee, accion nous est acru a demander les tenements en demene.—HOWARD. Statut de Gloucestre ne parle nent mes la ou la reversion &c. ; e le statut de Westminstre secunde voet qe en semblable cas semblable remedie soit done ; e ces deus reversion e remeindre ne sunt mie semblables.— Postea statutis inspectis per justiciarios, HENGHAM repetiit processum &c., E pur ceo qe nous veoms bien qe le entendement de statut de Gloucestre qe serroit garant de ceo bref ne mie de fee taille &c., si agarde &c. qe Laurence &c. ne preigne rien &c.

A.D. 1307.

§ STANTONE. T. porta le bref vers un J., qe fust somons &c. ; et aparust &c. ; et apres cele apparance fist defaute, par quei le petit cape &c. ; e pur ceo qe J. vient &c. e fut denz age, T. ne poeit par cele de-

Cosinage.

A.D. 1307. take any advantage of that default, but it was released: and J. answered and said that whereas T. took his title from the seisin of S. from whom descended &c. because he died without heir &c. of his body, she was daughter of the said S. and after his death as daughter and heir of S. entered &c. and claimed by the same descent: and she prayed judgment &c. And T. said that J. could not claim as heir of S.; because, six years before her birth, S., who she says was her father, went over the sea on a pilgrimage and never returned: and T. prayed judgment if she, as heir, &c. And because this exception is of so high a degree and goes to extinguish the right &c. and this J. who is under age can not properly be a party thereto, this court doth adjudge that the parole demur &c. until she attain her age &c.

When the writ said "which is vacant by reason of the "deprivation &c.," and was brought against the person deprived.

Quare impedit.

§ The prior &c. brought a writ of Quare impedit.—*Westcote.* Tortiously &c. presents &c., which is void by reason of the deprivation of &c.—*Hedone.* At present we do not claim anything in the right of patronage, but as vicar of the said church, and instituted on your presentation: judgment if this writ lie between us.—STAUNTON. What line of pleading do you take? First of all you say that you claim nothing in the right of patronage, and afterwards you plead to the plenarty.—*Herle.* He claims nothing &c.; we pray a writ to the bishop.—*Hedone.* We are vicars &c. and were instituted &c. under your patronage: judgment of this writ &c.—*Herle.* You are deprived.—*Hedone.* Not deprived: ready, where and how we ought.—And *Hedone* offered this averment wrongly: perceiving which, *Rostone* said, You say that we are deprived: how will you aver it?—*Herle.* I will aver that the vicarage is vacant.—BEREFORD. And he says that he is vicar by your patronage, and is there alive.—*Herle.* He is deprived.—BEREFORD. As to that, sue where you think you will best succeed; for this court has no cognizance thereof, and we will not send to faute nule avantage prendre, einz fut relesse; e J. respondi e dit qe la ou T. prist sun title de la seisine S. de qi descendi &c., pur ceo qil morust sanz heir &c. de son corps, ele fust fille mesme celui S.[1] e apres sa mort com fille e heir S. entra &c., e cleyma par mesme la descente, e demandoms jugement &c. Et T. dist qe J. ne poeit come heir S. clamer, car S., qi ele dit estre sun pere, cink anz avant sa nestre passa la mier en pilrinage sanz revenir; e demandoms jugement si ele com heir &c.: e pur ceo qe ceste excepcion est si haut en esteynant le droit &c. a la quele ceste denz age ne purra mie bien estre partie, si agarde &c. qe la parole remeigne &c. tant qe a sun age &c. A.D. 1307.

Sic, quæ vacat per privationem &c. Et fertur versus eundem privatum. Quare impedit de vicaragio.

§ Le priour &c. porta le bref.—*Wescote.* Atort &c. presente &c. qe voide est par la privacion &c.—*Hedone.* Nous clamoms rienz quant a ore en le avowerie, mes come vicaire de mesme la eglise, institut &c. par vostre presentement; jugement si ceo bref igise entre nous.—STANTONE. Coment pledez vous? primes ne clamez rienz en le avowerie, e pus pledez a la plenerete. —*Herle.* Il ne cleyme rienz &c.; nous prioms bref al eveske. — *Hedone.* Nous sumes vicaire &c. de vostre avowerie institut &c.; jugement si ceo bref &c.—*Herle.* Vous estes prive.—*Hedone.* Nent prive, prest, ou e quant nous devoms.—Et hanc verificationem male tendidit *Hedone*; quod percipiens,—*Rostone.* Vous dites qe nous sumes privez: coment le volez vous averer. — *Herle.* Jeo voille averer qe la vicare est voide.— BEREFORD. E il dit qil est vicare de vostre avowerie e est la en vie.—*Herle.* Il est prive.—BEREFORD. De ceo suez la ou vous quidrez espleiter; qe de ceo nad mie ceste court conissance, ne nous ne manderoms mie

[1] MS. G.

A.D. 1307. the bishop to ascertain if he be deprived: and as to your praying a writ to the bishop "non obstante reclamatione "&c.," that would be a false writ, for he claims nothing in the right of patronage, but admits that you are the patron, and says that he is your vicar and was instituted on your presentation; so it would be erroneous to say "non obstante reclamatione," when he claims nothing.—*Herle.* If we have not a remedy in this court we shall lose our presentation: for in the court Christian he claims something in the right of patronage and does not claim as vicar, by reason whereof the bishop does not receive our presentee; and in this court he claims as vicar, on our presentation &c.; by reason whereof we cannot have a writ to the bishop "non obstante reclamatione &c.;" and thus we are without remedy. And besides, if we sue before the bishop he will bring the Indicavit, whereupon the bishop will not dare to go further &c. and so without right &c. — BEREFORD. If the bishop decline to receive your presentee, on such a claim without more, he is not acting rightly.—*Herle.* The bishops do it every day.—BEREFORD. For every wrong that an ordinary does to you, you shall not have a remedy in this court: and according to law some will adjudge that neither an assise &c. nor this writ will lie against him. But if the bishop or any other person do you a wrong, bring against him what you shall think appropriate.

Dower. Dower, where the pleading went to vacate a fine which was in this form:—

Roger &c. acknowledges the tenements &c. to be the right of Guy Feire, and for that consideration Guy granted &c. to Roger for his life and that after the death of Roger the tenements were to return to Guy &c., to have and to hold to the said Guy and one J. his wife and to the heirs of their bodies begotten, and if they should die without heirs &c., that the tenements should remain to the right heirs of Roger &c. Thereupon came the wife of Roger and demanded dower &c. — *Westcote.*

al eveske de saver mou sil soit prive; e de ceo qe vous priez bref al Eveske non obstante reclamatione &c., ceo serreit un faux bref, qar il ne cleyme rienz en le avowerie, einz vous grante estre patron, e dist qil est vostre vikere institut a vostre presentement; dount il serreit malement dit non obstante reclamatione, del houre qil ne cleyme rienz.—*Herle.* Si nous ne eyoms remedie de ceste court nous perdroms nostre presentement: qar en la court Cristiene il cleime en le avowerie e nent com vicaire, par quei leveske ne resceit mie nostre presente, e en ceste court com vicaire de nostre presentement &c.; par quei nous ne poums nent aver bref al eveske non obstante reclamatione &c. &c.; e issi sanz remedie. E dautre part si nous suioms devant leveske il portera le Indicavit par quei leveske ne osera avant aler &c. e issi sanz reson &c. — BEREFORD. Si leveske deneye resceivre vostre presente pur tiel clame sanz plus, il ne fet mie reson. —*Herle.* Issi font eveskes chescon jour. —BEREFORD. E de chescon tort qe ordinaire vous fet vous naverez mie remedie en ceste court; e lealment nul home agardera qe ne assise &c. ne ceo bref ne gise vers luy: mes si leveske ou autre vous face tort, portez vers lui ceo qe vous quidrez bien faire. A.D. 1307.

De dote ubi placitatur ad vacuationem finis cujus forma talis fuit:— De dote.

§ Roger &c. conuse les tenements &c. estre le droit Gwy Feire, e pur ceste reson Gwy graunta &c. a Roger a terme de sa vie, e apres le deces Roger qe les tenements returnassent a Gwy &c., aver e tenir au dit Gwy e a une J. sa femme e as heirs de lour corps engendrez, e si eux deviassent sanz heirs &c., qe les tenements demorassent a dreiz heirs Roger &c.: e sur ceo vient la femme Roger e demanda dowere &c. — *Wescote.*

A.D. 1307. She ought not to have dower; for her husband from whom &c. had nothing in &c. except for his life, by the terms of this fine which was levied before she was married: judgment. — *Herle.* Piers, the grandfather of Roger was seised in his demesne as of fee of the tenements &c. whereof &c.: after whose death they descended to Osbern as son &c., and from Osbern to Roger; and that estate Roger had on the day when he married us, and of that estate he was seised, and never by transmutation of possession changed his estate; but he died &c. seised; ready &c. — BEREFORD. First of all be agreed as to the fine. Was the fine levied in the form &c.? — *Herle.* It is not for us to admit or deny it; we are not parties to it; nor are we privies in blood to any of the parties thereto: but the court may hold what it pleases on that head. — BEREFORD. Then, by God, since you do not deny it we will suppose that it was so levied. Now say if the fine was levied after the marriage or before. — *Herle.* Of a surety it was levied before; but by that fine he did not destroy the estate by which he was competent to endow us; for at the time of the levying of the fine he was seised &c. in his demesne as of fee and of right; now at the very beginning of the fine he acknowledged the right &c. to be Guy's, and nevertheless the fee and demesne remained in his person, since there was no possession transmuted from his person, and then that right which is acknowledged to be only an entail, is on failure of the entail brought back in fee into his own blood; and so ever since he married us he was seised &c. in his demesne as of fee: judgment &c. — STAUTNON. Then you want to avoid the fine. That would be against the statute.[1] — *Passeley.* No it would not; for the statute speaks of "a fine duly levied"; and this is not so, for it is all out of form and against the law first to acknowledge the right to be in, and then to limit it to the

[1] 27 Edw. I. st. 1. c. 1.

Dowere ne deit ele aver; car sun baron de qi &c. ne avoit &c. mes qe a terme de vie par la forme de ceste fin, qe se leva avant qe ele fu espose; jugement.—*Herle.* Peres le ael Roger des tenements &c. dount &c. fu seisi en demene com de fee; apres qi mort descendi a Osbern com a fiz &c., de Osbern a Roger, e tiel estat avoit Roger le jour qil nous esposa, e de tiel estat fut seisi, qi par transmutacion de sa possession unqes son estat changa, einz morust &c. seisi; prest &c. — BEREFORD. Seiez primes a un de la fin: se leva la fin en la forme &c.? — *Herle.* A nous est a granter ne a dedire; nous ne sumes pas a cele partie, ne a nulle des parties prive du saunk; mes la tiegne la court auxi com ele voudra. —BEREFORD. De par Deux, de pus ke vous ne le dedites pas, nous supposoms qil est issi; e se leva cele fin pus les esposailles ou avant? — *Herle.* Certes avant, mes par cele fin ne lui destrut mie estat qil nous poeit dowere: car au temps qe la fin leva si fust il seisi &c. en sun demene com de fee e de droit; dount a prime chief de la fin si conust il le droit &c. a Gwy, e jatardeys le fee e le demene demorerent en sa persone, del hour qe il ny avoit nule possession hors de sa persone transmute, e pus ceo droit qest conu simple taille, e pus, en defaute de la taille, le remette simple en sun sank; e issi tut temps pus qil nous esposa il fust seisi &c. en sun demene come de fee; jugement &c.—STANTONE. Donqe volez voider la fin, qe serra contre statut — *Passeley.* Noun serreit pas; qe statut parle "de "fine rite levato;" e cele nest pas, qe ele est tut hors de forme, encountre ley, primes a conustre le droit A.D. 1307

A.D. 1307. person to whom the acknowledgment is made.—STAUNTON, HENGHAM and BEREFORD having inspected the fine, asserted it to be in bad form, for the cause aforesaid. —*Herle*. A fine which is levied on words without deed is defeasible, just as a fine which witnesses only a release and quit-claim; if one say that he to whom the release and quit-claim be made was not seised at the time of the fine &c. it is void; but a fine levied on render where there is transmutation of possession, and so upon a deed, is not so voidable: then, since in this fine there is no render we think that it is voidable.

One under age being vouched to warranty as if he were of full age &c. challenged it. And nevertheless the voucher stood &c.

Voucher. § A tenant vouched &c. an infant under age just as if he were of full age, who came &c. —*Roistone*. Judgment of this voucher; for he has vouched as if the vouchee were of full age &c. — *Passeley*. Let him be viewed.— And the court viewed him and it was considered that he was under age. — *Passeley*. Let the parole then remain until he be of age. — *Hedone* (for the demandant). We pray seisin &c. since the tenant has badly vouched. – STAUNTON. Do you think for this cause to have seisin. And after consulting with HENHAM and HOWARD he decided that the parole should remain without day until the age &c. notwithstanding he was badly vouched.

Those who were to be received in defence of their right made an attorney before they were received &c.

§ A writ was brought against a man and his wife and their son who was under age. The husband made default; whereupon the Grand Cape to take the entirety &c.; and on the day when the Cape was returned he again made default; and thereupon came the wife and son to be received to defend for the entirety; and the demandant essoigned himself. — *Herle* rehearsed sur, e pus tailler le en sa persone a qi il est conu.— STANTONE, HENGHAM, e BEREFORD, inspectâ fine, asserebant esse de malâ formâ causâ prenotatâ. — *Herle.* Fin qe est leve sur paroles sanz fet, est defessable auxicom fin qe temoigne mes qe relees e quiteclamanz; si home die qe celui a qi le relees e la quiteclamanz se fit ne fu pas seisi au temps de la fin &c., ele est voide; mes fin qe se leve sur rendre ou ili ad transmutacion de possession e issi sur fet, nest pas issi voidable; dount del houre qe en ceste fin ny ad il nul rendre, nous entendoms qele soit voidable. A.D. 1307.

Existens infra etatem vocatus ad warrantiam sicut plenæ etatis &c., hoc calumpniavit. Et tunc stetit vocatio &c.

§ Un tenant voucha &c. un enfant denz age auxicom il fust de plein age, qe vient &c.—*Roistone.* Jugement de ceo voucher; qe ili ad vouche com de plein age &c. — *Passeley.* Soit veu. Et fuit visus curiæ et consideratus fore infra etatem. — *Passeley.* Remeigne donqes la parole tant qe a son age. — *Hedone* (pro petente). Nous prioms seisine &c. del hour qe le tenant ad malementes vouche. — STANTONE. Quidez vous par ceste cause aver seisine?—Et consultis HENGHAM et HOWARD consideratur qe la parole remaneret sine die usque ad etatem &c., non obstante quod male vocatum fuit &c. Voucher.

Admittendi in defensionem juris sui fecerunt attornatum antequam admissi fuerant &c.

Un bref porte vers un home e sa femme e un lour fiz qe fust denz age. Le baroun fit defaute, par quei le grant cape del entier prendre &c.; e au jour del cape returne derichief fit defaute; e sur ceo viendrent la femme e sun fiz pur estre receux a defendre del entier, e le demandant se fist essoigner. — *Herle* repetiit pre-

A.D. 1307. the aforesaid process; and prayed that if the court could allow it, the wife and son might make an attorney. STAUNTON (having consulted HENGHAM and HOWARD) The attorney may well be. And afterwards the demandant did not prosecute.

Dower; where the writ was brought against two jointly by one præcipe, who made default, whereupon the Grand Cape &c. which was no obstacle to them because they held severally.

§ The writ &c. against two, as against joint-tenants, by one præcipe, who made default, whereupon the Grand Cape &c. and on the day of its return they came.—*The attorney* for the demandant rehearsed the process and prayed seisin.—*Hedone.* Each of us holds his purparty in severalty apart from the other, and we did so on the day of the purchase of this writ; judgment of the writ. *The attorney.* We hold to the default.—BEREFORD. If he tells the truth, yet although you should hold seven years to the default, you shall get nothing; and a short folly is better than a long one.—*The attorney.* They held jointly on the day of the purchase of the writ, ready &c. —BEREFORD. If you join that inquest and it passes against you you will lose dower for ever &c.—And she afterwards prayed leave to retire from the writ.

Where the vouchee said he ought not to warrant, because the vouchor did not hold &c. at the time when he vouched &c.

Dower. § A writ of Dower was brought against a tenant, who vouched to warranty &c., and put forward the deed of his father &c. which witnessed it.—*Willoughby* (for the vouchee). We ought not to warrant: for on the day when he vouched us he was not tenant &c. neither in demesne nor by his warranty, ready &c.; nor is he now. —HOWARD. He himself acknowledged himself tenant, and he answers as tenant. Do you wish to be received to aver that he was not tenant, when he is not willing dictum processum e pria qe si la court poeit suffrir qe la femme e sun fiz poeint fere atturne. — STANTONE consultis HENGHAM e HOWARD. Le attorne gist bien; et post petens non est prosecutus. A.D. 1307.

De dote, ubi breve fertur versus duos conjunctim per unum precipe, qui fecerunt defaltam, per quod magnum cape &c. quod eis non obfuit quia seperatim tenuerunt. De dote.

§ Le bref &c. vers deus com vers joint tenants par un precipe, qe fesoient defaute, par quei le grant cape &c.; au jour de ceo retourne viendrent.—*Attornatus* pro petente recitavit processum e pria seisine.—*Hedone.* Chascon de nous tient sa purpartie en severalte de autre; e feimes le jour du bref purchace; jugement de ceo bref.—*Attorne.* Nous pernoms a la defaute.—BEREFORD. Sil soit veirs ceo qil dit, tut preissez vous touz ces vii. anz a la defaute vous gagnerez rienz; e meuz valt courte folie qe longe.—*Attorne.* Eux tyendrent joynt le jour du bref purchace, prest &c.—BEREFORD. Si vous joignez cele enqueste e il passe contre vous, vous perdrez dowere pur touz jours &c.—Et postea petiit licentiam recedendi de brevi &c.

Ubi vocatus dixit se non warrantizare, eo quod vocator non tenuit &c. tempore quo vocavit &c.

§ Un bref de dowere vers un tenant qe voucha a garant &c., e mist avant le fet sun pere &c. qe testmoigne.—*Willuby* (pro vocato). Garantir ne devoms; qar le jour qil nous voucha il ne fu pas tenant &c. ne en demene ne par sa garantie, prest &c., ne uncore est.—HOWARD. Il mesme se conust tenant e respond com tenant; voillez vous estre receu de averrer qil nestoit pas tenant del houre qil le ne voille pas de- De dote.

A.D. 1307. to deny it.—*Willoughby.* That he did not deny it was to our damage, for when he vouched us he had yielded dower to the demandant, and then lately by collusion he sued out his voucher.—BEREFORD. Admit it, and in answering the demandant say that. —*Willoughby.* One ought to warrant the tenant: for I will not warrant to him what he has not.—BEREFORD. Was he not tenant when the original writ was purchased?—*Willoughby.* We do not know.—BEREFORD. Since you will neither know nor deny nor admit this, we take it for granted. And your answer extends to both the vouchor and the demandant; for when you say, He was not tenant &c. on the day when he vouched us, that is to the vouchor; and when you say besides, For he had rendered to the demandant &c., that is to the demandant, and makes thereby to be understood that she is seised of what she demands, so an issue is to be had only against one of them. And I put the case that after the original writ &c. the tenant had alienated, and the demandant had so straitly sued him that she had brought him into court, and he had answered as he was bound to do, because he was tenant on the day when the writ &c., and were to vouch to warranty, should the vouchee not warrant because he was not tenant? (intimating that he should).—HOWARD. If the tenant after the original writ &c. be disseised, shall that be a reason for his vouchee not warranting? (intimating that he should warrant).—Afterwards he warranted, and said that the demandant detained from him certain charters; and the demandant said that she delivered to him the said charters in the presence of &c. Therefore BEREFORD issued an order for those to come in whose presence &c., in like manner with the others.

Record of an assise of novel disseisin where it was held that a grant of the right without attornment is insufficient &c.

Novel disseisin. § STAUNTON. Philip son of Elis brought the assise against William de la Bere &c. and complained &c.

dire ? — *Willuby*. Ceo qil ne le dedit pas fut a nostre damage, qar en ceo qil nous voucha il avoit rendu a la demandante dowere, e pus jatardeys par collusion suist sun voucher. — BEREFORD. Grantez, e en respo-nante le demandante dites ceo. — *Willuby*. Garantir deit homme au tenant, qar jeo ne lui garanteray point ceo qil nad pas. — BEREFORD. Ne fust il pas te-nant &c. quant le bref original fu purchace ?— *Willuby*. Nous ne savoms. — BEREFORD. Pus qe vous ceo ne volez saver ne dedire ne graunter, nous le tenoms agraunte ; e vostre respons se estend ambedeux al vouchour e a la demandante ; qe quant vous dites il ne fu mie tenant &c. le jour qil nous voucha, ceo est a voucheor, e pus outre qar il avoit rendu a la de-mandante &c., ceo est a cele demandante, e fet de ceo a entendre qele est seisie de ceo qe ele demande, dount il eurent aver issue soulment vers un de eux ; e jatardeis jeo pose qe apres le bref original &c. le tenant eust aliene e la demandante tant eust suy par force qe ily eust menc en court, e il eust respondu auxicom fere ly covendreit, pur ceo qil fust tenant le jour du bref &c., e vouche a garantie, ne luy garantereit mie le vouche pur ceo qil ne fu mie tenant ? quasi diceret sic.—HOWARD. Si le tenant apres le bref original &c. soit disseisi, ne luy garantera mie pur ceo sun vouche ? quasi diceret sic.—Postea warantizavit, et dixit quod petens detinebat sibi quasdam cartas ; et petens dixit quod liberavit ei predictas cartas in presentia &c.— Ideo par BEREFORD. Venire facias illos in quorum presentia &c. ; similiter cum aliis. A.D. 1307.

Recordum assisæ novæ disseisinæ ubi percipitur quod concessio juris sine attornamento &c. est insufficiens &c.

§ STANTONE. Philip fiz Elis porta lassise vers Willem de la Bere &c. e se pleint &c. Willem dit qe assise Novele disseisine.

A.D. 1307. *William* said that there ought not to be an assise, for he said that one Henry le Fevre acknowledged the right of the tenements &c. to belong to John de la Bere, whose heir William is, by fine &c., and granted that the tenements which ought to revert to him after the death of one Emma &c. should remain to him in fee simple; and so he entered after the death of the said Emma: and he prayed judgment if in opposition to that fine there ought to be an assise. And Philip said that one Emma (she who held for term of life) enfeoffed him of these tenements in fee simple by her charter, which he produced, and put him in seisin, and so he was seised until William and the others tortiously &c. The Assise said that Henry le Fevre to whom the fee and the right of these tenements belonged granted them to John de la Bere brother of William &c. whose heir &c. and by fine &c.; but that Emma who was tenant of the freehold for term of her life did not ever attorn to John; but they said that Emma held only for life by lease from the said Henry, which Emma, after the grant and acknowledgment which the said Henry had made to the said John, enfeoffed the said Philip in fee simple of the said tenements, and put him in seisin, which seisin he continued until William &c. ousted him. The court doth adjudge &c. and that Philip do recover his seisin of that estate which he first had, and let William have his recovery out of the note &c. if he please &c.

Taking of beasts.

§ *Wescote* &c. counted &c.—*Passeley.* We avow the taking &c., for you yourself hold of us two virgates of land, of which the place &c., by homage fealty and the services of &c. of rent by the year, of which services we were seised by the hand of one Helewyse, as by the hand of &c., which Helewyse enfeoffed you of these tenements, to hold of the chief lords &c.; on which you attorned to us for your fealty and for the rent &c.; and for that the rent was in arrear to us &c.—Bereford. Accord-ne devoit estre, car il dist qe un Henri le Fevre conussoit le droit des tenements &c. estre a Johan de la Bere, qi heir Willem est, par fin &c. granta qe ces tenementz qe a lui devoient revertir apres la mort une Emme &c. a luy remenassent en fee simple, e issi fust il entre apres la mort la dite Emme; e demanda jugement si encontre cele fin assise devoit estre. Et Philip dist qe une Emme (et memorandum quod illa fuit quæ tenuit ad terminum vitæ) de ces tenements lui enfeffa en fee simple par sa chartre, qil moustra, e lui mist en seisine, e issi fut seisi tant qe Willem e les autres atort &c. LASSISE dist qe Henri le Fevre, a qi le fee e le droit de ces tenementz fust, le granta a Johan de la Bere, frere Willem &c., qi heir, e par fin &c., mes Emme tenante del franc tenement a terme de sa vie ne se atturna unkes a Johan; mes ele dist qe Emme ne avoit mes qe a terme de vie du lees le dit Henri, la quele Emme, apres ceu grante e reconissance qe le dit Henri avoit fet [1] au dit Johan, enfeffa en fee simple le dit Phelipe des avantdiz tenements e lui mist en seisine, la quele seisine il continua taunke Willem &c. luy ousta. Si agarde &c., e qe Phelipe rescovere sa seisine de tel estat qe primes avoit, e eit Willem sun rescoverer hors de la note &c. sil voille &c. A.D. 1307.

Prise des avers.

§ *Wescote* &c. conta &c.—*Passeley.* Nous avowoms la prise &c., qe vous mesmes tenez de nous deus vergez de terre, dount le leu &c., par homage, fealte e par les services de &c. de rente par an, des queux services nous fumes seisi par my la mayn une Helewyse com par my la main &c., la quele Helewyse de ces tenements vous enfeffa a tenir des chief seignours &c.; par quei vous atturnastes a nous de vostre fealte e de la rente &c.; e pur ceo qe la rente nous fut arere &c.—

[1] MS. fu.

A.D. 1307. ing to your statement you ought not to have spoken of Helewyse when you were seised by the hand of the feoffee on whom you avow.—*Passeley*. But for the remainder of the services, of which services we were not seised by her hand, namely homage &c.—BEREFORD. You do not avow for these services. -- *Herle* repeated the avowry &c., and, said he, We tell you that we only hold a virgate of land of the land which Helewyse held, ready &c.; and as to that we tell you that neither he nor any of his ancestors &c. was seised &c. of any service since the time which is given for making avowry on seisin.—*Passeley*. You plead under a disguise, for Helewyse held two virgates &c. one in demesne and the other in fee, so that you have entirely her estate and the tenancy which she had.—*Herle*. We do not hold more than one carucate of land either in demesne or in service.—*Passeley*. Disclaim then.—*Herle*. The tenant shall disclaim, and we are not tenant &c., nor shall we disclaim for another's tenancy; and besides, disclaimer does not lie for a parcel.—*Passeley*. It often happens that one disclaims for another man's tenancy; and to neither of the two issues which you offer shall you be admitted; for since we allege seisin by your hands of services issuing from these tenements as by the hands of a tenant, we make you our tenant, from which position you can not retire except by disclaimer; for just as I claim you shall disclaim; and in right of the other, I do not affirm my estate, nor of the whole do I take my title of the seisin by your hands but by the hands of Helewyse; and that seisin you cannot counterplead you who are stranger to her; wherefore &c.—BEREFORD. The tenant must have some way in such a case against his lord; for otherwise where I hold of a man only one acre of land, he shall make himself my lord for three carucates, if I have them, against my will: wherefore &c.

BEREFORD. Solom vostre dit il ne covendra ja qe vous A.D. 1307. eussez parle de Helewise quant vous esteiez seisi par la main le feffe sur qi vous avowez.—*Passeley.* Mes pur le oel des services, des queux services nous ne esteimes pas seisi par sa mayn, saver homage &c. — BEREFORD. Vous ne avowez pas pur ces services. — *Herle* repetiit advocationem &c., e vous dioms qe nous ne tenoms qe une verge de tere de la tere qe Helewys tient, prest &c.; e de ceo vous dioms qe lui ne nul de ces auncestres &c. seisi &c. de nul service pus le temps qe done est de fere avowerie de seisine. — *Passeley.* Vous pledez suz une coverture; car Helewys tient deus vergez &c. la une en demene, e lautre en fee, issi qe vous avez purement sun estat e cele tenance qe ele avoit. — *Herle.* Nous ne tenoms mes qe une carue de terre ne en demene ne en service, prest. — *Passeley.* Desclamez donqes. — *Herle.* Tenant desclamera, e nous ne sumes nent tenant &c., ne nous descleymeroms point de autri tenance; e jatardeis desclamer ne gist point de parcele. — *Passeley.* Sovent avent qe daltri tenance home descleyme; e a nul des deus issues qe vous tendez ne serrez accepte; car del hour qe nous alleggoms seisine par my vos meins des services issanz des ces tenements com par my meinz de tenant, nous vous fessoms nostre tenant, de quei vous ne vous ostrez mie sil ne soit par desclamer; car auxicom jeo cleime vous descleymerez; e en droit del autre, jeo ne afferme mie mon estat ne del tut ne preigne mon title de la seisine par my vos meins, einz par les meins Helewyse, e quele seisine contrepleder ne poez pas vous, qe estes a lui estraunge; par quei. — BEREFORD. Ascune veye covent qe le tenant eit en teu cas contre sun seignour; car autrement ou jeo tendray de un home mes qe une acre de tere, il se fra mon seignur de treis carues si jeo les eusse, maugre mien; par quei &c.

A.D. 1307. Taking of beasts; where is treated of the pasture of a vill and its hamlet.

Taking of beasts.

§ John de Cogeshale complained that John de Brekles tortiously took his beasts in Strepham. — *Passeley.* We avow &c. in the same place &c., and for the reason that this place is within the bounds of the field of Brekles which is a hamlet of Strepham, within which bounds no terre-tenant reseant in the vill of Strepham ought to common; and for that we found them there, damage &c., in our common, &c. — *Herle.* Do you claim any common in Strepham? — *Passeley.* We are not now to plead about that. — HOWARD. How, will you have lands severed from theirs, and yet common with them in their lands in their pasture? I have well seen that in a vill one part of the vill does not common with the other part, but that each pasture has been severed from the other. — *Herle.* Now we pray judgment, since this is all one vill, and the pasture is one, and those of Brekles common with us, if he can, without showing some specialty for it, oust us from our common. — *Passeley.* The pasture and the field of Brekles are bounded, beyond which bounds neither you nor any reseant of Strepham ever had common, or pastured your beasts without your being caught and paying amends for it. — HOWARD. I have pasture where I never yet pastured; but for all that it does not follow that I have no pasture there. — BEREFORD to *Passeley.* Is the pasture one, or is it not? — *Passeley.* It is so severed that those of Strepham ought not to common beyond the bounds, as we have said. — HOWARD. Do you claim any common in Strepham? — *Passeley.* We are not now to plead of our claim about that. — HOWARD. Surely you are; for if you common in Strepham by reason of any tenements which you have in Brekles, the common is not severed, but one. — *Passeley.* Our common of Brekles is severed and bounded; beyond which bounds those of Strepham ought not to come; ready &c. — *Herle.* The pasture

Prise des avers, ubi loquitur de pastura villæ et ejus hameletti. A.D. 1307. Prise des avers.

§ Johan de Cogeshale se pleint qe Johan de Brekles atort prist ces avers en Strepham. — *Passeley*. Nous avowoms &c. en mesme le leu &c.; e par la reson qe ceo leu si est denz les boundes du champ de Brekles, qe est hamelet de Strepham, denz quels boundes nul terre tenant reseant en la ville de Strepham ne deit comuner; e pur ceo qe nous les trovames illoqes, damage &c. en nostre comune &c. —*Herle*. Clamez vous nule comune en Strepham? — *Passeley*. De ceo ne sumes nent ore a pleder. — HOWARD. Coment, volez vous terres aver severez de lours, e jatardeys comuner ove eux en lour terres en lour pasture? Jeo ay bien veu qe en une ville la une partie de la ville ne comune pas ove lautre, einz ad este la pasture severe chescon de autre. — *Herle*. Ore demandoms jugement, del houre qe ceo est tut une ville, e la pasture une, e ceux de Brekles comunent ove nous, si il nous puisse, sanz de ceo moustrer especialte, de nostre comune oster. — *Passeley*. La pasture e le chaump de Brekles sunt boundes, outre queles boundes vous ne nule reseant &c. de Strepham unqes comune ne aviez, ne vos avers pesates sanz ceo qe vous ne estoiez engage e feites les amendes. — HOWARD. Jeo en ay pasture ou jeo ne pesay unqes, e pur ceo nensuit il point qe nen ay pasture. — BEREFORD a *Passeley*. Est la pasture une ou ne mie? — *Passeley*. Ele est issi severe qe[1] ceux de Strepham ne deivent comuner outre les boundes qe nous avoms dit. — HOWARD. Clamez vous nulle comune en Strepham?—*Passeley*. De nostre clamer par la ne sumes ore a pleder. — HOWARD. Si estes certes, qar si vous comunez en Strepham par reson des tenements qe vous avez en Brekles, la comune nest pas severe einz une.—*Passeley*. Nostre comune de Brekles severe e bounde; outre qeles boundes ceux de Strephen ne deivent venir; prest.—*Herle*. La

[1] MS. par.

A.D. 1307. of Strepham is all one and not severed, ready &c. — *Passeley.* It is so severed that you ought not to common beyond the bounds &c.; ready &c. —BEREFORD. You are at issue; and what you will not reveal in pleading a good jury will reveal and will tell the truth, to wit, if the pasture is one or severed; and will tell us all about it.

That a wife &c. not named in the writ shall not be received &c.

§ The husband made default after appearance, and the Petit Cape issued against him, and was returned and served: his wife came and said by *Lanfare* that the tenements were her joint purchase &c., and prayed to be received.—STAUNTON. She is not named in the writ, and we are agreed that whereas she is not named in the writ, she shall not be received, but may have her recovery after the death of her husband by a "cui in vita" if she will; and because S. her husband has made default after default, this court adjudges that &c. do recover seisin &c.

Debt: where the writ was brought against a prior and one of his brethren.

§ Master John de Eversons brought a writ against W. de Totenhale, prior of the hospital of St. John of Jerusalem &c. and against one Brother John &c.—*Hedone.* Tortiously he has detained from and has not paid to him 160 marks &c.; and tortiously for this, that whereas this John, at a certain year, day and place, demised to them his church of Kemeseye to farm, that is to say to take the fruits of the said church for the term of two years thence next ensuing, for fourscore pounds each year, at certain terms; and that for the first year 60 marks, and for the second year the whole payment was in arrear &c.; and he offered suit &c.—*Herle* defended &c.; and said, he has counted and demanded &c. by reason of a delivery of a farm, and he does not say that we are seised by means of his delivery, which would much affirm his pasture de Strepham tut une e nent severe; prest.—*Passeley.* Issi severe qe vous ne devez comuner outre les boundes &c., prest.—BEREFORD. Vous estes a issue; e ceo qe vous ne volez descoverer enpledant une bone xij[ne] descovera e dirra la verite, videlicet de ceo, si la pasture une ou severe, e nous dirra tut coment il est. A.D. 1307.

Quod uxor &c. non nominata in brevi non admittitur &c.

§ Le baroun fit defaute apres apparance, e le petit cape sur ly &c., e returne, e servy; vient sa femme e par *Lanfare* dit qe ces tenements furent sun joint purchace &c., e pria estre receu.—STANTONE. Ele nest mie nome en le bref, e nous sumes acordez qe la ou ele nest mie nome, ele ne serra mie receu, einz eit sun rescoverer apres la mort sun baroun par "cui in vita" si ele voille; e pur ceo qe S. son baroun ad fet defaute apres defaute, si agarde &c. qe &c. rescovere seisine &c.

Debitum ubi fertur breve versus priorem et ejus fratrem.

§ Mestre Johan de Eversons porta bref vers W. de Totenhale priour del Hospital de Seint Johan de Jerusalem &c. e vers un Frere Johan &c.—*Hedone.* Atort lui detient e pas ne luy rendi clx. marcs &c., e pur ceo atort qe la ou mesme celui Johan lour bailla certein an jour e leu sa eglise de Kemeseye aferme, ceo est a saver a prendre les fruz de mesme la eglise tant qe a terme de deus anz prochein suianz pur iiii.[xx]. livres chascon an e certeinz termes; issi qe del primer an luy furent arere lx. marcs, e del secunde tote la paie &c.; e tendi suite &c.—*Herle* defendi &c.; il ad conte e demande &c. par reson de un baile de une ferme, e ne dit pas qe nous sumes seisi par my sun baile, qe afermereit mult sa accion; par quei si nous

A.D. 1307. action; therefore if we should not have the thing in respect of which he demands this debt, he would not be received to have the debt; judgment if on such a count &c.—*Hedone.* Say that you did not have it.—And he (*Herle*) was by judgment ousted from the exception.—*Herle.* What have you to show the debt?—*Hedone.* Good suit.—*Herle.* Have you anything else?—BEREFORD. If you have anything besides suit, plead it now, at your peril; for when he has defended against you and against your suit, and waged his law, perhaps you will not then get to put forward your deed.—*Hedone.* We have only suit.—*Herle* denied &c. and repeated the count, and said, W. tells you that neither on the day or year that you have counted, nor any year or day afterwards was he prior; ready &c., and we pray judgment if without a specialty showing a contract made at a time before he was prior, he ought to challenge this debt against him. —*Hedone.* What does Brother John answer?—BEREFORD. First answer to what he tells you: is not Brother John of the house of which W. is prior? and if his prior be absolved from this debt, he will discharge himself of it entirely if you will not say that he was then of such a condition that he could charge the house.—*Hedone.* Since John, against whom we have counted as well as against W., does not answer anything, we pray judgment &c. as of undefended.—BEREFORD. Be it as it may as to John; but if you do not answer to what they say to you, we shall take it for granted.—*Hedone.* He was prior at that time.—*Herle.* Not so.—*Hedone.* John answers nothing; judgment &c.—*Wescote.* By that answer you have enough for one and for the other.—BEREFORD affirmed this.—*Hedone.* Then that will serve for both. —BEREFORD. Yes, certainly.—Therefore &c.—And it is to be remembered that John leased his said church to the said prior &c. and to the said Brother John, as is aforesaid, by a writing indented between them, whereof the said Master John had one part in his possession, ne seussoms pas la chose pur quei il demande ceste dette, il ne serreit pas receu qil eust la dette, jugement si a teu counte &c. — *Hedone.* Dites qe vous ne le aviez pas: e fust oste par agard de la excepcion.— *Herle.* Quei avez de la dette ?—*Hedone.*—Suite bone. —*Herle.* Avez nule autre chose ?—BEREFORD. Si vous avez nul autre chose qe suite, dites ore en vostre peril; qe quant il avera defendu encontre vous e encontre vostre suite e tendra sa lei, par cas vous ne avendrez mie adonke de mettre avant fet.—*Hedone.* Nous navoms me qe suite.—*Herle* defendi &c. et repetiit narrationem; e W. vous dit qe le jour nel an qe vous avez conte, ne anz ne jours apres, si ne fu il pas priour, prest; e demandoms jugement si sanz especialte de contrat fet en temps devant qil estoit priour deive vers luy dette dereigner.—*Hedone.* Quei respont Frere Johan ?— BEREFORD. Responez primes a ceo qil vous dist; nest Frere Johan frere de la mesoun dount W. est priour; e si sun priour seit assouz de ceste dette, il se desafeblera tut si vous ne voillez dire qil fut tel au teu temps qil purra la meson charger. — *Hedone.* Del houre qe Johan, vers qi nous avoms conte auxibien com vers W., ne respont nent, jugement &c. com de noun defendu.—BEREFORD. Soit de Johan com estre purra; mes si vous ne responez a ceo qe eux vous dient, nous le tendroms agrante.—*Hedone.* Il fut priour a ceu temps.—*Herle.* Qe noun.—*Hedone.* Johan ne respond rienz, jugement.—*Wescote.* De ceo respons avez assez pur lun e pur lautre. — BEREFORD hoc affirmavit.—*Hedone.* Donqe servira cel pur ambedeux.—BEREFORD. Certes oil. Ideo &c.—Et memorandum qe Johan lessa sa eglise avantdite au priour &c. e au dit Frere Johan auxicom est avant dit, par un escrist endente entre eux, dount le dit Mestre Johan avoit la une par- A.D. 1307.

A.D. 1307. which sufficiently proved the debt; which Master John, within the term &c. resigned his church, whereby the said prior and Brother John lost their term; and they brought a writ of covenant against the said Master John, on which writ *Herle* wished he had then pleaded with them, because by reason of the breach of covenant they would have answered to the debt: and Master John would not plead, but made default; neither would he use the writing indented which he had, because it showed the covenant &c. for the term.

Debt, for money told delivered in charge.

§ *Willuby.* Philip the son of Thomas of Graham [complains] that Master Gilbert de Segrave tortiously detains from him and will not restore 60 marks and 11 marks which he owes him; and for this &c. that whereas &c. he bailed &c. to keep until he asked for them &c.—And the writ ran "which he owes and unjustly detains;" and neither the writ nor the count was challenged; which was wondered at, since naturally a debt ought to be demanded by a creditor, and the said Philip was not a creditor &c.—And yet *Herle* and *Passeley* were for the said Gilbert.

§ It may be said in an assise of Utrum "and if it be "found &c." although it be a writ of Right, in which one ought to lay a title of right, to wit, seisin of a predecessor or of an ancestor.—*Hedone.* R. tells you that of only so much &c.; and if it be found &c. tenant, he is ready to hear the jury. Nor is it necessary to say "the "esplees &c." but only that ancestor or the predecessor was seised &c. in the time of such a king.

Nuper obiit; where one of the parceners claimed as a stranger.

§ *Lanfare* (for the tenant). One J. and Alice his wife who were seised of these tenements, leased these tenements to us for the life of Alice, against whom we have tie vers lui qe assez temoigna la dette; le quel Mestre Johan denz le terme &c. resigna sa eglise, par quei les dis priour e Frere Johan perdirent lour terme; e porterent bref de covenant vers le dit Mestre Johan, a quei bref *Herle* voleit qil eust plede ov eux adonke, pur ceo qe par le covenant enfreint le eussont eux respondux a la dette; e Mestre Johan ne voleit mie pleder, einz fit defaute, ne le escrist endente qil avoit ne voleit il user, pur ceo qil testmoigna le covenant &c. du terme. A.D. 1307.

Debitum de denariis numeratis traditis in custodiam.

§ *Willuby.* Phelipe le fiz Thomas de Graham qe Mestre Gilbert de Segrave atort lui detient e pas ne lui rendent lx. marcs e xi. marcs les queux ily deit; e pur ceo &c., qe la ou &c. il bailla &c. agarder tant qil les demandast &c. Et fuit breve "quas ei debet [et] "injuste detinet;" et non fuit calumpniatum breve nec narratio; super quod miratur, cum naturaliter debitum debeat peti a creditore; ac idem Philippus[1] non erat creditor &c. Et tamen *Herle* et *Passeley* fuerunt cum predicto Gilberto.

§ Dici potest jurata de utrum, "Et si trove soit &c." tut soit il bref de dreit, en le quel home deit prendre title de dreit, saver seisine de predecessour ou de auncestre.—*Hedone.* R. vous dist qil mes qe de tant &c.; e si trove soit &c. tenant, il est prest de oier la jure: nec oportet dicere les esplez &c. sed solummodo le auncestre ou le predecessour &c. seisi &c. en temps de teu roi.

Nuper obiit ubi una participum clamavit ut extranea.

§ *Lanfare* (pro tenente). Un J. e Alice sa femme, qe furent seisis de ces tenements, ces tenements nous lesserent a terme de la vie Alice, vers queux nous avom

---

[1] MS. Gilbertus.

A.D. 1307. our voucher for our estate; and so we entered by way of purchase for the term of Alice's life; judgment if this writ lie against us.—BEREFORD. You wish to put him to his writ "de rationabili parte" if you can, and to oust him from this writ; but you do not show any reason why. —*Lanfare.* The writ of Mordancester would lie, which is in the possession; and in this writ we could vouch. — BEREFORD. Would you have him bring the Mordancester against you who are his parcener? He says that your common ancestor lately died seised. What say you? — *Lanfare.* The common ancestor was seised; and inasmuch as the tenements are devisable according to the custom of York, he devised them &c. to Alice for the term of her life; which Alice, together with her husband, leased to us her estate &c. — *Middeltone.* He did not devise them to Alice; ready &c.—And the other side said the contrary.—Therefore &c.—BEREFORD to *Lanfare.* At least you have disclaimed as to the parcenary: if the inquest go against you, your part of the heritage is null. — *Lanfare.* She demands nothing but two parts &c.; she will have no more than she demands. —BEREFORD. However that may be, you will not have it, for you do not claim to be her parcener. — *Lanfare.* Alice has only for the term of her life, and her estate we have; after her death the reversion is ours in common. —HOWARD. Do you think now to claim at first as a stranger, and then, if that fail you, to be aided by the estate of a parcener?

Quod permittat, for a bridge.

§ Command the prior of Bern[well] that &c. he permit &c. to throw down a certain bridge &c. which J. formerly prior, predecessor &c., raised to the nuisance of the frank tenement of A. &c. father of the said R., whose heir he is. —*Lanfare* counted and assigned three nuisances, to wit, whereas the filum aquæ &c. was used rightfully to run by the water which is between the vills of T. and A., so that it prevented the animals of T. from passing into the corn and grass of the plaintiff in A there had &c. raised

nostre voucher de nostre estat, e issint sumes entrez A.D. 1307
par voye de purchaz a terme de la vie Alice; jugement si cesti bref igise entre nous. — BEREFORD. Vous lui voillez mettre au bref de renable partie si vous puissez, e oster lui de ceo bref; mes vous ne mustrez mie reson pur quei. — *Lanfare.* Il igireit le mortdauncestre qest en la possession, e en ceo bref purrioms nous voucher. — BEREFORD. Voillez vous qil portast le mortdauncestre vers vous qe estes sun parcener? Il dit qe vostre comune auncestre morust seisi nadgers; qei dites vous?—Le comune auncestre fust seisi, e pur ceo qe les tenements sunt devissables, solom la coustume de Everwyk, il les devisa &c. a Alice a terme de sa vie; la quele Alice ove sun baroun sun estat nous lesserent &c. — *Middeltone.* Il ne le devisa pas a Alice, prest &c. — Et alii e contra.—Ideo &c.—BEREFORD a *Lanfare.* Au meinz vous avez desclame en la parcenerie; si enqueste die contre vous vostre parte de ceste heritage est nule. —*Lanfare.* Ele ne demande fors qe les deus parties &c.; ele navera nent plus qe ele ne demande.—BEREFORD. Coment qe soit, vous ne le averez pas, car vous ne clamez pas estre sa parcenere. *Lanfare.* Alice nad fors qe a terme de sa vie, qi estat nous avoms; apres qi mort la reversion est nostre en comune.—HOWARD. Quidez ore estre a primes clamer com estraunge, e pus estre eide par estat de parcener si ceo vous faille &c.?

Quod permittat de ponte.

§ Precipe priori de Bern. quod &c. permittat &c. prosternere quemdam pontem &c. quem J. quondam prior predecessor &c. levavit ad nocumentum liberi tenementi A. &c. patris predicti R. cujus heres &c.— *Lanfare* conta e assigna treis nussances, saver, la ou le fil del ewe &c. soleit adres coure par le ewe qe est entre la ville de T. e A. issi qe il desturba qe le aumail de T. ny passat en les blees ne en la herbe le pleintif

A.D. 1307. a bridge whereby they passed &c.; and also that whereas the plaintiff had no need to keep guard &c.; and also that by reason of that bridge the water &c. flows back and floods his meadows &c., tortiously and to his damage. — *Hedone* denied &c. He has assigned three nuisances, and if the inquest acquit us of one, yet they must inquire of the others. And so of each, as in a plea of assise; judgment &c. — Of this he was ousted by HOWARD. — *Kinge.* Judgment of the variance between the writ and the count; for he has counted by way of damage, and the writ does not state it; and nevertheless this is a writ of Right.—HOWARD. So is the "Ne vexes" every "Quod "permittat" and the "Quo jure," in which one counts by way of damages. — BEREFORD. He has said what ought to be said, and one word more; and if by chance the court decides that they shall not have damages, what have you to say to the disturbance.—*King.* We pray a view.—HOWARD to *Kinge.* We did not oust you by judgment from your exception. — *Wescote.* He now ousts himself since he has prayed the view; and we wish to imparl, if he ought to have the view, or not.—BEREFORD. If you do not grant him the view we will put you back into the condition in which you were at first. — *Westcote.* Nay, we will rather grant him the view. — And afterwards, J. of Cambridge, who was of counsel for the prior, came and said that they did not pray the view, but held still to the exception &c.—BEREFORD. Then do you disavow Adam de Kinge.—And afterwards, lest he should be disavowed, the attorney granted the view to the prior. And nevertheless, as it was thought, the exception was of force to have quashed the writ, if it had been better worded, thus, He counts by way of damage for a nuisance done to another; judgment if, for trespass done to another, he ought to recover damages:—which exception goes in full to the count. But it seems that it is not of force, because by reason that he is not suffered to throw down, he suffers damage; therefore &c. By en A., la avoit &c. leve un pount par ou il passa &c.; A.D. 1307. e ensi la ou le pleintif ne estovereit aver messer pur fere la garde &c.; e ensi qe par cel pount lewe &c. refoule e surunde ces preez &c., atort e a ces damages. —*Hedone* defendi &c. Il ad assigna treis nussances, dount si enqueste nous aquitast de la une, uncore covendra enquerer del autre. Et sic de singulis auxi com en play de assise; jugement &c. E fust oste par HOWARD. — *Kinge.* Jugement de la variance entre le bref e le counte; qil ad conte par my damage, e le bref ne le voet pas; e jatardeis ceo est un bref de dreit.— HOWARD. Auxi est le "ne vexes," chescon "quod per-"mittat," e le "quo jure," en les queux homme count par my damages.—BEREFORD. Il ad dit quant qe fet a dire, e une parole plus; e si par cas avis fut a la court qe eux ne en avereient mie damage, quei dites vous al destourber.—*Kinge.* Nous demandoms la vewe. — HOWARD a *Kinge.* Nous ne vous ostames mie de vostre excepcion par agarde.—*Wescote.* Il se ouste ore, del houre qil ad demande la vewe; e nous voloms enparler sil deive aver la vewe ou noun. —BEREFORD. Si vous ne lui grantez la vewe, nous vous remettroms en lestat qe vous estoiez adeprimes. — *Wescote.* Nay, plus tost lui granteroms la vewe.—Et postea J. de Cantebregge, qui fuit de consilio prioris, venit et dixit quod non petierunt visum, immo se tenent adhuc ad exceptionem &c. — BEREFORD. Donqe desavowez vous *Ad. de Kinge.* — Et postea ne disvocaretur attornatus prioris concessit visum: et tamen ut credebatur exceptio fuit valida pro brevi cassasse, quæ poterit dari sub meliori formâ sic, il count par my damage de annussance fet a autre, jugement si de trespas a autre fet damage deive rescoverer; quæ exceptio totaliter tendit ad narracionem; videtur tamen quod non valet, quia de hoc quod non patitur prosternere patitur dampnum,

A.D. 1307. this it is ascertained that if he were to recover damages, they would be adjudged from the time of the commencement of the nuisance; which could not be, for the reason aforesaid.

Cessavit. Aid is granted in a Cessavit &c.

§ The tenant said that he had only a term for life &c., and prayed aid &c. — *Hedone.* We have made you our very tenant, and we are seised by your own hands, and by your cesser this action has accrued to us; judgment if, on your cesser, aid &c. — *Warwick* (sitting in the Bench). Do you wish to have the land? — *Hedone.* Yes. — *Warwick.* And do you think to dereign it from a tenant for a term, since he prays aid of him &c., without the other being warned &c. — And the aid was awarded by HENGHAM.

A case where a tenant by the law of England alleged against the plaintiff that she detained the charters &c., and it was not allowed.

§ The widow of Robert Bardolf brought &c. against Ingeran Belet. — *Hedone.* She detains from us certain charters &c.; (and he specified &c.;) which if she will give up to us, we are ready to endow her, and we always have been. — *Herle.* How do the charters belong to you — *Hedone.* We have espoused Avice daughter and heir of Robert Bardolf, by whom we have issue, by reason of which issue we hold the tenements whereof &c. by the law of England, and we have the heir in our ward; and often during the life of Avice our wife we tendered your dower to you by such and such persons, so that you would restore the charters to us. — *Herle.* Nay, now here is another thing; now Avice is dead, what are you doing now? — *Hedone.* We still tender it to you in form aforesaid. — *Herle.* And we pray judgment, since it does not belong to you to have the charters &c., if you can &c. delay our dower. — *Warr.* to *Hedone.* Even if you had the charters, the heir of Avice would dereign them out of your hand in spite of ergo &c. Solvitur per hoc quod si recuperaret dampna adjudicanda essent a tempore nocumenti incepti; quod non poterit, ratione prius dicta. A.D. 1307

Auxilium concedetur en le cessavit &c.

§ Le tenant dit qil ne avoit mes qe a terme de vie &c., e pria aide &c. — *Hedone.* Nous vous avom fet nostre verrei tenant, e par vos meins demene seisi, e par vostre cesser nous est ceste accion acru; jugement si de vostre cesser eide &c.—*Warr.* (sedens in Banco). Volez aver la terre?—*Hedone.* Oil.—*Warr.* E quidez vous dereigner du tenant a terme, del houre qil prie aide de celui &c., sanz ceo qe lautre soit garni &c. — E leide fut agarde par HENGHAM.

Ubi tenens per legem Angliæ allegavit contra petentem quod detinuit cartas &c., et non allocatur.

§ La femme Robert Bardolf porta &c. vers Ingeran Belet. — *Hedone.* Ele nous detient certeines chartres &c., et nominavit &c., les queles si ele nous voudra rendre, nous la sumes prest de dowere, e tut temps avom este. — *Herle.* Coment apendent les chartres a vous? — *Hedone.* Nous avioms espose Avice fille e heir Robert Bardolf, de qi nous avoms issue, par reson de quel issue nous tenoms les tenements dount &c. par la lei dengletere, e avoms le heir en nostre garde, e sovent vostre dowere vivant Avice nostre femme vous tendimes par teles qe vous nous eussez les chartres renduz.—*Herle.* Nay, ore est autre chose[1]; Avice morte, qe fetes vous ore? — *Hedone.* Uncore vous tendoms en la forme avant.—*Herle.* E nous jugement, del houre qe a vous ne apent point de aver les chartres &c., si vous nous puissez &c. nostre dowere delaier.— *Warr.* a *Hedone.* Tut eussez vous les chartres le heir, Avice les dereignereit hors de vostre mayn maugre le vostre; par

[1] MS. ore.

A.D. 1307. you; wherefore it appears that they do not belong to you. — HENGHAM (ad idem). And at least if the heir &c. asked them of the woman, it would not be a good reason for her to say that she had delivered them to you.—And it was decided that the plaintiff should recover, notwithstanding &c.—Afterwards the said Ingelran complained to W HOWARD (who was not then in the Bench) that he was not able to be heard in that plea; and he (HOWARD) recalled the parties.— And *Hedone* pleaded his exception &c. — *Herle.* I answer him as W. but not as party. — HOWARD. Why? — *Herle.* Because judgment has been given; but for your satisfaction I tell you that about the charters he says what he wishes: we have them not, but they are in another person's keeping, and under his own seal. — *Ingeram.* You have forbidden him who has them to deliver them to us. — HOWARD. You are sufficiently in possession of them, since they are under your seal; and if she forbad him to eat; what of that? And *Hedone* was stopped by BEREFORD because he began again to plead thereon.

quei il piert qe eles ne apent mie. — HENGHAM (ad idem). E jatardeys si heir &c. les demanda de la femme, il ne serreit mie bone reson pur lui a dire qele les vous avoit baille. Et consideratur quod petens recuperet dotem non obstante &c. Postea predictus Ingelranus conquestus fuit W. HOWARD, qui tunc non fuit in Banco, quod non potuit audiri in isto placito, qui fecit revocare partes. Et *Hedone* recitavit excepcionem suam &c. — *Herle.* Jeo lui respond com W. mes noun pas com partie. — HOWARD. Par quei? — *Herle.* Pur ceo qe le jugement est rendu: mes pur mover vous vous dy jeo qil dist sun talent des chartres; nous ne les avoms pas, einz sunt en altri garde, e suz sun seal demene. — *Ingeram.* Vous avez defendu celi qe les ad qil ne les nous livre pas. — HOWARD. Assez le avez vous de pus qe eles sunt suz vostre seal; e si ele lui defend de manger, de ceo quei. Et *Hedone* fuit s^s quia inde reincipit placitare, per BEREFORD. A.D. 1307.

EASTER TERM IN THE THIRTY-FIFTH YEAR.

EASTER TERM IN THE THIRTY FIFTH YEAR.

A.D. 1307. Case where the tenant claimed only for a term of years.

Entry sur disseisin. § A writ of Entry founded on disseisin in the degrees was brought against the prior of Kenilworth.—*Herle.* We have nothing &c. but for a term of years by lease from Sir W. de Bereford, according to the form of this writing; and we had no other estate on the day when the writ &c.; judgment &c.—*Willeby.* Our writ says that you have entry by Simond Basset, and this is true, since he entered you have always been seised &c.—*Toudeby.* And although you had since alienated &c. the estate which you had by Simon, and afterwards retaken the estate, that contrivance, since you are in your first estate, will not hold as a degree.—STAUNTON said the same. —*Herle.* Yes, it certainly will, since we have nothing &c. except for a term of years; we never were in a former estate where we had a freehold. — *Willeby* offered to aver what he first said.—*Herle.* We can not with you join an averment of another person's freehold.—*Willeby.* W. de Bereford will perhaps give such an answer, if we bring a writ against him.—*Warr.* Since there is no tenant, and consequently no deforceant, put yourself in. —*Willeby.* He is a poor man, who can not enter against the will of the prior.

Cosinage, where the resort was challenged because it was not made in the whole blood.

§ One Isabel, who was under age, brought the writ against Thomas Corbet; and Thomas said that he had these tenements by lease from the king, whose charter he showed, and said that he ought not to answer on

DE TERMINO PASCHE ANNO XXXV°.

Ubi tenens nihil clamavit nisi ad terminum annorum. A.D. 1307.

§ Bref dentre fondu sur la disseisine en les degrez fust porte vers le priour de Kenlinworthe. —*Herle.* Nous neams rienz &c. mes qe a terme des anz du les Sire W. de Bereford, solom la forme de ceste escrit, ne riens ne aveiums le jour de bref &c., jugement &c. —*Willeby.* Nostre bref dist qe vous avez entre par Simond Basset; e ceo est verite, pus qil entra vous avez tut temps este seisi &c. — *Toudeby.* E tut ussez vous puis le estat qe vous avez par Simon aliene &c. e puis repris estat, cele makement del oure qe vous estes a vostre primer estat ne leztentdra mie desgre. —STANTONE idem dixit.—*Herle.* Si fra certes, del oure qe nous ne avoums riens &c. mes qe a terme des aunz, nous ne fumes nient a primer estat ou nous avoms fraunc tenement.—*Willeby* tendi de averrer quod primo dixit.—*Herle.* Nous ne poums a vous jondre nul averement de autri fraunc tenement.—*Willeby.* Tiel respuns par cas dorra W. de Bereford, si nous portasoums bref ver luy. —*Warr.* Del oure qil ni ad nul tenant, e par consequens nul deforceour, mettez vous einz.—*Willeby.* Cest un povres homme qe ne put pas entrer countre le volunte le priour.

Entre sur disseisine.

Cosinage ubi calumpniatur resorcio quia non fiebat in sanguine integro.

§ Une Isabele que fust deinz age porta le bref ver Thomas Corbet; e Thomas autrefoiz dit qil avoit ces tenements du lees le roi, dont il moustra sa chartre, e dit qil ne devoit de ces, rege inconsulto, respondre:

A.D. 1307. this matter, without the king's concurrence. And Isabel sued to the king, and the king ordered the Justices that, notwithstanding &c., they should proceed according to law and custom &c. And Isabel counted of the seisin of one John, and that from John it resorted to Margery as aunt, being sister of Isabel who was mother of John, and from Margery descended &c. — *Toudeby*. In Margery's blood you can not make any resort, nor can you demand anything through her blood; for king Henry gave these tenements to one Reymond de Luke, by which gift he was seised in his demesne as of fee; which Reymond took to wife one Elise who never had anything in these tenements except as wife of Reymond, and she afterwards married one Geoffrey, who begot on her that Margery to whom they make their resort. John the son of Isabel the daughter of Reymond died without heir of his body, wherefore our lord the king, for default of blood of John, seized &c. the tenements as his escheat, and gave them to Thomas Corbet: thus is Margery &c. a stranger in blood to Reymond, and we pray judgment if by her blood you can demand anything &c.—*Passeley*. Elise, the mother of Isabel and Margery, survived Reymond and died seised in her demesne as of fee.—*Passeley*. We are not in a writ of right, but in a possessory writ, where it is sufficient to maintain the possession.—*Toudeby*. And inasmuch as against our plea that you are a stranger both as to the possession and as to the right, which right we are ready to aver by the Chancery roll, you show no title to affirm your estate, we pray judgment if anything &c. you can demand.—*Passeley*. Elise survived Reymond for 40 years, and during all that time she &c. was seised, which seisin would give her an estate even though she had entered by abatement; and after her death, Isabel, mother of John, entered as heir, ready &c. by the country. — STAUNTON. Why then were not the tenements divided between Isabel and Margery?—*Passeley*. Margery had other tenements in satisfaction &c.—HOWARD.

e Isabele suist au rei, e le roi manda a les justices quod non obstante &c. procederent secundum legem et consuetudinem &c. Et Isabele conta de la seisine un Johan, de Johan &c. resorti a Margerie cum a aunte soer Isabele mere Johan; de Margerie descendi &c.—*Toudeby.* En le saunk[1] Margerie ne poez nul resorte fere, ne par soun saunk rens demander; qar le roi Henri dona ces tenements a un Reymound de Luke, par quel doun il fust seisi en son demene cum de fe; le quel Reymound prist femme une Elyse, qe en ceux tenements unkes rien ne out mes cum fe mme Reymound, sei lessa esposer a un Geffrey &c., qe de lui engendra cele Margerie a qi eux font lor resort. Johan le fiz Isabele la file Reymound devia sanz heir de son cors, par quei nostre seignour le rei par defaute de sank Johan seisi &c. les tenements cum sa escheyte, e les dona a Thomas Corbet; issi est Margerie &c. estraunge al sank Reymound, e demandoms jugement si par son sank rens &c. puisset demander.—*Passeley.* Elise mere Isabele e Margerie survesqui Reymound, e morust seisie en son demene cum de fe.—*Passeley.* Nous ne sumes point a le bref de dreit einz a la possession, ou suffit de maintenir la possession.—*Toudeby.* E desicom encountre nostre dit qe vous estes estraunge e en la possessioun e en la dreit, quel dreit nous prest de averrer par roule de la chancelerie, de afermer vostre estat nul title ne mustrez, jugement si riens &c. puissez demander.—*Passeley.* Elise survesqui Reymound .xl. aunz, e tut cele temps fust ele &c. seisie, quele seisine la dureit estat, mes qe ele fust entre par abatement; apres qi mort Isabele mere Johan entra cum heyr, prest &c. par pais. — STAUNTONE. Pur quei dunke ne furent les tenements departiz entre Isabele e Margerie?—*Passeley.* Margerie avoit autre tenements en allowaunce &c. — HOWARD. Le estat qe Thomas ad A.D. 1307.

[1] MS. sarreik.

A.D. 1307. The estate which Thomas has is from the king, and he is now to be pleaded with just as if the king was seised thereof; and if the king were seised thereof, and you were party with him, it would avail you nothing without title; no more &c.—STAUNTON (to the same effect). Passeley, you are a lawyer, and there is a written law which speaks of this matter; "the person in possession is "to be compelled &c.;" and he is in; and if you wish to have him out and to have the land, show and make your title.—*Passeley*. It is sufficient title for us in this possessory writ to aver the possession; and how will he aver his statement that Reymond was sole feoffee of the king, to him and his heirs?—STAUNTON. By the Chancery roll.—*Passeley*. Let him have his record.—*Toudeby*. To what purpose? You have not yet denied it: deny it first and we shall willingly have it.—*Passeley*. We are pleading for an infant under age, to whom the court will be more tender and the law more favourable, and we can not know anything of the records of Chancery; but we are willing to aver the possession &c. by a good jury, and we pray judgment. And on the other hand, in old times every writ, whether of right or of the possession, lay well against the king, and nothing is now changed except that one must now sue against him by bill where formerly one sued by writ: and since we offer to aver the possession &c., which averment they refuse, we pray judgment &c.—HOWARD. You say so much to demonstrate the title of Elise that I think the case is this, that Reymond &c. without the king's license enfeoffed some one &c. who re-enfeoffed him and Elise, in consequence whereof the king seized these tenements as forfeited, because they were alienated without his license.—*Passeley*. Such an alienation would not work a forfeiture.—HOWARD. If the heir of the first feoffor had entered, the feoffee would not oust him from the tenement by way of law, since he had nothing by way of license &c.—And so they remain, saving to each party his arguments, until the octaves of St. Michael.

ceo est par le roi, e est ore a pleder ove ly auxi cum le roi en fust seisi; e si le roi en fust seisi, e vous fuset partie a ly, il vous ne freit rens saun title; nent plus &c. — STAUNTONE (ad idem). Passeley, vouse ts legister, e il ad un tel lay escrit qe parle de cete matere, cogi possessorem re &c.; e il est einz, e si vous voilez aver le hors e aver la terre, mustrez et fetes vous title.—*Passeley.* Assez nous est title en cest bref possessorie de averer la possessioun; e coment voet il son dit verrer qe Reymound fust soul feffe du roi a ly e a ces heires?—STAUNTONE. Par roule de chauncelerie.—*Passeley.* Eit son record.—*Toudeby.* A quel oes; vous ne avez pas uncore dedist; dedites le primes, e nous le averons volunteres.—*Passeley.* Nous pledoms pur un enfaunt deinz age, a qi la curt serra plus tendre, e la ley plus favourable; e nous ne pouns nent saver record de la chauncelerie; einz voloms averrer la possessioun &c. par bon pais, e demandoms jugement: e dautre part, en auncien temps chescun bref e de dreit e de possessioun girreit ben ver le roi, de quei nest ore rens raunge mes qe tant qil voet qe home siwe ver luy par bille ou home siwist avant par bref; e del oure qe nous[1] voloms la possessioun &c. averrer, qele averement eux refusent, demaundoms jugement &c.—HOWARD. Vous ditez taunt de moustrer le title Elyse qe jeo crey qe il seit tiel, qe Reymound &c. saunz conge le roi enfeffa ascun &c., qe ly e Elise refeffa, par quei le roi seisie ces tenements cum forfes, pur ceo qil estoient alienez saunz son conge.—*Passeley.* Tiel alienacion ne freit pas forfeture.—HOWARD. Si leir le primer feoffour fust entre, le feffe ne luy outereit mie de tenement[2] par voie de lei, del oure qil navoit rens de counge &c.—Et sic commorantur salvis utrique parti rationibus suis usque in octabis Michaelis. A.D. 1307.

[1] MS. vous. [2] M.S. le serement.

A.D. 1307. Of a writ of Right removed into the Bench by the Recordari &c., where the tenant &c. at first recovered by " Jure de utrum."

Right. § The writ was brought against a parson of York for tenements which he himself had recovered by a " Jure de " utrum," and the plea was removed out of the court of York at the suit of the said parson by Recordari, with the cause, which was this, " because the said &c. who is " tenant &c. says that he recovered the said tenements " before Ralph de Hengham &c. Justices &c. by judg- " ment of the said court, on account whereof the afore- " said plea cannot be brought on in the said court. Let " there be done &c."—*Rostone.* We pray the view &c.—*Wileby.* You demanded it in the court of York, and there you had it; wherefore &c. — TRIKINGHAM. The record would be necessary to prove that, and we have nothing of the record; nor will we make the suitors come here to record that; for it would be for you a less hardship of law to grant the view &c.—STAUNTON. You have removed the plea &c. for a certain cause, to wit because you recovered the &c.; by which cause it well appears that you are certified of what tenements you are impleaded; wherefore the view is not necessary.—And he was ousted of it, by judgment.—*Rostone.* These tenements are frank-almoign of our church &c.; we pray aid of the prior of the Holy Trinity of York, our patron, and of the bishop of York our ordinary, without whom we cannot answer &c. — *Frisqeney.* You say nothing why you ought to have aid, for you do not make the tenements to be frank-almoign by your saying so &c.: you do not say that you found your church seised; and at least by your writ you suppose you yourself to be the purchaser of these tenements; wherefore &c.—STAUNTON. If he purchased them as the right of his church, that purchase will make him sooner to have aid than not.—It was adjudged that he should have the aid &c.

De breve de recto ammoto in Bancum per recordari &c., ubi tenens &c. primo recuperavit per jure de utrum. A.D. 1307.

§ Le bref fust porte ver une persone de Everwike des tenements qe il mesme avoit recovere par une jure de utrum, e la parole fust remue hors de la court de Everwike a la suite la dite persone par record ove cause, qe fust tiele, "quia idem &c. qui tenens &c. "dicit se predicta tenementa recuperasse coram R. de "Hengham &c. justiciariis &c. per judicium ejusdem curiæ "nostræ, propter quod loquela predicta in curia illa de- "duci non potest. Fiat &c."—*Rostone.* La vewe &c.—*Wileby.* Vous la avez demande en la court de Everwike, e la aviez, par quei &c.—TRIKINGHAM. A ceo prover besoignereit record, e nous ne avoms renz qe la record; ne nous ne from pas les suters vener cy pur cele recorder; qar meinder duresce de lay vous serreit a granter la vewe &c.—STAUNTONE. Vous avet fet remuer la parole &c. par certeine cause, scilicet pur ceo qe vous les recoverastes &c.; par quele cause il pert bien qe vous estes ascerte de queux tenements vous estes enplede; par quei la vewe nest mie necessarie: e fust oute par agarde.—*Rostone.* Ces tenements sunt fraunchez almoigne de nostre[1] eglise &c., prioms ayde del priour de la Seinte Trinite de Everwike, nostre patroun, e del evesqe de Everwike nostre ordener, saunz queux nous ne poums respondre &c.—*Frisqeney.* Vous ne ditez[2] renz pur quei[3] vous devez eide aver, qar vous ne fetes mie les tenements uncore fraunche almoigne par vostre dit &c., qe vous ne ditz pas qe vous trovastes vostre eglise seisie; e jatardays par vostre bref supposez vous mesme de ces tenements estre purchasour; par quei &c.—STAUNTONE. Si les purchasa cum la dreit de sa eglise, cel purchace li fra plus tost aver eyde qe noun. Et consideratum est quod habeat De recto.

[1] MS. vostre.

[2] MS. devez.

[3] The words "pur quei" are repeated.

A.D. 1307. And note that here in counting he offered suit and proof according to the custom of the court &c.

Waste. Where the tenant claimed the fee; also where after the inquest had passed against a man and his wife the woman sought to be received &c.

§ The writ was brought against a man and his wife who claimed the fee &c., and the plaintiff said that they had only a freehold for term of life, and upon that an inquest was joined between them, which passed in the country against the tenant.—And now, the verdict of the inquest being inspected by the Justices, *Passeley*, for the plaintiff, prayed judgment.—HENGHAM. Do you not wish to have your damages?—*Passeley*. Sir, we do wish it.—HENGHAM. Then it is necessary that they be inquired of by the inquest.—*Passeley*. It is not necessary, but they are to be assessed at your discretion, according to what we counted against them, since in pleading they did not deny the waste &c.—MALORE. If we now take an inquest for the damages, it will perchance be found by that inquest that they had committed waste in a moiety of the tenements; by that inquest, according to the law of the land, you will only recover the half, to wit the tenements wasted, and by this you recover the whole, and so the one inquest will be contrary to the other.—STAUNTON. It would not be; for in that inquest, the inquiry would be not of the quantity of the tenements wasted but only of the damage done by the waste.—*Passeley*. By the false claim, to our disheritance, the tenements are forfeited; and we pray judgment &c.—And the parties being interrogated about this, the wife appearing but the husband not appearing,—*Hedone* said, You have here Idonea the wife of &c., and she tells you that that tenement is her freehold, which her husband wishes for his own pleasure to lose, and she has come forward; judgment; and she prays to be received, auxilium &c.—Et nota quod hic in narrando il tendi sute e dereigne solom la custume de la curte &c. A.D. 1307.

Ubi tenens clamavit feodum, etiam ubi post inquisitionem transitam contra virum et uxorem mulier petiit se admitti &c. De vasto.

§ Le bref fust porte vers un home e sa femme qe clamerent fe &c.; e le pleintif diseit qe eles ne avoient mes qe franc tenement a terme de vie, e de ceo se joint entre eux un enqueste qe passa en pais e encontre le tenant.—Et nunc, veredicto inquisitionis per justiciarios inspecto, *Passeley*, pro querente, pria jugement.—HENGHAM. Ne volez pas aver vos damages?—*Passeley*. Si voloms sire.—HENGHAM. Dount covent il qe homme enquerge de ces par enqueste.—*Passeley*. Noun covent pas, einz sunt a juger par voz descrecions solom nostre demostrance qe nous countames vers eux, del oure qe enpledaunt e eux ne dediseient point le vast &c.—MALLORE. Si nous pernoms ore enqueste des damages trove serra par cas par cele qe eaux averent fest le vast en la moite des tenements, par quele enqueste solom lei de terre vous ne recoverez mes qe la moite, saver les tenementz waste e par ceste lenter, e issi la une enqueste contrariant al autre.—STAUNTONE. Noun freit; qe en cest enqueste home ne enquerreit pas de la quantite de tenements wastez einz solumes des damages fetz par le wast.—*Passeley*. Par lor faux clamance en nostre desheritance sount les tenements forfetz, e prioms jugement &c.—Et super hoc, partibus interrogatis, uxore comparente viro vero non,—*Hedone*. Vous avez ci Ydoine la femme &c., e vous dit qe cele tenement si est son franc tenement, lequel son baroun voleit de gre perdre, e est venuz avaunt jugement, e prie estre rescu &c. par

A.D. 1307. by statute.[1]—*Passeley.* It does not avail for you, for the judgment is not to be given on his default; and at least the meaning of the statute is that where a man and his wife demand tenements &c., and by this writ we do not demand against you any tenements.—*Rostone.* The statute speaks of three things, to wit, if a man &c. makes default, or feintly defends, or is desirous to surrender in the life of his wife; and we tell you that our husband defended feintly &c., and we pray &c.—STAUNTON. If you should be received, what would you say?—*Hedone.* The plaintiff is under coverture of a husband not named &c.; judgment of the writ: thereby it appears well that your husband, who for that reason might have abated the writ, pleaded feintly.—STAUNTON. Nay, he would not have done so now.—*Passeley.* The phrase "ita ficte" is not in that statute but in another,[2] to wit where a writ of dower is brought against a guardian who makes default or feintly defends by collusion &c.: so that by that phrase you have no advantage.—On another day *Rostone* for the woman, prayed that she might be received, as before &c.—*Malmesthorpe.* You ought not to be received, for the reason aforesaid &c.—STAUNTON. A case of this kind has been formerly seen in this court, where the woman was received; wherefore &c.—And she was received, as customary.—*Rostone* (for the woman). She has not committed any waste ready, &c.—*Toudeby.* Now she wishes to cover herself, inasmuch as what she has done is the act of her husband.—STAUNTON. It will not do; for if waste be found, it will fall on her neck just as fully as if she were sole and as if she while sole had committed the waste.—*Hedone.* She ought not rightly to be suffered to plead without her husband, wherefore we think that the writ should abate.—*Wileby* (not being on either side). You are pleading against your estate and to your disadvantage; for although the inquest pass against you, yet before judgment

[1] 13 Edw. I. (Westm. 2), c. 3.

[2] 13 Edw. I. (Westm. 2), c. 4.

statut &c.—*Passeley.* Ne overe mie pur vous, qar le A.D. 1307. jugement nest pas a rendre sur sa defaute; e jatardeis lentendement de statut est la ou homme e sa femme e demaundent tenements &c., e par cest bref ne demaundames vers vous nul tenements.—*Rostone.* Statut dit treis choses, silicet "si vir &c. defaltam fecerit, vel "ficte defendit, vel in vita uxoris reddere voluerit"; e vous diouns qe nostre baron defendi feintement &c., e prioms &c. — STAUNTONE. Si vous fuissez receive, qe dirreiet vous? — *Hedone.* La pleintive est coverte de baroun nent nome &c., jugement de bref, en par taunt pert il bien qe vostre baroun, qe par ceste cause le poeit aver abatu, pleda feintement.—STAUNTONE. Nay cele ne avereit pas a ore.—*Passeley.* Ceste parole "ita "ficte &c." nest pas en cel statut einz en un autre saver la ou bref de dowere est porte vers le gardein qe fet defaute ou feintement defende par collusioun &c., par quei par cele parole ne avez nul avanttage.—Ad alium diem *Rostone* pria pur la femme qe el poeit estre rescu, ut prius &c. — *Malmesthorpe.* Receive ne devez estre, ratione qua prius &c.—STAUNTONE. Home ad veu en ceste matere ceins avaunt ces houres ou la femme ad este rescu, par quei &c. — Et fuit admissa per consuetudinem.—*Rostone* (pro illa). Ele ne ad fet nul wast, prest &c.—*Toudeby.* Ore se voit ele coverer, par taunt qe ceo qe il ad fet est le fet son baron. — STAUNTONE. Noun fra, qar si il ieit wast trove il cherra en son col taunt avaunt cum si ele fust sole e hust fet le wast sole.—*Hedone.* Ele ne deit mie de resun estre suffert de pleder saunz sun barun, pur quei nous entendoms qe le bref sei abatereit.—*Wileby* (non existens cum aliquo partium). Vous pledez encountre votre estat e encuntre vostre avauntage; qar tut sei le enqueste passe contre vous, avaunt juge-

A.D. 1307. you can by this exception to wit that she is under coverture &c. abate their writ. And it was adjudged that the inquest &c.

Annuity without a specialty.

Where the plaintiff had no deed to show the annuity.

§ The prior of Lungeville brought the writ against the parson of Westone, and demanded twelve marks, as arrears of an annuity of six marks; and tortiously for this that he was seised of it in right of his church &c., by the hand of the same parson, and that all his predecessors were seised by the hands of all the parsons &c. until now for two years before the writ &c. — *Herle* denied &c. and the damages &c., and (said he) we do not think that on such a count this court can take cognisance of the plea, since for that annuity claimed they do not show any legal specialty or contract, such as grant by the patron with the assent of the bishop witnessing the thing which they demand; and for anything which they have shown in their count it is a pension, and a spiritual thing turned into a temporal thing; and we pray judgment if this court ought to take cognisance of the plea. — *Toudeby.* He is seised as in right of our church of a spiritual thing; and in this form in which we demand might a fine be levied. — *Herle.* That is the truth, and then the fine would make it a temporal thing and pleadable here. — *Toudeby.* We ourselves are patron &c., and that annuity was anciently reserved in right of our patronage, which makes it a temporal thing. — *Herle.* The statute of "Circumspecte "agatis"[1] applies in that case, it is a pension, and pleadable in the court Christian. — *Toudeby.* The assent of the bishop does not make it a temporal thing nor an annuity; and we ourselves are patrons &c., and we and our predecessors have been patrons from time whereof memory &c., and this it is which also proves the assent,

[1] 13 Edw. I. st. 4.

ment si poez par cest excepcion, sciant qe ele est coverte de baroun &c., lur bref abatre—Et consideratum est inquisitio &c. A.D. 1307.

Ou le pleintif ne avoit nul fet de annuyte.

Annuyte saunz especialte.

§ Le priour de Lungeville porta le bref vers la persone de Westone, e demanda xii. marcs qe arrere ly furent de un annuelte de vi. marcs; e pur ceo atort, qe il mesme en fut seisi com du droit de sa eglise &c. par mi la meyne mesme ceti persone, e touz ces predecessours &c. seisiz par mi les meins totes les persones &c., jeke ore a deus aunz avant le bref &c. — *Herle* defendi &c., e les damages &c.; entendoms mie qe sur tiel demoustrance cest court eit conisaunce de cele ple, del oure qe a ceste annuelte dreigner eux ne mustrent nul especial de lay contract cum du graunt le patroun ove le assent de evesqe, qe ceste chose qe eux demaundent tesmoygne; qe pur renz qe eux ount moustre en le moustrance ele est une enpensioun, e chose espiritele tornast en chose temporel, e demaundoms jugement si ceost court de cele ple deyve conustre. — *Toudeby.* Est seisi cum du dreit de nostre eglise chose espiritele; e jatardeys en ceste forme qe nous demandoms poeit fin estre leve. — *Herle.* Ceo est verite, e adunqes le fin ly freit temporel e pledable ceinz. — *Toudeby.* Nous mesme sumes patroun &c., e cele annuyte de antiquite retenu au droit de nostre patronage, qe la fet temporel. — *Herle.* Le statut Circumspecte agatis leu tent en tel cas, estre un pensioun e pledable en la court Christiene. — *Toudeby.* Assent de evesqe ne le fet pas temporel ne annuyte, e nous mesme sumes patroun &c., e avoms aste nous e nous predecessours patrouns de tut temps dount memorie, e est qe auxy

A.D. 1307. which assent sufficiently makes it a temporal thing &c., and we pray judgment. — HOWARD. In old times men could give their tithes where they thought fit; and it appears that since the patron by whom the church was first endowed reserved the six marks to his patronage as in right of his patronage, it is sufficiently a temporal thing. — *Toudeby.* If we were to implead him in Court Christian, and the Prohibition were brought, we should not have the Consultation on the demand for this annuity; therefore &c.: nevertheless, neither the assent of the bishop nor of the parson &c. makes such a thing a lay matter, but only the assent and deed of the patron, because the estates of these persons, namely the bishop and the parson, are spiritual, and the estate of the patron, namely the patronage, although the patron be a man of holy church, is a temporal thing; therefore by his assent, this thing is sufficiently temporal &c.— Afterwards they came to terms, so that the parson admitted that he had paid &c. and was to pay in the time which &c., saying nothing of his predecessors; which acknowledgment the prior admitted, and so the admission by the parson in no way burdens the church.

Mesne. Where the tenant held of the mesne lord by the same services as the chief lord of the mesne demanded of the tenant, and whereof the said mesne lord stood seised by &c.

§ Philip Walrand brought the writ against one Piers &c., and counted that tortiously he did not acquit him of the services which Ralph de Monthermer, earl of &c. and Joan his wife &c.: and tortiously for this, that whereas he holds of him &c. by homage and fealty, suit to his court every three weeks, and by the service of half a knight's fee, to wit, 20*s*. when the escuage is at 40*s*., and when more &c., for all services, there come the said Ralph &c. and Joan &c., and demand of him escuage &c. and suit &c., namely in such a year &c., and to compel prove assent, le queles asentement assez le fet temporel &c., e demaundoms jugement. — HOWARD. En anxien temps hom poet doner lour dimes ou beau lour fut, e pert del houre qe le patron par quei la eglise fut primes dowe retint a sa avowerie cum droit de sa avouerie le sis marcs assez est il temporel. — *Toudeby*. Si nous luy apledasoms en court Christiene e la prohibicion fust porte, nous ne averoms pas consultacion de la demaunde de cest annuite, ergo &c.; jatardys ne le assent de evesqe ne de persone &c. ne fet mie tiel chose laye, einz solement assent e fet de patroun, pur ceo qe les estat cesteseux persons, saver de evesqe e de persone, sount espiritels, e le estat le patroun, saver le patronage, tut seit patroun home de Seint Eglise, si est temporel; ergo, de soun assent assez est cest chose temporel &c. Postea concordatum, ita quod persona concessit se solvisse &c. et fore soliturum tempore quo, nihil loquens de predecessoribus suis, quam cognitionem admisit prior, et ita concessio personæ nihil onerat ecclesiam.

A.D. 1307.

Nota assent de patron fet chose temporel e annuite.

Ubi tenens tenuit de medio per eadem servitia que capitalis domini medii poscebat de tenente, et inde idem medius extitit seysitus per &c.

De medio.

§ Philep Walrand porta le bref vers un Pers &c., e conta qe atort ne ly aquite des services &c., qui Rauf de Mounthermer counte &c. e Jone sa femme &c.: e pur ceo atort, qe la ou il tent de ly &c. par homage e fealte, sute a sa curt &c. de treis semeynes e treis semeynes, e par les services de demy fee de chivaler, saver quant le escu curt e .xl. soz .xx. soz, e a plus &c., pur tous services, la venent les avaundiz Rauf &c. e Johane &c. e ly demandent sute &c. e escuage &c., cest a saver de tiel an &c., a ceo fere ly destreinent &c.,

A.D. 1307. him to do this they distrein &c., and the said Piers is mesne between them, and thereof ought to acquit him &c.—*Mutford* denied &c. and asked what they had to show the right to acquittance.—*Passeley.* We hold of you by the same services, and you thereof are seised at our hands, and you and your ancestors have acquitted us and our ancestors from time whereof there is no memory; judgment &c.—*Mutford.* Of the fealty and the suit we are seised, and thereof we have acquitted you, so that for those things you are not distreined; and as to the homage, we are not seised of your homage, wherefore of homage we are not bound to acquit you against others; and as to the escuage you yourself have voluntarily paid it to the earl, so that the default lies not on us.—*Passeley.* For the fealty and the suit we were distreined by your default, ready &c.; and we have often tendered you our homage, so that it is not our fault &c. ready &c.; and we are still ready to do it.—*Mutford.* And we are ready to receive it.—And he [the plaintiff] did homage &c.—*Passeley.* And as to the escuage, we never paid escuage to the earl, but what we paid was when he offered to distrein, ready &c. if he will deny it; and we pray our damages &c.—HENGHAM. For what do you pray your damages? Now for the first time he receives your homage, and now first of all have you become his man.—*Passeley.* That is not our fault, since we tendered it to him; and of the escuage he is &c. of us.—HENGHAM rehearsed &c., and said The court adjudges that you be henceforth bound to acquittance &c.—But nothing was adjudged as to damages; which seemed strange.

Notice of this matter will be found in last Hilary Term in a record of an assise of novel disseisin.

Scire facias.

§ William de la Bere brought the writ against Henry the son of Eliz &c. saying that after the death of one Edmund who held certain tenements for the term of his e dount mesme celi Pers meen est entre eaux e de ceo aquiter ly deit &c. — *Motford* defendi e demanda ceo qil aveiount del aquitance.—*Passeley.* Nous tenoms de vous par mesmes les services, e vous de ces estes seisi par my nous[1] meynz, e vous e vous auncestres nous e nous auncestres avez aquitez du temps dount il niad memorie; jugement &c.—*Motford.* De la fealte e de la sute sumes nous seisi, de quei nous vous avioms aquite, issi qe pur ces nestes mie destreint; e quant a le homage, nous ne sumes pas seisi de vostre homage, par quei de homage vers autres ne sumes pas tenuz de vous aquiter; e quant al escuage vous memes de gre lavez paiie au counte, issi qe defaute nest mie en nous. — *Passeley.* Pur la fealte e la sute destreint par vostre defaute, prest &c.; e nostre homage sovent nous avums tendu, issi qe en nous[1] ne remist mie &c., prest &c., e uncore sumes prest de fere le.—*Motford.* Et nous[1] prest del receivere:—et fecit homagium &c.—*Passeley.* E quant al escuage, nous ne payames unqes escuage au counte, einz ceo qe nous luy feimes fust pur ouffrant aver de destreiner, prest &c. sil le voile dedire; e prioms noz damages &c.—Hengham. De quei priez vous voz dammages? ore adeprimes resceiit il vostre homage, e ore aprimes estes vous devenu son homme.—*Passeley.* Ceo ne remist pas en nous[1] del oure qe nous ly tendimes; e si est de escuage &c. de nous.[1] —Hengham rehercia &c. Si agarde &c. qe desoremes ly seiitz tenuz a laquitance &c.: sed non consideratum est de dampnis quod videbatur mirum. A.D. 1307. Judicium.

Invenietur de ista materia in Termino Hillarii ultimo ubi recordum assisæ novæ dissesinæ &c.

§ Willem de la Bere porta le bref ver Henri le fiz Eliz &c. qe apres le mort un Emunde qe certeinz tenements tint a terme de sa vie del heritage Henri, Scire facias.

[1] MS. vous.

A.D. 1307. life, of the heritage of Henry, the reversion of the said tenements by fine &c. to John de la Bere brother of the said William, whose heir William is &c., in court &c., before Sir J. de Metingham &c., and that after the fine was recorded &c. before Sir Ralph de Hengham &c. in form aforesaid, occupied these tenements.—*Herle.* Where is the fine which is the warrant for this writ ? — STAUNTON. See here the note of it.—*Herle.* Is there any other warrant ? — *King.* That is sufficient. — *Herle.* Now we pray judgment, — since the writ says that that fine was recorded, and thereby it is to be supposed that it was ingrossed, after which ingrossment the note lost its force, —if that note can now be a warrant for any writ. On the other hand you will not find any fine levied between Henry &c. and John de la Bere.—STAUNTON. There is no other record than what is endorsed on that note ;— which was in this form.—And afterwards before &c. was &c. recorded between the aforesaid Henry and William de la Bere &c. in the form aforesaid.—*Herle.* That is no warrant for this writ, nor, any more, is the note, for the reason aforesaid &c. ; therefore &c. And it is a common phrase in this court to say that the fine is recorded when it is ingrossed, and not otherwise.—STAUNTON. We know all about the case between you ; it is this, Henry &c. granted &c. the reversion of the tenements which Edmund held &c. to John de la Bere by a fine &c. as it appears, and before John could make Edmund come and acknowledge his estate and attorn &c., John died ; then was recorded this note between the said Henry and William brother and heir of the said John, according &c., and Edmund of those tenements enfeoffed Henry the son of P. the son of Eliz in fee ; Edmund died ; after whose death William entered &c. and put out Henry the son of P. the son of Eliz, and was seised ; in whose seisin Henry released and quit-claimed &c. by fine &c. ; and then Henry the son of Eliz recovered &c. from William by assise.—*Herle.* Although you know the case, yet John has a bad case because the qe la reversioun de memes ceux tenements par fin &c. a Johan de la Bere frere le dist Willem, qi heyr Willem &c., en court &c. devaunt Sire J. de Metingham &c., e pus cele fin recorde &c. devaunt Sire Rauf de Hengham &c. in forma predicta, mesmes ces tenements ocupat.—*Herle.* Ou est la fin qe est garaunt de cesti bref? — STAUNTONE. Veez si la note. — *Herle.* I ad il autre garaunt? — *Kinge.* Cele suffit. — *Herle.* Ore demandoms jugement, del oure qe le bref dit qe cele fin fut recorde, e par taunt fet a supposer qe ele fust engrosse, apres qele engrosser la note perdi sa force, si cele note a ore puise estre garaunt de nul bref; e dautre part, si ne troverez nul fin leve entre Henri &c. e Johan de la Bere. — STAUNTONE. Il ni ad autre record qe ne seit endose en sele note la: quod fuit de tali forma; Et postea coram &c. fuit &c. recordata inter predictum Henricum et Willielmum de la Bere &c. in forma predicta.—*Herle.* Cel la nest mie garaunt de ceo bref, ne la note ne le plus, ratione qua prius &c., ergo &c. Et ceo est comune terme de ceinz a dire qe la fin seit recorde quant ele est engrosse, e ne mie autrement.—STAUNTONE. Nous savoms le cas qe est entre vous, qe est tiel, qe Henri &c. granta &c. la reversioun de tenements qe Emue tint &c. a Johan de la Bere par fin &c., auxi cum il pert M., e einz qe Johan poeit fere Emue venir a conustre son estat e aturner &c., Johan morust; e puis fut cele note recorde entre le dit Henri e Willem frere e heyr le dit Johan solom &c., e Emue[1] de ces tenements enfeffa Henri le fiz P. le fiz Eliz en fee. Emue[1] morust, apres qi mort Willem entra &c. et debita Henri le fiz P. le fiz Eliz, e seisi fust; en qi seisine Henri relessa e quiteclama &c. par fin &c.; e pus Henri le fiz Eliz recoveri &c. de Willem par assise.—*Herle.* Tut sachet vous le cas, uncore Johan ad il maues, pur ceo qe le court ne A.D. 1307.

[1] Here and sometimes afterwards this name is in the MS. spelt *Emme*.

A.D. 1307. court ought not to maintain or suffer it. And besides, by that fine which was levied on that release and quit-claim the writ is not warranted; for it was not levied according to the form of the note; and the writ says "in "the form aforesaid"; neither is there any other fine; wherefore &c.; nor [is it warranted] by the note &c., for the reason aforesaid; therefore &c. and we pray judgment. —STAUNTON. Do you think it not to be a fine until it be ingrossed? It certainly is so as soon as the concord is drawn.—And afterwards the writ was by the court adjudged to be good; and nevertheless the reasons against it were subtle and strong.—*Herle.* The writ says "which after the death of Edmund &c. he occupied," thereby supposing that Henry the son of P. the son of Eliz, had nothing in the lifetime of Edmund; and we tell you that the said William in this court in the lifetime of Edmund brought a writ against us, as against the tenants of these same tenements, namely a "quid juris clamat," which suit you will find continued in this court by process; and we pray judgment of the writ.—MALLORE. We find that the fine which was levied was not accordant with the note, wherefore the fine was not warranted by the note; and we find that William de la Bere sued the "quid juris &c." against Henry the son of Philip &c. and against Edmund as against tenants &c.; and truly that writ was not warranted by that note; for in the note only three persons were named, to wit, Henry the conusor and John to whom &c. and Edmund &c., and no more; wherefore &c. And because we find such an error in that process we annul it entirely: and you may sue out another writ on the footing of the first note, if you please, &c.

Right. Where the lord to whom the original writ is directed dies, the plea is afterwards removed from his court by the Recordari: and the cause was that the ancestor of deyt meintenir ne soffrer. E dautre part, par cele fin qe se leva sur cele reles e quite clamanz nost mie le bref garanti; qar ele ne est pas leve solom la forme de la note; e le bref dit "in forma predicta"; ne autre fin ne ad il pas; par quei &c.; ne par la note &c. ratione qua supra; ergo &c., e demandoms jugement.—STAUNTONE. Ne qidez pas qe ele seit fin taunt qe ele seit engrosse? si est certes a plutost qe la pes est retrete. Et postea breve consideratum fuit bonum per curiam; et tamen rationes in contrarium fuerunt suptiles et validæ.—*Herle.* Le bref dit qe "post mortem "Emue &c. occupavit," en taunt supposaunt qe Henri le fiz P. le fiz Elys vivant Emue rens ny avait; e nous dioms qe meme cesti Willem en ceste court vivaunt Emue suist[1] bref vers nous cum vers tenaunz de memes ceux tenements, ceo est a saver un[2] "quid "juris clamat," qele sute vous troverez continue ceinz par proces, e demandoms jugement du bref &c.—MALLORE. Nous trovoms qe la fin qe est lewe ne sa acorda mie a la note, par quei la fin par la note ne pas garanti; e nous trovom qe Willem de la Bere suist le quid juris &c. vers Henri le fiz Phylip &c. e vers Emue cum vers tenaunz &c.; et verrement cel bref ne fust pas garaunti par cele note: qar en la note ne furent mes qe treis persons nomes, saver Henri qe conuseit e Johan a qi &c., e Emue &c., e nerunt plus; par quei &c. E pur ceo qe nous trovoms tiel errour en cele process nous le anentisoms tut; e suwez autre bref hors de la primer note si vous voilez &c. A.D. 1307.

Ubi dominus cui originale breve dirigitur moritur, post removetur placitum a curia sua per recordari: et De recto.

1 MS. si. | 2 MS. ut.

A.D. 1307. the demandant had released and quit-claimed the thing to him whose assignee the tenant was.

§ Piers de Neorford brought the writ to Ralph de Monthermer and Joan his wife against Isabel la Denee and Nicolas her son, which Isabel and Nicolas, tenants, removed the plea by a Recordari for a certain cause, namely, because the ancestor of the demandant released and quit-claimed to him whose assignee the tenants were, by fine &c.—*Friskeney* defended, and (said he) We tell you that Joan, countess &c., to whom the original, which is the foundation of this plea, came, is dead; judgment if that plea on that original can stand any longer in this court.--The objection was not allowed because the plea was not in that court &c. — *Friskeney.* We pray the view.—*Toudeby.* You had it in the court &c.—*Herle.* The suitors have not made any record on this Recordari whereby one can now be certified, nor can the court in any other manner have knowledge; and we pray the view &c.—*Toudeby.* In their Recordari whereby the plea is removed a certain cause is stated, whereby it appears that they have sufficient knowledge of the tenements &c.—MALLORE. I advise that you grant him the view of your free will.—And the view was granted: which seemed strange and contrary to another plea in a writ of Right under similar circumstances.

Cessavit. Where the count was challenged because a certain number of masses, matins or prayers was not named therein.

§ The writ was brought against the prior of the Friars Preachers of Salisbury. And the writ said that so-and-so gave so much &c. for celebrating divine offices every day in the monastery. And he counted thus,--to celebrate every day divine offices,, namely matins, hours, masses and other prayers &c. — *Westcote* denied &c., and said We do not think that on that count &c.; for he does not name any certain number of masses or prayers; and if perchance we are to do the arrears, it is fuit causa quod launcestre le demandant avoit relesse e quiteclame tiel a cely, qi asingne le tenant est. A.D. 1307.

§ Pers de Neorford porta le bref a Raulf de Monthermer e Johane sa femme vers Isabele la Denee e Nycol son fiz, les queux Isabele e Nychol tenauns feseiint remuer la parole par un recordare par certeyn cause, saver, pur ceo qe launcestre le demaundaunt avoit relesse e quitclame a cely qi assingne le tenantz fut par fin &c.—*Fryskeney* defendi; e vous dioms qe Johane cuntesse &c., a qi le original qe est fundement de ceu ple vint, est morte; jugement si cele plee sour cele original puise outre estre ceinz. Nec allocatur, quia placitum non est in curia illa &c.—*Friskeney.* La vewe. —*Toudeby.* Vous la avez en la court &c.—*Herle.* Les suters unt fet nul record a ceo recordare, par quei home purra de ore estre certe, ne en autre manere poet la court de ceo asserter, e demaundoms la vewe &c.—*Toudeby.* Il i ad certeyn cause en lor recordare par quei la parole est remue, par la quele il pert qe il ount assez conisance de tenements &c.—MALLORE. Jeo lo qe vous ly grantez la vewe de bone volunte.—Et fuit visus concessus: quod videbatur mirum et contrarium alio placito in brevi de recto quod est in simili precedenti.

Ubi narratio calumpniatur quia certus numerus missarum, matutinorum nec orationum non datur in eodem. Cessavit.

§ Le bref fut porte ver le priour del ordre de Freres Prechours de Saloburi. Et fuit breve quod talis dedit &c. ad divina officia singulis diebus celebranda [ad] monasterium. Counta sic, a divine offices chescun jour celebrer, cest a saver, matins, oures, messes, e autre orisouns &c.—*Westcot* defendi &c. e nentent pas que a cel counte &c.; qar il ne noume mie certeyn nombre de messes, ne de orisouns; e si par cas nous ly froms

A.D. 1307. necessary that it be a thing certain; and we pray judgment.—*Malmesthorpe.* We say "every day," which is sufficiently certain &c.—And the count was adjudged good by the court &c.

Note. Taking of beasts in ancient demesne.

§ In a plea of taking of beasts where the abbat of Bortone complained of the earl of Lancaster, who said that the place where the taking &c. was of the ancient demesne &c., and that the abbat was tenant to the earl for the same manor; and (said he) we pray judgment if this court ought to take cognisance of any taking made within that manor. And the abbat put forward charters whereby divers persons had enfeoffed &c. to hold of the chief lords by the services &c.: and in addition, the grant and confirmation of earl Edmund, who confirmed those feoffments, and gave leave to the abbat to make that purchase, as far as in him lay, without &c. customs and services &c.; and, together with that, a grant and confirmation by the king, who granted and confirmed "saving &c. to the chief lords to be done;" and thus this place was his freehold; and (said he) we pray judgment if the court ought to take cognizance of this question, and especially in this plea of taking of beasts.—BRABAZON. It may be ancient demesne with respect to the person of the lord, and frank-fee as to you; but it does not follow that because it is freehold there fore it is frank-fee; and you have not yet made out by anything that you have shown that this is frank-fee; for no deed that you show ousts it from its first estate.—And afterwards the abbat was nonsuit. And therefore &c. And it is to be known that the earl's confirmation also gave leave to the abbat to purchase the homage of one T., which was not included in the king's confirmation.—MALLORE. You have purchased that homage without warrant; you shall tell us why; we take it into the king's hands. And he said to *Warwick*, Take suit thereof for the king.—*Passeley.* Nay, that homage is not of the ancient demesne nor held of the king.

les areres, ceo covenderit estre de chose certeyne; e demaundoms jugement.—*Marm.* Nous dioms "chescun "jour," que assez est certeyn &c. — E le counte fut agarde bon per curiam &c. A.D. 1307.

§ En play de prise des avers, ou le abbe de Bortone se pleynt del counte de Launcastre, qe dit qe le lu de la prise &c. si fut del auncien demene &c., e le abbe tenant le counte de mesme le manere, e demaundoms jugement si cest court de nul prise fete deinz cel maner deveyt conustrer. Et labbe mist avaunt chartres par le queux diverse gent enfefferent &c. a tenir des chef seynourage par le service &c.; e estre ceo, le graunt e le confermement le counte Edmund qe conferma ceux feffemens, e dona cunge a le abbe de fere cel purchace, quant qe en ly fut, sauns &c. coustumes e service &c.; et ovesqe ceo grant e confermement du roy, qe ensi conferma e granta "salvis &c. capita"libus dominis faciendis;" e issi fut cele lu soun fraunc tenement, e demaundoms jugement si cesti question[1] devoit conustre, e nomement en ceo play de prise des avers.—Brabazoun. Il porra estre auncyene demeyne respective a la persone le seignour, et franc fe quant a vous; mes il nensuit pas franc tenement ergo franc fee; e vous navez pas fet uncore, par rens qe vous avez moustre, qe ceo est franc fee; qar nul fet qe vous moustres ne ly oute de sun primer estat. Et postea abbas non est prosecutus. Et ideo &c. Et sciendum qe les confermemens le conte qil dona auxy cunge al abbe de purchaser le homage un T. qe ne fut mie compris denz le confermement du rey.—Mallore. Vous avez purchace cel homage saunz garant; dirrez par quei; nous le pernoms en la mayn le roy. Idem a *Warr.* Pernez la sute pur le roi.—*Passeley.* Nay, cele homage nest mie del auunciene demene ne tenuz du rey.

Nota. Prise des avers den lancyen demene.

[1] MS. cuiciun.

A.D. 1307. Cessavit. Note, of the essoin by the demandant after the tenant waged his law for non-summons.

Where the demandant on the fifth day after wager of law for non-summons, when the tenant came with his law, caused himself to be essoined.

§ The abbat of Lextone brought the writ against John de Blunville who waged his law for non-summons. and had a day; John came ready with his law, and the abbat essoined himself and had a day; both came, and John had not his law ready &c., and the abbat prayed seisin &c. because John failed of his law &c.—*Launfar.* Nay, we came on such a day ready with our law, on which day you essoined yourself, and thereby we are absolved from our law, and we pray judgment how we ought to depart.—MALLORE. Have you your law ready or not? Be sure that if you have it not, you will lose the land. — *Lanfar.* We have it not now, but we offered it heretofore &c.; wherefore we are absolved &c., and we pray judgment &c.—And thus they remained until the octaves of St. Michael. And the opinion of STAUNTON was here in opposition to the opinion of MALLORE.

Formedon: in the reverter.

Where it was said that land given in frank-marriage may be limited at the will of the donor otherwise than in the blood of the male and female donees.

§ One R. brought the writ against T. Launf. (and said) and tortiously for this that it is his right, for the reason that one Ralph grandfather of the said R., who of these tenements was seised in his demesne as of fee and of right, in time of &c., and the esplees &c., gave these tenements to one Adam &c., together with one Janette his wife in frank-marriage, by which gift the said Adam and Janette were seised of these tenements &c. according to the form of the aforesaid gift; and that from Adam and Janette, because they died without heir of their bodies, the right of these tenements reverted and ought to revert to Ralph as donor, according to the form &c. — *Toudeby.* What have you to show the form? — *Westcot.* Ready to aver it &c. — *Toudeby.* You shall not get to

Ubi petens quinto die post legem vadiatam de non summonitione, quando tenens venit cum lege sua, fecit se assoniari. A.D. 1307. Cessavit. Nota de essonio petentis postquam tenens vadiavit legem de non summonitione.

§ Le abbe de Lextone porta le bref ver Johan de Blunville, qe gaia sa ley de la noun sumonse, e avoit jour ; Johan vint prest ove sa ley, e le abbe se fit essoner, et avoyt jour ; le un e lautre vindrent, e Jon ne avoit mie sa ley prest &c., e le abbe pria seisine &c., pur ceo qe Johan fayly de sa ley &c. — *Launfar.* Nay, nous venimes au tel jour prest ove nostre ley, a quel jour vous feistes essoner, e par taunt sumes de cele ley assonez, e demaundoms jugement coment nous devomes departir. — MALLORE. Avez vostre ley prest ou noun ? qe seet certeyn si vous ne la eiez vous perderez la terre. — *Lanfare.* Ne ne lavons point a ore, einz la tendimes autrefoiz &c. ; par quei nous sumes assouz &c., e demaundoms jugement &c. Et sic commorantur usque in octabis Sancti Michaelis ; et oppinio de STAUNTONE fuit hic contra oppinioni MALLORE.

Ubi dicebatur quod terra data in liberum maritagium potest alio quam in sanguine donatarii et donatariæ talliari secundum voluntatem donatoris. Forma donacionis en le reverti.

§ Un R. porta le bref vers T. Launf. Et pur ceo atort, qe ceo est son dreit, par la resoun qe un Rauf &c., aele meme ceti R., qe de ces tenements en fut seisi en son demene cum de fee e de droit en temps &c., e tel explez &c., meme ceux tenements dona a un Adam &c. ove un Jonette sa femme en franc mariage, par quel doun les avanditiz Adam e Jonette furent de ces tenements seisi &c. solom la forme du doun avaundit ; de Adam e de Jonette, pur ceo qe il morirent saunz heyr de lour corps &c., reverti le droit de ces tenements e devoit revertir a Rauf cum a donour, solom la forme &c. — *Toudeby.* Qi avez de la forme ? — *Westcot.* Prest del laverer &c.—*Toudeby.* Vous ne avendrez point ; qar

A.D. 1307. that: for see here the charter of Ralph your grandfather of whom you speak, by which he enfeoffed the said Adam and Janette in frank-marriage, to have and to hold to Adam and Janette and to the heirs of the body of Janette begotten, and bound himself and his heirs to warranty. Adam died without issue by Janette; and she took another husband who begot on her Thomas who is now tenant, and we pray judgment if you as heir of Ralph and who by this charter are bound to warrant us against others, can demand anything against us.— *Westcot.* It amounts to this, that he did not give them simply in frank-marriage to Adam and Janette, but limited them further on &c. than he gave them in frank-marriage &c. —MALLORE. You will get no advantage against this charter; is it your grandfather's deed or not?—And, against his will, he was made by the court to answer this. And he denied the deed.—Therefore &c.

Taking of beasts.

The lord can not avow &c. for customs and services in the common pasture, or in any other place than in that or in parcel of that whence the services issue.

§ Adam de Bentleye avowed the taking &c. on an abbat &c. in the same place of which the abbat counted &c.; and for the reason that the abbat held of him two tofts by certain services, and for the services &c. he avowed &c., and in the place, which was not within the two tofts aforesaid. And the abbat prayed judgment inasmuch as he had avowed for rent-service issuing out of certain tenements, outside which tenements he has made the avowry, which is not avowable by him, and (said he) we pray judgment.— And Adam said that he is chief lord of the said vill, and that the place of the taking is common of pasture to the said vill, and he says that it is well lawful for him to distrein for rent in arrear on the common &c. appendant to the soil whereout his rent issues; and (said he) we pray judgment.— And for that Adam avowed elsewhere than in the place veet si la chartre Rauf vostre ael de qi vous parlez, par la quele il enfeffa les avaundiz Adam e Jonette en franc mariage, a aver e a tenir a Adam e a Jonette e as heyrs du corps Jonete engendrez, e oblige luy e ces heyrs a la garantie ; issi qe Adam devia sanz engendrure de Jonete ; ele prist autre baroun qe de ly engendra Thomas qe ore est tenaunt, e demaundoms jugement si vous cum heyr Rauf, qe par ceste chartre vers autre vous serriez lye a la garauntie &c., ver nous pussez ren demaunder.—*Westcot.* Taunt amounte qil ne les dona mie purement en franc-mariage a Adam e a Jonette, einz les tayla plus avant &c. qil lor dona en franc-mariage &c. — MALLORE. Vous ne avendrez pas encontre cest chartre : est ceo le fet vostre ael ou noun ? Et ad hoc positus fuit se invito ad respondendum per curiam ; et cartam dedixit. Ideo &c. A.D. 1307.

Quod dominus non potest advocare &c. pro consuetudinibus et servitiis in communi pastura nec in alio loco quam in illo seu aliquo percello unde servitia pervenerint. Prise des avers.

§ Adam de Benteleye avowa la prise &c. sur un abbe &c. en meme le lu qe le abbe counta &c., e par la reson qe labbe tynt de ly deus toftes par certeyns services, e pur les services &c. si auvoua &c. en le lu, qe ne fu pas deinz les deus toftes avandiz. E le abbe demaunda jugement desicum il avoit avoue pur rente service issaunt de certeinz tenements hors des queux tenements il ad fet le auvouerie qe nest mie de luy avouable, e demaunda jugement. Et Adam dit qil est chef seignour de meme la ville, e qe le lu de la prise si est comune de pasture a tyele ville, e dit qe byen ly list afere destresse pur rente arere en la comune &c. appendaunt a soyl dount sa rent ist e demaunda jugement. E pur ceo qe Adam avowa aylours qe en la lu

A.D. 1307. whence his rent arose, it was adjudged that the abbat should have his beasts quit, and his damages &c.—And it well seems that this last reason that Adam urged is worthless, since the common pasture was not so appendant to the tofts: but it was the common opinion and the opinion of the court and of the pleaders that although the tofts were land to which the common pasture was appurtenant yet he could not avow &c. in the said common outside the said land &c.

Formedon. Where the issue of the persons to whom &c. was given in fee-tail was received in defence of the right &c., and vouched to warranty the donor in the lifetime of the mother of the person who was tenant in tail.

§ A writ of formedon was brought by two sisters against Agnes who was the wife of Thomas Picot, who made default after default, wherefore &c.; and thereupon came one R. who was the son of Thomas and Agnes, and was under age.—*Rostone.* You have here R., the son and heir of Thomas Pycot and Agnes his wife, and he tells you that these tenements &c. were given in tail to Thomas and to Agnes and to the heirs of their bodies &c., and Thomas is dead, so that Agnes has only a freehold, and the right &c. is in the person of R., according to the form &c.; and he comes before judgment &c. and prays to be received &c., by statute.—*Malmesthorpe.* You pray to be received as heir of Thomas and Agnes by descent, and that by the statute[1] which says "Let the heirs be admitted, and those to whom the "reversion belongs;" now by the "heirs" are meant the heirs of the reversion, and by the "and those to "whom &c." are meant the donors; and there is nothing to mean the heir in the descent. And by the words "and they to whom the &c. belongs," are meant the donors and their heirs; so we think, and we pray judgment.—*Friskeney.* If Agnes had prayed aid of you, the aid would not have been granted, because she is party

[1] 13 Edw. I. (Westm. 2.) c. 3.

dount sa rente surdy, fust agarde qe le abbe hust ces avers quites e ces damages &c. Et bene videtur quod ista ultima ratio quam Adam pro se allegavit nihil valet, cum toftis non sit comunis pastura appendens: fuit tamen comunis oppinio et curiæ et narratoris quod licet tofti fuerat terra &c. cui communis pastura fuerat pertinens, non in eodem communi extra eandem terram potuit advocare &c. A.D. 1307.

Ubi exitus illorum quibus &c. datur in feodum talliatum admittebatur in defensionem juris &c., et vocaverunt ad warrantiam donatorem vivente matre partis talliati. Forme de doun.

§ Bref de forme de doun fut porte par deus souers vers Agnes qe fu la femme Thomas Picot, qe fit defaute apres defaute, par qi &c.; e sur ceo vint un R., le fiz Thomas e Agnes, qe fut de deinz age.—*Rostone.* Vous avez ci R., fiz e heir Thomas Pycot e Agnes sa femme, e vous dit qe ces tenements &c. furent donez en forme talle a Thomas e a Agnes e a lor heyrs de lor corps &c., e Thomas est mort, issi qe Agnes ne ad mes franc tenement, e le droit &c. est en la persone R. solom la forme &c.; e vent avaunt jugement &c. e prie estre rescu &c. par statut.—*Marm.* Vous priez estre rescu cum eyr Thomas e Agnes en la descente, e ceo par statut qe dit issi, "Admittantur heredes et illi "ad quos spectat reversio;" dount par le "heredes" si sunt entendu les heyrs de la reversion, e par le "et illi ad quos &c." les donours; issi qe nul entende-"ment est del heyr en la descente. Et par le "et illi "ad quos spectat &c." e les donours e lor heyres; e issi lentendoms nous, e demaundoms jugement.—*Friskeney.* Si Agnes hust prie ayde de vous, le eyde ne ust pas este grauntable, pur ceo qe ele est partie a

A.D. 1307. to the entail, and you are party to that through her; therefore in default of him who has as high an estate as you have, and for this first and chiefly, you ought not to be received.—STAUNTON. His condition is now better for being received than it would be if Thomas his father were alive; for at the present moment between Thomas and Agnes there cannot be any other heir; wherefore &c.—*King.* We tell you that Agnes had only a freehold for the term of her life, and the right entirely remained with our father, according to the form of this charter, and we pray judgment if we ought to be received to defend our right. And the charter stated that John had given these tenements to Thomas Picot and Agnes his wife, to them and to the heirs of their bodies begotten, and that if they died without heirs of their bodies begotten the tenements should remain to the right heirs of Thomas; and it is well admitted that he shall be received, and specially because his father who was party to the entail is dead.—And he was received, by judgment &c.—*Rostone.* We vouch to warranty the donor who is named in that charter.—STAUNTON (to the plaintiff). He vouches and he cannot serve you better. —*Malmesthorpe.* It seems to us that he shall not be received to that voucher, for that donor whom he vouches will not damage his tenant Agnes who is alive and in tenancy, and will warrant to her heir who holds nothing; wherefore it seems that this voucher is only for delaying our right; wherefore &c.—*Friskeney* (to the same purpose). If the vouchee warrant R., and by chance we were to recover, out of the tenancy, the woman would have to the value of her tenancy, and thus, although she was neither voucher nor warranted, she would recover to the value, which would be contrary to law; wherefore &c. — *Malmesthorpe.* One well sees how a woman is received to vouch on default by her husband and it is properly allowable, because she is party to the gift; wherefore &c.—STAUNTON (having consulted with la tayille, e vous a[1] cele partie par my luy; ergo en defaute de ly qi ad auxi haust estat cum vous, et, hoc primo et principaliter, rescu ne devez estre. — STAUNTONE. Sun estat est ore meylor de estre rescu qe ne serreit si Thomas soun pere fust en vie; qar a ore ne porra il entre Thomas e Agnes estre autre heyr, par quei &c.—*King*. Nous vous dioms qe Agnes ne out mes qe franc tenement a terme de sa vie, e le dreit enterement demora ov nostre pere, solom la forme de ceste chartre, e demaundoms jugement si nous devoms estre rescu pur nostre droit defendre. Et la chartre fut tiele, qe un Johan avoit done ces tes tenements a Thomas Picot e Agnes sa femme, a eux e a lor heyrs de lor corps engendrez, e si eux devieassent sanz heir de lor cors engendrez qe les tenements demorassent a dreit heyr Thomas; e est been rescu qil seit rescu, e nomement de puis qe sun pere partie a la taylle est mort: e fut rescu par agarde &c. — *Rostone*. Nous vouchoms a garrantie le donour qe est nome en cele chartre.—STAUNTONE (ad partem petentem). Il vouche, e il ne vous purra meuz server.—*Marm*. Il nous semble qil ne[2] serra pas rescu a cel voucher, qar cely donour qil vouche ne tresallera mie soun feffe Agnes qe est en pleyn vie en tenaunce, e garrauntira a son heyr qe rens ne tent; par quei il semble qe cele voucher vest mes qe en delayaunt nostre droit; par quei &c.—*Friskeney* (ad idem). Si le vouche garantit a R., e par cas par defit nous recoverioms hors de la tenaunce, la femme avereit a la vaylaunce de sa tenance, e issi ou ele ne avereit vouche ne garauntie ne fut, recovereit a la vaylance, qe serreit encontre ley; par quei &c. — *Marmesthorpe*. Home veit ben coment qe femme est receue, e defaute de sun baron voche, e ceo est ben suffrable, pur ceo qe ele est partie au doun; par qi &c.—STAUNTONE (consulto HENGHAM). R. A.D. 1307.

[1] MS. e.

[2] MS. nous.

A.D. 1307. HENGHAM). R. is received now as tenant of the tenements, because Agnes has lost whatever was in her; and this is a common reason to the tenant for vouching; wherefore it does not seem to us that your reasons bind him.—And he vouched, by judgment &c.

Per quæ servitia.

§ Henry de Ysham was made to come to acknowledge by what services he held &c. of Ralph de Hoe and his wife &c., which services the aforesaid Ralph and his wife had by fine granted to W. de Langetone; and he came and acknowledged to hold &c. by homage and by the service of one knight's fee &c.—STAUNTON. Ralph and his wife have granted &c. to W. &c.; will you attorn &c. —*Hamptone.* Yes, Sir; but we must have the like acquittance warranty and defence from W., as we had from Ralph and his wife.—STAUNTON. What have you to show that Ralph and his wife were bound to acquit you &c.—*Hamptone.* We and our ancestors have holden &c. of Ralph's wife and of her ancestors by the services aforesaid since the Conquest.—STAUNTON. Then have you nothing else &c. than the homage.—*Hampton.* No, Sir. —STAUNTON. The homage will be the same in the person of W. as it was in the person of Ralph's wife or of her ancestors &c.—And he did fealty, but not homage, because W. was not there except by attorney who is incapable of taking homage.

And so note that an attorney cannot receive homage: the nature of homage does not allow it.

Writ of debt against a termor.

Where the defendant after the expiration of the term was not received to aver by the country that there was nothing in arrear.

§ A woman brought the writ against Ralph de Ry., and counted that tortiously he detained from her 20*l.*: and tortiously for this, that whereas she &c. on a certain day and year delivered to the said Ralph the third part &c. for the term of &c. paying therefor every year &c. at the terms &c., which rent this said Ralph readily paid to her every year, until at such a term in such a year he est rescu ore cum tenaunt des tenements, pur ceo qe Agnes ad perdu quant que en ly fut; e ceo est un comune resun[1] au tenaunt de voucher; par quei il nous semble mie qe voz resuns lyent cuntre luy. Et fecit vocacionem par agarde &c. A.D. 1307.

§ Henri de Ysham fut fet venir a conustre par queux services il tint &c. de Rauf de Hoe [e] de sa femme &c., queux services les avandiz Rauf e sa femme par fin avoiient grante a W. de Langetone, qe vint e conust tenir &c. par homage e par le service de un fee de chivaler &c.—STAUNTONE. Rauf e sa femme hount graunte &c. a W. &c.; volez atturner &c.?—*Hamptone.* Sire, oyl, mes qe nous eiums tiel aquitance garauntie e defense de W. cum nous aveimes de Rauf e de sa femme.—STAUNTONE. Quei avez vous de Rauf e sa femme qe eux vous furent a le aquitance &c. tenuz.—*Hamptone.* Nous e noz auncestres avoms tenu &c. de la femme Rauf e de ces auncestres par les services &c. avaundiz puis le Conquest.—STAUNTONE. Dunqes navez autre chose &c. mes qe le homage.—*Hamptone.* Sire, noun.—STAUNTONE. Cel homage serra autiel en la persone W. cum il fut en la persone la femme R. ou ces auncestres &c. Et fecit fidelitatem set non homagium quia W. non fuit ibi nisi per attornatum qui hec rescipere nequivit.

Per que servicia.

Et sic nota quod attornatus non potest recipere homagium, et natura de homagio nec inferet.

Ubi defendens post terminum elapsum non potuit admitti sd verificandum per patriam quod nil fuit aretro.

§ Une femme porta le bref vers Rauf de Ry, e counta qe atort ly detint xx. livres. E pur ceo atort, la ou ele &c. certeyn jour e an, luy bayla a meme cesti Rauf la terce partie &c. a terme &c. a payer chescun an &c. a termes &c., la quel ferme mesme cesti Rauf prestement ly paya chescun an taunt qe a tiel

Breve de debito versus terminarium de redditu post terminum.

[1] MS. rens.

A.D. 1307. paid her nothing, nor has he paid anything at any other term in any following year of the whole term &c., which amounts &c. to 20*l.*; and that she has often requested him &c.—*Willeby* denied &c. and put forward an acquittance for part; and as to the remainder (said he) we tell you that this same &c., at certain terms within, &c., did during the term cause this ferm to be levied from us by her bailiffs, so that nothing is in arrear, ready &c. —MALLORE. She could not make the levy; it would have been a felony.—*Willuby.* One commonly distreins for rent in arrear all over the land.—HOWARD (thinking that it was a plea of taking of beasts, and that *Willeby* was pleading by way of avowry), said, Let your client come and avow what you say; (intimating that this thing was not avowable), and there is a case where the statute is referred to. MALLORE. I saw a case, before Sir J. de Vaux &c. in the eyre of Leicester, where one R., because his rent was in arrear, took his farmer's corn and carried it off, and disposed of it at his pleasure, and he was hung for that deed.—*Malmesthorpe.* It is not to be wondered at; we are speaking of a distress &c.; but in your case he committed a robbery.—*Herle.* We can not deny the acquittance; and for the remainder we pray judgment, since you can not deny the deed which we put forward and which proves our statement, (Memorandum that that writing was indented &c. and was of the term aforesaid) and you have fully admitted it, if you ought to get to any averment against it.—*Malmesthorpe.* This action is now given to you &c. because by way of distress &c. you can not succeed; but if during the term you had distreined &c. this averment would have been receivable against you, therefore now &c.—MALLORE (having consulted HOWARD, HENGHAM and STAUNTON) rehearsed &c.; and (said he) for what you have an acquittance you shall be allowed; and from the remainder you have nothing to deliver or acquit you in opposition to this deed which you have admitted, but you only offer to aver by the country &c.,

terme en tel an qe renz ly paya, ne a nul autre terme ne an suaunt de tut le terme &c., qe amounte &c. a xx. livres; dount ele ly ad sovent prie &c.—*Willuby* defendi, e mist avaunt aquitance de partie; e del remenant vous dioms qe mesme cesti &c. a termes dedeinz &c. fit lever cele ferme de nous par ces baylifs duraunt le terme: issi qil nad rens arere, e prest &c. —MALLORE. Fere la lever ne poet ele mie, qe ceo serreit fet de felonie.—*Willuby*. Homme destrein communement pur la ferme arere par tut la tere.—HOWARD, putans illud placitum esse de captione averiorum, et quod *Wileby* dixerat advocando &c., Lessez venir voster client e avower ceo qe vous dites; quasi diceret hoc non esse advocabile, et casus ibi relato statuto. — MALLORE. Jeo vi devant Sire J. de Vaus &c. en leyr de Leycestre un R., pur [1] ceo qe sa ferme ly fut arere prist les blez son fermer e les enporta e fit de ces sa volunte, e fust pendu pur le fet. — *Marm.* Ceo ne fust mie mervoyle; nous parloms de destresse &c., e en vostre cas il fit roberie. — *Herle.* Nous ne pooms dedire les aquitances, e de el demaundoms jugement del oure qe vous ne poet dedire le fet qe nous mettoms avant qe testmoyne nostre dit (et memorandum quod scriptum illud fuit indentatum &c. de termino predicto) einz le avez pleynement graunte, si countre cele a nul averement devez avenir.—*Marmesthorpe.* Cest accion vous est ore done &c. pur ceo qe par voie [de] destresse &c. ne poez avenir; mes si duraunt la terme ussez destreint &c. cest averement ust este resceivable countre vous; ergo a ore &c. — MALLORE (consulto HOWARD HENGHAM e STAUNTONE) recitavit &c.; e de ceo qe vous avez aquitance vous seriz alowe; e del el avez renz de vous deliverer ne acquiter encountre cest fest qe vous avez graunte, mes qe vous tendez de averer par pais A.D. 1307.

[1] MS. poez.

A.D. 1307. to which averment you shall not get, in opposition to your own deed; the court adjudges that she do recover &c.

Right. Præcipe in capite.

§ Robert de Tony brought the writ against John Pride, who vouched to warranty Fulk Fitz-Warin, who on the day for which he was summoned essoined himself de malo veniendi, and he had a day &c.; on which day he made default, wherefore the Cape ad valentiam &c. returnable &c., at which day he essoined him as being in the king's service, and he had a day until now.—STAUNTON (to the attorney of Fulk). Will you warrant?—*The Attorney.* Yes, sir.—*Herle* rehearsed the aforesaid process &c., and (said he) because the tenant had not sued his vouchee on these defaults, we pray judgment of the tenant.—*Toudeby.* The tenant is warranted and he is without day; if you wish to say anything against Fulk, see him here, ready &c; and why did you not sue against the vouchee?—*Herle.* Nay, this is your suit, and if the Petit Cape had issued against him, before the warranty had been terminated between you, it would have belonged to you to sue, and if he would have saved his default, you and not we, ought to have counterpleaded him.—STAUNTON. That step has passed you: he is warranted.—*Westcote* counted &c. that Fulk, by his warranty &c. deforces him; and he took title from the seisin of one of his ancestors named Ralph, from Ralph descending to Roger as son and heir, from Roger to Ralph as son, and from Ralph to Robert who now is &c.; suit and proof &c.—*Willeby* denied &c., and (said he) we tell you that he cannot now demand anything &c.; for one William &c. gave these tenements to that Ralph, of whose seisin &c., in frank-marriage with Peronel his wife, before the statute,[1] from whom issued Roger &c.: Peronel survived, and before the statute gave those tenements to this same Fulk and to Constance his wife and to the

[1] 13 Edw. I. De donis.

&c. a quel averement vous ne avendrez mie countre vostre fet; si agarde &c qe ele recovere &c. A.D. 1307.

§ Robert de Tony porta le bref ver Johan Pride, qe vouche a garantie Fulk le fiz Waryn, qe a jour qil fut somons se fit essoner de mal de venue, e avoyt jour &c.; a quel jour il fit defaute, par que le Cape ad valentiam &c. retournable &c.; a quel jour il se fit essoner du service le roy, e avoyt jour taunt qe ore. —STAUNTONE (a le atourne Fouke). Volez garantir?—*Le Attourne.* Sire, oyl.—*Herle* recitavit processum predictum &c., e de ceo qe le tenant nad mie ver son vouche de cestes defaute suy, demaundoms jugement du tenant. — *Toudeby.* Le tenant[1] est garanti e est saunz jour; si vous volez renz dire vers Fulk, veez le icy, prest &c.; e qe ne ussez vous sui vers le voucher. —*Herle.* Nay, ceo est vostre sute, e si le petit cape hust este a sure vers ly avaunt qe la garantie ust este termine entre vous, ceo apendereit a vous de sure, e sil voleit haver sauve sa defaute, vous ly deveriez haver contreplede e non pas nous.—STAUNTONE. Vous est passe le pas; il est garaunti. — *Westcote* counta &c. qe Fuke li deforce par sa garantie &c., e prist title de la seisine un son antecessour Rauf, de Rauf descendant a Roger cum a fiz e heir, de Roger a Rauf cum a fiz, de Rauf a Robert qe ore est &c. sute e dereigne &c. — *Willeby* defendi, e vous dioms qil ne put ore rens demaunder &c., qar un W &c. ces tenements dona a cely Rauf, de qi seisine &c., en fraunc mariage ove Pyronele sa femme, avaunt statut, de queux issi Roger &c.: Peronele survesqui, e meme ceux tenements avaunt statut dona a meme cest Fouk e a Custaunce sa femme, a haver e a tenir a Fouke e a

De recto: precipe in capite.

[1] MS. tenements.

A.D. 1307. heirs which the said Fulk should beget on Constance; and if Fulk and Constance should die without &c. begotten &c. that the tenements should return to Peronel and to her heirs; and she bound herself, to warranty, by this charter; now if we were impleaded by another you would be bound to warrant us &c., and in you is the reversion; and we pray judgment if now &c.—*Westcote.* We are in a writ of Right where they ought to give one answer in bar of our action; and now they &c. which is double, one for the reversion and the other for the warranty: and we pray that the court will oblige them to hold to one.—*Toudeby.* This is a deed, on which deed we take our answer, and we will not parcel it out or use it by pieces, but in its entirety.—And HENGHAM said the same thing.— *Herle.* In the deed &c. there are three things which can be counter-pleaded by us; one is the gift before the statute, another is the reversion, and the third is the warranty: whereof one perchance may be a matter of law and may go to judgment, and another may be the subject of an averment &c., which would be divers issues in this writ of Right; wherefore &c.—HOWARD. None of the points in the charter by which they wish to aid themselves is contrary to another, but they all depend on the right which is in the warranty; for they wish to be warranted according to the points placed in the charter; so that the greatest obstacle to you is the warranty.—Afterwards the parties took a day at the quinzein of St. Michael, and it is thought that the said R. will not further prosecute his writ.

Avowry. In right of a freehold in one vill one may have common &c. in another vill as appendant &c.

§ *Willeby.* We avow the taking &c., for the reason that we found his beasts &c., which were agisted in Wileby, a hamlet of T., feeding on and trampling down the grass in our common of Hongton where &c. he has no common, nor any land to which common is appen-

Custaunce e as heyrs qe le dit Fouk de Custaunce engendreit. E si Fouk e E. deviasent sanz &c. engendrez &c. qe les tenements retournassent a Peronele e a ces heyrs; e obliga &c. a la garauntie, e par cest chartre; dount si nous fusouns de autre enplede, vous nous serriez lie a la garantie &c., e a vous est la reversion, e demaundoms jugement si a ore &c. — *Westcote.* Nous sumes a un bref de dreit, ou il devent un response en barre de nostre accion; a ore &c. qe est dubble, le un pur la reversion, e lautre pur la garauntie; e prioms qe la court lor mette a tenir a le un.— *Toudeby.* Ceo est un fet, sur quel fet nous pernoms nostre respons; e nous ne parceleroms point, ne le useroms par peces, einz enterement. Hoc idem dixit HENGHAM.—*Herle.* En le fet &c. sunt treis choses qe pount par nous estre countrepledez; le un de le doun avaunt statut, autre de la reversion, la terce de la garantie; dount le un par cas poet[1] cheire en ley e en voie jugement, lautre en averement &c., qe serreient divers issues a ceo bref de dreit; par quei &c. — HOWARD. Nul dez poinz contenuz en la chartre par quei il se voilent eyder ne contrarie a autre, einz touz dependent del dreit qe est en la garantie; qar solom les poinz metez en la chartre voilent eux estre garantez, issi qe la greignure obstacle cuntre vous si est la garantie. Postea partes ceperunt diem usque in .xv. Sancti Michaelis, et creditur dictum R. breve suum ulterius nolle sequi. A.D. 1307.

Ratione liberi tenementi existentis in una villa potest quis habere comunam &c. in alia villa tanquam appendens &c. Advocacio.

§ *Willeby.* Nous avouoms la prise &c., e par la resoun qe nous trovames ces avers &c. qe agistez en Wileby qe est hamele de T., pessauns e defolauns le herbe de nostre comune de Hongtone ou &c. nad nule comune &c. ne tere a quei comune est apendant.—

[1] MS. poez.

A.D. 1307. dant. —*Malmesthorpe.* We have in Wileby which is a hamlet of T. a messuage and a virgate of land, and we tell you that our father and our grandfather, tenants &c., have always used to have their common &c. in Hongthon, as appendant to their land &c. in Wileby. — *Toudeby.* Your father and your grandfather were only seised of using the common within three years, and that time can not give you a title to have the common; but you must show a longer seisin.—*Malmesthorpe.* We and our ancestors and all the terre-tenants have been seised of the said common &c. as appendant &c. from the time of the limitation of the writ of Novel disseisin.—*Willeby.* Never seised as appendant, but only by your own taking, ready &c.—And the other side said the contrary.—Therefore &c.—In this case he did not take a title further back than the writ of Novel disseisin is limited, because he said that the common was appendant to the land, and so for it he might use the writ of Novel disseisin, which if he should not do, he must take his title from time whereof there is no memory.

Dower. Where the tenant vouched to warranty one other than the husband of the woman &c. and his heir, which voucher the demandant counter-pleaded, because she said that the tenant had entry by her husband.

§ A woman brought the writ against Stephen son of Benet, who vouched to warranty John the Clerk.—*Lanfar.* To that voucher you ought not to be received, for you yourself entered by our husband to whom the said John is not heir nor in any way privy in blood: and if it were a writ of Entry in the degrees, and we had said that you had entered by our husband, you would not be received to vouch out of the degrees; no more in this writ. —*Hegham.* These things may stand together, viz. that we entered by your husband &c., and that the voucher is yet receivable in this writ; and we tell you that after the death of your husband, John the Clerk was seised &c., and en-

Marm. Nous avoms en Willeby qe est hamele de T. un mees e une verge de tere, e nous dioums qe nostre pere e nostre ael, y tenauns &c., ount en use de haver lor comune &c. en Hongthone cum apendant a la tere &c. in Willeby. -- *Toudeby.* Vostre pere e vostre ael point de user denz treys auns, e cel temps ne vous poiez pas doner title de cele comune haver, einz covendreit plus lunge seisine aver.[1]-- *Malmesthorp.* Nous e noz auncestres e toz les teres tenauns de meme la comune seisi &c. cum appendant &c. du temps de la limitacion de bref de novele disseisine. --*Willeby.* Unqes seisi cum appendant, einz pur le vostre donaunt, prest &c. Et alii e contra. Ideo &c. Et in ista casu non cepit titulum ulterius quam breve novæ disseisinæ limitatur, quia dixit comunam esse appendentem terræ, e sic de ea posset uti brevi novæ disseisinæ, quod nisi fecerit, oporteret titulum capere de tempore a quo non exstat memoria. A.D. 1307

Ubi tenens vocavit ad warrantiam alium quam virum mulieris &c. et ejus heredem, quam vocationem petens contra placitavit eo quod dixit tenentem habere ingressum per virum suum. De dote.

§ Une femme porte le bref ver Estevene le fiz Benet qe voucha a garantie Johan le Clerk.—*Lanfar.* A cele voucher ne devez estre rescu, qar vous mesme entrastes par nostre baron, a qui le dit Johan nest eyr ne rens prive de sank; e sil fut un bref de entre en les degrez, e nous ussoms dit qe vous ussez entre par nostre baron, vous ne serriez mie rescu de voucher hors de les grez; nent plus en ceste bref.—*Hegham.* Stant simul qe nous entrames par vostre baron &c. e qe le voucher est uncore receyvable en ceste bref; e nous dioms qe apres la mort vostre baron, Johan le Clerk

[1] MS. vous.

A.D. 1307. feoffed us; ready &c.—MALLORE. The husband &c. may have enfeoffed Stephen and John and then have re-enfeoffed Stephen; wherefore &c.—*Lanfar.* Then Stephen is in his first estate, in which case he ought to answer just as much as if John had been dead ever since the purchase of his first estate.—STAUNTON. Your writ does not name any degrees, so it can not by this voucher be abated; wherefore &c.; nor is the voucher contrary to any point in your writ.—And the voucher stood, by the authority of HENGHAM, MALLORE and STAUNTON.

Covenant. Where the master of an hospital &c. and one of his brethren brought the writ.

§ Command Master John de Everose formerly parson of the church of Kemesheye that he perform to the prior of the hospital of St. John of Jerusalem in England and to John of London, a brother of the said hospital, the agreement made between the said Master John and the said Brother John concerning the fruits of the church of Kemeseye for four years.—*Rostone.* This court has no cognisance &c.; for the fruit of a church is a thing purely spiritual; judgment &c.—MALLORE. By the buying and the selling would it be spiritual?—*Rostone.* The form of the Chancery "is &c. to the co-brother of the said master," whereas the writ says "to the brother of the said hospital &c.;" judgment &c.—But this objection was not allowed.—*Rostone.* We formerly brought against the prior &c. a writ for a debt due to us on the same contract, and we put therein the same time as they do now; on which occasion the prior said that we ought not to challenge against him as our prior a debt for a contract made in that time; for at that time he was not prior; judgment if he as prior, on a contract made during that time, in opposition to his own acknowledgment, can claim damages against us.—*Herle.* That is to the action. Be avowed. —*Hedone.* We gave him another writ, and thereof we made protestation.—MALLORE. Although you made protestation, the court fut seisi &c., e nous enfeffa; prest &c.—MALLORE. Le baron &c. poez aver feffe Estevene [e] Johan, e pus refeffe Estefne, par quei &c.—*Lanfare.* Dunke est Estevene a son primer estat ou il deit taunt avaunt respondre cum si Johan ust tut temps pus soun primer purchas devie. —STAUNTON. Vostre bref ne nome nulz degrez, par quei il ne porra mie par cel voucher estre abatu; par quei &c.; ne le voucher nest mie encontre nul point qe est en vostre breve. Et stetit vocacio per HENGHAM, MALLORE, STANTONE. A.D. 1307.

Ubi magister hospitalis &c. et suus frater tulerunt breve. De conventione.

§ Precipe magistro Johanni de Everose quondam personæ ecclesiæ de Kemesheye quod teneat priori hospitalis Sancti Johannis Jerusalem in Anglia et Johanni de Londonia fratri ejusdem hospitalis convensionem factam inter predictum magistrum Johannem et prefatum fratrem Johannem de fructibus ecclesiæ de Kemeseye per quatuor annos. — *Rostone.* Ceste curt nad mie conisaunce &c.; qar fructus ecclesiæ est chose mere espiritele; jugement &c. — MALLORE. Per emptionem et vendicionem spirituale fuerit? — *Rostone.* Forme de la Chancelerie est &c. "confratri ejusdem magis-" tri," ou le bref dit "fratri ejusdem hospitalis &c." jugement &c. Nec allocatur. — *Rostone.* Autrefez portames nous vers le priour &c. le bref de dette qe nous fut due de meme le contracte, e omuttames de meme ceux temps qe eux fount ore, ou le priour dit qe nous ne devyoms ver luy cum nostre priour dette de contracte de teu temps dereigner, qar a cel temps ne estoit il pas priour, jugement sil cum priour, de contracte fet en tel temps, encontre sa conisance demene, vers nous damages [pusse] deregner. — *Herle.* Ceo est al accion; seez avowe. — *Hedone.* Nous le devoimes autre bref, e de ceo femes prodestacion. — MALLORE. Coment qe vous fistes prodestacion, la cour

A.D. 1307. will understand it as it really is, and not according to your wish: this goes purely to the action; for by your exception you think your intention to be this, that if he were not prior &c. he as prior could not have an action. —*Rostone* (the last exception having been written down) said, They were not ousted by our default, ready &c.—*Toudeby.* Let us get now to inquire about our term.—*Rostone.* As before; not ousted by our act &c.—*Herle.* You resigned the church to the bishop, as we have stated, whereby we were ousted, ready &c. — MALLORE. The resigning is an act, and if it was by your resignation, then it was by your act. Therefore &c. (It is to be noticed that the writing of the covenant was thus "I "have let to farm my church &c.")—*Rostone.* Judgment of the variance: the writ says "agreement about the "fruits &c." and the delivery was, as the writing testifies, of the church. — *Toudeby.* Nay there is a clause therein which contains a covenant, "so that they may "lawfully take the fruits of his aforesaid church for four "years &c."

Where two married men jointly purchased and jointly alienated, after whose deaths their wives brought the writ of Dower.

Where a woman was barred of her dower for that her husband had a joint estate.

§ Walter le Gleuman and John le Gleuman purchased &c. jointly &c. and then jointly alienated and died; and after their deaths Alice &c. the wife of Walter and Agnes &c. the wife of John brought their writ &c. — *Hedone* (to each plaintiff separately). Your husband &c. was never solely seised &c. so that &c., but jointly &c.; and he disclosed the facts of the case. — *Lanfar.* You have acknowledged that he was seised in his demesne as of fee &c., judgment &c.; and as to Agnes, in order better to affirm her estate, we tell you that John her husband survived &c. — MALLORE. According to what he says they had previously jointly alienated; and if that la entendra a ceo qe ele est, e noun pas a vostre voler; cele est purement al accion, qar par vostre excepcion entendez vostre entendement estre tiel, qe sil ne fut priour &c. il com priour ne poet[1] pas accion aver.—*Rostone* (scripta illa ultima[2] excepcione). Il ne furent pas oustez par nostre defaute, prest &c. — *Toudeby.* Aveimes nous de inquiser nostre terme. — *Rostone.* Ut prius, nent[3] oustez par nostre[4] fet &c.—*Herle.* Qe vous resingnastes le eglise al evesqe, cum nous avoms dit, par quei nous fumes outez, prest &c. — MALLORE. Resingnement est un fet, e si par vostre resingnement ergo par vostre fet, ideo &c. — Sciendum qe lescrit de covenaunt fut tiel "dimisi ad firmam ecclesiam meam "&c."—*Rostone.* Jugement de la variance; le bref dit "conventionem de fructibus &c." e le baylif est, prout scriptum testatur, de le eglise. — *Toudeby.* Nay il yad une clause leinz ou conventio se tayle, "Ita quod licite "percipiant fructus ecclesiæ suæ predictæ per quatuor "annos &c." A.D. 1307.

Ubi duo sponsi conjunctim perquisierunt et conjunctim alienaverunt, post quorum mortem uxores eorum tulerunt breve de dote &c.

§ Wauter le Gleuman e Johan le Gleuman purchaserente &c. jointement &c. e puis jointement alienerent, e devierent, e apres lor desces Alice &c. la femme Wauter &c., e Agnes &c. le femme Johan porterent lor bref &c. — *Hedone* (sigillatim ad utramque). Vostre baroun &c. ne fut unqes soul seisi &c. issi &c., einz jointement &c.; e desclosa le cas.—*Lanfar.* Vous avez conu qe il fut seisi en sun demeine cum de fe &c., jugement &c.; e quant a Agnes, pur muz afirmer soun estat, vous dioms qe Johan son baroun survesqui &c. — MALLORE. De ceo qil dit qe einz alienerent jointement; e

Ou femme est barre deo soun dower pur ceo qe soun baroun avoit joynt estat.

[1] MS. poez.
[2] MS. ultimis.
[3] MS. vent
[4] MS. vostre.

A.D. 1307. be true, John was not solely seised of anything.—And he said to *Lanfar*, Is it as he says or not? — *Lanfar* could not deny this. — MALLORE (having consulted HENGHAM and STAUNTON). The court adjudges that neither one nor the other takes anything &c.

That tenements holden by knight's service may be partible.

§ In a writ of Ael which Hugh son of Robert of Great Wodington brought against Nicholas la Grandame he counted of the seisin of Agnes his grandmother. — *Willeby.* The tenements of the demandants are partible and have been divided between &c., and we are issue of that Agnes of whose &c., so that against us, in the possession you can not have any writ except the Nuper obiit; judgment of this writ.—*Hedone.* They are holden by knight's service, ready &c. — STAUNTON. It may be that they are holden by knight's service and yet are partible. — *Willeby.* The tenements &c. were in the seisin of R. who had issue Thomas and Delfin, between whom the tenements &c. were divided; after whose deaths, because they died without heir &c., they descended to Reynilda as sister, and from Reynilda to Agnes, of whose seisin &c. — *Hedone.* They were not rightfully partible, ready &c. — STAUNTON. Nay, by God, you shall not say any thing about right, but only that they are not partible. — *Hedone.* They are not partible, ready &c. — STAUNTON. Nor divided. — *Hedone.* I answer higher up, wherefore &c. — *Warr.* You answer to one head but not to the other; admit then that they have been divided, and abide judgment. — STAUNTON. The division makes them partible, wherefore&c.—And at last he was driven to answer as to the division; and he denied it. Therefore &c.

si ceo sei verite, Johan ne fu soul seisi de rens. IDEM a *Lanfar*. E est ceo issi cum il dit ou noun ? — *Lanfar* hoc non potuit dedicere.—MALLORE consulto HENGHAM e STANTONE. Si agarde la court qe le un ne lautre ne pregne renz &c.

A.D. 1307.

Judicum.

Quod tenementa tenta per servitium militare possunt esse partibilia.

§ En un bref de ael qe Hugche le fiz Robert de la Graunt Wodingtone porta ver Nichole la Grandame e counta de la seisine Agnes sa ael. — *Welleby*. Les tenements de demaundanz sount departables, e ount este departiz entre &c., e nous sumes issue de cele Agnes de qi &c., issi qe vers nous en la possessioun ne poetz aver[1] nul bref mes qe le nuper obiit ; jugement de ceste bref. — *Hedone*. Tenuz par service de chivaler, prest &c. — STANTONE. Il porra estre qe ceaux sunt tenuz par service de chivaler e jatardis departables.—*Willeby*. Les tenements&c. furent en la seisine R., qe avoit issue Thomas e Delfin, entre quex les tenements &c. furent departiz ; apres qi mort, pur ceo qe eux devierent sanz heir &c., descendi a Rexnilde cum a sour, de Reynilde a Agnes de qi seisine &c. — *Hedone*. Nent departable de dreit, prest &c. — STANTONE. Nay, par Deu, vous nous ne averez nent de dreit, mes "quod non sunt "partibilia." — *Hedone*. Nent departables, prest &c. — STANTONE. Ne departiz.—*Hedone*. Jeo respound de plus aust, par quei &c. — *Warr*. Vous responez al un teste e noun pas al autre ; grauntez donqes qe il unt este departiz, e demorez en jugement. — STAUNTONE. Le departizon les fet departables, par quei &c.—Et ad ultimum fut chace a response a la departizon ; e il la dedit. Ideo &c.

---

[1] MS. vers.

A.D. 1307. Allegation of joint-feoffment, where the clause of the habendum et tenendum and the clause of warranty did not agree with the clause of gift.

§ One Annabel brought the writ against Richard of Lutlingthe, parson &c., to wit the Cui in vitâ &c.—*Toudeby.* We have nothing in those tenements except as joint feoffee with one Joan &c. according to the form of this charter, and he is not named in the writ; judgment &c. And he put forward the charter the tenor whereof &c. "I have given &c. and to Joan my daughter &c. to have &c. to the aforesaid Richard for the whole of his life and after the decease of the said Richard the tenements shall remain to the said Joan and the heirs of her body begotten. And I. &c. the said tenements to the said Richard for the whole of his life and after his death to the said Joan and the heirs &c. will warrant &c. —*Friskeney.* By the form of that charter Richard is only tenant for life, as appears by that clause "to have "&c.," and also by the clause of warranty; and your writ also speaks of tenements in T. and the charter speaks of tenements in E. — *Hales.* It may be that that S. is a hamlet of T.; and if you will say that these are not the tenements comprised in the charter &c. you can. — And they would not. —*Toudeby.* The gift was made jointly &c., and the charter shows it; judgment &c. — Mallore. The court adjudges that she do take nothing &c., and that Richard do go without day &c.

Dower. Where it was objected to a man and his wife plaintiffs that the same man had formerly in an assise of Mordancester claimed the fee, by which now &c. And also where the same tenants say they recovered on a higher title.

§ William Charles and Isabel his wife brought the writ against Henry de Rale and Mabel his wife and others by divers præcipes, and they demanded &c. of the freehold &c. and of John Pinchardon &c.—*Malmesthorpe*

Allegacio conjuncti feoffamenti ubi illa clausa, scilicet, habendum et tenendum, et clausa warrantiæ non concordans cum clausa doni. A.D. 1307.

§ Un Anable porta le bref ver Richard de Lutlingthe persone &c. saver "cui in vita" &c. — *Toudeby.* Nous ne avoms rens en cel tenements sinoun cum joint feffe ove un Johan &c., solom la forme de ceste chartre, nent nome en bref de jugement &c.: e mist avant la chartre unde tenor &c. "dedi &c. et Johannæ filiæ meæ " &c. habendum &c. predicto Ricardo ad totam vitam " suam et post decessum ipsius Ricardi, predicta tene- " menta remaneant predictæ Johannæ et heredibus de " corpore suo procreatis. Et ego &c. predicta tenementa " predicto Ricardo ad totam vitam suam &c. et post " decessum ipsius predictæ Johannæ et heredibus &c. " warrantizabo &c." — *Friskeney.* Par la forme de tel chartre Richard ad tenance soleyne a terme de sa vie, qe pert par cest clause habendum &c., e auxi par la clause de garantie, e auxi parle vostre bref de tenements en T., e la chartre de tenements en E. — *Hales.* Porra estre qe S. est haynel a T., e si vous voilez dire qe ces ne sunt pas les tenements contenuz en la chartre &c. vous poez.—Et noluere. — *Toudeby.* Le doun fut fet jointement &c., e ceo testmoigne la chartre; jugement &c. — Mallore. Si agarde &c. qele ne pregne renz &c., e Richard sanz jour &c.

Ubi obiit viro et mulieri petentibus quod idem vir alias in assisa mortis antecessoris clamavit feodum per quod modo &c. Et etiam ubi iidem tenentes dicunt se recuperasse de alteriori titulo.

§ Willam Charles e Isabele sa femme porterent le bref ver Henri de Rale e Mabile sa femme e autres par divers precipes, e demanderent &c. del fraunc tenement &c. et Johannis[1] Pinchardun &c. — *Malm.* (pur

[1] MS. Johanna.

A.D. 1307. (for Henry and Mabel). On this writ or on this demand you ought not now to be answered; for heretofore these same Henry and Mabel and the other parceners of Mabel brought a writ of Mordancester against the said William and Isabel, before &c, justices &c., on the death of Pinchardon of whose endowment &c., in which assise the said William counterpleaded us, and said that John's ancestor did not die seised, claiming the fee to our disheritance; which assise was assembled and passed, by which it was found that he died seised &c., wherefore &c.; now since he heretofore claimed the fee &c. to our disheritance &c., we pray judgment if he ought to be answered &c.—*Friskeney.* That is all to William.—*Warr.* It is to William and Isabel; for Isabel will not be received without William.— *Westcot.* And we pray judgment,—since in that assise Isabel claimed nothing, nor against her as a tortious deforcer were any damages recovered, as you will find, and she long time before that assise acquired her right to dower,—if by anything they say they can bar us from dower &c.—*Warr.* You have counterpleaded our exception, and we pray judgment &c. —MALLORE to *Westcot.* If the husband had released and quit-claimed &c., would not that be a bar &c. he being living?—*Westcot.* That is a different thing. — MALLORE. But it is a little like. — And in another præcipe the tenant vouched &c. the said Henry and Mabel, who warranted him &c.—*Friskeney.* Answer, now that you have warranted. — *Malmesthorpe.* Of these &c. you ought not to have dower; for John Pinchardon, of whose endowment &c., long time before he married you enfeoffed William Pinchardon his son of these tenements, by which feoffment he was seised, and he died seised: after whose death the said John in his time abated &c., and we ourselves with the parceners of the said Mabel at the time aforesaid before the same justices brought against you the Mordancester on the death of the said William Pinchardon,

Henri e Mabyle). Vous ne devez ore a cesti bref ne a ceste demande estre respondu; qar autrefez memes ceux Henri e Mabile e les autres parceners Mabile porterent bref de mordauncestre vers les avaunditz Willam e Isabele devaunt &c., justices &c., de la mort Pinchardone de qi dowement &c., a quele assise le dit Willam nous contrepleda, e dit qe launcestre Johan ne morust pas seisi, en clamant fee a nostre desheritaunces; la quele assise fust arrame e passa, par laquele fust trove qil morust seisi &c., par quei &c.; dount del oure qe autrefez a nostre[1] desheritacions &c., clama fee &c. demaundoms jugement sil le deive estre respondu &c. —*Friskeney.* Cet tut a Willam.—*Warr.* Cest a Willam e Isabele, qar Isabele ne serra mie rescue sanz Willam. —*Westcote.* E nous jugement, del oure qe a cele assise Isabele rien ne cleime ne ver luy cum vers deforceour tortenouse nul damage ne estoient recoverez solom ceo qe vous itroverez, e ele long temps avant cele assise cele douere out deservi, si par rens qe eux diount nous pussent de dowere &c. a[2] ore forbarrer.—*Warr.* Vous avez contre[plede] nostre excepcion, e demaundoms jugement &c. — MALLORE (a[2] *Westoft*). Si le baron eust relesse e quiteclame &c., ne serreit ceo mie barre &c. ly vivant?—*Westoft.* Cest autre. — MALLORE. Einz est apoy au tiel. E e[n] un autre precipe le tenaunt voucha &c. les avandiz Henri e Mabyle, qe ly garantirent &c. — *Friskeney.* Respondez la ou vous avez garanti. — *Marm.* De ces &c. ne devez dowere aver; qar Johan Ponchardoun, de qi dowement &c., avant ceo qil vous esposa longe temps, de ces tenements enfeffa Willam Ponchardoun sun fiz, par quele feffement il estoit seisi, e morust seisi: apres qi mort le dit Johan en ces temps se abbati &c., issi qe nous meme ensement ou les parceners la dite Mabile au temps avantdit e devant memes les justices portames devers vous le mortdauncestre de la mort le dit Willam A.D. 1307.

[1] MS. autre.

[2] MS. e.

A.D. 1307. by which assise it was found that he died seised &c. whereby we recovered on a higher &c.; and we pray judgment if you, on the endowment or the estate of him who had nothing except as an abater &c., can rightfully claim dower &c. —*Friskeney*. Isabel was the wife of John Pinchardon, and joined to him in lawful matrimony before he enfeoffed the said William Pinchardon, ready &c.—And the other side said the contrary.—Therefore &c.

It is not necessary that the defendant be seised of the annuity where by the deed a certain tenement is bound to distress.

§ In a plea of taking of beasts, *Ormesby* avowed the taking &c.; and for the reason that the plaintiff had granted and bound himself to the defendant in so many shillings yearly for his services done and to be done, and granted that if anything was in arrear he might distrein in all his tenements in C. and in T.; and for that &c.—*Lanfar*. He has not said that he was seised &c., judgment &c.—*Herle*. You admit the deed which gives us power to distrein this Henry &c.; judgment, and if you will, we will abide there boldly.—*Lanfar*. At the time of the making of this deed we were not seised of the tenements where the taking &c.—*Malmesthorpe*. He does not deny that he is now seised of them; wherefore &c.—STAUNTON. He says quite enough and you well know it.—*Malmesthorpe*. Seised &c., ready.

Ponchardoun, par quele assise fut trove qil morust A.D. 1307.
seisi &c., para quei nous recoverames de plus &c.; a juger si vous del dowement ou del estat celuy qe rienz navoit mes cum abater &c., dower &c. puissez demander. — *Friskeney.* Isabele fut la femme Johan Punchardoun, couple a luy en leal matrimonie, einz qil enfeffa le dit Willam Ponchardoun prest &c.—Et alii e contra.—Ideo &c.

Non indiget quod defendens seisietur de annuitate ubi per factum certum tenementum obligatur ad districtionem.

§ En[1] play de prise des avers, *Orm.* avouua la prise &c.; e par la reson qe le pleintif avoit grante e sei fut oblige al defendant en souz par an pur son service fet e a fere, e granta qe si rienz ly fut arere qil poit destreindre en touz ces tenements en C. e en T.; e pur ceo &c.—*Lanfar.* Il nad pas dit qil fut seisi &c., jugement &c.—*Herle.* Vous conussez le fet qe nous[2] doune poer a destreindre quel Henri &c., jugement; e si vous volez, demoroms la hardiement.—*Lanfar.* Au temps de la confeccion de cest fet nous ne esteimes pas seisi de ceux tenements ou la prise &c. — *Marm.* Il ne dedist pas qil ne est ore seisie; par quei &c. — STANTONE. Il vous dist assez e ore savez bien.—*Marm.* Seisei &c., prest.

---

[1] MS. Ceo.

[2] MS. vous.

PLEAS IN TRINITY TERM

IN THE XXXVTH YEAR OF THE REIGN OF KING EDWARD.

PLEAS IN TRINITY TERM IN THE XXXVTH YEAR OF THE REIGN OF KING EDWARD.

A.D. 1367. Dower. Where was vouched to warranty one who was not the husband of the plaintiff nor his heir, and the voucher was counterpleaded.

§ The countess Marshal brought the writ against Ralph de Mountchesney and demanded the moiety of the manor of F.—*Herle.* You ought not to recover a moiety &c. by way of dower, for this manor is held by knight's service, and there has never been dower of a moiety of this manor, ready &c.—*Toudeby.* Of what then ?—*Herle.* See you to that; we have answered your demand.—*Toudeby.* In this case the form of pleading should be this—"Never was lady endowed of the moiety &c. but of "the third part;—and we yield it to her;" if there were not an obstacle to her having dower: and inasmuch as you do not state anything which forecloses her of dower, we pray judgment &c.—*Herle.* To that demand which you have made we have answered, and if you will still make your demand of the third part, perchance we shall answer in another way.—*Toudeby.* A writ of Dower was never abated for defect in the demand.—HOWARD. He offers to aver that you ought not to be endowed according to your demand, and you will not make any other demand; then let the averment run.—*Toudeby.* He says nothing whereby we ought not to be endowed of the third part.—*Herle.* You do not demand it.—STAUNTON to *Toudeby.* If he were still to say, A lady &c. of the moiety of this manor &c., ready &c., and as to the third part were to vouch &c., the court would not now receive such an answer of divers issues; and yet I lately saw it received in fact in a suit between the abbat of Saint

DE TERMINO SANCTÆ TRINITATIS ANNO REGNI REGIS EDWARDI TRICESIMO QUINTO.

De dote ubi vocatur ad warrantiam alius quam vir mulieris petentis vel ejus heres, et contraplacitatur. A.D. 1307.

§ La contesse Mareschale porta le bref vers Randolf de Montchanesiz, e demanda la moite du maner de F.—*Herle.* Vous ne devez moite &c. en noun de dowere rescoverer, car ceo maner si est tenuz par fee de chivaler, e est a la comune lei, e si ne fust pas onqes nule dame de moite de ceu maner dowe, prest &c.—*Toudeby.* De qi donqes?—*Herle.* Veez vous; nous avom respondu a vostre demaunde.—*Toudeby.* Manere de pleder serreit en teu cas ceste, "unqes dame ne fust dowe de la moite "&c. einz de la terce partie; e cele luy rendoms," si obstacle ne fust pur quei ele ne deit dowere avoir; et desicom vous ne dites[1] rienz qe de dowere la forclost, demandoms jugement &c.—*Herle.* A tele demaunde com vous avez fet nous avoms respondu; e si uncore volez vostre demaunde de la terce partie fere, par cas nous respondroms par altre veie.—*Toudeby.* Bref de dowere ne fust onqes abatu pur defaute en la demaunde.—Howard. Il voet averer qe vous ne devez solom vostre demaunde estre dowe, e vous ne volez autre demaunde faire; courge donqes laverement. —*Toudeby.* Il ne dist rienz pur quei nous ne devoms estre dowe de la terce partie.—*Herle.* Vous ne la demandez mie.—Stantone a *Toudeby.* Sil deit uncore dame &c. de moite de ceu maner &c. prest &c., et quant a la terce partie vouchast &c., la court ne acceptreit mie tel respons de divers issues a ore; e jatardeis jeo le vy estre receu de fet entre labbe de Seint

---

[1] MS. dedites.

A.D. 1307. Edmund &c.—*Toudeby.* No, but he can yield the third part.—STAUNTON. He does not wish to lose his voucher, nor does the law will that one should drive him to do that.—*Toudeby*, being driven to this by the court, or the averment would have run,—amended his demand, and made it for the third part &c.—*Friskeney.* We vouch to warranty Giles de Mountpinzon and Cristiana his wife &c.—*Toudeby.* You entered by our husband, to whom the said Giles and Cristiana are not heirs, neither are they at all privy in blood, ready &c.—*Friskeney.* We hold only for life, and the reversion is theirs according to the form of a fine which was levied between them and W. de Langeton, by virtue of which fine we attorned to them, judgment &c.; and in a writ of Entry in the degrees the voucher would be receivable.—*Toudeby.* In this writ the law is more tender and favourable to enable the demandant to obtain her demand than in other writs &c.; wherefore &c.

Entry. Entry &c., where the reversion of the right of the woman was in the writ made to belong to her husband as well as to her, on account of which &c.

§ A man and his wife and the wife's cousin brought the writ &c. in this form, "into which he has not entry "unless by G. to whom D., grandfather of the said C. "and great-grandfather of the said A., demised them for "a term which has passed; and which after the said "term to the said B. and C. his wife and A. ought to "revert."—*Lanfar.* Judgment of the writ; for he makes the reversion of the right of the woman belong to her husband, who cannot with her be heir to any heritage. —And the writ was abated by STAUNTON and HENGHAM.

§ The prioress of Markyate heretofore brought a writ against Robert de Kendale, and said that the tenements were &c. her right and her escheat &c., for that one S. who held these tenements of her was a bastard and died

Edmund &c.—*Toudeby.* Noun, mes il poeit rendre la terce partie.—STANTONE. Il ne voet pas perdre sun voucher, ne lei ne voet pas qe home lui chace de ceo fere. — *Toudeby* (ad hoc positus per curiam vel quod verificacio curreret[1]) amenda sa demaunde, e la fist de la terce partie &c.—*Friskeney.* Nous vouchoms a garantie Giles de Mounpinzon e Cristiene sa femme &c.—*Toudeby.* Vous entrastes par nostre baroun, a qi les avantdiz Giles ne Cristiene ne sunt heirs ne rienz prive du saunk, prest &c.—*Friskeney.* Nous ne avoms mes qe a terme de vie, e la reversion est lour solom la forme qe se leva entre eaux e W. de Langetone par vertu de quele fin nous atturnames a eux, jugement &c.; e en bref dentre en degreez serreit le voucher resceivable.—*Toudeby.* En ceo bref est lei plus tendre e favorable de fere la demaundante atteyndre a sa demaunde qil ne soit en altres; par quei &c. A.D. 1307.

De ingressu &c., ubi reversio de jure mulieris facta fuit in brevi tam viro suo quam sibi, propter quod &c.

§ Un homme e sa femme e le cosin la femme porterent le bref &c. sic, "in quas non habet ingressum "nisi per G, cui D. avus predictæ C. et proavus pre- "dicti A. illas dimisit ad terminum qui preteriit; et "quæ post prefatum terminum ad predictos B. et C. "uxorem ejus et A. reverti debent."—*Lanfare.* Jugement du bref; car il fet la reversion du droit la femme a sun baroun, qe ne purra ove li estre heir de nule heritage; e le bref se abati par STANTONE e HENGHAM.

§ La prioresse de Markiate autrefoiz porta bref vers Robert de Kendale, e dist qe les tenements furent &c. sun droit e sa eschete &c., pur ceo qe un S. qe ces tenements tient de luy fust bastard e morust sanz heir

[1] MS. careret.

A.D. 1307. without heir of his body. And Robert said that the said S. held of him and not of &c.; and on this they went down to an inquest, which now came.—*Toudeby.* There is no need to have this inquest which now comes. —*Toudeby.* There is no need to have this inquest, for a thing which can be averred by the judgment and record of the court is not to be tried by an inquest; and we tell you that in this court &c. a fine was levied between Jordan de Kendale, father of Robert whose heir &c., and the said S., of the same tenements, by which fine the said Jordan rendered to S. the same tenements, to have and to hold of him and his heirs, before the statute,[1] and doing to the chief lords the services &c. for him and for his heirs; and see here the part of the fine &c., and we vouch the concord at our peril, and we pray judgment.—*Herle.* We have pleaded to the inquest, and we pray the inquest, and if you do not wish it, say so, and let us go to judgment: and if you in pleading left out a thing which might avail, yet for that we will not replead.—HOWARD. He says that there is no need to take the inquest &c., and it may perchance operate to defeat the fine.—*Herle.* It is not yet admitted that there is a fine.—HOWARD. We have pleaded and are at an issue in the plea, and this answer was entered.—The parties and also the inquest were adjourned to the morrow of All Souls.

§ Alice, who was the wife of Richard de Wodeward, brought the writ against Robert Fitz-Walter in these words, namely, "Whereas Alice &c. in our court in the " 27th year &c. recovered &c. against Robert &c. guardian " of the land and of the heir &c. of Richard le Wode- " ward, and we have heretofore commanded you that " you cause the said Alice to have full seisin thereof, and " yet you have not done it, we command you that you " warn the said Robert, tenant &c., that he be &c. to

[1] 18 Edw. I. Quia emptores.

de son corps; e Robert dist qe celui S. tient de lui e noun pas &c.: e de ceo descendirent en enqueste, qe ore vient.—*Toudeby.* Nest pas mester de prendre ceste enqueste qe ore vient.—*Toudeby.* Nest pas mester de prendre ceste enqueste, car chose qe puet estre avere par jugement e record de cort nert pas trie par enqueste; ore vous dioms nous qe en ceste cort &c. se leva une fin entre Jordan de Kendale, pere Robert, qi heir &c., e celui S., de mesme ces tenements, par quele fin le dist Jordan rendi a S. mesmes les tenements, a aver e tenir de lui e de ces heirs, avant statut, e fessant au chiefs seignours les services &c. pur lui e pur ces heirs; e veez icy la partie de la fin &c., e vouchoms le pee en nostre peril, e demandoms jugement. —*Herle.* Nous avoms plede al enqueste e prioms lenqueste, e si vous ne la volez pas, dites, e seoms a jugement; e si vous entrelessates chose qe valer vous poeit au pleder, pur ceo ne replederoms pas.—HOWARD. Il dist qil ceo nert pas mestier de prendre enqueste &c., e jatardeis ceo ert par cas a defere la fin.—*Herle.* Uncore nest pas grante qe ceo soit fin. — HOWARD. Nous avoms plede, e sumes a issue de play, e cest respons entres.—Adjornentur partes et etiam inquisitio in crastinum animarum. A.D. 1307.

§ Alice ke fut la femme Richard de Wodeward porta le bref vers Robert le fiz Wauter sic, scilicet "Cum
" Alice &c. en nostre court lan xxvii. &c. rescoveri &c.
" vers Robert &c. gardein de la tere e del heir &c.
" Richard le Wodeward, e a vous einz ces houres eoms
" comande qe al avantdite Alice plenere seisine de ceo
" enfeissez aver, vous de ceo uncore rien ne feistes,
" vous comandoms qe vous facez a saver al avantdit
" Robert tenant &c. qil soit &c. a moustrer sil sache

A.D. 1307. "show if he has anything to say why &c., seisin &c." —*Toudeby.* The writ is not consistent; for it first calls Robert guardian &c. and at the end does not call him guardian; judgment &c.—*Malmesthorpe.* The writ says at the end "the aforesaid Robert."—[*Toudeby.*] We have nothing in the wardship, nor had we on the day when the writ was purchased, nor ever since, judgment &c.—*Friskeney.* How then; are you not tenant &c.—*Toudeby.* Yes, we are; but not as guardian.—*Friskeney.* Say then how.—And he was made to do this by the court.—*Toudeby.* As our right and our escheat; for such an one &c. our tenant &c., committed felony, for which he was hung, and the king had the year and waste, after which time we entered as upon our escheat.—*Friskeney.* Now we pray judgment, since heretofore when we brought &c. our writ of Dower against you, you as guardian rendered it to us, suuposing and acknowledging the freehold to be in another person,—if you in opposition to that acknowledgment can get to such an averment in this writ which depends on that original.—*Herle.* You do not find that he rendered in his own person.—STAUNTON, having looked at the inrolment, found that the render &c. was by his attorney John de Jakele.—*Herle.* Still, we tell you that at the time of the render, that is to say the 27th year, the tenements were in the king's hands; ready &c.—MALLORE (to *Friskeney*). Was the king seised at the time of that render, as he says, or not?—*Friskeney.* As before; we abide your judgment.—HOWARD. If the king were seised when he rendered to you, what could you have? (intimating nothing).—MALLORE. Or if he had answered in the time of the king's seisin that the husband was not ever seised &c., and inquest on that had passed against him, what could you have answered? (intimating nothing). And perchance the king's seisin was the cause why the execution was not had: wherefore it is necessary that you should answer to what they allege; was the king seised or not?—*Friskeney* said as "rien dire pur quei &c. seisine &c."—*Toudeby.* Le bref nest pas pursuant, qar primes nome il Robert gardein &c., e en la fin ne lui nome pas gardein; jugement &c. —*Marm.* Le bref dist en la fin "predictum Robertum;" qe nous ne avoms rienz en la garde, ne aveymes le jour de cestui bref purchace, ne unqes pus; jugement &c.—*Friskeney.* Coment donqes, nestes mie tenant &c.? —*Toudeby.* Si sumes; mes noun pas en garde.—*Friskeney.* Dites donqes coment. E a ceo dire fust mys par la court.—*Toudeby.* Com nostre droit e nostre eschete; qar un tel &c., nostre tenant &c., fist felonie, pur la quele il fust pendue, e le roi avoit lan e le wast; apres queu temps nous entrames com nostre eschete.—*Friskeney.* Ore demandoms nous jugement, de pus qe autrefoiz quant nous portames &c. nostre bref de dowere vers vous,[1] rendistes com gardeyn, en supposant e conissant le franc tenement en altre persone, si vous encontre cele conisance a tel averement en cestui bref qe depent de cel original devez atteyndre.—*Herle.* Vous ne trovez pas qil rendi en propre persone.—STANTONE, irrotulamento inspecto, invenit redditionem &c. per attornatum suum Johannem de Jakele.—*Herle.* E uncore vous dioms qe au temps de rendre, saver lan .xxvii., furent les tenements en la mayn le roi, prest &c.—MALORRE a *Friskeney.* Fust le roi seisi au temps de cel rendre, sicom il dist, ou noun?—*Friskeney.* Ut prius, nous demoroms en vos jugements.—HOWARD. Si le roi fust seisi e il vous eust rendu, qe eussez vous eu? quasi diceret nil.—MALLORE. Ou sil eust respondu en temps de la seisine le roi qe le baroun ne fust onqes seisi &c., e enquest de ceo eust passe contre lui, quei eussez vous respondu? quasi diceret nil; e par cas la seisine le roi fust cause par quei la execucion ne se fist pas; par quei il vous covendreit respondre a ceo qe eux dyent; si le roi fut seisi ou noun.—*Friskeney.* A.D. 1307.

[1] MS. nous.

A.D. 1307. before.—MALLORE. You do not deny the king's seisin &c.; therefore we take it for granted.—And they had a day to hear judgment in the quinzein of St. Michael.

Where against the exception that the wife left her husband and remained with the adulterer, it was replied that the husband drove her from him.

§ A. who was the wife of Robert, baron of Greystoke, brought the writ against Ralph Fitz-William and demanded the third part of the manor of Greystoke.—*Malmesthorpe.* You ought not to have dower; for ten years before the death of Robert, of whose endowment &c., you went with your adulterer Simon, he who has now married you, without being reconciled during the whole of your life &c.—*Passeley.* The statute [1] gives this exception, saying "&c. of her own free will leaves her husband;" now we tell you that we were staying at Robert's manor of T., and living there as his wife, when he came with force and arms and saddled horses and drove us off from him, ready &c., and we pray judgment &c.—*Herle.* Then are we at one, viz. that you remained with your adulterer.—*Passeley.* You aid yourself by the words of the statute, and we deny them; that is enough for us.—*Herle.* Although she was driven off &c., there was no necessity for her to go to her adulterer and live with him; nothing shows a person's will better than his own act; and with this we tell you that she married her adulterer in the lifetime of her husband Robert, of whose endowment &c.; so her free will is sufficiently shown.—*Passeley.* Grant then that you drove her off, and then let us go to judgment.—*Herle.* And you admit that you remained with your adulterer.—STAUNTON (having looked at the statute and consulted with HENGHAM). This exception is given by statute, and in like manner as the statute gives it, it is necessary that

[1] 13 Edw. I. (Westm. 2.), c. 34.

Ut prius. — MALLORRE. Vous ne dedites pas la seisine le roi &c., par quei nous la tenoms a graunte. Et habent diem de audiendo judicio in quindenis Michaelis. A.D. 1307.

Ubi contra istam exceptionem, scilicet quod mulier reliquit virum suum et morabatur cum adultero, replicatur quod vir ab ipso eam fugavit.

§ A., qe fust la femme Robert baron de Greistoke, porta le bref vers Rauf fiz Willem, e demanda la terce partie du maner de Greistoke.—*Marm.* Vous ne devez dowere aver; car dis anz avant la mort Robert, de qi dowement &c., vous alastes od vostre avouter Simon, celi qe ore vous ad espose, sanz estre reconsille en tote vostre vie &c.—*Passeley.* Statut donne ceste excepcion qe dist &c. "sponte sua reliquerit virum suum;" ore vous dioms nous ke nous esteymes au maner Robert &c. de T., demorant com sa femme, ou il vient a force e armes e as chivaux covers, e nous enchasa de luy, e prest &c., e demandoms jugement &c.—*Herle.* Donqes sumes a un, qe vous demorastes ove vostre avouter.—*Passeley.* Vous eydez par paroles de statut, e nous les dedioms, qe nous suffit.—*Herle.* Tut eust ele este enchace &c. il ne la covendreit mie aler a sun avouter e demorer ove luy; e rienz ne prove meuz volonte de home fors son fet demene; e oveske ceo vous dioms qe ele se fist esposer a son avouter vivant sun baron Robert de qi dowement &c.; dount assez est sa volente prove.—*Passeleyghe.* Grauntez donqe qe vous la enchaceastes, e seoms pus a jugement.—*Herle.* E vous la demore ove vostre avouter.—STAUNTONE (viso statuto et consulto HENGHAM). Cest excepcion est done par statut, e auxi com statut la donne auxi la covent home

A.D. 1307. one should oppose it; for the quitting willingly without remaining, nor the remaining without the quitting, is not a cause given by statute, by itself; but there must be both; so we wish to inquire of this thing.—*Passeley.* He drove us from N. which is in the county of L., and we pray a jury of that neighbourhood &c.—*Herle.* The force is not there, but where you remained with your adulterer at Ripon in the county of York, from which neighbourhood we pray a jury.—So a jury from each neighbourhood came &c., by judgment &c.

Dower.

Where one other than the husband &c. or his heir was vouched, and the voucher was counterpleaded.

§ The wife of John Doun brought the writ against R. de Hengham, who said that he had nothing but for the term of his life by lease from one Richard de Hamptone, according to the form of a fine, whereof he showed one part, and he vouched &c. the said Richard. —*Lanfar.* Our husband John leased &c. to you for the term of your life, and you have always since continued without change in that estate, ready &c.; and the said Richard de Hampton is not the heir of John &c.; wherefore &c.—MALLORE. Do you wish to avoid the fine by averment of the country? this is not a writ of Entry in the degrees, and nothing leaves you although he have his voucher.—*Lanfar.* In order to have the good will of the gentleman she admits it.—MALLORE. It must needs be admitted in spite of her and you too: henceforth take care of that exception.

Quid juris clamat.

Where the conusees claimed another estate than what the conusor said they had &c.

§ A. granted that certain tenements which one J. and C. his wife held for a term of years &c. and which &c. to him ought to revert, should remain to B.; and B. sued out the Quid juris clamat against the aforesaid J. and C., who came, and C. answered that she had nothing &c.

contrarier; car le deguerpir de gree sanz la demore, ne la demore sanz deguerpir, nest cause done par statut par luy, mes lun ove lautre; e issi voloms nous de ceste chose enquere.—*Passeley.* Il nous enchacea de N. qe est en le conte de L., e prioms pais de visneto &c. —*Herle.* La force nest pas la [mes la] ou vous demorastes ove vostre avouter a Rypoun en le conte de E. de quele visne nous prioms pais.—Ideo venit jurata de utrisque visnetis &c. per considerationem &c. A.D. 1307.

Ubi vocatur aliquis quam vir &c. vel heres ejus, et contraplacitatur. De dote.

§ La femme Johan Doun porta le bref vers R. de Hengham, qe dist qil navoit rienz si noun a terme de vie du lees un Ricard de Hamptone, solom la forme de une fin dount il mustra la une partie, e voucha &c. le dit Ricard. — *Lanfare.* Johan nostre baroun vous lessa &c. a terme de vostre vie, e vous cel estat tut temps pus avez continue, prest &c. sanz remuement, e le dit Ricard de Hamptone nest pas heir Johan &c., par quei &c.— MALORRE. Voillez voider la fin par averement de pays? e ceo nest pas bref dentre en degreez, e rienz ne vous depart, tut eit il sun voucher.—*Lanfare.* Pur aver la bone volente du prod home ele ly grante.—MALLORRE. Il la covendreit graunter maugre le soen e le vostre auxi; e gardez desormes de tele excepcion.

Ubi recognitores clamavere alium statum quam recognoscens dicit illos habuisse &c. Quid juris clamat.

§ A. granta ke certeinz tenements qe un J. e C. sa femme tiendrent a terme des anz &c., e les queux &c. a luy devoient revertir, remanissent a B.; e B. suist le quid juris clamat vers les avantdiz J. e C., qe viendrent, e C. respondi qe ele ne avoit rienz &c.

A.D. 1307. except as wife of J.—*Lanfar.* What does J. answer?—*Passeley.* He tells you that A. leased to him these tenements for the term of six years; and, besides this, granted that he should hold the tenements to him and his heirs until the said A. or his heirs should pay him a certain sum;—and he put forward a deed which showed this, and he prayed judgment, inasmuch as his estate was non-certain, and attornment ought to be on a point certain, if &c. he ought to attorn.—*Spigurnel.* The fine can not be engrossed from that concord, for the concord states that J. and C. hold &c., and that is false, for she holds nothing; wherefore you must seek a new writ and draw a new concord, on account of the statute[1] which says "duly levied &c.": and the court is to see if the fine ought to be engrossed on such a concord, and one may as well abate a note as a writ. And he said moreover that a concord was drawn 12 years ago in this court of tenements which a woman held for the term of her life, as he who made the grant supposed, and she came into court by the Quid juris clamat, and said that she held by way of dower; and it was adjudged that she should go home, without attorning &c., because her acknowledgment was contrary to the concord as drawn.—Thereupon came A., who granted &c. and joined himself &c. And HENGHAM asked him if it was his deed: and he said Yes.—HENGHAM. Is the term past or not?—*Lanfar.* The term is not past; but we have paid the money &c., so that his estate is certain, and we pray judgment if he ought not to attorn.—HENGHAM. What have you to show that you have paid him?—*Lanfar.* Nothing &c.—*Spigurnel.* You ought to have an acquittance for the payment.—*Lanfar.* We will aver the payment to have been made &c.—HENGHAM. You have admitted the deed put forward by J. against you which states that he is to hold until you have paid him, and you have nothing which

[1] 27 Edw. I. st. 1. c. 1.

si noun com femme J.—*Lanfare.* Quei respond J.?— A.D. 1307.
Passeley. Il vous dist qe A. li lessa ces tenements a terme de seis anz. E estre ceo granta qil tendreit les tenements a lui e a ces heirs tant qe le dit A. ou ces heirs lui paiassent une certeine summe de aver; e mist avant fet qe ceo testmoigna; e demandoms jugement desicom sun estat est en noun certein e attornement covent qe soit sur certein point, jugement &c. sil &c. se devoit attorner.—*Spigurnel.* La fin ne se puet engrosser sur cele pees retrete, car la pees voet qe J. e C. tenent &c., e ceo est faux, qele ne tient rienz; par quei il covent quere novel bref e trere novele pees pur lestatut qe parle "rite levate &c.," e la court fet a vere si la fin deive engrosser sur tele pees retrete; e auxi bien puet home abatre note com bref: e dist outre qe une pees fust retrete a xii. anz de cy en ceste court des tenements qe une femme tient a terme de vie, a ceo qe celi qe grant supposa e ele vient en cort par le "Quid juris clamat," e dit qe ele tint en noun de dowere; e agarde fust qe ele alast a lostel sanz atturner &c., pur ceo qe sa conissance fust contrariant a la pees retrete.—E sur ceo vient A. qe graunta &c. e se joint &c.—Et Hengham lui demanda si ceo fust sun fet.—E il dist qe oil.—Hengham. Le quel est le terme passe ou noun?—*Lanfare.* Le terme nest mie passe, mes nous lui avoms paie les deners &c., issi qe sun estat est en certein, e demandoms jugement sil ne se deive atturner.—Hengham. Quei avez de ceo qe vous lui avez paie?—*Lanfare.* Rienz &c.—*Spigurnel.* Il vous covendreit aver aquitance de la paye.—*Lanfare.* Nous voloms averer la paye estre fet &c.—Hengham. Vous avez conu le fet qe J. met contre vous, qe voet qil tiegne tant qe vous luy eez paee, e vous navez rienz qe la

A.D. 1307. shows the payment: this court adjudges that J. do go, adieu, without day without attorning &c.

Essoin de malo veniendi cast after an inquest taken in a plea of dower, for the tenant &c.

§ A woman brought her writ of Dower against J., who came and pleaded to the inquest, which passed for the woman at the quinzein of Easter. And the parties were adjourned to hear their judgment on the verdict &c. to the octaves of Trinity, at which day he essoined himself de malo veniendi.—*Wileby.* The essoin does not lie after the verdict of an inquest has passed.—And nevertheless, HALES by general assent adjourned the essoin.

Where the demandant took title from the seisin of his ancestor in the time of king Henry, and the tenant said that king Richard enfeoffed &c. his ancestor, whose heir &c.; in consequence of which the matter did not proceed until the king was consulted.

§ John brought his writ of Cosinage against B. de Neville.—*Malmesthorpe.* King Richard was once on a time seised of the manor of C., of which manor these tenements are parcel, and he gave the manor with the appurtenances to H. de C., whose heir &c., to hold to him and his heirs for ever; and he bound &c.; and we do not think that you will hold this plea in the absence of the king;—and he put forward the charter of king Richard &c.—*Herle.* We have counted of the seisin of our ancestor in the time of king Henry; judgment if you ought to delay our plea by a deed of earlier date &c.—HENGHAM adjudged that the plea should remain without day until they had spoken with the king.

paie testmoigne; si agarde &c. qe J. aille a Deu sanz jour sanz atturner &c. A.D. 1307.

Essonium de malo veniendi jactum post inquisitionem captam in placito dotis pro tenente &c.

§ Une femme porta sun bref de dowere vers J., qe vient e pleda al enqueste, qe passa pur la femme a la quinzeine de Pasche. Et furent ajornez de oier lour jugement sur le verdit &c. as utaves de la Trinite, a quel jour se fist essoner de mal de venue.—*Willuby.* Lassoigne ne gist nent apres verdist denqueste passe: e nepurquant, HALES, de comune assent, adjorna lassoigne &c.

Ubi petens cepit titulum de seisina antecessoris sui de tempore regis Henrici, et tenens dicit regem Ricardum feoffasse &c. antecessorem suum, cujus heres &c., per quod non procedatur rege inconsulto.

§ Johan porta sun bref de cosinage vers B. de Neville.—*Malm.* Le roi Richard fust en ascon temps seisi del maner de C., de quel maner ceux tenements sunt parcele, e dona le maner ove les apurtenances a H. de C., qi heir &c., a tenir a luy e e ces heirs a touz jours, e obliga &c.; e nentendoms mye qe vous voillez ceo plee tenir sanz le roi; e mist avant la chartre le roi Ricard &c. — *Herle.* Nous avoms conte de la seisine nostre auncestre du temps le roi Henri; jugement si vous devez nostre plee targer par fet de plus haut temps &c.—HENGHAM agarda qe le plee demorast sanz jor tant qil eussent parle ove le roi.

A.D. 1307. Where, on avowry made upon a stranger, the plaintiff prayed aid of his wife who was not privy in any wise to that stranger.

§ A. brought a writ against C. who avowed &c. upon B. for rent &c.—*Willuby* (for A.). The tenement where the distress was made is my wife's purchase, without whom &c.: and we pray aid.—*Wescote.* Your wife is as much a stranger to our avowry as you are; judgment if aid &c.—*Willuby.* She was enfeoffed to her and her heirs, since the statute,[1] to hold of the chief lord &c.—STAUNTON. Where is the charter &c.—*Willuby.* It is not here, but we will bring it on another day.—STAUNTON. This is not properly aid; for aid is between privies &c.; but you pray that in order to charge or discharge the right of your wife you may bring her; wherefore, at your peril, bring her &c. on such a day.

Process in a writ of Right, after the tenant vouched a foreigner and brought the Supersedeas.

§ A man brought the writ in the city of London, and the tenant vouched to warranty, by aid of the king's court, John of Oxford, who was to be summoned in the county of Oxford; and on another day he brought the Supersedeas to the bailiffs &c., and sued out a writ of Warranty of charters in the Bench; the vouchee summoned did not come, on which day the tenant did not sue out any writ, and he had a day &c., on which day the sheriff returned a writ, and the party demandant came by writ of Right, and showed this process to the court; and it was said to the tenant that he should sue at his peril; and they had a day; the sheriff returned that the vouchee had neither lands nor tenements in his bailiwick &c.—*Herle* showed this thing to the court, and prayed that the tenant should be called for; and he made default.—STAUNTON (to the demandant). Sue a

---

[1] 18 Edw. I. Quia emptores.

Ubi, facta advocacione super extraneum, querens petit auxilium de uxore sua quæ illi extraneo in nullo fuit privata. A.D. 1307.

§ A. porta bref vers C. qe avowa &c. sur B.[1] pur rente &c.—*Willuby* (pur A.). Le tenement ou la destresse fust fete si est le purchas ma femme, sanz qi &c., e prioms aide.—*Wescote.* Vostre femme est auxi estraunge a nostre avowerie com vous; jugement si aide &c.—*Willuby.* Ele est feffe a luy e a ces heirs, pus le statut, a tenir del chief seignour &c.—STANTONE. Ou est la chartre &c.?—*Willuby.* Ele nest pas, mes nous la porteroms a un autre jour.—STANTONE. Ceo nest par proprement aide; qe aide est entre privez &c.; einz priez qe a charger ou descharger le dreit vostre femme vous la puisez amener; par quei en vostre peril amenez la &c. a tel jour.

Processus in brevi de recto, postquam tenens vocavit forinsecum et tulit le supersedeas.

§ Un homme porta le bref en la cite de Londres, e le tenant voucha a garantie, par eide de la cort le roi, Johan de Oxon, qe serra somons en le conte de Oxon; e al autre jour porta le supersedeas as baillifs &c., e suy bref de garantie de chartre en baunck; le vouche somons ne vynt point, a quel jour le tenant ne suy nul bref. e avoit jour &c., a quel jour le viconte retorna nul bref, e vient la partie demande par bref de droit e mustra ceo proces a la court; e dist fust au tenant qil suisit en sun peril; e avoient jour; le viconte retorna qe le vouche ne aveit terres ne tenements en sa baillye &c.—*Herle* moustra ceste chose a la cort, e pria qe le tenant fust demande; e il fist defaute.—STANTONE (ad petentem). Suiez bref hors

---

[1] MS. A.

A.D. 1307. writ, out of the rolls, to the mayor and to the bailiffs, as the statute directs &c.

An inquest regarding waste challenged.

§ *Roistone.* The sheriff was not personally present. — It was found by the sheriff's return that he was &c; so Roistone took nothing by that. — *Roistone.* He has returned that waste was done in hedges, where no waste ought to be adjudged; judgment. — MALLORE. We will forgive you that. — *Roistone.* He makes a return of waste committed in wood, namely 50 turf, where he should naturally have said oaks or an oak, and of waste in turf houses.— *Herle.* Be that as it may, there is other waste of wood found and returned. — MALLORE (having looked at the inquisition). We find in one place 50 turf, and in another place 10 oaks; what say you to that? — *Roistone.* This is a plaint which shall be disposed of by an inquest. — The justices having looked at the inquisiton, — STAUNTON said to *Herle,* Do you wish a new inquest? — *Herle* prayed that there might be one. — And he had it.

Where a man and his wife were vouched to warranty by their charter of a tenement which was the right of the wife.

§ One R. purchased tenements of a man and his wife, which were the right of the woman; and because the wife did not assent to levy the fine, he caused one Roger de Bykebyle to implead him &c., and he vouched to warranty the feoffor and his wife; and at the summons the husband made default, whereupon the Cape ad valentiam &c. of the whole, returnable now; again the husband made default, and the writ was served; and thereupon the wife came and said that the land taken was her right &c., and she prayed to be received; and she was received; and she asked by virtue of what he vouched her. — *Roistone* put forward a des roulles au meire e au baillifs, auxi com le statut voet &c. A.D. 1307.

Inquisicio de vasto calumpniata.

§ *Roistone.* Le viconte ne fut pas en propre persone. Et conpertum fuit per returnum vicecomitis quod sic &c.; nihil per hoc.—*Rostone.* Il ad returne de wast fet en hayes, ou nul wast deit estre ajuge; jugement. — MALLORRE. Ceo vous perdorroms. — *Roistone.* Il returne de wast fet en boys, saver l. bletrons, ou naturement serroit a dire cheines ou chene, e de wast en mesons bletrons. — *Herle.* De ceo soit com estre puet, il y ad autre wast de boys trove e returne.—MALORRE (inspecta inquisicione). Nous trovoms en un lu l. bletrons e en un altre leu x. cheynes; quei dites vous de ceo?—*Roistone.* Ceo est un pleinte qe serra servy par une enqueste. Et justiciarius visa inquisicione, — STANTONE a *Herle.* Volez novel enqueste? — *Herle* pria qe oil. Et habuit.

Ubi vir et uxor vocantur ad warrantiam per cartam suam de tenemento quod fuit jus uxoris.

§ Un R. purchassa tenements de un home e sa femme qe furent du droit la femme; e pur ceo qe la femme ne se assenti pas de lever la fin, il fist qe un Roger de Bykebyle li pleda &c., e il voucha a garantie le feffour e sa femme; e a la somonse le baron fist defaute, par quei le cape ad valentiam &c. del enter returnable a ore; derichief le baron fist defaute, e le bref fust servi; e sur ceo vient la femme e dist qe la terre prise fust sun droit &c., e pria estre receu; e fust receu; e demanda par quei il la voucha. — *Rostone* mist avant

A.D. 1307. charter which witnessed that her husband and she had given &c. and bound &c. to warranty &c. — STAUNTON. That is only the deed of her husband, and she by that deed ought not to be bound. — *Roistone.* It will not avail us as to the husband. — STAUNTON. You have vouched the husband and wife, and you have nothing to bind the wife, wherefore your voucher is worth nothing: you might have vouched the husband solely—*Roistone.* That would not have been in accordance with our specialty; and yet if two joint feoffees enfeoffed me and I vouched them &c.; although one of them has not &c. to recompense in value, I shall recover against the other who has &c.—STAUNTON. The case of joint feoffees is not similar to that of a man and his wife; for the wife is never vouched together with her husband unless she enfeoffed while sole, or came in by succession &c., or by fine levied &c.; and yet if you recover to the value, that will be of tenements taken &c.; and that you can not do, for they are the right of the wife who is not bound, and who will not warrant, for she has an action for the same tenements for which you wish to be warranted; nevertheless it is possible that the husband purchased; wherefore &c. — At another day MALLORE repeated &c., and said, For that you have nothing to bind &c. the woman except only this deed which was made by her under coverture and out of court, and relates to the right of the wife, for which an action remains &c., this court adjudges that as to the warranty she go quit, and that the demandant do recover seisin against the tenant, and that the tenant do recover in value against the husband if he have tenements which are not of the right of his wife, and if he have not, then let the tenant wait until such fall in &c.

Cui in vitâ. Where the writ was brought jointly against two, and one disclaimed in the freehold.

§ A woman brought &c. against A. and B.—*The Attorney* (for the tenants). A. tells you that he has nothing une chartre qe testmoigna qe sun baroun e il avoint done &c., e oblige &c. a la garrantie &c. — STANTONE. Cele nest mes qe le fet sun baroun, e ele par cel fet ne deit estre lye. — *Rostone.* Il ne nous vaudra en droit de sun baroun. — STANTONE. Vous avez vouche le baron e la femme, e a lier la femme ne avez rienz, par quei vostre voucher ne vaut rienz, e vous puissez aver vouche soulement le baron. — *Rostone.* Ceo eust este desacordant a nostre especialte; e jatardeis, deus joint feffez me enfeffereint, jeo les vouche &c., e tut ne eit lun &c. de faire a la value, jeo rescoveray vers lautre qe avera &c. — STANTONE. Non est simile en droit de joint feffez e un home e sa femme; qar la femme nert jammes vouche ove sun baron si ele sole ne enfeffast, ou par succession &c., ou par fin leve &c.; e jatardeys si vous rescoverez a la value, ceo ert des tenements pris &c., e ceo ne poez nent, qe eux sunt le droit la femme qe nest pas lye ne qe ne voet pas garantir, car ele ad accion a mesme les tenements des queux vous voillez estre garanti; nepurquant il est possible qe le baron purchasa; par quei &c. — Ad alium diem MALORRE repeta; E pur ceo qe vous navez rienz de lier &c. la femme fors qe soulement ceo fet qe fut fet suz la coverture sun baron e hors du court, e du dreit la femme dount accion la demoert &c., si agarde &c. qe en droit de ceste garantie ele aille quites, e qe le demandant rescovere seisine vers le tenant, e le tenant eit a la value del baron sil eit tenements qe ne seient pas du dreit sa femme, e si noun, attende donec acciderint &c. A.D. 1307.

Ubi breve fertur conjunctim versus duos, unus disclamat in libero tenemento. Cui in vita.

§ Une femme porta &c. vers A. e B. — *Attornatus pro tenentibus.* A. vous dist qil nad rienz &c. ne rienz

A.D. 1307. &c., nor does he now claim anything &c.; and B. tells you that he had entry by C. and not by her husband.—STAUNTON. Say it again.—*The Attorney.* Whereas she brings this writ jointly against A. and B., A. neither has anything, nor claims anything, nor ever had anything &c., judgment of the writ &c. — STAUNTON. This is another way of pleading.—*The woman.* He was joint tenant as the writ &c., on the day &c., ready &c.—*The Attorney.* Not so, ready &c.—And afterwards she prayed leave &c. for a writ &c.

Debt. Where, one executor being dead, the other executor sued without the executor of his co-executor.

§ Leonard le Tavener, executor &c., brought the writ against R. son of Matthew, and demanded 50*l.*—*Hunte.* Show that you are executor.—And he showed the testament, in which one John was named as the other executor. —*Hedone.* He is dead; wherefore &c.—*Hunte.* His executors are alive; judgment if without them &c.—And it was adjudged by HENGHAM and SPIGURNEL that that exception was of no avail to quash the writ, and that one executor may in such a cause well sue.—*Hedone* put forward a deed &c.—*Hunte.* In satisfaction of that debt, we, at such a time, leased to your testator our manor of T. in the county of Southampton to hold &c., and this writing was by the assent &c. delivered to one John, to hold the same until the end of the term, which manor your testator had for the whole of the term, and after his death, John &c., to whom the writing &c., by collusion &c. delivered that writing to the executors &c.; judgment &c.—*Herle.* All the force of the argument is that he had the manor in satisfaction. And inasmuch as we allege a thing of which the country can have cognisance, and not a payment of money made in a room, and are ready to aver, judgment &c. — *Spigurnel.* Why did not you take back the writing when &c.?—*Hunte.* We have told how by deceit he came by the writing.—HENGHAM. You ne cleime &c. a ore; e B. vous dist qil avoit entre par C[1] e noun pas par son baron.—STANTONE. Dites uncore. *Attorne.* La ou ele porte cestui bref joyntement vers A. e B., A. nad rienz, ne rienz ne cleime, ne rienz ne avoit &c., jugement du bref &c.—STANTONE. Ceo est un autre manere de pleder.—*La femme.* Tenant joyntement auxi com le bref &c. le jour &c. prest &c.—*Attorne.* Qe noun, prest &c. Et postea petiit licentiam &c. de brevi &c. A.D. 1307.

Ubi, mortuo uno executore, alter executor petiit sine executore sui co-executoris.

§ Leonard le Taverner, executour &c., porta le bref vers R. le fiz Matheu, e demanda .l. livres &c.—*Hunte.* Mustrez qe vous estes executour.—Et monstravit testamentum in quo nominabatur quod Johannes alter executor.—*Hedone.* Il est mort, par quei &c.—*Hunte.* Ces executours sunt en vie; jugement si sanz eux &c.: e fust agarde par HENGHAM SPIGURNEL quod illa exceptio non valuit pro brevi cassando, et quod satis bene potest unus executor in tali casu petere.—*Hedone* mist avant fet &c.—*Hunte.* En allowance de cele dette, teu temps &c. lessames a vostre testator nostre maner de T. en le conte de Suthampton, a tenir &c.; issi qe cest escrist fust par assent &c. livere a un Johan, a tenir tant qe au fin du terme, le quel maner vostre testator avoit tut le terme, e apres sa mort, Johan &c., a qi lescrist &c., par collusion &c. cel escrist livera as executours &c.; jugement &c.—*Herle.* Tote la force est qil avoit le maner en allowance. E desicom nous aleggoms chose de quei pays puet aver conissance, e noun pas suite de deners fet en chambre, e sumes prest daverer, jugement &c.—*Spigurnel.* Qe neussez vous pris lescrist devers vous quant &c.?—*Hunte.* Nous avom dist coment par desceite il avynt De debito.

[1] MS. B.

A.D. 1307. cannot deny that this is the deed of your testator, and you have nothing shewing payment which can be received against the writing; this court adjudges that Leonard &c. do recover his damages taxed by the Court &c.

Replevin. Avowry for escuage was made by the heir, and the tenant alleged that he was assigned in respect of his services to a certain woman tenant in dower &c., so &c.

§ The prior of Tanrigge complained that Martin Scheuche and Clarice his wife tortiously took his beasts &c.—*Passeley.* We avow the taking &c., for the reason that the prior holds of one Roland &c. a messuage, three virgates and a half of land, by homage fealty and escuage &c., and relief after the death of each prior, that is to say &c., and by suit &c; of which services &c. the said R. was seised &c.; then after the death of the said R. these services descended to Clarice our wife and Avice and two other sisters (whom he named) as sisters &c., which two others died without heirs of their bodies, and their shares descended to Clarice and Avice, and Avice granted her purparty to Martin and Clarice &c., on which grant the said prior attorned for his services, by which attornment we ourselves are seised at the hand of the prior &c. of the fealty suit and the rent &c.; and for that the escuage for the 31st year was in arrear to us, that is to say &c., and we had a writ &c. and did the service in Scotland, we avow the taking &c.—*Toudeby.* You can not avow on us for escuage for the 31st year, for at that time we performed our services to one Christiana who was the wife of Roland, to whom our services were assigned &c. for dower.—*Passeley.* At the time when the king granted to us his writ to take escuage from our tenants when the escuage was assessed by the king and earls and barons, you were our tenant; ready &c.—STAUNTON. Although you were well enough in respect of your services assigned to Chritiana who held in dower, she of those services, to wit the escuage, al escrist.—Hengham. Vous ne poez dedire qe ceo nest le fet vostre testator, ne rienz ne moustrez de la suite qe contre lescrist soit acceptable; si agarde &c. qe Leonard &c. rescovere ces damages taxez par la cort &c. A.D. 1307.

Advocacio pro scutagio facta per heredem, et tenens allegavit se fore assignatum de servitiis suis cuidam mulieri tenenti in dote &c., ideo &c. **Replegiare.**

§ Le priour de Tanrigge se pleint ke Martin Scheuche e Clarice sa femme atort pristrent ces avers &c.—*Passeley.* Nous avowoms la prise &c., par la reson qe le priour entyent de un Rouland &c. un mees, treis vergez de terre e demi, par homage fealte e escuage &c., e relef apres le desces de chescon priour, ceo est a saver &c., e par suite &c., des queux services &c. mesme celui R. fut seisi &c.; dount apres le deces le dist R., ces services descendirent a Clarice nostre femme e Avice e altres deus soers, quas nominavit, com as soers &c.; les queles deus &c. devierent sanz heir de lour corps; dount descendirent lour purparties a Clarice e a Avice, [e Avice] sa purpartie granta a Martin e a Clarice &c., par quel grant le dit priour se atturna de ces services, par quel atturnement nous meme sumes seisi par my la main le priour &c. de la fealte, suite, e de la rente &c.; e pur ceo qe lescuage del an .xxxi. nous est arere, cest a saver &c., e nous avioms bref &c. e feymes les services en Escoce, si avowoms la prise &c.—*Toudeby.* Del an .xxxi. ne poez sur nous pur escuage avowerie faire, car a teu temps esteymes de nos services entendanz a une Christiene qe fust la femme Roland a qi nos services furent assignez &c. en dowere. — *Passeley.* Au temps qe le roi nous granta sun bref del escuage aver de nos tenants quant lescuage fust assis par le roi e countes e barons, vous fustes nostre tenant; prest &c. —Stantone. Tut fuissez vous assez vous assigne de vos services a Christiene qe tyent en dowere, ele de teux services, saver escuage, ne poez rien demander; e eux

A.D. 1307. can not demand anything; and they say that Christiana held her dower of those who of this were warrantors to her; and escuage is a royal service which naturally shall be given to him who does the services for which it is given, and this is his fee, and the services will not be extinguished; wherefore it seems that he ought to have it.—*Toudeby.* Our services are not extinguished since we are assigned to Christiana, for she will take them; or if they were to be in arrear in her life, for her time, her executors will have them.—HENGHAM. Not the escuage. —*Toudeby.* Neither at the time of the assessing of the escuage nor at the time when the king granted to him his writ &c., did we hold of him; ready &c.; and he avows as purchaser, which is very different from his avowing as heir.—*Passeley.* We are partly purchasers and partly heir; and what you say cannot be; for eight years ago Avice acknowledged her purparty of the manor of T. to be the right of Martin and Clarice, and yielded it to them by fine in this court, and granted that her purparty of these services which Christiana held in dower, and ought to revert to her, should remain to Martin and Clarice; on which grant Christiana attorned to us for her fealty for the whole of her dower; and so this Christiana held wholly &c. of us; judgment &c.—*Toudeby.* You are wrong; for after the death of Christiana, the division of that dower was made between you, and our services, in satisfaction of others &c., were assigned to John de Haume and to this Avice his wife who you say granted to you &c., and we in respect of that were intendant to them until within this year when they granted to you by fine &c.; ready &c.—STAUNTON. Do you wish to defeat the first fine whereof they speak?—*Willeby.* We speak ex post facto.—*Passeley.* We are one of the heirs, and you can not by any other way escape &c.; but for that you say that at the time &c. you were intendant to Christiana who held in dower, [we say] that she can not demand those services nor do they belong to her, but dient qe Christiene entynt sun dowere de eux qe de ceo lui furent garaunz; e escuage si est real service qe naturelment serra done a lui qe fet les services par quei il est done, e ceo est sun fee, e les services ne serra mie esteinz; par quei il semble qil le deit aver.—*Toudeby.* Nos services ne sunt mie esteinz quaunt nous sumes assignez a Christiene, car ele les prendra; ou sil la furent arere en sa vie de son temps, ces executours les averont.—HENGHAM. Noun pas escuage.—*Toudeby.* Ne au temps del asseer del escuage ne au temps qe le roi lui granta sun bref &c. nous ne tenimes pas de lui, prest &c.; e il avowe com purchassour, qe mult ert autre qe sil ne eust avowe com heir.—*Passeley.* De partie sumes nous purchasors e de partie heir; e ceo qe vous dites ne puet estre; car passez .viii. anz Avice conussoit sa purpartie du maner de T. estre le dreit Martin e Clarice, e ceo lour rendy par fin en ceste cort, e granta qe sa purpartie de ces services qe Christiene tyent en dowere e a lui devoit revertir remanissent a Martin e a Clarice; par queu graunt Christiene se atturna a nous de sa fealte pur lenter de son dowere, e issint tint ceste Cristiene enterement &c. de nous; jugement &c.—*Toudeby.* Vous dites mal; qar apres la mort Cristiene la purpartie de cel dowere fust fete entre vous, e nos services en allowance de autres &c. assignez a Johan de Haume e a cesti Avice sa femme qe vous dites qe vous graunta &c., e nous de ceo a eux fumes entendanz tant ke denz cest an ke eux vous graunterent par fin &c., e prest &c.—STAUNTONE. Volez defere la primere fin dount eux parlent?—*Willuby.* Nous parloms ex post facto.—*Passeley.* Nous sumes un des heirs, e vous ne poez par autre veye esturtre &c.; mes pur ceo qe vous dites qe au temps &c. vous estoiez entendant a Cristiene qe tyent en dowere, qe ceux services ne poet demander ne a lui ne affereit, einz naturel- A.D. 1307.

A.D. 1307. naturally belong to the heirs, and we pray judgment &c. --*Toudeby.* Still you can not avow for the whole.—*Passeley.* We had the whole by heritage and by the grant of Avice, ready &c.—*Toudeby.* After Christiana's death our services were assigned to John and to Avice, as Avice's share, in satisfaction of the other &c., and to them have we been intendant until a year ago when they granted those services to you, ready &c.—And the other side said the contrary; therefore &c.

Jure de utrum.

§ In a writ of Utrum, *Roistone* said, Whereas he calls it a church, it is only a chapel, and if it be found &c. we say that it is not frank-almoigne &c.; and that our father gave these tenements to one T. to find a chantry in the said chapel on this condition that whenever the chantry ceased it should be lawful for him or his heirs to enter that land &c. And for that the chantry is not kept up, he has entered as heir. — *Spigurnel.* You have at least granted possession to the church: what have you to show the form whereof you speak ?—*Roistone.* The main matter of my plea falls within the cognisance of a jury; and it is that the tenements are not frank-almoigne &c. — *Spigurnel.* Then the other is only an evidence. — And nevertheless if the plaintiff had held well to the challenge which Spigurnel &c., it seems because he had at first put the church in possession, he could not turn her out of that possession without a special deed.

Where one coming in who was not named in the writ was received to defend his right &c.

§ The tenant made default after default, wherefore &c.; and there came one W. who said that the tenant had nothing &c. except at his will, and that he had delivered the said land to him for the purpose of sowing it, and he prayed that for any default &c., and prayed to be received &c. — *Stapeltone.* Tenant of the freehold on the day when the writ was purchased, ready &c. — *Trig.* Had he no other thing but the freehold ? for although ment as heirs, e demandoms jugement &c. — *Toudeby.* Uncore ne poez pas avower pur lenter.—*Passeley.* Nous aviom lenter qe de heritage qe de grant Avice, prest &c. — *Toudeby.* Apres la mort Cristiene nos services esteinz assignez a Johan e a Avice &c., cum purpartie Avice, en allowance de altres &c., e a eux sumes entendanz tant ke ore a un an ke eux ceux services vous graunterent, prest &c. Et alii e contra. Ideo &c. A.D. 1307.

§ *Roistone.* La ou il la nome eglise, ele nest mes chapele, e si trove soit, vous dioms qe ceo nest pas franche aumoingne &c.; qe nostre pere dona ceux tenements a un T. a trover un chanterie en la dite chapele sur tele condicion qe a quele houre qe home de ceste chanterie cessereit, a lui ou a ces heirs cele terre entrer &c. E pur ceo qe cele chanterie nest mes sustenue, si est il entre come heir. — *Spigurnel.* Vous avez au meynz grante possession al eglise; quei avez vous de cele forme dount vous parlez? — *Roistone.* Le gros de mon dist cheit en conissance de jure, qe est qe les tenements ne sunt pas franche aumoingne &c. — *Spigurnel.* Donqes nest lautre mes qe une evidence. Et tamen si pars petens bene se tenuisset ad calumpniam quam Spigurnel &c., videtur quod ex quo primo ecclesiam in possessione induxit, illam ab illa possessione sine facto speciali non potest ejicere. De jure de utrum.

Ubi superveniens non nominatus in brevi admittebatur pro jure defendendo &c.

§ Le tenant fist defaute apres defaute, par quei &c.; e survyent en W. qe dist tenant navoit rienz &c. mes qe a sa volente, e qe il lui avoit la dite terre baille a semer a champt, e pria qe par nule defaute &c., e pria estre receu &c.—*Stapeltone.* Tenant de franc tenement le jour du bref purchace prest &c. — *Trig.* Navoit il autre chose mes qe le franc tenement? car tut eust il

A.D. 1307. he had had the freehold &c. and not the fee, he in whom the fee &c. ought to be received. — *Willuby.* W. who prays to be received has nothing now in the freehold, ready &c. — *Hamptone.* Nor had he on the day when the writ was purchased. — *Willuby.* We have nothing to do with that; he now prays to be received, and it is sufficient for us to make him now of such an estate that he ought not to be received.—And this averment was admitted in the same way in which Willuby offered it, and W. found security for the mesne profits in accordance with the statute [1] &c.

Of tenements given in fee-tail, where it was excepted against a tenant alleging non-tenure &c.

§ The countess Marshal brought her writ against Nicholas de Segrave and Alice his wife, and demanded the manor of F.—*Toudeby* did not count otherwise than in this way, Seised in the time of the present king &c. —*Tiltone.* We can not yield it up; for on the day of the purchase of the writ and down to this day one John del Idle was and is tenant of a carucate of land of the demesne of the said manor; judgment &c.—*Toudeby.* By whose lease? — *Tiltone.* By John's lease. — *Toudeby.* To hold of whom? — *Tiltone.* What is that to you? he has the freehold, and is tenant, and was on the day &c., and that you can not deny; judgment &c. — *Toudeby.* It is something to us; for if he be enfeoffed to hold of you &c., thereby is not the description of the manor changed, for you are not tenant thereof in demesne and in service, and we demand it as a manor. — MALLORE asserted this, and wished to drive the party to answer. —*John de K.* John was enfeoffed.—*Herle.* There is no need; for before the statute [2] it was lawful for any one to enfeoff &c. to hold of himself, and at that time he might allege non-tenure. — *Passeley* (on the same side).

---

[1] 20 Edw. I. st. 3.

[2] 18 Edw. I. Quia emptores.

eu le franc tenement &c. e noun pas le fee, celuy en qi le fee &c. debet admitti.—*Willuby.* W. qe prie estre receu nad rienz en le franc tenement a ore, prest &c. —*Hamptone.* Ne navoit le jour du bref purchace.—*Willuby.* De ceo navoms qe faire; ore prie il estre receu, e de luy fere ore de tel estat qil ne deit estre receu nous suffit. Et admittebatur ista verificacio eodem modo quo Willuby pretendit, et W. invenit securitatem de exitibus medii temporis prout statutum &c. A.D. 1307.

De tenementis datis in feodum talliatum, ubi excipitur contra tenentem allegantem non tenuram &c.

§ La contesse Mareschal porta sun bref vers Nichol de Segrave e Alice sa femme, e demanda le maner de F.—*Toudeby* non narravit[1] aliter quam sic, seisi en le temps le roi qe ore est &c.—*Tiltone.* Nous ne poms rendre; car le jour du bref purchace e hui ceo jour si en est un Johan del Idle tenant de une carue de terre del demeyne de mesme le maner; jugement &c.—*Toudeby.* De qi lees?—*Tiltone.* Du lees Johan.—*Toudeby.* A tenir de qi?—*Tiltone.* Qe est ceo a vous? il ad le franc tenement, e est tenant, e fust le jour &c., e ceo ne poez dedire; jugement &c.—*Toudeby.* Si est; qar sil soit feffe a tenir de vous &c., par tant nest pas noun de maner change, qe vous nestes de cel tenant en demeyne e en service, e nous demandoms par maner.—MALLORRE hoc asserebat, e voleit aver chace la partie a respondre.—*Johan de K.* Johan fust feffe.—*Herle.* Nest pas mester; car avant statut bien lireit a chescon home feffer &c. a tenir de luy meyme, e en tel temps poeit alegger noun-tenure.—*Passeley* (ad

[1] MS. variavit.

A.D. 1307. If John were enfeoffed to hold of us by the services of 20*s*., and she were to recover of us as against the tenant of the manor of F., she would recover also the rent of 20*s*. whereof she was not ever seised; and she counts of her own seisin. —*Scotre* (on the same side). If she had recovered the manor, what avowry would she make for the 20*s*., since according to her statement she was purchaser of the manor, and she can not be aided by the estate of any of her ancestors. — *Toudeby.* On the day &c., tenant of the whole &c. according as it was in our seisin, ready &c.—And the other side said the contrary.—Therefore &c.

Writ of Right according to the custom of a manor, by Recordari &c.

William of Wykeham brought the writ against the abbat of Chichester, who caused the plea to be removed into the Bench by a Recordari, of which the cause ran thus,—because the said abbat holds these tenements by the gift of king John our grandfather &c.—*Lanfar* counted, and offered suit and proof according to the custom of the manor.—*Passeley* denied &c., and (said he) we tell you that this is our frank fee, whereof the king &c. enfeoffed &c., by this charter, one &c. our predecessor; judgment of the writ.—*Lanfar.* Our ancestor, of whose seisin we have counted, was &c. seised since that time, and held it in sokemanry; ready &c.; and although the services &c. issuing out of those tenements are comprised in that charter, yet the soil is not.—STAUNTON. If a rent were given &c., then were those tenements holden of his predecessor; and if they were held of him, and are now come into his hands by escheat or otherwise, now it is frank-fee in his person.—*Herle.* It must needs be frank-fee in the person of him who can make it frank-fee, that is the lord of the tenements &c.; it was not comprised in the charter, ready &c.—*Toudeby.* With what object idem). Si Johan fust feffe a tenir de nous par les services de .xx. souz, e ele rescoverast de nous com vers tenant du maner de F., e ele rescovereit issint la rente de .xx. souz dount ele nestoit unqes seisie; e ele counte de sa seisine demene.—*Scotre* (ad idem). Si ele eust rescovere le maner, quele avowerie freit ele pur les .xx. souz, del houre qele, a son dist, fust purchaceresse du maner, e par estat de nul de ces auncestres purra estre aide.—*Toudeby.* Le jour &c. tenant del enter &c. solom ceo qil fust en nostre seisine, prest &c.—Et alii e contra.—Ideo &c. A.D. 1307.

De recto secundum consuetudinem manerii per recordari &c.

§ Willem de Wykham porta le bref vers labbe de Cycestre, qe fist cele parole remuer en Baunk par un recordari dount la cause fust tele,—pur ceo qe le dit abbe tyent ces tenements de doun le roi Johan nostre ael &c.—*Lanfare* conta, e tendi suite e dreigne solom la coustume du maner.—*Passeley* defendi &c., e vous dioms qe ceo est nostre franc fee, e dount le roi &c. enfeffa &c. par ceste chartre un &c. nostre predecessour; jugement du bref.—*Lanfare.* Nostre auncestre, de qi seisine nous avom conte, fust &c. seisi pus cel temps, e le tyent en sokemanerie, prest &c.; e tut seont les services &c. issanz de ceux tenements comprises denz cele chartre, jatardeis le soil ne i est pas. —Stantone. Si une rente fust done &c., donqes furent ceux tenements tenuz de son predecessour; e si eux furent tenux de luy, e a ore devenuz en sa mayn par eschete ou par altre veie, ore est il franc fee en sa persone.—*Herle.* Il covent qil soit franc fee en la persone celi qe le purra fere franc fee, qe est le seignour les tenements &c.; noun pas comprise denz la chartre, prest &c. — *Toudeby.* A quel fet qe se ten-

A.D. 1307. is that averment offered?—STAUNTON. If it be found that it is not comprised, the plea will not be pleadable.—*Toudeby.* He admits that it is pleadable so far as he has counted against us, judgment &c.; and at least by his statement, that the services were comprised in the charter &c., and so that the seignory belonged to the abbat, which tenements are now come into the hands of the abbat &c., and he has made them frank-fee; for if the tenant in sokemanry were to purchase against his lord in whose person the tenement is frank-fee, he would not purchase by such a writ.—*Lanfar.* Still I did not admit that the rent &c. was comprised &c.—*Friskeney.* He offered suit and proof according to the custom; wherefore, it does not seem that by his count he admits it to be frank-fee. — STAUNTON. If he affirmed it by his count, what need had you to have put forward the king's charter, after the count &c., to prove it to be frank-fee. —*Herle.* Although we put forward a thing which proves what he admitted, that does not matter, and he ought at first to have made protestation that he was not obliged to plead thereto.—Afterwards STAUNTON (having consulted HENGHAM) said, Although he has pleaded foolishly, it is for us to look at our power, and we will not part with this business without trying the truth.—And it was adjudged that the averment should go in the form before mentioned. — *Lanfar* pretended that if the averment went against the abbat, the plea would return, but if for him, that the writ would abate.—*Lanfar.* We think &c. that if against the abbat, we shall recover seisin &c. —STAUNTON. Never by this court and by this writ.—In a similar writ the sheriff did not return the original; so the parties could do nothing; but HENGHAM ordered that the demandant should have a writ out of the rolls to cause the original to come &c.

dreit cel averement?—STANTONE. Si trove soit qe ne mye compris, le plee ne serreit mie pledable.—*Toudeby.* Il grante qe soit pledable si par tant qil ad conte vers vous, jugement &c.; e jadumeynz par sun dist qil dist qe les services furent compris denz la chartre &c., e issint qe la seignourye &c. fust al abbe, queux tenements sunt ore devenuz en la mayn labbe &c. e si les ad il fet franc; qar si le tenant en sokemanerye se purchacereit vers sun seignour en qi persone le tenement est franc fee, il ne se purchacereit par tiel bref.—*Lanfare.* Uncore ne grantay jeo pas qe la rente &c. fust compris &c.—*Friskeney.* Il tendi suite e dreine solom la coustume; pur quei il ne semble pas qe par counte le eit grante estre franc fee. —STANTONE. Sil afferma par counte, quel mestier aviez vous de aver mys avant chartre le roi, pus le counte &c., de prover les estre franc fee.—*Herle.* Tut meissoms nous avant chose qe prove ceo qil granta, ceo ne mist pas, e il devoit a deprimes aver fet protestacion qil ne devoit mie si pleder.—Postea STANTONE, consulto HENGHAM. Tut eit il folement plede, a nous est de vere nostre poer, e nous ne voloms nent ceste chose tresailler sanz la verite trier. Et consideratur verificacionem fieri in forma qua prius &c.—*Lanfare* pretend issint, qe si le averement passe encontre labbe, la parole retornereit; si pur luy, le bref abatereit.—*Lanfare.* Nous entendoms &c. qe si contre labbe, de rescoverir seisine &c.—STANTONE. Jammes par ceste cort e par ceo bref.—A un autel bref le viconte ne retornera mye le original; par quei les parties ne poeint rienz faire, einz fust agarde par HENGHAM qe le demandant eust bref hors des roulles de fere venir le original &c. A.D. 1307.

A.D. 1307. Where he who brought the writ, in his own right claimed nothing in the wardship but claimed as a buyer, of which the writ spoke nothing, and so it was challenged.

Ravishment of ward.

§ William son of Matthew brought the writ against Marmaduke de Tweng and others named &c.: and it was in accordance with the statute of Westminster,[1] thus, "to show why, with force and arms, William son " and heir &c. under the age &c., whose marriage to the " said William belongs, found at T., they ravished."—*Lanfar.* Tortiously they came with force &c. and William son and heir &c. whose marriage to the said W. belongs, and for the reason that Walter de Fauconberg, of whom S. the father of the said William held such and such tenements by knight-service (and he specified the tenements and the services) leased it to him, by which lease he was seised of the wardship &c., and in his seisin &c. found at T., they ravished &c. — *Herle.* The writ says, " whose marriage to him belongs," which implies that it is his in his own right, and in counting he says that it belongs to him by reason of the lease &c.; judgment of the variance.—*Tiltone.* We cannot in our case have any other writ in the Chancery; and the writ says that the marriage belongs to us, and that is the truth, and by what way we will in counting show to you. — *Herle.* The statute says that "if the plaintiff die before the " plea be determined, and the marriage belong to him by " reason of his own fee, the plea shall be resummoned at " the suit of the heir; but if the right belong to him by " title of gift or sale, it shall be resummoned at the suit " of his executors." If then this writ be good which does not make mention of the title of the plaintiff, but gives ground to suppose that it was by a gift &c., if he were to die the writ of resummons would have to be granted, and his heir might use it, which is against the statute; wherefore &c.—Hengham. The statute which

[1] 13 Edw. I. (Westm. 2), c. 35.

Ubi ille qui tulit breve jure suo nil clamavit in custodia, sed emptione, de qua nihil loquitur breve: Et ideo fuit calumpniatum &c. A.D. 1307.

Ravissement de garde.

§ Willem le fiz Matheu porta bref vers Marmaduke de Tweng e autres nomez &c. Et fuit forma secundum statutum Westminstriæ sic, "ostensurus quare vi "et armis Willielmum filium et heredem &c., infra "etatem &c., cujus maritagium ad ipsum Willielmum "pertinet, apud T. inventum, rapuere."—*Lanfare.* Atort vyendrent a force &c., e Willem fiz e heir &c. qi maria[ge] a mesme celui [W.] apent, e par la resoun qe Wauter de Facomberge de qi S. pere le dit Willem tient taunt des tenements par service de chivaler (et nominavit quæ tenementa et per quæ servitia &c.) celui lessa, par quel lees il fust seisi de la garde &c., e en sa seisine &c. a T. trove ravirent &c.—*Herle.* Le bref dist "cujus maritagium ad ipsum pertinet," qe donne entendement qe ceo est de sun droit demeyne, e en contant dist il qe a lui apent par reson du lees &c.; jugement de la variance.—*Tiltone.* Nous ne poums autre bref aver en nostre cas en la Chancelerie, e le bref dist qe le mariage a nous apent, e ceo est la verite, e par quele veie nous le moustroms en contant.—*Herle.* Le statut dit "quod si querens obierit ante placitum "deductum, et maritagium ei competebat ratione pro-"prii feodi, resummoneatur loquela ad sectam heredis "sui; si titulo donationis seu venditionis, resummone-"atur ad sectam executorum suorum;" si donqe cest bref soit bon qe ne fet mye mencion de title le pleintif, eynz fet a supposer qe de doun &c., sil morust, bref de resumons ert a graunter, e user le poeit sun heir, quod est contra statutum; par quei &c. — HENGHAM. Statut qe lui taille ceste accion lui donne sur cele

A.D. 1307. frames this action for him, gives him such a writ on that action; wherefore we think it to be in good form.—*Single.* We did not come with force or with arms or against the peace, but with the peace; and for the reason that the said S., father of William, held &c., and of Alice our wife &c. by knight-service &c., of which services we &c. seised, and he died in our homage, and we immediately after the death of the said S. our tenant, seized the body of the said William &c., because the marriage &c., and we brought him, as well &c., without tort &c.—*Tiltone.* It may be that S. held by knight-service of Walter our feoffor and of them divers tenements; then, since in avowry he can allege priority of seignory in their persons, judgment &c.—HENGHAM. Allege it, if you think it well to do so; he says that the wardship belongs to him; make then, in order to have the wardship, your estate better if you can than his.—*Tiltone.* S. &c. held the tenements &c. of Walter our lessor by priority to them, ready &c.—STAUNTON. You plead closely: in what writ are you that you do not aver your writ?—*Tiltone.* Whereas he says that freshly after the death of S. &c. he seized &c., he says wrongly: Walter our lessor was seised of him, and we after his lease were seised of him, until by force he ravished him, as our writ states, ready &c.—*Herle.* We have pleaded, and although it were so as you say, which we do not admit, we were well entitled to do so since we had right to the wardship.—STAUNTON. In a "command that he yield up the wardship &c." would not the defendant have his voucher?—*Herle.* He would.—STAUNTON. And it may be that his lessor had no right in the wardship; and though he have not a recovery against him by his voucher, of which recovery if you oust him by your ravishment, do you not work a tort against him? to which tort, according to what you say, there is no need to answer.—*Herle.* If I have right I do him no wrong; and in the case of which you speak he will have his recovery against the lessor when he is ousted accion tel bref; par quei nous le entendoms estre de bone forme.—*Single.* Nous ne venymes pas a force ne a armes ne encontre la pees, einz ove la pees, e par la reson qe meisme celi S. pere W. &c. entyent &c., et de Alice nostre femme &c. par service de chivaler &c., des queux service nous &c. seisi, e morust en nostre homage; e nous, meyntenant apres la mort le dit S. nostre tenant, seisimes le corps le dist W. &c. pur ceo qe le mariage &c., e luy amenames, com bien &c. sanz tort &c.—*Tiltone.* Il purra estre qe S. tient par service de chivaler e de Wauter nostre lessour e de eux divers tenements; dount del houre qe en avowerie il puet alegger priorite de seignourye en lour persones, jugement &c. — HENGHAM. Alleggez vous si vous quidez bien faire; il dist qe la garde a lui apent; fetes vous donqes vostre estat meillour si vous poez pur ceste garde aver qe soen.—*Tiltone.* S. &c. tient par priorite les tenements &c., de Wauter nostre lessour qe de eux, prest &c.—STANTONE. Vous pledez nycement: en quel bref estes vous qe naverez vostre bref?—*Tiltone.* La ou il dist qe freschement apres la mort S. &c. seisi &c., il dist mal: Wauter nostre lessour esteit seisi de lui demene, e nous pus sun lessour demene, tant qe a force le ravist com nostre bref dist, prest &c. — *Herle.* Nous avoms plede, e tut fut il issi com vous dites, qe nous ne grantoms pas, nous le poems bien faire del houre qe nous avioms droit en la garde.—STANTONE. A un precipe quod reddat custodiam &c. ne avereit le defendant sun voucher? — *Herle.* Si avera.—STANTONE. E purra estre qe sun lessour ne avoit nul dreit en la garde; e tut ne eit il vers luy rescoverer par sun voucher, de quel rescoverer si vous luy ostez par vostre ravissement, ne luy fetes vous tort, a quel tort, a ceo qe vous dites, nest pas mester de respondre.—*Herle.* Si jeo ey dreit jeo ne ly face nul tort; e en le cas de quei vous parlez il avera sun rescoverir vers le lessour A.D. 1307.

A.D. 1307. of his . . . by writ of covenant.—*Warr.* (sitting in the Bench). He who has right &c. never does ravishment or tort when he seizes the infant &c. whilst he is under age.—*Herle.* We will not replead; we have rejoined the averment. And the averment stood, in the way in which *Tilton* before offered it, to wit regarding the priority &c.

[Annuity.] Where the defendant said that his father was in prison when he made the deed &c.

§ In a writ of Annuity which was brought against W. de Meuille, — *Hedone* counted the common count, and to affirm his count put forward a deed in these terms, viz. that Henry the father, whose heir &c., had granted and given 100*s*., and bound his lands &c. to distress, and that if it happened that he could not &c. find a distress, then he bound himself and his heirs to pay the said annuity out of his coffers. — *Herle.* The deed which he puts forward does not state that he is to have an action whilst he can find a distress &c., and he has not said, in counting, that he can not find a distress; judgment &c. — *Scotre.* When there are two ways he may use which he pleases; now although he may take steps by way of distress, nevertheless, there is the annuity. — *Herle.* By that deed he can not demand anything, for at the time of the making &c. he who made it was in prison at Ripon, ready &c. — *Scotre.* What we have said is sufficient, and if you think it is not, admit our statement and let us go to judgment. — And it was adjudged that the answer was sufficient. — *Hedone.* He was not in prison on the day of which we have counted, which is stated in the date of the writing. — *Herle.* You may put what date you please, but whatever date &c. we tell you that at the time of the making &c. we were in prison &c. ready &c. — STAUNTON. Our style of entry is to say "at the time of quant il est oste de sun . . . . [1] par bref de covenant.—*Warr.* (sedens in banco). Celui qi ad dreit &c. ne fet jammes ravissement ne tort quel houre quil seisi lenfant &c. de taunt com il soit denz age.—*Herle.* Nous ne repledroms, nous avoms rejoynt le averement. Et stetit verificacio modo quo prius *Tiltone* pretendit, saver de priorite &c. A.D. 1307.

Ubi defendens dixit patrem suum esse in prisona quando fecit factum &c. per quod &c. interrogante querente in curia prisoñ, ad quod non est necesse respondere.

§ En le bref dannuyte qe fust porte vers W. de Meuille, — *Hedone* conta comune counte, e de affermer sun counte mist avant tel fet, scilicet qe le pere Henri, qi heir, avoit grante e done cent souz e oblige ces terres &c. a la destresse, e sil avyent qil ne poeit &c. destresse trover, adonqes il [obliga] lui e ces heirs a paier hors de ces coffres la dite annuite. — *Herle.* Le fet qil met avant ne voet pas qil eit accion &c. tant qil puisse destresse trover &c. &c., e il nad pas dist en contant qil ne purra destresse trover, jugement &c. — *Scotre.* Quant ily ad deus veies &c. il purra user la quele qe voudra; dount tut puet il avener par veye de destresse, jatardeys il lui ad annuite. — *Herle.* Par cel fet ne puet il rien demander, car en temps de la confeccion &c. si fut il qe fit &c. enprisone a Ripon, prest &c. — *Scotre.* Ceo qe nous avoms dist suffit; e si vous quidez qe noun, grantez nostre dist e seoms a jugement. Et consideratur responsionem fore sufficientem. —*Hedone.* Noun pas en prisone au jour qe nous avoms conte qe est nome en la date del escrist.—*Herle.*[2] Vous i purriez mettre quel date qe vous volez, mes quele date &c. vous dioms qe au temps de la confeccion &c. nous estoms en prisone &c. prest &c. — STANTONE. Nostre

---

[1] A blank in the MS.

[2] The MS. has "enprisone," which seems to be a mistake for the name of *Herle* the defendant's counsel.

A.D. 1307. "the making," and not to speak of the day, and so the entry shall be. — TRIKINGHAM. It may be that he was in prison and released on one and the same day, wherefore the averment of the day is not receivable &c.

Where &c. wished to have excluded the plaintiff because he received rent when he was of full age.

§ *Toudeby.* We make protestation that we did not know that the deed was made when you were under age; but we tell you that we hold the same tenements by lease from you for the term of our life, for which we paid to you beforehand 20*l.*, and we pay yearly 4*l.* which is the true value &c.; and we tell you that you, being of full age, have received the same rent from us; and see here your acquittances for that receipt which witness it, and the cause why &c. to wit, for the tenements which you leased to us for the term of our life: judgment if you ought to be answered. — *Hedone.* It is not a similar case: for where a tenement is given in exchange one may vouch, and one shall recompense in value for the exchange &c.; and not so in this case: and yet the receipt of rent or of any other service except homage does not take away the action in such a case. — *Roistone.* Inasmuch as he does not deny the cause of our action, which is the lease made while we were under age, or say anything which forecloses us of this action, judgment &c. — Afterwards the tenant, being by the court put to this, said, Of full age at the time of the making of the lease &c. ready &c. — Therefore &c.

Debt against an abbat and his monk on the writing only of the monk &c.

Debt. § *Hedone* counted that whereas he had lent to the said monk so much money and sold him a horse for so much &c., to be paid &c., at which day he came to the abbat and to the monk &c. —*Toudeby.* Is that your count ?—*Hedone* amended it in this way,—" which " money and horse came to the profit of the house manere dentre est a dire tempore confeccionis non loquendo die, e issi serra il entre. — TRIKINGHAM. Il purra estre qil fust enprisone e delivers tut en un jour; par quei laverement du jour nest pas resceivable &c. A.D. 1307.

Ubi &c. voluit exclusisse petentem quia plenæ etatis recepit redditum.

§ *Toudeby.* Nous fessoms protestacion qe nous ne conussoms pas qe le fet fut fete tant com vous fustes denz age, einz vous dioms qe nous tenoms mesme les tenements de vostre lees a terme de nostre vie, pur queles nous vous payames avaunt mayn xx. livres, e fessoms par an iiii. livres, qest a la verrei value &c.; e vous dioms qe vous esteant de plein age mesme la rente de nous aver receu; e veez icy vos aquitances de cele receite qe la testmoignent, e la cause pur quei &c., scilicet pur les tenements qe vous nous lessates a terme de nostre vie; jugement si vous devez estre respondu. — *Hedone.* Nest pas semblable; qe la ou tenement est done en eschange puet home voucher, e si fra home a la value pur les eschanges &c., et non in isto casu; e jatardeis resceite de rente ne de nul service forpris homage ne tout accion en tel cas. — *Roistone.* Desicom il ne dedit pas la cause de nostre accion, qest le lees denz age, ne rien ne dist qe de cele accion nous forclot, jugement &c.—Postea tenens, ad hoc positus per curiam, De plein age au temps du lees &c., prest &c. — Ideo &c.

Debitum versus abbatem et ejus monachum tantummodo per scriptum monachi &c.

§ *Hedone* conta qil la ou il avoit apreste au dist moingne tant deners e lui vendi un chival pur tant &c. a rendre &c., a quel jour il vient al abbe e al moigne &c. — *Toudeby.* Volez le counte? — *Hedone* se amenda de tant, les queux deners e chival viendrent

A.D. 1307. " &c.:" (and yet there was not very great need of the amendment, for he might have said that in his reply). —*Toudeby.* One can never charge an abbat on the deed of his monk unless the goods have come to the profit of his house; for you have no other cause in this case for demanding against the abbat. Also he was an escaped monk, and he carried off the money with him, so that it never came to the profit of the house, ready &c.—HENGHAM. What situation had he in the house?—*Hedone.* He held an office there. — STAUNTON (having consulted with HENGHAM). Do you wish on both sides that this averment should run.—The same to *Hedone.* Do you admit that he is an escaped &c.—*Toudeby.* He sued a writ to distrein the abbat "so that he have his monk," and he can not have him, since he is escaped. — STAUNTON. Therefore I say, that if the party will admit that he is escaped, the averment shall run, as aforesaid, but if otherwise it shall not. — *Toudeby.* Judgment then if by the deed of an escaped monk you can demand anything against the abbat.—STAUNTON. Nay, you have pleaded and offered an averment, and are at issue. — And the averment stood.

Where a tenant by a fine wished to have vouched out of the degrees, and in like manner prayed aid of him who was out of the degrees, and was not admitted to do so &c.

Entry sur disseisin.

§ Walter de Hose brought the writ against Henry Finche and Isabel his wife thus, "into which he had not " entry unless by Geoffrey de la Hose who thereof un- " justly &c. disseised the said Walter &c." And Henry prayed the view; and in the writ which issued to make him have the view he was named Henry Finche; and in the essoin after the view, in the same way; and now they had a day by the essoin.—*Toudeby.* We pray the view.—*Hedone.* You have had it; and that is witnessed by the sheriff, and you in agreeing thereto might have been essoined; wherefore &c. — *Toudeby.* The original a profit de la meson &c.; et jatardeis ceo ne fist mie mult grant mester a dire qar il poeit aver dist en repliant.—*Toudeby.* Home ne puet jammes charger abbe par fet de sun moingne si les biens ne devyndrent a profit de sa meson ; car autre cause ne avez en ceo cas a demander vers labbe.—*Idem.* Ceo est un moingne eschape, e il ad aporte ove lui les deners, issint qe eux ne viendront unqes a prou de la meson, prest &c.—HENGHAM. De quel mestier fust il en la meson?—*Hedone.* Un office de leinz.—STANTONE consulto HENGHAM. Volez de ambepars qe ceste averement courge.—DEM a *Hedone.* Grauntez vous qil est un eschape &c.?—*Toudeby.* Il suit bref a destreindre labbe "Ita quod 'habeat monachum suum" e il ne le puet pas aver del houre qil est eschape.—STANTONE. Pur ceo dye jeo, si la partie le voille granter qil est eschape, la verement curra ut predicitur, e autrement ne mie.—*Hedone.* Jeo ne le dedie pas.—*Toudeby.* Jugement donqe si par le fet de un eschape vers labbe rien puissez demander.—STANTONE. Nay, vous avez plede e tendu averement, e estes a issue.—Et stetit verificatio. A.D. 1307.

Ubi tenens per finem voluit vocasse extra gradus et similiter petiit auxilium de illo qui fuit extra gradus, nec admittitur &c.

§ Wauter de Hose porta le bref vers Henri Finche e Isabele sa femme sic, "in quas non habuit ingressum "nisi per Gaufridum de la Hose qui inde injuste &c. "disseisivit predictum Galfridum &c." Et Henri demanda la vewe; e en le bref qe issit de fere luy aver la vewe fust il nome issint Henri Finche; e en la essone apres la vewe en mesme la forme, e a ore avoient jour par essone.—*Toudeby.* Nous demandoms la vewe.—*Hedone.* Vous lavez eu, e ceo est testmoigne par viconte, e vous en agreant ceo puisse[z] aver este essone; par quei &c.—*Toudeby.* Le original dist H. Suthe,

De ingressu super disseisinam.

A.D. 1307. says H. Suthe, and you do not find that he had the view, but that Henry Fynche had it; wherefore &c.—STAUNTON. We have not by that a mistake.—*Toudeby.* We will not that it be annulled but that it be amended, and let Henry Fynche have the view, which he has not had.—STAUNTON. Whatever the writ of view says, the sheriff returned that Henry Finche had the view &c.—*Toudeby.* Then he did it without warrant; for the writ does not state that he is to cause him to have it.—STAUNTON. You are here; if you will answer, do so; if you will not, leave us: we see well that you have a day.—*Toudeby.* Henry Fynche has not a day.—STAUNTON. Let him go home then.—*Toudeby.* We have nothing &c. except for the term of our life by lease from John de Papenham, according to the form of this fine, and we vouch him to warranty &c.—*Hedone.* You shall not get to that, for that would be to abate our writ which is given in the degrees.—*Toudeby.* The fine was levied before your writ was purchased.—*Hedone.* What of that? although there were such plots among you to eloign our right, you are now in your first estate.—And he was ousted from the voucher, by judgment.—*Toudeby.* We have nothing &c. except for the term of our life, and the reversion is in John de Papenham, without whom &c., and we pray aid &c.—STAUNTON. You shall not have it, for their writ would abate by one way as well as by the other.—*Toudeby.* And if we plead without him in whose person the fee and the right are, to his disheritance, he will perchance oust us; and that is all our doubt.—HENGHAM. If you doubt of that, go to the Chancery and purchase for yourself against him a writ of warranty of charter.—And he was ousted of the aid, by judgment.—*Friskeney.* Whereas the writ says that we had not entry unless by Geoffrey &c., we say that we found our wife Isabel seised &c.; judgment of this writ.—And the demandant could not deny this. So it was adjudged that he should take nothing by his writ &c.

e vous ne trovez pas qe celuy out la vewe, einz la out Henri Fynche ; par quei &c.—STANTONE. Nous navoms pas cel par cele[1] mesprision.—*Toudeby.* Nous ne voloms pas qil soit anenti, einz soit amende, e eit Henri Fynche la vewe qe nel ad pas eu.—STANTONE. Coment qe le bref de vewe parle, le viconte retorna qe Henri Finche avoit la vewe &c.—*Toudeby.* Donqes le fist il sanz garant, car le bref ne voet qe il luy face aver.—STANTONE. Vous estes icy ; si vous volez respondre, fetes, si noun lessez ; nous veoms[2] bien ke vous avez jour. — *Toudeby.* Henri Fynche nad nul jour. — STANTONE. Aille donqes a lostel. — *Toudeby.* Nous navoms rienz &c. si noun a terme de nostre vie du lees Johan de Papenham solom la forme de ceste fin, e lui vouchoms a garantie &c.—*Hedone.* A ceo ne avendrez pas ; car ceo serreit de abatre nostre bref qest done en les degreez.—*Toudeby.* La fin se leva avant vostre bref purchace.—*Hedone.* De ceo quei ? tut furent teux makemenz entre vous pur nostre droit aloigner, vous estes ore a vostre primer estat. E il fust oste del voucher par agarde.—*Toudeby.* Nous ne avom rien &c. si noun a terme de nostre vie, dount la reversion est a Johan de Pakenham sanz qi &c., e prioms aide &c. — STANTONE. Vous nel averez pas, car tant bien abatereit lour bref par la une veye com par lautre. — *Toudeby.* E si nous pledoms sanz celi en qi persone le fee e le droit, en desheriteson de luy, il nous ostera par cas ; e ceo est tut nostre doute.—HENGHAM. Si vous dotez de ceo, alez a la Chancelerie purchacer vous de vers lui par bref de garanti de chartre.—E il fust oste del eide par agard.—*Friskeney.* La ou le bref dist qe nous navioms entre si noun par Geffrey &c., nous trovames nostre femme Isabele seisie &c., jugement de cestui bref.—Et petens non potuit hoc dedicere. Ideo consideratum est quod nil capiat per breve &c.

A.D. 1307.

[1] The words "par cele" are in the margin immediately following, and seem to be in substitution for, "pas cel."

[2] MS. nous voloms nous veoms.

A.D. 1307. Judgment in a writ of Besael in recovering damages, where the parties were at issue whether the great-grandfather died seised &c.

§ MALLORE. Because it is found that he died seised, this court adjudges that he do recover &c. against the tenant, and the tenant against Ernard de Percy his warrantor, to the value &c.—*Toudeby*. We pray our damages &c.— MALLORE. You will have them by the Statute of Gloucester.[1] — HALES. Yes, and they shall be adjudged since the death of your last ancestor, after whose death this action accrued to you; for from any other time you ought not to recover damages. — *Toudeby*. The land is worth 30*s*. yearly. — HALES. Which he takes from him from the time of the last ancestor.—And upon this the damages were awarded to the demandant.

Dower. § Rose, who was the wife of William Peche, brought the writ against the bishop of Norwich, and demanded the moiety of the manor of P. by way of dower. — *Malmesthorpe*. The manor is holden by knight-service, so only the third part is to be assigned in dower; now if you will amend your demand and make it for the third part, we will answer you.—*Hedone*. We hold to the demand which we have made.—*Malmesthorpe*. Then, whatever becomes of this dower, we make protestation, and we pray that the court will record it, that even if she ought to be endowed, she can only demand the third part &c.; and neither of so much nor of any part of this manor ought she to have dower; for her husband William &c., of whose endowment &c., was indicted for the death of John de Draytone before Sir Henry Spigurnel and his companions, justices assigned to hear and terminate &c. in the county of Norfolk, and there, before them, was put in exigent, and was demanded from county court to county court, until by process and according to the law

[1] 6 Edw. I. c. 1.

Judicium in brevi de proavo in dampnis recuperandis, ou les parties furent a travers qe le besael ne morust mie seisi &c. A.D. 1307.

§ MALLORE. Pur ceo qe trove est quil morust seisi, si agarde &c. qil rescovere &c. vers le tenant [e le tenant] vers Ernard de Percy sun garant a la vaillance &c.—*Toudeby*. Nous prioms nos damages &c.—MALORRE. Vous les averez par le statut de Gloucestre. — HALES. Oil, e serront agardez pus la mort vostre drein auncestre, apres qi mort ceste accion vous acrust; qar de autre temps ne devez damage rescoverer.—*Toudeby*. La terre vaut .xxx. souz par an. — HALES. Quæ sumit ab ipso de spatio ultimi antecessoris &c. Et super hoc fuerunt petenti dampna adjudicata.

§ Rose ke fu la femme Willem Peche porta bref vers leveske de Norwyche, e demanda la moite du maner de P. en noun de dowere.—*Malm*. Le maner est tenu par fee de chivaler dount nest de assigner en dowere mes qe la terce partie, e si vous volez amender vostre demande e fere la de la terce partie, nous vous respondroms.—*Hedone*. Nous tenoms a la demande qe nous avoms fet.—*Malm*. Adonqe, coment qe avyegne de cest dowere, nous fessoms protestacion, e ceo prioms qe la court recorde, qe tut devoit ele estre dowe, ele ne poeit demander mes qe la terce partie &c.; e de tant ne de renz de cest maner ne deit ele dower aver, car sun baron Willem &c., de qi dowement &c., fust endite de la mort Johan de Draytone devant Sire Henri Spigurnel e ces compaignon, justices assignez a oier e a terminer &c., en le conte de Norfolk, e illoeke devant eux mys en exigende, e demande de conte en conte, tanke par proces e solum lei de terre fust utlaghe, e prest De dote.

A.D. 1307. of the land he was outlawed, ready &c. how &c.; and then our lord the king had the year and waste, and the bishop, of whom this manor was holden, after that entered thereon as his escheat; and we pray judgment if she ought to have dower of this manor.—*Friskeney.* Our husband William died in the faith and in the peace of our lord the king, ready &c.; and we pray judgment &c. —HENGHAM. Answer this shortly: was he outlawed or nor?—*Friskeney.* Then let them say where and when and at whose suit he was outlawed.—*Herle* wanted to begin the whole process how he was first of all demanded in the county court &c. and so on down to the outlawry.—STAUNTON. We are not here to undo the outlawry after his death, so it is only necessary that you state the day on which he was outlawed.—*Herle.* In the county of Norfolk on Thursday [Nov. 24] in the beginning of the 30th year, and at the suit of the king.—*Friskeney.* We can not deny that he was outlawed, as they say; but we tell you that our lord the king did by his charter pardon him that outlawry; so that he was thereby restored to the peace, and he died in the peace; and we pray judgment if by such an outlawry which was only for contumacy and where he was not attainted of the fact, we ought to be barred of our dower.—*Malmesthorpe.* And we pray judgment, since you have admitted that outlawry which originated from a felony, and which naturally gives an escheat, and you do not allege anything in your favour but only that as you say the king pardoned you the suit of his peace, which we do not admit, and moreover a pardon does not deprive others of their right,—if you ought to have dower.—*Toudeby.* From him if he were alive and from his heir that outlawry would take away an action against us, therefore, much more, from his wife.—HENGHAM to *Friskeney.* You have admitted that your husband was outlawed; what have you to evidence your statement that he was restored to the peace?—*Friskeney.* Ready &c. by the rolls of the

&c., par quant &c.; e dount nostre seignour le roi en avoit lan e le wast, e levesko de qi ceo maner fust tenuz apres ceo est entre leinz com en sa eschete; e demandoms jugement si ele de ceo maner deyve dowere aver.—*Friskeney.* Nostre baron Willem morust a la foy e a la pees nostre seignour le roi, e prest &c.; e demandoms jugement &c.—HENGHAM. Responez a ceo brevement: fut il utlaghe ou ne mye?—*Friskeney.* Dyent donqes ou e quant e a qi suite utlaghe.—*Herle* voluit incepisse totum processum qualiter primo fuit exactus in comitatu &c. et sic usque ad utlagariam.—STANTONE. Nous ne sumes pas icy a defere la utlagerie apres sa mort, dount il ne covent mye qe vous dyez mes qe soulement le jour qil fust utlaghe.—*Herle.* En le conte de Norfolk le joeudi en la renef lan xxxme, e a la suite le roi.—*Frisqeney.* Nous ne poms dedire qil ne fust utlaghe auxicom eus dyent; mes nous vous dyoms qe nostre seignour le roi lui perdona cele uthlagarie par sa chartre, issint qil fust de tant resuscite a la pees, e a la pees morust; e demandoms jugement si, par cele utlagarie qe ne fust mes pur sa contumacie, ou il ne fust mie atteint du fet, devoms de dowere estre forclos.—*Malm.* E nous jugement, del houre qe vous avez grante cele utlagarie qe se prist sur cause de felonie e qe naturelment donne eschete, e rien aleggez pur vous mes qe soulement, a ceo qe vous dites, qe le roi vous perdona la suite de sa pees, quei nous ne grantoms pas, uncore qe en perdoun ne tout mye a autres lour droit, si vous devez dowere aver.—*Toudeby.* A lui meymes sil fust en vie e a sun heir tolereit cele utlagerie accion vers nous, ergo de plus force a sa femme. HENGHAM a *Friskeney.* Vous avez grante qe vostre baron fust uthlage; quei avez de ceo qe vous dites qil fust resuscite a la pees?—*Friskeney.* Prest &c. par A.D. 1307.

A.D. 1307. Chancery.—*Warr.* Since you have admitted the outlawry, it will be necessary to see by what words he was restored to the peace &c.—STAUNTON. If you have anything which can avail you, have it ready to-morrow &c.

YET OF TRINITY TERM IN THE 35TH YEAR OF KING EDWARD.

Before BRABAZON. At the quinzein of St. Hilary last[1] past, John Bygot brought the writ against John de Ferrers, tenant of the manor of Bukebroke, in this form, namely, to show if he had or could say anything why execution of a fine which was levied between John Bigot, father &c., whose heir &c., plaintiff, and Godfrey de Beaumond and Cecily his wife deforceants, of the aforesaid manor of Bukebroke, ought not to be had according to the form of the said fine. — *Herle.* As John Bygot you ought not to have execution, for you are a bastard &c. -- *John.* Mulier; ready &c. when and where &c.; and we pray a writ to the bishop.—And thereupon came one Ralph Bygot who said that he was son and heir of the said John Bygot the elder; and he said by *Willeby,* We have purchased the like writ against the said John de Ferrers and others &c., for the same manor, returnable at three weeks of Easter, by virtue of the same fine; and we pray that he may not have a writ to the bishop until he has pleaded the writ with us: for it is a truth that he is a bastard, and in deceit and fraud of us he made this suit against the said John de Ferrers, so that if by any false way he might legitimate himself, he would deprive us of our right of action. And it was decided by the court that he should not have the writ &c. to the bishop until that day in three weeks of

[1] See Abbreviatio Placitorum, p. 260.

roulles de la Chancelerie. — *Warr.* Del houre ke vous avez graunte la utlagerie il convendra vere par queles paroles il fust resuscite &c. — STANTONE. Si vous avez rien qe valer vous puet, eiez le prest demein &c. A.D. 1307.

ADHUC DE TERMINO TRINITATIS ANNO REGNI REGIS EDWARDI XXXV^TO^.

Coram BRABANZONE. A la quinezeine de Seint Hillari passe, Johan Bygot porta le bref vers Johan de Ferers tenant du maner de Bukebroke, saver sic, a moustrer se rienz eit ou dire savoit pur quei execucion de une fin qe se leva entre Johan Bigot, pere &c., qi heir &c., pleintif, e Godefre de Beaumond e Cecile sa femme deforceants, du maner de Bukebroke avantdit, ne se devoit fere solom la forme de la dite fin. — *Herle.* Com Johan Bygot ne devez execucion aver, car vous estes bastard &c. — *Johan.* Moellere, prest &c. ou e quant &c.; eprioms bref al eveske. — E sur ceo vyent un Rauf Bygot, qe se dist estre fiz e heir le dit Johan Bygot leygne, e dist par *Willuby,* Nous avom purchace autel bref vers le dit Johan de Ferers e autres &c. de mesme le maner, retornable a treis semeynes de Pasche, par vertu de mesme la fin; e prioms qil neit pas bref al eveske taunt qil eit a nostre bref plede ove nous; qar il est verite qil est bastard, e en deceite e en collusion de nous fet ceste suite vers le dist Johan de Ferers, issi qe si par nule faus veie se poet legitimier, nous tolereit nostre droit [de] accion.— Et consideratur per curiam quod non haberet breve &c. episcopo quousque illa dies de tribus sep-

A.D. 1307. Easter should come. And the said Ralph was told that he should well sue at his peril that his writ should then be returned and executed. — In the mesne time the said John Bygot and Ralph came to terms, so that at the three weeks of Easter the said John Bygot came and withdrew from his writ, and Ralph sued his writ in which were named John de Ferrers and Hawise his wife, John de Anesle and Simond de Julee, who were warned &c. And they came, and Simond answered as tenant of the freehold by *Herle*: Simond tells you that he has in that manor a joint-tenancy with John le Kyng of Godingtone and Thomas de la Forde, for the term of their lives, by lease from Sir John de Ferrers, and they are not warned, nor named in this writ, and without them this execution can not be allowed; and we pray judgment of the writ. — *Toudeby.* What have you to show this joint-tenancy ?—*Herle.* Ready to aver it &c.—*Toudeby.* You shall not get to that; for so would say those who you say hold jointly with you, when they shall come; and that would be to give a process without end; then unless you· support your statement by a deed, we pray judgment &c. — *Herle.* Before the statute[1] of joint-feoffees, such an averment was receivable in every writ, and by that statute it is not taken away; but the statute only says that in opposition to the deed which the tenant shall put forward, the demandant may join an averment in disproof of the deed of joint-tenure; wherefore a fortiori it seems that our averment is receivable.—Then they were driven by the court to put forward a deed; and they put forward a deed which witnessed &c.; and they prayed judgment of the writ, as before.—*Toudeby.* This is a judicial writ, which will not abate by the joint-feoffment.—SPIGURNEL. It does not seem that this writ should abate; for Simon has answered as tenant of the freehold; and if the writ were to abate, it would be necessary for him to be re-warned; and that would seem to be a hardship, since he

[1] 34 Edw. I. st. 1.

timanis Paschæ venerit. Et dictum fuit eidem Radulfo quod bene sequatur suo pericolo quod breve suum ad tunc fuerat retornatum et executum.—E en le meen temps le dit Johan Bygot e Rauf se acorderent, issi qe a treis semeynes de Pasche le dist Johan Bygot vient e se retreit de son bref, e Rauf suist son bref, en le quel furent nomez Johan de Ferers e Hawyse sa femme, Johan de Anesle, e Simond de Julee, qe furent garniz &c. Et viendrent, e Simond respont com tenant du franc tenement par *Herle.* Simond vous dist qil en ad en teu maner joint tenance ove Johan le Kyng de Codingtone, e Thomas de la Forde, a terme de lour vies, du lees Sire Johan de Ferers, qe ne sunt pas garniz ne nomez en cesti bref, sanz les queux il ne poet suffrir ceste execucion; e demandoms jugement du bref.—*Toudeby.* Quei avez de ceo qe vous [avez] tiel joint tenance?—*Herle.* Prest del averer &c.—*Toudeby.* A ceo ne avendrez vous mie; qar ensi dirreint ceux qe vous dites qe sunt joint ove vous quant eux veudront; e ceo serroit a doner proces sanz fin; dount sanz ceo qe vous provez vostre dist par fet, demandoms jugement &c.—*Herle.* Avant lestatut de joynt feffes fust tel averement resceivable en chescon bref, qe par cel statut ne pas defet; einz voet soulement lestatut qe encontre le fet qe le tenant mettra avant puisse le demandaunt joyndre averement en desprove de cel fet de jointe tenure; par quei de plus forte semble il qe nostre averement soit resceivable.—Puis furent chacez par la court de mettre avant fet; e mistrent avant fet qe testmoigna &c., e demaunderent jugement du bref com avant. *Toudeby.* Cest un bref de jugement qe ne se abatra mye par joint feffement.—SPIGURNEL. Il ne semble pas qe cestui bref se abatereit; car Simond ad respondu com tenant du franc tenement; e si le bref se abatesit, si lui covendreit il estre regarny; e ceo semblereit dures, del houre qil est encontre e ad re- A.D. 1307.

A.D. 1307. is in opposition and has answered; and nevertheless we do not yet know what estate John de Ferrers and the other persons named claim &c.: so we do not know if it would be necessary to warn them or not; wherefore &c.—He (SPIGURNEL) asked John de Ferrers what he claimed.—*Herle.* There is no need that he claim now, since the tenant of the freehold has given an answer which abates the writ.—SPIGURNEL. If he is warned to show &c. and is in court, let him claim if he will for his benefit; if not, let him cease.—*Herle.* If you adjudge that we must claim now if we wish to claim anything, we will do it &c.—SPIGURNEL. You are warned &c.; we will not give any judgment thereon.—*Herle.* John de Ferrers claims the reversion after the death of the joint feoffees named in that writing, and he has now the fee and the right, and Hawise has nothing &c.—[SPIGURNEL.] For that it seems to us it is not necessary that those who are named in this writ, and have showed their estate and have answered in part, should be again warned, we are of opinion that this writ shall not abate; but do you, Ralph, sue a writ to warn the other joint-tenants that they be &c. at the quinzein of Trinity to show why &c. And let Simond and John keep the same day.—And in the mesne time Simond de Julee died. On which day John de Ferrers came in his proper person and John Kynge and Thomas.—[*Herle.*] And this writ directs that John Kinge and Thomas be &c. to show together with Simond de Julee &c.; now we tell you that together with him they cannot show &c., for the said Simond is dead; judgment of the writ.—*Toudeby.* You shall not thereby abate our writ; for although he were alive and made default, that would not hurt us; no more &c.: and since you do not show anything, we pray execution &c. —*Herle.* We are speaking of what the writ says, "to "show if &c.," which cannot be, since he is dead.—SPIGURNEL. If you could say that the estate which Simond had was now by way of succession come into the person spondu, e jatardeis nous ne savoms uncore quel estat Johan de Ferers e les autres nomez cleiment &c.; e dount nous ne savoms si mester ert de garnir eux ou ne mye; par quei &c. IDEM demaunda a Johan de Ferers ceo qil clame.—*Herle.* Nest pas mester qil cleime a ore, del houre qe tenant del franc tenement ad done respons qe abate le bref. SPIGURNEL. Sil est garny a moustrer &c. e est en cort, e cleime sil voille pur son profit, e si noun, cesse.—*Herle.* Si vous agardez qil nous covendra a ore clamer si rien clamer voloms nous le froms &c.—SPIGURNEL. Vous estes garniz &c., nous ne froms de ceo nule agard.—*Herle.* Johan de Ferers cleime la reversion apres la mort de joinz feffez nomez en cel escrit, e a ore ad le fee e le dreit, et Hawys rien nad &c., breviter.—[SPIGURNEL.] E pur ceo qil nous semble pas mestier qe ceux qe sunt nomez en cestui bref e ount moustre lour estat e respondu en partie seient derichief garniz, si nous est il avis qe cestui bref ne se abatera pas; mes vous Rauf suez bref de garnir les autres joint tenans qil seient &c. a la quinezeine de la Trinite, ostensuri scilicet quare &c. Et Simond e Johan gardent mesme le jour.—Et illo medio tempore Simond de Julee obiit. A quel jour Johan de Ferers vient en propre persone, e Johan Kynge e Thomas,[1] e ceo bref voet qe Johan Kinge e Thomas seyent &c. a moustrer ensemblement ove Simond de Julee &c.; ore vous dioms qe ensemblement ove luy ne poient eux moustrer &c., qar le dist Simond est mort; jugement du bref.—*Toudeby.* Par tant ne abaterez pas nostre bref; car tut fust il en vie e feist defaute, ceo nous ne nuyreit pas; nent plus &c.; e del houre qe vous moustrez rienz, prioms execucion &c.—*Herle.* Nous parloms a ceo qe le bref doune, ad ostendendum sil &c., qe ne purra mie estre, del houre qil est mort.—SPIGURNEL. Si vous puissez dire qe lestat qe Simond A.D. 1307.

[1] The name of a counsel seems to be omitted here.

A.D. 1307. of his heir, so that the heir ought to be warned, you would say well: but since, according to what the deed which he formerly put forward witnesses, you have a joint-tenancy, so that after his death the entirety remains in you, without anything that was in his person being able to be vest in any other person than you, it does not seem that by that way you can abate this writ. —*Herle.* If you adjudge &c.—BRABAZON. We will not give any judgment; you are warned; answer as you think best.—*Herle.* Then we tell you that we have nothing except for the term of life by lease from John de Ferrers, in whose person the fee and the right &c., and without whom we cannot answer or show &c., and we pray aid of him.—*Toudeby.* John de Ferrers has a day now by appointment, and he is there; let him join &c. and say what he will.—*Herle.* Although he has a day now by appointment, yet he has not a day as he who is now prayed in aid, of which aid-prayer, since it is grantable by law, there will be a process.—*Wescote.* Backwards the process is continued against John de Ferrers, as against the tenant; and since those tenants have now prayed aid of him, if they perchance should lose and at another time were to bring their writ of warranty of charter against John, they would recover to the value; and that would be a marvellous thing, that tenant should recover against tenant.—*Malmesthorpe.* Aid is grantable in favour of him who is prayed in aid, so that he may save his right; and he himself is there of whom aid &c.; and he may now maintain his right if he have any; then since he is there present, it does not seem that, in delay of this exception, he ought to have aid.—*Toudeby.* Heretofore by his claim he drove us to sue out a writ of warning against other tenants of the freehold who were not named in our writ, and he still remains in that writ a party by appointment; wherefore it does not seem that by that aid-prayer those tenants shall drive us again to rewarn him who is in court and avoit fust a ore par veie de succession en la persone A.D. 1307 sun heir devenuz, qe leir covendreit estre garny, vous deissez bien: mes del houre a ceo qe le fet qil autrefoiz mist avant testmoigne vous avez joynt tenance, issint qe apres sa mort tut lenter vous demoert, sanz ceo qe rienz en sa persone fust en autre qe les voz purra vestier, ne semble pas qe par cele voie puissez cesti bref abatre.—*Herle.* Si vous agardez &c.—BRABANZONE. Nous ne froms nul agard; vous estes garny; responez a meuz qe vous quidez faire.—*Herle.* Donqe vous dioms nous qe nous navom rienz si noun a terme de vie du lees Johan de Ferers, en qi persone le fee e le droit &c., sanz qi nous ne poms respondre ne moustrer &c., e prioms aide de lui.—*Toudeby.* Johan de Ferrers ad jour a ore par prefixcion, e est la; se joigne &c., e dye ceo qil voudra.—*Herle.* Tut eit il jour a ore par prefixcion, il nad mye jour com celui qe a ore est prie en aide, de quel prier, del houre qil est grantable de lei, ert proces.—*Wescote.* Cea en arere est le proces continue vers Johan de Ferers com vers tenant; e del houre qe ceux tenants ore lui ount prie en aide, e si eux par cas perdissent e autre foiz portassent lour bref de garantie de chartre vers Johan, eux rescovereient a la vaillance, e ceo serreit merveillouse chose, qe tenant rescovereit vers tenant.—*Malm.* Eide est grantable en favour de celi qe est prie en aide, issi qil pusse sun droit sauver; e il est meme la de quei aide &c., e sun droit meyntener a ore purra si nul en eit; dount del houre qil est la en present, ne semble pas qe en targant ceste excepcion eide deive aver.—*Toudeby.* Autrefoiz par sun clamance nous chasa il a suyre bref de garnissement vers autre tenant de franc tenement qe ne furent pas nomez en nostre bref, e il uncore demoert en cel bref partie par prefixion; par quei il ne semble pas qe ceux tenans nous rechaceront mie par cel eide prier de regarnir celui qe est en

A.D. 1307. warned.—*Herle.* The claim of John de Ferrers did not drive you, but on the contrary Simond de Julee did; for what John then claimed, where he said nothing, the court drove him to do.—SPIGURNEL. You are here to a writ which issues out of the fine and is originated by the statute, to which writ you shall not have your delays as in other writs pleadable &c.; since you are warned, and have now a day by appointment, it does not seem &c.—*Inge.* This writ serves for nothing else but to warn &c. that he be &c. to show if he know how to say anything why execution &c., and not to answer to any party, as in any other writ where voucher or other delays lie: and you are there, and have a day &c.; wherefore &c.—BRABAZON. Before the statute, in order to do that, the demandant had another mode of purchase, and this is now given by statute, and we are not well satisfied about it: therefore we wish to advise on this matter with our companions who were at the making of the statute.—On another day BRABAZON rehearsed the matter briefly and in conclusion said, And we well see that John de Ferrers has a day and is warned and in court &c., wherefore &c., if he wish to say anything let him say it.—*Wescote.* We do not think that by that fine the court has power to cause them to have such execution &c.; for when the fine says "between John Bigot plaintiff and Godfrey de Beaumond "and Cecily his wife deforceants," it supposes that John Bygot is out of possession, which thing is also affirmed by the fact that in the acknowledging part of the writ what is acknowledged to him is not said to be "as that which he has of any ones gift" &c. And on the other hand you do not find in the said fine that John Bygot, as he who was seised of this manor, did render it to Godfrey and Cecily, but that he only granted it; then, since you do not find, by any word in the fine, that John Bygot had any estate of seisin &c., it does not seem that, by virtue of that fine, his heir ought by resummons cort e garny.—*Herle.* Le clamance Johan de Ferers ne vous chasa pas, einz fist le revers Simond de Julee: car ceo qe Johan a donqe clamer, ou rien diseit, la court lui chasa de ceo faire.—SPIGURNEL. Vous estes issi au bref qe ist hors de la fin, e est conceu par statut, a quel bref vous naverez mie vos delayes com en autres brefs pledables &c.; del houre qe vous estes garny, e ore avez jour par prefixion, ne semble pas &c.—*Inge.* Ceo bref de autre rien ne sert mes a garnir &c. qil soit &c. a moustrer sil sache rienz dire pur quei execucion, e noun pas a respondre a nule partie com en autre bref ou voucher ou autres delayes gisent; e vous estes la e avez jour &c.; par quei &c.—BRABANZONE. Avant statut a cel afere fust autre voye de purchaz pur le demaundant, e ceste si est ore done par statut; dount nous ne sumes pas bien avisez: e pur ceo voloms de ceste chose conseiller ove nos compaig[n]ons qe furent al statut fere.—Ad alium diem BRABANZONE repetiit breviter, et in fine, E veoms bien qe Johan de Ferers ad jour e est garny e en cort &c., par quei &c. sil voudra rien dire dye.—*Wescote.* Nous ne entendoms mie qe par cele fin court eit poer de fere lour aver tele execucion &c.; car par tant qe la fin dist entre Johan Bigot pleignant e Godefre de Beaumond e Cecile sa femme deforceants, suppose ele en luy meyme Johan Bygot estre hors, quele chose est auxi afferme, e par taunt qen la conissance du bref qe luy est conu nest pas dist com ceo qil ad de nuly doun. Et de autre part, vous ne trovez pas en la dite fin qe Johan Bygot, com celui qe de ces seisi fust, ceo maner rendi a Godefre e a Cecile, einz soulment granta; dount del houre qe vous ne trovez pas par nule parole de la fin qe Johan Bygot nul estat de seisine &c. ne out, il ne semble pas qe, par vertue de cele fin, sun heir par resomons de

A.D. 1307.

A.D. 1307. to have seisin of the reversion.—*Malmesthorpe.* At the time of the levying of that fine, such was the manner of levying a fine, although it happened that he who granted was seised; and it is quite as possible to understand by the fine that John Bygot was in seisin as out of seisin; then, since you do not by anything you say show that at the time &c. he was out of seisin, and the fine is in good form and accepted by the court &c., we ask judgment and pray execution.—*Herle.* Then you do admit that it is possible to understand, by the words of the fine, that he was out &c.—*Toudeby.* We say that the fine is accepted by the court, and levied according to the mode which then obtained &c., which fine is not to be annulled in any way, and we pray execution of it.—*Westcote* repeated his last reason and only added, And for the greater enlightenment of the court we are ready to aver by a good jury that John Bygot never had anything.—*Toudeby* repeated his last argument.—ROUBYRI. And what say you of the averment which he offers? Will not you accept it?—*Toudeby.* No, sir; it is not receivable against the fine or to impeach it.—*Herle.* It is well receivable at common law; then there are only two statutes which touch this matter; one is Westminster 2nd [1] which now gives process after a judgment of the court and a fine levied,

the other is the statute *Quia fines &c.*[2] which states that I shall not have an averment against the words of the fine; in which statute . . .

[1] 13 Edw. I. c. 45.

[2] 27 Edw. I. c. 1.

reversion seisine deyve aver. — *Malm.* Au temps del lever de cele fin fust la manere tele de fin lever, tut fust il issint qe celuy qe granta fust seisi; e si est il tant possible de entendre par la fin qe Johan Bygot fust en seisine com hors de seisine; dount del houre qe par rienz qe vous dites ne luy mustrez mye au temps &c. estre hors de seisine, e la fin est de bone forme e accepte de cort &c., demaundoms jugement e prioms execucion. — *Herle.* Donqe grantez vous qil est possible de entendre par paroles de la fin qil fust hors &c. — *Toudeby.* Nous dioms qe la fin est accepte de court, e leve solom la manere qe adonke fust &c., quele fin nest pas anyentissable par nule veye, e prioms de cele execucion. — *Westcote* repetiit rationem suam ultimam et addidit tantum, E pur [1] greyndre aveyement faire a la court, si sumes nous prest del averer par bon pays qe Johan Bygot ne out unkes rien. — *Toudeby* repetiit rationem suam ultimam. — ROUBYRI. E del averement qil vous tend quei dites vous? nel volez pas? — *Toudeby.* Noun, sire; ele nest pas contre la fin ne pur cele effreyndre resceivable. — *Herle.* Qil est resceivable bien de comune ley; dount il ne sunt mes qe deus statuz qe touchent ceste matere, le un le secunde de Westminstre qe oredeyne proces apres jugement de court e fin leve, e cel ne estes mie &c.; lautre est quia fines &c. qe voet qe jeo ne eye mie averement encontre paroles de la fin; en quel estatut . . . A.D. 1307.

[1] MS. pus.

INDEX.

INDEX.

A.

E.

F.

H.

I.

P.

Q.

R.

T.

V.

W.

Y.

LONDON:
Printed by GEORGE E. EYRE and WILLIAM SPOTTISWOODE
Printers to the Queen's most Excellent Majesty.
For Her Majesty's Stationery Office.
[B 410.—750.—3/79.]

ENGLAND.

CATALOGUE

OF

RECORD PUBLICATIONS

ON SALE

BY

Messrs. Longman & Co., and Messrs. Trübner & Co., London;
Messrs. James Parker & Co., Oxford and London;
Messrs. Macmillan & Co., Cambridge and London;
Messrs. A. & C. Black, and Messrs. Douglas and Foulis, Edinburgh;
and Mr. A. Thom, Dublin.

CATALOGUE.

CONTENTS.

CALENDARS OF STATE PAPERS, &c.

[Imperial 8vo., cloth. *Price* 15*s*. each Volume or Part.]

As far back as the year 1800, a Committee of the House of Commons recommended that Indexes and Calendars should be made to the Public Records, and thirty-six years afterwards another Committee of the House of Commons reiterated that recommendation in more forcible words; but it was not until the incorporation of the State Paper Office with the Public Record Office that the Master of the Rolls found himself in a position to take the necessary steps for carrying out the wishes of the House of Commons.

On 7 December 1855, he stated to the Lords of the Treasury that although "the Records, State Papers, and Documents in his charge constitute the most "complete and perfect series of their kind in the civilized world," and although "they are of the greatest value in a historical and constitutional "point of view, yet they are comparatively useless to the public, from the "want of proper Calendars and Indexes."

Acting upon the recommendations of the Committees of the House of Commons above referred to, he suggested to the Lords of the Treasury that to effect the object he had in view it would be necessary for him to employ a few Persons fully qualified to perform the work which he contemplated.

Their Lordships assented to the necessity of having Calendars prepared and printed, and empowered the Master of the Rolls to take such steps as might be necessary for this purpose.

The following Works have been already published under the direction of the Master of the Rolls:—

Calendarium Genealogicum; for the Reigns of Henry III. and Edward I. *Edited by* Charles Roberts, Esq., Secretary of the Public Record Office. 2 Vols. 1865.

This is a work of great value for elucidating the early history of our nobility and landed gentry.

CALENDAR OF STATE PAPERS, DOMESTIC SERIES, OF THE REIGNS OF EDWARD VI., MARY, ELIZABETH, and JAMES I., preserved in Her Majesty's Public Record Office. *Edited by* ROBERT LEMON, Esq., F.S.A., (Vols. I. and II.), and MARY ANNE EVERETT GREEN, (Vols. III.-XII.). 1856-1872.

Vol. I.—1547-1580.
Vol. II.—1581-1590.
Vol. III.—1591-1594.
Vol. IV.—1595-1597.
Vol. V.—1598-1601.
Vol. VI.—1601-1603, with Addenda, 1547-1565.
Vol. VII.—Addenda, 1566-1579.
Vol. VIII.—1603-1610.
Vol. IX.—1611-1618.
Vol. X.—1619-1623.
Vol. XI.—1623-1625, with Addenda, 1603-1625.
Vol. XII.—Addenda, 1580-1625.

These Calendars render accessible to investigation a large and important mass of historical materials. The Northern Rebellion of 1566-67; the plots of the Catholic fugitives in the Low Countries; the numerous designs against Queen Elizabeth and in favour of a Catholic succession; the Gunpowder-plot; the rise and fall of Somerset; the Overbury murder; the disgrace of Sir Edward Coke; the rise of the Duke of Buckingham, &c. Numerous other subjects are illustrated by these Papers, few of which have been previously known.

CALENDAR OF STATE PAPERS, DOMESTIC SERIES, OF THE REIGN OF CHARLES I., preserved in Her Majesty's Public Record Office. *Edited by* JOHN BRUCE, Esq., F.S.A., (Vols. I.-XII.); *by* JOHN BRUCE, Esq., F.S.A., and WILLIAM DOUGLAS HAMILTON, Esq., F.S.A., (Vol. XIII.), and *by* WILLIAM DOUGLAS HAMILTON, Esq., F.S.A., (Vols. XIV.-XV.) 1858-1877.

Vol. I.—1625-1626.
Vol. II.—1627-1628.
Vol. III.—1628-1629.
Vol. IV.—1629-1631.
Vol. V.—1631-1633.
Vol. VI.—1633-1634.
Vol. VII.—1634-1635.
Vol. VIII.—1635.
Vol. IX.—1635-1636.
Vol. X.—1636-1637.
Vol. XI.—1637.
Vol. XII.—1637-1638.
Vol. XIII.—1638-1639.
Vol. XIV.—1639.
Vol. XV.—1639-1640.

This Calendar presents notices of a large number of original documents of great value to all inquirers relative to the history of the period to which it refers. Many of them have been hitherto unknown.

CALENDAR OF STATE PAPERS, DOMESTIC SERIES, DURING THE COMMONWEALTH, preserved in Her Majesty's Public Record Office. *Edited by* MARY ANNE EVERETT GREEN. 1875-1878.

Vol. I.—1649-1650.
Vol. II.—1650.
Vol. III.—1651.
Vol. IV.—1651-1652.
Vol. V.—1652-1653.

This Calendar is in continuation of those during the reigns from Edward VI. to Charles I., and contains a mass of new information.

CALENDAR OF STATE PAPERS, DOMESTIC SERIES, OF THE REIGN OF CHARLES II., preserved in Her Majesty's Public Record Office. *Edited by* MARY ANNE EVERETT GREEN. 1860-1866.

Vol. I.—1660-1661.
Vol. II.—1661-1662.
Vol. III.—1663-1664.
Vol. IV.—1664-1665.
Vol. V.—1665-1666.
Vol. VI.—1666-1667.
Vol. VII.—1667.

Seven volumes of this Calendar, of the period between 1660 and 1667, have been published.

CALENDAR OF HOME OFFICE PAPERS OF THE REIGN OF GEORGE III., preserved in Her Majesty's Public Record Office. 1760 (25 Oct.)–1765. *Edited by* JOSEPH REDINGTON, Esq., 1878.

This is the first volume of the modern series of Domestic Papers, commencing with the accession of George III.

CALENDAR OF STATE PAPERS relating to SCOTLAND, preserved in Her Majesty's Public Record Office. *Edited by* MARKHAM JOHN THORPE, Esq., of St. Edmund Hall, Oxford. 1858.

Vol. I., the Scottish Series, of the Reigns of Henry VIII., Edward VI., Mary, and Elizabeth, 1509–1589.

Vol. II., the Scottish Series, of the Reign of Elizabeth, 1589–1603; an Appendix to the Scottish Series, 1543–1592; and the State Papers relating to Mary Queen of Scots during her Detention in England, 1568–1587.

These two volumes of State Papers relate to Scotland, and embrace the period between 1509 and 1603. In the second volume are notices of the State Papers relating to Mary Queen of Scots.

CALENDAR OF DOCUMENTS relating to IRELAND, preserved in Her Majesty's Public Record Office, London. *Edited by* HENRY SAVAGE SWEETMAN, Esq., B.A., Trinity College, Dublin, Barrister-at-Law (Ireland). 1875–1877.

Vol. I.—1171–1251. | Vol. II. 1252–1284.

These volumes contain a Calendar of all documents relating to Ireland, preserved in the Public Record Office, London; the work is to be continued to the end of the reign of Henry VII.

CALENDAR OF STATE PAPERS relating to IRELAND, OF THE REIGNS OF HENRY VIII., EDWARD VI., MARY, AND ELIZABETH, preserved in Her Majesty's Public Record Office. *Edited by* HANS CLAUDE HAMILTON, Esq., F.S.A. 1860–1877.

Vol. I.—1509–1573.
Vol. II.—1574–1585.
Vol. III.—1586–1588.

The above have been published under the editorship of Mr. Hans Claude Hamilton.

CALENDAR OF STATE PAPERS relating to IRELAND, OF THE REIGN OF JAMES I., preserved in Her Majesty's Public Record Office, and elsewhere. *Edited by* the Rev. C. W. RUSSELL, D.D., and JOHN P. PRENDERGAST, Esq., Barrister-at-Law. 1872–1877.

Vol. I.—1603–1606.
Vol. II.—1606–1608.
Vol. III.—1608–1610.
Vol. IV.—1611–1614.

This series is in continuation of the Irish State Papers commencing with the reign of Henry VIII.; but, for the reign of James I., the Papers are not confined to those in the Public Record Office, London.

CALENDAR OF STATE PAPERS, COLONIAL SERIES, preserved in Her Majesty's Public Record Office, and elsewhere. *Edited by* W. NOEL SAINSBURY, Esq. 1860–1878.

Vol. I.—America and West Indies, 1574–1660.
Vol. II.—East Indies, China, and Japan, 1513–1616.
Vol. III.—East Indies, China, and Japan, 1617–1621.
Vol. IV.—East Indies, China, and Japan, 1622–1624.

These volumes include an analysis of early Colonial Papers in the Public Record Office, the India Office, and the British Museum.

CALENDAR OF LETTERS AND PAPERS, FOREIGN AND DOMESTIC, OF THE REIGN OF HENRY VIII., preserved in Her Majesty's Public Record

Office, the British Museum, &c. *Edited by* J. S. BREWER, M.A., Professor of English Literature, King's College, London. 1862-1876.

Vol. I.—1509-1514.	Vol. IV.—Introduction.
Vol. II. (in Two Parts)—1515-1518.	Vol. IV., Part 1.—1524-1526.
Vol. III. (in Two Parts)—1519-1523.	Vol. IV., Part 2.—1526-1528.
	Vol. IV., Part 3.—1529-1530.

These volumes contain summaries of all State Papers and Correspondence relating to the reign of Henry VIII., in the Public Record Office, of those formerly in the State Paper Office, in the British Museum, the Libraries of Oxford and Cambridge, and other Public Libraries; and of all letters that have appeared in print in the works of Burnet, Strype, and others. Whatever authentic original material exists in England relative to the religious, political, parliamentary, or social history of the country during the reign of Henry VIII., whether despatches of ambassadors, or proceedings of the army, navy, treasury, or ordnance, or records of Parliament, appointments of officers, grants from the Crown, &c., will be found calendared in these volumes.

CALENDAR OF STATE PAPERS, FOREIGN SERIES, OF THE REIGN OF EDWARD VI., preserved in Her Majesty's Public Record Office. 1547-1553. *Edited by* W. B. TURNBULL, Esq., of Lincoln's Inn, Barrister-at-Law, and Correspondant du Comité Impérial des Travaux Historiques et des Sociétés Savantes de France. 1861.

CALENDAR OF STATE PAPERS, FOREIGN SERIES, OF THE REIGN OF MARY, preserved in Her Majesty's Public Record Office. 1553-1558. *Edited by* W. B. TURNBULL, Esq., of Lincoln's Inn, Barrister-at-Law and Correspondant du Comité Impérial des Travaux Historiques et des Sociétés Savantes de France. 1861.

The two preceding volumes exhibit the negotiations of the English ambassadors with the courts of the Emperor Charles V. of Germany, of Henry II. of France, and of Philip II. of Spain. The affairs of several of the minor continental states also find various incidental illustrations of much interest.

A valuable series of Papers descriptive of the circumstances which attended the loss of Calais merits a special notice; while the progress of the wars in the north of France, into which England was dragged by her union with Spain, is narrated at some length. The domestic affairs of England are of course passed over in these volumes, which treat only of its relations with foreign powers.

CALENDAR OF STATE PAPERS, FOREIGN SERIES, OF THE REIGN OF ELIZABETH, preserved in Her Majesty's Public Record Office, &c. *Edited by* the Rev. JOSEPH STEVENSON, M.A., of University College, Durham, (Vols. I.-VII.), and ALLAN JAMES CROSBY, Esq., M.A., Barrister-at-Law, (Vols. VIII.-X.) 1863-1876.

Vol. I.—1558-1559.	Vol. VI.—1563.
Vol. II.—1559-1560.	Vol. VII.—1564-1565.
Vol. III.—1560-1561.	Vol. VIII.—1566-1568.
Vol. IV.—1561-1562.	Vol. IX.—1569-1571.
Vol. V.—1562.	Vol. X.—1572-1574.

These volumes contain a Calendar of the Foreign Correspondence during the early portion of the reign of Queen Elizabeth, deposited in the Public Record Office, &c. They illustrate not only the external but also the domestic affairs of Foreign Countries during that period.

CALENDAR OF TREASURY PAPERS, preserved in Her Majesty's Public Record Office. *Edited by* JOSEPH REDINGTON, Esq. 1868-1879.

Vol. I.—1557-1696.	Vol. III.—1702-1707.
Vol. II.—1697-1702.	Vol. IV.—1708-1714.

The above Papers connected with the affairs of the Treasury comprise petitions, reports, and other documents relating to services rendered to the State, grants of money and pensions, appointments to offices, remissions of fines and duties, &c. They illustrate civil and military events, finance, the administration in Ireland and the Colonies, &c., and afford information nowhere else recorded.

CALENDAR OF THE CAREW PAPERS, preserved in the Lambeth Library. *Edited by* J. S. BREWER, M.A., Professor of English Literature, King's College, London ; and WILLIAM BULLEN, Esq. 1867–1873.

Vol. I.—1515–1574.
Vol. II.—1575–1588.
Vol. III.—1589–1600.
Vol. IV.—1601–1603.
Vol. V.—Book of Howth ; Miscellaneous.
Vol. VI.—1603–1624.

The Carew Papers relating to Ireland, deposited in the Lambeth Library, are unique, and of great importance. The Calendar (now completed) cannot fail to be welcome to all students of Irish history.

CALENDAR OF LETTERS, DESPATCHES, AND STATE PAPERS, relating to the Negotiations between England and Spain, preserved in the Archives at Simancas, and elsewhere. *Edited by* G. A. BERGENROTH. 1862–1868.

Vol. I.—Hen. VII.—1485–1509.
Vol. II.—Hen. VIII.—1509–1525.
Supplement to Vol. I. and Vol. II.

Mr. Bergenroth was engaged in compiling a Calendar of the Papers relating to England preserved in the archives of Simancas in Spain, and the corresponding portion removed from Simancas to Paris. Mr. Bergenroth also visited Madrid, and examined the Papers there, bearing on the reign of Henry VIII. The first volume contains the Spanish Papers of the reign of Henry VII. ; the second volume, those of the first portion of the reign of Henry VIII. The Supplement contains new information relating to the private life of Queen Katharine of England ; and to the projected marriage of Henry VII. with Queen Juana, widow of King Philip of Castile, and mother of the Emperor Charles V.

CALENDAR OF LETTERS, DESPATCHES, AND STATE PAPERS, relating to the Negotiations between England and Spain, preserved in the Archives at Simancas, and elsewhere. *Edited by* DON PASCUAL DE GAYANGOS. 1873–1877.

Vol. III., Part 1.—Hen. VIII.—1525–1526.
Vol. III., Part 2.—Hen. VIII.—1527–1529.

Upon the death of Mr. Bergenroth, Don Pascual de Gayangos was appointed to continue the Calendar of the Spanish State Papers. He has pursued a similar plan to that of his predecessor, but has been able to add much valuable matter from Brussels and Vienna, with which Mr. Bergenroth was unacquainted.

CALENDAR OF STATE PAPERS AND MANUSCRIPTS, relating to ENGLISH AFFAIRS, preserved in the Archives of Venice, &c. *Edited by* RAWDON BROWN, Esq. 1864–1877.

Vol. I.—1202–1509.
Vol. II.—1509–1519.
Vol. III.—1520–1526.
Vol. IV.—1527–1533.
Vol. V.—1534–1554.
Vol. VI., Part I.—1555–1556.

Mr. Rawdon Brown's researches have brought to light a number of valuable documents relating to various periods of English history ; his contributions to historical literature are of the most interesting and important character.

SYLLABUS, IN ENGLISH, OF RYMER'S FŒDERA. *By* Sir THOMAS DUFFUS HARDY, D.C.L., Deputy Keeper of the Public Records. Vol. I.—Will. I.–Edw. III. ; 1066–1377. Vol. II.—Ric. II.–Chas. II. ; 1377–1654. 1869–1873.

The "Fœdera," or "Rymer's Fœdera," is a collection of miscellaneous documents illustrative of the History of Great Britain and Ireland, from the Norman

Conquest to the reign of Charles II. Several editions of the "Fœdera" have been published, and the present Syllabus was undertaken to make the contents of this great National Work more generally known.

REPORT OF THE DEPUTY KEEPER OF THE PUBLIC RECORDS AND THE REV. J. S. BREWER TO THE MASTER OF THE ROLLS, upon the Carte and Carew Papers in the Bodleian and Lambeth Libraries. 1864. *Price* 2*s*. 6*d*.

REPORT OF THE DEPUTY KEEPER OF THE PUBLIC RECORDS TO THE MASTER OF THE ROLLS, upon the Documents in the Archives and Public Libraries of Venice. 1866. *Price* 2*s*. 6*d*.

In the Press.

SYLLABUS, IN ENGLISH, OF RYMER'S FŒDERA. *By* Sir THOMAS DUFFUS HARDY, D.C.L., Deputy Keeper of the Public Records. Vol. III.—Appendix and Index.

CALENDAR OF LETTERS AND PAPERS, FOREIGN AND DOMESTIC, OF THE REIGN OF HENRY VIII., preserved in Her Majesty's Public Record Office, the British Museum, &c. *Edited by* J. S. BREWER, M.A., Preacher at the Rolls, and Rector of Toppesfield. Vol. V.—1531, &c.

CALENDAR OF STATE PAPERS, COLONIAL SERIES, preserved in Her Majesty's Public Record Office, and elsewhere. *Edited by* W. NOEL SAINSBURY, Esq. Vol. V.—America and West Indies, 1661–1670.

CALENDAR OF STATE PAPERS relating to IRELAND, OF THE REIGN OF JAMES I., preserved in Her Majesty's Public Record Office, and elsewhere. *Edited by* the Rev. C. W. RUSSELL, D.D., and JOHN P. PRENDERGAST, Esq., Barrister-at-Law. Vol. V.—1615—1625.

CALENDAR OF STATE PAPERS AND MANUSCRIPTS, relating to ENGLISH AFFAIRS, preserved in the Archives of Venice, &c. *Edited by* RAWDON BROWN, Esq. Vol. VI., Part II.—1556–1558.

CALENDAR OF LETTERS, DESPATCHES, AND STATE PAPERS, relating to the Negotiations between England and Spain, preserved in the Archives at Simancas, and elsewhere. *Edited by* DON PASCUAL DE GAYANGOS. Vol. IV., Part I.—Hen. VIII. 1529–1530.

CALENDAR OF DOCUMENTS relating to IRELAND, preserved in Her Majesty's Public Record Office, London. *Edited by* HENRY SAVAGE SWEETMAN, Esq., B.A., Trinity College, Dublin, Barrister-at-Law (Ireland). Vol. III.—1285–1292.

CALENDAR OF STATE PAPERS, DOMESTIC SERIES, DURING THE COMMONWEALTH, preserved in Her Majesty's Public Record Office. *Edited by* MARY ANNE EVERETT GREEN. Vol. VI.—1653, &c.

In Progress.

Calendar of State Papers, Colonial Series, preserved in Her Majesty's Public Record Office, and elsewhere. *Edited by* W. Noel Sainsbury, Esq. Vol. VI.—East Indies, 1625, &c. Vol. VII.—America and West Indies, 1671, &c.

Calendar of State Papers, Foreign Series, of the Reign of Elizabeth, preserved in Her Majesty's Public Record Office. *Edited by* Allan James Crosby, Esq., M.A., Barrister-at-Law. Vol. XI.—1575, &c.

Calendar of State Papers, Domestic Series, of the Reign of Charles I.; preserved in Her Majesty's Public Record Office. *Edited by* William Douglas Hamilton, Esq., F.S.A. Vol. XVI.—1640.

Calendar of State Papers relating to Ireland, of the Reign of Elizabeth, preserved in Her Majesty's Public Record Office. *Edited by* Hans Claude Hamilton, Esq., F.S.A. Vol. IV.—1588, &c.

Calendar of Home Office Papers of the Reign of George III., preserved in Her Majesty's Public Record Office. 1766, &c. *Edited by* Joseph Redington, Esq.

Calendar of Treasury Papers, preserved in Her Majesty's Public Record Office. *Edited by* Joseph Redington, Esq. Vol. V.—1714, &c.

THE CHRONICLES AND MEMORIALS OF GREAT BRITAIN AND IRELAND DURING THE MIDDLE AGES.

[ROYAL 8vo. half-bound. *Price* 10*s*. each Volume or Part.]

On 25 July 1822, the House of Commons presented an address to the Crown, stating that the editions of the works of our ancient historians were inconvenient and defective; that many of their writings still remained in manuscript, and, in some cases, in a single copy only. They added, "that an "uniform and convenient edition of the whole, published under His Majesty's "royal sanction, would be an undertaking honourable to His Majesty's reign, "and conducive to the advancement of historical and constitutional know- "ledge; that the House therefore humbly besought His Majesty, that He "would be graciously pleased to give such directions as His Majesty, in His "wisdom, might think fit, for the publication of a complete edition of the "ancient historians of this realm, and assured His Majesty that whatever "expense might be necessary for this purpose would be made good."

The Master of the Rolls, being very desirous that effect should be given to the resolution of the House of Commons, submitted to Her Majesty's Treasury in 1857 a plan for the publication of the ancient chronicles and memorials of the United Kingdom, and it was adopted accordingly. In selecting these works, it was considered right, in the first instance, to give preference to those of which the manuscripts were unique, or the materials of which would help to fill up blanks in English history for which no satisfactory and authentic information hitherto existed in any accessible form. One great object the Master of the Rolls had in view was to form a *corpus historicum* within reasonable limits, and which should be as complete as possible. In a subject of so vast a range, it was important that the historical student should be able to select such volumes as conformed with his own peculiar tastes and studies, and not be put to the expense of purchasing the whole collection; an inconvenience inseparable from any other plan than that which has been in this instance adopted.

Of the Chronicles and Memorials, the following volumes have been published. They embrace the period from the earliest time of British history down to the end of the reign of Henry VII.

1. THE CHRONICLE OF ENGLAND, by JOHN CAPGRAVE. *Edited by* the Rev. F. C. HINGESTON, M.A., of Exeter College, Oxford. 1858.

Capgrave was prior of Lynn, in Norfolk, and provincial of the order of the Friars Hermits of England shortly before the year 1464. His Chronicle extends from the creation of the world to the year 1417. As a record of the language spoken in Norfolk (being written in English), it is of considerable value.

2. CHRONICON MONASTERII DE ABINGDON. Vols. I. and II. *Edited by* the Rev. JOSEPH STEVENSON, M.A., of University College, Durham, and Vicar of Leighton Buzzard. 1858.

This Chronicle traces the history of the great Benedictine monastery of Abingdon in Berkshire, from its foundation by King Ina of Wessex, to the reign of Richard I., shortly after which period the present narrative was drawn up by an inmate of the establishment. The author had access to the title-deeds of the house; and incorporates into his history various charters of the Saxon kings, of great importance as illustrating not only the history of the locality but that of the kingdom. The work is printed for the first time.

3. LIVES OF EDWARD THE CONFESSOR. I.—La Estoire de Seint Aedward le Rei. II.—Vita Beati Edvardi Regis et Confessoris. III.—Vita Æduuardi Regis qui apud Westmonasterium requiescit. *Edited by* HENRY RICHARDS LUARD, M.A., Fellow and Assistant Tutor of Trinity College, Cambridge. 1858.

The first is a poem in Norman French, containing 4,686 lines, addressed to Alianor, Queen of Henry III., and probably written in the year 1245, on the occasion of the restoration of the church of Westminster. Nothing is known of the author. The second is an anonymous poem, containing 536 lines, written between the years 1440 and 1450, by command of Henry VI., to whom it is dedicated. It does not throw any new light on the reign of Edward the Confessor, but is valuable as a specimen of the Latin poetry of the time. The third, also by an anonymous author, was apparently written for Queen Edith, between the years 1066 and 1074, during the pressure of the suffering brought on the Saxons by the Norman conquest. It notices many facts not found in other writers, and some which differ considerably from the usual accounts.

4. MONUMENTA FRANCISCANA; scilicet, I.—Thomas de Eccleston de Adventu Fratrum Minorum in Angliam. II.—Adæ de Marisco Epistolæ. III.—Registrum Fratrum Minorum Londoniæ. *Edited by* J. S. BREWER, M.A., Professor of English Literature, King's College, London. 1858.

This volume contains original materials for the history of the settlement of the order of Saint Francis in England, the letters of Adam de Marisco, and other papers connected with the foundation and diffusion of this great body. It has been the aim of the editor to collect whatever historical information could be found in this country, towards illustrating a period of the national history for which only scanty materials exist. None of these have been before printed.

5. FASCICULI ZIZANIORUM MAGISTRI JOHANNIS WYCLIF CUM TRITICO. Ascribed to THOMAS NETTER, of WALDEN, Provincial of the Carmelite Order in England, and Confessor to King Henry the Fifth. *Edited by* the Rev. W. W. SHIRLEY, M.A., Tutor and late Fellow of Wadham College, Oxford. 1858.

This work derives its principal value from being the only contemporaneous account of the rise of the Lollards. When written the disputes of the schoolmen had been extended to the field of theology, and they appear both in the writings of Wycliff and in those of his adversaries. Wycliff's little bundles of tares are not less metaphysical than theological, and the conflict between Nominalists and Realists rages side by side with the conflict between the different interpreters of Scripture. The work gives a good idea of the controversies at the end of the 14th and the beginning of the 15th centuries.

6. THE BUIK OF THE CRONICLIS OF SCOTLAND ; or, A Metrical Version of the History of Hector Boece ; by WILLIAM STEWART. Vols. I., II., and III. *Edited by* W. B. TURNBULL, Esq., of Lincoln's Inn, Barrister-at-Law. 1858.

This is a metrical translation of a Latin Prose Chronicle, and was written in the first half of the 16th century. The narrative begins with the earliest legends, and ends with the death of James I. of Scotland, and the "evil ending of the traitors that slew him." Strict accuracy of statement is not to be looked for in such a work as this ; but the stories of the colonization of Spain, Ireland, and Scotland are interesting if not true ; and the chronicle is valuable as a reflection of the manners, sentiments, and character of the age in which it was composed. The peculiarities of the Scottish dialect are well illustrated in this metrical version, and the student of language will find ample materials for comparison with the English dialects of the same period, and with modern lowland Scotch.

7. JOHANNIS CAPGRAVE LIBER DE ILLUSTRIBUS HENRICIS. *Edited by* the Rev. F. C. HINGESTON, M.A., of Exeter College, Oxford. 1858.

This work is dedicated to Henry VI. of England, who appears to have been, in the author's estimation, the greatest of all the Henries. It is divided into three distinct parts, each having its own separate dedication. The first part relates only to the history of the Empire, and extends from the election of Henry I., the Fowler, to the end of the reign of the Emperor Henry VI. The second part is devoted to English history, and extends from the accession of Henry I in the year 1100, to the year 1446, which was the twenty-fourth year of the reign of King Henry VI. The third part contains the lives of illustrious men who have borne the name of Henry in various parts of the world.

Capgrave was born in 1393, in the reign of Richard II., and lived during the Wars of the Roses, for the history of which period his work is of some value.

8. HISTORIA MONASTERII S. AUGUSTINI CANTUARIENSIS, by THOMAS OF ELMHAM, formerly Monk and Treasurer of that Foundation. *Edited by* CHARLES HARDWICK, M.A., Fellow of St. Catharine's Hall, and Christian Advocate in the University of Cambridge. 1858.

This history extends from the arrival of St. Augustine in Kent until 1191. Prefixed is a chronology as far as 1418, which shows in outline what was to have been the character of the work when completed. The only copy known is in the possession of Trinity Hall, Cambridge. The author was connected with Norfolk, and most probably with Elmham, whence he derived his name.

9. EULOGIUM (HISTORIARUM SIVE TEMPORIS) : Chronicon ab Orbe condito usque ad Annum Domini 1366 ; a Monacho quodam Malmesbiriensi exaratum. Vols. I., II., and III. *Edited by* F. S. HAYDON, Esq., B.A. 1858–1863.

This is a Latin Chronicle extending from the Creation to the latter part of the reign of Edward III., and written by a monk of the Abbey of Malmesbury, in Wiltshire, about the year 1367. A continuation, carrying the history of England down to the year 1413, was added in the former half of the fifteenth century by an author whose name is not known. The original Chronicle is divided into five books, and contains a history of the world generally, but more especially of England to the year 1366. The continuation extends the history down to the coronation of Henry V. The Eulogium itself is chiefly valuable as containing a history, by a contemporary, of the period between 1356 and 1366. The notices of events appear to have been written very soon after their occurrence. Among other interesting matter, the Chronicle contains a diary of the Poitiers campaign, evidently furnished by some person who accompanied the army of the Black Prince. The continuation of the Chronicle is also the work of a contemporary, and gives a very interesting account of the reigns of Richard II. and Henry IV. It is believed to be the earliest authority for the statement that the latter monarch died in the Jerusalem Chamber at Westminster.

10. MEMORIALS OF HENRY THE SEVENTH: Bernardi Andreæ Tholosatis Vita Regis Henrici Septimi; necnon alia quædam ad eundem Regem spectantia. *Edited by* JAMES GAIRDNER, Esq. 1858.

The contents of this volume are—(1) a life of Henry VII., by his poet laureate and historiographer, Bernard André, of Toulouse, with some compositions in verse, of which he is supposed to have been the author; (2) the journals of Roger Machado during certain embassies on which he was sent by Henry VII. to Spain and Brittany, the first of which had reference to the marriage of the King's son, Arthur, with Catharine of Arragon; (3) two curious reports by envoys sent to Spain in the year 1505 touching the succession to the Crown of Castile, and a project of marriage between Henry VII. and the Queen of Naples; and (4) an account of Philip of Castile's reception in England in 1506. Other documents of interest in connexion with the period are given in an appendix.

11. MEMORIALS OF HENRY THE FIFTH. I.—Vita Henrici Quinti, Roberto Redmanno auctore. II.—Versus Rhythmici in laudem Regis Henrici Quinti. III.—Elmhami Liber Metricus de Henrico V. *Edited by* CHARLES A. COLE, Esq. 1858.

This volume contains three treatises which more or less illustrate the history of the reign of Henry V., viz.: A Life by Robert Redman; a Metrical Chronicle by Thomas Elmham, prior of Lenton, a contemporary author; Versus Rhythmici, written apparently by a monk of Westminster Abbey, who was also a contemporary of Henry V. These works are printed for the first time.

12. MUNIMENTA GILDHALLÆ LONDONIENSIS; Liber Albus, Liber Custumarum, et Liber Horn, in archivis Gildhallæ asservati. Vol. I., Liber Albus. Vol. II. (in Two Parts), Liber Custumarum. Vol. III. Translation of the Anglo-Norman Passages in Liber Albus, Glossaries, Appendices, and Index. *Edited by* HENRY THOMAS RILEY, Esq., M.A., Barrister-at-Law. 1859–1862.

The manuscript of the *Liber Albus*, compiled by John Carpenter, Common Clerk of the City of London in the year 1419, a large folio volume, is preserved in the Record Room of the City of London. It gives an account of the laws, regulations, and institutions of that City in the twelfth, thirteenth, fourteenth, and early part of the fifteenth centuries.

The *Liber Custumarum* was compiled probably by various hands in the early part of the fourteenth century during the reign of Edward II. The manuscript, a folio volume, is also preserved in the Record Room of the City of London, though some portion in its original state, borrowed from the City in the reign of Queen Elizabeth and never returned, forms part of the Cottonian MS. Claudius D. II. in the British Museum. It also gives an account of the laws, regulations, and institutions of the City of London in the twelfth, thirteenth, and early part of the fourteenth centuries.

13. CHRONICA JOHANNIS DE OXENEDES. *Edited by* Sir HENRY ELLIS, K.H. 1859.

Although this Chronicle tells of the arrival of Hengist and Horsa in England in the year 449, yet it substantially begins with the reign of King Alfred, and comes down to the year 1292, where it ends abruptly. The history is particularly valuable for notices of events in the eastern portions of the kingdom, which are not to be elsewhere obtained, and some curious facts are mentioned relative to the floods in that part of England, which are confirmed in the Friesland Chronicle of Anthony Heinrich, pastor of the Island of Mohr.

14. A COLLECTION OF POLITICAL POEMS AND SONGS RELATING TO ENGLISH HISTORY, FROM THE ACCESSION OF EDWARD III. TO THE REIGN OF HENRY VIII. Vols. I. and II. *Edited by* THOMAS WRIGHT, Esq., M.A. 1859–1861.

These Poems are perhaps the most interesting of all the historical writings of the period, though they cannot be relied on for accuracy of statement. They are various in character; some are upon religious subjects, some may be called satires, and some give no more than a court scandal; but as a whole they present a very fair picture of society, and of the relations of the different classes to one another. The period comprised is in itself interesting, and brings us, through the decline of the feudal system, to the beginning of our modern history. The songs in old English are of considerable value to the philologist.

15. The "OPUS TERTIUM," "OPUS MINUS," &c., of ROGER BACON. *Edited by* J. S. BREWER, M.A., Professor of English Literature, King's College, London. 1859.

This is the celebrated treatise—never before printed—so frequently referred to by the great philosopher in his works. It contains the fullest details we possess of the life and labours of Roger Bacon: also a fragment by the same author, supposed to be unique, the "*Compendium Studii Theologiæ.*"

16. BARTHOLOMÆI DE COTTON, MONACHI NORWICENSIS, HISTORIA ANGLICANA; 449–1298: necnon ejusdem Liber de Archiepiscopis et Episcopis Angliæ. *Edited by* HENRY RICHARDS LUARD, M.A., Fellow and Assistant Tutor of Trinity College, Cambridge. 1859.

The author, a monk of Norwich, has here given us a Chronicle of England from the arrival of the Saxons in 449 to the year 1298, in or about which year it appears that he died. The latter portion of this history (the whole of the reign of Edward I. more especially) is of great value, as the writer was contemporary with the events which he records. An Appendix contains several illustrative documents connected with the previous narrative.

17. BRUT Y TYWYSOGION; or, The Chronicle of the Princes of Wales. *Edited by* the Rev. JOHN WILLIAMS AB ITHEL, M.A. 1860.

This work, also known as "The Chronicle of the Princes of Wales," has been attributed to Caradoc of Llancarvan, who flourished about the middle of the twelfth century. It is written in the ancient Welsh language, begins with the abdication and death of Caedwala at Rome, in the year 681, and continues the history down to the subjugation of Wales by Edward I., about the year 1282.

18. A COLLECTION OF ROYAL AND HISTORICAL LETTERS DURING THE REIGN OF HENRY IV. 1399–1404. *Edited by* the Rev. F. C. HINGESTON, M.A., of Exeter College, Oxford. 1860.

This volume, like all the others in the series containing a miscellaneous selection of letters, is valuable on account of the light it throws upon biographical history, and the familiar view it presents of characters, manners, and events. The period requires much elucidation; to which it will materially contribute.

19. THE REPRESSOR OF OVER MUCH BLAMING OF THE CLERGY. By REGINALD PECOCK, sometime Bishop of Chichester. Vols. I. and II. *Edited by* CHURCHILL BABINGTON, B.D., Fellow of St. John's College, Cambridge. 1860.

The "Repressor" may be considered the earliest piece of good theological disquisition of which our English prose literature can boast. The author was born about the end of the fourteenth century, consecrated Bishop of St. Asaph in the year 1444, and translated to the see of Chichester in 1450. While Bishop of St. Asaph, he zealously defended his brother prelates from the attacks of those who censured the bishops for their neglect of duty. He maintained that it was no part of a bishop's functions to appear in the pulpit, and that his time might be more profitably spent, and his dignity better maintained, in the performance of works of a higher character. Among those who thought differently were the Lollards, and against their general doctrines the "Repressor" is directed. Pecock took up a position midway between that of the Roman Church and that of the modern Anglican Church; but his work is interesting chiefly because it gives a full account of the views of the Lollards and of the arguments by which they were supported, and because it assists us to ascertain the state of feeling which ultimately led to the Reformation. Apart from religious matters, the light thrown upon contemporaneous history is very small, but the "Repressor" has great value for the philologist, as it tells us what were the characteristics of the language in use among the cultivated Englishmen of the fifteenth century. Pecock, though an opponent of the Lollards, showed a certain spirit of toleration, for which he received, towards the end of his life, the usual mediæval reward—persecution.

20. Annales Cambriæ. *Edited by* the Rev. John Williams ab Ithel, M.A. 1860.

These annals, which are in Latin, commence in the year 447, and come down to the year 1288. The earlier portion appears to be taken from an Irish Chronicle, which was also used by Tigernach, and by the compiler of the Annals of Ulster. During its first century it contains scarcely anything relating to Britain, the earliest direct concurrence with English history is relative to the mission of Augustine. Its notices throughout, though brief, are valuable. The annals were probably written at St. Davids, by Blegewryd, Archdeacon of Llandaff, the most learned man in his day in all Cymru.

21. The Works of Giraldus Cambrensis. Vols. I., II., III., and IV. *Edited by* J. S. Brewer, M.A., Professor of English Literature, King's College, London. Vols. V., VI., and VII. *Edited by* the Rev. James F. Dimock, M.A., Rector of Barnburgh, Yorkshire. 1861–1877.

These volumes contain the historical works of Gerald du Barry, who lived in the reigns of Henry II., Richard I., and John, and attempted to re-establish the independence of Wales by restoring the see of St. Davids to its ancient primacy. His works are of a very miscellaneous nature, both in prose and verse, and are remarkable chiefly for the racy and original anecdotes which they contain relating to contemporaries. He is the only Welsh writer of any importance who has contributed so much to the mediæval literature of this country, or assumed, in consequence of his nationality, so free and independent a tone. His frequent travels in Italy, in France, in Ireland, and in Wales, gave him opportunities for observation which did not generally fall to the lot of mediæval writers in the twelfth and thirteenth centuries, and of these observations Giraldus has made due use. Only extracts from these treatises have been printed before, and almost all of them are taken from unique manuscripts.

The Topographia Hibernica (in Vol. V.) is the result of Giraldus' two visits to Ireland. The first in the year 1183, the second in 1185–6, when he accompanied Prince John into that country. Curious as this treatise is, Mr. Dimock is of opinion that it ought not to be accepted as sober truthful history, for Giraldus himself states that truth was not his main object, and that he compiled the work for the purpose of sounding the praises of Henry the Second. Elsewhere, however, he declares that he had stated nothing in the Topographia of the truth of which he was not well assured, either by his own eyesight or by the testimony, with all diligence elicited, of the most trustworthy and authentic men in the country; that though he did not put just the same full faith in their reports as in what he had himself seen, yet, as they only related what they had themselves seen, he could not but believe such credible witnesses. A very interesting portion of this treatise is devoted to the animals of Ireland. It shows that he was a very accurate and acute observer, and his descriptions are given in a way that a scientific naturalist of the present day could hardly improve upon. The Expugnatio Hibernica was written about the year 1188 and may be regarded rather as a great epic than a sober relation of acts occurring in his own days. No one can peruse it without coming to the conclusion that it is rather a poetical fiction than a prosaic truthful history.

Vol. VI. contains the Itinerarium Kambriæ et Descriptio Kambriæ: and Vol. VII., the lives of S. Remigius and S. Hugh.

22. Letters and Papers illustrative of the Wars of the English in France during the Reign of Henry the Sixth, King of England. Vol. I., and Vol. II. (in Two Parts). *Edited by* the Rev. Joseph Stevenson, M.A., of University College, Durham, and Vicar of Leighton Buzzard. 1861–1864.

The letters and papers contained in these volumes are derived chiefly from originals or contemporary copies extant in the Bibliothèque Impériale, and the Depôt des Archives, in Paris. They illustrate the line of policy adopted by John Duke of Bedford and his successors during their government of Normandy, and such other provinces of France as had been acquired by Henry V. We may here trace, step by step, the gradual declension of the English power, until we are prepared to read of its final overthrow.

23. The Anglo-Saxon Chronicle, according to the several Original Authorities. Vol. I., Original Texts. Vol. II., Translation. *Edited and translated by* Benjamin Thorpe, Esq., Member of the Royal Academy of Sciences at Munich, and of the Society of Netherlandish Literature at Leyden. 1861.

This Chronicle, extending from the earliest history of Britain to the year 1154, is justly the boast of England; for no other nation can produce any history, written in its own vernacular, at all approaching it, either in antiquity, truthfulness, or extent, the historical books of the Bible alone excepted. There are at present six independent manuscripts of the Saxon Chronicle, ending in different years, and written in different parts of the country. In this edition, the text of each manuscript is printed in columns on the same page, so that the student may see at a glance the various changes which occur in orthography, whether arising from locality or age.

24. Letters and Papers illustrative of the Reigns of Richard III. and Henry VII. Vols. I. and II. *Edited by* James Gairdner, Esq. 1861–1863.

The Papers are derived from MSS. in the Public Record Office, the British Museum, and other repositories. The period to which they refer is unusually destitute of chronicles and other sources of historical information, so that the light obtained from these documents is of special importance. The principal contents of the volumes are some diplomatic Papers of Richard III.; correspondence between Henry VII. and Ferdinand and Isabella of Spain; documents relating to Edmund de la Pole, Earl of Suffolk; and a portion of the correspondence of James IV. of Scotland.

25. Letters of Bishop Grosseteste, illustrative of the Social Condition of his Time. *Edited by* Henry Richards Luard, M.A., Fellow and Assistant Tutor of Trinity College, Cambridge. 1861.

The Letters of Robert Grosseteste (131 in number) are here collected from various sources, and a large portion of them is printed for the first time. They range in date from about 1210 to 1253, and relate to various matters connected not only with the political history of England during the reign of Henry III., but with its ecclesiastical condition. They refer especially to the diocese of Lincoln, of which Grosseteste was bishop.

26. Descriptive Catalogue of Manuscripts relating to the History of Great Britain and Ireland. Vol. I. (in Two Parts); Anterior to the Norman Invasion. Vol. II.; 1066–1200. Vol. III.; 1200–1327. *By* Sir Thomas Duffus Hardy, D.C.L., Deputy Keeper of the Public Records. 1862–1871.

The object of this work is to publish notices of all known sources of British history, both printed and unprinted, in one continued sequence. The materials, when historical (as distinguished from biographical), are arranged under the year in which the latest event is recorded in the chronicle or history, and not under the period in which its author, real or supposed, flourished. Biographies are enumerated under the year in which the person commemorated died, and not under the year in which the life was written. This arrangement has two advantages; the materials for any given period may be seen at a glance; and if the reader knows the time when an author wrote, and the number of years that had elapsed between the date of the events and the time the writer flourished, he will generally be enabled to form a fair estimate of the comparative value of the narrative itself. A brief analysis of each work has been added when deserving it, in which the original portions are distinguished from those which are mere compilations. When possible, the sources are indicated from which such compilations have been derived. A biographical sketch of the author of each piece has been added, and a brief notice has also been given of such British authors as have written on historical subjects.

27. ROYAL AND OTHER HISTORICAL LETTERS ILLUSTRATIVE OF THE REIGN OF HENRY III. Vol. I., 1216–1235. Vol. II., 1236–1272. *Selected and edited by* the Rev. W. W. SHIRLEY, D.D., Regius Professor in Ecclesiastical History, and Canon of Christ Church, Oxford. 1862–1866.

The letters contained in these volumes are derived chiefly from the ancient correspondence formerly in the Tower of London, and now in the Public Record Office. They illustrate the political history of England during the growth of its liberties, and throw considerable light upon the personal history of Simon de Montfort. The affairs of France form the subject of many of them, especially in regard to the province of Gascony. The entire collection consists of nearly 700 documents, the greater portion of which is printed for the first time.

28. CHRONICA MONASTERII S. ALBANI.—1. THOMÆ WALSINGHAM HISTORIA ANGLICANA; Vol. I., 1272–1381: Vol. II., 1381–1422. 2. WILLELMI RISHANGER CHRONICA ET ANNALES, 1259–1307. 3. JOHANNIS DE TROKELOWE ET HENRICI DE BLANEFORDE CHRONICA ET ANNALES, 1259–1296; 1307–1324; 1392–1406. 4. GESTA ABBATUM MONASTERII S. ALBANI, A THOMA WALSINGHAM, REGNANTE RICARDO SECUNDO, EJUSDEM ECCLESIÆ PRÆCENTORE, COMPILATA; Vol. I., 793–1290: Vol. II., 1290–1349: Vol. III., 1349–1411. 5. JOHANNIS AMUNDESHAM, MONACHI MONASTERII S. ALBANI, UT VIDETUR, ANNALES; Vols. I. and II. 6. REGISTRA QUORUNDAM ABBATUM MONASTERII S. ALBANI, QUI SÆCULO XV^{mo} FLORUERE; Vol. I., REGISTRUM ABBATIÆ JOHANNIS WHETHAMSTEDE, ABBATIS MONASTERII SANCTI ALBANI, ITERUM SUSCEPTÆ; ROBERTO BLAKENEY, CAPELLANO, QUONDAM ADSCRIPTUM: Vol. II., REGISTRA JOHANNIS WHETHAMSTEDE, WILLELMI ALBON, ET WILLELMI WALINGFORDE, ABBATUM MONASTERII SANCTI ALBANI, CUM APPENDICE, CONTINENTE QUASDAM EPISTOLAS, A JOHANNE WHETHAMSTEDE CONSCRIPTAS. 7. YPODIGMA NEUSTRIÆ, A THOMA WALSINGHAM, QUONDAM MONACHO MONASTERII S. ALBANI, CONSCRIPTUM. *Edited by* HENRY THOMAS RILEY, Esq., M.A., Cambridge and Oxford; and of the Inner Temple, Barrister-at-Law. 1863–1876.

In the first two volumes is a History of England, from the death of Henry III. to the death of Henry V., by Thomas Walsingham, Precentor of St. Albans, from MS. VII. in the Arundel Collection in the College of Arms, London, a manuscript of the fifteenth century, collated with MS. 13 E. IX. in the King's Library in the British Museum, and MS. VII. in the Parker Collection of Manuscripts at Corpus Christi College, Cambridge.

In the third volume is a Chronicle of English History, attributed to William Rishanger, who lived in the reign of Edward I., from the Cotton. MS. Faustina B. IX. in the British Museum, collated with MS. 14 C. VII. (fols. 219–231) in the King's Library, British Museum, and the Cotton MS. Claudius E. III., fols. 306–331: an account of transactions attending the award of the kingdom of Scotland to John Balliol, 1291–1292, from MS. Cotton. Claudius D. VI., also attributed to William Rishanger, but on no sufficient ground: a short Chronicle of English History, 1292 to 1300, by an unknown hand, from MS. Cotton. Claudius D. VI.: a short Chronicle, Willelmi Rishanger Gesta Edwardi Primi, Regis Angliæ, from MS. 14 C. I. in the Royal Library, and MS. Cotton. Claudius D. VI., with Annales Regum Angliæ, probably by the same hand: and fragments of three Chronicles of English History, 1285 to 1307.

In the fourth volume is a Chronicle of English History, 1259 to 1296, from MS. Cotton. Claudius D. VI.: Annals of Edward II., 1307 to 1323, by John de Trokelowe, a monk of St. Albans, and a continuation of Trokelowe's Annals, 1323, 1324, by Henry de Blaneforde, both from MS. Cotton. Claudius D. VI.: a full Chronicle of English History, 1392 to 1406, from MS. VII. in the Library of Corpus Christi College, Cambridge; and an account of the Benefactors of St. Albans, written in the early part of the fifteenth century, from MS. VI. in the same Library.

The fifth, sixth, and seventh volumes contain a history of the Abbots of St. Albans, 793 to 1411, mainly compiled by Thomas Walsingham, from MS. Cotton. Claudius E. IV., in the British Museum: with a Continuation, from the closing pages of Parker MS. VII., in the Library of Corpus Christi College, Cambridge.

The eighth and ninth volumes, in continuation of the Annals, contain a Chronicle, probably by John Amundesham, a monk of St. Albans.

The tenth and eleventh volumes relate especially to the acts and proceedings of Abbots Whethamstede, Albon, and Wallingford, and may be considered as a memorial of the chief historical and domestic events during those periods.

The twelfth volume contains a compendious History of England to the reign of Henry V., and of Normandy in early times, also by Thomas Walsingham, and dedicated to Henry V. The compiler has often substituted other authorities in place of those consulted in the preparation of his larger work.

29. Chronicon Abbatiæ Eveshamensis, Auctoribus Dominico Priore Eveshamiæ et Thoma de Marleberge Abbate, a Fundatione ad Annum 1213, una cum Continuatione ad Annum 1418. *Edited by* the Rev. W. D. Macray, M.A., Bodleian Library, Oxford. 1863.

The Chronicle of Evesham illustrates the history of that important monastery from its foundation by Egwin, about 690, to the year 1418. Its chief feature is an autobiography, which makes us acquainted with the inner daily life of a great abbey, such as but rarely has been recorded. Interspersed are many notices of general, personal, and local history which will be read with much interest. This work exists in a single MS., and is for the first time printed.

30. Ricardi de Cirencestria Speculum Historiale de Gestis Regum Angliæ. Vol. I., 447–871. Vol. II., 872–1066. *Edited by* John E. B. Mayor, M.A., Fellow of St. John's College, Cambridge. 1863–1869.

The compiler, Richard of Cirencester, was a monk of Westminster, 1355–1400. In 1391 he obtained a licence to make a pilgrimage to Rome. His history, in four books, extends from 447 to 1066. He announces his intention of continuing it, but there is no evidence that he completed any more. This chronicle gives many charters in favour of Westminster Abbey, and a very full account of the lives and miracles of the saints, especially of Edward the Confessor, whose reign occupies the fourth book. A treatise on the Coronation, by William of Sudbury, a monk of Westminster, fills book iii. c. 3. It was on this author that C. J. Bertram fathered his forgery, *De Situ Brittaniæ*, in 1747.

31. Year Books of the Reign of Edward the First. Years 20–21, 21–22, 30–31, 32–33, and 33–35. *Edited and translated by* Alfred John Horwood, Esq., of the Middle Temple, Barrister-at-Law. 1863–1879.

The volumes known as the "Year Books" contain reports in Norman-French of cases argued and decided in the Courts of Common Law. They may be considered to a great extent as the "lex non scripta" of England, and have been held in the highest veneration by the ancient sages of the law, and were received by them as the repositories of the first recorded judgments and dicta of the great legal luminaries of past ages. They are also worthy of the attention of the general reader on account of the historical information and the notices of public and private persons which they contain, as well as the light which they throw on ancient manners and customs.

32. Narratives of the Expulsion of the English from Normandy, 1449–1450.—Robertus Blondelli de Reductione Normanniæ: Le Recouvrement de Normendie, par Berry, Hérault du Roy: Conferences between the Ambassadors of France and England. *Edited, from MSS. in the Imperial Library at Paris, by* the Rev. Joseph Stevenson, M.A., of University College, Durham. 1863.

This volume contains the narrative of an eye-witness who details with considerable power and minuteness the circumstances which attended the final expulsion of the English from Normandy in the year 1450. The history commences with the infringement of the truce by the capture of Fougères, and ends with the battle of Formigny and the embarkation of the Duke of Somerset. The whole period embraced is less than two years.

33. Historia et Cartularium Monasterii S. Petri Gloucestriæ. Vols. I., II., and III. *Edited by* W. H. Hart, Esq., F.S.A., Membre correspondant de la Société des Antiquaires de Normandie. 1863–1867.

This work consists of two parts, the History and the Cartulary of the Monastery of St. Peter, Gloucester. The history furnishes an account of the monastery from its foundation, in the year 681, to the early part of the reign of Richard II., together with a calendar of donations and benefactions. It treats principally of the affairs of the monastery, but occasionally matters of general history are introduced. Its authorship has generally been assigned to Walter Froucester, the twentieth abbot, but without any foundation.

34. Alexandri Neckam de Naturis Rerum libri duo; with Neckam's Poem, De Laudibus Divinæ Sapientiæ. *Edited by* Thomas Wright, Esq., M.A. 1863.

Neckam was a man who devoted himself to science, such as it was in the twelfth century. In the "De Naturis Rerum" are to be found what may be called the rudiments of many sciences mixed up with much error and ignorance. Neckam was not thought infallible, even by his contemporaries, for Roger Bacon remarks of him, "this Alexander in many things wrote what was true and useful; "but he neither can nor ought by just title to be reckoned among authorities." Neckam, however, had sufficient independence of thought to differ from some of the schoolmen who in his time considered themselves the only judges of literature. He had his own views in morals, and in giving us a glimpse of them, as well as of his other opinions, he throws much light upon the manners, customs, and general tone of thought prevalent in the twelfth century. The poem entitled "De Laudibus Divinæ Sapientiæ" appears to be a metrical paraphrase or abridgment of the "De Naturis Rerum." It is written in the elegiac metre; and though there are many lines which violate classical rules, it is, as a whole above the ordinary standard of mediæval Latin.

35. Leechdoms, Wortcunning, and Starcraft of Early England; being a Collection of Documents illustrating the History of Science in this Country before the Norman Conquest. Vols. I., II., and III. *Collected and edited by* the Rev. T. Oswald Cockayne, M.A., of St. John's College, Cambridge. 1864–1866.

This work illustrates not only the history of science, but the history of superstition. In addition to the information bearing directly upon the medical skill and medical faith of the times, there are many passages which incidentally throw light upon the general mode of life and ordinary diet. The volumes are interesting not only in their scientific, but also in their social aspect. The manuscripts from which they have been printed are valuable to the Anglo-Saxon scholar for the illustrations they afford of Anglo-Saxon orthography.

36. Annales Monastici. Vol. I.:—Annales de Margan, 1066–1232; Annales de Theokesberia, 1066–1263; Annales de Burton, 1004–1263. Vol. II.:—Annales Monasterii de Wintonia, 519–1277; Annales Monasterii de Waverleia, 1–1291. Vol. III.:—Annales Prioratus de Dunstaplia, 1–1297; Annales Monasterii de Bermundeseia, 1042–

1432. Vol. IV.:—Annales Monasterii de Oseneia, 1016–1347; Chronicon vulgo dictum Chronicon Thomæ Wykes, 1066–1289; Annales Prioratus de Wigornia, 1–1377. Vol. V.:—Index and Glossary. *Edited by* Henry Richards Luard, M.A., Fellow and Assistant Tutor of Trinity College, and Registrary of the University, Cambridge. 1864–1869.

The present collection of Monastic Annals embraces all the more important chronicles compiled in religious houses in England during the thirteenth century. These distinct works are ten in number. The extreme period which they embrace ranges from the year 1 to 1432, although they refer more especially to the reigns of John, Henry III., and Edward I. Some of these narratives have already appeared in print, but others are printed for the first time.

37. Magna Vita S. Hugonis Episcopi Lincolniensis. From Manuscripts in the Bodleian Library, Oxford, and the Imperial Library, Paris. *Edited by* the Rev. James F. Dimock, M.A., Rector of Barnburgh, Yorkshire. 1864.

This work contains a number of very curious and interesting incidents, and being the work of a contemporary, is very valuable, not only as a truthful biography of a celebrated ecclesiastic, but as the work of a man, who, from personal knowledge, gives notices of passing events, as well as of individuals who were then taking active part in public affairs. The author, in all probability, was Adam Abbot of Evesham. He was domestic chaplain and private confessor of Bishop Hugh, and in these capacities was admitted to the closest intimacy. Bishop Hugh was Prior of Witham for 11 years before he became Bishop of Lincoln. His consecration took place on the 21st September 1186; he died on the 16th of November 1200; and was canonized in 1220.

38. Chronicles and Memorials of the Reign of Richard the First. Vol. I.:—Itinerarium Peregrinorum et Gesta Regis Ricardi. Vol. II.:—Epistolæ Cantuarienses; the Letters of the Prior and Convent of Christ Church, Canterbury; 1187 to 1199. *Edited by* William Stubbs, M.A., Vicar of Navestock, Essex, and Lambeth Librarian. 1864–1865.

The authorship of the Chronicle in Vol. I., hitherto ascribed to Geoffrey Vinesauf, is now more correctly ascribed to Richard, Canon of the Holy Trinity of London. The narrative extends from 1187 to 1199; but its chief interest consists in the minute and authentic narrative which it furnishes of the exploits of Richard I., from his departure from England in December 1189 to his death in 1199. The author states in his prologue that he was an eye-witness of much that he records; and various incidental circumstances which occur in the course of the narrative confirm this assertion.

The letters in Vol. II., written between 1187 and 1199, are of value as furnishing authentic materials for the history of the ecclesiastical condition of England during the reign of Richard I. They had their origin in a dispute which arose from the attempts of Baldwin and Hubert, archbishops of Canterbury, to found a college of secular canons, a project which gave great umbrage to the monks of Canterbury, who saw in it a design to supplant them in their function of metropolitan chapter. These letters are printed, for the first time, from a MS. belonging to the archiepiscopal library at Lambeth.

39. Recueil des Croniques et anchiennes Istories de la Grant Bretaigne a present nomme Engleterre, par Jehan de Waurin. Vol. I. Albina to 688. Vol. II., 1399–1422. *Edited by* William Hardy, Esq., F.S.A. 1864–1868.

40. A Collection of the Chronicles and ancient Histories of Great Britain, now called England, by John de Wavrin. Albina to 688. (Translation of the preceding Vol. I.) *Edited and translated by* William Hardy, Esq., F.S.A. 1864.

This curious chronicle extends from the fabulous period of history down to the return of Edward IV. to England in the year 1471, after the second deposition of

Henry VI. The manuscript from which the text of the work is taken is preserved in the Imperial Library at Paris, and is believed to be the only complete and nearly contemporary copy in existence. The work, as originally bound, was comprised in six volumes, since rebound in morocco in 12 volumes, folio maximo, vellum, and is illustrated with exquisite miniatures, vignettes, and initial letters. It was written towards the end of the fifteenth century, having been expressly executed for Louis de Bruges, Seigneur de la Gruthuyse and Earl of Winchester, from whose cabinet it passed into the library of Louis XII. at Blois.

41. Polychronicon Ranulphi Higden, with Trevisa's Translation. Vols. I. and II. *Edited by* Churchill Babington, B.D., Senior Fellow of St. John's College, Cambridge. Vols. III., IV., V., and VI. *Edited by* the Rev. Joseph Rawson Lumby, B.D., Vicar of St. Edward's, Fellow of St. Catharine's College, and late Fellow of Magdalene College, Cambridge. 1865–1876.

This is one of the many mediæval chronicles which assume the character of a history of the world. It begins with the creation, and is brought down to the author's own time, the reign of Edward III. Prefixed to the historical portion, is a chapter devoted to geography, in which is given a description of every known land. To say that the Polychronicon was written in the fourteenth century is to say that it is not free from inaccuracies. It has, however, a value apart from its intrinsic merits. It enables us to form a very fair estimate of the knowledge of history and geography which well-informed readers of the fourteenth and fifteenth centuries possessed, for it was then the standard work on general history.

The two English translations, which are printed with the original Latin, afford interesting illustrations of the gradual change of our language, for one was made in the fourteenth century, the other in the fifteenth. The differences between Trevisa's version and that of the unknown writer are often considerable.

42. Le Livere de Reis de Brittanie e Le Livere de Reis de Engletere. *Edited by* John Glover, M.A., Vicar of Brading, Isle of Wight, formerly Librarian of Trinity College, Cambridge. 1865.

These two treatises, though they cannot rank as independent narratives, are nevertheless valuable as careful abstracts of previous historians, especially "Le Livere de Reis de Engletere." Some various readings are given which are interesting to the philologist as instances of semi-Saxonized French.

It is supposed that Peter of Ickham must have been the author, but no certain conclusion on that point has been arrived at.

43. Chronica Monasterii de Melsa, ab Anno 1150 usque ad Annum 1406. Vols. I., II., and III. *Edited by* Edward Augustus Bond, Esq., Assistant Keeper of the Manuscripts, and Egerton Librarian, British Museum. 1866–1868.

The Abbey of Meaux was a Cistercian house, and the work of its abbot is both curious and valuable. It is a faithful and often minute record of the establishment of a religious community, of its progress in forming an ample revenue, of its struggles to maintain its acquisitions, and of its relations to the governing institutions of the country. In addition to the private affairs of the monastery, some light is thrown upon the public events of the time, which are however kept distinct, and appear at the end of the history of each abbot's administration. The text has been printed from what is said to be the autograph of the original compiler, Thomas de Burton, the nineteenth abbot.

44. Matthæi Parisiensis Historia Anglorum, sive, ut vulgo dicitur, Historia Minor. Vols. I., II., and III. 1067–1253. *Edited by* Sir Frederic Madden, K.H., Keeper of the Department of Manuscripts, British Museum. 1866–1869.

The exact date at which this work was written is, according to the chronicler, 1250. The history is of considerable value as an illustration of the period during which the author lived, and contains a good summary of the events which followed the Conquest. This minor chronicle is, however, based on another work (also written by Matthew Paris) giving fuller details, which has been called the "Historia Major." The chronicle here published, nevertheless, gives some information not to be found in the greater history.

45. LIBER MONASTERII DE HYDA: A CHRONICLE AND CHARTULARY OF HYDE ABBEY, WINCHESTER, 455–1023. *Edited, from a Manuscript in the Library of the Earl of Macclesfield, by* EDWARD EDWARDS, Esq. 1866.

The "Book of Hyde" is a compilation from much earlier sources which are usually indicated with considerable care and precision. In many cases, however, the Hyde chronicler appears to correct, to qualify, or to amplify—either from tradition or from sources of information not now discoverable—the statements, which, in substance, he adopts. He also mentions, and frequently quotes from writers whose works are either entirely lost or at present known only by fragments.

There is to be found, in the "Book of Hyde," much information relating to the reign of King Alfred which is not known to exist elsewhere. The volume contains some curious specimens of Anglo-Saxon and Mediæval English.

46. CHRONICON SCOTORUM: A CHRONICLE OF IRISH AFFAIRS, from the EARLIEST TIMES to 1135; with a SUPPLEMENT, containing the Events from 1141 to 1150 *Edited, with a Translation, by* WILLIAM MAUNSELL HENNESSY, Esq., M.R.I.A. 1866.

There is, in this volume, a legendary account of the peopling of Ireland and of the adventures which befell the various heroes who are said to have been connected with Irish history. The details are, however, very meagre both for this period and for the time when history becomes more authentic. The plan adopted in the chronicle gives the appearance of an accuracy to which the earlier portions of the work cannot have any claim. The succession of events is marked, year by year, from A.M. 1599 to A.D. 1150. The principal events narrated in the later portion of the work are, the invasions of foreigners, and the wars of the Irish among themselves. The text has been printed from a MS. preserved in the library of Trinity College, Dublin, written partly in Latin, partly in Irish.

47. THE CHRONICLE OF PIERRE DE LANGTOFT, IN FRENCH VERSE, FROM THE EARLIEST PERIOD TO THE DEATH OF EDWARD I. Vols. I. and II. *Edited by* THOMAS WRIGHT, Esq., M.A. 1866–1868.

It is probable that Pierre de Langtoft was a canon of Bridlington, in Yorkshire, and that he lived in the reign of Edward I., and during a portion of the reign of Edward II. This chronicle is divided into three parts; in the first is an abridgment of Geoffrey of Monmouth's "Historia Britonum," in the second, a history of the Anglo-Saxon and Norman kings, down to the death of Henry III., and in the third a history of the reign of Edward I. The principal object of the work was apparently to show the justice of Edward's Scottish wars. The language is singularly corrupt, and a curious specimen of the French of Yorkshire.

48. THE WAR OF THE GAEDHIL WITH THE GAILL, or, THE INVASIONS OF IRELAND BY THE DANES AND OTHER NORSEMEN. *Edited, with a Translation, by* JAMES HENTHORN TODD, D.D., Senior Fellow of Trinity College, and Regius Professor of Hebrew in the University, Dublin. 1867.

The work in its present form, in the editor's opinion, is a comparatively modern version of an undoubtedly ancient original. That it was compiled from contemporary materials has been proved by curious incidental evidence. It is stated in the account given of the battle of Clontarf that the full tide in Dublin Bay on the day of the battle (23 April 1014) coincided with sunrise; and that the returning tide in the evening aided considerably in the defeat of the Danes. The fact has been verified by astronomical calculations, and the inference is that the author of the chronicle, if not himself an eye-witness, must have derived his information from those who were eye-witnesses. The contents of the work are sufficiently described in its title. The story is told after the manner of the Scandinavian Sagas, with poems and fragments of poems introduced into the prose narrative.

49. GESTA REGIS HENRICI SECUNDI BENEDICTI ABBATIS. THE CHRONICLE OF THE REIGNS OF HENRY II. AND RICHARD I., 1169–1192; known

under the name of BENEDICT OF PETERBOROUGH. Vols. I. and II. *Edited by* WILLIAM STUBBS, M.A., Regius Professor of Modern History, Oxford, and Lambeth Librarian. 1867.

This chronicle of the reigns of Henry II. and Richard I., known commonly under the name of Benedict of Peterborough, is one of the best existing specimens of a class of historical compositions of the first importance to the student.

50. MUNIMENTA ACADEMICA, OR, DOCUMENTS ILLUSTRATIVE OF ACADEMICAL LIFE AND STUDIES AT OXFORD (in Two Parts). *Edited by* the Rev. HENRY ANSTEY, M.A., Vicar of St. Wendron, Cornwall, and lately Vice-Principal of St. Mary Hall, Oxford. 1868.

This work will supply materials for a History of Academical Life and Studies in the University of Oxford during the 13th, 14th, and 15th centuries.

51. CHRONICA MAGISTRI ROGERI DE HOUEDENE. Vols. I., II., III., and IV. *Edited by* WILLIAM STUBBS, M.A., Regius Professor of Modern History, and Fellow of Oriel College, Oxford. 1868–1871.

This work has long been justly celebrated, but not thoroughly understood until Mr. Stubbs' edition. The earlier portion, extending from 732 to 1148, appears to be a copy of a compilation made in Northumbria about 1161, to which Hoveden added little. From 1148 to 1169—a very valuable portion of this work—the matter is derived from another source, to which Hoveden appears to have supplied little, and not always judiciously. From 1170 to 1192 is the portion which corresponds with the Chronicle known under the name of Benedict of Peterborough (*see* No. 49); but it is not a copy, being sometimes an abridgment, at others a paraphrase; occasionally the two works entirely agree; showing that both writers had access to the same materials, but dealt with them differently. From 1192 to 1201 may be said to be wholly Hoveden's work: it is extremely valuable, and an authority of the first importance.

52. WILLELMI MALMESBIRIENSIS MONACHI DE GESTIS PONTIFICUM ANGLORUM LIBRI QUINQUE. *Edited, from William of Malmesbury's Autograph MS., by* N. E. S. A. HAMILTON, Esq., of the Department of Manuscripts, British Museum. 1870.

William of Malmesbury's "Gesta Pontificum" is the principal foundation of English Ecclesiastical Biography, down to the year 1122. The manuscript which has been followed in this Edition is supposed by Mr. Hamilton to be the author's autograph, containing his latest additions and amendments.

53. HISTORIC AND MUNICIPAL DOCUMENTS OF IRELAND, FROM THE ARCHIVES OF THE CITY OF DUBLIN, &c. 1172–1320. *Edited by* JOHN T. GILBERT, Esq., F.S.A., Secretary of the Public Record Office of Ireland. 1870.

A collection of original documents, elucidating mainly the history and condition of the municipal, middle, and trading classes under or in relation with the rule of England in Ireland,—a subject hitherto in almost total obscurity. Extending over the first hundred and fifty years of the Anglo-Norman settlement, the series includes charters, municipal laws and regulations, rolls of names of citizens and members of merchant-guilds, lists of commodities with their rates, correspondence, illustrations of relations between ecclesiastics and laity; together with many documents exhibiting the state of Ireland during the presence there of the Scots under Robert and Edward Bruce.

54. THE ANNALS OF LOCH CÉ. A CHRONICLE OF IRISH AFFAIRS, FROM 1014 to 1590. Vols. I. and II. *Edited, with a Translation, by* WILLIAM MAUNSELL HENNESSY, Esq., M.R.I.A. 1871.

The original of this chronicle has passed under various names. The title of "Annals of Loch Cé" was given to it by Professor O'Curry, on the ground that it was transcribed for Brian Mac Dermot, an Irish chieftain, who resided on the island in Loch Cé, in the county of Roscommon. It adds much to the materials for the civil and ecclesiastical history of Ireland; and contains many curious references to English and foreign affairs, not noticed in any other chronicle.

55. MONUMENTA JURIDICA. THE BLACK BOOK OF THE ADMIRALTY, WITH APPENDICES. Vols. I., II., III., and IV. *Edited by* SIR TRAVERS TWISS, Q.C., D.C.L. 1871–1876.

This book contains the ancient ordinances and laws relating to the navy, and was probably compiled for the use of the Lord High Admiral of England. Selden calls it the "jewel of the Admiralty Records." Prynne ascribes to the Black Book the same authority in the Admiralty as the Black and Red Books have in the Court of Exchequer, and most English writers on maritime law recognize its importance.

56. MEMORIALS OF THE REIGN OF HENRY VI.:—OFFICIAL CORRESPONDENCE OF THOMAS BEKYNTON, SECRETARY TO HENRY VI., AND BISHOP OF BATH AND WELLS. *Edited, from a MS. in the Archiepiscopal Library at Lambeth, with an Appendix of Illustrative Documents, by* the Rev. GEORGE WILLIAMS, B.D., Vicar of Ringwood, late Fellow of King's College, Cambridge. Vols. I. and II. 1872.

These curious volumes are of a miscellaneous character, and were probably compiled under the immediate direction of Bekynton before he had attained to the Episcopate. They contain many of the Bishop's own letters, and several written by him in the King's name; also letters to himself while Royal Secretary, and others addressed to the King. This work elucidates some points in the history of the nation during the first half of the fifteenth century.

57. MATTHÆI PARISIENSIS, MONACHI SANCTI ALBANI, CHRONICA MAJORA. Vol. I. The Creation to A.D. 1066. Vol. II. A.D. 1067 to A.D. 1216. Vol. III. A.D. 1216 to A.D. 1239. Vol. IV. A.D. 1240 to A.D. 1247. *Edited by* HENRY RICHARDS LUARD, D.D., Fellow of Trinity College, Registrary of the University, and Vicar of Great St. Mary's, Cambridge. 1872–1877.

This work contains the "Chronica Majora" of Matthew Paris, one of the most valuable and frequently consulted of the ancient English Chronicles. It is published from its commencement, for the first time. The editions by Archbishop Parker, and William Wats, severally begin at the Norman Conquest.

58. MEMORIALE FRATRIS WALTERI DE COVENTRIA.—THE HISTORICAL COLLECTIONS OF WALTER OF COVENTRY. Vols. I. and II. *Edited, from the MS. in the Library of Corpus Christi College, Cambridge, by* WILLIAM STUBBS, M.A., Regius Professor of Modern History, and Fellow of Oriel College, Oxford. 1872–1873.

This work, now printed in full for the first time, has long been a *desideratum* by Historical Scholars. The first portion, however, is not of much importance, being only a compilation from earlier writers. The part relating to the first quarter of the thirteenth century is the most valuable and interesting.

59. THE ANGLO-LATIN SATIRICAL POETS AND EPIGRAMMATISTS OF THE TWELFTH CENTURY. Vols. I. and II. *Now first collected and edited by* THOMAS WRIGHT, Esq., M.A., Corresponding Member of the National Institute of France (Académie des Inscriptions et Belles-Lettres). 1872.

The Poems contained in these volumes have long been known and appreciated as the best satires of the age in which their authors flourished, and were deservedly popular during the 13th and 14th centuries.

60. MATERIALS FOR A HISTORY OF THE REIGN OF HENRY VII., FROM ORIGINAL DOCUMENTS PRESERVED IN THE PUBLIC RECORD OFFICE. Vols. I. and II. *Edited by* the Rev. WILLIAM CAMPBELL, M.A., one of Her Majesty's Inspectors of Schools. 1873–1877.

These volumes are valuable as illustrating the acts and proceedings of Henry VII. on ascending the throne, and shadow out the policy he afterwards adopted.

61. Historical Papers and Letters from the Northern Registers. *Edited by* James Raine, M.A., Canon of York, and Secretary of the Surtees Society. 1873.

The documents in this volume illustrate, for the most part, the general history of the north of England, particularly in its relation to Scotland.

62. Registrum Palatinum Dunelmense. The Register of Richard de Kellawe, Lord Palatine and Bishop of Durham; 1311–1316. Vols. I., II., III., and IV. *Edited by* Sir Thomas Duffus Hardy, D.C.L., Deputy Keeper of the Public Records. 1873–1878.

Bishop Kellawe's Register contains the proceedings of his prelacy, both lay and ecclesiastical, and is the earliest Register of the Palatinate of Durham.

63. Memorials of Saint Dunstan Archbishop of Canterbury. *Edited, from various MSS., by* William Stubbs, M.A., Regius Professor of Modern History, and Fellow of Oriel College, Oxford. 1874.

This volume contains several lives of Archbishop Dunstan, one of the most celebrated Primates of Canterbury. They open various points of Historical and Literary interest, without which our knowledge of the period would be more incomplete than it is at present.

64. Chronicon Angliæ, ab Anno Domini 1328 usque ad Annum 1388, auctore Monacho quodam Sancti Albani. *Edited by* Edward Maunde Thompson, Esq., Barrister-at-Law, and Assistant-Keeper of the Manuscripts in the British Museum. 1874.

This chronicle gives a circumstantial history of the close of the reign of Edward III. which has hitherto been considered lost.

65. Thómas Saga Erkibyskups. A Life of Archbishop Thomas Becket, in Icelandic. Vol. I. *Edited, with English Translation, Notes, and Glossary, by* M. Eiríkr Magnússon, Sub-Librarian of the University Library, Cambridge. 1875.

This work is derived from the Life of Becket written by Benedict of Peterborough, and apparently supplies the missing portions in Benedict's biography.

66. Radulphi de Coggeshall Chronicon Anglicanum. *Edited by* the Rev. Joseph Stevenson, M.A. 1875.

This volume contains the "Chronicon Anglicanum," by Ralph of Coggeshall, the "Libellus de Expugnatione Terræ Sanctæ per Saladinum," usually ascribed to the same author, and other pieces of an interesting character.

67. Materials for the History of Thomas Becket, Archbishop of Canterbury. Vols. I., II., and III. *Edited by* the Rev. James Craigie Robertson, M.A., Canon of Canterbury. 1875–1877.

This Publication will comprise all contemporary materials for the history of Archbishop Thomas Becket. The first volume contains the life of that celebrated man, and the miracles after his death, by William, a monk of Canterbury. The second, the life by Benedict of Peterborough; John of Salisbury; Alan of Tewkesbury; and Edward Grim. The third, the life by William Fitzstephen; and Herbert of Bosham.

68. Radulfi de Diceto Decani Lundoniensis Opera Historica. The Historical Works of Master Ralph de Diceto, Dean of London. Vols. I. and II. *Edited, from the Original Manuscripts, by* William Stubbs, M.A., Regius Professor of Modern History, and Fellow of Oriel College, Oxford. 1876.

The Historical Works of Ralph de Diceto are some of the most valuable materials for British History. The Abbreviationes Chronicorum extend from the Creation to 1147, and the Ymagines Historiarum to 1201.

69. ROLL OF THE PROCEEDINGS OF THE KING'S COUNCIL IN IRELAND, FOR A PORTION OF THE 16TH YEAR OF THE REIGN OF RICHARD II. 1392–93. *Edited by* the Rev. JAMES GRAVES, A.B. 1877.

The Roll printed in this volume throws considerable light on the History of Ireland at a period when little is known of it, and seems to be the only document of the kind extant.

70. HENRICI DE BRACTON DE LEGIBUS ET CONSUETUDINIBUS ANGLIÆ. LIBRI QUINQUE IN VARIOS TRACTATUS DISTINCTI. AD DIVERSORUM ET VETUSTISSIMORUM CODICUM COLLATIONEM TYPIS VULGATI. Vols. I. and II. *Edited by* SIR TRAVERS TWISS, Q.C., D.C.L. 1878–1879.

This is a new edition of Bracton's celebrated work, collated with MSS. in the British Museum; the Libraries of Lincoln's Inn, the Middle Temple, and Gray's Inn; the Bodleian Library, Oxford; the Bibliothèque Nationale, Paris; &c. &c.

In the Press.

CHRONICLE OF ROBERT OF BRUNNE. *Edited by* FREDERICK JAMES FURNIVALL, Esq., M.A., of Trinity Hall, Cambridge, Barrister-at-Law.

CORPUS HISTORICUM EBORACENSE. CHRONICA PONTIFICUM ECCLESIÆ EBORACI AUCTORE THOMA STUBBS DOMINICANO; and other Documents relating to the Primacy of York. *Edited by* JAMES RAINE, M.A., Canon of York, and Secretary of the Surtees Society.

REGISTER OF MALMESBURY ABBEY: PRESERVED IN THE PUBLIC RECORD OFFICE. *Edited by* J. S. BREWER, M.A., Preacher at the Rolls, and Rector of Toppesfield.

THE METRICAL CHRONICLE OF ROBERT OF GLOUCESTER. *Edited by* WILLIAM ALDIS WRIGHT, Esq., M.A.

A COLLECTION OF SAGAS AND OTHER HISTORICAL DOCUMENTS relating to the Settlements and Descents of the Northmen on the British Isles. *Edited by* Sir GEORGE WEBBE DASENT, D.C.L., Oxon., and M. GUDBRAND VIGFUSSON, M.A.

THÓMAS SAGA ERKIBYSKUPS. A LIFE OF ARCHBISHOP THOMAS BECKET, IN ICELANDIC. Vol. II. *Edited, with English Translation, Notes, and Glossary, by* M. EIRÍKR MAGNÚSSON, M.A., Sub-Librarian of the University Library, Cambridge.

POLYCHRONICON RANULPHI HIGDEN, with Trevisa's Translation. Vol. VII. *Edited by* the Rev. JOSEPH RAWSON LUMBY, D.D., Vicar of St. Edward's, Fellow of St. Catharine's College, and late Fellow of Magdalene College, Cambridge.

RECUEIL DES CRONIQUES ET ANCHIENNES ISTORIES DE LA GRANT BRETAIGNE A PRESENT NOMME ENGLETERRE, par JEHAN DE WAURIN. Vol. III. *Edited by* WILLIAM HARDY, Esq., F.S.A.

GERVASII MONACHI DOROBERNENSIS CHRONICA DE TEMPORE REGUM ANGLIÆ STEPHANI, HENRICI II., ET RICARDI I. *Edited by* WILLIAM STUBBS, M.A., Regius Professor of Modern History, and Fellow of Oriel College, Oxford; and Canon of St. Paul's, London.

MATTHÆI PARISIENSIS, MONACHI SANCTI ALBANI, CHRONICA MAJORA. Vol. V. *Edited by* HENRY RICHARDS LUARD, D.D., Fellow of Trinity College, Registrary of the University and Vicar of Great St. Mary's, Cambridge.

LESTORIE DES ENGLES SOLUM GEFFREI GAIMAR. *Edited by* SIR THOMAS DUFFUS HARDY, D.C.L., Deputy Keeper of the Public Records.

HISTORIA ANGLORUM HENRICI HUNTENDUNENSIS. *Edited by* THOMAS ARNOLD, ESQ.

MATERIALS FOR THE HISTORY OF THOMAS BECKET, ARCHBISHOP OF CANTERBURY. Vol. IV. *Edited by* the Rev. JAMES CRAIGIE ROBERTSON, M.A., Canon of Canterbury.

In Progress.

DESCRIPTIVE CATALOGUE OF MANUSCRIPTS RELATING TO THE HISTORY OF GREAT BRITAIN AND IRELAND. Vol. IV.; 1327, &c. *By* Sir THOMAS DUFFUS HARDY, D.C.L., Deputy Keeper of the Public Records.

REGISTRUM EPISTOLARUM FRATRIS JOHANNIS PECKHAM, ARCHIEPISCOPI CANTUARIENSIS. *Edited, from MS. in All Souls' College, Oxford, by* CHARLES TRICE MARTIN, ESQ., B.A.

HENRICI DE BRACTON DE LEGIBUS ET CONSUETUDINIBUS ANGLIÆ. LIBRI QUINQUE IN VARIOS TRACTATUS DISTINCTI. AD DIVERSORUM ET VETUSTISSIMORUM CODICUM COLLATIONEM TYPIS VULGATI. Vol. III. *Edited by* SIR TRAVERS TWISS, Q.C., D.C.L.

PUBLICATIONS

OF

THE RECORD COMMISSIONERS, &c.

ROTULORUM ORIGINALIUM IN CURIÂ SCACCARII ABBREVIATIO. Henry III.—Edward III. *Edited by* HENRY PLAYFORD, Esq. 2 Vols. folio (1805—1810). *Price* 25*s*. boards, or 12*s*. 6*d*. each.

CALENDARIUM INQUISITIONUM POST MORTEM SIVE ESCAETARUM. Henry III.—Richard III. *Edited by* JOHN CALEY and JOHN BAYLEY, Esqrs. Vols. 3 and 4, folio (1821—1828), boards: Vol. 3, *price* 21*s*.; Vol. 4, *price* 24*s*.

LIBRORUM MANUSCRIPTORUM BIBLIOTHECÆ HARLEIANÆ CATALOGUS. Vol. 4. *Edited by* the Rev. T. HARTWELL HORNE. Folio (1812), boards. *Price* 18*s*.

ABBREVIATIO PLACITORUM. Richard I.—Edward II. *Edited by* the Right Hon. GEORGE ROSE and W. ILLINGWORTH, Esq. 1 Vol. folio (1811), boards. *Price* 18*s*.

LIBRI CENSUALIS vocati DOMESDAY-BOOK, INDICES. *Edited by* Sir HENRY ELLIS. Folio (1816), boards, (Domesday-Book, Vol. 3). *Price* 21*s*.

LIBRI CENSUALIS vocati DOMESDAY-BOOK, ADDITAMENTA EX CODIC. ANTIQUISS. *Edited by* Sir HENRY ELLIS. Folio (1816), boards (Domesday-Book, Vol. 4). *Price* 21*s*.

STATUTES OF THE REALM. *Edited by* Sir T. E. TOMLINS, JOHN RAITHBY, JOHN CALEY, and WM. ELLIOTT, Esqrs. Vols. 7, 8, 9, 10, and 11, including 2 Vols. of Indices, large folio (1819—1828). *Price* 31*s*. 6*d*. each ; except the Indices, *price* 30*s*. each.

VALOR ECCLESIASTICUS, temp. Hen. VIII., Auctoritate Regia institutus. *Edited by* JOHN CALEY, Esq., and the Rev. JOSEPH HUNTER. Vols. 3 to 6, folio (1817-1834), boards. *Price* 25*s*. each.

*** The Introduction, separately, 8vo., cloth. *Price* 2*s*. 6*d*.

ROTULI SCOTIÆ IN TURRI LONDINENSI ET IN DOMO CAPITULARI WESTMONASTERIENSI ASSERVATI. 19 Edward I.—Henry VIII. *Edited by* DAVID MACPHERSON, JOHN CALEY, and W. ILLINGWORTH, Esqrs., and the Rev. T. HARTWELL HORNE. Vol. 2, folio (1819), boards. *Price* 21*s*.

FŒDERA, CONVENTIONES, LITTERÆ, &c. ; or, RYMER'S FŒDERA, New Edition, folio. Vol. 3, Part 2, 1361—1377 (1830) : Vol. 4, 1377—1383 (1869). *Edited by* JOHN CALEY and FRED. HOLBROOKE, Esqrs. Vol. 3, Part 2, *price* 21*s*. ; Vol. 4, *price* 6*s*.

DUCATUS LANCASTRIÆ CALENDARIUM INQUISITIONUM POST MORTEM, &c. Part 3, Calendar to the Pleadings, &c., Henry VII.—13 Elizabeth. Part 4, Calendar to the Pleadings, to end of Elizabeth. (1827—1834.) *Edited by* R. J. HARPER, JOHN CALEY, and WM. MINCHIN, Esqrs. Folio, boards, Part 3 (or Vol. 2), *price* 31*s*. 6*d*.; Part 4 (or Vol. 3), *price* 21*s*.

CALENDARS OF THE PROCEEDINGS IN CHANCERY, IN THE REIGN OF QUEEN ELIZABETH; with Examples of earlier Proceedings from Richard II. *Edited by* JOHN BAYLEY, Esq. Vols. 2 and 3 (1830—1832), folio, boards, *price* 21*s.* each.

PARLIAMENTARY WRITS AND WRITS OF MILITARY SUMMONS, together with the Records and Muniments relating to the Suit and Service due and performed to the King's High Court of Parliament and the Councils of the Realm. *Edited by* Sir FRANCIS PALGRAVE. (1830—1834.) Folio, boards, Vol. 2, Division 1, Edward II., *price* 21*s.*; Vol. 2, Division 2, *price* 21*s.*; Vol. 2, Division 3, *price* 42*s.*

ROTULI LITTERARUM CLAUSARUM IN TURRI LONDINENSI ASSERVATI. 2 Vols. folio (1833, 1844). Vol. 1, 1204—1224. Vol. 2, 1224—1227. *Edited by* THOMAS DUFFUS HARDY, Esq. *Price* 81*s.*, cloth; or separately, Vol. 1, *price* 63*s.*; Vol. 2, *price* 18*s.*

PROCEEDINGS AND ORDINANCES OF THE PRIVY COUNCIL OF ENGLAND. 10 Richard II.—33 Henry VIII. *Edited by* Sir NICHOLAS HARRIS NICOLAS. 7 Vols. royal 8vo. (1834—1837), cloth. *Price* 98*s.*; or separately, 14*s.* each.

ROTULI LITTERARUM PATENTIUM IN TURRI LONDINENSI ASSERVATI. 1201—1216. *Edited by* THOMAS DUFFUS HARDY, Esq. 1 Vol. folio (1835), cloth. *Price* 31*s.* 6*d.*

*** The Introduction, separately, 8vo., cloth. *Price* 9*s.*

ROTULI CURIÆ REGIS. Rolls and Records of the Court held before the King's Justiciars or Justices. 6 Richard I.—1 John. *Edited by* Sir FRANCIS PALGRAVE. 2 Vols. royal 8vo. (1835), cloth. *Price* 28*s.*

ROTULI NORMANNIÆ IN TURRI LONDINENSI ASSERVATI. 1200—1205; also, 1417 to 1418. *Edited by* THOMAS DUFFUS HARDY, Esq. 1 Vol. royal 8vo. (1835), cloth. *Price* 12*s.* 6*d.*

ROTULI DE OBLATIS ET FINIBUS IN TURRI LONDINENSI ASSERVATI, tempore Regis Johannis. *Edited by* THOMAS DUFFUS HARDY, Esq. 1 Vol. royal 8vo. (1835), cloth. *Price* 18*s.*

EXCERPTA E ROTULIS FINIUM IN TURRI LONDINENSI ASSERVATIS. Henry III., 1216—1272. *Edited by* CHARLES ROBERTS, Esq. 2 Vols. royal 8vo. (1835, 1836), cloth, *price* 32*s.*; or separately Vol. 1, *price* 14*s.*; Vol. 2, *price* 18*s.*

FINES, SIVE PEDES FINIUM; SIVE FINALES CONCORDIÆ IN CURIÂ DOMINI REGIS. 7 Richard I.—16 John, 1195—1214. *Edited by* the Rev. JOSEPH HUNTER. In Counties. 2 Vols. royal 8vo. (1835—1844), cloth, *price* 11*s.*; or separately, Vol. 1, *price* 8*s.* 6*d.*; Vol. 2, *price* 2*s.* 6*d.*

ANCIENT KALENDARS AND INVENTORIES OF THE TREASURY OF HIS MAJESTY'S EXCHEQUER; together with Documents illustrating the History of that Repository. *Edited by* Sir FRANCIS PALGRAVE. 3 Vols. royal 8vo. (1836), cloth. *Price* 42*s.*

DOCUMENTS AND RECORDS illustrating the History of Scotland, and the Transactions between the Crowns of Scotland and England; preserved in the Treasury of Her Majesty's Exchequer. *Edited by* Sir FRANCIS PALGRAVE. 1 Vol. royal 8vo. (1837), cloth. *Price* 18*s.*

ROTULI CHARTARUM IN TURRI LONDINENSI ASSERVATI. 1199—1216. *Edited by* THOMAS DUFFUS HARDY, Esq. 1 Vol. folio (1837), cloth. *Price* 30*s*.

REPORT OF THE PROCEEDINGS OF THE RECORD COMMISSIONERS, 1831—1837. 1 Vol. folio (1837), boards. *Price* 8*s*.

REGISTRUM vulgariter nuncupatum "The Record of Caernarvon," e codice MS. Harleiano, 696, descriptum. *Edited by* Sir HENRY ELLIS. 1 Vol. folio (1838), cloth. *Price* 31*s*. 6*d*.

ANCIENT LAWS AND INSTITUTES OF ENGLAND; comprising Laws enacted under the Anglo-Saxon Kings, from Æthelbirht to Cnut, with a Translation of the Saxon; the Laws called Edward the Confessor's; the Laws of William the Conqueror, and those ascribed to Henry the First; Monumenta Ecclesiastica Anglicana, from 7th to 10th century; and Ancient Latin Version of the Anglo-Saxon Laws; with Glossary, &c. *Edited by* BENJAMIN THORPE, Esq. 1 Vol. folio (1840), cloth. *Price* 40*s*. Or, 2 Vols. royal 8vo. cloth. *Price* 30*s*.

ANCIENT LAWS AND INSTITUTES OF WALES; comprising Laws supposed to be enacted by Howel the Good; modified by subsequent Regulations under the Native Princes, prior to the Conquest by Edward the First; and anomalous Laws, consisting principally of Institutions which, by the Statute of Ruddlan, continued in force. With a Translation of the Welsh. Also, a few Latin Transcripts, containing Digests of the Welsh Laws, principally of the Dimetian Code. With Glossary, &c. *Edited by* ANEURIN OWEN, Esq. 1 Vol. folio (1841), cloth. *Price* 44*s*. Or, 2 Vols. royal 8vo. cloth. *Price* 36*s*.

ROTULI DE LIBERATE AC DE MISIS ET PRÆSTITIS, Regnante Johanne. *Edited by* THOMAS DUFFUS HARDY, Esq. 1 Vol. royal 8vo. (1844), cloth. *Price* 6*s*.

THE GREAT ROLLS OF THE PIPE, 2, 3, 4 HEN. II., 1155—1158. *Edited by* the Rev. JOSEPH HUNTER. 1 Vol. royal 8vo. (1844), cloth. *Price* 4*s*. 6*d*.

THE GREAT ROLL OF THE PIPE, 1 RIC. I., 1189—1190. *Edited by* the Rev. JOSEPH HUNTER. 1 Vol. royal 8vo. (1844), cloth. *Price* 6*s*.

DOCUMENTS ILLUSTRATIVE OF ENGLISH HISTORY in the 13th and 14th centuries, selected from the Records of the Department of the Queen's Remembrancer in the Exchequer. *Edited by* HENRY COLE, Esq. 1 Vol. fcp. folio (1844), cloth. *Price* 45*s*. 6*d*.

MODUS TENENDI PARLIAMENTUM. An Ancient Treatise on the Mode of holding the Parliament in England. *Edited by* THOMAS DUFFUS HARDY, Esq. 1 Vol. 8vo. (1846), cloth. *Price* 2*s*. 6*d*.

REGISTRUM MAGNI SIGILLI REGUM SCOTORUM in Archivis Publicis asservatum. 1306—1424. *Edited by* THOMAS THOMSON, Esq. Folio (1814). *Price* 10*s*. 6*d*.

THE ACTS OF THE PARLIAMENTS OF SCOTLAND. Folio (1814—1875). *Edited by* THOMAS THOMSON and COSMO INNES, Esqrs. Vol. 1, *price* 42*s*. Vols. 5 and 6 (in three Parts), *price* 21*s*. each Part; Vols. 4, 7, 8, 9, 10, and 11, *price* 10*s*. 6*d*. each Volume; Vol. 12 (Index), *price* 63*s*. Or, complete, 12 Volumes in 13, *price* 12*l*. 12*s*.

THE ACTS OF THE LORDS AUDITORS OF CAUSES AND COMPLAINTS (ACTA DOMINORUM AUDITORUM). 1466—1494. *Edited by* THOMAS THOMSON, Esq. Folio (1839). *Price* 10*s*. 6*d*.

THE ACTS OF THE LORDS OF COUNCIL IN CIVIL CAUSES (ACTA DOMINORUM CONCILII). 1478—1495. *Edited by* THOMAS THOMSON, Esq. Folio (1839). *Price* 10*s*. 6*d*.

ISSUE ROLL OF THOMAS DE BRANTINGHAM, Bishop of Exeter, Lord High Treasurer of England, containing Payments out of His Majesty's Revenue, 44 Edward III., 1370. *Edited by* FREDERICK DEVON, Esq. 1 Vol. 4to. (1835), cloth. *Price* 35*s*. Or, royal 8vo. cloth. *Price* 25*s*.

ISSUES OF THE EXCHEQUER, James I.; extracted from the Pell Records. *Edited by* FREDERICK DEVON, Esq. 1 Vol. 4to. (1836), cloth. *Price* 30*s*. Or, royal 8vo. cloth. *Price* 21*s*.

ISSUES OF THE EXCHEQUER, Henry III.—Henry VI.; extracted from the Pell Records. *Edited by* FREDERICK DEVON, Esq. 1 Vol. 4to. (1837), cloth. *Price* 40*s*. Or, royal 8vo. cloth. *Price* 30*s*.

HANDBOOK TO THE PUBLIC RECORDS. *By* F. S. THOMAS, Esq., Secretary of the Public Record Office. 1 Vol. royal 8vo. (1853), cloth. *Price* 12*s*.

HISTORICAL NOTES RELATIVE TO THE HISTORY OF ENGLAND. Henry VIII. —Anne (1509—1714). Designed as a Book of Reference for ascertaining the Dates of Events. *By* F. S. THOMAS, Esq. 3 Vols. 8vo. (1856), cloth. *Price* 40*s*.

STATE PAPERS, DURING THE REIGN OF HENRY THE EIGHTH: with Indices of Persons and Places. 11 Vols., 4to. (1830—1852), cloth. *Price* 5*l*. 15*s*. 6*d*.; or separately, *price* 10*s*. 6*d*. each.

Vol. I.—Domestic Correspondence.
Vols. II. & III.—Correspondence relating to Ireland.
Vols. IV. & V.—Correspondence relating to Scotland.
Vols. VI. to XI.—Correspondence between England and Foreign Courts.

WORKS PUBLISHED IN PHOTOZINCOGRAPHY.

DOMESDAY BOOK, or the GREAT SURVEY OF ENGLAND OF WILLIAM THE CONQUEROR, 1086; fac-simile of the Part relating to each county, separately (with a few exceptions of double counties). Photozincographed, by Her Majesty's Command, at the Ordnance Survey Office, Southampton, Colonel SIR HENRY JAMES, R.E., F.R.S., &c., Director. 35 Parts, imperial quarto and demy quarto (1861–1863) boards. *Price* 4*s*. 6*d*. to 1*l*. 1*s*. each Part, according to size; or, bound in 2 Vols., 18*l*. (*The edition in two volumes is out of print.*)

This important and unique survey of the greater portion of England* is the oldest and most valuable record in the national archives. It was commenced about the year 1084 and finished in 1086. Its compilation was determined upon at Gloucester by William the Conqueror, in council, in order that he might know what was due to him, in the way of tax, from his subjects, and that each at the same time might know what he had to pay. It was compiled as much for their protection as for the benefit of the sovereign. The nobility and people had been grievously distressed at the time by the king bringing over large numbers of French and Bretons, and quartering them on his subjects, "each according to the measure of his land," for the purpose of resisting the invasion of Cnut, King of Denmark, which was apprehended. The commissioners appointed to make the survey were to inquire the name of each place; who held it in the time of King Edward the Confessor; the present possessor; how many hides were in the manor; how many ploughs were in demesne; how many homagers; how many villeins; how many cottars; how many serving men; how many free tenants; how many tenants in soccage; how much wood, meadow, and pasture; the number of mills and fish-ponds; what had been added or taken away from the place; what was the gross value in the time of Edward the Confessor; the present value; and how much each free man or soc-man had, and whether any advance could be made in the value. Thus could be ascertained who held the estate in the time of King Edward; who then held it; its value in the time of the late king; and its value as it stood at the formation of the survey. So minute was the survey, that the writer of the contemporary portion of the Saxon Chronicle records, with some asperity—"So very narrowly he caused it to be traced out, that there was not a single hide, nor one virgate of land, nor even, it is shame to tell, though it seemed to him no shame to do, an ox, nor a cow, nor a swine was left, that was not set down."

Domesday Survey is in two parts or volumes. The first, in folio, contains the counties of Bedford, Berks, Bucks, Cambridge, Chester and Lancaster, Cornwall, Derby, Devon, Dorset, Gloucester, Hants, Hereford, Herts, Huntingdon, Kent, Leicester and Rutland, Lincoln, Middlesex, Northampton, Nottingham, Oxford, Salop, Somerset, Stafford, Surrey, Sussex, Warwick, Wilts, Worcester, and York. The second volume, in quarto, contains the counties of Essex, Norfolk, and Suffolk.

Domesday Book was printed *verbatim et literatim* during the last century, in consequence of an address of the House of Lords to King George III. in 1767. It was not, however, commenced until 1773, and was completed early in 1783. In 1860, Her Majesty's Government, with the concurrence of the Master of the Rolls, determined to apply the art of photozincography to the production of a fac-simile of Domesday Book, under the superintendence of Colonel Sir Henry James, R.E., Director of the Ordnance Survey, Southampton. The fac-simile was completed in 1863.

* For some reason left unexplained, many parts were left unsurveyed; Northumberland, Cumberland, Westmoreland, and Durham, are not described in the survey; nor does Lancashire appear under its proper name; but Furness, and the northern part of Lancashire, as well as the south of Westmoreland, with a part of Cumberland, are included within the West Riding of Yorkshire. That part of Lancashire which lies between the Ribble and Mersey, and which at the time of the survey comprehended 688 manors, is joined to Cheshire. Part of Rutland is described in the counties of Northampton and Lincoln.

FAC-SIMILES of NATIONAL MANUSCRIPTS, from WILLIAM THE CONQUEROR to QUEEN ANNE, selected under the direction of the Master of the Rolls, and Photozincographed, by Command of Her Majesty, by Colonel SIR HENRY JAMES, R.E., Director of the Ordnance Survey. *Price*, each Part, with translations and notes, double foolscap folio, 16*s*.

Part I. (William the Conqueror to Henry VII.). 1865.
Part II. (Henry VIII. and Edward VI.). 1866.
Part III. (Mary and Elizabeth). 1867.
Part IV. (James I. to Anne). 1868.

The first Part extends from William the Conqueror to Henry VII., and contains autographs of the kings of England, as well as of many other illustrious personages famous in history, and some interesting charters, letters patent, and state papers. The second Part, for the reigns of Henry VIII. and Edward VI., consists principally of holograph letters and autographs of kings, princes, statesmen, and other persons of great historical interest, who lived during those reigns. The third Part contains similar documents for the reigns of Mary and Elizabeth, including a signed bill of Lady Jane Grey. The fourth Part concludes the series, and comprises a number of documents taken from the originals belonging to the Constable of the Tower of London; also several records illustrative of the Gunpowder Plot, and a woodcut containing portraits of Mary Queen of Scots and James VI., circulated by their adherents in England, 1580-3.

Public Record Office,
March 1879.

SCOTLAND.

CATALOGUE OF SCOTCH RECORD PUBLICATIONS

PUBLISHED UNDER THE DIRECTION OF

THE LORD CLERK REGISTER OF SCOTLAND.

On Sale by—

MESSRS. LONGMAN & CO., AND MESSRS. TRÜBNER & CO., LONDON;
MESSRS. JAMES PARKER & CO., OXFORD AND LONDON;
MESSRS. MACMILLAN & CO., CAMBRIDGE AND LONDON;
MESSRS. A. & C. BLACK, AND MESSRS. DOUGLAS & FOULIS, EDINBURGH;
AND MR. A. THOM, DUBLIN.

CHRONICLES OF THE PICTS AND SCOTS, AND OTHER EARLY MEMORIALS OF SCOTTISH HISTORY. Royal 8vo., half bound (1867). *Edited by* WILLIAM F. SKENE, LL.D. *Price* 10*s.*

LEDGER OF ANDREW HALYBURTON, CONSERVATOR OF THE PRIVILEGES OF THE SCOTCH NATION IN THE NETHERLANDS (1492–1503); TOGETHER WITH THE BOOKS OF CUSTOMS AND VALUATION OF MERCHANDISES IN SCOTLAND. Royal 8vo., half bound (1867). *Price* 10*s.*

DOCUMENTS ILLUSTRATIVE OF THE HISTORY OF SCOTLAND FROM THE DEATH OF KING ALEXANDER THE THIRD TO THE ACCESSION OF ROBERT BRUCE, from original and authentic copies in London, Paris, Brussels, Lille, and Ghent. In 2 Vols, royal 8vo., half bound (1870). *Edited by* Rev. JOSEPH STEVENSON. *Price* 10*s. each.*

ACCOUNTS OF THE LORD HIGH TREASURER OF SCOTLAND. Vol. 1, A.D. 1473–1498. *Edited by* THOMAS DICKSON. 1877. *Price* 10*s.*

REGISTER OF THE PRIVY COUNCIL OF SCOTLAND. *Edited and arranged by* J. H. BURTON, LL.D. Vol. 1, 1545–1569. Vol. 2, 1569–1578. 1877. *Price* 15*s. each.*

ROTULI SCACCARII REGUM SCOTORUM. THE EXCHEQUER ROLLS OF SCOTLAND. Vol. 1, A.D. 1264–1359. Vol, 2, A.D. 1359–1379. *Edited by* JOHN STUART, LL.D., and GEORGE BURNETT, Lyon King of Arms. 1878. *Price* 10*s. each.*

FAC-SIMILES OF THE NATIONAL MSS. OF SCOTLAND. (*Out of print.*) Parts I., II., and III. *Price* 21*s. each.*

Stationery Office,
1*st January* 1879.

IRELAND.

CATALOGUE OF IRISH RECORD PUBLICATIONS.

On Sale by—

MESSRS. LONGMAN & CO., AND MESSRS. TRÜBNER & CO., LONDON
MESSRS. JAMES PARKER & CO., OXFORD AND LONDON;
MESSRS. MACMILLAN & CO., CAMBRIDGE AND LONDON;
MESSRS. A. & C. BLACK, AND MESSRS. DOUGLAS & FOULIS, EDINBURGH;
AND MR. A. THOM, DUBLIN.

CALENDAR OF THE PATENT AND CLOSE ROLLS OF CHANCERY IN IRELAND. HENRY VIII., EDWARD VI., MARY, AND ELIZABETH. Royal 8vo. (1861-3). Vols. 1, 2, and 3. *Price* 11*s*. each.

ANCIENT LAWS OF IRELAND.
Seuchus Mor. (1865–1873.) Vols. 1, 2, and 3. *Price* 10*s*. each.

FAC-SIMILES of NATIONAL MANUSCRIPTS of IRELAND. *Edited by* JOHN T. GILBERT, F.S.A., M.R.I.A. Parts I., II., III. (in the press), IV. (in progress). *Price*, 42*s*. each.

This work is intended to form a comprehensive Palæographic Series for Ireland. It will furnish characteristic specimens of the documents which have come down from each of the classes which, in past ages, formed principal elements in the population of Ireland, or exercised an influence in her affairs. With these reproductions will be combined fac-similes of writings connected with eminent personages or transactions of importance in the annals of the country to the end of the reign of Queen Anne.

The specimens are reproduced as nearly as possible in accordance with the originals, in dimensions, colouring, and general appearance. Characteristic examples of styles of writing and caligraphic ornamentation are, so far as practicable, associated with subjects of historic and linguistic interest. Descriptions of the various manuscripts are given by the Editor in the Introduction. The contents of the specimens are fully elucidated and printed in the original languages opposite to the Fac-similes—line for line—without contractions—thus facilitating reference and aiding effectively those interested in palæographic studies.

Part I. contains upwards of seventy coloured specimens, commencing with the earliest Irish MSS. extant.

Part II. extends from the Twelfth Century to A.D. 1299, and contains ninety specimens in colours.

In Part III.—now in the Press—the Work will be carried down to the end of the reign of Henry VIII.

(*This work is sold also by Letts, Son, & Co.*, 33, *King William Street; E. Stanford, Charing Cross; J. Wyld, Charing Cross; B. Quaritch*, 15, *Piccadilly; W. & A. K. Johnston, Edinburgh; and Hodges, Foster & Co., Dublin*).

Stationery Office,
1*st January* 1879.